Green Line
Oberstufe

Lehrerfassung

von

Dr. Steffen Brand
Prof. Dr. Peter Bruck
Ellen Butzko
Louise Carleton-Gertsch
Paul Dennis
Krista Eichler
Cornelia Kaminski
Nilgül Karabulut
Michael Kleis

Hartmut Klose
Silke Krieger
Berit Möckel
Corienne Naumann
Dr. Peter Naumann
Michael Rogge
Thomas Tepe
Alexandra Timm

Ernst Klett Verlag
Stuttgart · Leipzig

So lernen Sie mit Green Line

Start in ein Kapitel

Code z5e563

Auf einigen Seiten im Buch finden Sie Green Line-Codes. Diese führen Sie zu weiteren Informationen. Geben Sie den Code einfach in das Suchfeld auf www.klett.de ein.

Den Einstieg in ein *Topic* bildet die **Introduction**.

Fürs Abitur trainieren

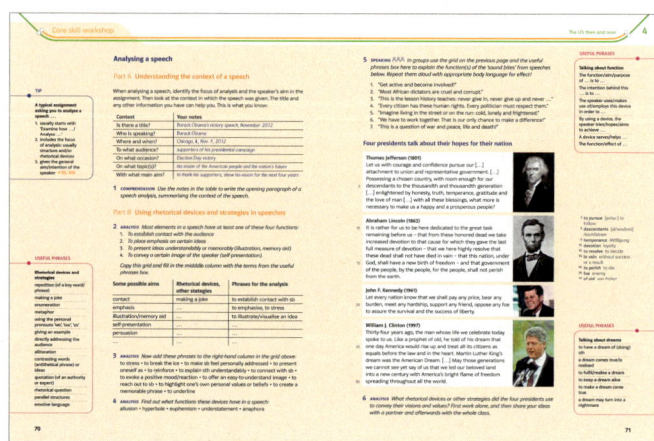

Im **Core skill workshop** können Sie eine abiturrelevante *Skill* wiederholen und trainieren.

Thema erarbeiten und vertiefen

Im weiteren Kapitel finden Sie Texte und Materialien für die Erarbeitung des Themas auf zwei verschiedenen Niveaus: **Texts** und **Advanced texts**.
Die *Tasks* orientieren sich an den Aufgaben, die Sie im Abitur erwarten und bereiten Sie optimal darauf vor.

Fördern, fordern, differenzieren

Die roten Dreiecke verweisen auf Hilfen (△) und zusätzliche Aufgaben (▲) im **Diff pool**-Anhang.

Überprüfen

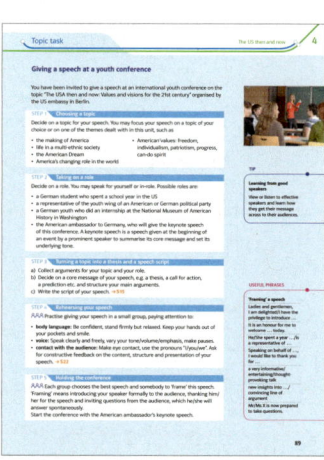

Den Abschluss jedes *Topics* bildet die **Topic task**: Die Aufgabe führt die inhaltlichen Schwerpunkte und die *Core skill* zusammen.

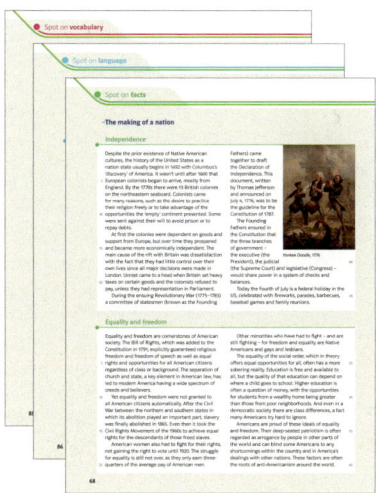

INNERHALB EINES KAPITELS

Zum Wiederholen kurz vor dem Abitur

Die *Spot on*-Seiten bieten auf einen Blick das inhaltliche **Basiswissen** des *Topics*, den themenspezifischen **Wortschatz** und wichtige **sprachliche Strukturen** mit jeweils passenden Aufgaben. Sie eignen sich auch besonders zum selbstständigen Arbeiten bzw. Wiederholen, denn die Lösungen zu diesen Seiten finden Sie unter dem jeweiligen Green Line-Code des Topics.

CD-ROM

Die Schüler-CD (◎) enthält *Vocabulary sheets* mit Lernwortschatz zu allen Texten im Buch. Zu den *Spot on*-Seiten und zu *Intercultural communication* enthält sie zusätzlich die Audios und Videos.

AM ENDE DES BUCHES

Üben, nachschlagen, sicher kommunizieren

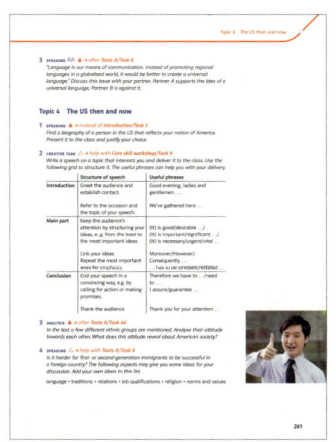

Der **Diff pool** bietet die Möglichkeit, Aufgaben mit Hilfen zu lösen oder anspruchsvollere Aufgaben zu bearbeiten.

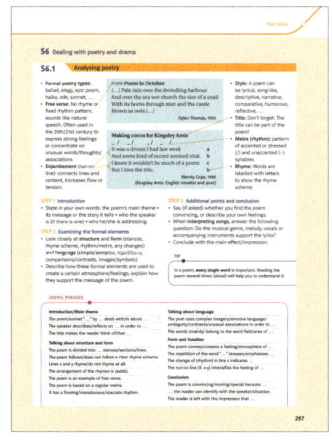

Hier finden Sie alle wichtigen **Skills** auf einen Blick mit zusätzlichen Erläuterungen, Tipps und *Useful phrases*.

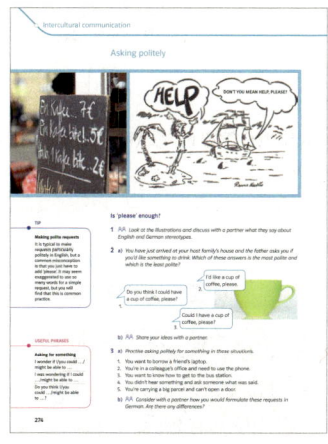

Auf den **Intercultural communication**-Seiten trainieren Sie sicher und souverän auf Englisch zu interagieren.

SYMBOLE

→△1	Verweis auf leichtere Aufgaben / Hilfen im *Diff pool*	
→▲2	Verweis auf anspruchsvollere Aufgaben im *Diff pool*	
→S28	Verweis auf den Skillsanhang	
👥	Partnerarbeit	
👥👥	Gruppenarbeit	
◎S	Verweis auf die Schüler-CD (Audio, Video, …)	
◎L1/1	Verweis auf die Lehrer-Audio-CDs (z. B. L1/1 = CD1/Track 1)	
📀L	Verweis auf die Lehrer-Film-DVD (Film)	
🌐	Verweis auf Green Line-Code mit weiteren Materialien	

ABKÜRZUNGEN

adj	adjective		*infml*	informal
adv	adverb		*n*	noun, substantive
AE	American English		*pej*	pejorative
↔	antonym		*pl*	plural
BE	British English		*sg*	singular
coll	collocation		*sb*	somebody
disappr	disapproving		*sl*	slang
e.g.	*exempli gratia* (Lat.) = for example		*sth*	something
			syn	synonym
esp	especially		*v*	verb
fml	formal		*vlg*	vulgar
hum	humorous		*vs*	versus
i.e.	*id est* (Lat.) = that is			

Green Line Oberstufe
Lehrerfassung
Ausgabe für Baden-Württemberg

Autorinnen und Autoren: Dr. Steffen Brand, Grünkraut; Prof. Dr. Peter Bruck, Lüdinghausen; Ellen Butzko, Tübingen; Louise Carleton-Gertsch, München; Paul Dennis, Lahnstein; Krista Eichler, Weil der Stadt; Cornelia Kaminski, Fulda; Nilgül Karabulut, Aachen; Michael Kleis, Geltendorf; Hartmut Klose, Seevetal; Silke Krieger, Castrop-Rauxel; Berit Möckel, Nürnberg; Corienne Naumann, Erlangen; Dr. Peter Naumann, Erlangen; Michael Rogge, Essen; Thomas Tepe, Münster; Alexandra Timm, Kasel

Beratung: Anette Christiani, Dortmund; Cornelia Kaminski, Fulda; Michael Kleis, Geltendorf; Hartmut Klose, Seevetal; Heike Piornak, Dessau-Roßlau; Dr. Stephan Schüller, Norheim; Dr. Christine Tiefenthal, Hamburg; Harald Weisshaar, Bisingen; Bernd Wick, Neckartenzlingen

Zusätzliche Hinweise in Ihrer Lehrerfassung

Native American • **Markierter Lernwortschatz** aus den Vocabulary sheets

Avoiding mistakes
Aussprache
¹⁵technology [tekˈnɒlədʒi]
• Hinweise zu ergänzenden und weiterführenden **Zusatzmaterialien**, Informationen zu **Bildinhalten, Praxistipps** in „Avoiding mistakes" und viele weitere Verweise

Hinweis: Auch als Hausaufgabe geeignet • Hinweise in Form von geeigneten **Unterrichtsmethoden, Zusatzmaterialien,** Inhalten im **Differenzierungsanhang** und Hausaufgabenvorschläge direkt an den Tasks

1. Auflage   1 5 4 3 2 1 | 2019 18 17 16 15

Alle Drucke dieser Auflage sind unverändert und können im Unterricht nebeneinander verwendet werden.
Die letzte Zahl bezeichnet das Jahr des Druckes.
Das Werk und seine Teile sind urheberrechtlich geschützt. Jede Nutzung in anderen als den gesetzlich zugelassenen Fällen bedarf der vorherigen schriftlichen Einwilligung des Verlages. Hinweis § 52 a UrhG: Weder das Werk noch seine Teile dürfen ohne eine solche Einwilligung eingescannt und in ein Netzwerk eingestellt werden. Dies gilt auch für Intranets von Schulen und sonstigen Bildungseinrichtungen. Fotomechanische oder andere Wiedergabeverfahren nur mit Genehmigung des Verlages.

© Ernst Klett Verlag GmbH, Stuttgart 2015. Alle Rechte vorbehalten.
www.klett.de

Redaktion: Melissa Braun-Keller; Jim Martin; Peter Cole, Stuttgart
Herstellung: Marietta Heymann
Gestaltung: normaldesign GbR, Schwäbisch Gmünd
Titelbild: Getty Images RF (Photodisc), München
Illustrationen: Virginia Romo, Stuttgart (Illustrationen); Christian Dekelver, Weinstadt (Landkarten)
Satz: Wiebke Hengst, Ostfildern
Druck: PASSAVIA Druckservice GmbH & Co. KG, Passau

Printed in Germany
ISBN 978-3-12-530480-2

CD-ROM
Diesem Schülerbuch liegt eine CD-ROM bei. Die Urheber und Mitwirkenden sind den entsprechenden Verzeichnissen auf der CD-ROM oder im Anhang dieses Buches zu entnehmen. Sollten Sie Probleme mit dem vorliegenden Programm haben, finden Sie in der Datei „Hotline.txt", die sich auf der obersten Ebene der CD-ROM befindet, unsere Kontaktdaten und weitere Hilfestellungen. Auf der CD-ROM befindet sich ein ausführliches Handbuch zum Programm.

Aufnahmeleitung: Ernst Klett Verlag GmbH
Produktion: John Green TEFL Audio, London; RBA Productions, Andrew Branch, Brighton
Sprecherinnen und Sprecher: Max Berendt, Elaine Claxton, Teresa Gallagher, James Goode, Abigail Hardiman, Jonathan Keeble, Harriet Kershaw, Kate Lock, Rachael Louise Miller, Richard Pearce, Nigel Pilkington, Bill Roberts, Martin Sherman
Vocabulary sheets: Lektorat editoria, Fellbach; Anja Treinies, Düsseldorf
Quellen: Ein ausführliches Quellenverzeichnis finden Sie bei den Text- und Bildquellen.
Presswerk: Osswald GmbH & Co., Leinfelden-Echterdingen

Inhaltsverzeichnis

Section	Text theme	Media/Type of text

1 The individual and society 🌐 6wi4eu

Page	Section	Text theme	Media/Type of text
12	Introduction	Social developments and human rights	L Pictures/Quotations
14	Spot on facts	The make-up of society	Informative texts/Graphs
16	Core skill workshop	**Analysing a film** Side Effected **17**	L Film
19	Texts A **A question of class**	A new class system in the UK **19** A better society? (Veronica Roth) **20**	Internet article Novel extract
	B **Generations apart**	The young versus the old (Fay Weldon) **22**	Newspaper article
24	Advanced texts C **Social attitudes**	A generation of individualists **24** Richard Cory (Edwin A. Robinson) **26**	Newspaper article Poem
	D **How technology is changing society**	No hiding place (Dave Eggers) **27** How not to be alone (Jonathan Safran Foer) **30**	Novel extract Newspaper article
32	Spot on language	„Work and travel" auf Hallig Hooge: Schuften bei den Schafen **33**	Mediation text
34	Spot on vocabulary		
35	Topic task	**Producing a short film**	

2 The United Kingdom 🌐 ny56ij

Page	Section	Text theme	Media/Type of text
36	Introduction	Britishness	Pictures/Quotations
38	Spot on facts	The United Kingdom – a 'united' kingdom?	Informative texts
40	Core skill workshop	**Analysing a newspaper article** London riots – one year on **41**	Newspaper article
43	Texts A **The English, the Scots, the Welsh and the Irish**	How British do you feel? **43**	Quotations
	B **Britain and the rest of the world**	Play no. 77 **44**	L Play
	C **Britain and Europe**	Views of three politicians: Churchill, Cook, Cameron **45**	L Speech extracts
	D **London and the rest of Britain**	The global city **46**	L Newspaper article
48	Advanced texts E **The North and the South**	"Dark and true and tender is the north" **48**	L Newspaper article
	F **People at the top and the bottom**	The Royals **50** Welfare recipients – a speech by David Cameron **52**	L Newspaper article L Speech extract
	G **City boys**	Growing up in Hackney **54** City Boy (Peter Daniels) **55**	Book extract Poem
56	Spot on language	Warum wir Deutschen die Royals so lieben **57**	Mediation text
58	Spot on vocabulary		
59	Topic task	**Creating a class newspaper**	

Inhaltsverzeichnis

Section	Text theme	Media/Type of text

3 Regional identities ⊕ ts2m7y

60 **Introduction**	Defining regional identity	Pictures/Quotations
61 **Spot on facts**	Regionalism in the UK and the US	Maps/Informative texts
62 **Texts**		
A Identities in the UK – tradition and change	Shipyard (Sting) **62** Gaelic will only be a hobby language **63**	⊙L Song Newspaper article
B Rural and urban identities in the US	Red state, blue city **64**	Map/Newspaper article

4 The US then and now ⊕ z5e563

66 **Introduction**	Abstract ideas and American life American Dream or American nightmare? **67**	Pictures Quotations
68 **Spot on facts**	The making of a nation	⊙S ⊙L Informative texts
70 **Core skill workshop**	**Analysing a speech** Four presidents talk about their hopes for their nation **71** Barack Obama's victory speech, November 2012 **72**	Speech extracts Speech extract
73 **Texts**		
A The immigrant experience	Welcome to all! **73** Native Speaker (Chang-Rae Lee) **74** Responding to 9/11 – A mosque near Ground Zero? **76**	Cartoon 📖L Novel extract Speech extract
78 **Advanced texts** B Equality and the Dream	Liberty and justice for all? (Harper Lee) **78** A dream deferred **80**	📖L Novel extract Newspaper article
C An ongoing debate: America's gun culture	America's poorly regulated gun culture **81** Do we have the courage to stop this? **82**	Pictures Newspaper article
D Ethnic minorities	As I Grew Older (Langston Hughes) **84** stupid america (Abelardo Delgado) **85**	📖L Poem Poem
86 **Spot on language**	Wie Träume unser Wirtschaftsleben beeinflussen **87**	Mediation text
88 **Spot on vocabulary**		
89 **Topic task**	Giving a speech at a youth conference	

5 International relations ⊕ jy9z2b

90 **Introduction**	Trouble spots	Maps
91 **Spot on facts**	The European Union	Informative text
92 **Texts** A Military power	Can the EU become the world's policeman? **92**	Newspaper article/Graph
B The EU and the UK – another special relationship?	"EU treatment of human rights is second to none" **94** "If we left, we would get back our democracy" **94**	Cartoon/Speech 📖L extracts
C The new old anti-Americanism	Der neue alte Antiamerikanismus **95**	⊙L Mediation text

Section	Text theme	Media/Type of text

6 Migration and diversity 🌐 92pp34

96	Introduction	Diversity in the English-speaking world National identity **97**	Pictures Informative text
98	Spot on facts	The consequences of migration	⊙s 📖L Informative texts
100	Core skill workshop	**Practising for oral exams** Review: Vauxhall **100**	Role cards Review
103	Texts A Diversity and identity	Diverse City **103** What does a true German look like? **104** Black, British and proud **105**	⊙L Song Internet article Newspaper article
	B Crossing borders	The Tortilla Curtain (T.C. Boyle) **106**	📖L Novel extract/Film posters
108	Advanced texts C Immigration policy	Immigration, integration and British values **108**	Speech
	D Dealing with prejudice	Disgraced (Ayad Akhtar) **110** The fashion industry's problem with race **112**	⊙L Play Newspaper article
	E Immigration in Australia and Canada	From: A short history of immigration **113** This is who I am, an immigrant **114**	Poem Internet article
116	Spot on language	Almanya – Willkommen in Deutschland **117**	Mediation text
118	Spot on vocabulary		
119	Topic task	**Staging a talk show**	

7 Faith and religion 🌐 sq36ms

120	Introduction	The importance of religion	Pictures/Cartoon
121	Spot on facts	Religion in Great Britain and the US	Informative texts/Graph
122	Texts A Feelings and facts	Young Americans' religious attitudes today **122**	⊙L Picture/Interview/Graph
	B Living with religion today	One nation under God? **124** How Christian fundamentalism feeds the divide **125**	Newspaper article Newspaper article

8 Political systems 🌐 us23yz

126	Introduction	Young people and politics	📖L Pictures/Statistics
127	Texts A Young people and politics	Teen "rights" of passage **127**	Internet article
128	Spot on facts	Political systems in the US and the UK	Informative texts/Diagram
130	Texts B Old characteristics and new political developments	The Negotiator (Frederick Forsyth) **130** Open government **131**	Novel extract/Quotations

Inhaltsverzeichnis

Section	Text theme	Media/Type of text

9 Globalisation 7wi6zu

Page	Section	Text theme	Media/Type of text
132	Introduction	Global perspectives	L Pictures/Quotations
134	Spot on facts	Chances and challenges of globalisation	Informative texts/Cartoons
136	**Core skill workshop**	**Dealing with mediation tasks**	
		Straßenfußball verbindet **136**	Mediation text
		Kickfair **138**	Mediation text
139	**Texts**	The world until yesterday **139**	Book extract
	A Different cultures and lifestyles	Why IKEA took China by storm **140**	Newspaper article
	B Global production and its consequences	Textile workers in Bangladesh **141**	L Internet article/Graph
	C Limited resources	The Aqueduct (Ray Bradbury) **142**	L Short story/Cartoon
144	**Advanced texts**	Working for an NGO **144**	Interview
	D NGOs, civil society and global players	Are NGOs fit for their purpose? **145**	Newspaper article
		Starbucks celebrates record revenues **146**	Newspaper article
		Capital has a nationality **146**	Book extract
	E Developing and developed world	West African nations pay a price for EU e-waste **147**	Internet article
		Reshoring manufacturing: Coming home **148**	L Newspaper article
		Global learning **149**	Internet article
	F The individual in a global world	Over the mountains my true love waits **150**	Short story extract
152	Spot on language	Globalisierung am Scheideweg **153**	Mediation text
154	Spot on vocabulary		
155	Topic task	Creating a special issue of the school newspaper	

10 India bq83i8

Page	Section	Text theme	Media/Type of text
156	Introduction	Aspects of India	Pictures/Map
158	Spot on facts	India – an overview	Informative texts
160	**Core skill workshop**	**Analysing an extract from a novel**	
		Extract from The Accidental Apprentice (Vikas Swarup) **161**	Novel extract
163	**Texts**	Street-smart **163**	L Book extract
	A A nation of entrepreneurs	A competitive edge **164**	L Book extract
	B The rich-poor divide	Slums in Vakola (Aravind Adiga) **165**	Novel extract
		India has one third of the world's poorest, says World Bank **166**	Newspaper article
	C Popular culture	Cricket – India's national sport **167**	Informative text
		Bollywood **167**	Newspaper article
168	**Advanced texts**		
	D Hinduism and India's caste system	Interview with Tarquin Hall **168**	L Interview
	E Tradition and gender roles	India dishonoured? **170**	Book extract
		Cartoons for change in the New Delhi metro **172**	Internet article/Cartoons
	F The history of India	The sun sets on the British Empire **173**	L Book extract
		Train to Pakistan (Kushwant Singh) **174**	Novel extract
176	Spot on language	India holidays **176**	Advertisement
		15 Tage Indien **177**	Mediation text
178	Spot on vocabulary		
179	Topic task	Organising an Indian literature festival	

Section	Text theme	Media/Type of text

11 The media ⊕ 2ta7fs

180 Introduction	Recent history of the media	Pictures/Timeline/Quotations
182 Spot on facts	Developments in the media	Graphs/Cartoons/Informative texts
184 **Core skill workshop**	**Analysing visuals**	Photo/Cartoon/Advertisement
187 Texts		
A Reality TV	Reality TV: a ghastly plague upon modern society 187	Blog
B The meaning of reality	Sharing is caring (Dave Eggers) 189	Novel extract
	Second-hand experiences (Gillian Flynn) 190	Novel extract
192 Advanced texts		
C Journalism in the twenty-first century	Open journalism 192	Blog
	Citizen journalists 193	🎞L Newspaper article
D The whistle-blower	Marcus's dilemma (Cory Doctorow) 194	⊙L Novel extract
E Etiquette, ethics and the media	Mobile phone use by many is outrageously rude 196	Newspaper article
	Phubbing/Online safety 197	Advertisements
F The power of transmedia	The death of a friend 198	Book extract
	Transmedia and marketing 199	Interview
200 Spot on language	Du steckst in einer Seifenblase 201	Mediation text
202 Spot on vocabulary		
203 Topic task	**Creating a marketing campaign**	

12 The arts ⊕ mn6bv5

204 Introduction	Works of art from different periods	Pictures/Quotations
205 Texts	Diane Young (Vampire Weekend) 205	⊙L Song
A Combining visual art and music	A musician as portrait photographer 206	Newspaper article/Pictures
B Art in various locations	A controversial work of art 207	Informative text
	Anger at Walmart heiress's $1.4bn gallery as art market becomes focus for protest 208	Newspaper article
	Street art: Beauty or Beast? 209	Pictures

13 The Englishes ⊕ g77e4v

210 Introduction	The role of English in the world	⊙L Pictures/Cartoon Graph
212 Spot on facts	English	⊙s 🎞L Informative texts
214 **Core skill workshop**	**Analysing a listening text**	⊙s ⊙L Interviews/Song
217 Texts	English – the global language of pop music? 217	Newspaper article
A The global spread of English	Why diet is a four-letter word in Germany 218	Newspaper article
B Language and cultural identity	Learn English online: How the internet is changing language 219	Newspaper article
	The other hand (Chris Cleave) 220	⊙L Novel extract
222 Advanced texts	Voices from Britain 222	⊙L Interviews
C Dialects of English	The history and future of British dialects 222	⊙L Interviews
	Mind your language 222	⊙L Interviews
D Linguistic imperialism	Linguistic imperialism – Just speak English? 223	Newspaper article

Inhaltsverzeichnis

Section	Text theme	Media/Type of text
E **All the Englishes**	Mother Tongue (Amy Tan) 224	Memoir
F **English worldwide**	Six countries 227	⊙L Interviews
G **The future of English**	English will die out like Latin 228 English on the internet 229	Newspaper article Graphs
230 **Spot on language**	Warum Denglish Sprachmüll ist 231	Mediation text
232 **Spot on vocabulary**		
233 **Topic task**	**Creating a podcast**	

14 Shakespeare ⊕ h4e4bt

234 **Introduction**	Theatre and entertainment – then and now	🎬L Pictures/Quotations
236 **Spot on facts**	Shakespeare's life and times	⊙s ⊙L Informative texts
238 **Core skill workshop**	**Analysing a scene from a play** Scenes from: The Taming of the Shrew, A Midsummer Night's Dream, Much Ado About Nothing 238 Othello: Planting the seeds of doubt 240	⊙L Play ⊙L Play
241 **Texts**		
A **On the stage**	It was hard being an Elizabethan actor (Bill Bryson) 241	Book extract
B **The way to success**	Macbeth: The opening scene 243 Othello: The opening scene 244	⊙L Graphic novel ⊙L Play
C **Shakespeare in film**	Shakespeare in Love 245	Film script
246 **Advanced texts**	Macbeth: Power and ambition 246	🎬L ⊙L Play
D **Insights into the human mind**	Othello: Manipulation 247	⊙L Play
E **Shakespeare – fame and fortune?**	Writing Shakespeare (Stephen Greenblatt) 248 Sonnet 91 249 Fear no more 250 How could a commoner write such great plays? 251	Book extract ⊙L Poem ⊙L Poem Film review
F **Not for an age, but for all time**	Shakespeare: A life on stage 252	Newspaper article
254 **Spot on language**	Shakespeares „Homies" reden jetzt Jugendslang 255	Mediation text
256 **Spot on vocabulary**		
257 **Topic task**	**Filming a scene from Shakespeare**	

Diff pool

258
1 **The individual and society** 258
2 **The United Kingdom** 259
3 **Regional identities** 260
4 **The US then and now** 261
5 **International relations** 262
6 **Migration and diversity** 263
7 **Faith and religion** 265
8 **Political systems** 265
9 **Globalisation** 266
10 **India** 267
11 **The media** 268
12 **The arts** 269
13 **The Englishes** 269
14 **Shakespeare** 271

Section		Text theme	Media/Type of text

Intercultural communication

Page	Section	Text theme	Media/Type of text
273	**Introduction**	Intercultural communication and intercultural competence	Informative text
274	**Asking politely**	Is 'please' enough?; Saying 'yes' and 'no'	⊙s ⊙L Dialogues
276	**Opinions and criticisms**	Saying what you think	⊙s ⊙L Dialogues
278	**Making a complaint**	Complaining politely	⊙s ⊙L Dialogues
280	**Register**	How formal do you need to be?; Formal and informal situations	⊙s ⊙L Dialogues
282	**Small talk (I)**	You actually talk to strangers?; Ice-breakers; What can you do if you don't know the person?; Keeping small talk small	⊙s ⊙L Dialogues
284	**Small talk (II)**	How to keep the conversation going; How can I end the conversation or tell when the conversation is over?	⊙s ⊙L Dialogues
286	**Negotiating**	The fine art of negotiation; Negotiation tactics; Language for negotiation	⊙s ⊙L Dialogues
288	**Watch your English!**	Bad influences and false conceptions; English as a lingua franca; Adjusting to the situation	⊙s ⊙L Dialogues

Skills

Page	Section	Content
290	**Table of contents**	
291	**Word skills**	**S1** Learning vocabulary with vocabulary sheets; **S2** Guessing new words; **S3** Working with a dictionary
293	**Text skills**	**S4** Dealing with non-fictional texts; **S5** Dealing with narrative texts; **S6** Dealing with poetry and drama; **S7** Characterisation; **S8** Narrative perspectives; **S9** Narrative techniques; **S10** Style and stylistic devices; **S11** Skimming, scanning and taking notes
304	**Writing skills**	**S12** Creative writing; **S13** Summary; **S14** Essay; **S15** Speech; **S16** Review; **S17** Newspaper article; **S18** Letter; **S19** Term paper and quoting; **S20** Paragraphs, editing and checking
318	**Listening skills**	**S21** Listening comprehension
319	**Speaking skills**	**S22** Presentation; **S23** Dialogue; **S24** Discussion and debate; **S25** Interview
324	**Mediating skills**	**S26** Mediating and translating skills
326	**Special skills**	**S27** Statistics, diagrams and maps; **S28** Working with visuals; **S29** Working with films; **S30** Making a survey; **S31** Advertising; **S32** Doing research; **S33** Peer evaluation; **S34** Dealing with exam tasks (with *Operatoren*)

Appendix

Page	Section
338	**Glossary of literary terms**
343	**Classroom methods**

1 The individual and society
Introduction

Code
6wi4eu

Extended family: Father, mother and nine children

Young father and his son slicing up vegetables in the kitchen

"There is no such thing as society. There are individual men and women, and there are families."
Margaret Thatcher (1925–2013), former British Prime Minister

"If a free society cannot help the many who are poor, it cannot save the few who are rich."
John F. Kennedy (1917–1963), former US President

Two men working in a field and two horses pulling a plough

Young men and women in business attire sitting around a table and talking to each other

1 VISUALS
  a) Describe and analyse the photos, explaining how they illustrate changes that society has undergone and discuss whether these changes have been positive or not. → **S28.1**
  b) In small groups make a list of other important social developments. Then discuss your findings with the rest of the class.
  c) Choose the quotation you like best and explain why. **Geeignete Methode:** Placemat

2 RESEARCH
  a) Make a list of the human rights a person should have to be able to live in dignity and justice.
  b) Compare your list of rights with those in the UN Declaration of Human Rights. Where there are differences, think about the reasons behind them. Share your findings with a partner.

Large rainbow flag (gay pride flag) during a parade in London

"A society grows great when old men plant trees whose shade they know they will never sit in."

Greek proverb

"I don't want to live in a world where everything that I say, everything I do, everyone I talk to, every expression of creativity or love or friendship is recorded."

Edward Snowden,
former NSA employee

"Individual commitment to a group effort – that is what makes a team work, a company work, a society work, a civilization work."

Vince Lombardi (1913–1970),
US football player and coach

Environmentalists planting trees in a park

3 EVALUATION
a) 👥 In pairs think about what a society needs to offer to make human rights flourish. The expressions in the box will help you.
b) Outline the responsibilities individuals have towards society. Do children and adults have the same responsibilities? Explain why (not). **Hinweis:** auch schriftl. HA
c) **Think:** Which two rights and responsibilities are the most important for you? **Pair:** Discuss your ideas with a partner and find a consensus. **Share:** Then do the same in class.
Zusatzmaterial WB Task 1: Collocations; **KV 1:** Make a Difference Day

⊙ L2/8 4 LISTENING
a) Listen to a radio report about a new trend in the US. Describe the set-up in the Ruggles/Dusseault household, outlining the reasons for it. Explain how builders are reacting to the change. → **S21**
b) Which of the changes outlined above could possibly be affected by this new trend?

Zusatzmaterial WB
Task 5: Speaking

USEFUL PHRASES

Talking about human rights

welfare state
legal system
social security
the disadvantaged
to provide a safety net
to protect one's citizens
to govern justly
to address inequality
to meet the needs of the old/ill/poor

Spot on facts

The make-up of society

What is social class?

Social class refers to the grouping of people in society according to their social and economic status, e.g. lower class, middle class and upper class. A person's social class is affected by their income (money earned through a job), wealth (accumulation of assets), family background, education, attitudes and hopes.

Social inequality describes the unequal opportunities and rewards available to different groups within society. It can influence different areas of people's lives, such as health, education, jobs etc.

Social mobility is the term we use when an individual, family or group moves up or down the social hierarchy.

Social class in the US

Although the US does not have any titled nobility or royalty unlike many European countries, US society is still divided into different social classes: the upper class or elite, the upper middle class, the middle class, the lower middle class and the poor. Yet upward social mobility – from 'rags to riches' – is an integral part of the American Dream. As President Obama said, "Here in America, our success should depend not on accident of birth, but the strength of our work ethic and the scope of our dreams. That's what drew our forebears here. It's how the daughter of a factory worker is CEO of America's largest automaker; how the son of a barkeeper is Speaker of the House; how the son of a single mom can be President of the greatest nation on Earth."

However, since the 1970s the gap between the rich and poor has been growing, fuelled in recent years by the economic downturn. Income inequality is growing and it has become increasingly difficult for the poor to move up into the middle class and more precarious for those who remain there. This trend is reflected in a survey by the Pew Research Center:

What class do you belong in?

%	2008	2012
Lower (NET)	25	32
Lower class	6	7
Lower middle class	19	25
Middle class	53	49
Upper (NET)	21	17
Upper middle class	19	15
Upper class	2	2
Don't know/Refused	1	1

Pew Research survey, 2014

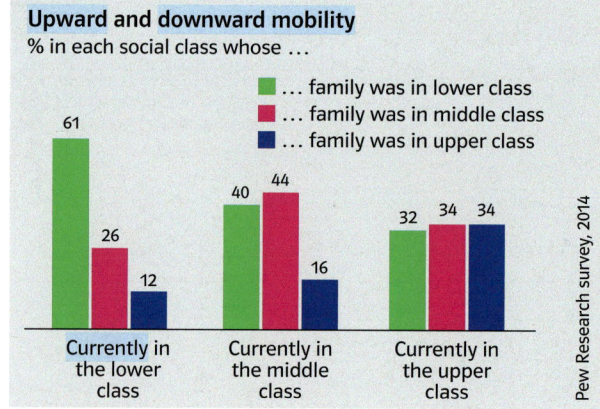

Upward and downward mobility
% in each social class whose …

- … family was in lower class
- … family was in middle class
- … family was in upper class

Currently in the lower class: 61, 26, 12
Currently in the middle class: 40, 44, 16
Currently in the upper class: 32, 34, 34

Pew Research survey, 2014

In 2014 President Obama laid out plans to reverse the "stalled" American Dream, promising "a set of concrete, practical proposals to speed up growth, strengthen the middle class, and build new ladders of opportunity into the middle class."

The generations

At present there are five main generations in the US and other Western countries, all of whom have their own likes, dislikes, values and attributes. Although researchers do not always agree on the exact dates, they are categorised as follows: the Silent Generation (born between 1927 and 1943), Baby Boomers (born between 1944 and the early 1960s), Generation X (born between the early 1960s and the early 1980s), Generation Y, also known as the Millennials, (born between the early 1980s and the the late 1990s), and Generation Z (born between the late 1990s and the present day).

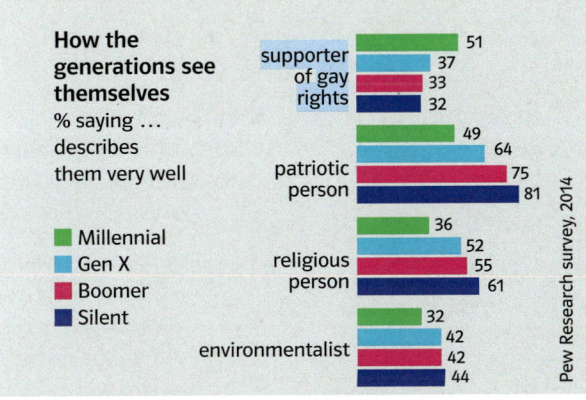

What makes your generation unique?	Millennial	Gen X	Boomer	Silent
1.	Technology use (24%)	Technology use (12%)	Work ethic (17%)	WWI/Great Depression (14%)
2.	Music/pop culture (11%)	Work ethic (11%)	Respectful (14%)	Smarter (13%)
3.	Liberal/tolerant (7%)	Conservative/trad'l (7%)	Values/morals (8%)	Honest (12%)
4.	Smarter (6%)	Smarter (6%)	"Baby Boomers" (6%)	Work ethic (10%)
5.	Clothes (5%)	Respectful (5%)	Smarter (5%)	Values/morals (10%)

The Millennials

The Millennials are characterised as being confident, self-expressive, liberal, upbeat and open to change. As a generation they are ethnically and racially more diverse than the previous generations, which explains the fact that they are racially more tolerant than previous generations. Four out of ten have at least one tattoo, although about three quarters of them say that their tattoo is hidden by clothing.

They consider themselves to be more technologically savvy than their parents. According to a survey by the Pew Research Center, three-quarters of them have a profile on a social networking site, and one in five have posted a video of themselves online. They are concerned about their privacy and have applied privacy settings to their social media profiles.

Generation Z

Generation Z is the first generation to grow up truly mobile, and they take smartphones, tablets, high-speed wireless connections for granted. For them, online and offline technologies are becoming increasingly blurred, and they are the most connected of all the generations. They are constantly multitasking, using assorted electronic devices. On the downside, their attention spans are getting shorter – which is also seen as being a greater challenge for those seeking to market products to them. Their communication is 'bite-size' and images such as emoticons play an important role.

Studies show that this generation is more realistic than the previous one, having grown up in a post 9/11 world and in the wake of the Great Recession. Yet instead of hiding behind these and other problems, they are eager to confront them. Unlike the Millennials they are more concerned about man's impact on the planet and are more socially active – slacktivism is out and volunteering is back in. At the same time, they are physically less active than their parents' generation, spending less time outside and doing sports and more in front of different screens.

1 RESEARCH In small groups choose one of the generations above and find out more about it. Then find two people who belong to that generation and interview them about their generation and its values and views. Compare what they say with your findings. Think of how best to show the information and present it to the other groups. → S22

Zusatzmaterial WB/KV
WB Task 2: Comparisons
KV 2: Creating a mind map on the concept of social class

Core skill workshop

Analysing a film

Part A Introduction to film analysis

1 BRAINSTORMING
a) Make a list of all of the different types of film genres you can think of.
b) Read the descriptions of the film genres below and identify them. Find an example of a film for each one. Discuss your findings in class.

- A film with a light-hearted plot that aims to amuse the audience
- A film that focuses on a love affair
- A film designed to create feelings of fear, alarm or panic in the audience
- A film that employs black humour to get its point across
- A film with a fast-moving plot and fight scenes, violence, car chases, etc.
- A film focusing on realistic characters and emotionally-charged events

c) Make a note of what films and narrative texts (e.g. novels, short stories) have in common. Then discuss the differences between them. → △1
Diff (help with): Vorgabe möglicher Aspekte

2 VISUALS In a film the camera acts as the narrator as it guides us through the story, defining the point of view from which we see what is going on. Different camera shots are used to create different effects. → S29.1
Hinweis: Auch als schriftliche Hausaufgabe geeignet
a) Match the pictures with the camera shot or camera angle:

close-up – extreme close-up – medium shot – long/wide shot – full shot – eye-level shot – high-angle shot – low angle shot – over-the-shoulder shot

b) Now match the type of shot with the description:

- shows the location and the context of the situation
- shows most of a person's body or part of an object but also some of the background – the most common kind of shot in films
- shows a person's face
- shows all of a person's body or a complete object
- shows a small detail that would otherwise be lost

c) What effect can be created by the five different camera angles described?

1 The individual and society

3 CREATIVE TASK *Sound plays a vital role in films. Soundtracks are made up of the following elements: music (theme music, background music), sound effects (birdsong, sirens) and voice(s). Atmosphere can also be created through silence. Discuss the sound effects you would use if you were filming the following:*

- romantic comedy – when the protagonist is about to fall into a swimming pool by accident when he meets his girlfriend's family for the first time
- thriller – when the police officer is about to turn around and stare into the criminal's face
- action film – a car chase through the streets of Manhattan

Part B Analysing a short film

4 VIEWING Watch the short film *Side Effected*. *(The annotations in the margin will help you with a few key expressions.)* Then do the tasks below.

5 COMPREHENSION
  a) Briefly outline the plot.
  b) Say which genre the film belongs to.
  c) Outline the themes and issues addressed in the film.

6 ANALYSIS
  a) Describe the setting and think why the location was chosen. Identify the key props and explain their significance.
  b) Explain what happens at the end. Say whether you find the ending convincing or not.

7 SPEAKING
  a) Make notes about the characters in a grid like the one below and then discuss the relationship between them.

  What do the following aspects tell us about Mason and his boss and the kind of people they are?

	Mason	Boss
Physical appearance (age, clothes, facial or other distinguishing features)	…	…
Voice (words and tone)	…	…
Behaviour (mannerisms, gestures)	…	…

  b) Watch the film again and at important points in the action, pause the film and discuss what the characters might be feeling. Explain how their facial expressions and their body language reflect this.
  c) Just as there are round and flat characters in narrative texts, the same can be said of characters in a film. How would you describe the characters in this film? Find evidence in the film. → **S7**
  d) Do you identify with one of the characters? Explain why (not).

side effect Nebenwirkung
peripheral vision part of your vision that occurs out of the centre of your gaze
drug trial Arzneimitteltest
rat man man testing a drug on rats
colour blindness here: not able to see differences between red and green
condition illness
appendage body part attached to the main part of the body

Mason

Boss

17

Core skill workshop

8 ANALYSIS The way the camera is used influences how the viewer sees the action and identifies with the characters. This cinematic point of view can either be objective or subjective, meaning that we see the events through the eyes of one particular character. It can also change from shot to shot. → **S29.1**

a) Watch the opening of the film. What kind of shots are used? How does the director already give hints as to the relationship between the two characters through the different shots used?

USEFUL PHRASES

Talking about camera work

to tilt up/down

to zoom in/out

There is a long shot/medium shot/(extreme) close-up of …

We see … from the front/above/behind.

We see a close-up of …

The film opens with a close-up/medium shot/long shot of …

b) As the conversation progresses, the shots rapidly change from one character to another as they speak. Identify the type of shot used and describe the effect it creates.

c) The camera focuses on the employee's face as we hear the boss continuing to talk. Why might the director do this?

d) Identify the first time we see the two characters together in one shot. In retrospect, why is this significant? Halfway through the film the director shows the two characters from the side in a shot together. What else can we see in this shot? Explain the significance.

9 ANALYSIS Lighting and sounds are also important for creating atmosphere in a film. Different audio elements are used, such as sounds, voices and music.

a) What kind of lighting does the director use in the film? Is it realistic, natural or artificial? Is it used to create a special atmosphere or effect?

b) Identify the sounds used in the short film. Why do you think further possibilties were not used? What effect is created by this?

Part C Evaluation

TIP

You can find film reviews on the internet. Note that they always refer to the actors and director by name, information that can be found in the credits at the end of the film.

10 SPEAKING Discuss how convincing you find the film as a whole – consider the actors, the camera work, the plot, the soundtrack etc.

11 CREATIVE TASK Write a short review of the film for an online website, outlining the film's strengths and weaknesses. → **S29.2** → ▲2 **Diff** (instead of): Einen
Hinweis: Auch als schriftliche Hausaufgabe geeignet   inneren Monolog schreiben

12 SPEAKING Hold a debate on the following motion:
"The film Side Effected is about society's responsibility towards the individual."

A A question of class

A new class system in the UK

People in the UK now fit into seven social classes, a major survey conducted by the BBC suggests. It says the traditional categories of working, middle and upper class are outdated, fitting 39% of people. It found a new model of seven social classes ranging from the elite at the top to a "precariat" – the poor, precarious proletariat –
5 at the bottom. More than 161,000 people took part in the Great British Class Survey, the largest study of class in the UK.
The new classes are defined as:
- **Elite** – the most privileged group in the UK, distinct from the other six classes through its wealth. This group has the highest levels of all three capitals
10 - **Established middle class** – the second wealthiest, scoring highly on all three capitals. The largest and most gregarious group, scoring second highest for cultural capital
- **Technical middle class** – a small, distinctive new class group which is prosperous but scores low for social and cultural capital. Distinguished by its social isolation
15 and cultural apathy
- **New affluent workers** – a young class group which is socially and culturally active, with middling levels of economic capital
- **Traditional working class** – scores low on all forms of capital, but is not completely deprived. Its members have reasonably high house values, explained
20 by this group having the oldest average age at 66
- **Emergent service workers** – a new, young, urban group which is relatively poor but has high social and cultural capital
- **Precariat**, or precarious proletariat – the poorest, most deprived class, scoring low for social and cultural capital

25 Professor of sociology at Manchester University, Fiona Devine, said the survey really gave a sense of class in 21st Century Britain.
   "It's what's in the middle which is really interesting and exciting, there's a much more fuzzy area between the traditional working class and traditional middle class. There's the emergent workers and the new affluent workers who are different
30 groups of people who won't necessarily see themselves as working or middle class. The survey has really allowed us to drill down and get a much more complete picture of class in modern Britain."
   The researchers say the new affluent workers and emergent service workers appear to be the children of
35 the "traditional working class", which they say has been fragmented by de-industrialisation, mass unemployment, immigration and the restructuring of urban space.

BBC website, 2013

FACT FILE

The Great British Class Survey (2011) measured people's **economic capital** (income, savings, house value); **social capital** (number and status of people a person knows) and **cultural capital** (type and extent of cultural interests and activities).

4 **precarious** uncertain
11 **gregarious** sociable
13 **prosperous** doing well financially
16 **affluent** wealthy
21 **emergent** beginning to exist or be noticed
21 **service worker** person who works with customers (sales, food service, social work etc.)
23 **deprived** lacking basic or essential things

Zusatzmaterial WB
Tasks 6–7: Listening

---

1 COMPREHENSION Sum up the new findings about class in Britain that came to light in this survey.
Hinweis: Auch als schriftliche Hausaufgabe geeignet

2 VISUALS Look at the cartoon. Identify the new social classes and say which stereotypes the cartoonist is highlighting. Discuss your ideas with a partner. → **S28.2**
Zusatzmaterial WB Task 3: Prepositions
Geeignete Methode: Speed dating

Cartoon illustrating British class distinctions

Texts

A better society?

In this extract from Divergent, *Beatrice, who grew up with her parents and brother Caleb in Abnegation, is about to select her future faction during the Choosing Ceremony. She is torn between staying in her current faction and moving to Dauntless, to whom she also feels drawn.*

My mother hugs me, and what little resolve I have left almost breaks. I clench my jaw and stare up at the ceiling, where globe lanterns hang and fill the room with blue light. She holds me for what feels like a long time, even after I let my hands fall. Before she pulls away, she turns her head and whispers in my ear, "I love you. No matter what."

I frown at her back as she walks away. She knows what I might do. She must know, or she wouldn't feel the need to say that.

Caleb grabs my hand, squeezing my palm so tightly it hurts, but I don't let go. The last time we held hands was at my uncle's funeral, as my father cried. We need each other's strength now, just as we did then.

The room slowly comes to order. I should be observing the Dauntless; I should be taking in as much information as I can, but I can only stare at the lanterns across the room. I try to lose myself in the blue glow.

Marcus stands at the podium between the Erudite and the Dauntless and clears his throat into the microphone. "Welcome," he says. "Welcome to the Choosing Ceremony. Welcome to the day we honor the democratic philosophy of our ancestors, which tells us that every man has the right to choose his own way in this world."

Or, it occurs to me, one of five predetermined ways. I squeeze Caleb's fingers as hard as he is squeezing mine.

"Our dependents are now sixteen. They stand on the precipice of adulthood, and it is now up to them to decide what kind of people they will be." Marcus's voice is solemn and gives equal weight to each word. "Decades ago our ancestors realized that it is not political ideology, religious belief, race, or nationalism that is to blame for a warring world. Rather, they determined that it was the fault of human personality – of humankind's inclination toward evil, in whatever form that is. They divided into factions that sought to eradicate those qualities they believed responsible for the world's disarray."

My eyes shift to the bowls in the center of the room. What do I believe? I do not know; I do not know; I do not know.

"Those who blamed aggression formed Amity."

The Amity exchange smiles. They are dressed comfortably, in red or yellow. Every time I see them, they seem kind, loving, free. But joining them has never been an option for me.

"Those who blamed ignorance became the Erudite."

Ruling out Erudite was the only part of my choice that was easy.

"Those who blamed duplicity created Candor."

I have never liked Candor.

"Those who blamed selfishness made Abnegation."

I blame selfishness; I do.

"And those who blamed cowardice were the Dauntless."

But I am not selfless enough. Sixteen years of trying and I am not enough.

My legs go numb, like the life has gone out of them, and I wonder how I will walk when my name is called.

"Working together, these five factions have lived in peace for many years, each contributing to a different sector of society. Abnegation has fulfilled our need for

---

VIP FILE

Veronica Roth (born 1988) is a US writer. The *Divergent* trilogy was her debut work. She sums up the action in *Divergent* as follows: "In Beatrice Prior's dystopian Chicago world, society is divided into five factions, each dedicated to the cultivation of a particular virtue – Candor (the honest), Abnegation (the selfless), Dauntless (the brave), Amity (the peaceful), and Erudite (the intelligent)".

5 **resolve** firm determination to do sth
5 **to clench one's jaw** to tightly close one's jaw *(Kiefer)* to avoid showing emotion
21 **ancestor** sb related to you who lived a long time ago
25 **precipice** very steep rock face, *here:* edge
29 **to be to blame for sth** to be held responsible for a bad situation or problem
29 **fault** responsibility for sth bad
30 **inclination** tendency or urge to act in a particular way
31 **to seek/sought/sought to do sth** to try to do sth
32 **disarray** chaotic situation
41 **duplicity** dishonest behaviour, deceitfulness
45 **cowardice** lack of courage or bravery

The individual and society   1

Still from the film *Divergent*

selfless leaders in government; Candor has provided us with trustworthy and sound leaders in law; Erudite has supplied us with intelligent teachers and researchers; Amity has given us understanding counselors and caretakers; and Dauntless provides us with protection from threats both within and without. But the reach of
55 each faction is not limited to these areas. We give one another far more than can be adequately summarized. In our factions, we find meaning, we find purpose, we find life."

I think of the motto I read in my Faction History textbook: *Faction before blood*. More than family, our factions are where we belong. Can that possibly be right?
60 Marcus adds, "Apart from them, we would not survive."

The silence that follows his words is heavier than other silences. It is heavy with our worst fear, greater even than the fear of death: to be factionless.

Marcus continues, "Therefore this day marks a happy occasion – the day on which we receive our new initiates, who will work with us toward a better society
65 and a better world."

From: Veronica Roth, *Divergent*, 2011

51 **sound** competent
53 **counselor** advisor
64 **initiate** new member

3 COMPREHENSION
 a) *Collect information about the five factions in a table. Then explain why each was created and what purpose it has in society.*
 b) *What do we learn about Beatrice in this extract? Make notes and compare your findings with those of a partner.* → **S11.2**
 Zusatzmaterial WB Task 4: Talking about characteristics
4 ANALYSIS *How does the narrative perspective influence our view of Beatrice and the Choosing Ceremony?* → **S8**   → ▲**3 Diff** (instead of): Änderung der Erzählperspektive
 Hinweis: Auch als schriftliche Hausaufgabe geeignet
5 CREATIVE TASK *In groups choose a faction and design a poster to attract people to it. Think about the personality traits you are looking for and the message you want to send. Display your posters and organise a gallery walk. Be prepared to answer questions and justify your designs.*

6 SPEAKING *What similarities and differences can you identify between our society and the one in which Beatrice lives? Discuss your ideas in class.*

Zusatzmaterial WB
Tasks 8–14: Reading and writing

B Generations apart

1 BEFORE YOU READ *Make a note of the differences between your generation and that of your grandparents.*

The young versus the old

The other day I came face to face with untrammelled youth and realised the true contempt in which society now seems to hold the elderly.

I'd just disembarked the 3.50pm train home from London's Waterloo to Dorset and was waiting to climb the steps across the tracks by the stone bridge.

The old and infirm, those with bicycles or heavy bags, take time and wait politely so as not to hold others up; we're very mannerly here in Dorset.

I made it up, and then conscious of a hip that needs replacing, I started my descent somewhat gingerly. I had only eight steps to go when a youth bounded up the stairs on my side.

Instead of dodging aside and back as the young usually do, he stopped in front of me, stared and waited for me to move out of his way. He was not aggressive; the light in his eye was not so much hostile as aflame with self-righteousness.

The problem was I am 81, he was 18, I was just in his way. He was declaring war. I was taken by surprise.

"Just you wait," I almost said, but didn't. Instead I stood aside, understanding my defeat before the words formed. I was the one to move, and he bounded on, triumphant.

It was a clash of wills; age lost and youth won, as in the end I suppose it must.

[…] I hope the young man caught his train, I really do. The old are living ten years longer than they used to, which is, of course, at the root of the trouble. There are too many of us and we won't get out of the young's way.

We postpone our retirement, block promotion, use up the benefit budget and don't look good on camera. What's the use of us?

We hold the young up at the supermarket, fumbling for coins or offering cheques, unable to use touch screens, too often grumpy and ungrateful. Our mobility scooters are a real danger on the pavements.

On the media we're portrayed as victims: helpless and abused, kept alive by the medical profession when we've mislaid our marbles, staring glassy-eyed into space.

And so a new generation gap is born. Last time it was this acute was in the Sixties, when the parental generation had to come to terms with the new sexual freedom of the young, their long hair, torn jeans and a whole raft of radical ideas.

It was a sudden shift in the zeitgeist, blown up out of nowhere. We're seeing the same again, with the Facebook generation. We don't understand them: they don't understand us.

The young live in a fast, global but self-referential, world; the old still live in a slow one which values national identity, the sanctity of marriage, the existence of God, the different roles of men and women.

No wonder that an 18-year-old wouldn't step aside. No wonder that I, an 81-year-old, did. For a moment I saw things from his point of view.

Fay Weldon, *Daily Mail*, 2013

VIP FILE

Fay Weldon (born 1931) English novelist and playwright whose works have been associated with feminism.

---

¹ **untrammelled** not restricted in thought or action
² **contempt** *Verachtung*
⁵ **infirm** weak due to age or illness
⁶ **to hold sb up** to keep sb waiting
⁶ **mannerly** polite
⁸ **gingerly** slowly and carefully
⁸ **to bound up** to run up energetically
¹² **self-righteousness** *Selbstgerechtigkeit*
¹⁸ **clash of wills** situation in which two people try to defeat each other by refusing to give up their standpoint
²² **to postpone sth** to delay sth
²² **benefit budget** *Sozialkasse*
²⁷ **abused** treated very badly
²⁸ **to mislay** (usually **lose**) **one's marbles** (*infml*) to become confused and no longer reason properly
³¹ **raft** (*infml*) large amount
³⁵ **self-referential** concerned with oneself
³⁶ **sanctity** holiness

The individual and society 1

 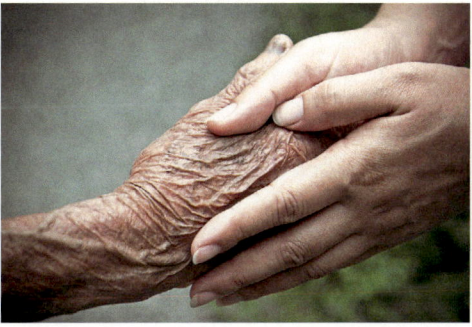 

2 **COMPREHENSION** *Sum up what the article is about in two or three sentences.*

3 **ANALYSIS** *What does Weldon mean when she says, "It was a clash of wills; age lost and youth won, as in the end I suppose it must"? Explain why you agree or disagree with her statement.* **Hinweis:** Auch als schriftliche Hausaufgabe geeignet

4 **LANGUAGE** *Examine the style and tone in which the article is written. What means does the author use to get her point across? Say whether you find it effective or not.* → **S10.1**

5 **EVALUATION** *Weldon asks, "What's the use of us?" What can the older generation offer society? What challenges does our ageing society pose? Discuss your ideas in class.*

6 **VISUALS**
   a) *The 'Campaign to End Loneliness' was set up in the UK to try to tackle loneliness amongst older people. Look at the statistics below. Does anything surprise you? In pairs, discuss why (not).*

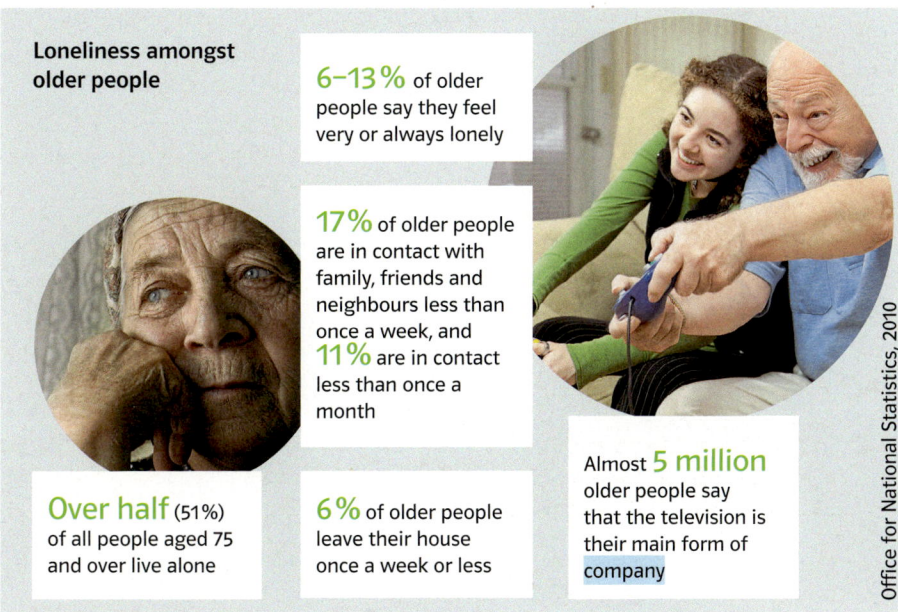

Loneliness amongst older people

6–13 % of older people say they feel very or always lonely

17 % of older people are in contact with family, friends and neighbours less than once a week, and **11 %** are in contact less than once a month

Over half (51%) of all people aged 75 and over live alone

6 % of older people leave their house once a week or less

Almost **5 million** older people say that the television is their main form of company

Office for National Statistics, 2010

   b) *What can we do as a society to try to solve this problem? And what can we do as individuals? Discuss your ideas in class.*
   Geeignete Methode: Fishbowl discussion

C Social attitudes

1 BEFORE YOU READ How do you see your generation in comparison to other ones? Which issues are important to you, and to what extent do they differ from the ones that are important to your parents or grandparents? Discuss your ideas with a partner.

A generation of individualists

Britain's youth are not just more liberal than their elders. They are also more liberal than any previous generation. [...]

A group of 17- and 18-year-olds assembled in their lunch hour at a diverse London school offers a cross-section of political views. Some are more left-wing than others; some are more apathetic. But they are not as different as they seem. When pushed to describe their politics, they agree that the state's primary role is to protect individual freedom. For them, social and moral causes such as gay rights and sex equality loom larger than things like welfare and health. Asked whether any had joined recent protests against government spending cuts, they respond with raised eyebrows, laughter and effusive denials. [...]

The young are less likely than their elders to consider themselves part of any particular religion, less likely to join a political party or a trade union and, according to the long-running British Social Attitudes survey (BSA), less likely to have a "high or very high opinion" of the armed forces. As far as they are concerned, people have a right to express themselves by what they consume and how they choose to live.

Predictably, that translates into a tolerance for social and cultural difference. Polls show that the young are more relaxed than others about drugs, sex, alcohol, euthanasia and non-traditional family structures. They dislike immigration, but not as strongly as do their elders. And they are becoming ever more liberal. The BSA has tracked attitudes for three decades. It shows that the young are now far more tolerant of homosexuality, for example, than were previous generations at the same age.

Experimenters with new technologies, fashions and ideas, young people in Britain and elsewhere have long tweaked established social institutions. But their iconoclasm goes further than this. Young Britons are classical liberals: as well as prizing social freedom, they believe in low taxes, limited welfare and personal responsibility. In America they would be called libertarians.

More than two-thirds of people born before 1939 consider the welfare state "one of Britain's proudest achievements". Less than one-third of those born after 1979 say the same. According to the BSA, members of Generation Y are not just half as likely as older people to consider it the state's responsibility to cover the costs of residential care in old age. They are also more likely to take such a hard-hearted view than were members of the famously jaded Generation X (born between 1966 and 1979) at the same stage of life.

"Every successive generation is less collectivist than the last," says Ben Page of Ipsos MORI, a pollster. All age groups are becoming more socially and economically liberal. But the young are ahead of the general trend. They have a more sceptical view of state transfers, even allowing for the general shift in attitudes (see chart).

Polling by YouGov shows that those aged 18 to 24 are also more likely than older people to consider social problems the responsibility of individuals rather than government. [...] They care about the environment, but are also keen on commerce: more supportive of the privatisation of utilities, more likely to reject

---

FACT FILE

Britain's Welfare State
In 1942 a Liberal politician, William Beveridge, proposed setting up a welfare state to provide social care "from the cradle to the grave". The idea was to ensure an acceptable minimum standard of living for everyone in Britain. It was to be financed by compulsory National Insurance contributions to be paid each week. Over the following years legislation was passed to cover: free health care, free education, council housing for those in need, social security as well as measures to support full employment. The welfare state is now in decline and many people are questioning its continued viability.

---

⁶ **to push sb** *here:* to urge or compel sb to do sth
⁸ **to loom large** to be important
¹⁰ **effusive** very enthusiastic
¹² **trade union** *Gewerkschaft*
¹⁴ **armed forces** military
²⁴ **to tweak sth** (*infml*) to make small changes to improve sth
²⁵ **iconoclasm** *Bildersturm*
²⁷ **libertarian** sb who thinks that people should be allowed to do and think what they want
³³ **jaded** bored, lacking enthusiasm
³⁶ **pollster** *Meinungsforscher*
³⁸ **shift** change
⁴² **commerce** *Handel*
⁴² **utilities** *Leistungen der öffentlichen Vorsorgungsbetriebe*
⁴² **to reject** to refuse to accept sth

government attempts to ban branding on cigarette packets and more likely to agree
45 that Tesco, Britain's supermarket giant, "has only become so large by offering customers what they want".

Why the shift? History is one explanation. Today's young people
50 grew up in a period of relatively low unemployment, after the removal of the contributory elements of the welfare system and long after the collectivist afterglow of the second world war had
55 faded.

But their attitudes also reflect the hardships they face today. The economic slowdown and government cuts have hit them harder than most. The coalition
60 has trimmed the support paid to those who stay in school between the ages of 16 and 18, raised university tuition fees and axed a temporary employment scheme for those aged 18 to 24. Although overall joblessness is lower than in most European countries, youth unemployment has increased by half since 2008: an advertisement of eight vacancies at a Nottingham coffee shop recently drew 1,700 applications.
65 Just as the construction of the post-war welfare state helps to explain the collectivist instincts of the old, today's economic adversity and dwindling welfare payments appear to be forging a generation of dogged individualists. Rosina St James, a 22-year-old student who chairs the British Youth Council, a network of 230 organisations, describes a sense that "you're running against the person next to
70 you". "People in our generation are incredibly competitive with each other," she says.

The Economist, 2013

Young people at cash point machines in London

59 **coalition** *here:* between the Conservative Party and the Liberal Democrats
60 **to trim sth** *here:* to reduce the size or cost of sth
61 **to axe** to get rid of
66 **adversity** a difficult period
66 **to dwindle** to become gradually less or smaller
67 **dogged** *hartnäckig*

Avoiding mistakes
Aussprache
18**euthanasia** [ˌjuːθəˈneɪzə]
61**scheme** [skiːm]

2 COMPREHENSION *Sum up the changes in attitude amongst young people compared to those of past generations. Describe what explanations are given for these changes in the text.*
Hinweis: Auch als schriftliche Hausaufgabe geeignet

3 ANALYSIS *Analyse the language and the style of the article, using your findings to say how sympathetic the article is towards young people.* → S10

4 EVALUATION *Imagine you have read this article online. Write a comment to post underneath it, reacting to the final statement: "People in our generation are incredibly competitive with each other." Remember to remain polite and make sure that you can justify your point of view.* **Hinweis:** Auch als schriftliche Hausaufgabe geeignet
Zusatzmaterial WB Task 16: Tenses; **KV 3:** The Nobel Peace Prize

Zusatzmaterial WB
Task 15: Mediation

FACT FILE

Margret Thatcher (1925–2013) UK Conservative Prime Minister from 1979–1990, nicknamed 'The Iron Lady' for her uncompromising politics and hard leadership style.

Children of Thatcher

The government should spend more money on welfare benefits for the poor, even if it leads to higher taxes, % agree

— Pre-war *(born before 1945)*
— Baby-boomers *(born 1945–1965)*
— Generation X *(born 1966–79)*
— Generation Y *(born after 1979)*

Ipsos MORI; British Social Attitudes Survey

Advanced texts

Richard Cory

Whenever Richard Cory went down town,
We people on the pavement looked at him:
He was a gentleman from sole to crown,
Clean favored, and imperially slim.

And he was always quietly arrayed, 5
And he was always human when he talked;
But still he fluttered pulses when he said,
"Good-morning," and he glittered when he walked.

And he was rich – yes, richer than a king –
And admirably schooled in every grace: 10
In fine, we thought that he was everything
To make us wish that we were in his place.

So on we worked, and waited for the light,
And went without the meat, and cursed the bread;
And Richard Cory, one calm summer night, 15
Went home and put a bullet through his head.

Edwin A. Robinson

4 **clean favored** clean through privilege
4 **imperially** in the manner of an emperor or king
5 **quietly arrayed** dressed in good but not ostentatious clothes
11 **in fine** in short

VIP FILE

Edwin Arlington Robinson (1869–1935) was an American poet who won three Pulitzer Prizes for his work. "Richard Cory" is one of Robinson's most popular poems and was written during the economic depression of 1893.

Hinweis
Weiterführend kann mit Adaptionen gearbeitet werden
Musik: z. B. *Richard Cory* von Simon and Garfunkel oder Them
Kurzgeschichte: z. B. *Poetic Justice* von Carolyn Mullen

5 COMPREHENSION Briefly outline what the poem is about in your own words.

6 ANALYSIS What three themes are addressed in the poem? Find quotations to back up your answer.

7 ANALYSIS
a) Explain who the "we" in the poem refers to. Describe their feelings towards Richard Cory.
b) Analyse the pattern of the poem (metre, rhyme scheme). → S6.1
c) What figures of speech does the poet use and to what effect?

8 LANGUAGE Describe Richard Cory's appearance in your own words. Some of the language used to describe him is unusual. Explain why you think the poet might have used it.

9 CREATIVE TASK On the morning after Cory's suicide, this information spreads quickly in the neighbourhood. Three people Cory always passed by in the street talk about their feelings caused by this event and speculate on Cory's motive(s). What do they say? Write this dialogue and present it to the class.
Geeignete Methode zur weiteren Analyse des Charakters Richard Cory: Hot seat

10 SPEAKING To what extent are the themes in the poem still relevant today? Discuss your ideas in class. **Geeignete Methode:** Fish bowl discussion

D How technology is changing society

1 BEFORE YOU READ What does the expression "the ultimate search tool" bring to mind?

No hiding place

In this extract from The Circle, *Mae is giving a demonstration of SoulSearch, a recently developed online search tool, to people at the company. She describes it as being "the ultimate search tool".*

"In seconds, the computer will select, at random, a fugitive from justice. I don't know who it will be. No one does. Whoever it is, though, he's been proven a menace to our global community, and our assertion is that whoever he or she is, SoulSearch will locate him or her within twenty minutes. Ready?"

Murmurs filled the room, followed by scattered applause.

"Good," Mae said. "Let's select that fugitive."

Pixel by pixel, the silhouette slowly became an actual and specific person, and when the selection was finished, a face had emerged, and Mae was shocked to find it was a woman. A hard-looking face, squinting into a police camera. Something about this woman, her small eyes and straight mouth, brought to mind the photography of Dorothea Lange – those sun-scarred faces of the Dust Bowl. But as the profile data appeared beneath this photo, Mae realized the woman was British and very much alive. She scanned the information onscreen and focused the audience on the essentials.

"Okay. This is Fiona Highbridge. Forty-four years old. Born in Manchester, England. She was convicted of triple murder in 2002. She locked her three children in a closet and went to Spain for a month. They all starved. They were all under five. She was sent to prison in England but escaped, with the help of a guard who she apparently seduced. It's been a decade since anyone's seen her, and police have all but given up on finding her. But I believe we can, now that we have the tools and the participation of the Circle."

"Good," Stenton said into Mae's ear. "Let's focus now on the UK."

"As you all know, yesterday we alerted all three billion Circle users that today we'd have a world-changing announcement. So we currently have this many people watching the live feed." Mae turned back to the screen and watched a counter tick up to 1,109,001,887. "Okay, over a billion people are watching. And now let's see how many we have in the UK." A second counter spun, and landed on 14,028,981. "All right. The information we have says that her passport was revoked years ago, so Fiona is probably still in the UK. Do you all think fourteen million Brits and a billion global participants can find Fiona Highbridge in twenty minutes?"

The audience roared, but Mae didn't, in fact, know if it would work. She wouldn't have been surprised, actually, if it didn't – or if it took thirty minutes, an hour. But then again, there was always something unexpected, something miraculous about the outcomes when the full power of the Circle's users was brought to bear. She was sure it would be done by the end of lunch.

"Okay, everyone ready? Let's bring up the clock." A giant six-digit timer appeared in the corner of the screen, indicating hours, minutes, and seconds.

"Let me show you some of the groups we have working together on this. Let's see the University of East Anglia." A feed showing many hundreds of students, in a large auditorium, appeared. They cheered. "Let's see the city of Leeds." Now a shot of a public square, full of people, bundled up in what appeared to be cold

---

VIP FILE

Dave Eggers (born 1970) is a US writer, editor and publisher. His novel *The Circle* is a dystopian novel reminiscent of George Orwell's *1984*. A young woman, Mae Holland, gets a job at the influential and powerful Circle, a tech company with over a billion users that combines elements of Google and Facebook in a sinister manner.

Avoiding mistakes
Wortschatz
¹⁹**murder** the crime of killing sb deliberately
murderer so who has killed another person

⁴ **at random** *wahllos, zufällig*
⁴ **fugitive from justice** person who has done sth illegal and is trying to avoid being caught by the authorities
⁵ **menace** threat
⁶ **assertion** claim
¹¹ **to emerge** *here:* to become visible
¹² **to squint** *schielen*
¹⁴ **Dorothea Lange** (1895–1965) US documentary photographer
¹⁴ **Dust Bowl** period of severe dust storms in parts of the US in the 1930s
²² **to seduce** *verführen*
²⁶ **to alert sb** to tell sb about a danger or a problem
³¹ **to revoke sth** to officially say that sth is no longer valid or legal
³⁷ **to bring to bear** *zum Tragen bringen*

Advanced texts

and blustery weather. "We have dozens of groups all over the country, who will be banding together, in addition to the power of the network as a whole. Everyone ready?" The Manchester crowd raised their hands and cheered, and the students of East Anglia did, too.

"Good," Mae said. "Now on your mark, get set. Go."

Mae drew her hand down, next to the photo of Fiona Highbridge, a series of columns showed the comment feed, the highest-ranked appearing at the top. The most popular thus far was from a man named Simon Hensley, from Brighton: Are we sure we want to find this hag? She looks like the Scarecrow from Wizard of Oz.

There were laughs throughout the auditorium.

"Okay. Time to get serious," Mae said.

Another column featured users' own photos, posted according to relevance. Within three minutes, there were 201 photos posted, most of them close corollaries to the face of Fiona Highbridge. On screen, votes were tallying, indicating which of the photos were most likely her. In four minutes it was down to five prime candidates. One was in Bend, Oregon. Another was in Banff, Canada. Another in Glasgow. Then something magical happened, something only possible when the full Circle was working toward a single goal: two of the photos, the crowd realized, were taken in the same town: Carmarthen, in Wales. Both looked like the same woman, and both looked exactly like Fiona Highbridge.

In another ninety seconds someone identified this woman. She was known as Fatima Hilensky, which the crowd voted was a promising indicator. Would someone trying to disappear change their name completely, or would they feel safer with the same initials, with a name like this – different enough to throw off any casual pursuers, but allowing her to use a slight variation on her old signature?

Seventy-nine watchers lived in or near Carmarthen, and three of them posted messages claiming they saw her more or less daily. This was promising enough, but then, in a comment that quickly shot to the top with hundreds of thousands of votes, a woman, Gretchen Karapcek, posting from her mobile phone, said she worked with the woman in the photo, at a commercial laundry outside Swansea. The crowd urged Gretchen to find her, there and then, and capture her by photo or video. Immediately, Gretchen turned on the video function on her phone and – though there were still millions of people investigating other leads – most viewers were convinced Gretchen had the right person. Mae, and most watchers, were riveted, watching Gretchen's camera weave through enormous, steaming machines, co-workers looking curiously at her as she passed quickly through the cavernous space and ever-closer to a woman in the distance, thin and bent, feeding a bedsheet between two massive wheels.

Mae checked the clock. Six minutes, 33 seconds. She was sure this was Fiona Highbridge. There was something in the shape of her head, something in her mannerisms, and now, as she raised her eyes and caught sight of Gretchen's camera gliding toward her, a clear recognition that something very serious was happening. It was not a look of pure surprise or bewilderment. It was the look of an

---

45 **blustery** very windy
53 **hag** (*infml*) ugly, unpleasant old woman
53 **scarecrow** *Vogelscheuche*
58 **to tally** to register (as a score)
59 **prime** *here:* top
69 **pursuer** sb who is chasing another person
74 **laundry** place where clothes are cleaned
79 **riveted** paying complete attention to sth
81 **cavernous** very large and dark
87 **bewilderment** confusion

animal caught rooting through the garbage. A feral look of guilt and recognition.

For a second, Mae held her breath, and it seemed that the woman would give
up, and would speak to the camera, admitting her crimes and acknowledging she'd
been found.

Instead, she ran.

For a long moment, the holder of the camera stood, and her camera showed
only Fiona Highbridge – for there was no doubt now that it was her – as she fled
quickly through the room and up the stairs.

"Follow her!" Mae finally yelled, and Gretchen Karapcek and her camera began
pursuit. Mae worried, momentarily, that this would be some botched effort, a
fugitive found but then quickly lost by a fumbling co-worker. The camera jostled
wildly, up the concrete stairs, through a cinderblock hallway, and finally approached
a door, the white sky visible through its small square window.

And when the door broke open, Mae saw, with great relief, that Fiona Highbridge
was trapped against a wall, surrounded by a dozen people, most of them holding
their phones to her, aiming them at her. There was no possibility of escape. Her face
was wild, at once terrified and defiant. She seemed to be looking for gaps in the
throng, some hole she could slip through. "Gotcha, kid-killer," someone in the crowd
said, and Fiona Highbridge collapsed, sliding to the ground, covering her face.

In seconds, most of the crowd's video feeds were available on the Great Room
screen, and the audience could see a mosaic of Fiona Highbridge, her cold hard
face from ten angles, all of them confirming her guilt.

"She must be kept safe," Stenton hissed into Mae's ear.

"Keep her safe," Mae pleaded with the mob. "Has someone called the police – the
constables?"

In a few seconds, sirens could be heard, and when Mae saw the two cars race
across the parking lot, she checked the time again. When the four officers reached
Fiona Highbridge and applied handcuffs to her, the clock on the Great Room screen
read 10 minutes, 26 seconds.

"I guess that's it," Mae said, and stopped the clock.

The audience exploded with cheers, and the participants who had trapped Fiona
Highbridge were congratulated worldwide in seconds.

"Let's cut the video feed," Stenton said to Mae, "in the interest of allowing her
some dignity."

Mae repeated the directive to the techs. The feeds showing Highbridge dropped
out, and the screen went black again.

"Well," Mae said to the audience. "That was actually a lot easier than even
I thought it would be. And we only needed a few of the tools now at the world's
disposal."

From: Dave Eggers, *The Circle*, 2013

88 **feral** behaving in a wild, animal-like way
97 **botched** badly planned and unsuccessful
98 **fumbling** clumsy
104 **defiant** refusing to be beaten
105 **throng** crowd
121 **dignity** *Würde*

TIP

Herd or mob mentality describes how people are influenced by their peers to adopt certain behaviours or trends without thinking.

"I'm a natural leader. I was the first one over the cliff."

2 COMPREHENSION Explain what SoulSearch is and describe how it works. → △4
   Diff (help with): Vorgabe von zwei Zusammenfassungen
3 ANALYSIS → S10 → △5 **Diff** (help with): Vorgabe möglicher Aspekte
   a) Examine the language and tone Mae uses to manipulate the audience.
   b) Find an example of irony in the text and explain the meaning behind it.
   Hinweis: Auch als schriftliche Hausaufgabe geeignet
4 VISUALS Read the tip box, then describe and interpret the cartoon. → S28.2
   Zusatzmaterial WB Task 17: Idioms and phrasal verbs
5 SPEAKING Social media has helped society by enabling individuals to find a collective voice. At the same time it has encouraged the rise of herd behaviour. Find examples for both sides and hold a mobile debate on the benefits and risks of social media for the individual. → S24.1 → ▲6
   Diff (instead of): Anstoß für eine Diskussion zum Thema soziale Medien und Menschenrechte

Advanced texts

Young woman crying in public

Young man sitting on a bench and looking at a skyline

Avoiding mistakes
Aussprache/Betonung
[28] **psychologist**
[saɪˈkɑːlədʒɪst]
[30] **psychological**
[ˌsaɪkəˈlɑːdʒɪkl]

[14] **boundary** Grenze
[16] **affluent** wealthy
[20] **to retreat into sth** to avoid an unpleasant, dangerous situation by doing sth else
[21] **distraction** Ablenkung
[28] **compassion** feeling of sympathy for sb who is in a bad situation
[31] **at the expense of sth** auf Kosten von etw
[37] **miserly** geizig
[38] **substitute** replacement
[42] **to originate** to begin
[44] **burdensome** difficult to carry out
[44] **to facilitate sth** to make sth possible
[46] **declension** here: related group
[46] **diminished** reduced in size or importance

6 BEFORE YOU READ *Describe the first photo. What would you do if you saw a stranger crying in public?* → **S28.1**

How not to be alone

A couple of weeks ago, I saw a stranger crying in public. I was in Brooklyn's Fort Greene neighborhood, waiting to meet a friend for breakfast. I arrived at the restaurant a few minutes early and was sitting on the bench outside, scrolling through my contact list. A girl, maybe 15 years old, was sitting on the bench opposite me, crying into her phone. I heard her say, "I know, I know, I know" over and over.

What did she know? Had she done something wrong? Was she being comforted? And then she said, "Mama, I know," and the tears came harder.

What was her mother telling her? Never to stay out all night again? That everybody fails? Is it possible that no one was on the other end of the call, and that the girl was merely rehearsing a difficult conversation?

"Mama, I know," she said, and hung up, placing her phone on her lap.

I was faced with a choice: I could interject myself into her life, or I could respect the boundaries between us. Intervening might make her feel worse, or be inappropriate. But then, it might ease her pain, or be helpful in some straightforward logistical way. An affluent neighborhood at the beginning of the day is not the same as a dangerous one as night is falling. And I was me, and not someone else. There was a lot of human computing to be done.

It is harder to intervene than not to, but it is vastly harder to choose to do either than to retreat into the scrolling names of one's contact list, or whatever one's favorite iDistraction happens to be. Technology celebrates connectedness, but encourages retreat. The phone didn't make me avoid the human connection, but it did make ignoring her easier in that moment, and more likely, by comfortably encouraging me to forget my choice to do so. My daily use of technological communication has been shaping me into someone more likely to forget others. The flow of water carves rock, a little bit at a time. And our personhood is carved, too, by the flow of our habits.

Psychologists who study empathy and compassion are finding that unlike our almost instantaneous responses to physical pain, it takes time for the brain to comprehend the psychological and moral dimensions of a situation. The more distracted we become, and the more emphasis we place on speed at the expense of depth, the less likely and able we are to care.

Everyone wants his parent's, or friend's, or partner's undivided attention – even if many of us, especially children, are getting used to far less. Simone Weil wrote, "Attention is the rarest and purest form of generosity." By this definition, our relationships to the world, and to one another, and to ourselves, are becoming increasingly miserly.

Most of our communication technologies began as diminished substitutes for an impossible activity. We couldn't always see one another face to face, so the telephone made it possible to keep in touch at a distance. One is not always home, so the answering machine made a kind of interaction possible without the person being near his phone. Online communication originated as a substitute for telephonic communication, which was considered, for whatever reasons, too burdensome or inconvenient. And then texting, which facilitated yet faster, and more mobile, messaging. These inventions were not created to be improvements upon face-to-face communication, but a declension of acceptable, if diminished, substitutes for it.

But then a funny thing happened: we began to prefer the diminished substitutes. It's easier to make a phone call than to schlep to see someone in person. Leaving a message on someone's machine is easier than having a phone conversation – you can say what you need to say without a response; hard news is easier to leave; it's easier to check in without becoming entangled. So we began calling when we knew no one would pick up.

Shooting off an e-mail is easier, still, because one can hide behind the absence of vocal inflection, and of course there's no chance of accidentally catching someone. And texting is even easier, as the expectation for articulateness is further reduced, and another shell is offered to hide in. Each step "forward" has made it easier, just a little, to avoid the emotional work of being present, to convey information rather than humanity.

The problem with accepting – with preferring – diminished substitutes is that over time, we, too, become diminished substitutes. People who become used to saying little become used to feeling little. […]

We often use technology to save time, but increasingly, it either takes the saved time along with it, or makes the saved time less present, intimate and rich. I worry that the closer the world gets to our fingertips, the further it gets from our hearts. It's not an either/or – being "anti-technology" is perhaps the only thing more foolish than being unquestioningly "pro-technology" – but a question of balance that our lives hang upon.

Most of the time, most people are not crying in public, but everyone is always in need of something that another person can give, be it undivided attention, a kind word or deep empathy. There is no better use of a life than to be attentive to such needs. There are as many ways to do this as there are kinds of loneliness, but all of them require attentiveness, all of them require the hard work of emotional computation and corporeal compassion. All of them require the human processing of the only animal who risks "getting it wrong" and whose dreams provide shelters and vaccines and words to crying strangers.

We live in a world made up more of story than stuff. We are creatures of memory more than reminders, of love more than likes. Being attentive to the needs of others might not be the point of life, but it is the work of life. It can be messy, and painful, and almost impossibly difficult. But it is not something we give. It is what we get in exchange for having to die.

Jonathan Safran Foer, *New York Times*, 2013

VIP FILE

Jonathan Safran Foer (born 1977) is a US writer; best known for his two novels *Everything is Illuminated* and *Extremely Loud and Incredibly Close*.

52 **entangled** involved in a difficult or complicated situation
55 **inflection** the way in which the voice goes up and down when you speak
56 **articulateness** ability to speak in a fluent and coherent manner
58 **to convey sth** to make an idea or feeling known
71 **attentive** paying close attention
74 **corporeal** (fml) relating to the physical world
76 **vaccine** *Impfung*

7 *COMPREHENSION   Hinweis: Auch als schriftliche Hausaufgabe geeignet
   a) What is the point of the anecdote at the beginning of this essay?
   b) Outline the criticism Foer levels at modern-day technology.

8 ANALYSIS   Analyse the stylistic devices Foer uses in the text and explain how effective you think they are. → S10   Zusatzmaterial WB Task 18: Stylistic devices

9 EVALUATION   Lines 64–65: "I worry that the closer the world gets to our fingertips, the further it gets from our hearts." Do you agree with what the author is saying? Write a comment on the article explaining why (not). → S14.2
   Hinweis: Auch als schriftliche Hausaufgabe oder mündliche Diskussion geeignet

10 SPEAKING   *Think – Pair – Share:* Discuss what you think society will be like in 25 years' time. To what extent do you think the role of the individual will have changed?

Spot on language

> **Hinweis**
> Selbstevaluation für Schüler über Green Line-Code

Talking about the past

1 *Complete the text, deciding whether to use the past simple or present perfect in each case.*

> Times **(change)** since I **(be)** your age! In those days we **(not have)** computers, let alone the internet or mobile phones. People **(seem)** to spend more time talking to each other and **(not sit)** looking at their phones all the time! On the other hand, I really appreciate new technology, as it **(make)** it much easier to stay in contact with people. Even though I **(not have)** the chance to visit them yet, I regularly skype with my grandchildren in New Zealand. In fact the last time I **(speak)** to them **(be)** only yesterday!

Children communicating online

Using connectives

2 a) *Read the two sentences and decide which of the connectives could be used to link them (not all of them will make sense). Then say how the meaning is changed each time.*

and • although • whereas • since • then • afterwards • meanwhile • so • firstly • but

Tris's eyes move to the bowls in the centre of the room. She feels scared.

b) *How does the placement of the connective change the meaning of the sentence?*

As Tris's eyes move to the bowls in the centre of the room, she feels scared.
Tris's eyes move to the bowls in the centre of the room, as she feels scared.

c) *If you change the placement of the connectives in your sentences from a), say whether the sentence still makes sense and how the meaning changes.*

3 a) *Sort the following connectives according to their function. Add any others that you can think of.*

Function	Connectives
giving your opinion • comparing • opposing • showing cause and effect • adding more information • giving examples • making a point • generalising • summing up • listing arguments	although • but • as • since • then • on the contrary • firstly, secondly, thirdly • finally • furthermore • in addition • similarly • in my view • I believe • as a rule • therefore • in general • in conclusion • an example of this is • for this reason • for instance • in contrast • unlike • having said this • whereas • in the same way • yet • unless • as long as • nevertheless

b) *Using the connectives above, write a paragraph outlining the effect of an ageing population on society. You could include the following ideas.* → **S20.1**

put pressure on social services • affect economic growth • people are living longer and are healthier • help for younger family members • challenges for family members due to health issues

The individual and society

Mediation

4 Your British friend and you are both interested in doing voluntary work after leaving school. You have just read an article about a project on Hallig Hooge, an island in the North Sea. Write an email to your friend describing the project and saying whether you would want to apply for it or not. → S26.1

„Work and Travel" auf Hallig Hooge: Schuften bei den Schafen

Der Motor brummt monoton, die Fähre schiebt sich durch die stockdunkle Nordsee. Es ist eiskalt an Deck, die Temperatur liegt um den Gefrierpunkt. In wenigen Minuten wird das Schiff den Anleger erreichen, der von Scheinwerfern angestrahlt wird und das Tor zur Hallig Hooge ist. Die Marschinsel ist nicht einmal sechs Quadratkilometer groß, zu Fuß ist sie in drei Stunden umrundet. Dauerhaft leben 100 Menschen hier, verteilt auf zehn Warften – jenen künstlichen Erdhügeln, die Häuser und Menschen bei Sturmflut und „Landunter" schützen.

Eine freundliche Frau mit Brille hat mich schon auf der Fähre begrüßt und mit drei weiteren Halligbewohnern sowie einem Hund bekannt gemacht, während die Mannschaft das Anlegemanöver vorbereitet. Die Dame vom Touristikbüro wird während meines „Hand gegen Koje"-Aufenthalts meine Kollegin sein. Das Ferienprojekt gibt es seit vier Jahren. Rund 250 Menschen haben bisher daran teilgenommen. Mindestens zwei Wochen müssen sie bleiben.

So lange werde auch ich auf der Hallig wohnen – und arbeiten. Meine Unterkunft ist eine Dachgeschosswohnung auf der Hanswarft. Die Idee zu dem Projekt „Hand gegen Koje" hatte Hooges Bürgermeister Matthias Piepgras. „Wir haben gemeindeeigene Wohnungen, die wir aus verschiedenen Gründen nicht dauerhaft vermieten wollen", so Piepgras. Da man diese aber auch nicht leerstehen lassen wollte, sei die Idee entstanden, ehrenamtliche Mitarbeiter darin wohnen zu lassen.

Am Morgen nach der Ankunft trete ich um 10 Uhr meinen Dienst im Touristikbüro an. „Im Sommer sind die Einsatzmöglichkeiten vielfältiger", erklärt mir Gemeindemitarbeiter Erco Jacobsen, „Rasen mähen, Bänke streichen, Zäune reparieren, Unkraut zupfen". Im Winter sei wohl eher Büroarbeit angesagt. Angesichts der Schneeflocken, die waagerecht über die Hallig stürmen, eine gute Idee.

Täglich sitze ich nun vier Stunden ehrenamtlich am Schreibtisch, mache Pressearbeit für die Gemeinde, Telefondienst, koche Kaffee. Der Rest des Tages ist für lange Spaziergänge da, bei denen man mehr Schafe als Menschen trifft, für gute Bücher und Schlaf. Das Freizeitangebot auf Hooge ist begrenzt – die Infrastruktur auch: Es gibt eine Schule mit vier Schülern, eine Kirche, einen Kaufmannsladen und einen Krankenpfleger. Wird ein Arzt benötigt, kommt der per Rettungshubschrauber oder Seenotkreuzer.

„10 bis 15 Bewerbungen gehen jeden Monat ein", sagt Erco Jacobsen über das Ferienprojekt. Drei „Hand gegen Koje"-Plätze könnten parallel vergeben werden, außerdem werde genau geschaut, womit der Bewerber das Halligleben bereichern könne. „Durch das Projekt profitieren wir von den unterschiedlichsten Fähigkeiten, wir können nur lernen von den Teilnehmern." Nicht alle Interessenten bekämen einen Platz, so der Gemeindemitarbeiter. Entscheidend seien Kapazität und Qualifikation.

Die Teilnehmer würden mehr als Kollege denn als Gast aufgenommen, erklärt Erco Jacobsen. „Es ist ein Geben und Nehmen, die Besucher können hinter die Kulissen des Halliglebens blicken." Auch Freundschaften seien schon entstanden.

Die bisherigen „Hand gegen Koje"-Teilnehmer waren zwischen 18 und 80 Jahre alt. „Bei dem 80-Jährigen fragte ich mich erst, was das soll", sagt Piepgras und schmunzelt, „aber der Mann war jahrzehntelang Bausachverständiger, und er hat uns mit einem Mängelbericht zum Schulbau sehr geholfen."

Spiegel Online, 2013

Spot on vocabulary

Describing people

1 a) *The following adjectives are used to describe a person's characteristics. These can either have a positive or negative effect on society. Sort them, thinking why you put them into each category, then discuss your groupings in class. Be prepared to justify your choices.*

> aggressive • ignorant • compassionate • empathetic • cowardly • generous • enthusiastic • contemptuous • selfless • trustworthy • honest • confident • liberal • tolerant • realistic • idealistic • apathetic • materialistic • sensitive • understanding • selfish • sensible • competitive • defiant • attentive • dogged • self-righteous

b) *Add any others that you come across or that you think are important.*

Discussing social topics

2 a) *Choose three collocations from the list below and write a definition for each one. Then exchange lists with a partner and see if you can guess their words (without referring back to the list below!).*

> welfare state • mass unemployment • spending cuts • trade union • economic slowdown • economic opportunities • work ethic • income equality • welfare benefits

b) *Match the noun 'class' and the adjective 'social' with the words on the right to form collocations.*

> social • class | system • class • status • inequality • problem • mobility • hierarchy • consciousness

c) *Complete the following sentences using the collocations from above.*

1. Our ageing society is one of the most pressing ▨ facing us today.
2. ▨ refers to people's movement up or down within society.
3. According to a recent survey, the ▨ in the UK has expanded; instead of there being three ▨ there are now seven.
4. Members of the aristocracy used to enjoy a higher ▨ than the rest of the population, but nowadays there is less ▨ and more flexibility within the ▨.
5. Immigrants to the US in the nineteenth century were hoping to leave ▨ behind them.

d) *Using a dictionary, make a list of other words that can collocate with 'social' and 'class'.* → **S3**

Writing about the generation gap

3 a) *Complete these collocations with the correct preposition.*

- to believe … a fair society
- to be concerned … a problem
- to be tolerant … others
- to blame sb … sth
- to show a lack … understanding
- to come to terms … sth
- to rebel … authority
- to be … the root of a problem
- to discriminate … older people
- to be sensitive … other people's values
- to depend … sth
- to live … a different world
- to be faced … a choice
- to see sth … sb else's point of view

b) *Use the expressions and your own ideas to write a paragraph on the generation gap.*

> **TIP**
> First work on the vocab sheets; then test yourself here!

Topic task

The individual and society · **1**

Producing a short film

In small groups you are going to produce a three-minute film. → S29.3

STEP 1 — Choosing a theme
Your theme should relate to an aspect of the Topic, e.g.:
Alone in society • The lonely man/woman • Young and old • I'm different

STEP 2 — Brainstorming ideas
Note down your first ideas: Storyline? Narrative elements? Number of characters? Setting? Location?

STEP 3 — Allocating tasks
You will need at least one scriptwriter, someone who likes drawing to do the storyboard, a director, a soundtrack designer, a camera operator and of course actors. Some of you may have more than one task. Concentrate on your own tasks, but involve the whole group in decision-making.

STEP 4 — Next steps
a) Start with the **script** for your film. Think about how many scenes you will need and write the dialogue.
b) Next prepare **storyboard** panels so you can see what each shot will look like in advance. The person drawing these can find information and help on the internet, including ready-made templates.
c) The director needs to think about the **casting**. What kind of actors do you want? Do they need special talents or have to look a certain way?
d) The **soundtrack** is more than just music. What kind of sounds will be needed? Director and soundtrack designer should work together.
e) The **shooting script** breaks the script down into shots. Each shot should be described in detail, e.g.

Shot no.	Setting/characters/ action/props	Dialogue	Camera	Lighting/ effects	Sound/ Music
1	EXT. Billy standing in front of closed school	--------	Wide shot, slowly zooming in to show a close-up of Billy's face	Overcast day, evening	Silence

STEP 5 — Shooting
Shoot the film, then edit it, cutting out anything that does not serve your purpose. Then add the soundtrack.

STEP 6 — Screening
After finishing your films, organise a screening in class. If you have time, design a poster for your film. While watching the other films, note down positive or negative points. Then vote on the following:
Best film • Best script • Best director • Best actor • Best soundtrack

TIP

Look for a website such as the Internet Movie Script Database (IMSDb) to see what professional film scripts look like.

They include information about
- the action (in italics), the setting and props, who is in the scene and what is happening,
- the dialogue (with names of characters),
- the scene number
- the location (e.g. INT = interior; EXT = exterior) and the time.

2   The United Kingdom
Introduction

Code
ny56ij

Souvenirs celebrating typical London tourist attractions

Front of Buckingham Palace with an illumination of the Queen

Girls in headscarves waving Union Jacks

"The British experiment has been the most influential partnership in history, (…) creating the most successful nation-state the world has ever seen."
Dominic Sandbrook

"For me, Britishness means the Royal Family and tradition."
David Sinclair-Benstead, 67, retired hospital chef

"I feel British rather than English. If you say English, you really segregate to the white, English people. Britain is more inclusive."
Hilda Nenohwe, 19, student

"I was once proud to be British. As a Scot I felt I was an equal part of the best country in the world. But as I grew older I understood the English did not see the UK as a partnership of equals."
"lisalane"

1 COMPREHENSION *National identity and the concept of 'Britishness' have been debated for years in the UK. Go through the quotes and make a chart.*

- positive associations with 'Britishness'
- criticism of the term 'British' or 'Britishness'
- alternatives to 'Britishness'

"We've lost our Britishness. We are now multi-faith, and the tragedy is that the people coming in don't respect our culture."

Christine Fish, 67, former nurse

"I don't like the term 'United Kingdom'. I would prefer it to be the 'countries of Britain' rather than a kingdom."

Selwyn Jones, 57, architect and bookseller

"I can envision a new 'British' akin to Scandinavian identity. British, to me, will mean the British Isles (…). Shetlanders, Scots, Manx, Irish, Welsh and English can start to celebrate our similarities without having it forced upon us."

"Mick McNemesis"

"Can you be Scottish and British? (…) Can we find a way to appreciate what is separate and unique about us and still think that what we have in common with others matters more?"

Bill Clinton, former US President

Two people holding the Union Jack and the Scottish flag (with the St. Andrew's Cross)

Two teams playing Rugby; the game was invented in the UK

Diverse police force

Union Flag protest in Belfast

Stonehenge, famous remnant of Britain's Celtic heritage

2 **VISUALS** *Choose one picture and interpret it in the context of Britishness.* → **S28**
   Geeignete Methode: Think – Pair – Share
3 **SPEAKING** *What does Germanness mean to you?*
   a) *Make a mind map as preparation for the speaking activity. Include those aspects the quotes refer to (i.e. system of government, national pride etc.) and add your own.*
   b) *Prepare a one- or two-minute statement about what Germanness means to you. Concentrate on two or three aspects from the mind map. Then listen to the other statements within your group. Share your ideas in class.*

The United Kingdom – a 'united' kingdom?

The Kingdom unites (and 'disunites'?)

England, Scotland, Wales and Ireland were originally independent countries. England came to dominate the others and over a period of several hundred years a political union was gradually formed: In 1301
5 the English King Edward I made his Welsh-born son Prince of Wales, and by 1542 Wales had been fully annexed by England. In 1604 the king of Scotland became also the king of England, the union of the two countries taking place in 1707. The 'Parliament of
10 Great Britain', however, remained in London.

In 1535 Henry III brought Ireland under English control for the first time and founded the Kingdom of Ireland. This provoked repeated unrest in the country. The union between Ireland and Great Britain came
15 into effect in 1801, creating the 'United Kingdom of Great Britain and Ireland'.

As a reaction to subsequent movements to establish home rule in Scotland, Wales and Ireland, Parliament in London set up government offices in
20 these regions to grant them more political authority. After the Irish War of Independence (1919–1921) Ireland was divided, leaving only Northern Ireland as part of the United Kingdom.

In 1998 Ireland, Scotland and Wales were granted
25 their own law-making institutions in areas of regional interest (parliaments in Edinburgh and Belfast, an assembly in Cardiff). This transfer of political powers from the centre to the regions is called devolution.

In 2014 a referendum in Scotland on independence
30 was narrowly defeated. Nevertheless, it triggered a debate on more devolved power to Scotland, Wales and Northern Ireland as well as more autonomy to the regions and the larger cities in England.

A 'disunited' England? – the North-South divide

The North-South divide in England refers to differences within the country, such as climate, landscape, mentality or wealth. People in the North are generally poorer but quite often seen as more
5 warm-hearted than southerners. Northerners are more often working-class people, whereas southerners tend to be middle-class, white-collar workers.

Where does the line between the North and the South run? Research based on statistics suggests
10 that the dividing line goes from the mouth of the river Humber in the Northeast to the Bristol Channel in the Southwest (a more or less diagonal line).

Historically, the North developed differently from the South: it was the heartland of industrialisation, with mines in Lancashire, Yorkshire and Durham 15 and heavy industry concentrated in cities such as Sheffield, Manchester, and Newcastle.

In the second half of the 20th century those industries went into decline, leaving the cities partly derelict. In recent years northern cities have undergone major redevelopment and minor 20 economic booms, but in all of them the industrial past is still clearly visible.

The gap between the rich and the poor

Traditionally, Britain has always been a class-ridden society, the rich and the poor leading very different lives (and even speaking different 'languages', i.e. accents).
   As a result of the Industrial Revolution the cities expanded with the influx of working-class people from the countryside, but slums grew too. In the Victorian age the slums were notorious for their poverty, their crime, their brutality, their lack of sanitation. Private charities or individuals felt the need to help the less privileged, which eventually led the government to set up welfare policies (e.g. benefits for the poor).
   1942 saw the beginning of the comprehensive welfare state, which aimed at security for the individual from the cradle to the grave.
   In recent decades this system has come under attack, and successive Conservative governments have introduced measures to cut back welfare and encourage more self-reliance.

Empire and Commonwealth

From the 16th century British companies set up trading posts around the world to ensure the supply of much needed goods, e.g. tea, sugar, teak, rubber etc. Often these posts came to hold political power over large areas of land and over time became colonies attracting settlers (such as North America, South Africa).
   The British government controlled the colonies with the help of governors, administrators and armies, but they often clashed with local powers. One of these clashes lead to the loss of the North American colonies, which became the United States of America. In the 18th century Britain expanded its colonial power to the southern hemisphere and with the acquisition of political power in India and Africa in the 19th century the United Kingdom became the most powerful nation on earth.
   The British Empire ruled roughly one quarter of the world's population, and its capital, London, became "the greatest city of any age or country". During the 20th century most former colonies gained independence, but the legacy of the British Empire is still alive today. English has become the world language, and the UK still has close ties with most of its former colonies through the Commonwealth, an association of 54 nations.

The United Kingdom as part of a United States of Europe?

World War II and its aftermath turned out to be a turning-point for Britain: India, the biggest and richest colony, gained independence, marking the beginning decline of the British Empire. Winston Churchill (Prime Minister during and after WW II) was haunted by the idea of a European continent in ruins; he called for a "United States of Europe", hoping to ensure peace and cooperation.
   But the UK only joined the EU in 1973, and remained sceptical about a European parliament which was perceived as threatening the sovereignty of the nation state.
   In addition, Britain adamantly refused to introduce the euro in 2002 and since then governments have repeatedly rejected membership of the eurozone.
   Criticism of the EU has continued to grow, with the foundation of an anti-European party (UKIP in 1993) and serious demands to hold a nationwide referendum on a possible exit from the EU.

---

1 COMPREHENSION *Create a timeline of British history with the information given. You may do further research and add more dates.* **Hinweis:** Auch als Hausaufgabe geeignet

2 SPEAKING → S32
   a) *Research one of these topics in detail and give a short talk.*
   b) *Research the most recent developments in the devolution process.*

Core skill workshop

> **Hinweis**
> Bei der Bearbeitung dieses Core skill workshops bietet es sich an, auch tagesaktuelle Artikel einzubeziehen bzw. verschiedene englischsprachige Zeitungen in den Unterricht mitzubringen

Analysing a newspaper article

Part A Broadsheet or tabloid?

When analysing a newspaper article, you should first identify what type of newspaper it is, broadsheet or tabloid. Compare how a story about two runaway teenagers is reported in two different papers:

Broadsheet newspaper *(Guardian)*	Tabloid newspaper *(Daily Mail)*
Headline: *Teenage runaways fly to Dominican Republic*	Headline: *Lovers, 16, flee public school at night and fly to Caribbean*
Two teenagers have disappeared from their boarding school in the middle of the night - and flown to the Caribbean together. Edward Bunyan and Indira Gainiyeva, both 16, are thought to have vanished at around 3am from Stonyhurst College in Clitheroe, Lancashire.	Two sixth-form lovers have jetted off to the Caribbean after sneaking out of their public school in the middle of the night. […] They waited until staff on night duty had gone to bed and fellow pupils were asleep in their dorms before grabbing their bags and sneaking out.
The Daily Telegraph reported that police were searching for the couple in the Caribbean and quoted a school spokesman who said the two families were "desperately concerned".	Sources said their parents were sick with worry, but were trying to resolve the drama with minimal police involvement.
Stonyhurst College, a Catholic day and boarding school, was founded in 1593, and proudly bills itself as one of Britain's leading Catholic boarding schools.	Stonyhurst College, originally founded in 1593 in France, is a Catholic school that accepts pupils from other Christian traditions. […] a lot of the pupils at Stonyhurst come from very wealthy families. […] In 2009 a girl and a boy, aged 16 and 17, were expelled after they were caught in bed together.

> **TIP**
>
> Newspaper articles in **broadsheet** or quality papers are typically written for an educated readership. They use formal language and provide comprehensive information, analysis, and critical insight into complex issues.
>
> A **tabloid** or popular newspaper is written for a mass readership, it often makes events appear sensationalist and dramatic. Complex issues are frequently simplified.

1 ANALYSIS → S4
   a) *Compare the excerpts of the two articles, looking at content and use of language.*
   b) *Examine the additional information on the school the* Daily Mail *provides and comment on it.*
   c) *Analyse how the reporter of the quality paper makes it clear where exactly the information is from and where he has relied on speculation.*
   d) *Discuss the differences between tabloid and broadsheet newspapers.*

Part B Types of newspaper article

- **News report:** A relatively short article about a recent event presenting facts only (who? what? when? where? etc.). The essential information is in the first paragraph of the article (for people who don't have much time). Less important details, figures, statements etc. are presented in the following paragraphs
- **News story/feature story:** A longer article about a recent event (for people who are interested). Unlike the news report it often provides analysis and background information and often begins with a story-like introduction about one individual to arouse interest. Feature stories are typically written in a personal or emotional style, e.g. to arouse sympathy.

The United Kingdom

- **Editorial/column:** They express views and opinions on current events. An editorial usually represents the newspaper's position, whereas a column reflects one (often well-known) journalist's opinion.
- **Letter to the editor:** Letters written by readers to give their personal opinion on newspaper articles or parts of articles. They are often written in order to criticise the paper for incorrect or one-sided information or views and typically start with 'Dear Sir/Dear Madam' (meaning the editor).

2 ANALYSIS Look at each of the following excerpts from newspapers and establish what type of article it is:

> **EU flag rules ...**
> "Regarding your front page of today, only two buildings in the UK are expected to fly the European flag for Europe Day ..."

> **Enough is enough – let's leave the EU ...**
> "Several experiences have left me disillusioned about the EU's approach to effecting change ..."

> **Romanian immigrants to be deported ...**
> "one [...] said she came to Britain to get free hospital treatment on the NHS. Daniella, dressed head-to-toe in black and holding a plastic bag full of NHS medicines and papers, said: 'I'm from Romania, I came for the hospital."

> **Drop in UK staff in Brussels ...**
> "While the UK accounts for 12.5% of the EU's total population, the number of British staff working for the European Commission has fallen ... to 4.6% in the last seven years."

3 CREATIVE TASK Experiment with the different types of articles. Use the story of the teenage runaways to write one or two paragraphs for a feature story and an editorial. → **S12.2** *Hinweis:* Auch als Hausaufgabe geeignet **Zusatzmaterial KV 1:** Checklist

Part C Structure of a newspaper article – train of thought

London riots – one year on

Jahmal was born into the ranks of Britain's [...] working poor: his mother is a personal assistant who is studying part-time for a psychology degree. Before the riots, he was a man with little hope. "Things were tough. I didn't see much of a future. All I've got going for me is music." DJing is his passion but – like
5 the majority of young black people in austerity Britain – he was out of work. "I've been trying to get a job for over two years now," he says. He applied for apprenticeships in construction and the London Underground, but was rejected.
   So what made this young man throw two bottles at the police on 8 August
10 2011, as the turmoil that erupted in Tottenham spread to nearby Hackney? Fury at perceived police harassment – a worryingly familiar tale among young black men I've spoken to – certainly played a part. "I see the police as a 'legit' gang," Jahmal says. "They bully people, they harass people. My mum's been raided three times for no reason at all. Each time they raided they found nothing." He
15 claims that his cousin was slammed against a wall and injured after a police officer objected to an unwanted stare.
   "Some police officers are alright," he says. "But some will talk to you like you're a dog." The riots, then, he says, were partly about turning the tables on despised representatives of authority. "It was to give them a taste of their own
20 medicine," he claims.

FACT FILE

London riots 2011
After the police had shot a man in Tottenham, London, in August 2011 young people all over London attacked the police, burned cars, broke into stores and stole goods such as hi-fi equipment and trendy clothes. These riots then spread to other cities in England. Britain's politicians were quick to blame these riots as 'mindless criminality'.

5 **austerity Britain** *here:* where the government is cutting back on social welfare programmes
10 **turmoil** trouble, violence
11 **harassment** misbehaviour, aggression
12 **legit** short for: legitimate
13 **to raid** *here:* to check and search
19 **to despise** to hate, to detest

Core skill workshop

23 **lethal** deadly
26 **to condemn** to criticise, to damn
33 **borough** part of a city
33 **to soar** to grow dramatically

USEFUL PHRASES

Structure of an article

the first/second/… paragraph

presents a typical example

illustrates a general problem or broad issue

provides facts and figures

analyses underlying reasons

shows the link between cause and effect

outlines possible consequences

presents sth in a chronological order

contrasts two issues or sides

Zusatzmaterial WB
Tasks 1, 2: Formal and informal language
Task 8: Listening
Task 16: Mediation

FACT FILE

Characteristics
- political, social, global issues
- reliable information
- comprehensive information
- objectivity: separating fact from opinion or speculation

USEFUL PHRASES

Talking about headlines

precise – informative – succinct – dramatic – sensational – puzzling – playful – emotional

sum up the article/ provide background information on/arouse interest/make curious/ trigger emotions

---

But Jahmal – who after spending months locked away in jail wants to rebuild his life, and who spoke on condition that his surname and picture would not be used – argues that a lethal combination lay behind the riots: a sense that young people had little future to look forward to.

"If you go through proper channels, people don't really listen to you. They brush it under the carpet." Jahmal says he cannot bring himself to condemn the disorder. "I'm not saying the riots were a good thing, but in a way they had to happen," he argues. "I can't state it enough: there has to be a lot more opportunities for kids, to keep them off the street, to keep them focused. Otherwise it's going to happen again."

Hackney showcases the divisions of one of the most unequal cities in the Western world. In the year following May 2011, long-term youth unemployment in the borough soared by a stunning 186.4 per cent. "There are some of the richest people in Britain in Hackney, and there are some of the highest levels of youth unemployment, and they're all living next to each other," […].

Owen Jones, *The Independent*, 2012

4 COMPREHENSION There are six paragraphs in this news story. Sum up each paragraph in one or two sentences.

5 ANALYSIS Explain the structure of the article – what is the logical connection between the paragraphs. Make use of the word bank.

6 CREATIVE TASK Rewrite the article into a feature story for a tabloid paper:
   a) Decide how you can make it more dramatic and emotional.
   b) Decide in which order you will present the events mentioned above and the language you will use.
   Hinweis: Auch als Hausaufgabe geeignet

Part D Characteristics of broadsheet newspapers

Broadsheet newspapers take great care to inform their readership objectively and separate fact from opinion or speculation. Re-read the article in section C and analyse some of the strategies broadsheet papers employ:

7 ANALYSIS Explain how the story of one man, Jahmal, is used in order to write about more general issues.

8 ANALYSIS → S4.2
   a) Where did the writer get his information from? Assess how reliable the informant is.
   b) At times the writer appears to be critical or sceptical about what his informant says. Find examples in the text.
   c) What is the underlying attitude towards the issues he writes about?

9 ANALYSIS Broadsheet papers aim at providing comprehensive information. Compare the information below and explain the details and nuances of the original version:
   a) Fury at police harassment (ll. 11/12)
   b) Jahmal won't condemn the riots (ll. 27/28)
   c) Youth unemployment (ll. 33/34)

10 ANALYSIS Analyse the headline – what is its function?

A The English, the Scots, the Welsh and the Irish

How British do you feel?

"I was born in Godalming. [...] I feel English rather than British. Every time someone blinks, I understand what they mean, which I don't in Scotland and Wales."
Michael Hill, 50, Hastings

5 "I'm Scottish, and when I travel abroad and people ask, "What nationality are you?", I always say, "I'm Scottish" before I'd ever say "I'm British", even though I've lived in England for more than 30 years. But when talking about the island that we live in, I always call it Britain. So our identity is a dual one."
Anne McNeill, 51, Bradford

"I would say I was Scottish first, but I don't think we should be independent. I just don't think it would work. We don't have enough money and we'd end up 10 like Ireland, skint. We've been OK so far – being proudly Scottish but also part of the UK. Scotland is different from the other countries in the UK, and we've always managed to avoid being overwhelmed by England. If it's not broke, why fix it?"
Nicola Butler, 27, Edinburgh

"I'm definitely more Welsh than British, but I'm not sure about separation. 15 That would depend on economics and whether the benefits outweighed the disadvantages. I'm a Welsh speaker and so is my wife, though we talk English to each other. She's from an English-speaking area, and when I first got to know her we spoke English. [...] I think we have a different identity to English people, and even if I move away I think I'd come back and settle down 20 here. I'd want my kids to go to a Welsh school. It's important the language continues and grows."
Gwion Thomas, 27, Caernarfon

"The school I went to was very Protestant. It had real loyalist leanings and everyone loved the monarchy. But even there we felt that Northern Ireland had a bit-part in Britain, and if they could get rid of us they'd be quite happy 25 to. We need to get past traditional points of view when it comes to loyalism and republicanism, and really do what's best economically for us as a country. And whether that's creating a unified Ireland, or remaining part of the UK, or Northern Ireland moving more towards home rule in a real, dedicated sense, should be an economic judgment. Politics shouldn't play a 30 part of it."
Scott Johnson, 23, Belfast

FACT FILE

Regional identity in Great Britain is quite strong. Scotland and Wales have their own football teams, languages, pound coins and patron saints.

[1] **Godalming** approx. 30 miles southwest of London
[7] **dual** consisting of two parts
[10] **skint** (sl) bankrupt, without money
[22] **loyalism** supporting the union with the UK
[24] **bit-part** (theatre) very small role
[26] **republicanism** supporting the idea of a unified Ireland
[28] **home rule** political authority in one's own region or territory
[29] **dedicated** here: taken seriously

Zusatzmaterial WB
Task 3: Past tenses

1 **COMPREHENSION Hinweis:** Auch als Hausaufgabe geeignet
   a) Look up which part of the UK the interviewees live in.
   b) A united kingdom or separate identities? Make a chart and sum up briefly why people feel they are part of the UK or identify with one of the four countries in it.

2 **ANALYSIS** Examine the people's attitudes towards complete independence. Can you find an overall tendency towards unity or towards separation?

3 **CREATIVE TASK** You work for a broadsheet newspaper. You are to turn four of the above statements into a feature story with the headline 'A United Kingdom?'
   → S12.2

TIP

A united kingdom	Separate identities
…	M. Hill – feels unspoken understanding only with other English people

Texts

Hinweis
Die Erstbegegnung mit dem Text als Hörverstehen gestalten

B Britain and the rest of the world

1 BEFORE YOU READ 👥 *In pairs prepare your roles and act this play.*

🔊 L3/18 **Play no. 77**

LIONEL	I do apologise. So you're actually staying here?	
JIM	Oh yep.	
LIONEL	Really? And you're paying?	
JIM	According to my credit card.	
LIONEL	If you're guests, then please disregard what I said about my shoes. I wouldn't expect you to clean them.	5
JIM	Yeah. You've got to talk to someone at the desk about that.	
LIONEL	Lovely. And which part of Africa?	
JIM	I'm sorry? I'm not catching what you're saying. Your accent.	
LIONEL	You're not from Tanganyika, are you?	10
JIM	No, we're all from Philadelphia.	
LIONEL	You see, my wife's eldest brother was posted to Tanganyika and had the most wonderful experience. Of course, we don't have colonies now. We're quite worthless.	
JIM	Not to us. You're important. You're with us.	15
LIONEL	We certainly had the discipline to run Tanganyika well.	
JIM	Well, it's all running well here.	
LIONEL	My wife's brother even had a special cane, you see. He brought it back with him. So I hope you're not one of those ones who's running the place into the ground.	20
JIM	Philly's got its problems, but we're trying our best.	
LIONEL	You hear such terrible things from over there, don't you?	
JIM	Sure, but we've got some excellent sports teams.	
LIONEL	We worked bloody hard. There was stability when we were there. My brother-in-law used to say, 'You can trust a white face.'	25
JIM	Is that an English expression? Is that English?	
LIONEL	Well, it's been a pleasure speaking with you. I wish I knew how to say goodbye in your language.	
JIM	It's just 'goodbye'.	
LIONEL	That's very good. Well said. You've learned, haven't you?	30

From: Craig Taylor, *A Million Tiny Plays About Britain*, 2012

The Ritz London

⁵ **to disregard** to ignore, to take no notice
¹² **to be posted** to be sent to (a country)
¹⁸ **cane** *here:* stick for beating natives
¹⁹ **to run sth into the ground** to mismanage
²¹ **Philly** short form for Philadelphia

Zusatzmaterial WB
Task 4: Commenting

TIP

Caricature in literature works similarly to caricature in drawing: the author reduces protagonists to a few main traits and exaggerates them.

2 COMPREHENSION *Describe the context of this 'tiny play' – who are the two protagonists, and where are they?*

3 ANALYSIS *Examine how Lionel portrays the British Empire and the men who worked for it. Analyse his attitude towards Jim.* → ▲1
Diff (after): Analyse von Jims Reaktion auf Lionels Einstellung

4 CREATIVE TASK *Imagine an American journalist has accidentally overheard the conversation. Write an article 'Black in Britain' for his column, in which you present the above conversation and give your opinion on it.* → S12.2

5 EVALUATION *Interpret this play as a caricature – what point is the playwright trying to make?* → △2 **Diff** (instead of): Einen Dialog zwischen Jim und seiner Frau über die Begegnung mit Lionel schreiben

44

C Britain and Europe

Views of three politicians: Churchill, Cook, Cameron

> **Avoiding mistakes**
> Aussprache
> ⁵ancient ['eɪnʃənt]

This noble continent, comprising on the whole the fairest and the most cultivated regions of the earth; enjoying a temperate and equable climate, is the home of all the great parent races of the western world. It is the fountain of Christian faith and Christian ethics. It is the origin of most of the culture, arts,
5 philosophy and science both of ancient and modern times.
If Europe were once united in the sharing of its common inheritance, there would be no limit to the happiness, to the prosperity and glory which its three or four hundred million people would enjoy. […] We must build a kind of United States of Europe. […]

Winston Churchill, 1946

Winston Churchill (1874–1965), British Prime Minister (1940–45, 1951–55), Nobel Prize in Literature 1953

To deny that Britain is European is to deny both our geography and our
10 history. Our culture, our security, and our prosperity, are inseparable from the continent of Europe. […] Europe is where our domestic quality of life is most directly at stake, whether the issue is environmental standards, the fight against organised crime, policy on asylum or stability on the continent. But it
15 is not simply a question of economic and political realism that ties Britain to Europe, compelling as those arguments are. Britain is also a European country in the more profound sense of sharing European assumptions about how society should be organised. […] I do not accept that to acknowledge our European identity diminishes our Britishness. Nor do I accept that membership
20 of the European Union is a threat to our national identity. […] Britain has everything to gain from being a leading partner in a strong Europe.

Robin Cook, 2001

Robin Cook (1946–2005), Labour politician, UK Foreign Secretary 1997–2001

I know that the United Kingdom is sometimes seen as an argumentative and rather strong-minded member of the family of European nations. And it's true that our geography has shaped our psychology. We have the character
25 of an island nation – independent, forthright, passionate in defence of our sovereignty. We can no more change this British sensibility than we can drain the English Channel. And because of this sensibility, we come to the European Union with a frame of mind that is more practical than emotional. For us, the European Union is a means to an end - prosperity, stability, the anchor of
30 freedom and democracy both within Europe and beyond her shores - not an end in itself. […] I don't just want a better deal for Britain. I want a better deal for Europe too. So I speak as British Prime Minister with a positive vision for the future of the European Union. A future in which Britain wants, and should want, to play a committed and active part. Some might then ask: why raise
35 fundamental questions about the future of Europe when Europe is already in the midst of a deep crisis? Why raise questions about Britain's role when support in Britain is already so thin? There are always voices saying "don't ask the difficult questions." […] If we don't address these challenges, the danger is that Europe will fail and the British people will drift towards the exit.

David Cameron, 2013

David Cameron, born in 1966, British Prime Minister since 2010

Texts

TIP

Comparing language
- length of sentences
- sentence structure (main clause, lots of subordinate clauses)
- tone of speech
- emotional language
- register (i.e. formal, casual, poetic etc.)
- use of pronouns
- rhetoric devices (e.g. contrast/antithesis, alliteration, repetition, parallelism, metaphors)
- humour

Zusatzmaterial WB
Task 5: Conditionals
Task 7: Speaking

1 COMPREHENSION *Compare what the British politicians said about Britain as part of a European Union. Complete the following table:*
Hinweis: Auch als Hausaufgabe geeignet

	Churchill	Cook	Cameron
Situation in Europe at the time	…	…	…
General ideas about a European Union	…	…	…
Britain's role in a/the European Union	…	…	…

2 ANALYSIS *Compare and contrast how the politicians use language and rhetorical devices to persuade their audiences.*

3 EVALUATION *Write a personal column of about 200 words on some of the consequences for the EU if the UK were to withdraw from the Union.*
→ **S14.2** → △3 **Diff** (instead of): Leserbrief (Letter to the editor) zum Volksentscheid über den Verbleib in der EU schreiben

○ L3/19 **4 LISTENING** *Comment on how the leader of the UK Independence Party (which calls for a complete withdrawal of the UK from the EU) characterises the European Union.*

D London and the rest of Britain

Commuters at Oxford Circus tube station

View over London

The global city

London is the British city which joined the super-league, the world capital which ranks with Paris, New York and Tokyo. It is the epicentre of Britain's political, economic and cultural life, the seat of our government, hub of our media and home to one of the world's biggest financial markets. […] in a global context, London is the exception rather than the rule. The East Coast of the US has New York – the capital of media and commerce – and Washington DC – the capital of government. Australia has Sydney, Melbourne and Canberra; Spain has Barcelona and Madrid. And Britain has … London, the sprawling, unrivalled capital whose gravitational force exerts a distorting effect on the rest of the country.

Londoners have to pay the price for the capital's status. Residents have sky-high house prices in many areas of the capital – the average house price is now over £1.25m in Kensington and Chelsea – and have high-cost travel, congestion, crime and grime.

² **epicentre** centre, middle
³ **hub** core, centre
⁸ **to sprawl** to spread out
⁸ **unrivalled** without a rival
⁸ **gravitational** *here:* like a magnet
⁹ **to distort** to deform, to damage
¹² **congestion** overcrowding, traffic jams
¹³ **grime** dirt

The United Kingdom 2

But what cost does the rest of the country pay for London? Talk to business
15 people and civic leaders around the UK and it is not hard to draw up a charge sheet
against the capital. Londoners are said to be rude and insular, and they look down
their nose at anyone from the provinces. "It's an unresolved issue," says Jude Kelly,
director of London's Southbank Centre. "Is London a rival to other cities in its own
nation, or a repository of their knowledge?"

20 Those trying to run businesses in the north of England or Scotland have to incur
serious expense to even make it to a meeting in the capital, leaving home at four in
the morning to make it to London for 9am. But the biggest charge against London
is that it sucks talent and resources out of the rest of the country. [...] Given the
concentration of power in London it's no surprise that since the 1960s successive
25 British governments have tried to move key government departments out of
London. The BBC is the latest public body to follow suit, with the relocation of key
staff and programmes to Salford Quays in Manchester.

But even devolution to Scotland, Wales and Northern Ireland has done little to
reduce London's power. The gravitational pull of the capital is hard to resist: not
30 least because many people who have made their career in London find it hard to
imagine life outside the M25. For many people in Britain's public life, London is the
only place to be.

But not so long ago the political and cultural landscape of Britain was a good
deal less uneven than today. In the Victorian era, Britain's economic landscape was
35 made up of powerful city states, with their own local governments, distinct political
cultures and vibrant economies. In the north of England, Manchester, Birmingham
and Liverpool were the workshops of the world. Further north, Glasgow described
itself as the "Second City of the Empire" and the mighty Clyde shipyards produced
vessels which sailed the seven seas.

40 But as the manufacturing bases of these other cities declined and London's
population and economy soared, London started to seem less and less like a big
British city and more and more like a global city which just happened to be based
in the south-east of England. It has amplified the faults – as well as the virtues –
of the capital. Now, as historian and politician Lord Hattersley puts it, London is
45 "hugely crowded, hugely busy and full of people who are not really interested in
each other".

The size of London's economy has led some to suggest that the capital should
go it alone, and declare independence from the rest of the country. There are plenty
in the rest of the country who might be glad to see it go.

David Stenhouse, *BBC News Magazine*, 2010

FACT FILE

London is a world capital
In terms of population, airports, universities and tourists it beats all other European cities. It is also the most expensive city in the world.

Zusatzmaterial WB
Task 6: Comparisons
Tasks 9–15: Reading and writing

15 **civic** of the community
15 **charge sheet** list of faults or problems
16 **insular** keeping to themselves
17 **unresolved** not having been solved
19 **repository** storehouse, warehouse
20 **to incur** to suffer
23 **to suck** to draw
26 **relocation** removal of people or institutions
31 **M25** motorway around Greater London
36 **vibrant** dynamic, energetic
39 **vessel** ship
41 **to soar** to boom, to increase
43 **to amplify** to increase, to boost

The Shard and Tower Bridge on the River Thames in London

---

1 **COMPREHENSION** Outline positive and negative aspects of London as mentioned in this article.

2 **ANALYSIS** Analyse the article's train of thought – why does the author arrive at the conclusion that London should declare independence?
Zusatzmaterial KV 2: Hilfestellung zur Analyseaufgabe

3 **EVALUATION** The author compares other world cities with London. Compare London with Berlin and comment on the situation in Germany. → △4
Diff (help with): Vorgabe von Aspekten

4 **VIEWING** Compare the advantages of London with those of Sheffield. Discuss with a partner where you would prefer to live, London or Sheffield.
Geeignete Methode: Speed dating

5 **CREATIVE TASK** Write a letter to the editor and comment on the idea that London should declare independence. Decide first whether you will write as a Londoner or as someone living outside of London. → S18.1
Hinweis: Auch als mündliche Diskussion geeignet (Methode: Thinking hats)

Zusatzmaterial WB Mock exam 3: British Postcolonialism – Pakistanis in England

Advanced texts

> **Hinweis**
> Die Erstbegegnung mit dem Text als Hörverstehen gestalten

E The North and the South

1 BEFORE YOU READ *Discuss typical differences between the North and the South of Germany with a partner.*

Regeneration projects at Salford Quays

Durham, England

⊙ L3/20 "Dark and true and tender is the north"

> **Avoiding mistakes**
> Aussprache/Betonung
> ⁴**inevitable** [ɪnˈevɪtəbl]

¹ **Wigan** a town near Manchester
³ **scrawl** disorderly mass
⁴ **litter** waste, rubbish
⁶ **bluster** roar, thundering
⁷ **to judder** to rattle, shake
¹⁴ **dour** harsh, gloomy
¹⁶ **scarred** damaged, injured
¹⁷ **towpath bridges** bridges along small rivers and canals lined by paths
¹⁷ **pit-shaft** tunnel into a coal-mine
¹⁷ **quarry** mine, gravel pit
¹⁸ **to burrow** to dig, to excavate
²⁰ **Tennyson** Alfred, Lord Tennyson (1809–1892); famous poet
²³ **to spruce up** to clean up, to brush up
²³ **gleam** shine, glitter

In the early summer of a decade ago, I stood on platform four of Wigan North Western station with my mother, waiting for the London train. We made a little light conversation, visited the buffet, looked out over the tracks across the scrawl of metal and litter and weeds to the opposite platform; filling time until the inevitable moment of departure. When the train finally pulled into the station, all noise and heat and bluster, my mother hugged me very, very tightly. I climbed aboard, the doors closed, the engine juddered, and as it sailed slowly towards Warrington Bank Quay, I remember looking through the carriage window and seeing her still standing there, small and wet-eyed on the platform. This was how I left the north. Slipping out quietly, with little fanfare and only a small, fierce goodbye. […] 10

Thousands of people leave the north each year. They head south in search of better job prospects, better weather – and sometimes they never return. Yet the north stays with us. […] I missed the colour of the leaves that seemed to grow a darker, dearer green than those of the south. I missed the dour beauty of a region that was once the nation's industrial heartland, the mills, the mines, the blackened 15 bricks, the canals, the way the landscape is scarred by the past – the rope-burns on the towpath bridges, the old pit-shafts, quarries, disused railways, the strange deformities of a land that has been tunnelled and burrowed and shifted and finally left to settle. I missed the voices. […] I missed its kindness. And often I thought of that line by Tennyson: "Bright and fierce and fickle is the south/ And dark and true 20 and tender is the north." […]

Ten years is a long time, and the north has changed since I left. They have spruced up our cities now, regeneration programmes have brought a gleam to Manchester and Leeds and Liverpool and Newcastle. They are shinier than I

> **Avoiding mistakes**
> **Wortschatz**
> [35]**to wonder at** to be very surprised by something
> [49]**to wonder if** to ask onself, to ask a question

25 remember them; the old mills and warehouses have been remodelled into luxury apartments, there are boutique hotels, fancy bars and restaurants, branches of Harvey Nichols and Space NK. Even Wigan has a new shopping centre these days, with a Costa Coffee and a Caffè Nero. And while I cannot quite shake a certain sadness about the fact that our former manufacturing heartland has been revived
30 through consumerism, it is a joy to see it flourish once more, to see it proud and exhilarated and glad.

But the south has changed too; or at least my opinion of it has softened. When I moved to London I had visited the city only a handful of times, and it seemed such a foreign land. It was a city that would never rest, that could never hold its tongue
35 like a northern town. I wondered at the heat and the noise and the dirt of this great city, at the sirens, and the shouts, and the babies crying long into the night. I wondered at all the people, living stacked atop of one another, flocking around tube stations and bus stops, fierce-eyed and determined as pigeons. I called my mother and told her about the stalls on the street corners that sold mangos and
40 avocados, about the smell of it all, and the hurry and the hugeness. I wondered if I would ever become one of these people.

Slowly, slowly, I began to learn its bus routes, short cuts, slang. I started to feel the ebb and flow of the city. And I hardened myself, too: I stopped looking people in the eye, I no longer struck up conversations with strangers, I began to walk
45 at a pace, head down, purposeful. […] And, little by little, I assimilated myself. Gradually, I became a southerner.

But still the north lingers in me, there in my bones and my blue-tinged skin, in my love of barm cakes and brass bands, of pies and pit-songs and pea-wet, and of the train that carries me home again, through Crewe and Warrington to Wigan; a
50 love that is dark and tender and true.

Laura Barton, *The Guardian*, 2010

[26] **boutique hotel** small hotel, designed for well-off customers
[27] **Harvey Nichols** luxury fashion store
[27] **Space NK** luxury beauty boutique
[30] **to flourish** to do well economically, to prosper
[31] **exhilarated** thrilled, happy
[37] **stacked** piled up, crowded
[37] **to flock** to gather, to assemble
[38] **fierce-eyed** looking fiercely, aggressively
[43] **ebb and flow** tide flowing back and forth
[44] **to strike (struck/ struck) up a conversation** to start talking to sb
[47] **to linger** to remain, to stay
[47] **tinged** coloured, stained
[48] **barm cake** soft bread roll with flour on top
[48] **brass band** group of musicians playing brass instruments (like trumpets)
[48] **pit-song** song sung by miners
[48] **pea-wet** liquid left behind by mushy peas (poor man's food)

2 COMPREHENSION
a) Outline the major differences between the North and the South of England as presented by the author. **Hinweis:** Auch als Hausaufgabe geeignet
b) Describe how the North has changed according to the author.

3 ANALYSIS The author writes about very personal experiences. Analyse how she manages to make her writing entertaining for a larger audience. Consider content and language. → **S10**
Zusatzmaterial KV 3: Hilfestellung zur Analyseaufgabe

4 CREATIVE TASK Imagine you have left your home region. Write a short autobiographical feature story (similar to the one above) about what you would miss. → **S12**
Zusatzmaterial WB Task 17: Rhetorical devices

5 VISUALS Interpret how the cartoonist sees the difference between northerners and southerners in the UK. Pay attention to body language. → **S28.2**

L3/21 **6 LISTENING** Outline why it is justified to talk about a revival of the North in recent years. → △**5**
Diff (help with): Geschlossene Aufgabe zum Hörverstehen

TIP

Leaving home
- Decide about the circumstances of your departure (and where you went).
- Think about what you would miss: colours/landscape/ songs and music/ mentality/buildings, shops, streets/accent or language/food/…
- Decide whether you want to write about the new place you live in.

Advanced texts

Avoiding mistakes
Wortschatz
¹**to give birth to a baby**,
to have a baby ein Baby
bekommen
NICHT: to become a baby

Prince William, his wife
Catherine and baby George

Baby George

Prince William
Catherine, Duchess of Cambridge

Prince Charles
Princess Diana †

Queen Elizabeth
Prince Philip

⁵ **to embrace** accept, welcome
⁸ **obediently** obeying dutifully
¹⁵ **to champion** to promote
¹⁷ **to desist** to cease, to stop
³³ **to exemplify** to act as an example for others
³⁵ **amorphous** without a clear shape
³⁵ **cumbersome** awkward, difficult
³⁶ **Tea Party** very right-wing political movement in the US
³⁷ **grassroots** ordinary people at the local level
³⁸ **unaccountable** irresponsible
⁴⁰ **sovereign body** supreme ruling institution
⁴³ **benign** kind
⁴³ **paternal** father-like
⁴⁴ **devotion** dedication, loyalty

F People at the top and the bottom

1 BEFORE YOU READ Have you ever wondered what life would be like if you were a member of the British Royal Family? Exchange your views with a partner.

The Royals

Kate, Duchess of Cambridge, has given birth to a prince. […] The new prince is third in line to the throne, after Prince Charles, Prince of Wales, and Prince William, Duke of Cambridge, bumping Prince Harry into fourth place. Like them, he will have no power but considerable influence. As the personification of the British state, he will be taught to embrace the virtues of good government. Like his father and 5 grandfather and great-grandfather, he will be expected to serve in uniform, most likely in the Royal Navy.

When his time comes, he will obediently read out the government's legislative program as if it were his own and sign every law put before him without demurring. Like his great-grandmother Queen Elizabeth, he will soon discover that 10 the rich life he inherits comes with a high price tag: selfless, untiring public service and a continuous invasion of his personal privacy.

It is increasingly difficult for any member of the Royal Family to have views of any kind. Once it was apolitical to promote population control and wildlife protection, as championed for years by the Duke of Edinburgh before he was told 15 to stop interfering in politics. Prince Charles, too, tried to take an interest in organic farming and architecture until he, too, was urged to desist. Everything is political today, except perhaps stamp collecting and shuffleboard.

Such a strict regime is not for everyone. Princess Diana, beloved around the world for her photogenic fashion sense, discovered too late that the job of being 20 married to the heir to the throne was not all about her. She had married into a hard-nosed business where everyone is expected to do their bit, charming the less fortunate and acting as an unpaid extra during national ceremonies.

Kate has learned the hard lessons of the glamorous mother-in-law she never knew and has democratized the monarchy by buying clothes off the peg and 25 performing the daily chore of shaking thousands of hands without complaint. She will no doubt instruct her son in the art of being the center of attention without hogging the limelight.

Is there anything we can learn from the birth of the new prince? Britain's constitutional monarchy is a system of government that few drafters of 30 constitutions would choose, but it has its advantages. […] In Britain, the Royals personify the state, making it more human, understandable and likeable. The new prince will one day be called upon to represent the whole of Britain and exemplify its eternal values. In America, the state is thought of as little more than the federal government, an anonymous, amorphous, cumbersome body that has few 35 friends even among those who believe it a force for good. The Tea Party is just the latest in a series of grassroots movements that suspect the American state for its unaccountable use of power against citizens. […]

While Britain's monarchy is no more than a front for parliament, which is the nation's sovereign body, its traditional relationship with the people informs the 40 nature of the connection between the government and the governed. The link between the British state and its citizens is one of a monarch with his or her subjects, which is a benign, paternal, responsible association that exchanges concern for devotion.

Here [in the US], the state intervenes between citizens and the guarantees of their rights expressed in the Constitution, which is far from the warm-hearted, trusting relationship that exists in Britain. On acceding the throne, Queen Elizabeth, like the monarchs before her, pledged a lifetime of service to her people. No such personal oath reassures Americans that their lives are important to the keepers of the state.

None of these constitutional niceties will be of any interest to the latest Windsor baby until, at some time in the future, he discovers what fate, or act of God if you will, has conferred on him. He will enjoy a charmed life until the day dawns he is not so much a king in waiting as a prisoner in a constitutional arrangement not of his choosing.

There are many arguments for republicanism, but perhaps the most persuasive for those expected to act out the rich tapestry of the British monarchy is that, despite their immense wealth and privilege, they have been given a life sentence they did nothing to deserve. For that the Windsor family, in its moment of happiness, should be both thanked and pitied.

Nicholas Wapshott, *Reuters Agency website*, 2013

47 **to acccede the throne** to become king or queen
48 **to pledge** to promise
49 **oath** binding promise
53 **to confer** to give
53 **the day dawns** the day begins
54 **not of his choosing** which he didn't choose
56 **republicanism** political system without a monarch
57 **tapestry** *here:* tradition
58 **life sentence** punishment for the rest of one's lifetime

2 COMPREHENSION Describe in detail what is expected from the Royals and what mistakes some of them have made in the past. → ▲6
Diff (after): Analyseaufgabe zur Darstellung der königlichen Familie
3 ANALYSIS Compare the system of government in Britain with that in the US as the author sees it.
4 LISTENING Listen to the interview and outline what 'invasion of privacy' means with respect to servants.
5 SPEAKING Read the fact file and keep in mind what you learnt from the text and the audio. Then carry out a debate on the motion 'Becoming a prince or princess in the Royal Family is not really desirable.' → S24.1
Zusatzmaterial KV 4: Role cards
6 CREATIVE TASK Read the fact file. Write a letter to the editor criticising some of Nicholas Wapshott's opinions and arguing that a monarch basically leads an easy, luxurious and carefree life. → S18.1
Hinweis: Auch als Hausaufgabe geeignet

Zusatzmaterial WB
Task 18: The passive voice

Prince Charles

FACT FILE

A typical day in the life of the Queen

Morning: The Queen reads and answers letters. After that she reads and signs official papers. Later in the morning she has meetings ('audiences') with an overseas ambassador, a newly appointed member of the army and a judge. Then she has invited about a dozen guests for an informal lunch.

Afternoon: The Queen and the Duke of Edinburgh fly by helicopter to two engagements outside London – at a school and a hospital.

Evening: The Queen receives a report on the parliamentary proceedings of the day. Later she holds a reception at Buckingham Palace for 'The Queen's Award for Industry'. Before she goes to bed she finishes reading some official papers.

Advanced texts

Welfare recipients – a speech by David Cameron

FACT FILE

David Cameron was on a tour through Kent, a properous county southeast of London with good employment opportunities, when he delivered this speech in a huge shopping centre.

3 **frail** *here:* weak
19 **Job Seeker's Allowance** welfare payments for jobless people
20 **to be entitled** to have a right
20 **Housing Benefit** welfare payment to cover the rent
26 **to take out** *here:* to get money
30 **resentment** bad feeling, bitterness
34 **complacent** overly confident and relaxed
34 **patronising** snobbish, condescending
36 **self-reliance** willingness to rely on one's own strengths and abilities
36 **industry** *here:* willingness to work hard
36 **aspiration** hope to improve one's life
37 **write-off** without worth
38 **to deliver** to realise, to make it happen

"On my first night as Prime Minister, I said we would build a more responsible society. Where we back those who work hard and do the right thing. Where we look after the elderly and frail. Where – as I put it – those who can, should; and those who can't, we will always help.

Building that society is simply not possible without radically reforming welfare. Today, almost one pound in every three spent by the Government goes on welfare. In a world of fierce competitiveness – a world where no-one is owed a living – we need to have a welfare system that the country can properly afford. The system we inherited was not only unaffordable. It also trapped people in poverty and encouraged irresponsibility. […]

Take two young women living on the same street in London. One studied hard at college for three years and found herself a full-time job – say as a receptionist – on £18,000 a year, or about £1200 take-home pay a month. She'd love to get her own place with a friend – but with high rents in her area, the petrol to get to work and all the bills, she just can't afford it. So she's living at home with her mum and dad and is saving up desperately to move out. Then there's another woman living down the street. She's only 19 years old and doesn't have a job but is already living in a house with her friends. How? Because when she left college and went down to the Job Centre to sign on for Job Seeker's Allowance, she found out that if she moved out of her parents' place, she was automatically entitled to Housing Benefit, so that's exactly what she did.

[…] What these examples show is that we have, in some ways, created a welfare gap in this country – between those living long-term in the welfare system and those outside it. Those within it grow up with a series of expectations: you can have a home of your own, the state will support you whatever decisions you make, you will always be able to take out no matter what you put in.

This has sent out some incredibly damaging signals. That it pays not to work. That you are owed something for nothing. It gave us millions of working-age people sitting at home on benefits even before the recession hit. It created a culture of entitlement. And it has led to huge resentment amongst those who pay into the system, because they feel that what they're having to work hard for, others are getting without having to put in the effort.

[…] That's what our reforms are all about. Transforming lives. Helping people walk taller. Attacking the complacent, patronising view that said all millions of working-age people were good for was receiving from the state. And saying: no – self-reliance is in everyone. Industry is in everyone. Aspiration is in everyone. No-one is a write-off. That's why getting people into jobs is central to our vision for making this country stronger and we need to keep building a system that delivers

this vision. […] it follows from this that we need to think harder about who receives
40 it. If it is a real safety net, then clearly it's principally for people who have no other means of support, or who have fallen on hard times. But there are many receiving today who do not necessarily fall into these camps.

For example, the state spends almost £2 billion a year on housing benefit for under-25s. There are currently 210,000 people aged 16-24 who are social housing
45 tenants. Some of these young people will genuinely have nowhere else to live – but many will. And this is happening when there is a growing phenomenon of young people living with their parents into their 30s because they can't afford their own place, almost 3 million between the ages of 20 and 34. So for literally millions, the passage to independence is several years living in their childhood bedroom as they
50 save up to move out – while for many others, it's a trip to the council where they can get housing benefit at 18 or 19 – even if they're not actively seeking work.

Again, I want to stress that a lot of these young people will genuinely need a roof over their head, like those leaving foster care, or those with a terrible, destructive home life and we must always be there for them. But there are many
55 who will have a parental home and somewhere to stay – they just want more independence. The point is this: the system we inherited encourages them to grab that independence, rather than earn it. Perversely, the benefits system encourages this process from one generation to the next. […]

Raising big questions on welfare, as I have today – it might not win the
60 government support. Frankly a lot of it might rub people up the wrong way. But as I've argued, the reform of welfare isn't some technocratic issue. It's about the kind of country we want to be – who we back, who we reward, what we expect of people, the kind of signals we send to the next generation. So no matter how tough it is, we are going to ask the big questions. Because governing is not a popularity
65 contest. It's about doing what is right for our country not just for today but for the long-term – and that is what we are determined to do."

David Cameron, from the UK government website, 2012

45 **tenant** someone living in a rented apartment or house
49 **passage** *here:* move
50 **council** the local governing authority of a town
53 **foster care** care for children without parents or in destructive families, provided and paid for by the community
60 **to rub sb up the wrong way** to make sb angry
61 **technocratic** *here:* something designed by technicians (without emotions)

Zusatzmaterial WB
Task 19: Reporting

7 COMPREHENSION *Explain Cameron's assertion that Britain's welfare system does not encourage self-reliance.*

8 ANALYSIS *Examine the language Cameron uses to persuade his audience.* → S10

9 EVALUATION *Prime Minister David Cameron argues that his ideas for welfare reform (i.e. cutting benefits for young people straight out of school) are 'right for our country'. Comment on this view.*
Hinweis: Auch als mündliche Diskussion geeignet, z. B. Fishbowl discussion

10 SPEAKING *A role-play:*
The two young women Cameron uses as an example meet in a pub.
The working woman: Try to convince the other woman to start working.
The jobless woman: Try to defend yourself. → △7
Diff (help with): Vorgabe von Argumenten

11 VIEWING *Watch the video and answer the following questions.*
 a) *Summarise the welfare reforms for young people.*
 b) *List the advantages and disadvantages of the reforms as mentioned in the video.*
 c) *Give your personal comment on the welfare reforms.*

12 CREATIVE TASK *Imagine you are a reporter and have heard Cameron's speech. Write one of the following articles:* → S4   **Hinweis:** Auch als Hausaufgabe geeignet
 a) *An objective summary of his central ideas for a broadsheet newspaper.*
 b) *An emotional summary of his speech for a tabloid newspaper.*
 c) *An editorial for the newsletter of the opposition (Labour Party).*

FACT FILE

Conservative Party (or Tories) centre-right political party, which traditionally favours private enterprise and tax reductions for businesses and households
Labour Party centre-left political party, which prides itself on having created the welfare state; its voters are traditionally working-class
System of government constitutional monarchy, i.e. the monarch is the head of state, the laws are made by parliament and the governing political party

Advanced texts

G City boys

Growing up in Hackney

Lucy Skilbeck talks about her teenage son, growing up in Hackney.

He's really confident to take on the world as it is. I mean, I worry about things that he refuses to worry about to do with teenagehood. You hear about all the stabbings, and I think that there is a media storm about that, but I also think there are kids who are being seriously hurt and killed. That's terrible, but I don't know that moving to the country is the solution. I don't think that middle-class families saying, 'Well, we don't want our kids growing up in these neighbourhoods so we'll take them out of here' is actually the solution to any of the kinds of social problems that need addressing. I'm not saying that I'm staying as some kind of social martyr. We love being here because it is so diverse and so interesting and it seems to be the meeting place of so many cultures: there's the mosque at the top of our street, there's the big Turkish community, just up the road is one of the largest Hasidic Jewish communities in London, and then there's the African community which is split between Muslim and Christian faiths. All those communities actually all work together peaceably and I think there's something really important about that.

The other thing that happens when you grow up in London, and maybe Hackney in particular, is that you learn how to manage social tensions and cope with them or deal with them or avoid them. There are all sorts of signals that he will pick up that I wouldn't pick up. There are all sorts of coded things that I would be oblivious to. Simple things like where people are standing in relations to other people, for instance, and not getting too close. Or like what it is to disrespect someone and who it is you mustn't disrespect. Making eye contact or not making eye contact. There's all sorts of things that he just knows. It seems innate, but obviously it's learned through many years. It think it is a real skill and it's something that children who grow up here have a particular gift for or understanding of. It's a survival mechanism, of course, but it is transferable. […]

Although everyone will tell you otherwise, there certainly is a class system, but here the class system is much more profound and deep-rooted and significant. I think accent is fundamentally attached to that, and that although regional dialects have become acceptable and in fact desirable in many ways, that London accent, with the wivs and whatevs, still connotes a lack of facility with language or something, which in itself then suggests that you're not as intellectually adept. […] So with Duncan, what I found difficult was when he started picking up those bad habits, the v instead of the th and things. Because that, to me, signalled that he wouldn't be taken seriously as he got older. And so I just made this deal with him and he's kind of stuck to it, although he still needs prompting, but much less than he used to. He can talk however he needs to with his friends, but he also has to learn to talk more correctly so that he can be taken seriously when he's older.

From: Craig Taylor, *Londoners*, 2011

FACT FILE

Hackney is an inner-city borough in London with two faces: There are large housing estates where gang violence and crime are big problems, and there are other parts that have become very trendy in recent years.

¹⁹ **to be oblivious to** not to know about, be ignorant of
²³ **innate** something a person is born with
²⁶ **transferable** *here:* useful in other situations
³¹ **wiv** London accent for with
³¹ **whatev** London accent for whatever
³² **adept** capable
³⁶ **to prompt** *here:* to remind

Zusatzmaterial WB
Task 20: Describing contrasts

---

1 COMPREHENSION List advantages and disadvantages of growing up in Hackney, London, as Lucy Skilbeck sees them.

2 EVALUATION Do you think Lucy Skilbeck is realistic or too optimistic in light of the recent developments in Hackney? Discuss.

3 CREATIVE TASK Write a news story for a tabloid newspaper: "Growing up in inner-city London". → S4   → ▲8   **Diff** (instead of): Einen Leitartikel (feature story) aus der Sicht von Duncan über seine Erfahrungen in Hackney schreiben

4 BEFORE YOU READ
a) Look at the photos and read the fact file. Then speculate: who is the 'City Boy' and what do you think happens to him? **Geeignete Methode:** Speed dating
b) If someone writes a poem about a financial district, what might it be about?

FACT FILE

The City of London is part of Greater London. It is in the centre of the city and is home to banks, financial firms and insurance companies. To distinguish it from the city as a whole, it is spelt wih a capital 'C'. London and New York are the most important financial centres worldwide.

City Boy

In a moment of love I caught a sense of money
and how they make it, and make it up. That city boy,
comfortable and sharp in a suit that fits him,
steers through the station when the city bars have closed,
5 and an evening of gin is a good anaesthetic
when he trips and smacks the concrete. He'll get home,
he'll recover in the faith that the concrete
is his dream of money: work and lust
made into metal and paper, made into numbers
10 that whisper to each other, transact and multiply.
Even after closing time, spreadsheets
are building up office blocks, and credit
that creates the pavement to land on.
I saw the drunken city exercise discretion, and
15 the sober city dream of how to keep it happening.
I watched the city boy get up and walk. I felt how this money
is part of us, and keeps ourselves within it. Some of it
has to be love, what we hope and where we're tender.
All we have is trust for it to care for us, curse us
20 and keep us in harness, to work for something in a city
made out of buildings and people standing up, or falling down.

From: Peter Daniels, *Counting Eggs*, 2012

⁴ **to steer** *here:* to try to walk straight
⁵ **anaesthetic** drug that kills pain
⁶ **to smack** to fall hard on sth
⁶ **concrete** 1. street, pavement; 2. opposite of abstract
¹⁰ **to transact** to do business, to deal
¹¹ **spreadsheet** chart used in bookkeeping to show profit and loss
¹⁴ **to exercise discretion** to remain quiet about sth
²⁰ **harness** gear put on horses to make them obey

5 COMPREHENSION → S6 Zusatzmaterial KV 5: Working with a poem
a) Sum up what happens to the 'City boy' one evening.
b) Explain the relationship between 'work and lust' or money and love as the speaker sees it.
c) Explain the significance, according to the speaker, of money for the City of London.
d) Discuss the significance of the last phrase in the poem: "in a city made out of buildings and people standing up, or falling down."

6 SPEAKING "Money makes the world go round." – In groups of four discuss to what extent you agree with this proverb.

7 CREATIVE TASK Choose one of the following:
a) Do some research and write a feature story: "A day in the life of a London banker." Decide on the sort of newspaper you are writing for.
b) During the financial crisis (as of 2008) banks and bankers came under attack. Write a column: "We – the 99% – don't want to save bankrupt banks."
Geeignete Methode zur Präsentation und Auswertung: Gallery walk

FACT FILE

The 99%
During the financial crisis protesters used the slogan: "We are the 99%." The phrase refers to the ordinary people whose taxes saved banks which had engaged in risky financial transactions for rich clients (i.e. the 1%).

Spot on language

> **Hinweis**
> Selbstevaluation für Schüler
> über Green Line-Code

The language of newspapers

1 *In newspaper articles journalists frequently report what other people said – but do you remember how to use reported speech correctly? Check yourself and rewrite the sentences below in reported speech using an introductory verb in the past tense (i.e. Jahmal said …). Refer to a grammar book if you think you have forgotten the rules.*

1. **JAHMAL** I have been trying to get a job for over two years.
2. **A BLACK YOUTH** If you go through proper channels, people don't really listen to you.
3. **A PARENT** Even university graduates might not get a job in the end.
4. **A YOUTH WORKER** There must be more opportunities for kids.
5. **A SCHOOL LEAVER** I want to get a job abroad so I won't be staying in the UK when I leave uni.
6. **OPPOSITION SPOKESWOMAN** We'll be asking a question on this in Parliament the day after tomorrow.
7. **A TEACHER** Don't give up and try to work that little bit harder.

2 *If as a writer you don't want to name your source or if the witness or informant is unimportant, you can use a passive construction with the infinitive perfect. Look at the example:*

subject (who? What?)	passive + verb of saying or thinking	infinitive perfect (*to have* + past participle)	rest of sentence
Two teenagers	are thought	to have disappeared	at around 3 a.m. from their school.

Starting with "They are …" change the following sentences into passive constructions, using some of the following words:

believe • consider • estimate • expect • presume • report • rumour • say • suppose • think

1. **A FELLOW STUDENT** I think I saw them book their tickets online during study session.
2. **ANOTHER FELLOW STUDENT** Well, it seems that they were fed up with the awful weather here.
3. **GROUND STAFF AT THE AIRPORT** I am quite certain that I saw one young couple boarding the early morning flight to the Dominican Republic.
4. **RECEPTIONIST** It has been so busy lately, I don't remember exactly what happened. It could have been them. They seemed very excited when they checked into their suite on the top floor.
5. **WAITER AT RESTAURANT** I recognise them! They had a romantic dinner here by the beach.
6. **MEMBER OF STAFF** Obviously they decided they wanted to continue their schooling elsewhere.

3 *In order to appear objective it may be important to make use of adverbs or adverbial expressions to express finer shades of meaning. Rewrite the text below using expressions from the following list. Your goal is to tone down the expressions connoting a strong argument or a very important point.*

a bit • comparatively • gradually • partially • relatively • sensibly • somehow • somewhat • to a certain degree • to some extent • understandably

London is incredibly huge and houses or apartments in the city are terribly expensive. The city needs to radically reform its public transport system. The congestion, the noise, the crime – Londoners have to pay an awfully high price for living in the capital. Some economists are extremely concerned for the prosperity of other parts of Britain. In a fiercely competitive global economy British politicians cannot neglect the provinces.

4 Participle constructions are very common in German newspapers and a typical feature of formal language. In English, however, these constructions are quite different, since article and noun cannot be separated by a participle construction. Compare:

Nach einem	im vergangenen Jahr	vorgestellten	Bericht	der britischen Regierung …
According to a	report	presented	by the government	a year ago …

Translate the following sentences into English using participle constructions:

1. Eine im Mai veröffentlichte Studie der Universität von Leeds …
2. Der vor einem Jahr inhaftierte Hauptverdächtige …
3. Ein durch Gewalt und Kriminalität geprägter Stadtteil im Osten Londons …
4. … eine von der Opposition heftig kritisierte Maßnahme.

Mediation

5 Your class has an email project with a British school on 'Britishness – Germanness'. One question that your British partner asked was whether Germans would like to have a king or queen too. You decide to do some research and come across the following article. Referring to the content of the article, write an email answering your British partner's question and adding your personal opinion at the end. → S26.1

Warum wir Deutschen die Royals so lieben

[…] Die Royals erfüllen gleich mehrere deutsche Sehnsüchte auf einmal. […]
Die Sehnsucht nach kultureller Einheit: Die Royals – und vor allem die Queen – bilden den kulturellen Mittelpunkt Englands. „Man erlebt auf diese Weise eine tief befriedigende Zugehörigkeit, eine intensive Verbundenheit mit den anderen Menschen", erklärt der Berliner Kultursoziologe Frithjof Hager. Darum beneiden wir die Engländer, denn in Deutschland gibt's was Vergleichbares höchstens auf lokalem Niveau. Die Queen der Kölner ist zum Beispiel der Dom.
Die Sehnsucht nach Märchen: Als Deutsche wachsen wir mit Grimms Märchen auf. Froschkönig, Dornröschen und der schöne Königssohn. Das findet seine logische Fortsetzung bei Rosamunde Pilcher und im britischen Königshaus. Ja, natürlich, wir ahnen, dass das Inselvolk nicht nur aus Lordships und Butlern besteht. Wir könnten es besser wissen. Aber wir wollen es nicht.
Die Sehnsucht nach Stil: Wir machen zwar Witze darüber, aber insgeheim bewundern wir Deutschen die englische Aristokratie für ihren Stil und ihre wie selbstverständlich genossenen Vorrechte. Diese ganzen manierierten Sprach- und Verhaltenscodes, dieses unnachahmliche Originalgeschnösel der Upper Class, die in Eton antrainierte Selbstdisziplin – damit verglichen ist Deutschlands feine Gesellschaft ein Haufen auftrumpfender Neureicher.
Die Sehnsucht nach Pomp: […] Wir Deutschen lieben die Engländer für ihren ungebrochenen Patriotismus und den damit einhergehenden „Pomp and Circumstance". Keine andere Nation kann Staatsbegräbnisse so schön inszenieren. Und eine „Royal Wedding" ist natürlich noch besser. Eine Prinzenhochzeit mit Kutschen, berittenen Soldaten und ausstaffierten Gästen mit Federhüten, Uniformen und Schottenröcken kommt der tief in der deutschen Seele verankerten Leidenschaft für Rituale sehr entgegen. Was können wir dagegen aufbieten? Rosenmontagszug und Oktoberfest.
Die Sehnsucht nach der Romanze: Kate Middleton will es vermutlich noch nicht wahrhaben, aber die britische Monarchie ist im Grunde ein Big-Brother-Haus, aus dem man nie wieder rauskommt. Man steht unter ständiger Medienbeobachtung, und das ist der zwischenmenschlichen Beziehung nicht unbedingt förderlich. Bekanntermaßen ist da so einiges in die Brüche gegangen. Dennoch hoffen wir alle, dass William und Kate für immer zusammenbleiben, so wie wir das damals auch bei Charles und Diana gehofft haben. […] Wir Deutschen sind eben hoffnungslose Romantiker.

Christoph Driessen, *Mitteldeutsche Zeitung*, 2011

Spot on vocabulary

Writing a newspaper article

1 *Use synonyms from the word-field 'say' to summarise what somebody else wrote or said.*
Note: There is rarely only one solution.

to state • to declare • to claim • to argue • to observe • to assert • to admit • to emphasise • to stress • to point out • to mention • to specify • to hint (at) • to bring up (i.e. issues) • to complain • to regret • to maintain

1. Most of the people interviewed ▮ that they identified with their region. Some of them ▮ that they were still for a 'United Kingdom'.
2. In his speech Prime Minister David Cameron ▮ that he wanted to do the right thing for Britain. He ▮ that Britain would continue to play an active part in Europe.
3. One rioter ▮ that there might be more violence in the future. He ▮ that he had been unable to find a job.
4. Londoners ▮ that their city was the only good place to live in Britain. They ▮ that the benefits outweighed the disadvantages.

2 *Rewrite the following sentences by using the verbs below.*

to come under attack • to decline • to deny doing sth/having done sth • to disregard • to reject

1. The black teenager was accused of having thrown stones at the police, but said he was innocent.
2. A Welshman said: "The government in London doesn't care about our interests in Wales."
3. At first, the BBC didn't like the idea of moving departments out of London.
4. One Scottish lady said she was against the move for independence.
5. In recent years there has been a lot of criticism of the European Union in Britain.

3 a) *Study the vocab sheet 'Spot on facts' and complete the text with the appropriate words or expressions.*

Britain ▮ major changes after the Empire went into ▮ . Due to its close ▮ with its former colonies, it introduced ▮ to attract immigrants. They were ▮ the same rights as Britons, including ▮ and other social ▮ . This, however, ▮ resistance and ▮ heated debates among politicians. The ▮ of immigrants was ▮ as very negative by parts of British society.

b) *Use the following expressions to describe the political situation in the various parts of the United Kingdom, i.e. England, Scotland, Wales and Northern Ireland.*

assembly • capital • devolution • divide • home rule • seat of government • referendum • sovereignty

4 *Study the vocab sheets again and correct the eight mistakes in the following sentences.*

The Prime Minister said that he was comitted to the EU and that European history and British history were inseperable. He was also concerned because he felt prosperity was on stake for all of Europe. The European Union for him was a mean to an end, not an end for itself. In his opinion the British had always had an independent frame of thought, so it was no wonder that the majority drifted to exit.

> **TIP**
> First work on the vocab sheets; then test yourself here!

Topic task

The United Kingdom

Creating a class newspaper

As part of the writing assignments in this chapter, you have already written a number of newspaper articles. In groups choose the best ones, write new ones and as a class create your own newspaper.

STEP 1 Finding a title

Decide on the type of newspaper you want to produce (tabloid, broadsheet). Then brainstorm a title for your newspaper. In class, everybody writes down their suggestion(s) on separate slips of paper, which are then pinned on the board or laid out for everyone to read. Then every student can award two points for the best title and one point for the second best. The title with the highest number of points wins. → **S17**

STEP 2 Forming expert groups

Decide which newspaper section you would like to focus on and form groups of four to five students:
- front page
- culture
- society and lifestyle
- politics
- UK news
- comment

Each group will write and edit articles and create one page for your newspaper (i.e. layout, photos, headlines etc.)

STEP 3 Editorial meeting 1 (within your groups)

- Each group decides on a chief editor (who is in charge of the meeting).
- Choose a designer, who will do the page layout for the group. Discuss and decide on basic features (font, columns etc.).
- As a group brainstorm topics you would like to write articles on. Discuss which texts (from the writing assignments) you might want to use and how many new articles you will need.
- Decide which group member(s) will write which article.

STEP 4 Layout 1

Write your article at home and with the help of standard word processing programmes like Word, make your texts look really professional. Add photos where appropriate. Proofread it and check for mistakes. → **S20**

STEP 5 Editorial meeting 2 (within your groups)

- Each group member reads each article and correct mistakes in it.
- As a group, discuss whether the various articles need to be changed/revised/shortened; try to be specific.
- Discuss the headlines; if you are not happy with them, come up with alternatives.
- Choose the best photos.

STEP 6 Layout 2

Your designer will put together all the articles and the photos to create your newspaper page. Within your group discuss the final layout and make the necessary changes.
Your teacher will put all the pages together – and there's your newspaper.

3 Regional identities
Introduction

Code
ts2m7y

"I believe that one can never leave home. I believe that one carries the shadows, the dreams, the fears and the dragons of home under one's skin, at the extreme corners of one's eyes and possibly in the gristle of the earlobe."
Maya Angelou (1928–2014),
African American writer and civil rights activist

"Home is where my habits have a habitat."
Fiona Apple (born 1977),
American singer-songwriter and pianist

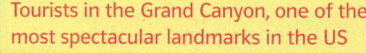
Tourists in the Grand Canyon, one of the most spectacular landmarks in the US

This is how the majority of Scots described themselves according to the last census

Oxford Circus Station; more than 40,000 pedestrians have been counted passing through the junction at the busiest times

1. **SPEAKING** Look at the pictures and quotations. Which factors define a region and its people? **Geeignete Methode:** Think – Pair – Share

2. **SPEAKING** Explain what is typical of the region you were born and/or live in. To what extent do you identify with this region?

3. **CREATIVE TASK**
   a) Examine how the US license plates present their regions. → S28.1
   b) Discuss what a license plate for your region could look like, design it and prepare a short 'promotion talk' for your plate.
   Geeignete Methode zur Präsentation und Auswertung: Gallery walk

Spot on **facts**

Regional identities 3

Regionalism in the UK and the US

Factors defining regional identity

A region can generally be defined as an area of land, but not always with exact limits or borders. It might be part of a country or include more than one. A region's identity is often shaped by its landscape – famous examples are the Peak District in England, the Scottish Highlands and the Great Plains in the US and Canada. Regional boundaries might also be drawn along historical or political lines. The American South, for example, mainly consists of the former Confederate states, which wanted to separate from the Union during the Civil War.

Language and its varieties can also define a region and bond people together. Frequently, the residents of a region speak a specific accent or dialect. Thus, varieties of Northern English differ in pronunciation, vocabulary and grammar from Standard English. Residents in some regions even speak their own language. Protecting these languages often means preserving a region's and its people's identity, as with the Celtic languages of the so-called Celtic Fringe: Wales (Welsh), Scotland, Northern Ireland and the Republic of Ireland (Scottish and Irish Gaelic), Cornwall (Cornish), the Isle of Man (Manx), and Brittany in the northwest of France (Breton).

Further defining factors can be an area's traditions, customs, cuisine, religion or economy.

Regional identities in the UK and the US

Almost 13 per cent of the British live in the area of Greater London, making it Britain's political, financial, cultural and economic centre. However, people living elsewhere show loyalty to the distinctive character of their local regions, defined by landscape, typical occupations, wealth and language differences, giving good reasons for increasing devolution (see Topic United Kingdom). England's South, with its mild climate, picturesque towns, fertile fields and seaside resorts, has always attracted tourists. The North has been marked by heavy coal mining, textile and shipbuilding industries and a harsher climate.

1 Greater London
2 South
3 East Anglia
4 Midlands
5 Wales
6 North
7 Lowland Scotland
8 Highland Scotland
9 Northern Ireland

The US is a federal union of 50 states including Alaska and Hawaii. Since the founding of the country, power has gradually shifted away from states towards the government in Washington DC, though state governments still decide on issues such as education, land and property laws.

Climate, geography and history have shaped people's attitudes. The rather densely populated states of the East Coast, the Great Lakes and California are considered progressive and vote mostly Democrat (the so-called blue states), the rural American South as well as the Midwest can be characterised as conservative and tend to vote Republican (the red states). However, Hispanic immigration has begun to change this balance in the south.

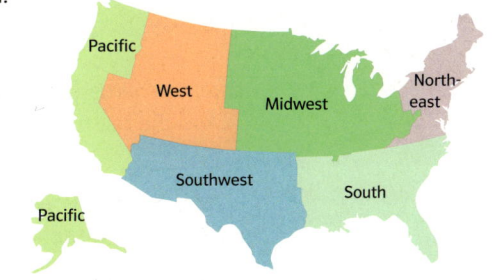

1 COMPREHENSION Read the texts, then close the book and explain the following terms: regional identity – Celtic fringe – England's North and South – blue/red states.

2 SPEAKING Look at the maps of the UK and the US. What do you associate with the different regions they show? Have you ever been to any of them? **Hinweis:** Auch als schriftliche Hausaufgabe geeignet

Zusatzmaterial WB
Task 1: Talking about regional identities

Texts

A Identities in the UK – tradition and change

1 BEFORE YOU READ Compare the two photos of Newcastle from the 1960s and today. What do they tell us about this northeastern English town? → **S28.1**
Geeignete Methode: Think – Pair – Share

Big tanker being built in a shipyard very close to a residential neighbourhood

Riverbank with old and new bridges and very modern buildings

Shipyard ⊙ L3/3

Ah, me name is Jackie White and I'm foreman of the yard,
And ye don't mess with Jackie on this quayside.
Why I'm as hard as iron plate, woe betide ye if yr late,
When we have to push the boat out on a spring tide.
5 Now ye could die and hope for Heaven, but ye'd need to work your shift,
And I'd expect ye's all to back us to the hilt.
And if St. Peter at his gate were to ask ye why yr late,
Why you'd tell him that ye had to get a ship built.
We built battleships and cruisers for Her Majesty the Queen,
10 Super tankers for Onassis, and all the classes in between,
We built the greatest shipping tonnage that the world has ever seen,
And the only life we've known is in the shipyard.

All the platers and the welders, and the boiler making crews,
When they see that bugger finished on the slipway,
15 All the hardship's soon forgot and we'll cheer as like as not,
And the bairns'll wave their Union Jacks all day.

[…] there's a mixture of emotions, hatred, gratitude and pride,
And you hate yourself for crying but it's difficult to hide,
For there's a sadness in the leavin' and ye worry what's ahead,
20 And that worry never leaves ye, keeps on nagging in yr head,
And so ye pray to God for orders, but ye'll worry till yr dead …
Until they bury your remains in the blacksmith's shed,
And the only life ye've known is in the shipyard.

Words and music: Sting

VIP FILE

Sting (born 1951 in Wallsend) is a British singer-songwriter. In 2013 his musical *The Last Ship*, which was inspired by his upbringing in Wallsend, opened on Broadway.

² **ye** *(archaic)* you
³ **woe betide ye** [wəʊ] *Wehe dir*
⁶ **to the hilt** completely
¹⁰ **Aristoteles Onassis** (1906–1975) Greek shipping magnate, billionaire
¹¹ **tonnage** *here:* number of big ships
¹³ **plater, welder** metalworking professions
¹⁴ **bugger** *(sl)* fellow
¹⁵ **as like as not** *(dialect)* probably
¹⁶ **bairn** *(dialect)* child
²⁰ **to nag** to bother

Regional identities 3

2 COMPREHENSION Summarise what you learn about Jackie White and about life in Newcastle at the end of its shipbuilding era.

3 LISTENING Listen to another part of the song. Outline what is said about the lives of Tommy Thompson, Peggy White and Davy Harrison. →S21 →△1
Zusatzmaterial KV 1: Vokabelhilfe   Diff (help with): True/False-Aufgaben

4 ANALYSIS Re-read the excerpt of the song and listen to the CD.
  a) Explain how the music and the language contribute to portray the people and to create a fuller picture of life in Newcastle. →△2 Diff (help with): Worthilfen
  b) Examine how the use of stylistic devices adds to the atmosphere.

5 CREATIVE TASK The chorus runs: "The only life we've known is in the shipyard." Imagine you worked at a shipyard in Newcastle. Write a letter to a friend, explaining what the loss of the shipbuilding industry means to you, your family and the city. **Hinweis:** Auch als Hausaufgabe geeignet

6 RESEARCH Can you think of any region or town in Germany which has been confronted with a similar transformation? Do some research and prepare a short presentation for your classmates. →S22, S32

FACT FILE

Newcastle upon Tyne is a northeastern English industrial town whose great shipbuilding era started with the first iron coal ship in 1852 and ended when the Swan Hunters shipyard closed in 1993. The area now suffers from the highest unemployment in England. However, in recent years, new technology businesses have emerged.

Gaelic will only be a hobby language

My father, in his old age, was asked if he would be wearing a kilt at a grandson's wedding. He replied, "I'm a Lowlander. I've never worn a kilt in my life". He had been born and brought up in Aberdeenshire, lived there till he went to Malaya as a very young man, and, like most Lowlanders of his generation, had no time for Gaelic.
5 He thought it nonsensical for public money to be spent keeping the language on a life-support machine. I suspect that even today, despite the pro-Gaelic propaganda to which we are subjected, and despite, or perhaps because of, the proliferation of signs in Gaelic, a majority of Lowland Scots would agree with him, believing that public money spent on Gaelic might be better spent elsewhere – or, of course, not
10 spent at all. [...]
  Unlike my late father, I don't dismiss Gaelic as an out-of-date and therefore useless language. I am sympathetic to those who want to learn it and promote it. What I object to is the hypocrisy and pretence that goes along with enthusiasm for Gaelic; hypocrisy and pretence that are encouraged by the Scottish Government
15 [...]. Successive Scottish governments, eager to emphasise our distinct national identity, have made Gaelic a key feature of our difference from England, and have fostered the pretence that we are a bilingual nation. We aren't.
  There are many different languages spoken here – apparently some 54,000 people speak Polish at home – but we are essentially an English-speaking people,
20 English being the language of public discourse, spoken by many with an admixture of old Scots and with a Scottish intonation. The several varieties of spoken Scots are in far more common use than Gaelic. [...]
  To subscribe to the official view that we are a bilingual English-and-Gaelic speaking nation is to indulge in cant. It is to practise intellectual dishonesty.

Allan Massie, The Scotsman, 2013

Avoiding mistakes
[11] **late** *formal, only before noun* no longer alive

[7] **to be subjected to sth** to be exposed to sth
[7] **proliferation** large increase
[11] **to dismiss** to disregard, to have a low opinion of sth
[13] **pretence** the act of pretending
[17] **to foster** to support
[24] **to indulge in sth** to allow yourself do sth you enjoy
[24] **cant** [kænt] hypocrisy

FACT FILE

Scottish Gaelic
Since 2005 Gaelic has been the second official language in Scotland, after English. About 58,000 Scots speak Gaelic, out of 5 million inhabitants. In comparison, 1.5 million people regularly speak the 'broad Scots' dialect of English. The use of Gaelic is actively promoted: Apart from bilingual road signs, there are several Gaelic schools, radio stations and a TV channel, BBC Alba (the Gaelic name for Scotland).

7 COMPREHENSION Describe the author's attitude towards Gaelic. Also consider the information given in the fact file.

8 EVALUATION Write a comment on the following statement: "Language is the only homeland." (Czesław Miłosz, Polish poet, 1911–2004) →S14.2 →▲3
Zusatzmaterial KV 2/2a: Mediation, Comment, Discussion   Diff (after): Pro-Kontra-Diskussion zur Frage einer Einheitssprache

Zusatzmaterial WB
Task 2: Tenses; Task 3: Mediation

Texts

B Rural and urban identities in the US

1 BEFORE YOU READ

a) Describe what the map shows. Give possible reasons for the differences in population density in the US, considering factors such as climate, landscape and history. →S27   Geeignete Methode: Think – Pair – Share

b) Discuss how living in a big city or in the countryside might influence people's lifestyle and attitudes.   Geeignete Methode: Speed dating

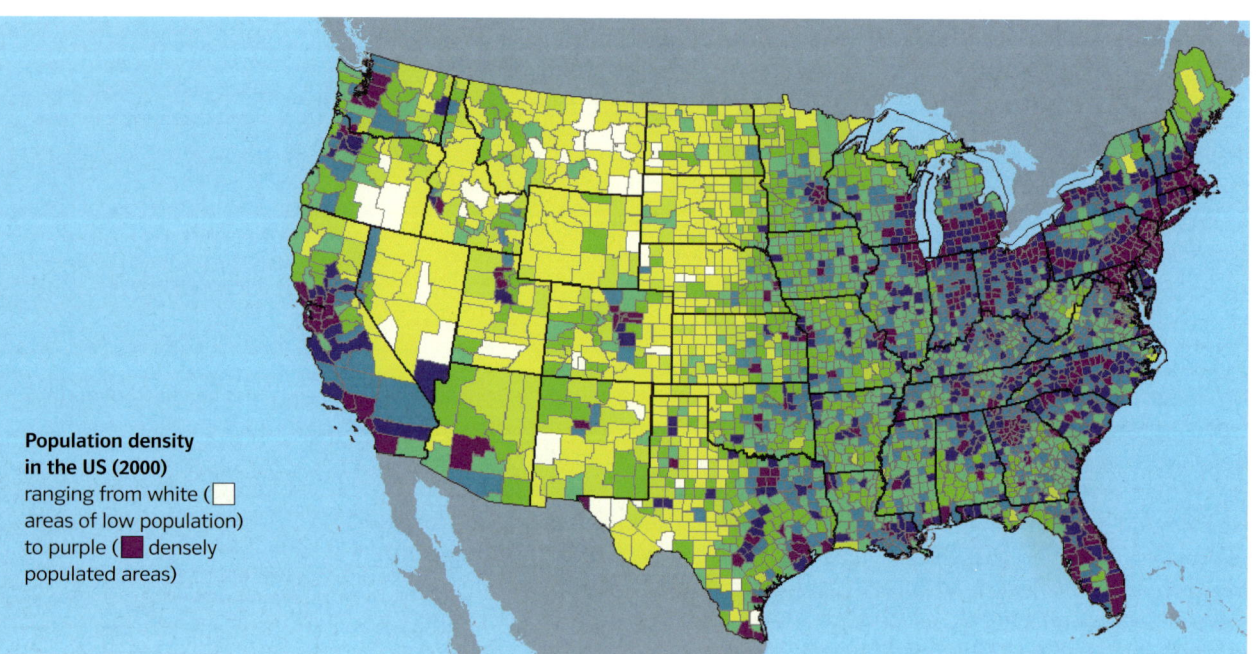

Population density in the US (2000) ranging from white (☐ areas of low population) to purple (■ densely populated areas)

Red state, blue city

Starting before the Civil War era, America's political dividing lines were drawn along state and regional borders. Cities and the then-extensive rural areas shared a worldview North and South of the Mason-Dixon line. While there was always tension within states, they were bound by a common politics. The city of Charleston, for example, was as rabidly anti-North as some inland plantation areas. Economic engines, ways of life, and moral philosophies changed at the 36th parallel, where the North began.

Today, that divide has vanished. The new political divide is a stark division between cities and what remains of the countryside. Not just some cities and some rural areas, either – virtually every major city (100,000-plus population) in the United States of America has a different outlook from the less populous areas that are closest to it. The difference is no longer about *where* people live, it's about *how* people live: in spread-out, open, low-density privacy – or amid rough-and-tumble, in-your-face population density and diverse communities that enforce a lower-common denominator of tolerance among inhabitants. The voting data suggest that people don't make cities liberal – cities make people liberal. […]

The gap is so stark that some of America's bluest cities are located in its reddest states. Every one of Texas' major cities – Austin, Dallas, Houston, and San Antonio – voted Democratic in 2012, the second consecutive presidential election in which they've done so. Other red-state cities that tipped blue include Atlanta,

---

³ **Mason-Dixon line** politically defined line symbolising the cultural boundary between the Northeastern and Southern states; historical demarcation line for the legality of slavery
⁵ **rabidly** fanatically
⁷ **parallel** *Breitengrad*
¹³ **rough-and-tumble** wild, tough, without rules
¹⁴ **to enforce** *here:* to give strength to
¹⁴ **lower-common denominator** *here: Mindestmaß*

Indianapolis, New Orleans, Birmingham, Tucson, Little Rock, and Charleston, S.C. – ironically, the site of the first battle of the Civil War. […]
This divide between blue city and red countryside has been growing for some time. Since 1984, more and more of America's major cities have voted blue each year,
25 culminating in 2012, when 27 out of the nation's 30 most populous cities voted Democratic. […]
In due course, these populous bastions of urban liberalism have helped spur state legislation and court rulings to create new laws, such as those permitting same sex marriage, that are often in direct conflict with federal laws and with the
30 majority of fellow state counties. These measures are not always controversial […] but the divisions are often stark: cities vs. everywhere else. […]
After this year's election, roughly half of the 50 states allow the practice of one, more, or all of the following: same-sex marriage, marijuana use or assisted suicide. Voters in Alabama, Missouri, Montana, and Wyoming passed largely symbolic laws
35 that would prohibit Obamacare, effectively another lifestyle law. Meanwhile, all of the states that voted against Obamacare also ban both same-sex marriage and marijuana use.

Josh Kron, *The Atlantic*, 2012

[27] **to spur** to encourage
[35] **Obamacare** refers to President Obama's 2010 law aiming at an affordable healthcare

2 COMPREHENSION Explain the title of the text by summing up the core ideas.
Hinweis: Auch als Hausaufgabe geeignet
3 ANALYSIS Compare the statements in the text about rural America with the experience described below.

Raccoons

Appalachian scene in North Georgia

People enjoy tubing in North Georgia

It might be hard walking ten minutes to get to your nearest neighbours. It might be hard if it takes twenty minutes by car to get to the next grocery store. But there is no place like the American countryside and there are so many beautiful things that completely make up for any negative aspects. I loved sitting outside enjoying the
5 good weather and the feeling of nature. At night I could hear the raccoons coming to the house and the crickets in the garden. But the best days were the family days at the river. We went swimming, hiking, met some friends or just had a picnic. The peacefulness is just incredible. Another point that really surprised me was the mentality of the people. They are just so friendly and helpful and they really stick
10 together. It was great to become a part of this community and really feel the team spirit. If there is one place I totally feel at home in and I would always go back to, it's the south of America.

Jule, German exchange student for five months near Elberton, Georgia

[5] **raccoon** Waschbär
[6] **cricket** Grille

USEFUL PHRASES

City vs. countryside
to have (easy) access to sth
a relaxed/hectic pace of life
to experience a sense of community
to be open-minded/narrow-minded/reserved
to enjoy/take in sth

4 EVALUATION In his article Josh Kron claims that "people don't make cities liberal – cities make people liberal" (l. 16). Comment on this statement.
Hinweis: Auch als Hausaufgabe geeignet
5 SPEAKING You have the chance to spend a gap year at a US high school. Discuss whether you would prefer to live in an urban or a rural area. → S23

4 The US then and now
Introduction

Code
z5e563

A tourist in front of the Statue of Liberty

Monument Valley, situated on the Arizona/Utah state line

Painting by John Trumbull called *The Committee of Five presenting their work to the Congress on June 28, 1776*

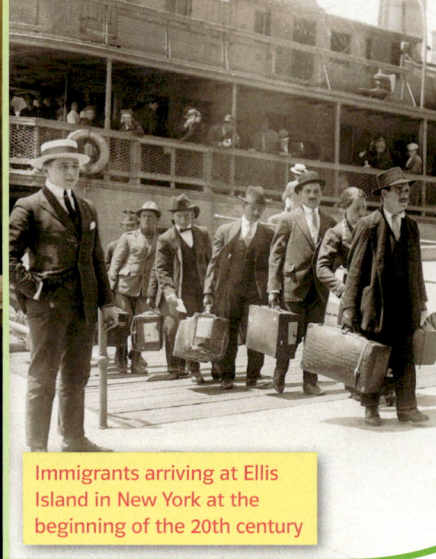
Immigrants arriving at Ellis Island in New York at the beginning of the 20th century

1 SPEAKING
  a) *Describe the pictures on these pages. Use the pictures to talk about the US. What abstract ideas does each image represent?* → **S28.1**
  b) *What do you know about life in the US?*

2 SPEAKING *In the Declaration of Independence America's Founding Fathers declared that God had given them all the right to "life, liberty and the pursuit of happiness". With a partner discuss what these rights mean to you.*
Geeignete Methode: Speed Dating

American Dream or American nightmare?

"Americans have so far put up with inequality because they felt they could change their status. They didn't mind others being rich, as long as they had a path to move up as well. The American Dream is all about social mobility in a sense – the idea that anyone can make it."
Fareed Zakaria, Indian-born US journalist and writer

"The American Dream is that dream of a land in which life should be better and richer and fuller for everyone, with opportunity for each according to ability or achievement."
James Truslow Adams (1878–1949), US writer and historian

"The story of the 20th century is one of the American Dream gradually being extended to more and more of the population. In 2009, President Barack Obama looked back across those past decades as he took the oath of office. He described his inauguration as a fulfillment of the American Dream."
Ari Shapiro, American radio journalist

"The American Dream has run out of gas. The car has stopped. It no longer supplies the world with its images, its dreams, its fantasies. No more. It's over. It supplies the world with its nightmares now: the Kennedy assassination, Watergate, Vietnam."
J. G. Ballard (1930–2009), English writer

"We must stop talking about the American Dream and start listening to the dreams of Americans."
Max Beerbohm (1872–1956), English writer and caricaturist

Cartoon by Michael Kichk; the people on the bus resemble Rosa Parks, Martin Luther King Jr and Barack Obama

People at a political rally

3 SPEAKING If you emigrated to America, what aspects of your life might be different? **Geeignete Methode:** Placemat

4 ANALYSIS From the quotations above and what you have already learned, write a list of some ideas that define the American Dream.

5 VISUALS Find both positive and negative pictures that represent America as you understand it. Show your pictures to the class and explain why you chose them.
→ S28 → ▲1 **Diff** (instead of): Präsentation einer Biographie

USEFUL PHRASES

Talking about cultures

to firmly believe in/to cling to dreams

fundamental human/civil rights

to put an end to

to force one's values on

to bring freedom to a country

of key importance

Spot on facts

The making of a nation

Independence

Despite the prior existence of Native American cultures, the history of the United States as a nation state usually begins in 1492 with Columbus's 'discovery' of America. It wasn't until after 1600 that European colonists began to arrive, mostly from England. By the 1770s there were 13 British colonies on the northeastern seaboard. Colonists came for many reasons, such as the desire to practice their religion freely or to take advantage of the opportunities the 'empty' continent presented. Some were sent against their will to avoid prison or to repay debts.

At first the colonies were dependent on goods and support from Europe, but over time they prospered and became more economically independent. The main cause of the rift with Britain was dissatisfaction with the fact that they had little control over their own lives since all major decisions were made in London. Unrest came to a head when Britain set heavy taxes on certain goods and the colonists refused to pay, unless they had representation in Parliament.

During the ensuing Revolutionary War (1775–1783) a committee of statesmen (known as the Founding Fathers) came together to draft the Declaration of Independence. This document, written by Thomas Jefferson and announced on July 4, 1776, was to be the guideline for the Constitution of 1787.

The Founding Fathers ensured in the Constitution that the three branches of government – the executive (the President), the judicial (the Supreme Court) and legislative (Congress) – would share power in a system of checks and balances.

Today the Fourth of July is a federal holiday in the US, celebrated with fireworks, parades, barbecues, baseball games and family reunions.

Yankee Doodle, 1776

Equality and freedom

Equality and freedom are cornerstones of American society. The Bill of Rights, which was added to the Constitution in 1791, explicitly guaranteed religious freedom and freedom of speech as well as equal rights and opportunities for all American citizens regardless of class or background. The separation of church and state, a key element in American law, has led to modern America having a wide spectrum of creeds and believers.

Yet equality and freedom were not granted to all American citizens automatically. After the Civil War between the northern and southern states in which its abolition played an important part, slavery was finally abolished in 1865. Even then it took the Civil Rights Movement of the 1960s to achieve equal rights for the descendants of those freed slaves.

American women also had to fight for their rights, not gaining the right to vote until 1920. The struggle for equality is still not over, as they only earn three-quarters of the average pay of American men.

Other minorities who have had to fight – and are still fighting – for freedom and equality are Native Americans and gays and lesbians.

The equality of the social order, which in theory offers equal opportunities for all, often has a more sobering reality. Education is free and available to all, but the quality of that education can depend on where a child goes to school. Higher education is often a question of money, with the opportunities for students from a wealthy home being greater than those from poor neighborhoods. And even in a democratic society there are class differences, a fact many Americans try hard to ignore.

Americans are proud of these ideals of equality and freedom. Their deep-seated patriotism is often regarded as arrogance by people in other parts of the world and can blind some Americans to any shortcomings within the country and in America's dealings with other nations. These factors are often the roots of anti-Americanism around the world.

Immigration

The first Europeans to come to America were colonists or settlers and were mainly from Britain, Spain, the Netherlands and France. They all had to survive an arduous journey across the Atlantic. Many were driven by the desire to escape from religious, political or economic oppression and the belief that America would offer them a better life.

The peak periods of immigration were the mid-19th century (mainly from Northern and Northwestern Europe, particularly Germans after the failed revolution of 1848 and Irish during the famine years of 1845–52), the early 20th century (mainly from Southern and Eastern Europe) and post-1965, when a change in the immigration laws led to more non-Europeans entering the country. This eventually changed the ethnic make-up of the nation. While European immigrants accounted for nearly 60% of the total foreign population in 1970, they made up only 15% in 2000. This is due to steadily increasing immigration from Latin America – mainly Mexico, but also Cuba, El Salvador and the Dominican Republic – and from Asian countries such as China, the Philippines and India.

America once saw itself as a melting pot in which these immigrants ideally gave up their way of life, language and culture and became part of a unified, monocultural American nation. But since 1970 this metaphor has largely been replaced by the idea of a multicultural and diverse America – a salad bowl in which different cultures mix, but remain different.

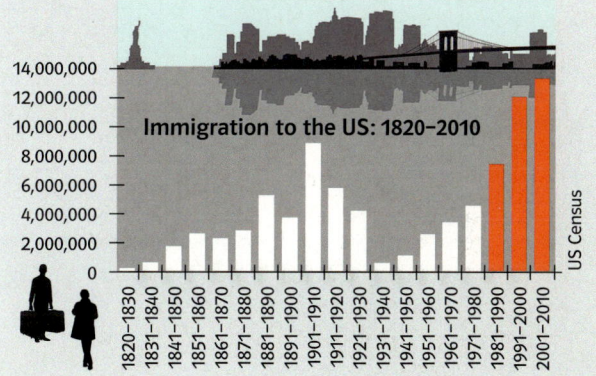

The American Dream

The American Dream is a set of beliefs and ideals which, in theory at least, allow every American the freedom to prosper and advance socially and financially through hard work. The concept is hard to pin down because there are individual interpretations. Some dream of fame and fortune; others of a fulfilled life or simply a life without state interference.

The idea of the American Dream probably began to take hold when Thomas Jefferson wrote in 1776 that Americans were born with the unalienable rights to "life, liberty and the pursuit of happiness." The phrase itself was actually coined by James Truslow Adams in his 1931 book *The Epic of America*: "The American Dream is that dream of a land in which life should be better and richer and fuller for everyone, with opportunity for each according to ability or achievement. […] It is not a dream of motor cars and high wages merely, but a dream of social order in which each man and each woman shall be able to attain to the fullest stature of which they are innately capable, and be recognised by others for what they are, regardless of […] birth or position."

For centuries people have come to America – and are still coming – attracted by the American Dream: the economic dream of success and prosperity ('from rags to riches'), the social dream of equality and opportunity, the political dream of democracy and justice, or the personal dream of freedom and self-realisation. While for many US citizens the dream is still alive, for many others it is an illusion or has – for whatever reason – even turned into a nightmare.

---

1 LISTENING Listen to the dialogue about the role of the frontier and then write a text about it similar in style to the fact files above. You may use additional research materials. → **S12.2**
Zusatzmaterial KV 1: Überprüfung des Hörverstehens mit Lückentext

2 SPEAKING Choose one of these topics or one of the other abstract ideas from Task 4 on the previous page and prepare a short talk on it.

3 RESEARCH Create a timeline of the US based on the dates and events in these texts. Then use the internet or other resources to add to your timeline. **Hinweis:** Auch als Hausaufgabe geeignet

Core skill workshop

Analysing a speech

Part A Understanding the context of a speech

When analysing a speech, identify the focus of analysis and the speaker's aim in the assignment. Then look at the context in which the speech was given. The title and any other information you have can help you. This is what you know:

Context	Your notes
Is there a title?	Barack Obama's victory speech, November 2012
Who is speaking?	Barack Obama
Where and when?	Chicago, IL, Nov. 7, 2012
To what audience?	supporters of his presidential campaign
On what occasion?	Election Day victory
On what topic(s)?	his vision of the American people and the nation's future
With what main aim?	to thank his supporters, show his vision for the next four years

1 COMPREHENSION Use the notes in the table to write the opening paragraph of a speech analysis, summarising the context of the speech.

Part B Using rhetorical devices and strategies in speeches

2 ANALYSIS Most elements in a speech have at least one of these four functions:
1. To establish contact with the audience
2. To place emphasis on certain ideas
3. To present ideas understandably or memorably (illustration, memory aid)
4. To convey a certain image of the speaker (self-presentation).

Copy this grid and fill in the middle column with the terms from the useful phrases box.

Some possible aims	Rhetorical devices, other strategies	Phrases for the analysis
contact	making a joke	to establish contact with sb
emphasis	…	to emphasise, to stress
illustration/memory aid	…	to illustrate/visualise an idea
self-presentation	…	…
persuasion	…	…
…	…	…

3 ANALYSIS Now add these phrases to the right-hand column in the grid above:
to stress • to break the ice • to make sb feel personally addressed • to present oneself as • to reinforce • to explain sth understandably • to connect with sb • to evoke a positive mood/reaction • to offer an easy-to-understand image • to reach out to sb • to highlight one's own personal values or beliefs • to create a memorable phrase • to underline

4 ANALYSIS Find out what functions these devices have in a speech:
allusion • hyperbole • euphemism • understatement • anaphora

TIP

A typical assignment asking you to analyse a speech …
1. usually starts with 'Examine how …/ Analyse …'
2. includes the focus of analysis: usually structure and/or rhetorical devices
3. gives the general aim/intention of the speaker → S5, S15

Avoiding mistakes
Wortschatz
Eine Rede halten: to give/make/deliver a speech
NICHT: to hold a speech

USEFUL PHRASES

Rhetorical devices and strategies

repetition (of a key word/phrase)
making a joke
enumeration
metaphor
using the personal pronouns 'we', 'our', 'us'
giving an example
directly addressing the audience
alliteration
contrasting words (antithetical phrase) or ideas
quotation (of an authority or expert)
rhetorical question
parallel structures
emotive language

The US then and now 4

5 SPEAKING *In groups use the grid on the previous page and the useful phrases box here to explain the function(s) of the 'sound bites' from speeches below. Repeat them aloud with appropriate body language for effect!*

1. "Get active and become involved!"
2. "Most African dictators are cruel and corrupt."
3. "This is the lesson history teaches: never give in, never give up and never …"
4. "Every citizen has these human rights. Every politician must respect them."
5. "Imagine living in the street or on the run: cold, lonely and frightened."
6. "We have to work together. That is our only chance to make a difference!"
7. "This is a question of war and peace, life and death!"

Four presidents talk about their hopes for their nation

Thomas Jefferson (1801)
Let us with courage and confidence pursue our […] attachment to union and representative government. […] Possessing a chosen country, with room enough for our descendants to the thousandth and thousandth generation […] enlightened by honesty, truth, temperance, gratitude and the love of man […] with all these blessings, what more is necessary to make us a happy and a prosperous people?

Abraham Lincoln (1863)
It is rather for us to be here dedicated to the great task remaining before us – that from these honored dead we take increased devotion to that cause for which they gave the last full measure of devotion – that we here highly resolve that these dead shall not have died in vain – that this nation, under God, shall have a new birth of freedom – and that government of the people, by the people, for the people, shall not perish from the earth.

John F. Kennedy (1961)
Let every nation know that we shall pay any price, bear any burden, meet any hardship, support any friend, oppose any foe to assure the survival and the success of liberty.

William J. Clinton (1997)
Thirty-four years ago, the man whose life we celebrate today spoke to us. Like a prophet of old, he told of his dream that one day America would rise up and treat all its citizens as equals before the law and in the heart. Martin Luther King's dream was the American Dream. […] May those generations we cannot see yet say of us that we led our beloved land into a new century with America's bright flame of freedom spreading throughout all the world.

6 ANALYSIS *What rhetorical devices or other strategies did the four presidents use to convey their visions and values? First work alone, and then share your ideas with a partner and afterwards with the whole class.*

USEFUL PHRASES

Talking about function

The function/aim/purpose of … is to …

The intention behind this … is to …

The speaker uses/makes use of/employs this device in order to …

By using a device, the speaker tries/hopes/aims to achieve …

A device serves/helps …

The function/effect of …

---

2 **to pursue** [pəˈsuː] to follow
5 **descendants** [dɪˈsendənt] *Nachfahren*
6 **temperance** *Mäßigung*
12 **devotion** loyalty
13 **to resolve** to decide
14 **in vain** without success or a result
16 **to perish** to die
20 **foe** enemy
24 **of old** *von früher*

USEFUL PHRASES

Talking about dreams

to have a dream of (doing) sth

a dream comes true/is realised

to fulfil/realise a dream

to keep a dream alive

to make a dream come true

a dream may turn into a nightmare

Core skill workshop

Part C Analysing an extract from a speech

Barack Obama's victory speech, November 2012

Tonight, more than 200 years after a former colony won the right to determine its own destiny, the task of perfecting our union moves forward.

It moves forward because of you. It moves forward because you reaffirmed the spirit that has triumphed over war and depression, the spirit that has lifted this country from the depths of despair to the great heights of hope, the belief that while each of us will pursue our own individual dreams, we are an American family, and we rise or fall together as one nation and as one people. 5

Tonight, in this election, you, the American people, reminded us that while our road has been hard, while our journey has been long, we have picked ourselves up, we have fought our way back, and we know in our hearts that for the United States of America, the best is yet to come. […] Despite all our differences, most of us share certain hopes for America's future. 10

We want our kids to grow up in a country where they have access to the best schools and the best teachers – a country that lives up to its legacy as the global leader in technology and discovery and innovation – with all of the good jobs and new businesses that follow. 15

We want our children to live in an America that isn't burdened by debt, that isn't weakened up by inequality, that isn't threatened by the destructive power of a warming planet.

We want to pass on a country that's safe and respected and admired around the world, a nation that is defended by the strongest military on Earth and the best troops this – this world has ever known – but also a country that moves with confidence beyond this time of war to shape a peace that is built on the promise of freedom and dignity for every human being. 20

We believe in a generous America, in a compassionate America, in a tolerant America open to the dreams of an immigrant's daughter who studies in our schools and pledges to our flag […]. That's the future we hope for. That's the vision we share. That's where we need to go – forward. That's where we need to go. […] 25

America, I believe we can build on the progress we've made and continue to fight for new jobs and new opportunities and new security for the middle class. I believe we can keep the promise of our founders, the idea that if you're willing to work hard, it doesn't matter who you are or where you come from or what you look like or who you love. It doesn't matter whether you're black or white or Hispanic or Asian or Native American or young or old or rich or poor, abled or disabled, gay or straight. You can make it here in America if you're willing to try. 30

35

USEFUL PHRASES

Talking about a line of argument

The speaker starts off with
points out that
claims
demands
provides information about
presents facts on
focuses on
offers solutions to/for
promises

Avoiding mistakes
Aussprache
¹⁵technology [tekˈnɒlədʒi]

President Obama with his wife Michelle, his elder daughter Malia and his younger daughter Sasha

⁵ **despair** loss of hope
¹⁴ **legacy** Erbe
²⁷ **to pledge** to solemnly promise

USEFUL PHRASES

Talking about body language

His (lack of) eye contact with the audience captivates (alienates) …

The speaker's erect/relaxed posture conveys the message …

His conscious use of hand gestures suggests …

---

7 ANALYSIS Examine how President Obama sends a message of shared values and hopes to his supporters after being declared the winner in the election. Consider his line of argument and use of rhetorical devices.

8 SPEAKING Practice presenting this speech in small groups. Pay attention to body language, voice inflection and maintaining contact with the audience. → S15

9 CREATIVE TASK Write a speech on a topic that interests you and deliver it to the class. →△2 **Diff** (help with): Vorgabe von Struktur und Redemitteln

Hinweis
Weiterführend können tagespolitsch aktuelle Reden in den Core skill workshop integriert werden

Texts

The US then and now — 4

A The immigrant experience

Welcome to all!

The sign to the left of Uncle Sam says: "Free education, free land, free speech, free ballot, free lunch."

The sign near the centre of the image says: "No oppressive taxes, no expensive kings, no compulsory military service, no knouts or dungeons."

knout heavy whip
to pave to cover a street with stones

1 **VISUALS** Re-read the box on 'immigration' in the Spot on facts. With this background in mind, describe and evaluate the cartoon 'Welcome to all!' by Joseph Keppler, published by the satirical American magazine Puck in 1880.
→ S28.2

2 **CREATIVE TASK** Write Uncle Sam's short welcoming speech to the immigrants. Consider the historical situation, the setting, the addressees and the messages on the two boards. → S15

3 **ANALYSIS** Explain the humour and message in the following joke:
Many immigrants came to America because of the stories they had heard that there the streets were paved with gold. When they got off the boat in New York, however, they discovered three things: first, that the streets were **not** paved with gold, second, that the streets were not paved **at all**, and third, that **they** were expected to pave them. **Hinweis:** Auch als Hausaufgabe geeignet

USEFUL PHRASES

Talking about hopes
to be hopeful, optimistic
to have high hopes
great expectations
to be disillusioned with sth
to be shocked by reality
sth does not meet one's expectations

FACT FILE

Uncle Sam is a national personification of the United States. He is usually portrayed as an old man with a white beard dressed in the stars, stripes and colours of the American flag.

Zusatzmaterial KV/WB
KV 2: Analyse eines Flussdiagramms
WB Tasks 10–11: Listening

Texts

4 SPEAKING *In the novel* Native Speaker, *the Korean first-person narrator remembers his father's immigrant story in the US. Read the following extract and then share with a partner what you have learned about the father's life in America.* → S8

An Asian-American working in a newspaper shop

Asian-American family

Native Speaker

I thought his life was all about money. He drew much energy and pride from his ability to make it almost at will. He was some kind of human annuity. He had no real cleverness or secrets for good business; he simply refused to fail, leaving absolutely nothing to luck or chance or something else. Of course, in his personal lore he would have said that he started with $200 in his pocket and a wife and baby and just a few words of English. Knowing what every native loves to hear, he would have offered the classic immigrant story, casting himself as the heroic newcomer, self-sufficient, resourceful.

The truth, though, is that my father got his first infusion of capital from a ggeh, a Korean "money club" in which members contributed to a pool that was given out on a rotating basis. Each week you gave the specified amount; and then one week in the cycle, all the money was yours.

His first ggeh was formed from a couple dozen storekeepers who knew each other through a fledgling Korean-American business association. In those early days he would take me to their meetings down in the city [...]. At the meetings the men would be smoking, talking loudly, almost shouting their opinions. There were arguments but only a few, mostly it was just all the hope and excitement. I remember my father as the funny one, he'd make them all laugh with an old Korean joke or his impressions of Americans who came into his store, doing their stiff nasal tone, their petty annoyances and complaints.

In the summers we'd all get together, these men and their families, drive up to Westchester to some park in Mount Kisco or Rye. In the high heat the men would set up cones and play a match of soccer, and even then I couldn't believe how hard they tried and how competitive they were, my father especially, who wasn't so skilled as ferocious, especially on defence. He'd tackle his good friend Mr. Oh so hard that I thought a fight might start, but then Mr. Oh was gentle, and quick on his feet, and he'd pull up my father and just keep working to the goal.

Sometimes they would group up and play a team of Hispanic men who were also picnicking with their families. Once, they even played some black men, though my father pointed out to us in the car home that they were African blacks. Somehow there were rarely white people in the park, never groups of their families,

² **at will** whenever one likes
² **annuity** [əˈnuːəti] *here:* money being earned regularly
⁵ **lore** stories
⁷ **to cast** to present
⁸ **self-sufficient** independent
⁹ **infusion of capital** *here:* money to start a business
¹⁴ **fledgling** newly founded
¹⁹ **impressions** imitations
²⁰ **petty annoyances** anger not to taken seriously
²² **Westchester** county in New York
²² **Mount Kisco, Rye** towns in Westchester County
²³ **cone** *Kegel*
²⁴ **competitive** playing to win
²⁵ **ferocious** [fəˈrəʊʃəs] aggressive

just young couples, if anything. After some iced barley tea and a quick snack my father and his friends would set up a volleyball net and start all over again. The mothers and us younger ones would sit and watch, the older kids playing their own
35 games, and when the athletics were done the mothers would set up the food and grill the ribs and the meat, and we'd eat and run and play until dark. And only when my father dumped the water from the cooler was it the final sign that we would go home.

I know over the years my father and his friends got together less and less.
40 Certainly, after my mother died, he didn't want to go to the gatherings anymore. But it wasn't just him. They all got busier and wealthier and lived farther and farther apart. Like us, their families moved to big houses with big yards to tend on weekends, they owned fancy cars that needed washing and waxing. They joined their own neighborhood pool and tennis clubs and were making drinking friends
45 with Americans. Some of them, too, were already dead, like Mr. Oh, who had a heart attack after being held up at his store in Hell's Kitchen. And in the end my father no longer belonged to any ggeh, he complained about all the disgraceful troubles that were now cropping up, people not paying on time or leaving too soon after their turn getting the money. In America, he said, it's even hard to stay Korean.
50 I wonder if my father, if given the chance, would have wished to go back to the time before he made all that money, when he had just one store and we rented a tiny apartment in Queens. He worked hard and had worries but he had a joy then that he never seemed to regain once the money started coming in. He might turn on the radio and dance cheek to cheek with my mother. He worked on his
55 car himself, a used green Impala with carburetor trouble. They had lots of Korean friends that they met at church and then even in the street, and when they talked in public there was a shared sense of how lucky they were, to be in America but still have countrymen near.

From: Chang-Rae Lee, *Native Speaker*, 1995

32 **barley** *Gerste*
37 **to dump** *here:* to empty
40 **gathering** meeting
42 **to tend** to take care of
46 **to be held up** *überfallen werden*
46 **Hell's Kitchen** (until the 1990s) poor neighbourhood of Manhattan, New York
52 **Queens** part of New York City
55 **Impala** middle-class car made by Chevrolet
55 **carburetor** [ˈkɑːrbəreɪtə] *Vergaser*

5 COMPREHENSION *Say whether the following statements are true, false or whether there is not enough information given in the text to determine the fact.*

1. The speaker's father made his money illegally.
2. The father shows some racist tendencies.
3. Money made his father happy.
4. The father was proud of his Korean heritage.
5. The father was very competitive.
6. The father was happier before his success.

6 ANALYSIS
a) *Outline the father's biography in America.*
b) *Analyse the extent to which the father's story is a classic American success story.*
c) *Characterise him by describing his personality, values and dreams.*
d) *What lesson do you think the son learned from his father's life?* →▲3
   Geeignete Methode zur weiteren Analyse: Hot seat

Diff (after): Analyse der Haltung der im Text erwähnten ethnischen Gruppen zueinander

7 VIEWING *Watch President Obama talking about the need for a new immigration policy to help second-generation immigrants. Describe how convincing his ideas seem to you.* →**S29.2**

8 SPEAKING *Discuss how hard it must be to succeed in a foreign country for first-generation compared with second-generation immigrants.* →△4
Diff (help with): Stichwörter als Argumentationshilfe

Zusatzmaterial WB
Task 1: Common mistakes
Task 2: Simple and progressive forms
Task 3: Paraphrasing
Task 4: Writing a letter
Task 5: Analysis
Task 6: Writing a dialogue

Texts

One of the pools of the National September 11 Memorial in lower Manhattan. The two pools are placed exactly where the Twin Towers once stood.

The names of the nearly 3,000 victims of the attacks on the WTC on September 11, 2001 and February 26, 1993 are inscribed on parapets surrounding the two pools

9 BEFORE YOU READ What happened on 9/11? What happened afterwards? What are the consequences of that day?

10 BEFORE YOU READ State why you think it could be controversial to build a mosque near Ground Zero.

Responding to 9/11 – A mosque near Ground Zero?

Since 2001, in the United States 'Ground Zero' is generally understood to mean the site of the World Trade Center in Manhattan, New York, which was destroyed in the September 11 attacks. After the decision in May 2010 to allow the building of a mosque two blocks away from the World Trade Center Site, Michael Bloomberg, the mayor of New York, defended the project. The following text is an extract from his speech on August 3, 2010.

We have come here to Governor's Island to stand where the earliest settlers first set foot in New Amsterdam, and where the seeds of religious tolerance were first planted. We've come here to see the inspiring symbol of liberty that, more than 250 years later, would greet millions of immigrants in the harbor, and we have come here to state as strongly as ever – this is the freest City in the world. That's what makes New York special and different and strong.

Our doors are open to everyone – everyone with a dream and a willingness to work hard and play by the rules. New York City was built by immigrants, and it is sustained by immigrants – by people from more than a hundred different countries speaking more than two hundred different languages and professing every faith. And whether your parents were born here, or you came yesterday, you are a New Yorker.

We may not always agree with every one of our neighbors. That's life and it's part of living in such a diverse and dense city. But we also recognize that part of being a New Yorker is living with your neighbors in mutual respect and tolerance. It was exactly that spirit of openness and acceptance that was attacked on 9/11. On that day 3,000 people were killed because some murderous fanatics didn't want us to enjoy the freedom to profess our own faiths, to speak our own minds, to follow our own dreams and to live our own lives. […]

The World Trade Center Site will forever hold a special place in our City, in our hearts. But we would be untrue to the best part of ourselves – and who we are as New Yorkers and Americans – if we said 'no' to a mosque in Lower Manhattan.

Let us not forget that Muslims were among those murdered on 9/11 and that

---

7 **Governor's Island** island very close to Manhattan
8 **New Amsterdam** old name for New York
8 **seed** *Saat*
15 **to sustain** to make strong
16 **faith** religious belief
21 **mutual** from both sides

our Muslim neighbors grieved with us as New Yorkers and as Americans. We would betray our values – and play into our enemies' hands – if we were to treat Muslims differently than anyone else. In fact, to cave to popular sentiment would be to hand a victory to the terrorists – and we should not stand for that.

For that reason, I believe that this is an important test of the separation of church and state as we may see in our lifetime – as important a test – and it is critically important that we get it right.

On September 11, 2001, thousands of first responders heroically rushed to the scene and saved tens of thousands of lives. More than 400 of those first responders did not make it out alive. In rushing into those burning buildings, not one of them asked, "What God do you pray to? What beliefs do you hold?"

The attack was an act of war – and our first responders defended not only our City but also our country and our Constitution. We do not honor their lives by denying the very Constitutional rights they died protecting. We honor their lives by defending those rights – and the freedoms that the terrorists attacked. [...]

The local community board in Lower Manhattan voted overwhelmingly to support the proposal and if it moves forward, I expect the community center and mosque will add to the life and vitality of the neighborhood and the entire City.

Political controversies come and go, but our values and our traditions endure – and there is no neighborhood in this City that is off limits to God's love and mercy, as the religious leaders here with us today can attest.

Michael R. Bloomberg, New York City website, 2010

30 **to grieve** to show sadness
32 **to cave** to give in
45 **community board** local political group
45 **overwhelmingly** with a big majority
48 **controversy** [ˈkɒntrəvɜːsi] discussion, debate
48 **to endure** [enˈdʊr] to keep on living
49 **off limits** not open

Avoiding mistakes
Hinweis auf amerikanische Schreibweise
10 **harbor**, 20 **recognize**, 21 **neighbor**, 42 **honor**, 46 **center**

11 COMPREHENSION Based on the speech, summarise why Bloomberg supports the building of a mosque close to Ground Zero.

12 ANALYSIS Analyse the way Bloomberg tries to win his audience to support the building of this mosque. → S4 **Hinweis:** Auch als Hausaufgabe geeignet

13 EVALUATION Do you think building a mosque in Germany would be controversial after such an event? Write a comment. → △5
Diff (help with): Hinweise zur Struktur eines Comments
Hinweis: Auch als mündliche Diskussion geeignet, z. B. Fishbowl discussion

Zusatzmaterial WB
Task 7: Writing the date
Task 8: Rewording
Tasks 12–16: Reading and writing
Task 17: Mediation

FACT FILE

War on terror

After the terrorist attacks of September 11, 2001, the Bush administration declared a worldwide 'War on Terror', involving military operations, new security legislation, efforts to block the financing of terrorism, and the elimination of al-Qaeda. Washington called on other states to join in the fight against terrorism, asserting that "either you are with us, or you are with the terrorists." Many governments joined this campaign, often adopting harsh new laws, lifting long-standing legal protections and stepping up domestic policing and intelligence work.

Critics charge that the 'War on Terror' is an ideology of fear and repression that creates enemies and promotes violence rather than preventing acts of terror and strengthening security. The worldwide campaign has too often become an excuse for governments to repress opposition groups and disregard international law and civil liberties.

Zusatzmaterial WB
Mock exam 1: American Dream – American realities

Advanced texts

B Equality and the Dream

1 BEFORE YOU READ In Germany, is everyone treated equally? In court? On the street? In stores? In schools? At the voting booth?

Liberty and justice for all?

Published in 1960 when segregation and discrimination against African Americans was widespread, Lee's novel describes the trial of a black man accused of raping a white woman. Despite evidence proving that he is innocent, the all-white jury wants to sentence the defendant Tom Robinson to death. Read how Atticus Finch, the defense attorney, defends Robinson during his closing arguments of the trial. 5

'Gentlemen,' he was saying, 'I shall be brief, but I would like to use my remaining time with you to remind you that this case is not a difficult one, it requires no minute sifting of complicated facts, but it does require you to be sure beyond all reasonable doubt as to the guilt of the defendant. To begin with, this case should never have come to trial. This case is as simple as black and white. 10

'The state has not produced one iota of medical evidence to the effect that the crime Tom Robinson is charged with ever took place. It has relied instead upon the testimony of two witnesses whose evidence has not only been called into serious question on cross-examination, but has been flatly contradicted by the defendant. The defendant is not guilty, but somebody in the courtroom is. 15

'I have nothing but pity in my heart for the chief witness for the state, but my pity does not extend so far as to her putting a man's life at stake, which she has done in an effort to get rid of her own guilt.

'I say guilt, gentlemen, because it was guilt that motivated her. She has committed no crime, she has merely broken a rigid and time-honored code of our 20 society, a code so severe that whoever breaks it is hounded from our midst as unfit to live with. She is the victim of cruel poverty and ignorance, but I cannot pity her: she is white. She knew full well the enormity of her offense, but because her desires were stronger than the code she was breaking, she persisted in breaking it. She persisted, and her subsequent reaction is something that all of us have known 25 at one time or another. She did something every child has done – she tried to put the evidence of her offense away from her. But in this case she was no child hiding stolen contraband: she struck out at her victim – of necessity she must put him away from her – he must be removed from her presence, from this world. She must destroy the evidence of her offense. 30

'What was the evidence of her offense? Tom Robinson, a human being. She must put Tom Robinson away from her. Tom Robinson was to her a daily reminder of what she did. What did she do? She tempted a Negro. She was white, and she tempted a Negro. She did something that in our society is unspeakable: she kissed a black man. Not an old Uncle, but a strong young Negro man. No code mattered to 35 her before she broke it, but it came crashing down on her afterwards.

'Her father saw it, and the defendant has testified as to his remarks. What did her father do? We don't know, but there is circumstantial evidence to indicate that Mayella Ewell was beaten savagely by someone who led almost exclusively with his left. We do know in part what Mr Ewell did: he did what any God-fearing, 40 persevering, respectable white man would do under the circumstances – he swore out a warrant, no doubt signing it with his left hand, and Tom Robinson now sits before you, having taken the oath with the only good hand he possesses – his right hand.

VIP FILE

Nelle Harper Lee (born April 28, 1926) is one of the most influential American novelists of the 20th century despite having published only one book, *To Kill a Mockingbird*. In 1961 she was awarded the Pulitzer Prize for the book, which deals with the daily occurances of racism that she observed in her hometown of Monroeville, Alabama, as a child.

Avoiding mistakes
Aussprache
[43] **oath** *BE* [əʊθ], *AE* [oʊð]

---

[1] **segregation** separating one kind of people from another
[4] **defendant** someone who has to defend himself in a court of law
[8] **minute** [mɪˈnuːt] small
[8] **sifting** exact studying
[11] **not one iota** not the slightest amount
[17] **at stake** at risk
[21] **hounded** chased
[22] **unfit** unsuitable
[23] **offense** wrong-doing
[25] **to persist** to continue
[25] **subsequent** following
[28] **contraband** illegal alcohol
[34] **to tempt** to attract or seduce
[35] **code** the accepted way of behaving in society
[37] **remarks** words
[39] **to lead with your left** to use your left fist when boxing
[41] **to persevere** *durchhalten*
[41] **to swear out a warrant** to make a statement on oath

Atticus Finch and Tom Robinson in the courtroom scene from *To Kill a Mockingbird*

45 'And so a quiet, respectable, humble Negro who had the unmitigated temerity to "feel sorry" for a white woman has had to put his word against two white people's. I need not remind you of their appearance and conduct on the stand – you saw them for yourselves. The witnesses for the state, with the exception of the sheriff of Maycomb County, have presented themselves to you gentlemen, to this court, in
50 the cynical confidence that their testimony would not be doubted, confident that you gentlemen would go along with them on the assumption – evil assumption – that all Negroes lie, that all Negroes are basically immoral beings, that all Negro men are not to be trusted around our women, an assumption one associates with minds of their caliber.
55 'Which, gentlemen, we know is in itself a lie as black as Tom Robinson's skin, a lie I do not have to point out to you. You know the truth, and the truth is this: some Negroes lie, some Negroes are immoral, some Negro men are not to be trusted around women – black and white. But this is a truth that applies to the human race and to no particular race of men. There is not a person in this courtroom who has
60 never told a lie, who has never done an immoral thing, and there is no man living who has never looked upon a woman with desire.' […]
'One more thing, gentlemen, before I quit. Thomas Jefferson once said that all men are created equal, a phrase that the Yankees and the distaff side of the Executive branch in Washington are fond of hurling at us. There is a tendency in
65 this year of grace 1935 for certain people to use this phrase out of context, to satisfy all conditions. We know that all men are not created equal in the sense that some people would have us believe. The most ridiculous example I can think of is that the people who run public education promote the stupid and idle along with the industrious – because all men are created equal, educators will gravely tell you,
70 the children left behind suffer terrible feelings of inferiority. We know all men are not created equal in the sense some people would have us believe – some people are smarter than others, some people have more opportunity because they're born with it, some men make more money than others, some ladies make better cakes than others – some people are born gifted beyond the normal scope of most men.
75 'But there is one way in this country in which all men are created equal – there is one human institution that makes a pauper the equal of a Rockefeller, the stupid man the equal of an Einstein, and the ignorant man the equal of any college president. That institution, gentlemen, is a court. It can be the Supreme Court of the United States or the humblest J.P. court in the land, or this honorable court which
80 you serve. Our courts have their faults, as does any human institution, but in this country our courts are the great levellers, and in our courts all men are created equal.'

From: Harper Lee, *To Kill a Mockingbird*, 1960

45 **unmitigated** complete, full
45 **temerity** audacity, boldness, courage
47 **conduct** behavior
48 **exception** Ausnahme
51 **assumption** thought
63 **distaff side** female side
64 **to hurl** to throw
68 **idle** lazy
69 **industrious** active
69 **gravely** seriously
70 **inferiority** not being good enough
74 **scope** capacity, reach
76 **pauper** beggar, bum
79 **J.P. court** justice of the peace court, the lowest court

2 COMPREHENSION Say what Mayella Ewell did wrong and how she dealt with it.

3 COMPREHENSION Summarise what Atticus Finch says in lines 62–82.

4 SPEAKING Define what 'true equality' means to you. Think about all the areas of society that need to be included so that the definition covers all aspects of life.
Hinweis: Auch als schriftliche Hausaufgabe geeignet

5 VIEWING Watch this news report on the motor industry in present-day urban America and answer the following questions:
a) One part of each generation's American Dream has always been the hope of doing better than one's parents did. Evaluate the chances of that happening to the current generation of Americans in light of the video clip.
b) Analyse the structure of the short video. To what extent is it objective?
Zusatzmaterial KV 3 Task 2: True/False-Aufgabe zur Überprüfung des Hörsehverstehens
Hinweis: Weiterführend kann die Lektüre des Romans oder die Analyse von Filmauszügen erfolgen

Zusatzmaterial KV/WB
KV 3 Task 1: Wortschatzarbeit
WB Task 18: Stylistic devices

Advanced texts

Hinweis
Alternativer Einstieg mit dem Gedicht *A dream deferred* von Langston Hughes

Avoiding mistakes
Betonung
⁵ambivalent [æmˈbɪvələnt]

A dream deferred

"Because differences in income in the US are believed to be related to skill and effort, and because social mobility is assumed to be high," Isabel Sawhill, co-director of the Center on Children and Families at the Brookings Institution, wrote recently, "inequality seems to be more acceptable than in Europe."

And yet the gap between those enduring beliefs and our more ambivalent modern realities is widening. The operative definition of the American Dream has long been: In every generation, children will live better than their parents did. Millions of Americans, no matter where they start on the income ladder, still clear that bar. But to a greater extent than our self-image allows, success in America is now a matter of choosing the right parents. As Sawhill and two colleagues have calculated, nearly two-thirds of children born to parents in the bottom fifth of income remain stuck in the lowest two-fifths as adults. […]

Although we consider mobility the heart of the American Dream, international studies find that, in most European countries, children born near the bottom now have a better chance of reaching the top than in the United States.

So far, these new trends haven't shattered the public's belief that success is earned, not inherited. In Allstate/National Journal Heartland Monitor polls over the past four years, a significant majority of Americans said they believe "the American Dream is still possible and achievable for … people like you." Most also think that their own efforts, not events beyond their control, will determine their success. […]

And yet these polls also point to cracks in that conviction. Nearly three-fifths of Hispanics and African-Americans, and about two-fifths of Asian-Americans, said last year that they believe their children will enjoy greater opportunities. Yet only about a fourth of whites agreed; more than two-fifths of whites feared their children would have fewer opportunities.

Ronald Brownstein, *National Journal Magazine*, 2012

to defer [dɪˈfɜːr] to delay until a later time
⁵ **enduring** continuing
⁸ **to clear a bar** *here:* to overcome a barrier
¹⁷ **to inherit** to pass down from one generation to the next

Zusatzmaterial WB
Task 19: Writing (letter to the editor)

6 COMPREHENSION
a) Explain the title 'A dream deferred'.
b) Sum up the findings presented in the text.

7 ANALYSIS On May 19, 2011, the Pew Economic Mobility Project conducted a national poll to assess the Americans' perceptions of economic mobility and the American Dream. Compare the information provided in the text from 2012 with the results of the poll as presented in the two graphs. → S27

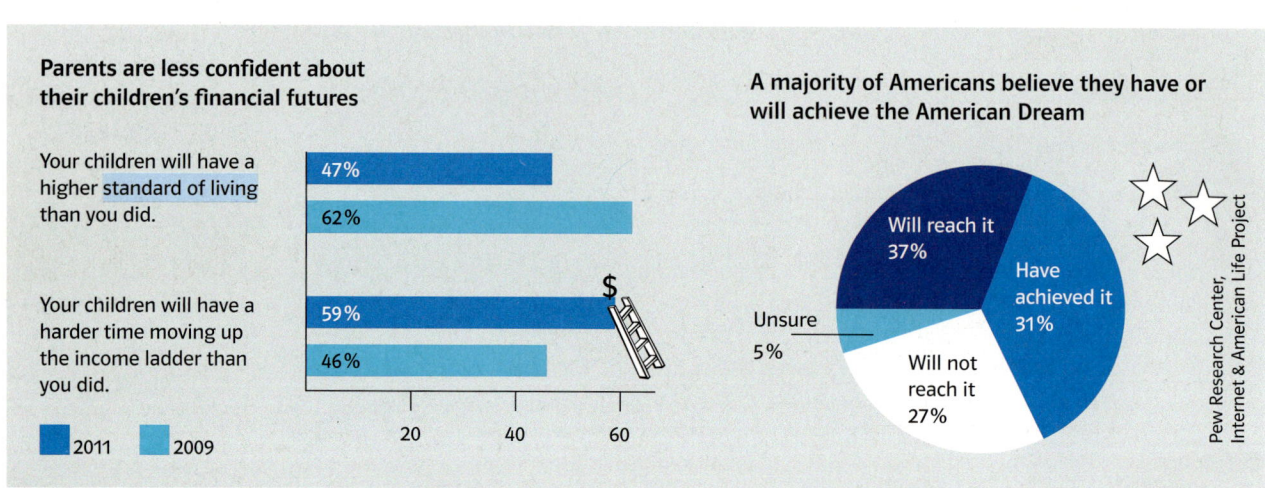

Parents are less confident about their children's financial futures

Your children will have a higher standard of living than you did.
2011: 47%
2009: 62%

Your children will have a harder time moving up the income ladder than you did.
2011: 59%
2009: 46%

A majority of Americans believe they have or will achieve the American Dream

Will reach it 37%
Have achieved it 31%
Will not reach it 27%
Unsure 5%

Pew Research Center, Internet & American Life Project

C An ongoing debate: America's gun culture

America's poorly regulated gun culture

Some statistics speak for themselves

A family visits a gun show together

1 SPEAKING
   a) Why are some people fascinated by guns? Who should have the right to buy firearms?
   b) What impression of America's attitude to guns do the photos convey?

2 ANALYSIS In June 2008 a Supreme Court decision upheld the right of individuals to possess and use firearms (see fact file), in particular handguns, for self-defence in the home. What could have been the reasons for granting this right in the US in the 18th century and now?

3 SPEAKING
   a) What would you think and feel if you heard this on the radio?

"Breaking News. Authorities say 20-year-old Adam Lanza blasted his way into Sandy Hook Elementary this morning in Newtown, Connecticut, and gunned down 26 people, including 20 children. He also killed his mother before the school attack, and later killed himself."

   b) What questions does this news story raise?

4 SPEAKING In 2014 a Gallup poll on gun laws came up with the following four key findings:

1. 37% of Americans had a gun in their home (down from 48% in 1990).
2. 49% of Americans wanted stricter laws covering the sale of firearms compared to 78% in 1990.
3. When asked what should be done to prevent mass shootings from occurring in the US, the most common answer was 'stricter gun control laws' (24%).
4. Of the 143 guns owned by the killers of 62 mass shootings in the US since 1982, three-quarters of the weapons were legally owned.

Discuss these statistics and what they tell you about the gun culture in America.
Geeignete Methode: Think – Pair – Share

FACT FILE

The Second Amendment to the US Constitution (1789) says, "A well regulated militia, being necessary to the security of a free state, the right of the people to keep and bear arms, shall not be infringed."

to bear *here:* to carry
to infringe to limit, to restrict

Zusatzmaterial WB
Task 9: Speaking

Advanced texts

FACT FILE

National Rifle Association (NRA), a powerful lobbying group in Washington that promotes the right of citizens to bear firearms in the United States. NRA membership reached 4.5 million in 2013.

¹ **harrowing** frightening, shocking
¹ **aftermath** [ˈæftəmæθ] period of time after a devastating event
² **to well** to come up
⁴ **lunatic** crazy person
¹¹ **carnage** [ˈkɑːnɪdʒ] blood bath
¹² **codes** *here:* regulations
¹² **to govern** to control
¹⁷ **to shrug** *die Achseln zucken*
¹⁷ **curb** restriction
¹⁹ **tip** *here:* front part
²⁰ **gumption** courage
²² **craven** without courage, cowardly
²² **feckless** *nichtsnutzig*
²⁵ **.22 rifle** long-barrel weapon with a relatively small opening
³³ **to deter** [dɪˈtɜːr] *abschrecken*
³⁵ **to pack heat** (*US slang*) to carry a hidden gun
³⁷ **unceasing** not ending
³⁷ **toll** *here:* number of deaths
³⁸ **homicide** [ˈhɒmɪsaɪd] murder
⁴¹ **purchase** [ˈpɜːrtʃəs] act of buying
⁴² **trafficker** trader, sb who buys and sells sth illegally
⁴⁴ **to impose** to introduce
⁴⁴ **background check** collection of relevant information
⁴⁵ **to back** to support
⁴⁶ **to require** *here:* to make it law
⁴⁶ **microstamp** very small mark
⁴⁶ **shell** *Patronenhülse*
⁴⁸ **road map** plan, concept
⁴⁹ **to galvanize** to shock sb so that he acts

Do we have the courage to stop this?

In the harrowing aftermath of the school shooting in Connecticut, one thought wells in my mind: Why can't we regulate guns as seriously as we do cars?

The fundamental reason kids are dying in massacres like this one is not that we have lunatics or criminals – all countries have them – but that we suffer from a political failure to regulate guns. 5

Children ages 5 to 14 in America are 13 times as likely to be murdered with guns as children in other industrialized countries, according to David Hemenway, a public health specialist at Harvard who has written an excellent book on gun violence.

So let's treat firearms rationally as the center of a public health crisis that claims one life every 20 minutes. The United States realistically isn't going to ban guns, but 10 we can take steps to reduce the carnage.

American schoolchildren are protected by building codes that govern stairways and windows. School buses must meet safety standards, and the bus drivers have to pass tests. Cafeteria food is regulated for safety. The only things we seem lax about are the things most likely to kill. 15

The Occupational Safety and Health Administration has five pages of regulations about ladders, while federal authorities shrug at serious curbs on firearms. Ladders kill around 300 Americans a year, and guns 30,000.

We even regulate toy guns, by requiring orange tips – but lawmakers don't have the gumption to stand up to National Rifle Association extremists and regulate real 20 guns as carefully as we do toys. What do we make of the contrast between heroic teachers who stand up to a gunman and craven, feckless politicians who won't stand up to the NRA? [...]

I grew up on an Oregon farm where guns were a part of life; and my dad gave me a .22 rifle for my 12th birthday. I understand: shooting is fun! But so is driving, 25 and we accept that we must wear seat belts, use headlights at night, and fill out forms to buy a car. Why can't we be equally adult about regulating guns?

And don't say that it won't make a difference because crazies will always be able to get a gun. We're not going to eliminate gun deaths, any more than we have eliminated auto accidents. But if we could reduce gun deaths by one-third, that 30 would be 10,000 lives saved annually.

Likewise, don't bother with the argument that if more people carried guns, they would deter shooters or interrupt them. Mass shooters typically kill themselves or are promptly caught, so it's hard to see what deterrence would be added by having more people pack heat. There have been few if any cases in the United States in 35 which an ordinary citizen with a gun stopped a mass shooting.

The tragedy isn't one school shooting, it's the unceasing toll across our country. More Americans die in gun homicides and suicides in six months than have died in the last 25 years in every terrorist attack and the wars in Afghanistan and Iraq combined. 40

So what can we do? A starting point would be to limit gun purchases to one a month, to curb gun traffickers. Likewise, we should restrict the sale of high-capacity magazines so that a shooter can't kill as many people without reloading.

We should impose a universal background check for gun buyers, even with private sales. Let's make serial numbers more difficult to erase, and back California 45 in its effort to require that new handguns imprint a microstamp on each shell so that it can be traced back to a particular gun. [...]

Other countries offer a road map. In Australia in 1996, a mass killing of 35 people galvanized the nation's conservative prime minister to ban certain rapid-fire long guns. The "national firearms agreement," as it was known, led to the buyback of 50

650,000 guns and to tighter rules for licensing and safe storage of those remaining in public hands.

The law did not end gun ownership in Australia. It reduced the number of firearms in private hands by one-fifth, and they were the kinds most likely to be used in mass shootings.

In the 18 years before the law, Australia suffered 13 mass shootings – but not one in the 14 years after the law took full effect. The murder rate with firearms has dropped by more than 40 percent, according to data compiled by the Harvard Injury Control Research Center, and the suicide rate with firearms has dropped by more than half.

Or we can look north to Canada. It now requires a 28-day waiting period to buy a handgun, and it imposes a clever safeguard: gun buyers should have the support of two people vouching for them.

For that matter, we can look for inspiration at our own history on auto safety. As with guns, some auto deaths are caused by people who break laws or behave irresponsibly. But we don't shrug and say, "Cars don't kill people, drunks do."

Instead, we have required seat belts, air bags, child seats and crash safety standards. We have introduced limited licenses for young drivers and tried to curb the use of mobile phones while driving. All this has reduced America's traffic fatality rate per mile driven by nearly 90 percent since the 1950s.

Some of you are alive today because of those auto safety regulations. And if we don't treat guns in the same serious way, some of you and some of your children will die because of our failure.

Nicholas D. Kristof, *New York Times*, 2012

⁶¹ **to compile** to collect
⁶⁷ **to vouch** [vaʊtʃ] *sich verbürgen*

Avoiding mistakes
Wortschatz
⁶⁰**data** Daten
   dates Termine

5 COMPREHENSION *Several numbers are mentioned in this article. Go through the text with a partner and find all the numbers. Then rewrite the phrase in which they are used.*
Example: (lines 6–7) Young American between the ages of 5 and 14 are murdered 13 times more frequently than children in other developed countries.

6 ANALYSIS *Divide the text into sections and give headings for each one. Write down keywords for each section, and summarise the author's argument.*
Hinweis: Auch als Hausaufgabe geeignet

7 ANALYSIS *Analyse how the author tries to convince his readers of the need to regulate guns. Consider the content, language and tone.* → S4

8 VISUALS *Interpret the cartoon above based on the information in Section C of this topic.* → S28.2

9 SPEAKING *Should guns be more strictly regulated in America? Conduct a panel discussion with*

- Nicholas Kristof, the author of the text above
- a representative of the NRA
- a member of the NGO Moms Demand Action
- a journalist from Germany (see Erfurt or Winnenden school shootings).

10 RESEARCH *Write a short fact box on 'Guns in Germany' based on your findings.*
→ **S32**   **Hinweis:** Auch als Hausaufgabe geeignet

FACT FILE

Guns in America
Today the United States has by far the highest rate of gun ownership in the world (90%). It also has the highest rate of murders among advanced countries. (11,000 in 2010). Fifteen of the 25 worst mass shootings in the last 50 years took place in the United States. The statistical probability that a person will be killed by a firearm is 16 times greater in the US than Germany.

Zusatzmaterial KV/WB
KV 4: Role play cards
WB Task 20: Idiomatic expressions

Advanced texts

D Ethnic minorities

As I Grew Older

It was a long time ago.
I have almost forgotten my dream.
But it was there then,
In front of me,
5 Bright like a sun –
My dream.

And then the wall rose,
Rose slowly,
Slowly,
10 Between me and my dream.
Rose until it touched the sky –
The wall.

Shadow.
I am black.
15 I lie down in the shadow.
No longer the light of my dream
before me,
Above me.
Only the thick wall.
20 Only the shadow.
My hands!
My dark hands!

Break through the wall!
Find my dream!
25 Help me to shatter this darkness,
To smash this night,
To break this shadow
Into a thousand lights of sun,
Into a thousand whirling dreams
30 Of sun!

Langston Hughes, 1925

25 **to shatter** to destroy
26 **to smash** to break into many pieces
29 **whirling** moving quickly

VIP FILE

Langston Hughes (1902–1967) was a writer who was part of the Harlem Renaissance of the 1920s, in which African American literature, art and music became increasingly popular in America.

USEFUL PHRASES

Talking about the African American experience

slavery
exploitation
racial segregation
black underclass vs black middle class
Rosa Parks
Civil Rights Movement
Martin Luther King
informal discrimination
ethnic prejudices
positive/reverse discrimination
success stories
Barack Obama

1 COMPREHENSION Describe the speaker's view of his early life and his present thoughts and feelings.

2 ANALYSIS
 a) What makes this poem effective? Analyse how the speaker conveys his message through figurative language and other poetic devices. → S10.2
 b) Recite the poem in a way which reflects the speaker's message.

3 EVALUATION Comment on the statement: "This poem is a timeless cross-cultural and cross-ethnic description of the experience of growing up across all cultures and ethnic backgrounds." → S14.2 → △6 **Diff** (help with): Definition der Schlüsselwörter

4 VIEWING
 a) View a news report to find out about African Americans in Harlem today and how they felt about immigration and the American Dream shortly before the 2012 election.
 b) To what extent have African American dreams come true?
 c) Using the news report as a guide, write the script for a TV commentary which places the current situation in Harlem into the wider context of African American history. In doing so, quote from the poem above and use as many of the keywords from the box as possible.

Zusatzmaterial WB
Task 21: Analysing poetry

stupid america

stupid america, see that chicano
with a big knife
on his steady hand
5 he doesn't want to knife you
he wants to sit on a bench
and carve christ figures
but you won't let him.

stupid america, hear that
10 chicano
shouting curses on the street
he is a poet without paper and pencil
and since he cannot write
he will explode.

15 stupid america, remember that chicanito
flunking math and english
he is the picasso
of your western states
20 but he will die
with one thousand masterpieces
hanging only from his mind.

From: Abelardo Delgado, *Chicano: 25 Pieces of a Chicano Mind*, 1969

10 **chicano** having to do with Mexican Americans
17 **to flunk** to fail

VIP FILE

Abelardo Delgado (1930–2004) was born in Mexico and moved to El Paso, Texas, with his mother in 1943. His life was spent working as an artist, activist and teacher. He helped develop many Chicano Studies programs in universities throughout the Western United States.

Zusatzmaterial WB
Task 22: Fine-tuning your vocabulary
Task 23: Writing poetry

5 **COMPREHENSION** State what image of the Hispanic minority the poem conveys.

6 **ANALYSIS** Explain how the speaker underlines the urgency of his warnings. Consider the structure of the poem, the use of imagery and the speaker's message. → S6.1 **Hinweis:** Auch als Hausaufgabe geeignet

7 **CREATIVE TASK** A publisher is planning an edition of the best multicultural American poems of the last century. The two poems here are shortlisted for that collection. Write a letter to the publisher in which you argue for or against each of these two poems. → S18.1 **Hinweis:** Auch als mündliche Diskussion geeignet

8 **CREATIVE TASK**
a) Write your own free verse or traditional poem about America. Use any knowledge gained in this unit to express your praise or criticism. Select useful rhetorical devices to get your message across effectively.
b) Practise reciting your poem first to yourself and then to a partner for constructive feedback. Present your poem in the class.

9 **ANALYSIS** Discuss the statistics below. What do they tell us about the comparative success of various ethnic groups in the US? → S27

Ethnic diversity in the US	Whites	Asian Americans	Native Americans	African Americans	Latinos/Hispanics
Less than high school	15.3%	19.5%	27.4%	29.1%	48.5%
College degree	25.3%	42.9%	10.8%	13.6%	9.9%
High skill occupation	21.4%	34.6%	11.9%	12.3%	9.6%
Married: spouse present	64.5%	74.9%	50.2%	38.0%	56.3%
Median personal income (US$)	23,640	20,200	14,500	16,300	14,400
Living in poverty	9.4%	11.5%	25.1%	24.9%	21.4%

US Census

Hispanics at a demonstration calling attention to the value of migrant workers in Washington

10 **RESEARCH** *"Has the American Dream come true for minorities?"* Research different ethnic/minority groups in the US. Focus on their history of immigration, living conditions today etc. Make a one-page fact file and give group presentations. Take notes during the other presentations. Compare your findings about ethnic groups with respect to the research question.

Spot on language

> **Hinweis**
> Selbstevaluation für Schüler über Green Line-Code

Using rhetorical devices effectively

1 *Write down rhetorical devices that you would use in a statement or speech and give an example of each device. Compare your results with those of a partner. Discuss which ones seem most effective to you at certain points in a speech (introduction/main body/conclusion) and why.*

2 *The text below is the beginning of a speech that is relatively lacking in rhetorical devices and coherence. Improve it by connecting the ideas and introducing some rhetorical devices.*

To most people the American Dream consists of owning your own home and a car. They dream of having a decent job and the prospect of a better future for their children. Many Americans wonder
5 if achieving this dream is still possible. Many of the cornerstones of the American Dream are under pressure or gone. Today the middle class, which best embodies the ideals of the American Dream, is shrinking. The poor and the super-rich are increasing
10 in number. Americans are too afraid to dream at all. They are afraid of terrorism, cheap immigrant labor and crazed gunmen. The country is divided to such an extent that there can be no one-size-fits-all American Dream any more.
   The Dream may be tough enough to withstand the 15 challenges of our times. It lives on in every citizen who works hard to provide for his/her family. The Dream is still alive in every soldier who fights abroad to protect his/her fellow Americans. It is visible in every citizen who speaks out for freedom and 20 equality. The Dream lives on in every American who brings up his/her children to cherish and perpetuate the values that have made this country great.

Writing and presenting an effective speech beginning

3 a) *Write the beginning of a speech about how the unit has changed your knowledge/view of the US. Use rhetorical devices for effect.*
   b) *Practise reading your speech beginnings out loud, paying attention to speed, pauses, emphasis and intonation.*
   c) *Listen to and comment on the beginning of your speeches.*

Talking optimistically about the future

4 *Copy the table below and fill it in with four useful phrases for each column from this list:*

I am very confident that … • in the near/foreseeable future • are working hard to … • to tackle a pressing problem • to overcome resistance • My hope for the future is that … • in the short/long term • have to ensure that … • There is no doubt that … • as a first step • to convince sceptics • will make every effort to … • I am cautiously optimistic that … • gain the support of … • are prepared to … • as a first concrete measure

Optimism	The future	Intention and initiative	Toward solving problems
…	…	…	…

5 *Imagine you are being interviewed for a new job or you have just arrived in a new country. Answer the following questions in a friendly and optimistic way using the phrases from the table above. Ask the other person questions as well.*

What are your plans for the first three months? • What will be your first priority in your job? • How do you feel about the many challenges you are facing? • …

Mediation

6 *Collect useful words and phrases for making comparisons.*

7 *Your American pen pal has told you about some relatives for whom the American Dream has not come true yet. He/She would like to know what young people in Germany expect of their future. On the basis of the article below, write an email in which you describe the 'German Dream' of young Germans and then compare it with the American Dream. Explain the conclusions the author draws from the differences in these two dreams.* → **S26.1**

Wie Träume unser Wirtschaftsleben beeinflussen

Was kommt nach dem *American Dream*? Wovon die Menschen in einem Land träumen, entscheidet auch über die Wirtschaftskraft eines Landes.

Stephan Grünewald hat kürzlich junge Deutsche auf die Couch gelegt und war am Ende etwas überrascht. Der Mann ist Trendforscher, er betreibt in Köln die Unternehmensberatungsfirma Rheingold und findet mit tiefenpsychologischen Methoden heraus, was die Menschen hierzulande wünschen, fürchten und träumen.

Als er das zuletzt bei jungen Erwachsenen erfragte, solchen im Berufsanfängeralter zwischen 18 und 21, staunte er: „Wir waren verblüfft, wie bürgerlich-konservativ die Lebensträume ausfallen". Die Traumberufe seien heute oft diejenigen, die in den siebziger Jahren eher noch ein niedriges Sozialprestige hatten: Beamter, Bankkaufmann, Versicherungsangestellter.

Der *German Dream* – für den Psychologen Grünewald ist er in dieser Generation ein Streben nach Sicherheit, nach Überschaubarkeit, nach „einer beständigen Welt, in der wieder Sekundärtugenden zählen". Nach solider, planbarer aber keineswegs aufregender beruflicher Laufbahn, nach einer guten Vereinbarkeit von Beruf und Familie. Risiko und Unternehmertum bleiben die Sache einer Minderheit.

[…] Ganz grob betrachtet und im Vergleich mit anderen Ländern ist da etwas dran: In Deutschland träumt man nicht den großen Traum von Wagnis, Abenteuer und Selbstverwirklichung als Unternehmer. Man will ein Einfamilienhaus.

Auf die Wirtschaftskraft und für die Neuerungsfähigkeit eines Landes haben solche Träume und Sehnsüchte einen Einfluss, sie übersetzen sich ja in unternehmerischen Wagemut, in Pflichtbewusstsein bei der Arbeit, in die Bereitschaft zur Anstrengung und Selbstausbeutung. […] Der Harvard-Historiker Niall Ferguson sah das nicht viel anders, als er kürzlich über Deutschland und seine europäischen Nachbarn bitter urteilte: „Europäer sind heute die Faulpelze der Welt. Im Durchschnitt arbeiten sie weniger als Amerikaner und viel weniger als Asiaten. […] Zwischen 2000 und 2009 arbeitete ein durchschnittlicher Amerikaner knapp 1.711 Stunden pro Jahr, aber der durchschnittliche Deutsche nur 1.437 Stunden". Seit 1979 klaffe diese Schere immer weiter auseinander, sagt Ferguson.

Aber warum wird in den USA im Vergleich so hart gearbeitet? Tatsächlich stoßen viele Forscher auf der Suche nach Erklärungsmustern auf das alte Klischee des *American Dream*. Eine hohe Zahl von Amerikanern bekennt sich in Umfragen bis heute zu diesem Set von Vorstellungen: dass in ihrem Land jedermann den Aufstieg schaffen könne, egal welcher Herkunft oder Hautfarbe, solange er hart genug arbeite und ein ordentliches Leben führe. Wenn man an so etwas wirklich glaubt, ist das eine wunderbare Voraussetzung dafür, dass man sich für die Arbeit maximal aufopfert. Dass man Rückschläge wegsteckt, wieder auf die Beine kommt und etwas Neues anfängt.

Die Zeit, 2012

8 *Comment on Grünewald's findings and conclusions. How does your personal dream compare with the German and American Dreams described in the article?*

Spot on vocabulary

Writing about the American Dream and nightmare

1 *Use the English equivalents of these German words to complete the text.*

> überfüllt • Möglichkeiten • verdoppeln • Anhänger • Gelegenheit • begegnen • verstört

After the east coast had become too `1`, Americans headed west where more freedom, fistfuls of gold and `2` supposedly awaited them. Jefferson's Louisiana Purchase of 1803 `3` the size of the nation. His `4` applauded the `5` to create millions of new farms. But as the settlers moved west, they `6` Native Americans who were `7` by their lack of respect for nature.

2 a) *Find the missing forms.*

verb	noun	adjective
to theorise	a new ▭ about the frontier	▭ ideas
settlers ▭ the West	we saw her ▭ as she grew	transformational
live long and ▭	prosperity	to run a ▭ business
to commit oneself	to demand total ▭	to be ▭ to the cause
▭ different groups of people	equality	▭ opportunity
to separate	▭ of church and state	▭ but equal
they ▭ production	individual	▭ attitude toward one's goals

b) *Form adjectives from these words.*

> support • opportunity • possibility • diversity • persistence • ethnicity • invention • spectacle • difference

c) 👥 *Write sentences using the nouns and adjectives. Leave blanks and have a partner fill them in.*

3 *Find the antonyms and write informative sentences with them.*

> advocate *(n)* • indifference • to discriminate against • to reduce • to immigrate • minimal

4 *Match the pairs and use them in sentences about the US.*

| to conduct • minimum • to offer • per capita • assault • mortgage • to hold • election | **+** | an incentive • income • campaign • wage • a rally • payments • a poll • weapon |

5 *Compose a short essay called "The American Nightmare" using most of these expressions.*

> to strike out • to be at stake • to renege on promises • minimum wage • homeless shelter • up in the air • reality • flee • hope

TIP

🔘 First work on the vocab sheets; then test yourself here!

Topic task

The US then and now 4

Giving a speech at a youth conference

You have been invited to give a speech at an international youth conference on the topic "The USA then and now: Values and visions for the 21st century" organised by the US embassy in Berlin.

STEP 1 — Choosing a topic

Decide on a topic for your speech. You may focus your speech on a topic of your choice or on one of the themes dealt with in this unit, such as

- the making of America
- life in a multi-ethnic society
- the American Dream
- America's changing role in the world
- American values: freedom, individualism, patriotism, progress, can-do spirit

STEP 2 — Taking on a role

Decide on a role. You may speak for yourself or in-role. Possible roles are:

- a German student who spent a school year in the US
- a representative of the youth wing of an American or German political party
- a German youth who did an internship at the National Museum of American History in Washington
- the American ambassador to Germany, who will give the keynote speech of this conference. A keynote speech is a speech given at the beginning of an event by a prominent speaker to summarise its core message and set its underlying tone.

STEP 3 — Turning a topic into a thesis and a speech script

a) Collect arguments for your topic and your role.
b) Decide on a core message of your speech, e.g. a thesis, a call for action, a prediction etc. and structure your main arguments.
c) Write the script of your speech. → S15

STEP 4 — Rehearsing your speech

Practise giving your speech in a small group, paying attention to:

- **body language:** Be confident, stand firmly but relaxed. Keep your hands out of your pockets and smile.
- **voice:** Speak clearly and freely, vary your tone/volume/emphasis, make pauses.
- **contact with the audience:** Make eye contact, use the pronouns "I/you/we". Ask for constructive feedback on the content, structure and presentation of your speech. → S22

STEP 5 — Holding the conference

Each group chooses the best speech and somebody to 'frame' this speech. 'Framing' means introducing your speaker formally to the audience, thanking him/her for the speech and inviting questions from the audience, which he/she will answer spontaneously.
Start the conference with the American ambassador's keynote speech.

TIP

Learning from good speakers

View or listen to effective speakers and learn how they get their message across to their audiences.

USEFUL PHRASES

'Framing' a speech

Ladies and gentlemen, I am delighted/I have the privilege to introduce …

It is an honour for me to welcome … today.

He/She spent a year …/is a representative of …

Speaking on behalf of …, I would like to thank you for …

a very informative/entertaining/thought-provoking talk

new insights into …/convincing line of argument

Mr/Ms X is now prepared to take questions.

5 International relations
Introduction

Code jy9z2b

UN peacekeeper, often called Blue Helmets because of their headgear

Trouble spots worldwide

Trouble spots around Europe

USEFUL PHRASES

Talking about international relations

on the local/national/international level

source of the conflict, ethnic/religious tensions/turmoil, conflicting parties

reconciliation, separation, border, barbed wire, use of force, relief work/efforts

1 SPEAKING Describe the state of the world we live in. Then share your assessment with your group.

2 VISUALS Describe the map and identify the various crisis regions. → S27

3 ANALYSIS
  a) List possible causes for international conflicts and suggest ways to resolve them. **Zusatzmaterial KV 1:** Speaking prompts
  b) Which role do international organisations like NATO, the UN, or the EU play in conflict resolution? → △1 **Diff** (help with): Vorgabe möglicher Aspekte
  c) What requirements have to be met in order for a resolution to be successful?

Spot on **facts**

International relations **5**

The **European Union**

> **Avoiding mistakes**
> Wortschatz
> [27]**still** nevertheless, in spite of that

1 BEFORE YOU READ What does the European Union mean to you? How does it affect your everyday life?
Geeignete Methode: Think – Pair – Share

A growing supranational organisation

The European Union is a political and economic union, whose goal it is to secure peace and prosperity in Europe. Its roots lie in the European Coal and Steel Community (with coal and steel at that time being key war industries), which was founded by Belgium, France, West Germany, the Netherlands, Italy and Luxemburg. Over the many decades of its existence, this supranational organisation has increased both in size, from the six founding members to 28 member states in 2014, as well as in power and complexity with ever more competencies and institutions. Its main institutions include: the European Commission, which serves as the executive branch of the EU; the European Council and the European Parliament, which share the legislative power of the EU; and the European Court of Justice, which functions as the judiciary branch. The underlying goal of these institutions is to enact, create and govern the common legal framework in the EU. These legal policies aim at ensuring the free movement throughout the EU of people, goods, services, and capital as well as ensuring a wider and deeper integration of Europe.

Decision-making is a crucial issue for the EU. Over the years many reforms have had to be made in reaction to the growing number of member states and the resulting difficulties in decision-making. Still, the EU has proven its ability to pass legislation in all kinds of policy areas.

The most readily felt EU policies are most likely the common currency for member states of the monetary union and the freedom to work, study and travel anywhere in the EU, but there are numerous other initiatives the EU has undertaken that have a strong impact on our everyday lives, such as the regulation of roaming charges or its laws protecting the privacy of EU citizens.

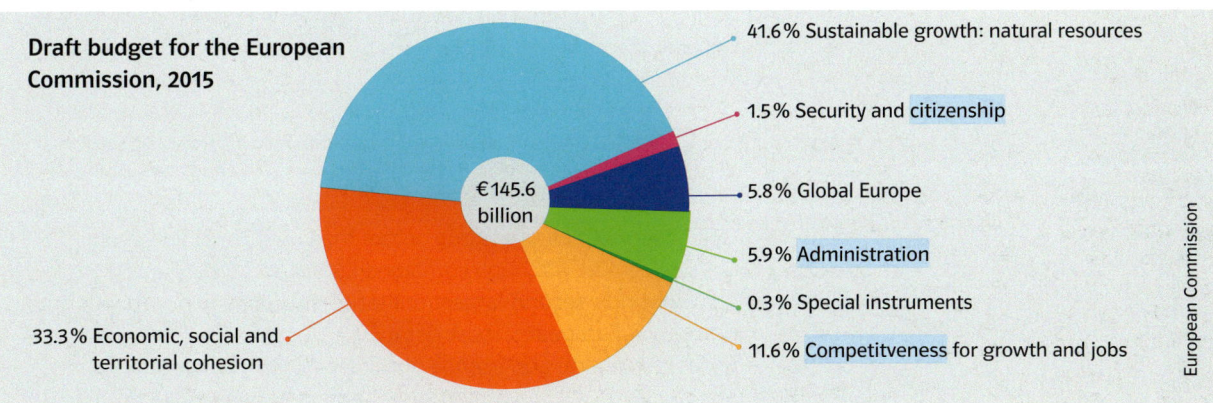

Draft budget for the European Commission, 2015
€145.6 billion
- 41.6% Sustainable growth: natural resources
- 1.5% Security and citizenship
- 5.8% Global Europe
- 5.9% Administration
- 0.3% Special instruments
- 11.6% Competitveness for growth and jobs
- 33.3% Economic, social and territorial cohesion

European Commission

2 ANALYSIS To what extent are the tasks and goals of the EU reflected in the budget of the European Commission?

Texts

A Military power

1 BEFORE YOU READ *Discuss whether you think there is a need for a world policeman.* **Geeignete Methode:** Speed dating

Can the EU become the world's policeman?

"A decade of war is now ending," President Obama declared Monday. Maybe that's true in America, but it isn't true anywhere else. Extremists are still plotting acts of terror. Authoritarian and autocratic regimes are still using violence to preserve their power. The United States can step back from international conflicts, but that won't make them disappear.

Fortunately, there is another power that shares our economic and political values, that possesses sophisticated military technology and is also very interested in stopping the progress of fanatical movements, especially in North Africa and the Middle East. That power is Europe.

Don't laugh! I realize that even a year ago, that statement would have seemed absurd. I certainly couldn't have written it in the immediate aftermath of the 2011 Libya operation, during which France, Britain and a dozen other nations were barely able to sustain a brief war, involving no ground troops, against a poorly armed and unpopular regime. Unverified reports at the time alleged that the French ran out of bombs and were dropping lumps of concrete. Without the intelligence and coordination provided by American warships and airplanes and the CIA, the French planes wouldn't even have known where to drop them.

Yet here we are in 2013, watching the French air force and troops come to the aid of the formerly democratic government of Mali, which is fighting for its life against a fanatical Islamist insurgency. Furthermore, this French intervention has (so far) broad national support. Although there have been public criticisms of the operation's logistics, preparation and ultimate goals, almost no one in France questions the need for intervention. Hardly anyone is even asking "Why France?"

[…O]ther Europeans are offering money and soldiers. The European Union has authorized funding to train African troops who will assist — and it does have more experience than you'd think. EU forces, operating far beneath the publicity radar, successfully attacked pirate bases on the Somali coast last spring. "They destroyed our equipment to ashes," a man described as a "pirate commander" told the Associated Press. All told, the European Union has intervened militarily in more than two dozen conflicts. Not quite as much as the French since 1960, but getting there.

A number of obstacles must be overcome before the European Union could become the world's policeman. Although combined European military spending does make the EU the world's second-largest military power, it still isn't enough for a sustained conflict. Some Europeans, most notably the Germans, would have to overcome their post-World War II abhorrence of soldiers. Other Europeans, most notably the British, would have to be convinced, as others have concluded, that Americans just aren't that interested in NATO anymore. An added complication emerged this week when British Prime Minister David Cameron announced his

---

Avoiding mistakes
Aussprache
²⁰**alleged** [əˈledʒd]

---

⁴ **to plot** to plan
⁴ **authoritarian** enforcing strict obedience
⁴ **autocratic** ruling with absolute power
⁵ **to preserve** to protect
¹⁸ **barely** almost not
¹⁸ **sustain** to keep going
¹⁸ **to allege** to claim
²⁶ **insurgency** Aufstand
³⁵ **all told** in total
³⁸ **overcome an obstacle** successfully deal with a problem
⁴² **abhorrence** Abscheu

intention to renegotiate his country's relationship with the European Union. However it unfolds, this process is unlikely to aid in the development of a common European foreign and defense policy.

These are big obstacles. But what's the alternative? If America is to enjoy "peace in our time" – an expression now deployed by both Barack Obama and Neville Chamberlain – while the rest of the world remains at war, then someone else will fill the vacuum. A glance at the other candidates – China, Russia, perhaps Qatar or another Gulf nation – ought to make us all stop giggling about cheese-eating surrender monkeys and start offering logistical and moral support. Europe may not be the best superpower. But it's the only one we've got.

Anne Applebaum, *The Washington Post*, 2013

52 **glance** quick look
53 **cheese-eating surrender monkeys** *here:* derogatory description of the French

2 COMPREHENSION
a) *Illustrate the development of European involvement in armed international conflicts.* → S4.1
b) *Explain the obstacles that have yet to be overcome for the EU to become the world's policeman.*

3 ANALYSIS
a) *Analyse the author's attitude toward the EU becoming the new world policeman.* → S4.2
b) *Analyse the language Applebaum uses to get her point across.*

4 ANALYSIS
Describe and analyse the graph. → S27   **Hinweis:** Auch als Hausaufgabe geeignet

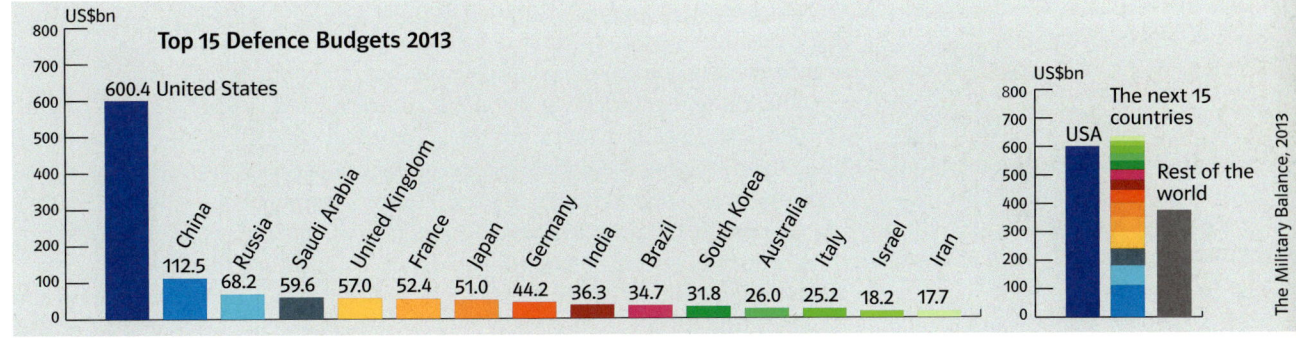

5 SPEAKING
a) *Discuss with your partner whether every country needs to have a military.*
b) *In percent, how much money should be spent on the military?* **Geeignete Methode:** Think – Pair – Share

6 EVALUATION → ▲2   **Diff** (instead of): Diskussion über die Einführung des UNICEF Programms „Learning for Peace" in Europa
a) *Discuss the following theses, taking the article and the graph into consideration:*

1. The EU has to become the next world's policeman.
2. The EU will never match the military power of the US.
3. The next logical step for a Common Security and Defence Policy would be a common military.
4. There are too many hindrances for a common military to be successful in the EU.
5. For the EU to do the job well, it should spend more money on the military.

b) *Formulate a joint position on the first thesis.*
c) *Form new groups and exchange your joint position with new people.*

Zusatzmaterial WB
Task 1: Collocations
Task 2: Working with cartoons
Task 3: Analysis
Task 4: Language awareness

Texts

B The EU and the UK – another special relationship?

1 VISUALS *Analyse the relationship between the EU and the UK as portrayed in this cartoon. Can you think of possible consequences of an increasing distance between the EU and the UK?* → **S28.2**

Just to make sure we keep our distance …

¹ **crossroads** *Scheideweg*
² **to ditch** to get rid of
³ **to opt** to decide
⁴ **to abandon** to give up
⁵ **entity** body
⁹ **to abdicate** to step down or not participate in

"EU treatment of human rights is second to none"

We are coming up to a major crossroads in the country's future and the heart of it is whether we are going to ditch an expansive vision and opt for a shrinking one. Do we want to become a medium-sized country with no great influence or responsibility in the world, abandoning our international role, or do we want to be part of a much bigger entity with far-reaching international influence in which we 5 would be a significant decision-maker?

The shrinking of the vision will also shrink our ideas, our attitudes and the scale of our innovations. It would be the cautious move of a relatively elderly society deciding to abdicate from any major global role. The once-upon-a-time alternative to the EU, our relationship with America, is no longer the option that it might have 10 been. Our most powerful ally is increasingly multicultural, rather than Anglo Saxon, and its major strategic interests lie predominantly in Asia.

Shirley Williams (Liberal Democrat MP), *The Observer*, 2014

"If we left, we would get back our democracy"

We can govern ourselves better than 27 other countries can do it for us. That is the positive and optimistic case for Britain leaving the EU and becoming an independent country, trading with Europe, but governing ourselves.

Of course, when exporting to the EU we would need to obey the rules of the single market, just as exporters to the US or Japan obey their rules, although many 5 trade rules are now set globally. However, we would no longer need to apply the vast regulatory superstructure of the EU to the majority of our exports which go outside the EU, or to the near three-quarters of our economy that is domestic trade.

In return for giving up one vote among 28 countries on EU rules, we would again have a national say on global rules, as Norway, Switzerland and South Korea 10 do, enjoy free trade with the EU as they do and govern our own domestic economy. Instead of having to obey rules set by the EU, we could set our own policies democratically. In some areas we might choose to allow greater flexibility, while in others, say in protecting animal welfare, we might regulate more strictly.

Mark Reckless (Tory MP), *The Observer*, 2014

⁴ **to obey** to do what you are told
⁷ **vast** very large
¹⁰ **to have a say** to have power to decide

2 COMPREHENSION *Compare and contrast these two MPs' positions.* → **S4**

3 SPEAKING *Slip into the role of either Williams or Reckless and argue your case against the other.* → **S24** **Zusatzmaterial KV 2:** Role cards

4 EVALUATION *Write a letter to either Williams or Reckless in which you argue against their position.* → **S18.1** **Hinweis:** Auch als Hausaufgabe geeignet

5 VIEWING *Watch the film clip "Flying the EU flag in the UK" and compare what the flagmaker says about the British flag as opposed to the EU flag. What do you notice with respect to his word choice?*

6 EVALUATION *"It's one thing to run something up a flagpole, another to salute it." Comment on this and explain what this means for the EU.*
Hinweis: Auch als Hausaufgabe geeignet

C The new old anti-Americanism

1 BEFORE YOU READ What comes to mind when you think of the US-German relationship? Take events such as the aftermath of 9/11 and the 2013 NSA scandal into account. **Geeignete Methode:** Placemat

Zusatzmaterial WB
Task 5: Speaking

◉ L2/9 **2 MEDIATION** Listen to a German Tagesschau podcast and write an email about its content to an American high school exchange student. → **S26.1** **Hinweis:** Auch als Hausaufgabe geeignet

3 MEDIATION The exchange student wants to find out more about German-American relations. Use the following article to explain the source of Anti-Americanism and the „Negativfolie der USA" in a second email. → △3 **Diff** (help with): Verbesserung eines Lösungsvorschlags

Der neue alte Antiamerikanismus

Die NSA-Affäre und ihre Folgen: Die USA werden hierzulande immer verhasster. Hinter der vermeintlichen Kritik verbergen sich jedoch oft muffigste Ressentiments.
Die transatlantischen Beziehungen liegen am Boden, mit jeder weiteren NSA-Enthüllung wächst das Misstrauen. Dass die Bundesregierung jetzt offenbar
5 sogar die Spionageabwehr gegen die USA ausbauen will, wäre vor Kurzem noch undenkbar gewesen – heute fügt es sich ins Bild. Inzwischen mehren sich selbst die Forderungen nach einem offenen Bruch. „Europa muss sich vom amerikanischen Einfluss endlich lösen", hieß es kürzlich auf Focus Online, nachdem die US-Diplomatin Victoria Nuland in einem öffentlich gewordenen Telefongespräch
10 polemisch über die Ukraine-Politik der Europäer hergezogen war („Fuck the EU"). […]
Da schreibt Jakob Augstein auf *Spiegel Online*, die rüpelhafte Äußerung der US-Diplomatin zeige einmal mehr, dass Europa gegenüber den USA gestärkt werden müsse. Dies könne aber nur funktionieren, wenn das Europäische Parlament mehr
15 Macht erhalte. Recht so! Doch dann kommt's. Augstein entwirft sein Wunschbild von Europa nämlich vor der Negativfolie der USA. Dort sei „längst entschieden", wer die Macht habe: „Die wichtigen Weichen werden zwischen Big Money, Big Data und den Big Guns gestellt. Und der Wert eines Rechts entspricht den technologischen Kosten, es zu brechen. Europa hat noch die Wahl, einen anderen Weg zu gehen."
20 Das ist Antiamerikanismus pur. Denn die Kritik verkehrt sich hier in ein stereotypes Welterklärungsmuster, in dem alles Negative – ob Kapitalmacht, Waffengewalt, Überwachungsstaat oder Rechtsdefizite – auf die USA projiziert wird. Und das nur, um sich eine europäische Identität herbeizufantasieren, die dazu im Gegensatz steht: moralisch höherwertig, gut. Dies ist heuchlerisch. Denn
25 Augstein gesteht ja selbst ein, dass es mit der Demokratie in Europa nicht zum Besten steht. […]
Es sind muffigste Ressentiments, die da zum Vorschein kommen. Das alte dualistische Bild: Ein degeneriertes, materialistisches und bigottes Amerika auf der einen Seite – und das kulturvolle, zivilisierte Europa auf der anderen. Transformiert
30 ins 21. Jahrhundert – der NSA-Skandal macht's möglich. Das ist der neue Antiamerikanismus: Die moralische Supermacht Europa erhebt sich gegen den Koloss USA. Dieser Antiamerikanismus ist brandgefährlich, weil er vordergründig zwar ein gutes Gefühl verschaffen mag, die eigenen Verfehlungen jedoch verdeckt und faktisch alles beim Alten lässt – ob Datenschnüffelei oder Demokratiedefizite.
35 Eine solche Haltung ist alles andere als kritisch, nämlich konformistisch und reaktionär.

Tobias Jaecker, *Die Zeit*, 2014

6 Migration and diversity
Introduction

Code
92pp34

Mohamad Farah, who was born in Mogadishu, waving the national flag of the UK (Union Jack)

Young boy with the national flag of Canada (Maple Leaf)

Girls wearing the national flag of Australia (Union Jack and Southern Cross) as headscarves

People celebrating in front of the American flag (Star-Spangled Banner/Stars and Stripes)

1 VISUALS
   a) Look at all the pictures on these two pages. Which of them affects you most? Share your first impressions with your partner.
   b) Take a closer look at the pictures and match them to the UK, the US, Canada and Australia or to all of them. Give reasons for your choices.

2 SPEAKING In small groups discuss what the pictures have in common and share your ideas in class. → **S24**

3 CREATIVE TASK How multi-ethnic is society in your country? Find pictures representing your ideals. Compare them in small groups and vote for the best picture and present it in class.

Brick Lane, famous street in East London

Demonstration in front of The East London Mosque

National identity

There are different concepts of national identity. One concept defines national identity as a person's sense of belonging to a nation, which is shaped by language and traditions. According to this idea, national identity is not an inborn trait and can change in the course of one's life.

The other concept of national identity is based on the idea of having the same ancestry or ethnicity. This idea reflects the original meaning of the word nationality. 'Nation' comes from the Latin word *natus*, which means 'born'. Therefore, the word nation can be understood as belonging to the same racial group. However, this concept is problematic and outdated, since nowadays every nation has a mixed population.

British police uniforms; Sikhs are allowed to wear a turban instead of the official police hat

4 COMPREHENSION *Sum up the text about national identity in your own words.*

5 EVALUATION
 a) *Which concept of national identity do you prefer? Give reasons.*
 b) *Tony Blair, a former British Prime Minister, said that "blood alone" does not define national identity and that modern Britain was shaped by a "rich mix of all different ethnic and religious origins". Look at the pictures and at the definitions of nationality and comment on Blair's statement.*

6 VISUALS *Describe and analyse the cartoon.* → S28.2
Hinweis: Auch als Hausaufgabe geeignet

● Spot on **facts**

> **Hinweis**
> Diese Doppelseite kann als Grundlage für Kurzvorträge mit aktuellen Entwicklungen und Zahlen dienen

The consequences of migration

Embracing diversity

Did you know that the 'World Day for Cultural Diversity for Dialogue and Development' is on 21st May? In an era of mass-immigration societies are becoming more and more diverse. We speak of cultural diversity
5 when people of different races, ethnicities, nationalities, languages, religions or sexual orientations live in a community. UNESCO adopted the Universal Declaration on Cultural Diversity in 2001.

The idea of World Diversity Day is to give us an
10 opportunity to become aware of the value of cultural diversity and lead the way to more harmony in our culturally diverse society by combatting polarisation and stereotypes.

Definitions
Ethnicity
belonging to a group of people who share a common culture, including their history, religion, language and traditions
Mass immigration
migration of large groups of people from one geographical area to another
Multi-ethnic
describing a society that includes various groups of people from different cultures
Race
the defining of people according to a variety of physical characteristics

1 BRAINSTORMING Before you look at the chart below, guess which are the top ten countries people migrate to.

Migration worldwide

Global migration continues to rise. In 2013 there were 232 million international migrants, more than half of which lived in just 10 host countries (see table on the right). Most migrants leave their country in search
5 of better opportunities for themselves and their families, but a large number of refugees are fleeing war and persecution.

International migration takes away a significant number of highly educated and skilled individuals
10 from developing countries. This 'brain drain' can harm the growth potential in the emigrants' home country, but the money they send back to help their relatives can also boost the economy. The figures in 2011 for the OECD (international economic
15 organisation including 34 developed countries) show that about 30 % of the immigrants were highly educated. This means, for example, that one in every nine people born in Africa with a university diploma or corresponding qualification lived in an OECD
20 country in 2010–11.

In addition to migrants who want to settle permanently in a new country, there are also millions of migrant workers who move to another country for specific projects or seasonal work, e.g. as unskilled
25 workers in construction and agriculture. Many of these are also undocumented, which is cheaper for the employer, but dangerous for the workers as they can be exploited more easily.

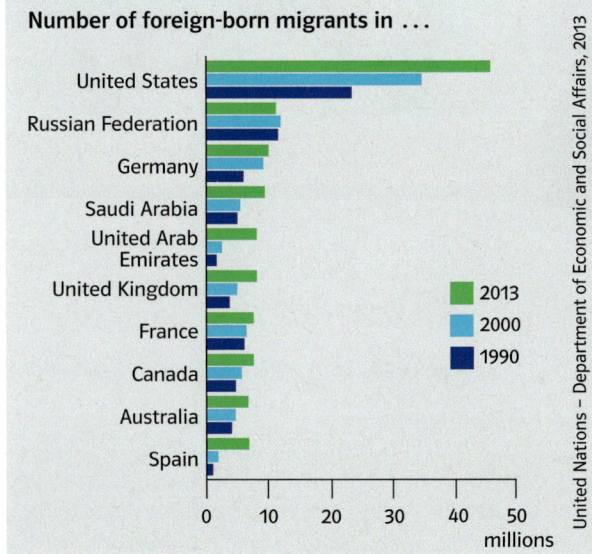

Number of foreign-born migrants in ...
(United States, Russian Federation, Germany, Saudi Arabia, United Arab Emirates, United Kingdom, France, Canada, Australia, Spain; years 2013, 2000, 1990)
United Nations – Department of Economic and Social Affairs, 2013

⊙S 2 VIEWING Watch the film about young people in Europe who are looking for job opportunities abroad. Compare their situation with that of someone migrating from a developing country to a highly developed one.

Migration and diversity

Immigration to the US

The US is, by definition, a nation of immigrants with a racially, ethnically and culturally diverse population. The most important ethnic groups are the following:

Whites are still the majority, but they are comprised of the descendants of a multitude of different nationalities and cultures. Britain, Ireland, Italy, Germany, Scandinavia, Eastern Europe etc. – throughout the last centuries war, religious persecution, hunger or poverty have sent waves of immigrants from each of these regions to seek a new life in the US.

The demographically most dynamic group are Latinos (from all Central and South American countries) or Hispanics (only from Spanish-speaking countries). Ongoing immigration from Latin America, often by illegal immigrants crossing the Mexican-American border, means that this group is growing rapidly in numbers and importance.

African Americans are the second-largest minority. Many are descended from Africans who were brought to the American colonies as slaves. After the abolition of slavery in 1865 they faced segregation and discrimination until the Civil Rights Movement of the 1960s. Anti-discrimination laws and programmes such as affirmative action (positive discrimination, i.e. giving advantages in education and employment to minorities) have improved the social situation of blacks, but the after-effects can still be felt today.

Asian Americans are a very diverse group, ranging from the descendants of Chinese railroad workers in the 18th century to relative newcomers, e.g. from Korea, Vietnam or India.

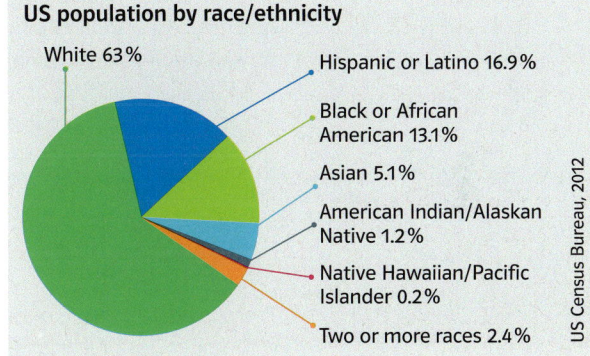

US population by race/ethnicity
- White 63%
- Hispanic or Latino 16.9%
- Black or African American 13.1%
- Asian 5.1%
- American Indian/Alaskan Native 1.2%
- Native Hawaiian/Pacific Islander 0.2%
- Two or more races 2.4%

US Census Bureau, 2012

Immigration to the UK

Since WWII the UK has become a much more ethnically and culturally diverse country. A significant number of immigrants from Commonwealth nations, e.g. India, Pakistan or the Caribbean were encouraged to come and work in the UK to overcome labour shortages in the 1950s and 1960s. Most of these settled in London and the industrial towns of the Midlands and the North, such as Birmingham or Leicester, where even today the number of British Asians or Black Britons is significantly higher than elsewhere in the country. In the 21st century many people from Eastern Europe have come to work in the UK.

There is an ongoing debate about the benefits and the limits of mass immigration to the UK. Many, especially on the political right, call for a more restrictive immigration policy. Terrorist attacks by religious fundamentalists who are second or third-generation immigrants have influenced public opinion negatively and increased the pressure on immigrant communities in the UK, especially Muslim ones, to integrate or even assimilate. Calls for a common British identity and common values and cultural norms have become more insistent. Nevertheless, there is a broad consensus that tolerance and diversity have profited the country and are now an integral part of Britishness.

Ethnic composition of the UK, based on the 2011 Census

Ethnic group	2011 population	%
White: Total	55,010,359	87.1
Asian or Asian British: Indian	1,412,958	2.3
Asian or Asian British: Pakistani	1,174,983	1.9
Asian or Asian British: Bangladeshi	451,529	0.7
Asian or Asian British: Chinese	433,150	0.7
Asian or Asian British: Other Asian	861,815	1.4
Asian or Asian British: Total	4,372,339	6.9
Black or Black British: Total	1,904,684	3.0
Mixed multiple: Total	1,250,229	2.0
Other ethnic groups: Total	643,567	1.0
Total	**63,182,178**	**100**

3 VISUALS Look at the two charts on this page and compare the composition of the population in the US and in the UK. From what you've learned on this page and your general knowledge, explain the differences.
Hinweis: Auch als Hausaufgabe geeignet

Core skill workshop

Practising for oral exams

Part A Oral exams in class

1 **BRAINSTORMING** Do you like the cartoon? Say why or why not.

2 **BRAINSTORMING**
   a) What are the differences and similarities between oral and written exams? Make a list.
   b) Compare your findings with a partner.

Oral communication skills, like presentation skills and discourse competence, have a high priority in real-life situations because most daily life communication is oral and not written. Speaking skills can be tested in oral exams. Their structure can vary. There are individual exams, partner exams and group exams. Usually, oral tests consist of two parts, a monologue and a dialogue with a partner or in small groups.

Most students find oral exams tougher than written ones because you need to think on your feet and react immediately in contrast to a written exam.

3 **SPEAKING** What kind of exam do you prefer? Discuss your preference.

"I hate taking a test without an eraser."

> **TIP**
>
> **Practising on your own**
> Record your voice when doing a speaking task, e.g. with a smartphone. Now you can listen as often as you want and work on your language use and speaking abilities.
>
> Use a mirror or film yourself to work on your body language and to check if you have any nervous habits.

Part B Presenting a monologue in an oral exam

There is a wide range of assignments for this part of an oral exam. The most common types of assignments are summaries, descriptions, comments and, of course, short presentations based on visuals or a text, or even both. But any kind of storytelling, analysing, comparing and mediating is possible as well.

Review: Vauxhall

> The novel *Vauxhall* by Gabriel Gbadamosi, a writer of Irish-Nigerian descent, touches your soul because it tells the story of Michael, an Irish-Nigerian schoolboy with a Catholic mother and a Muslim father, who grows up in a multi-ethnic area in the southwest of London, Vauxhall. With a child's innocent gaze Michael gives us an insight into his family life by describing his father's tribal scars and his brothers' circumcisions. But he also describes daily life in Vauxhall's neighbourhood from his perspective – including policemen who enjoy arresting black schoolchildren playing truant or actions of racism against immigrants. Gbadamosi's sense of humour in describing these multi-ethnic encounters makes this book a real page-turner.

4 **SPEAKING** Present the novel *Vauxhall* to a partner on the basis of the review and explain why you would or would not like to read it.
   a) First, read the review and make sure you understand the text. Take notes on the content or mark relevant information in the text. You need your notes to practise your presentation.
   b) Find arguments why you would or would not like to read this novel.
   c) Structure your information and present it to the listener.
   d) Now practise your presentation with your notes and at least once without using them. Speak clearly and vary your voice to make your presentation interesting for the listener.

Migration and diversity 6

5 SPEAKING
   a) As partner A give your presentation to your partner. If you use your notes, make sure that you look up and speak after looking at them.
   b) As partner B listen to the presentation and take notes on content, language and body language. Then give feedback to the presenter. → **S33**
   c) Switch roles.

6 EVALUATION Reflect on your working process. The grid can help you.

	☺	😐	☹
1. I had no problems taking notes for my presentation.	…	…	…
2. I had no problems structuring my presentation.	…	…	…
3. I had no problems using my own words.	…	…	…
4. I had no problems using linking words.	…	…	…
5. I had no problems with my pronunciation.	…	…	…
6. I had no problems with my body language.	…	…	…
7. I had no problems keeping eye contact.	…	…	…
8. …	…	…	…

Part C Speaking in an exam dialogue

Dialogues usually make up the second part of an oral exam. They can also be tested by a wide range of assignment types. The most common types are (controversial) discussions, debates, role-plays, telephone conversations and interviews. The correct register (the use of formal or informal language) depends on the context of the dialogue.

In a controversial discussion you have to be a good speaker and a good listener as well; otherwise, you cannot react to your partner's arguments and your interaction will fail.

7 BRAINSTORMING Prepare a controversial discussion on the issue "Diversity – boon or bane (blessing or curse)?" Find three or more arguments before you start. You are allowed to use the arguments below. Also think about possible counterarguments and your line of argumentation. Take notes. → **S24.3**

Partner A	Partner B
You are of the opinion that diversity is a boon because	You are of the opinion that diversity is a bane because
• Immigrants enrich for our diverse culture – think of food, for example!	• Diversity weakens national identity.
• We need skilled people for our economy so everyone benefits.	• Too many different cultures, languages and religions divide a country.
• …	• …

8 SPEAKING Practise what you want to say in a quiet voice, once while using your notes and at least once without them.

9 SPEAKING Act out the controversial discussion with your partner. Be a good speaker and listener. Do not interrupt each other.

USEFUL PHRASES

Structuring your monologue

First I am going to talk about…; then I will deal with…; after that I will analyse …; and finally I …

I would like to start with …

To begin with, …

Next I'd like to point out …

Another important argument …

On the one hand, … ; on the other hand, …

Furthermore, …/ Apart from that, …

To sum up, one can say …

Finally/Lastly …

On the whole, …

I'd like to finish/conclude by …

Putting/To put it in a nutshell, …

TIP

Be aware of the context of the dialogue and check whether you need **informal language** (e.g. in a telephone conversation with a friend) or **formal language** (e.g. in an interview with an official person).

Core skill workshop

USEFUL PHRASES

Turn-taking

Would you please be so kind as to let me finish my sentence?

Sorry to interrupt, but …

Arguing

I'm afraid I don't (quite) agree with you there.

I see what you mean, but …

I'd like to add an idea you haven't mentioned so far.

But I do think it's important to take … into consideration.

Although this is …, we mustn't forget that there is also …

In this context it's necessary to …

10 EVALUATION *Reflect on your working process. The grid can help you.*

	😊	😐	🙁
1. It was easy to argue from a certain point of view.	…	…	…
2. It was easy to listen to my partner and to react to him/her.	…	…	…
3. It was easy to keep the discussion going.	…	…	…
4. It was easy to express myself fluently.	…	…	…
5. It was easy to use body language.	…	…	…
6. It was easy to keep eye contact with my discussion partner.	…	…	…
7. …	…	…	…

Part D Conducting a mock exam

11 SPEAKING

a) Get together in groups of four. Two group members will act out the role of exam candidates A and B and two the role of the teachers.
b) The two candidates prepare their assignments, and the teachers agree on criteria for their feedback for the candidates. → S33
c) Act out the mock exam.
d) Reflect on the mock exam: What was easy and what was difficult? What have you learned in order to succeed in an oral exam?

Partner A — Monologue

Jessica Ennis, 26, has Jamaican roots and won a gold medal in the Olympic Games for Britain. Describe the picture based on your knowledge about immigration and diversity and comment on it.

Partner B — Monologue

The British National Football Team includes players with diverse ethnic backgrounds. Describe the picture based on your knowledge about immigration and diversity and comment on it.

Partner A+B — Dialogue

Germany's Chancellor Angela Merkel said about diversity in her country: "This multicultural approach, saying that we simply live side by side and live happily with each other, has failed. Utterly failed."
Partner A: You agree with Merkel's statement. Partner B: You disagree with Merkel's statement.
Think about arguments and examples and discuss this statement with your partner.

Texts

Migration and diversity 6

A Diversity and identity

1 BEFORE YOU READ Make a mind map for the word 'diversity'. → △1 **Diff** (help with): Vorgabe von möglichen Aspekten

Diverse City

They call us Diverse City, we're colorful good
It's like a freak show in your neighborhood
So, if you wanna praise you can come on down
Cause this freak show's leaving the ground
5 Up, up and away, baby we don't play,
Maybe you thought you was done for the day
He said, she said, I said this,
That you can't get away from your moment of bliss

Stirring, we'll lure you in
10 And we'll make room for the shade of skin
Short ones, tall ones, skinny ones, bigger,
Love is the gun and we pullin' that trigger

So you send me and I'll send you hope in the form of a new tattoo
Mine is the shiny city on a hill and yours, of course, is the colors that fill it
15 We'll take you high, we'll take you higher
Now come to the city where you can praise
If you're black, if you're white, if you're yellow or grey
In the morning, in the night, anytime of day
What's that place – Diverse City

20 With curls in your hair and braids on the side
Straight shake 'em loose, just come on and ride
We're a body with parts, like you and me
Together we make diversity

Welcome to Diverse City, we're colorful good
25 It's like a freak show in your neighborhood
So, if you wanna praise you can come on down
Cause this freak show's leaving the ground

Said we're Diverse City, we're colorful goods
It's just a state of mind, we gonna shine the way that we should, baby
30 So, if you wanna praise you can come on down
Cause this freak show's leaving the ground

You bring the heart, I'll bring the soul
I'll bring the flag, you bring the pole
We'll fly it high so the whole world knows
35 The dream of a king 'bout to unfold
We 'bout to do this thing for real
Diverse City got mass appeal
So put your hand in the hand of mine

And we'll spread this love like dandelions

Words and music: Toby McKeehan and Christopher Stevens, 2004

VIP FILE

tobyMac is the stage name of **Toby McKeehan** (born Kevin Michael McKeehan in 1964). He is a Christian recording artist, music producer, hip-hop/pop artist, singer-songwriter and author.

3 **to praise** to honour
8 **bliss** happiness, salvation
9 **stirring** moving, exciting
9 **to lure** [lʊə] to attract
12 **to pull the trigger** den Abzug drücken
14 **shiny city on a hill** biblical phrase often used to describe an ideal place blessed by God
29 **state of mind** attitude
33 **pole** Fahnenmast
35 **The dream of a king 'bout to unfold** reference to Dr Martin Luther King's speech "I have a dream", in which he dreamt of the end of segregation in the US
37 **appeal** attraction
39 **dandelion** ['dændɪlaɪən] Löwenzahn

Texts

Zusatzmaterial WB
Task 1: Talking about songs

2 COMPREHENSION **Zusatzmaterial KV 1:** Geschlossene Hörverstehensaufgaben zum Song
  a) *Sum up the concept of diversity as described in the song by tobyMac.*
  b) *Compare your mind map from Task 1 with his idea of diversity.*

3 ANALYSIS *Analyse the stylistic devices the songwriter uses to convey his message.* → **S10** **Hinweis:** Auch als Hausaufgabe geeignet

L3/1 **4 LISTENING** *Listen to the song and discuss whether the sound and the rhythm of the song emphasise the content.*

5 SPEAKING *Discuss with a partner whether this song has a positive impact on the listener.*

6 CREATIVE TASK *"Every line I write, I'm thinking about how to serve humankind, whether they're people who share in the faith I have or not," tobyMac says, citing one of his chief influences, reggae icon Bob Marley.*
Write a letter to tobyMac commenting on his statement. → **S18.1** → △2
Diff (instead of): Eine Rede schreiben
Hinweis: Auch als Hausaufgabe geeignet

7 BEFORE YOU READ *Do you think Germany is an ethnically diverse society?*

What does a true German look like?

The question is at the core of a debate which simmers – and occasionally boils over – as Germany tries to define itself in an age of migration.

Gunter Piening, for example, thinks his blond hair and blue eyes make him the picture of Germanness – but he doesn't like that perception. He is Berlin's Commissioner for Integration and Migration, and he told the BBC: "A lot of people think that 'German' is an ethnic category – that Germans are blond and blue eyed."

His department is waging a publicity campaign to show different faces of Germany – without blond hair and blue eyes.

"Too late, we have started to think about what our society is," he said.

Comparing Germany to Britain, he added: "Maybe one reason is that Great Britain was part of an empire so the British have had long, long experience dealing with different groups from all over the world.

We have problems with people accepting that a modern society is ethnically diverse. Maybe that is a difference to Great Britain or France or an immigration society like the United States." […]

"One difference is that immigrants are represented in Britain in the media. They are visible in the middle class," he said. […]

Mr Piening's angst about integration comes as Germany is undergoing a period of deep introspection about its identity.

President Christian Wulff said recently: "Islam is part of Germany."

That prompted Chancellor Angela Merkel to say that "multiculti" – she used the slightly disparaging term for multiculturalism – had "failed, utterly failed".

Stephen Evans, *BBC News*, 2010

5

10

15

20

¹ **core** center
¹ **to simmer** to boil gently
⁴ **perception** the way to see someone; view, picture
⁵ **commissioner** *Beauftragter*
⁷ **to wage a campaign** to lead a campaign
¹⁸ **angst** [æŋst] anxiety, fear
¹⁸ **to undergo** to go through
¹⁹ **introspection** self-analysis, self-examination
²¹ **to prompt** *here*: to stimulate, to encourage
²² **disparaging** *abwertend*
²² **to fail** to flop

Zusatzmaterial WB
Task 12: Mediation

8 COMPREHENSION *Sum up the differences between Germany, Britain, France and the US concerning diversity, according to Gunter Piening.*

9 SPEAKING *Do you agree with Gunter Piening's statement that immigrants are not represented in the German media? Discuss his statement in small groups and present your results in class.*
Geeignete Methode: Think – Pair – Share

6 Migration and diversity

10 BEFORE YOU READ *Are you proud of your nationality? Give reasons.*

Black, British and proud

The immigration debate misses a crucial point: those living here cannot help being shaped by the culture. They are British – like me.

I am black, the daughter of African immigrants who came to England in the 1970s. I am also British – and proudly so. British culture, values and ways of life are
5 an intrinsic part of my identity. […]

Having spent my entire life in England, I am as much immersed in English culture as any white English native. I am not particularly different, apart from on the most superficial basis: the colour of my skin.

When abroad, I am even more aware of how my Britishness defines me. In
10 America I am referred to as "the English girl". Black, but English nonetheless. At "home" in Nigeria, my strong English accent sets me apart as an "oyinbo" – a Yoruba word for an English person. On the other hand, there are Nigerian customs and traditions that I just don't get because I filter them through British eyes.

Like other immigrants, my parents have maintained aspects of their African
15 traditions. They speak Yoruba, eat Nigerian food and socialise with other Nigerians. In spite of this, and the fact that they came to England as adults, they still have a hard time adjusting when they go to Nigeria because they have unwittingly, over time, become so accustomed to English ways. Other black Britons who have decided to go "back home" to Africa or the Caribbean after living in England for
20 many years, are realising that they are now much more English than they could ever have imagined. […]

Immigrants, and their children, have been – and still are – subject to economic, educational, legal and social inequalities. We all have a need to belong. […]

In the late 1990s my mother and younger sister were nearly deported to Nigeria
25 because they were not British citizens. I, as a citizen, was to be allowed to stay in England. My mother argued that, having spent the majority of her adult life in England, she, and my sister, felt British and deserved to remain in the country. Thankfully the judge realised that as a high-interest tax payer, with a successful job, paying through the nose for two young children to attend private school, my
30 mother – and sister – should be allowed to stay in England, a country to which they belonged and to which they were contributing greatly. […]

I'm black, I'm British, and I'm proud.

Lola Adesioye, *The Guardian*, 2008

proud self-assured, self-confident
1 **crucial** ['kruːʃl] vital, central
2 **to shape** to form
5 **intrinsic** essential, fundamental
6 **immersed** involved deeply
14 **to maintain** to keep, to conserve
16 **in spite of this** nevertheless
17 **to adjust** to adapt
17 **unwittingly** unintentionally, unconsciously
18 **to become accustomed to sth** to become familiar with sth
23 **inequalities** differences, discrimination
28 **high-interest tax payer** *Steuerzahler mit hohem Steuersatz*
29 **to pay through the nose** *here:* to pay a lot

Zusatzmaterial WB
Task 2: Adjectives with prepositions
Task 5: Listening
Tasks 6–11: Reading

VIP FILE

Lola Adesioye participated in the European Youth Parliament. She is politically active concerning anti-racism and treating ethnic minorities equally.

11 COMPREHENSION *Describe Adesioye's feelings about being British.*

12 ANALYSIS *How is she perceived by the British, the Americans and the Nigerians? Compare their perceptions with her own and comment on them.*

13 EVALUATION *Write a list of factors determining identity. Rank them in order of importance and assess what role ethnicity and nationality play in this.*
Geeignete Methode: Placemat

14 RESEARCH *Find out about one Briton who originally came to the UK as an immigrant. Give a two-minute presentation about him/her in front of the class.*
→ **S22, S32** **Zusatzmaterial KV 2:** Feedback sheet

Texts

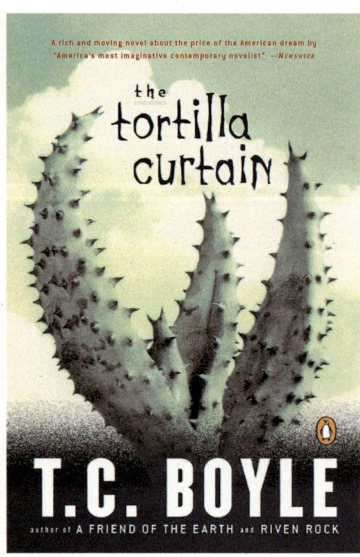

B Crossing borders

1 BEFORE YOU READ *Look at the book cover and brainstorm ideas about a possible plot. Share your ideas with a partner. Make notes.*

The Tortilla Curtain

América and her husband Cándido illegally crossed the border from Mexico to California, dreaming of a better future. Instead of living in a nice apartment, they are hiding in a canyon without food or water. Cándido has been hit hard by a car and is unable to move. Since he cannot work, América decides to find work in the city to make some money.

She walked aimlessly round the lot. Cars went by on the canyon road, but fewer of them now, and at greater intervals. There was a gas station, a secondhand-clothing store; across the street, the post office, and then the little shopping center where the *paisano* from Italy had his store. The men were staring at her openly now, and their stares were harder, hungrier. Most of them were here alone, separated from their families – and their wives – for months at a time, sometimes years. They were starving, and she was fresh meat.

The image spooked her, and she started off down the road, conscious of their eyes drilling into her. All the warmth she'd felt earlier, the familiarity, the brother- and sisterhood, was gone suddenly, and all she could think of, looming nightmarishly, was the faces of those animals at the border – *Mexican animals* – the ones who'd come out of the night to attack her and Cándido as they crossed over. Mexicans. Her own people. And when the light hit them their faces showed nothing – no respect, no mercy, nothing.

América had been terrified to begin with – what she and Cándido were doing was illegal, and she'd never done anything illegal in her life. Crouching there beside the corrugated iron fence, her mouth dry and heart racing, she waited through the long night till the *coyote* gave the word, and then she and Cándido and half a dozen others were running for their lives on the hard-baked earth of another country. Two-thirds of their savings had gone to this man, this *coyote*, this emissary between the two worlds, and he was either incompetent or he betrayed them. One minute he was there, hustling them through a gap in the fence, and the next minute he was gone, leaving them in a clump of bushes at the bottom of a ravine in a darkness so absolute it was like being thrust into the bottom of a well.

And then the animals jumped them. Just like that. A gang of them, armed with knives, baseball bats, a pistol. And how did they know that she and Cándido would be there beneath the particular bush – and at the ungodly hour of 4 a.m.? There were six or seven of them. They pinned Cándido down and cut the pockets from his trousers, and then, in that hot subterranean darkness, they went for her. A knife was in her face, their hands were all over her, and they jerked the clothes from her as if they were skinning a rabbit. Cándido cried out and they clubbed him; she screamed, and they laughed. But then, just as the first one loosened his belt, taking his time, enjoying it, the helicopter came with its lights and suddenly it was bright day and the vermin were scattering and Cándido had her and the wash of their propellers threw the dirt against her bare skin like a thousand hot needles. "Run!" Cándido screamed. "Run!" and she ran, naked, her feet sliced by the rocks and the stabbing talons of the desert plants, but she couldn't outrun a helicopter.

---

⁶ **lot** here: Parkplatz
⁹ **paisano** friend, countryman
⁹ **to stare** to look intensely
¹² **to starve** to be very hungry
¹³ **spooked** surprised, shocked
¹⁴ **to drill** bohren
¹⁵ **looming** approaching
¹⁹ **mercy** pity, sympathy
²¹ **to crouch** to duck
²² **corrugated iron** *Wellblech*
²³ **coyote** [kaɪˈəʊti] here: person who smuggles illegal immigrants across the Mexican border
²⁵ **emissary** [ˈemɪsri] messenger
²⁶ **to betray sb** to deceive sb
²⁸ **ravine** [rəˈviːn] *Schlucht*
³² **ungodly hour** *unchristliche Uhrzeit*
³³ **to pin sb down** to hold sb so he cannot move
³⁹ **vermin** *Ungeziefer*
⁴² **talon** claw

That was the most humiliating night of her life. She was herded along with a hundred other people toward a line of Border Patrol jeeps and she stood there
45 naked and bleeding, every eye on her, until someone gave her a blanket to cover herself. Twenty minutes later she was back on the other side of the fence.

From: T.C. Boyle, *The Tortilla Curtain*, 1995

43 **humiliating**
embarrassing, taking away sb's dignity

2 SPEAKING How do you feel after reading this excerpt? Share your feelings with your partner. Did you expect this plot? Compare your notes from Task 1 with what actually happens. **Geeignete Methode:** Speed dating

3 COMPREHENSION Summarise the plot and outline the setting and atmosphere.
Hinweis: Auch als Hausaufgabe geeignet

4 ANALYSIS
a) Analyse the stylistic devices the author uses to evoke the reader's emotions.
b) Which narrative perspective is used? Explain the effect it has on the information the reader receives. → **S8** Zusatzmaterial WB Task 3: Narrative perspectives

5 SPEAKING Cándido and his wife are back in Mexico. He calls an American friend and tells him what has happened. In pairs, write down the telephone conversation and practise your dialogue. Act out the telephone conversation in class. → **S12, S23** → ▲3 **Diff** (instead of): Tagebucheintrag

6 VIEWING Watch the clips and note the problems and limitations undocumented immigrants face in the US. Compare notes and discuss whether undocumented immigrants should be deported or made legal.

7 VISUALS Choose one of the film posters dealing with American immigrants trying to reach the US. Then describe it to your partner and analyse it. Afterwards, discuss which of the films you would rather watch in class. → △4
Diff (help with): Vorgabe möglicher Aspekte

TIP

Watch out! Do not mix up the **author** with the **narrator** when analysing a fictional text. The author writes the story and the narrator tells the story.

Zusatzmaterial WB
Task 4: Speaking

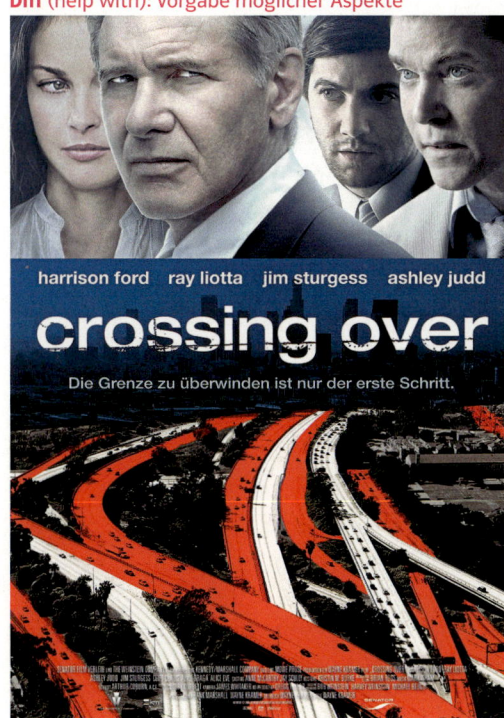

8 RESEARCH Find out about the history of legal and illegal immigration in America and prepare a short presentation. → **S32**
Hinweis: Auch als Hausaufgabe geeignet

Advanced texts

C Immigration policy

1 BEFORE YOU READ These excerpts are from a speech given by Liam Fox, a Conservative Member of Parliament, in 2014. Judging from this information and from the title, what do you expect the speech's main points to be?

Immigration, integration and British values

Immigrant children in front of the English flag

One of the most pressing needs in British politics is for an evidence based, grown up debate about immigration. Perhaps more than any other subject it is used as a totem for wider political views to be aired, motives impugned and facts to be distorted. When we talk about immigration we need to be aware of a particular danger and it is this: if we do not debate the issue rationally and reasonably then there will be plenty of people on the margins of our politics who will use the issue irresponsibly and unreasonably. It is the duty of those of us in the political mainstream to own this debate and not surrender it to the political fringe. [...]

So, how do we balance the economic, cultural and political considerations?

I believe that for immigration to be successful, there are two human prerequisites. The first is that there is a willingness among the host population to integrate those coming into the country. The second is that the immigrant population has to be willing to integrate into the legal and cultural systems of the host population. Unwillingness on the part of either group is likely to result in hostility to immigrant groups with an increased likelihood of consequent ghettoization. Ideas of commonality need to be fostered.

There has been a tendency – rightly and understandably – to celebrate the cultural diversity of the UK, but if we only cheer diversity and ignore commonality, then we are likely to achieve little more than fragmentation. The United Kingdom has had a history of successfully integrating many different groups over many years, but the rapid increase in immigrant numbers over the past decade or so has made the process more difficult as resistance among the host population has increased and immigrants have increasingly settled in large communities, often remaining culturally separate rather than simply retaining their cultural identity. Sadly, the debate has largely revolved around numbers of immigrants rather than who they are, where they come from and what their relationship with their new home will be, including whether they will be contributing to our economic well-being or becoming passengers on the welfare train.

So it is important to look in detail at what level and kind of immigration might be relevant and beneficial to the UK. [...]

Of course getting the right skills from abroad is only one of the options available; the other is an educational system in Britain that does not consistently fail those in the middle and lower social groups. [...]

UK immigration policy needs to be rebalanced so that those who come to our country are usefully economically active. There is neither the public appetite nor an economic case for allowing immigrants to come to the UK who will simply absorb our national wealth rather than helping to create it. Equally, we must develop policy that ensures that we are not turning away workers we need. Many of these will be skilled workers, a group currently in danger of being choked off, but it may

---

¹ **pressing** demanding, urgent
³ **totem** icon, symbol
⁴ **to impugn** [ɪmˈpjuːn] to question, doubt
⁵ **to distort** verdrehen
⁸ **margin** Rand
¹⁰ **to surrender** to capitulate
¹¹ **political fringe** political parties with extreme views
¹⁵ **prerequisites** requirements
¹⁶ **host population** population of the country being immigrated to
¹⁹ **hostility** aggression
²¹ **commonality** unity, harmony
²¹ **to foster** to cultivate, encourage
²⁹ **to retain** to keep
³⁰ **to revolve around sth** sich um etw. drehen
³³ **passenger on the welfare train** here: sb who takes advantage of the welfare system
³⁵ **beneficial** [ˌbenɪˈfɪʃl] good, useful, valuable
⁴⁴ **to choke off** here: to unnecessarily keep out

ultimately mean unskilled labour too. In short, I believe that we need to have what we might call an 'open and shut' immigration policy. That is, an approach that is open to those who are economically active and have the skills our economy requires but closed to those who will become dependent on the state or who possess skills we do not require for our economic well-being.

How do we construct and sell an economically effective and politically viable immigration policy in a Western country with adverse demographics and the need to produce greater wealth, all set against the background of a potentially incendiary political debate?

The key variables we have to keep in mind are the impact of immigration on national income and its distribution among non-migrants, the national labour market, the fiscal balance (including public services, social security, tax revenues, etc.), and the impact on national identity and the attitudes of the migrant and non-migrant population.

We must pay particular attention to the impact on public services. Although getting the right people into the economy as active participants should mean higher growth and tax receipts in the future, we need to be mindful of what our current infrastructure can actually handle.

One of the problems in recent years has been that an inadequate infrastructure combined with largely uncontrolled immigration has diminished appreciation of the benefits that immigration can bring – one of the reasons Britain has had a generally good record on assimilation and race relations in the past.

The impact of immigration on national identity should not be understated either. How much any society will find acceptable depends on the level of cultural diversity which it is willing to tolerate. […]

A properly balanced approach would ensure that the UK benefited economically from immigration but that it did not adversely affect national security, public order or the social and political stability of the country. Whether or not explicit protection of existing citizens' rights to employment (and other benefits) over those of potential citizens is required or desirable is an issue worthy of debate, a complex and contentious matter involving potentially competing ideas of the free market and national entitlements. The formulation of such policies will never be easy in a political environment which is more often knee-jerk than considered but, if done successfully, the outcomes will be better for all those involved. […]

Liam Fox, July 7, 2014

Young people from different cultural backgrounds in a chemistry lab

50 **viable** practical, feasible
51 **adverse demographics** *here:* the fact that there are increasingly fewer young and more and more old people
53 **incendiary** [ɪnˈsɛndɪəri] *here:* aggressive, destructive
56 **tax revenues** *Steuereinnahmen*
64 **appreciation** [əˌpriːʃɪˈeɪʃn] thankfulness
71 **adversely** harmfully
75 **contentious** controversial, quarrelsome
77 **knee-jerk** *reflexartig*
77 **considered** reflected

2 COMPREHENSION Sum up the speaker's idea of an 'open and shut' policy (ll. 45–49) in your own words.

3 COMPREHENSION 👥 List the positive and negative aspects of immigration in the text with your partner. Compare your results. → △5
Diff (help with): Vorgabe von Schlüsselwörtern

4 ANALYSIS How does the speaker try to convince his audience? Focus on the speaker's main argument and the line of argumentation as well as the use of language in this speech. → S10

5 EVALUATION Write a letter to the speaker saying whether his speech has convinced you. → S18.1 **Hinweis:** Auch als Hausaufgabe geeignet

6 SPEAKING 👥 With a partner discuss the speaker's idea controversially. Partner A is in favour and Partner B is against the speaker's 'open and shut' policy. Before you start your discussion think about convincing arguments to strengthen your line of argument. → S24.3 → ▲6
Diff (instead of): Interview schreiben

Avoiding mistakes
Aussprache
47**economy** [ɪˈkɒnəmi]
12**economic** [ˌiːkəˈnɒmɪk]

Zusatzmaterial WB
Task 13: Reported speech
Task 14: Vocabulary building

Hinweis
An dieser Stelle kann vertiefend mit aktuellen Reden von Politikern aus verschiedenen englischsprachigen Ländern zum Thema Migration gearbeitet und Vergleiche angestellt werden

Advanced texts

D Dealing with prejudice

1 BEFORE YOU READ Look at the pictures and describe how some Americans perceived Islam after the attacks of 9/11.

FACT FILE

On September 11, 2001 (also referred to as **9/11**), a series of four coordinated terrorist attacks were launched by the Islamic terrorist group Al-Qaeda upon the US in New York City, in the air over Pennsylvania and the Washington, D.C. metropolitan area.

Vanalism on the Islamic Center of America

Islamophobia after 9/11

Disgraced

The play *Disgraced* by Ayad Akhtar, winner of the 2013 Pulitzer prize for drama, is centred on socio-political themes such as Islamophobia in the US and how Muslim-American citizens see themselves. The play carefully depicts racial and ethnic prejudices Muslims had to face after 9/11 when the perception of Islam changed drastically in the US. It tells the story of Amir Kapoor, a successful Pakistani-American lawyer, who is distancing himself from his cultural and religious roots by changing his name and denying his Muslim faith.

EMILY	How is Mort?	
AMIR	Obsessed with the idea that meditation is going to bring down his cholesterol.	10
EMILY	Haven't seen him in ages.	
AMIR	I barely see him. He hardly comes in. A couple of hours a day at most when he does show up.	
EMILY	Pays to be the boss.	
AMIR	I mean, basically, I'm doing his job. I don't mind.	15
EMILY	He loves you.	
AMIR	He depends on me.	
EMILY	Okay. He spent I don't know how much on that birthday present for you?	
AMIR	Couple grand at least.	20
EMILY	Excuse me.	
AMIR	Honey, I really am pretty much doing his job.	
EMILY	So he gets you a book. Or a bottle of scotch. Or takes you to dinner. Why'd he get you a statue of Siva? *(Beat.)* He doesn't think you're Hindu, does he?	
AMIR	He may have mentioned something once … You realize I'm going to end up with my name on that firm?	25
EMILY	Leibowitz, Bernstein, Harris, and Kapoor.	
AMIR	My mother will roll over in her grave …	
EMILY	Your mother would be proud.	
AMIR	It's not the family name, so she might not care, seeing it alongside all those Jewish ones …	30
	From the kitchen: the intercom buzzes.	
AMIR	*Looks over, surprised.* EMILY *puts down her pencil. Heads for the kitchen.*	
EMILY	That'll be Abe.	

---

[1] **disgraced** shamed, dishonored
[9] **obsessed** besessen
[12] **barely** hardly
[17] **to depend on** abhängig sein von
[20] **grand** *infml* 1000 dollars
[24] **Siva** Shiva is an important Hindu god
[27] **Leibowitz, Bernstein, Harris** owners of Amir's law firm
[32] **intercom** Gegensprechanlage

6 Migration and diversity

35	AMIR	*(surprised)* Abe?
	EMILY	*(disappearing into the kitchen)* Your nephew?
	AMIR	Oh, right. Wait …
	EMILY	*(at the intercom, offstage)* Yes? Send him up.
		As EMILY *now returns:*
40	AMIR	You're not gonna let this thing go, are you?
	EMILY	I don't like what's happening. Somebody's gotta do something about it.
	AMIR	I went to see that guy in prison. What more do you two want?

There's a knocking on the door, as Amir starts putting on his pants. Amir's gotten to the door. Opening, it shows … ABE – twenty-two, of South Asian origin. But as
45 *American as American gets. Vibrant and endearing. He's wearing a KidRobot T-shirt under a hoodie, skinny jeans and high tops. As AMIR is buckling his belt:*

	ABE	*(looking over at EMILY, back to AMIR)* Should I come back?
	AMIR	No, no.
	ABE	You sure?
50	AMIR	Yeah. I'm sure. Come in, Hussein.
	ABE	Uncle.
	AMIR	What?
	ABE	Could you just call me –
	AMIR	*(finishing his thought)* I've known you your whole life as Hussein.
55		I'm not gonna start calling you Abe now.
	ABE	*shakes his head. Turning to EMILY.*
	EMILY	Hi, Abe.
	AMIR	Hi, Aunt Emily.
		He turns to AMIR, lighthearted.
60	ABE	*(pointing)* See? How hard can it be?
	AMIR	Abe Jensen? Really?
	ABE	You know how much easier things are for me since I changed my name? It's in the Quran. It says you can hide your religion if you have to.
	AMIR	I'm not talking about the Quran. I'm talking about you being called Abe
65		Jensen. Just lay off it with me and your folks at least.
	ABE	It's gotta be one thing or the other. I can't be all mixed up.
	EMILY	*(off Amir's reaction)* Amir. You changed your name, too.
	ABE	You got lucky. You didn't have to change your first name. Could be Christian. Jewish. Plus, you were born here. It's different.

From: Ayad Akhtar, *Disgraced*, 2013

42 **prison** jail
45 **vibrant** lively, energetic
45 **endearing** attractive, charming
46 **hoodie** *Kapuzenpullover*
46 **to buckle** to fasten
59 **to be lighthearted** to be cheerful
63 **Quran** central religious text of Islam
63 **to hide** to conceal

2 COMPREHENSION After having read this excerpt and looking at the pictures again, can you understand why Muslims change their names?

3 COMPREHENSION Describe Amir's reaction to Abe's decision to change his name from Hussein to Abe.

4 ANALYSIS Amir says, "My mother will roll over in her grave …" Compare this statement with his own reaction towards Abe's decision and comment on it.
Geeignete Methode zur weiteren Analyse: Freeze frame

5 LISTENING
a) Listen to an interview with Ayad Akhtar and sum it up. → S21
b) What inspired him to write this drama?

6 EVALUATION Akhtar says in this interview that after 9/11 "being Muslim is not a neutral fact." Comment on his statement. → S14.2
Hinweis: Auch als schriftliche Hausaufgabe geeignet

Advanced texts

7 BEFORE YOU READ *Have you ever watched* Germany's Next Topmodel? *Does the background of the models represent the cultural diversity in Germany? Discuss this question in small groups.*

The fashion industry's problem with race

Landing the front cover of British Vogue catapults a model to supermodel status, it is an integral part of being booked for the biggest catwalks and advertising campaigns. It is a gateway to stardom, a pinnacle of fashion modelling. It has also become resolutely white-only.

The August 2002 edition of British Vogue featured Naomi Campbell as the cover star – smiling and relaxed in boot cut jeans and a white vest. Since then, 12 years and 146 covers have been shot, edited and distributed to newsstands and not one has featured an individual black model.

In September 2013 Naomi Campbell, Iman, and Bethann Hardison wrote an open letter calling on designers to diversify their catwalks. "No matter the intention, the result is racism. Not accepting another based on the colour of their skin is clearly beyond aesthetic." […]

Carole White, founder of Premier Model Management and outspoken critic of the lack of diversity in the fashion industry, says: "I'm surprised that there has not been a black model on the cover of British Vogue for this amount of time as we are such a diverse country, but perhaps British Vogue think the calibre of black models are not out there?" […]

As well as 'there aren't any black models' or 'it's because of celebrity culture', there is another excuse for racism floating around the fashion industry: "There is this fallacy that 'black covers don't sell'" explains Furlong. "But how do you know? There hasn't been one for twelve years! You can't say people don't buy it when they're not given the chance to buy it."

As well as being deeply offensive to black women, being used as an excuse for racism is insulting to consumers of fashion magazines. The last 12 years of side-lining black models reflects the attitudes of those at the top of the fashion industry, not those of fashion fans. The fashion industry has a problem with race which goes far beyond just fashion magazine covers, however ending years of cover discrimination would be an important step. Based in London, one of the most multi-cultural cities in the world, British Vogue could be spearheading change.

"Treat black models the same as you would treat any other kind of model," states Furlong. "Jourdan Dunn is a household name, there has to have been a specific and conscious decision not to use her. If she was white, at her level, she would have had multiple Vogue covers by now – no doubt about it."

Tasny Hoskins, *The Guardian*, 2014

Supermodel Naomi Campbell on the catwalk

¹ *Vogue* very popular fashion magazine
² **catwalk** *Laufsteg*
³ **pinnacle** high point, peak
⁴ **resolutely** definitely
¹⁰ **to diversify** *here:* to expand in regard to ethnicity
¹³ **outspoken** open, frank, honest
¹⁶ **calibre** level of quality or ability
²⁰ **fallacy** ['fæləsi] erroneous belief, myth
²⁰ **Jody Furlong** founder of a casting agency
²³ **offensive** insulting, rude
²⁵ **to side-line sb** *jdn beiseiteschieben*
²⁹ **to spearhead** to initiate, to lead
³¹ **to be a household name** *überall bekannt sein*

Avoiding mistakes
Wortschatz
¹³**critic** Kritiker
  criticism Kritik

8 COMPREHENSION *Sum up the problem the author describes in her article.* → **S13**

9 ANALYSIS *How does the author try to convince the reader? Focus on the author's arguments and her use of language.*

10 SPEAKING *Discuss whether the fashion industry should introduce a quota for non-white models on the cover of magazines or on the catwalk.* → **S23**
Geeignete Methode: Thinking hats

11 CREATIVE TASK *Write a letter to the editorial board of the British Vogue magazine, commenting on their decision not to feature black models.* → **S18.1**
Hinweis: Auch als Hausaufgabe geeignet

Zusatzmaterial WB
Task 15: Past Tenses
Task 16: Synonyms

E Immigration in Australia and Canada

1 BEFORE YOU READ 👥 *What do you know about immigration to Australia? Make notes and share your findings with your partner.*
Geeignete Methode: Speed dating

From: A short history of immigration

'Oh, my God!' say the Eora.
'What's all that red/white/blue?'
'Oh, my God!' says Captain Phillip.
'We've brought the Irish too.'

5 'Oh, my God!' say London lags.
'Please send us no more thieves.'
'Begorrah, Lord!' the Irish say.
'Be sparin' us Chinese!'

'Bloody hell, send back Kanakas!'
10 our noble workers jeer.
'They cut the cane in half the time.
A man can't buy a beer.'

'Dear God of England,' Barton prays,
'do keep our country white …
15 and leave the heathen in his place,
far north and out of sight.'

'Oh, King of Jazz,' the twenties roar.
'It's Populate or Perish!
A country white as Reckitt's Blue's
20 the only one to cherish.'

'God help us quick,' says '42,
'We're damn well on our knees.
The Peril's here. Bring on the Yanks
to paste the Japanese.'

25 'And look, dear God, here come the Dagoes
bouncing off the boat.
We're nearly out of Dutch and Danes …
and Englishmen of note.'

'And now, dear God, here come the Balts
30 escaping Mother Russia.
Next week we'll have the Reds as well,
Ivan and Natasha.

From: Geoff Page, "A short history of immigration", *Agnostic skies*, 2006

---

¹ **Eora** Aboriginal people around Sydney
² **red/white/blue** colours of the British flag
³ **Captain Phillip** commander of the first fleet of British settlers, including many prisoners; established the first British colony in Australia in 1788
⁵ **lag** *(sl)* prisoner, convict
⁶ **thief** *Dieb*
⁷ **Begorrah** *(sl)* by God
⁸ **to spare** *ersparen*
⁹ **Kanakas** workers from various Pacific Islands
¹⁰ **to jeer** *höhnen*
¹³ **Edmund Barton** Prime Minister 1901–1903 who promoted a 'White Australia Policy'
¹⁵ **heathen** *Heide*
¹⁸ **Populate or Perish** slogan urging people to have more children to defend Australia against invasion during the World Wars
¹⁹ **Reckitt's Blue** soap used as a whitener for clothes
²⁰ **to cherish** to appreciate
²¹ **'God help us quick,' says '42** in 1942 Japan bombed Darwin in Northern Australia, causing significant damage
²³ **peril** danger *here:* the Yellow Peril, *(pej)* colonial term for China and Japan
²³ **Yanks** short form of Yankees, *here:* US military
²⁴ **to paste** *here:* to defeat
²⁵ **Dagoes** *(pej)* Italians, Spaniards or Portuguese

---

2 BRAINSTORMING Do you like the poem? Justify why or why not.

3 COMPREHENSION Sum up how the people who migrated to Australia react towards each new wave of immigrants.

4 ANALYSIS Analyse the use of personal pronouns in each stanza. → △7
Diff (instead of): Analyse der Darstellung verschiedener Migrantengruppen

5 EVALUATION Comment on the question about what the poem contributes to your understanding of Australian society.

6 RESEARCH Find out about migration to Australia and give a short presentation.

7 CREATIVE TASK This is the first part of the poem. Find out who else migrated to Australia and write two more stanzas about them. → **S6.1, S12.1**
Hinweis: Auch als Hausaufgabe geeignet
Geeignete Methode zur Präsentation und Auswertung: Gallery walk

> **VIP FILE**
>
> **Geoff Page** (born in 1940) is an Australian poet who has published sixteen collections of poetry as well as several prose and verse novels.

Advanced texts

8 BEFORE YOU READ Have you ever thought about how an immigrant feels in your country? Make a mind map and compare it with a partner.

This is who I am, an immigrant

Sitting in a West End Toronto coffee shop, I scan the street for a man wearing baggy jeans, dark sunglasses and sporting the kind of clunky gold necklaces that are often referred to as "bling." I've never met a rapper before and admit to having a preconceived image of the musician I'm scheduled to meet. I'm caught off guard when a poised man in a collared shirt and fitted pants reaches his hand over a stroller carrying the most adorable two-year-old boy with a head full of bouncing curls and a wide smile. I look for heavy gold rings before shaking his hand and immediately feel ashamed for my mischaracterization. The 31-year-old isn't the stereotypical rapper I expected.

Soft-spoken and humble, Chansa has a down-to-earth personality that's diametrically opposed to the loud arrogance I've come to associate with rap musicians. After politely correcting my pronunciation of his name – "it's with an '*ah*' sound: Chansa" – we proceed to talk about his life in Zambia, his move to Canada and his career as a performing artist and songwriter.

Born in Zambia, Chansa spent his elementary school years in Iowa, U.S.A., while his father was studying and teaching at Iowa State University. Upon returning to Africa, he travelled around the continent and even spent a year in Europe. […]

As a child in Iowa, Chansa felt ashamed by his ethnic name. "I wished my name was John, just so I wouldn't stand out," he says. After writing his debut single "Immigrant" – an homage to the struggles faced by newcomers in Canada – using his Zambian name was a way to reclaim his African roots and show the world he's proud of his heritage.

"Whenever I meet people the first thing that happens when I introduce myself is they say 'huh?' and then I have to spell it out. It's so ingrained in me now that usually I spell it before I say it and then the next question is where are you from?" laughs Chansa. "So, I thought what better way to proclaim my Zambian-ness that going by my name"; a name Chansa says would be easily recognized by any of his countrymen as clearly Zambian.

His single, "Immigrant," was released in July and is full of provocative lyrics that are sure to touch a chord with newcomers. The song describes the struggles immigrants face in Canada from culture shock and loneliness to financial sacrifices and dealing with prejudice. I ask him to explain his thoughts behind some of the song's most evocative lyrics:

Lord knows the struggles I've had to endure to get me here … here's a place that I'm still adjusting to, feeling' culture shock, seein' things that I'm not accustomed to.

"Where I come from, it's a very community-based society. Here, in Canada, it's all about personal space. Even when you're on the subway, people don't want to be spoken to. If someone's engaging with you, it has to be for a reason like I need directions or something. It can't just be saying hi for the reason of saying hi," he says.

I may be overseas, yeah, but don't get it twisted, money doesn't grow on trees here, but we sacrifice and send it, it's hard to comprehend it.

"When you're in Africa or Asia or Latin America and you're watching TV, you see the shine. So you come out here and you speak with people on the phone and say you're struggling [in Canada] and they say, 'Yeah, whatever, we see what the lifestyle is like.' When you leave the 'developing world' to go to the 'developed world,' there's an expectation that you're going to be the saviour for your family.

Avoiding mistakes
Aussprache
[4] **schedule** [ˈskedʒuːl]
Betonung
[29] **provocative** [prəˈvɒkətɪv]

---

[2] **baggy** loose-fitting
[2] **clunky** clumpy, heavy, solid
[2] **necklace** [ˈnekləs] *Halskette*
[4] **preconceived** prejudiced, fixed
[4] **to be caught off guard** *auf etwas nicht gefasst sein*
[5] **poised** self-assured
[6] **stroller** *Buggy, Kinderwagen*
[10] **soft-spoken** quiet
[10] **humble** unpretentious, modest
[11] **diametrically opposed to sth** the total opposite of sth
[13] **to proceed** to continue
[20] **homage** [ˈhɒmɪdʒ] tribute
[20] **struggles** problems
[20] **to face** to confront, to encounter
[21] **to reclaim** to regain, to get back
[22] **heritage** *Erbe*
[24] **to be ingrained** to be deep-rooted
[26] **to proclaim** to declare
[30] **to touch a chord** [kɔːd] to move sb emotionally
[33] **evocative** [ɪˈvɒkətɪv] *aufrüttelnd, bewegend*
[47] **saviour** rescuer, liberator

So when you come here and perhaps things aren't what you expected them to be, you're now stuck between a rock and a hard place. You can't go back because what
50 awaits you are people that are expecting a saviour and they don't want to hear that you came back empty-handed. At the same time, you're the lowest of the low here."

People look at us and judge us like we're repeat offenders … This is who I am, an immigrant, does that make me so evil?

"Any kind of discrimination usually comes from ignorance. I think the average
55 Canadian doesn't know what being an immigrant is like. Listening to the song [might] give them insight. They'll say, so this is what you guys go through, this is how you feel, tell me more. The purpose of any art is to initiate conversations. Whether some people really hate the song, but they talk about it or people who like the song and talk about it, then it's done its job."

60 Although "Immigrant" contains some truths about Chansa's personal experience in Canada, he says he didn't write it to be about himself, but wanted it to be a portrayal of the collective immigrant experience. "I would like for any immigrant who hears the song to say 'He articulated what we've been feeling,'" he says, adding he hopes the song will inspire others to share their stories and create an
65 open dialogue about the struggles of Canada's immigrant community.

Lisa Evans, *Canadian Immigrant* website, 2013

52 **repeat offender** *Wiederholungstäter*
56 **insight** *Einblick*

9 BRAINSTORMING Do you agree with Chansa that people do not know what being an immigrant is like? Discuss this with your partner. → S23

10 COMPREHENSION Sum up what Chansa's song "Immigrant" is about and what he wants to achieve with his song. → S13 **Hinweis:** Auch als Hausaufgabe geeignet

11 ANALYSIS
a) Describe Chansa's experiences and inner conflict concerning his Zambian name "Chansa". **Hinweis:** Auch als Hausaufgabe geeignet
b) Compare his experience with Amir's and Abe's in the play *Disgraced* earlier in this chapter.

12 EVALUATION Make a list and compare Chansa's life and experiences in the "developing" and the "developed" world and comment on them.

13 CREATIVE TASK
a) Describe and analyse the two stamps issued by Canada Post in 2014 to commemorate two communities of historic significance to black Canadians.
Hinweis: Auch als Hausaufgabe geeignet
b) Imagine the Deutsche Post wants to make similar stamps to commemorate famous immigrants or milestones in immigration to Germany. What themes could they represent and what might they look like? In your group write or draw a draft and present it in class, then cast a vote on the most promising idea.
Geeignete Methode zur Präsentation und Auswertung: Gallery walk

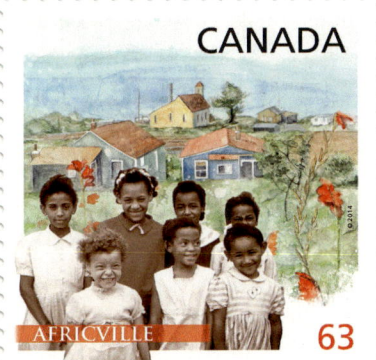

Spot on language

> Hinweis
> Selbstevaluation für Schüler über Green Line-Code

Avoiding biased or offensive language

Ethnically or racially biased language can create division, separation and tension between you and others. Therefore, use unbiased language when talking about ethnic or cultural groups and show respect to the people you are talking to or talking about. Avoiding language that could be interpreted as biased and offensive is no easy task for a learner of a foreign language. The best way to deal with this issue is to use
5 words that are inclusive and avoid unintended stereotypes.

Here are some examples:
- The term "Native American" has gained favour over "Indian". Depending on your knowledge about the person, you might more accurately refer to a specific tribe, like Cheyenne, Navajo, or Sioux.
- The native people of Canada are referred to as "Inuit" not "Eskimo".
10 - More and more people of mixed racial heritage want to be recognised as such, rather than being identified by a specific racial designation.

1 Have you personally ever experienced biased language? How did you feel?

2 Why is biased language unacceptable? Give reasons from the text and add more.

3 On your own collect biased words and think about what makes them offensive. Share your findings and feelings in small groups and find unbiased words to replace them.

4 Look at the list and match biased and unbiased phrases.

biased language

1 **Spanish people**
Only appropriate for people from Spain; and, therefore, imprecise when referring to people from Latin, Central or South America.

2 **coloured, non-white**

3 **negro, negroid, coloured person, dark**

4 **illegal alien**
Although preferable to just 'illegal' (when we call a person 'illegal', we imply that they are an object), this term lacks recognition of the person's humanity first.

5 **mulatto**

6 **Orientals**
Certain food may be labelled 'Oriental', and carpets may be 'Oriental', but not people's identities.

7 **Caucasian people**

unbiased language

a **white people, European American individuals**

b **bi-racial people, multi-racial individuals**
Only when it is relevant to state this in a communication.

c **Latino people** or **Latino/Latina, Hispanic Americans**

d **Asian people, Asian American individuals**

e **Black or African American**

f **people of color**
In the US context, 'people of color' usually refers to Asian/Pacific Islander, Native American, Latino/a, Hispanic, African American and biracial/multiracial people and should not be used synonymously with 'Black' or 'African American.'

g **undocumented immigrant** or **worker**; person seeking asylum, refugee

Migration and diversity

Mediation

5 *Your English friend tells you that there are many great movies in the UK about immigration like* East is East *and* Bend it like Beckham. *He asks you whether there are similar films about immigrants in Germany. You are not sure and check the internet. Read the movie review below and write an email summing up the plot of the film to your English friend.* → **S26.1**

6 *Exchange your email with a partner and check your partner's language and the content. Use a dictionary if necessary.* → **S33**

Almanya – Willkommen in Deutschland

„Wer oder was bin ich eigentlich – Deutscher oder Türke?" – Diese Frage stellt sich der kleine Cenk, Enkel des in den 60er Jahren nach Deutschland eingewanderten Gastarbeiters Hüseyin Yilmaz. Wie viele andere lebt seine Familie seit nunmehr 40 Jahren in Deutschland, die Frage nach dem „Zuhause" oder der „Heimat" ist deshalb nicht ganz so leicht zu beantworten. „Almanya – Willkommen in Deutschland" widmet sich dieser ganz besonderen Familiengeschichte humorvoll und ernsthaft zugleich. Doch statt eines schweren Dramas kann sich der Zuschauer auf eine frische Komödie mit Herz und einer gewaltigen Prise interkulturellem Tiefgang freuen, die seit Oktober als DVD und Blu-ray in den Ladenregalen steht.

Die Schwestern Yasemin und Nesrin Samdereli vollbringen mit „Almanya – Willkommen in Deutschland" ein kleines Kunststück: Wem es gelingt, Themen wie Migration, kulturelle wie religiöse Identität und Fragen nach Heimat und Staatsangehörigkeit humorvoll und doch absolut seriös, ernsthaft und vielschichtig zu behandeln, hat eine Leistung vollbracht, die aller Ehren wert ist. Bei der zumeist negativ behafteten, tristen und bekümmernden Berichterstattung in jeglichen Medien grenzt es an ein Wunder, dass diese „culture-clash"-Komödie entstehen konnte. Sie erzählt gefühlvoll, mit Wärme und Liebe zu den Figuren, die Familiengeschichte von Hüseyin Yilmaz (Vedat Erincin), der als einemillionunderster Gastarbeiter irgendwann in den Sechzigern nach Deutschland kommt und bald die Familie nachholt. Heute leben er und seine Frau Fatma (Lilay Huser) zusammen mit den vier Kindern und ihren beiden Enkeln noch immer in Deutschland. Cenk, der jüngste Spross, steht völlig zwischen den Stühlen. Während der Opa sich zweifelsohne als Türke sieht, wandeln Eltern, Onkel und Tante zwischen den Welten. Er selbst weiß einfach nicht, ob er nun Türke oder Deutscher ist. Als Hüseyin die ganze Familie zusammentrommelt um in die Türkei zu reisen, wo er ein Haus gekauft hat, will Cenk alles wissen. Wieso und weshalb Opa nach Deutschland kam, was die Türken von den Deutschen unterscheidet und und und …

Cousine Canan (Aylin Tezel) erzählt daraufhin die ganze Geschichte – von damals bis heute. Regisseurin Yasemin Samdereli verfilmt mit „Almanya" das Drehbuch ihrer Schwester Nesrin, die viele eigene Erfahrungen mit einfließen ließ. Völlig unbeschwert und doch aussagekräftig entsteht so eine tiefgreifende Erzählung, die zwischen köstlich amüsant als auch bitterernst und traurig pendelt. „Almanya" ist weitaus mehr als eine Komödie und doch bereitet sie die deutsch-türkischen Eigenarten mit einem ordentlichen Augenzwinkern auf. Aus heutiger Sicht wird die Ankunft des Familienoberhauptes im so fremden Deutschland gezeigt, die ersten Gehversuche und später die zögerliche Annäherung. Kulturelle Unterschiede wie auch religiöse und einfache Verhaltensunterschiede finden ihren Weg auf die Leinwand, wo sie zu einem tollen Mischmasch verbunden werden. Besonderer Kniff ist die Erzählung aus der Einwandererperspektive: Nicht nur die deutschen Sitten und Gegebenheiten erscheinen fremd, auch die Sprache hat ihre Tücken. Die Schwestern bieten auf diese Weise nicht nur eine emotionale Brücke zwischen Publikum und Charakteren, sondern vermitteln spannende wie heitere Eindrücke, wie der „Durchschnittsdeutsche" auf Fremde wirken muss.

Bei der Berlinale außer Konkurrenz gezeigt, konnte „Almanya" schon vor dem regulären Kinostart bei Kritik und Publikum punkten, später bezeichnete man die Geschichte als „Passender Film zur Integrationsdebatte". […]

Ruhr-Guide online magazine, 2011

Spot on **vocabulary**

Finding the core vocabulary

1 *On your own: Write down ten very important words in the context of migration and diversity.*

2 *In pairs: Compare your words and agree on 15 words. Justify your choice and discard the other words.*

3 *Now find another pair, and in groups of four compare your words and agree on 20 words. Justify your choice and discard the other words. The 20 remaining words are your core vocabulary.*

4 *In your group of four discuss how you decided on your core vocabulary. These questions can help you: Have you chosen the same words? How many? Did somebody have totally different words? Was it hard to agree on certain words?*

Talking about immigration

5 *Get together in small groups. Copy the words from the box below onto index cards. You can add more words. Mix the cards and put them face down in a pile on the table.*

a) **Touch – Turn – Talk:** Touch the card – turn it over – and talk for 30 seconds about the word in the context of migration and diversity. Be spontaneous! Take turns.

b) **Taboo:** Touch the card – look at it but don't let anybody else see what is on the card! Explain the word by paraphrasing it. The other group members have to guess the word. The winner gets the index card. Take turns. The group member with the most cards wins.

---

diversity • crossing borders • citizenship • multi-ethnic • integration • adapt to a culture • minority • enrichment • illegal alien • nationality • race • religious diversity • interfaith relationship • welfare • immigration • emigration • immigration law • identity • fear • mixed-race marriage • …

---

6 *Get together in small groups. Copy the words from the box below onto index cards. You can add more words. Mix the cards and put them face down in a pile on the table.*

Touch – Turn – Write: The youngest group member picks a card and puts it face up on the table. Everybody has two minutes to write a short text using the words in a meaningful context. Then pass your text to your neighbour on your left. Correct the text from your right-hand partner, then pass the text on and correct the next text until you have your own text in front of you. Check the corrections and ask questions if necessary. Take turns picking cards.

---

multicultural • world migration • deportation of illegal immigrants • Commonwealth migration • brain drain • diverse cities • cultural traditions from one's homeland • to be accepted • to adapt to a culture • …

---

7 *Use all of the vocabulary in the box to write a personal statement about the picture.*

ethnic backgrounds • immigrants • citizenship • proud • multi-racial • society • diversity

NHS National Health Service
(staatliches Gesundheitssystem des UK)

> **TIP**
>
> First work on the vocab sheets; then test yourself here!

Topic task

Migration and diversity — 6

Staging a talk show

There are heated debates about migration and diversity around the world. Discuss this issue by staging a talk show in class, following the steps below. Before you start, think about these questions: Have you ever been to a talk show? Do you watch talk shows on TV? Why do you like or dislike them? Do they have an influence on your opinion?

STEP 1 — Choose the topic

Agree on a name and exact topic for your talk show. Choose a controversial question, e.g.
a) Should immigration to the US/UK/Germany be limited by new laws?
b) Are immigrants a blessing or a curse?
c) Should illegal immigrants be deported?
d) …

STEP 2 — Assign and prepare the roles

You need the following roles for your talk show. Prepare each of them in small groups of four to five students:

- **One host group:** The host moderates the show. Think about how to introduce the topic and your four guests. Think about questions to keep the discussion going and how to close the discussion. → S24.2
- **Four guest groups:** Each group has four guests: Two who are in favour of the topic, and two who are against it. In each group, think of how to introduce yourself and prepare a short introductory statement expressing your point of view. Find convincing arguments. To do so, research necessary information like recent facts and figures. Anticipate arguments the other groups could use and be ready to give your opinion on them. Make notes for your discussion. → S24.3
- **One audience group:** Create an observation sheet to evaluate the discussion. Think of contents and (body) language.

STEP 3 — Stage your talk show

- Each guest group and the host group name a member (or two for tough issues), who acts out the role in the talk show. The other group members become part of the audience now. They can ask questions or make comments.
- Stage the talk show as authentically as possible. The seating arrangement should be in a semi-circle in front of the class. Do not forget to speak freely! Don't just read a prepared text aloud.

STEP 4 — Evaluate the talk show

- All participants of the talk show: Report your experiences and feelings.
- The audience: You observed the discussion. Were the roles presented convincingly? Did they stick to facts? What arguments were raised?
- Finally, discuss in class whether the talk show had any effect on your own opinion on the topic. (What have we learned? What convinced you most? Was it useful to look at the topic from different angles?)

President Obama as a guest on *The View*

USEFUL PHRASES

For the talk show host
Today's topic is …
I would like to welcome my guests …
Could you briefly introduce yourself and state your opinion on …
I would like to ask the audience for any questions or comments.
We have time for one last contribution/comment/question.
I'd like to thank my guests for …

USEFUL PHRASES

For the talk show guests
It's evident that …
These facts prove that …
This is convincing proof/evidence of …
Let me give you an example of …
Considering the fact that …
I'm referring to …
The point I'm trying to make is …

Zusatzmaterial KV 3/3a
Role cards

7 Faith and religion
Introduction

Code
sq36ms

Young African Americans in a gospel choir

Young pilgrims in front of the Cathedral of Santiago de Compostela

Church service in the Crystal Cathedral, Los Angeles

Two chocolate bars showing the symbols of a mosque and a Christian church

Drive-in church service, Daytona Beach

Couple at drive-up wedding chapel

1 SPEAKING Choose one of the pictures and describe it. What does it tell you about the importance of religion?

2 SPEAKING State your personal opinion about the concept of drive-in churches. Would you like to attend a service while sitting in a car?

3 VISUALS Analyse the message conveyed by the picture of the chocolate bars. → S28.2
Geeignete Methode: Think – Pair – Share

Spot on facts

Faith and religion — 7

Religion in Great Britain and the US

Religion in Great Britain

When Pope Clement VII refused to divorce King Henry VIII from his first wife, Henry VIII used this as an opportunity to separate from Rome in 1534. By the Act of Supremacy, he established himself, the monarch, as 'Supreme Head of the Church of England (C of E)'. Henry VIII became the legal authority of the new 'Anglican' church. Besides the divorce, he then dissolved the monasteries in England and Wales and confiscated their property.

The C of E has two branches: the High Church, with services similar to Catholic ceremonies, and the Low Church, which stresses simplicity of worship.

The C of E is led by two archbishops, appointed for life by the monarch. Together with 24 of the 42 Anglican bishops, they are also members of the House of Lords and take an active part in politics. If a bishop retires or dies, a new bishop is nominated by a Crown Commission and the British Prime Minister. Priests, deacons and lay ministers complete the hierarchy. The C of E has female priests (since 1994) and female bishops (since 2014).

Scotland has its own official Presbyterian church, 'the Kirk', which is democratically governed and stresses simplicity and preaching.

Free churches include Methodists and Baptists. These churches disagree with the doctrine and rituals of the High Church.

Other religious groups in Great Britain include Muslims, Jews, Roman Catholics, Sikhs and Hindus.

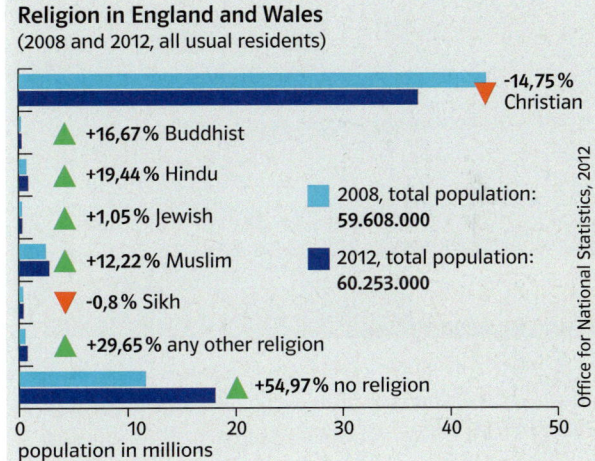

Religion in England and Wales
(2008 and 2012, all usual residents)

-14,75 % Christian
+16,67 % Buddhist
+19,44 % Hindu
+1,05 % Jewish
+12,22 % Muslim
-0,8 % Sikh
+29,65 % any other religion
+54,97 % no religion

2008, total population: 59.608.000
2012, total population: 60.253.000

population in millions

Office for National Statistics, 2012

Religion in the United States of America

In November 1620 the ship *Mayflower* arrived on the Massachusetts coast, chartered by Puritan families who were to become known as the Pilgrim Fathers. Driven by religious persecution in Europe, they hoped to find the 'promised land' in North America. Other Christian denominations such as the Quakers and Roman Catholics followed them on their search for a more tolerant home. The experience of religious persecution played a decisive part in creating the First Amendment to the US Constitution in 1791, which guarantees the complete separation of church and state and the free practice of religion. These two factors, the experience of religious persecution and the freedom of religious expression, led to a huge variety of religious groups in the US. Some of the largest religious minorities are Mormon, Jewish, Muslim, Buddhist and Hindu.

There are more Protestants than Catholics. The Protestants divide again into numerous denominations, such as the Baptist churches, the Methodists and the Presbyterians. Some denominations take a literal approach to the Bible. An important political aim of Christian fundamentalists is, for example, teaching Creationism instead of the theory of evolution in schools, a development that has received much attention in the press recently.

---

1 COMPREHENSION Describe the hierarchical structure of the Church of England.

2 ANALYSIS Describe and interpret the bar chart. → S27

3 EVALUATION Comment on the different relationships between church and state in the UK and the US and their consequences in politics and for society. → △1
Diff (help with): Strukturierungshilfe, Vorgabe möglicher Aspekte
Hinweis: Auch als schriftliche Hausaufgabe geeignet

Hinweis
Weiterführend können Recherchen zu den genannten religiösen Gruppierungen anschließen.

Texts

A Feelings and facts

1 BEFORE YOU READ
a) Describe, analyse and comment on the photo on the left. → S28.1
b) Discuss examples of how churches try to attract young people.

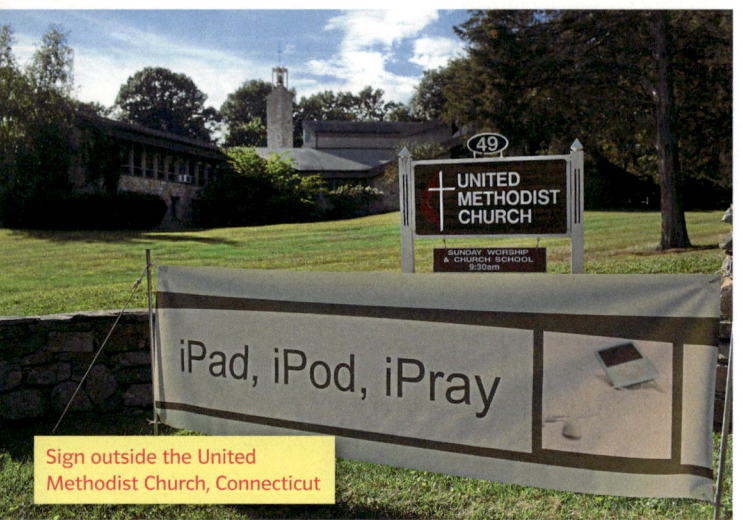

Sign outside the United Methodist Church, Connecticut

Young Americans' religious attitudes today

According to a study conducted by the Pew Research Center in 2012, one-fifth of Americans are religiously unaffiliated – higher than at any time in recent US history – and especially those younger than 30 seem to be drifting away from organized religion. The following statements were taken from a discussion among a group of young people and reveal some reasons why a third of young Americans say they don't belong to any religion.

Yusuf Ahmad, 33, raised Muslim, is now an atheist. His doubts set in as a child with sacred stories he just didn't believe: "Like the story of Abraham – his God tells him to sacrifice his son. Then he takes his son to sacrifice him, and he turns into a goat. I remember growing up, in like fifth [or] sixth grade I'd hear these stories and be like, 'That's crazy! Why would this guy do this? Just because he heard a voice in his head, he went to sacrifice his son and it turned into a goat?' There's no way that this happened. I wasn't buying it.
Today if some guy told you that I need to sacrifice my son because God told me to do it, he'd be locked up in a crazy institution."

Kyle Simpson, 27, raised Christian. He has a tattoo on the inside of his wrist that says "Salvation from the cross" in Latin: "[…] I don't [believe in God] but I really want to. The problem with questions like these is you don't have anything that clearly states, 'Yes, this is fact,' so I'm constantly struggling. But looking right at the facts – evolution and science – they're saying, no there is none. But what about love? What about the ideas of forgiveness? I like to believe they are true and they are meaningful. […]"

Melissa Adelman, 30, raised Catholic: "Starting in middle school we got the lessons about why premarital sex was not OK, why active homosexuality was not OK, and growing up in American culture, kids automatically pushed back on those things, and so we had some of those conversations in school with our theology teachers. The thing for me – a large part of the reason I moved away from Catholicism was because without accepting a lot of these core beliefs, I just didn't think that I could still be part of that community. I remember a theology test in eighth grade where there was a question about homosexuality, and the right answer was that if you are homosexual, then that is not a sin because that's how God made you, but acting upon it would be a sin. That's what I put down as the answer, but I vividly remember thinking to myself that that was not the right answer."

Lizz Reeves, 23, raised by a Jewish mother and a Christian father. She lost a brother to cancer: "I wanted so badly to believe in God and in heaven, and that's where he was going. I wanted to have some sort of purpose and meaning associated with

---

3 **unaffiliated** independent
here: not part of a religious community
12 In the original **story of Abraham**, his son did not *turn* into a goat but God *sent* an animal to reward his obedience.
13 **to sacrifice** to kill a person or an animal and offer them to a god in a religious ceremony
18 **to buy** *here:* not accept or believe
22 **salvation** being saved from evil
33 **core** fundamental

FACT FILE

The **Seventh-day Adventist** Church is a Protestant denomination which was established in the US in the 19th century. Its members emphasise the Second Coming or advent of Christ, and they regard Saturday as the Sabbath.

his passing. And ultimately the more time I spent thinking about it, I realized the purpose and meaning of his life had nothing to do with heaven, but it had to do with how I could make choices in my life that give his life meaning. […]"
Statements from a discussion on NPR, January 15, 2013

45 **Rigoberto Perez, 30, an Iraq War veteran who was raised as a Seventh-day Adventist:** "But you don't have to have a sense of community from religion. I don't get my sense of community from religion. I'm a veteran, I ride sport bikes. I'm a fan of a football team. People can get that sense of community from everywhere."
Statement from a discussion on NPR, January 17, 2013

42 **passing** death

Avoiding mistakes
Wortschatz
40**heaven** place believed to be the home of God, place of existence after mortal life
sky upper atmosphere of the earth

USEFUL PHRASES

Talking about religion
Biblical stories are legendary/unbelievable/inhumane/parables …
to search for certainty/for proof of God's existence/a purpose in life
to reject religious intolerance/implausible moral standards
to believe in Christ's life and teachings …
to find fulfillment …
to offer a guideline for one's own way of life

2 COMPREHENSION State the reasons given by each interviewee why he/she is no longer religiously committed.

3 CREATIVE TASK
   a) Decide in a team of four which person you would like to send an email to. Draft a response to that person. Your email should include support or criticism of the particular person's view of religion by presenting arguments and experiences of your own. Write your email and swap your answer with another group.
   b) Now read their text and prepare an answer from the point of view of the interviewed person dealt with. Discuss your answer with that group.

L1/22 **4 LISTENING**
   a) Listen to the next part of the discussion and describe the experiences of the first speakers, Melissa and Lizz, after leaving their religious communities.
   b) Point out the speakers' different attitudes to praying.

5 VISUALS Describe, analyse and interpret the statistics. → S27 **Hinweis:** Auch als Hausaufgabe geeignet

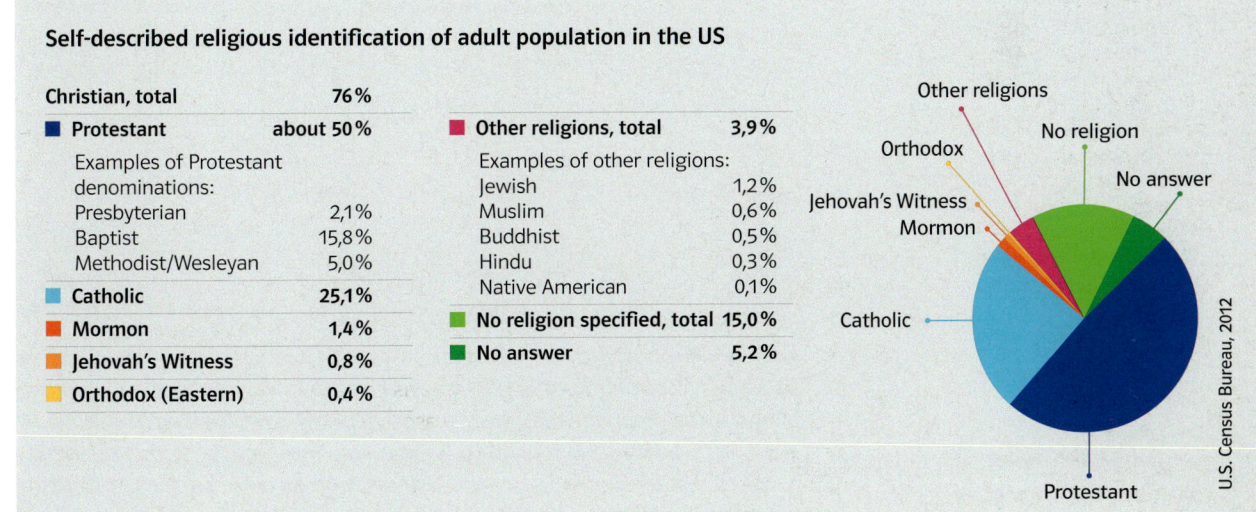

6 SPEAKING Prepare a short presentation on religious affiliation and demographic and ethnic groups in the US. Discuss your findings. Point out which particular finding surprised you and explain why. → S22 → ▲2
Diff (instead of): Vergleich zweier Statistiken (Zusammensetzung religiöser Gruppen in den USA und dem Vereinigten Königreich)

Zusatzmaterial WB
Task 1: Talking about religion
Task 2: Mediation

Texts

Avoiding mistakes
Aussprache
[15]**entrepreneur**
[ˌɒntrəprəˈnɜːr]

First Amendment
The First Amendment was adopted to the constitution in 1791 and guarantees the separation of church and state and the free exercise of religion.

[2] **pew** seat in a church
[5] **affiliation** connection
[7] **the narrative on the right** as the conservative Christians see it
[8] **to commission** to give sb the task of doing sth
[11] **to kowtow** (infml) to be very polite to
[15] **exasperated** angry, frustrated, upset
[15] **parson** priest
[17] **sterling** good, strong
[22] **God's New Israel** refers to the self-image of the early Pilgrim settlers who believed to have been called to establish the 'New Israel'
[23] **unprecedented** has never happened before

USEFUL PHRASES

Talking about secularisation

the separation of church and state

to support a secular state

a gap between Christians and a secular society

the process of secularisation of society

to share the same religion

atheist

religious pluralism is increasing

to belong to a denomination

to regard religion as a private matter

B Living with religion today

One nation under God?

This week millions of "Chreasters" – Americans who attend church only on Christmas and Easter – will crowd into pews to sing carols and renew their vague relationship with the Christian God. This year, there may be fewer Chreasters than ever. A growing number of "nones" live in our midst: those who say they have no religious affiliation at all. An October Pew Research Center poll revealed that they now account for 20 percent of the population, up from 16 percent in 2008. [...] 5

The narrative on the right is this: Once upon a time, Americans honored the Lord, and he commissioned their nation to welcome all faiths while commanding them to uphold Christian values. But in recent decades, the Supreme Court ruled against prayer in public schools, and legalized abortion, while politicians declared "war on 10
Christmas" and kowtowed to the "homosexual lobby."

America's rates of church affiliation have long been higher than those of Europe – perhaps because of the First Amendment, which permitted a religious "free market" that encouraged innovation and competition between spiritual entrepreneurs. Yet membership, as every exasperated parson knows, is not the 15
same as showing up on Sunday morning. Rates of church attendance have never been as sterling as the Christian Right's fable of national decline suggests. Before the Civil War, regular attendance probably never exceeded 30 percent, rising to a high of 40 percent around 1965 and declining to under 30 percent in recent years – even as 77 percent still identify as Christians and 69 percent say they are "very" or 20
"moderately" religious, according to a 2012 Gallup survey.

We know, then, that the good old days were not so good after all, even in God's New Israel. Today's spiritual independents are not unprecedented. What is new is their increasing visibility. "I like the fact that we're getting more 'nones' because it helps Christians realize that they're different," Stanley Hauerwas, a Protestant 25
theologian at Duke Divinity School, said when I asked for his thoughts on the Pew poll. "That's a crucial development. America produces people that say, 'I believe Jesus is Lord, but that's just my personal opinion.'"

Molly Worthen, *New York Times*, 2012

1 COMPREHENSION Find examples from the text to support the statement that common Christian values are becoming less important in American society.

2 ANALYSIS Explain why church affiliation in the US is higher than in Europe, according to the text, and compare the different situation for churches in the US and in Germany.

3 MEDIATION Your class is co-operating with an American high school on a project about the religious affiliations of young people in the US and in Germany. Collect information about church membership in Germany. Compare these figures to those given in the article and send an email of about 150 words to your partner school in America. Your email should include a short summary of the reasons given for the decline of church membership in Germany as well as a short comment on that decline. → **S26**

Geeignete Methode: Think – Pair – Share; **Zusatzmaterial KV 1:** Panel discussion

Hinweis
In diesem Zusammenhang kann auf den Text und die Bedeutung des allmorgendlichen Treueschwurs auf die Fahne und die Nation (Pledge of Allegiance) an amerikanischen Schulen eingegangen werden

How Christian fundamentalism feeds the divide

Mix It Up at Lunch Day is one of those programs that just seems like a nice thing to do.
   The idea is that on one day of the school year, kids are invited to have lunch with the kind of kids they don't usually hang out with: the jocks mix with the nerds,
5 lunch tables are racially integrated, et cetera.
   [...] You can argue about how permanent its effects are, or whether other approaches might be better, but the idea of making new friends in the lunchroom seems utterly benign. Right?
   Wrong, as it turns out – at least, according to the American Family Association
10 (AFA), a radical rightwing evangelical policy group. Mix It Up at Lunch Day is, in fact, part of "a nationwide push to promote the homosexual lifestyle in public schools", according to the AFA literature. The program "is an entry-level 'diversity' program designed specifically by the Southern Poverty Law Center to establish the acceptance of homosexuality into public schools, including elementary and junior
15 high schools," warns the AFA website. "See if your child's school is on the list."
   [...] So why does the form of religion that seeks to claim the term "Christian" in the political realm have to focus so relentlessly on a "gay conspiracy" – not to mention sexually active singles and the purely evil Muslims?
   I don't believe for a moment that this hysterical voice that screeches in
20 America's political sphere is the authentic voice of religion in America. Most religious Americans want to mix it up at lunch! They want to make friends across party lines, and they want to help people who are less fortunate. A survey by the Public Religious Research Institute, released on 24 October, reveals that 60% of Catholics believe the Church should place a greater emphasis on social justice
25 issues and their obligation to the poor, even if that means focusing less on culture war issues such as abortion and same-sex marriage.
   [...] Why is it that when politicians want to demonstrate just how religiously righteous they are, they talk about banning same-sex marriage and making contraceptives hard to get, instead of showing what they have done to protect the
30 weak?
   There is an obvious answer, and it is, in a sense, staring you in the face every time you watch a political debate or read about the latest antics of *Focus on the Family* and the AFA. The kind of religion that succeeds in politics tends to focus on the divisive element of religion. If you want to use religion to advance a partisan
35 political agenda, the main objective you use it for is to divide people between us and them, between the in-group and the out-group, the believers and the infidels.

Katherine Stewart, *The Guardian*, 2012

---

to feed to increase
[4] **jock** student athlete who is considered to be stupid
[8] **benign** harmless, good
[17] **relentlessly** endlessly
[17] **conspiracy** *Verschwörung*
[19] **to screech** *kreischen*
[28] **righteous** morally good and fair
[32] **antics** (*pl, n*) annoying, silly behaviour

---

4 COMPREHENSION *Point out what the Mix It Up program is and why it is opposed by the American Family Association.*

5 ANALYSIS *Examine the writer's attitude towards the AFA.* → △3
Diff (help with): Strukturierungshilfe, Vorgabe möglicher Aspekte   **Hinweis:** Auch als Hausaufgabe geeignet

6 RESEARCH *Do some research on the following controversial topic in US schools: the teaching of creationism/intelligent design vs. the theory of evolution. Point out what the controversy is.* → S32   **Hinweis:** Weiterführend kann eine Diskussion anschließen

Hinweis
Je nach aktueller politischer Situation kann diese Topic flexibel in die Oberstufenzeit integriert werden (z. B. Wahlen in USA, GB, D oder Europa)

8 Political systems
Introduction

Code
us23yz

Young woman voting in a polling place

Aaron Schock was, at 27, the youngest member elected to the US House of Representatives in 2009.

Pamela Nash was 25 when she was first elected to the UK House of Commons in 2010.

British Asian Muslims entering a polling station to vote in election

Support for key social and fiscal issues
Young voters in the 2012 Presidential Election

■ 30 years or more
■ 18–29 years old

Issue	30 years or more	18–29 years old
Same sex marriage – support legalizing	45%	66%
Taxes – increase on incomes $250,000 or more	46%	50%
Immigration – support a pathway to citizenship	64%	68%
Healthcare law – expand or leave as is	42%	53%
Abortion – should be legal	58%	64%

CIRCLE, Tufts University, US

USEFUL PHRASES

Talking about survey results

The results are worrying/ surprising/very varied/as we expected.

Some/Most/Not many respondents thought that …

The … result may be due to …

1 CREATIVE TASK Conduct a survey in your class using these questions:
1. Have you ever voted in an official election?
2. How many minutes do you watch or read political news per week?
3. Do you know enough about politics to vote responsibly in an election?
4. Do you feel strongly about any political topic? If so, which?
5. Would you consider becoming active in politics? If so, why? If not, why not?
6. Do you think that your vote can change anything?

Present your results to the class in an appropriate form. Use pie or bar charts for quantifiable answers. Make a statement about these results. → **S27, S30**

2 VIEWING
a) *Watch the interview with Aaron Schock. Sum up how he sees politics.*
b) ***Think-Pair-Share:*** *How much can young people influence politics? Take the film, the statistics and the pictures into account.*

A Young people and politics

Teen "rights" of passage

Registering to vote was very reminiscent of the day I got my driver's license.
   Right before my road test, I envisioned how my life would be different once I had the independence that came with driving a car. I had never been adept at navigation, but it seemed as if all drivers possessed an inherent knowledge of
5 every road, side street, highway and traffic circle within a 50-mile radius. […] But on my first joy ride alone, I realized that I was bestowed with no such internal GPS. The lack of divine intervention disappointed me, and after making several circles around my own town, I found myself exercising my new privilege with diminishing frequency. I had the entitlement, but none of the wisdom. Driving wasn't fun, but
10 rather a huge responsibility. […] I felt bizarrely unfulfilled and without direction.
   I had a comparable sense of anticlimax when I registered to vote in my government class last week. Though I knew I had a liberal standpoint, I didn't think I was politically savvy enough to align myself with a party. Beyond my fears of being incarcerated should my registration form prove invalid, affiliating myself with
15 any particular group screamed "slacktivism." I couldn't see the benefit of attaching my name to a cause I might have little or no involvement in […] Or maybe I would become so disillusioned by unyielding politicians and frustrated by their gridlock that I wouldn't make the effort to go out and vote.
   Despite my initial leanings, my teacher convinced me to select a party. I didn't
20 know if I'd ever be motivated to vote in a primary election, but I thought the option sounded somewhat appealing. Despite my shortage of knowledge, I felt it was my civic duty to take advantage of the liberties granted by the Constitution. […]
   Much like driving, I had always seen voting as fun. I loved stepping into the voting booth, watching my mom close the curtain and pull levers that were high
25 above my head. Though the system looked complicated at the time, I believed that the concept of voting would click for me once I could do it on my own. But much like driving, voting seemed like nothing but hype and confusion once I was finally given the opportunity.
   However, I have a renewed desire to learn. I never want to get lost on the
30 road, and I never want to vote for the politician just because she has the coolest name on the ballot. I want to be a better driver, and I want to be a more informed American. I want to reap the benefits of privileges that people of other nations can only dream of having. Maybe these responsibilities aren't what I originally thought them to be, but maybe I have to learn to embrace them in ways that don't
35 necessarily involve the notion of "fun." Most of all, I want to use my independence wisely.

Erica deMichiel, *Huffington Post*, 2013

"rights" of passage wordplay on 'rites of passage': transition rituals into adulthood
[1] **reminiscent** [remɪˈnɪsənt] reminding sb
[4] **inherent** [ɪnˈherənt] natural, built-in
[6] **to be bestowed with** given
[7] **lack of divine intervention** no help from God
[13] **savvy** knowledgeable
[14] **incarcerated** [ɪnˈkɑːsəreɪtəd] imprisoned
[15] **slacktivism** choosing the easy way without thinking
[19] **initial leanings** first tendency
[24] **pull levers** [ˈliːvəz] here: operate a voting machine
[32] **reap the benefits** profit from, enjoy

USEFUL PHRASES

Talking about politics
to (go out and) vote for …
to register to vote
to envision sth
to exercise a privilege
to be entitled to do sth
to have a responsibility/ civic duty to …
to affiliate oneself with sb
to be frustrated/ disillusioned by …
to experience gridlock
to select a party
to step into the voting booth

---

1 COMPREHENSION Outline similarities between driving and voting in the text.

2 ANALYSIS Explain why deMichiel has chosen the comparison between learning to drive and first-time voting to express her attitude to voting.

3 SPEAKING Compare the author's experience with your own experience of elections.

4 RESEARCH Find out about a political topic which affects you personally. Collect information and statistics for a classroom debate on your topic. → S24
Hinweis: Recherchearbeit auch als Hausaufgabe geeignet

Zusatzmaterial WB
Task 1: Indirect questions

Spot on facts

> **Avoiding mistakes**
> Wortschatz
> **politics:** politicians' work in general, including their election and legislative decision-making work → to go into/study politics, world politics
> **policy:** the plan of action chosen by a political party; a party line on an issue → foreign policy, to pursue a certain policy

Political systems in the US and the UK

The political system of the United States

The US federal constitutional republic dates back to the written US Constitution ratified in 1790, which gives the individual states great autonomy to prevent the federal government from becoming too powerful. However, in recent decades, the President's power has increased, both in American and in world politics.

The Constitution specifies three branches of government, the legislative (Congress), the judicial (the Supreme Court) and the executive branch (the Administration). A system of checks and balances prevents abuse of power by any branch. This means, however, that a President can find himself confronted by a majority in Congress for the opposition party, which can cause gridlock instead of progress.

The two parties in Congress are the Democratic Party (more liberal) and the Republican Party (more conservative). Each party's candidate for President is selected in a long process usually starting with primaries and ending with a state convention. Instead of voting for their President directly, US citizens elect members of the Electoral College, who have pledged to support a particular candidate, a method often regarded as unjust, as it does not always reflect the popular vote.

The people (electorate: all American citizens over 18)

| ... vote directly in Federal Elections for Representatives (every two years) and Senators (1/3 of the Senate every two years) | Each state has
- a number of representatives based on the size of the population
- exactly two senators | ... vote indirectly in Presidential Elections by electing members of the Electoral College (every four years), who then vote for President and Vice President | Electoral College |

United States Government

Legislative (makes laws)

Judicial (evaluates laws)

Executive (carries out laws)

TWO CHAMBERS OF CONGRESS

House of Representatives
435 Representatives (Congressmen, congresswomen) serve for two years

Senate
100 Senators serve for six years

Supreme Court
– nine Supreme Court Justices appointed for life
– highest court of appeal
– checks new laws for validity according to the Constitution

President
– Head of State & Government
– Commander-in-Chief of the US Armed Forces
– signs or vetoes Congress bills

Cabinet
– Vice President and heads of 15 executive departments

Checks and balances: Each part of the US government can check the others' decisions.

> **The Congress can**
– pass/veto/ratify laws and treaties and approve the appointment of justices
– override President's veto with a 2/3 majority vote
– regulate commerce, taxes, spending and military expenses and declare war

> **The Supreme Court can** declare executive actions and laws unconstitutional

> **The President can**
– propose/approve/veto laws
– make treaties with foreign governments
– nominate Supreme Court judges
– be impeached by Congress

> **Avoiding mistakes**
> Betonung/Aussprache: **politics** [ˈpɒlətɪks], **politician** [ˌpɒləˈtɪʃn], **political** [pəˈlɪtɪkl], **policy** [ˈpɒləsi]

8 Political systems

The political system of the United Kingdom

The UK political system is a constitutional monarchy with parliamentary democracy, based on a largely unwritten constitution that has evolved over centuries, gradually reducing the rights of
5 the monarch and strengthening Parliament. The sovereign is officially Head of State and appoints Supreme Court judges, who are independent from government, but he/she now represents rather than rules.
10 In a first-past-the-post election system, only one candidate in each constituency is elected and all other votes are 'wasted'. This benefits the two large parties, the Conservatives (Tories) and the Labour Party, while disadvantaging smaller ones. Recently, coalitions with the Liberal Democrats have been 15 formed. Advantages of first-past-the-post are that it is simple to understand, produces strong, mainly single-party governments and provides a close link between MPs and their constituencies.

Although many legislative powers in domestic 20 issues have been devolved to national assemblies in Scotland, Wales and Northern Ireland, Parliament (in Westminster, London) remains responsible for legislation affecting the UK as a whole, international relations and financial matters. 25

The people (electorate: all British nationals over 18, in 650 parliamentary constituencies of very different sizes) **vote directly in General Elections** in a first-past-the-post system for up to five years.

Government of the United Kingdom

THE HOUSES OF PARLIAMENT

House of Commons
650 Members of Parliament (MPs), one for each constituency
- examine the work of the Government
- debate and pass bills (drafts for laws)

House of Lords
About 760 members (life peers and 26 Anglican bishops)
- advise on/suggest changes of bills
- can delay most bills for up to a year
- hereditary peerage abolished in 1999

The Monarch/Sovereign

Official Head of State and the Commonwealth, Commander-in-Chief of the Armed Forces, Supreme Governor of the Church of England – hereditary and crowned for life.

- representational function; State Opening of Parliament each year in May/June
- appoints the Prime Minister and all Lords in the House of Lords
- bills approved by Commons and Lords receive Royal Assent, becoming Acts of Parliament, thereby law

Prime Minister
Leader of the party winning most seats in the House of Commons
- represents Government
- reports regularly to the monarch

Shadow Cabinet
- MPs and Lords from the second largest (official) Opposition party
- responsible for checking and questioning Cabinet's work

Cabinet
20 senior ministers appointed by Prime Minister, in charge of government departments

---

1 ANALYSIS Compare the UK and US political systems. Look, for example, at the balance of power, the roles of the monarch and the President, and the number of political parties most often in government. →△1
Diff (after): Vergleich mit deutschem System

Texts

Zusatzmaterial WB
Task 2: Conditionals

B Old characteristics and new political developments

The Negotiator

Washington insiders will sometimes, in complete privacy, admit to British friends that they would give their right arms for the British governmental system.

The British system is fairly simple. The Queen is the head of state and she stays in place. The head of government is the Prime Minister, who is always the leader of the party that wins the general election. This has two advantages. The nation's chief executive cannot be at loggerheads with a majority from the opposing political party in Parliament (which facilitates necessary, though not always popular, legislation) and the incoming prime minister after an election win is almost always a skilled and experienced politician at national level, and probably a former Cabinet minister in a previous administration. The experience, the knowhow, the awareness of how things happen and how to make them happen, is always there.

London has one third advantage. Behind the politicians stands an array of senior civil servants who probably served the previous administration, the one before that and the one before that. With a hundred years at the top between a dozen of them, these 'mandarins' are of vital help to the new winners. They know what happened last time and why, they keep the records, they know where the landmines are situated.

In Washington the outgoing incumbent takes almost everything with him – the experience, the advisers and the records, or at any rate those that some congenial colonel has not shredded. The incoming man starts cold, often with only experience in government at state level, bringing his own team of advisers, who may be as 'cold turkey' as he is, and not quite sure which are the footballs and which the landmines. It accounts for quite a few Washington reputations soon walking around with a permanent limp.

From: Frederick Forsyth, *The Negotiator*, 1989

² **to give one's right arm for sth** to want sth very much
⁶ **to be at loggerheads/ in gridlock with sth/ sb** sich streiten, einander blockieren
⁷ **to facilitate sth** [fəˈsɪlɪteɪt] make sth easier
⁸ **legislation** making laws
¹³ **civil servants** Staatsbeamten
¹⁵ **mandarin** *here:* wise, experienced, powerful person
¹⁸ **incumbent** [ɪnˈkʌmbənt] Amtsinhaber/in
¹⁹ **congenial colonel** [ˈkɜːnəl] *(ironic)* friendly military officer
²⁰ **to shred** destroy *(paper)*
²² **cold turkey** normally the unpleasant state that drug addicts experience after suddenly stopping taking drugs
²³ **reputation** Ruf
²⁴ **limp** Hinkefuß

VIP FILE

Frederick Forsyth (*1938) was the youngest British Royal Air Force pilot at 19 in 1956, then became a journalist for Reuters in Europe. He is the author of several political thrillers, including *The Day of the Jackal*, *The Negotiator* and *The Kill List*.

1 COMPREHENSION **Hinweis:** Auch als Hausaufgabe geeignet
   a) *Decide whether the following statements are true or false according to the text.*
   1. US politicians say the only advantage of the British system is that the monarch can advise all new prime ministers.
   2. The British Prime Minister can pass even unpopular laws because his party always has the majority in Parliament.
   3. Senior civil servants have often worked for the British administration through several changes of government.
   4. The US President leaves some government records for the next President.
   b) *Outline the three ways in which governing is easier for a British prime minister and the three corresponding problems a US president faces.*

2 ANALYSIS
   a) *Explain the meaning of 'cold turkey' and 'walking around with a permanent limp' in this context. Find some more examples of metaphors and personification in the text and explain their function.*
   b) *Point out, in contrast to the focus of the text, some advantages of the American change-of-office characteristics, considering its lack of 'mandarins'.* →△2 **Diff** (help with): Hinführung und Beispiele

3 EVALUATION *Use your knowledge of the different political systems in Germany, the UK and the US to discuss which system you find best.* **Geeignete Methode:** Fishbowl discussion

Hinweis Dieser Text kann als Ausgangspunkt für eine tiefergehende Auseinandersetzung mit unterschiedlichen politischen Systemen in Form einer Recherchearbeit dienen

Open government

One of the most noticeable trends in 21st century world politics is that many countries are introducing the three elements of open government into their political systems: transparency, open data and open participation.

Group 1 – Open data: visionary mission or dangerous risk?

Pro: Knowledge is power. With key information openly available, power can be held to account, inequality challenged, and inefficiencies exposed [...] Everyone has the potential to understand our world, and the knowledge they need to tackle major challenges such as poverty and climate change, and the findings of publicly-funded research, so we can start to understand these, tackle them, and know if our solutions are working. We see a world where information helps deliver a balance of power.
Open Knowledge Foundation, UK, 2014

Con: Openness can also be a threat in dangerous situations, whether that's being gay in a small town or during revolutionary times when confronting repressive states armed to the teeth. That [...] was a lesson learned the hard way by several people in North Africa and the Middle East during Arab Spring as well as the London Riots last summer when their posts to Facebook were used by the military and police, respectively, to track people down.
Prof. Dwayne Winseck, Canada, 2012

Group 2 – Open participation: perfect ... just for a few interested geeks?

Pro: What happens when half of the world's population lives in cities? When over three billion people are online? When there are more than 15 billion connected devices? Old organizational models hit end-of-life. People behave differently. [...] The world used to be about command and control. Someone told you what to do. There still is a lot of that. But collaborative innovation is taking over. [...] There is no significant distinction between the public good and the private good. It's just good.
Marten Mickos, US, 2012

Con: If online participation engages only a fraction of the population, but [...] starts influencing the way policies are developed and service designed and delivered, isn't this creating a new divide between those who do participate and those who do not? The latter would still express their opinion through periodic elections [...]. But the former would start influencing processes and positions along the way. Who would then ensure the balance?
Andrea di Maio, Italy, 2011

4 COMPREHENSION Divide into two groups. Create a table of advantages and disadvantages of either **1: open data** or **2: open participation**. Add your ideas.

5 SPEAKING In your groups choose one of the topics below:
making students pay for university education • declaring war on another country • more taxes for rich people • allowing same-sex marriage
   a) **Group 1:** Consider whether available statistics could improve public understanding of the topic. **Group 2:** Consider which members of the public would be most likely to participate in the debate on the topic.
   b) Come together to discuss whether a decision made by the public on these topics would be better than a decision made by elected representatives. →▲3
   Diff (after): Interpretation und Diskussion von zwei Zitaten in Gruppenarbeit

---

FACT FILE

Open government
Transparency means that information about decision processes, changes in law, and statistics on government spending is made available for everyone to see, often online.
Open data is the free-for-all publication of data and statistics by public government institutions, including election, scientific research and survey results, weather, environmental damage, maps and transport information.
Open participation enables citizens to be involved in political decision-making processes by communicating criticism, suggestions and petitions directly, often online, to government representatives.

[3] **to hold sb to account** to check and criticise someone's work if it's not good enough
[10] **publicly funded research** öffentlich finanzierte Forschung
[19] **repressive states armed to the teeth** schwer bewaffnete Diktaturen
[23] **Arab Spring** protests and demonstrations in the Arab world in 2010/11
[27] **to track down** aufspüren

Zusatzmaterial WB
Task 3: Mediation

Hinweis
Hier können weitere Projekte zu aktuellen politischen Entwicklungen anschließen

9 Globalisation
Introduction

Code
7wi6zu

President Obama speaking to sub-Saharan Africa's young leaders at a summit

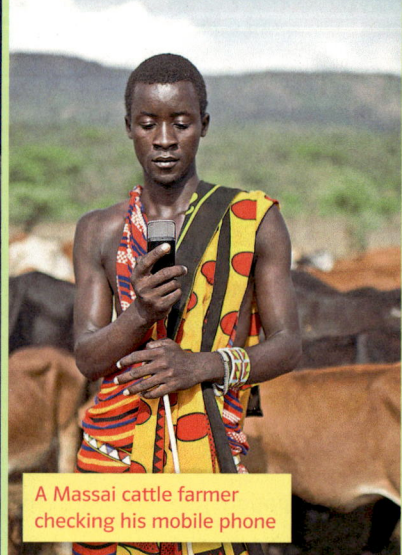
A Massai cattle farmer checking his mobile phone

John Naikasie, Kenya, upholds his traditional Massai values but wants his children to go to private schools

"I would like my own children to get higher than I did. So I would like them to have a real good education."

Christina Frias (37), USA, actress, criticises global consumerism

"It's very difficult on a daily level of basic survival to remember that the little I have is enough for most people in the world."

Martha Brim, Australia, is a professional dancer of traditional Aboriginal dances

"Drugs and alcohol is a main issue in our community and if you don't have that education how would you get a job in the main stream?"

1 **BRAINSTORMING** *How does globalisation affect you personally?*

2 **VISUALS** **Geeignete Methode:** Think – Pair – Share
   a) *Choose one of the photographs on these two pages and describe it to your partner.* → **S28.1**
   b) *For each of the photographs find a heading that reflects one aspect of globalisation.*

Billboard showing Santa Claus with a Coke bottle in Managua, Nicaragua

Hong Kong container port

Black Friday, a lowest-price sale day in the US

Female Chinese workers sewing clothes

Glezel Delos Reyes (23), Philippines, participates in the global labour market

"I sacrificed all my life to work here in Singapore."

Christian Corcoran, USA (30), is concerned about international politics

"George Washington said: 'Never get involved with other people's affairs.'"

Dulcie Isaro (63), Palm Island, lives in an Aboriginal community off the Australian coast

"I would like to see a lot of things happen on this island."

3 VIEWING *Watch the six short clips from* 7 Billion Others, *a multimedia website where hundreds of people from all over the world give their views on the world and their hopes and fears. Collect information about how globalisation has changed their lives and their communities.*

4 EVALUATION
   a) *Compare your results from Tasks 1–3. Are there any important aspects of globalisation that are missing? Add them.*
   b) *On the basis of your findings, decide on the five most important challenges and the five most promising opportunities of globalisation.*

Spot on facts

Chances and challenges of globalisation

Globalisation – a basic definition

Globalisation refers to the growing global network of trade, travel, knowledge and influence. It is possible today for individuals and groups of people to buy and sell products all over the world, to travel to any place and to exchange information across the planet.

This freedom, however, can also put human rights, the environment, individual cultures and financial security into danger. The advantages of the global network are great; but the challenges it brings could be greater. Interestingly, the global network will probably be the key not only to global problems, but also to their solutions.

"The internet means we can organise anti-globalisation demos across the planet."

People, cultures and lifestyles

Chances

Globalisation affects us all on a daily basis: People can move and travel freely, seeing more of the world and learning about other people. This increases cultural awareness and reduces the causes of conflict. Ongoing exchange between academics, experts or politically interested people all over the world makes research, protests and activism more effective, fostering the emergence of a global civil society. Migrants can move to different countries to find work and support their families, helping these countries to fill important labour gaps at the same time.

On a more official level, international government and non-government organisations (NGOs) can share knowledge and know-how and bring help to where it is needed. Help ranges from granting microcredit loans (to start a small business) or debt relief to providing technology, education, food and medicines. Similarly, conflicts between countries can be handled diplomatically and with a better understanding of the situation because more information is available than ever before.

All these possibilities contribute to a global 'togetherness'. Individual people, groups and even nations can find friends and partners with similar interests and ideas all over the globe. Traditions and regional and cultural identity can be shared, explained, continued and celebrated.

Challenges

Globalisation is often seen as synonymous with westernisation. Western culture, propagated by the media, serves as an example for many developing countries, but also endangers the cultural diversity of nations' languages, traditions, ways of life, values and beliefs.

Yet Western influence is not limited to culture. Developed countries are tempted to use their economic and political power to intervene in other countries' affairs. However, such interventions are not always welcome or beneficial and can cause a divide or even war. Moreover, help from the outside often hinders developing countries from building functional administrations and infrastructure of their own.

As a result of global consumption, travel and transport, limited resources are disappearing. The rapid economic growth of large emerging markets like China, India or Brazil, who are adopting the West's unsustainable lifestyle and consumerism, make the situation worse. The disposal of mountains of (often toxic) waste is often left to Third World workers – the result of the widespread "Not in my back yard" attitude. The availability of fresh water, which is becoming scarce, may be crucial in the future. Potential 'side effects' of increased migration are illegal immigration, people-smuggling and the frequently bad treatment of immigrant minorities.

1 VISUALS *Choose one of the cartoons. Describe it and interpret its message.* → **S 28.2**
Hinweis: Auch als Hausaufgabe geeignet

A network of products

Chances

First and foremost, globalisation means gaining access. People have access to essential products, specialities and medicines from all over the world, and both small and large companies have the chance to sell their products worldwide.

The **global market area** potentially secures jobs, livelihoods and economic stability, since customers and companies have access to (or can outsource) cheaper materials, products and labour, lowering costs and raising profits.

The **global trade** of goods supports poor communities especially in developing countries, giving people much-needed jobs and improving local infrastructure. **Fair trade** campaigns can help developing countries to get a fair share of the profits created.

"…But in the Global Marketplace you're only 650,247,555th."

Challenges

In theory, open markets and a globalised economy provide a level playing field for everybody. However, political interests, financial power and subsidisation contribute to an unfair distribution of wealth and power as well as the rise of **'global players'** (large international corporations), dominating market shares and lowering the chances of survival for small businesses. Apart from that, interdependent financial networks make economies increasingly vulnerable to financial disasters.

Outsourcing, offshoring and the global competition for cheap materials and labour undermine the standards of living and income, especially in poor countries. This often leads to horrendous working conditions, with many workers still not being able to afford basic essentials, and to the use of child labour. Developed countries, on the other hand, are affected by tax evasion and stagnating wages.

However, these production conditions are often 'invisible' to those who buy things. Customers are encouraged by advertising and peer pressure to consume more than they need without knowing how and where the things they buy have been produced.

The communication network

Chances

Access to global communication via **mobile and internet technology** is increasingly cheap and unrestricted. This means even people in remote or rural areas can communicate, be educated and work without an expensive landline infrastructure.

Global communication facilitates trade, travel and contact with friends, family and business partners. Developers can cooperate, e.g. in education, human rights and aid organisations. There is also a political dimension to the communication network: Anyone able to use a computer has a voice now, from young people or immigrants without voting rights to dissidents in dictatorships. News and instant information can save lives in a crisis or expose crime and propaganda.

Challenges

Concerns are voiced about **personal data**, which has become less secure, and the fact that data 'paper trails' can be used to track, observe, predict and control people's behaviour and movements. Non-democratic governments in particular may try to use the internet to control their citizens.

At the same time, large parts of the world like those in extreme poverty, remote places or war zones, still have little or no access to the global internet network. This great disadvantage may even threaten their existence.

Finally, the global **flood of information** can make it very difficult to find out which information is important and to assess the quality of the source.

2 SPEAKING Form groups of four or five. Choose five of the challenges mentioned on these two pages and discuss possible solutions. **Zusatzmaterial KV 1:** Peer conference/Placemat zum Thema Globalisierung

Zusatzmaterial WB
Tasks 9–14: Reading and writing

Core skill workshop

Dealing with mediation tasks

Part A Understanding the task

In contrast to translation, mediation means expressing specific ideas from a text in another language for another person (the addressee). Therefore, it is important to read the task carefully and to identify
- the addressee (the reader or listener of your text),
- the purpose (the information which is relevant for the addressee),
- the text type required,
- your relationship with the addressee (for appropriate register and style).

> **TIP**
> Sometimes **the addressee** is not explicitly stated but can be deduced from the information given in the task.

1 COMPREHENSION *For each of the following example tasks, note the addressee, the purpose, the required text type and register (formal or informal).*
   a) Your American pen pal is really fond of soccer. His/Her parents, however, consider it a waste of time. You think the information on the website of the network Fußball-Lernen-Global might help your pen pal convince them. Based on the article, write an email to him/her, outlining the chances street football provides for young people and the projects planned for 2014.
   b) You are doing an internship at an international media agency based in Berlin. Currently, you are writing contributions in English for their blog "Life in Germany". Based on the following interview, write a short article about the German football league, the 'Bundesliga', and its relevance for different regions in Germany.

Part B Finding relevant information

Before working on your mediation text, make sure you understand the original text, i.e. read it once for gist. Then scan it for the details as required in the task. → S11

2 COMPREHENSION *Skim the following text. State the text type, title, author/source and summarise its topic in one sentence.*

Straßenfußball verbindet

Jugendliche der Gesamtschule Wulfen und ihrer brasilianischen Partner-Schule CEMP hatten die Möglichkeit, globales Lernen im Rahmen einer Austauschbegegnung in Brasilien hautnah zu erfahren. Nach der Ankunft in São Luis, der Hauptstadt des Bundesstaates Maranhão, besuchte die Gruppe zunächst Formação[4] und wurde mit den verschiedenen Arbeitsfeldern und Strukturen der Organisation vertraut gemacht. Im Anschluss daran stand ein 12-tägiger Besuch in São Bento und der dortigen Partnerschule CEMP auf dem Programm.
   In diesen Tagen hatten die Jugendlichen die Möglichkeit, sich intensiv über ihre Erfahrungen mit Straßenfußball und über Möglichkeiten der Partizipation und Verantwortungsübernahme in der Kommune auszutauschen. Ganz praktisch wurde dies beim gemeinsamen Ausrichten eines Straßenfußballturniers auf dem 'Plaza de Eventus' mitten in São Bento, an dem verschiedene Schulen der Stadt teilnahmen. Ein Erfahrungsaustausch über die deutsche und die brasilianische Spielekultur bot zudem die Möglichkeit sich auch durch das gemeinsame Spielen näher zu kommen. Dabei stellten die Jugendlichen erstaunt fest, wie viele Spiele ihrer Länder ähnlich oder sogar gleich waren.

---

[4] (Instituto) Formaçao Brazilian NGO

Die gemeinsame Zeit wurde aber auch genutzt, um gemeinsame Inhalte und Projekte für die Zeit bis zum geplanten Gegenbesuch der Brasilianer in Deutschland 2014 festzulegen. Hierbei entstand die Idee, ein gemeinsames
20 Projekt zu den Lebensrealitäten umzusetzen und dabei über Präsentationen auf beiden Seiten auch die gesamte Schule einzubeziehen. Außerdem planen die Jugendlichen ein simultan in beiden Ländern stattfindendes Straßenfußballturnier. Die Jugendlichen beschlossen auch, die Kommunikation und die Zusammenarbeit durch das Einrichten eines gemeinsamen Blogs auch neben
25 den bereits stattfindenden Skype-Gesprächen weiter zu verbessern.

Ein Highlight der gemeinsamen Zeit war sicherlich der Besuch im Nationalpark Lençóis Maranhenses zum Abschluss der Begegnung. São Bento und Wulfen verbinden also mittlerweile neben dem Straßenfußball auch viele gemeinsame Erfahrungen, Projekte und Zukunftsvisionen, die in der kommenden
30 Zeit in die Praxis umgesetzt werden sollen. Die Begegnung wurde durch das ENSA-Programm gefördert und ist Teil einer langfristigen Lernpartnerschaft zwischen beiden Schulen, die bereits seit 2011 besteht.

Fussball-Lernen-Global website, 2013

3 LANGUAGE *Explain these words and phrases from the text in English:*
Möglichkeiten der Partizipation • Verantwortungsübernahme • gemeinsames Ausrichten eines Straßenfußballturniers • Spielekultur • Projekt zu Lebensrealitäten   **Hinweis:** Auch als Hausaufgabe geeignet

4 COMPREHENSION *Re-read Task 1a) on the previous page. Scan the text for the information the addressee (your pen pal) is interested in. Copy this grid and complete it with keywords in English:*

who takes part in the project	…
chances of street football	…
future common projects	…

Part C Writing your mediation text

5 MEDIATION *Write the email to your American pen pal. Follow these steps:*
a) *Start with an appropriate introduction. Which of these introductions fits the situation best? Why?*
   1. Young people from Wulfen and their partner school CEMP did a project on global learning in Sao Luis, Brazil. When …
   2. Dear XY, how are you? I think I've got some really interesting news. …
   3. Hey, here's something on soccer: Some guys from Wulfen …

b) *Using your notes from Task 4, think of how to structure your email. If necessary, change the structure of the original text for your purpose. Do not forget to give any information in your own words.*

c) *End the email appropriately.* → **S18.4**

6 LANGUAGE *Check your text for the following points:*
• logic and length (only relevant points included?)
• register and style
• language (sounds natural? matches the text type?)
• correctness (grammar, spelling, punctuation)

TIP

Scanning and note-taking
Mark only relevant points. Highlight keywords in the text. Use different colours for different themes. Translate or paraphrase/explain the keywords if necessary and note them next to the text.

TIP

Dealing with mediation situations
• Think of possible cultural and language differences (e.g. explain concepts or terms; use strategies to ask/react politely).
• Keep to the chosen register and style.
• The new text should usually be much shorter than the original.

Core skill workshop

7 MEDIATION Your school would like to take part in the KICKFAIR project together with your partner schools in the UK and Poland. You have been asked to present KICKFAIR to their teaching staff via Skype. Prepare a short statement in English (max 200 words). Explain how KICKFAIR works (their aims and partners) and why football is important for social and global learning.
Hinweis: Auch als Hausaufgabe geeignet

Kickfair

Fußball fasziniert, begeistert und verbindet Menschen auf der ganzen Welt – unabhängig von Alter, Geschlecht, sozialem Hintergrund oder kultureller Zugehörigkeit. Beim Fußball können Kinder und Jugendliche wichtige soziale Erfahrungen machen: Sie lernen im Team zu spielen, sich an Regeln zu halten, mit Sieg und Niederlage umzugehen und die Leistung des anderen anzuerkennen. Dieses Potential greift KICKFAIR seit mehreren Jahren auf und entwickelt über Fußball vielfältige Projekte in den Bereichen Bildung, Lernen und Erziehung. Im Mittelpunkt steht der junge Mensch – der Leitgedanke, an dem sich KICKFAIR orientiert. Über die Projekte werden Räume geschaffen, in denen junge Menschen gemeinsam Dinge in die Hand nehmen und entwickeln. Hier können sie miteinander lernen, ihr eigenes Lebensumfeld mitgestalten und so für sich und andere neue und positive Lebensperspektiven aufbauen. […]

Im Vordergrund steht das Entdecken und Entfalten von Stärken und Talenten. KICKFAIR schafft Räume, in denen junge Menschen Aufgaben finden, die sie fordern und fördern – unabhängig von Geschlecht, von Nationalität, von sozialer Herkunft, von ethnischer Zugehörigkeit oder von schulischer Bildung. Das Gefühl der Zugehörigkeit und der Aspekt des miteinander und voneinander Lernens ist dabei zentral. […] Im gemeinsamen Handeln und Entwickeln ergeben sich dabei vielfältige Lernmöglichkeiten. Die Jugendlichen lernen, im Team zu arbeiten, flexibel und selbständig zu arbeiten und können dabei wichtige Schlüsselkompetenzen erwerben. Das Lernen geschieht so in einer ganzheitlichen Form: auf der Basis eigenen Handelns und der eigener Erfahrungen, die im Projektverlauf immer wieder reflektiert werden. […]

Über Straßenfußball sollen attraktive Zugänge zu verschiedenen Themen geschaffen werden. Lernbereiche wie Demokratie-Lernen, Werteerziehung, Konfliktmanagement oder globales Lernen sollen nicht kognitiv, sondern ausgehend von den eigenen Erfahrungen auf dem Spielfeld geöffnet werden. […] In langfristig angelegten gemeinsamen Projekten haben die Jugendlichen die Möglichkeit, ihre Kompetenzen zu erweitern und neue Blickwinkel kennen zu lernen. Ziel ist es, über Straßenfußball eine gemeinsame Identität zu schaffen. Die Jugendlichen sollen so kulturelle Vielfalt als Bereicherung erkennen und Einblicke in globale Zusammenhänge bekommen. Globalisierung soll dadurch nicht als Bedrohung, sondern als Chance für die gemeinsame Entwicklung erkannt werden.

KICKFAIR arbeitet in einem Netzwerk aus internationalen Partnern. Diese Partner arbeiten ebenfalls über Fußball in den Bereichen Lernen, Bildung, Erziehung und Entwicklung. Zentrales Ziel der beteiligten Organisationen ist es, Kompetenzen und Erfahrungswissen aus den verschiedenen gesellschaftlichen Zusammenhängen zusammen zu bringen und zu systematisieren. Das gemeinsam entwickelte Wissen fließt in die jeweiligen Projekte zurück und gibt dort wichtige Impulse für die lokale Weiterentwicklung. Durch gemeinsame Veröffentlichungen wird es aber auch für andere zugänglich gemacht.

KICKFAIR e.V. website, 2007

A Different cultures and lifestyles

The world until yesterday

An American anthropologist recalls one of his many visits to New Guinea.

An airport scene

The most obvious difference between that 2006 check-in scene etched in my memory, and the 1931 photographs of "first contact," is that New Guinea Highlanders in 1931 were scantily clothed in grass skirts, net bags over their shoulders, and headdresses of bird feathers, but in 2006 they wore the standard international garb of shirts, trousers, skirts, shorts, and baseball caps. Within a generation or two, and within the individual lives of many people in that airport hall, New Guinea Highlanders learned to write, use computers, and fly airplanes. Some of the people in the hall might actually have been the first people in their tribe to have learned reading and writing.

[…] Another subtle difference between the 1931 and 2006 scenes was that the 2006 crowd included some New Guineans with an unfortunately common American body type: overweight people with "beer bellies" hanging over their belts. The photos of 75 years ago show not even a single overweight New Guinean: everybody was lean and muscular. If I could have interviewed the physicians of those airport passengers, then (to judge from modern New Guinea public health statistics) I would have been told of a growing number of cases of diabetes linked to being overweight, plus cases of hypertension, heart disease, stroke, and cancers unknown a generation ago.

From the jungle to the 405

Returning to urban life in the U.S. means returning to time pressures, schedules, and stress. Just the thought of it raises my pulse rate and my blood pressure. In New Guinea jungle there is no time pressure, no schedule. […]

A New Guinean from the nearest village may have promised me yesterday that he'll visit camp "tomorrow" to teach me bird names in his local language: but he doesn't have a wristwatch and can't tell me when he'll come, and perhaps he'll come another day instead. In Los Angeles, though, life is heavily scheduled. My pocket diary tells me what I shall be doing at what hour on what day, with many entries months or a year or more off in the future. E-mails and phone calls flood in all day every day, and have to be constantly re-prioritized into piles or numbered lists for responding. […]

Returning to Los Angeles from New Guinea jungle carries for me big changes in my social environment: much less constant, direct, and intense interactions with people. During my waking hours in New Guinea jungle, I'm almost constantly within a few feet of New Guineans and ready to talk with them, whether we are sitting in camp or out on a trail looking for birds. When we talk, we have each other's full attention; none of us is distracted by texting or checking e-mail on a cell phone.

Jared Diamond, *The World Until Yesterday*, 2012

New Guinea today

New Guinea Highlanders in traditional clothing

[1] **anthropologist** sb who studies human societes, customs and beliefs
[1] **New Guinea** [njuːˈɡɪni] large island in the Southwest Pacific Ocean, north of Australia
[3] **etched in** cut into
[5] **scantily clothed** wearing very little
[7] **garb** clothes in a special style
[12] **subtle** almost not noticeable
[19] **hypertension** high blood pressure
[19] **stroke** loss of blood supply to the brain
[21] **the 405** very busy and congested Interstate Highway in California
[31] **pile** things put on top of each other

Avoiding mistakes
Wortschatz
[17]**statistics** *plural noun + singular verb*, Statistik

Zusatzmaterial WB
Task 1: Word families

---

1 COMPREHENSION *Make a list with three columns noting down the features of life in New Guinea and Los Angeles today as well as in traditional New Guinea.* → ▲1
Diff (after): Dialog zwischen New Guinea Highlander und seinem Enkel verfassen
2 ANALYSIS *Examine the author's position between the two cultures.*
Hinweis: Auch als Hausaufgabe geeignet
3 CREATIVE TASK *Have you ever experienced a foreign culture radically different from Western life? Write a short text remembering your feelings then. If not, imagine such a situation and write a fictional account of the experience.* → △2
Diff (instead of): Comment (Entscheidung im traditionellen oder modernen New Guinea zu leben)
Zusatzmaterial KV 2: Partner discussion

Texts

Why IKEA took China by storm

Home Depot's big box stores have bombed in China, and lots of analysts and pundits have attributed the failure to the difference in culture – the Chinese simply don't like do-it-yourself. That's true, but it's not the whole story. It's not that simple. Look at IKEA. The furniture retail juggernaut from Sweden is killing it in China, and it's famous for making its customers put everything together themselves. In fact, CEO Mikael Ohlssen said in late 2011 that sales in China are growing faster than at the company as a whole. So, if the Chinese don't like do-it-yourself, what's the difference between Home Depot and IKEA? Helen H. Wang, an author and consultant on China's middle class, explained the concept in a column at Forbes last year:

"In the last fifteen years, home ownership has gone from practically zero to about 70 percent. However, many people have little sense of how to furnish or decorate a home. They are very eager to learn from the West. This is one of the reasons that IKEA is very popular in China. Their Western-style showrooms provide model bedrooms, dining rooms, and family rooms showing how to furnish them. Their stylish and functional modern furniture is particularly appealing to young couples. Chinese consumers need to be educated as they have no role models. They are eager to learn but they need guidance. Companies that invest in educating the market can expect to reap handsome rewards."

When you go to Home Depot, you're asking for help to solve an existing problem that you have – you want to install a ceiling fan, you want to put new windows in or you want to build a deck. The staff is helpful, and they'll help you figure out what you have to do for the project, but the project in it, of itself, isn't necessarily packed with Western culture. IKEA, on the other hand, teaches the consumer how to decorate their home, and thereby experience Western culture. The project – and the payoff, for that matter – lets consumers experience that culture. […]

Retailers often don't realize how complex things are in China. There are so many subcultures – after all, there's more than 1.3 billion people there – and so many things beyond a company's control. For instance, most Chinese live in condos and don't have garages to stockpile tools, points out Wang.

Dan Harris, an attorney who specializes in Chinese law, explained […] the lessons he learned about consumers there: "[…] Like consumers just about everywhere else in the world, China's are fickle, mercurial and unpredictable."

Kim Bhasin, *Business Insider*, 2012

---

¹ **Home Depot** *here:* American home improvement retailer
¹ **to bomb** *here:* to fail
² **pundit** expert
⁴ **to be killing it** *here:* to be very successful
⁴ **retail** Einzelhandel
⁴ **juggernaut** *here:* huge and powerful company
³³ **condo** [ˈkɑːndoʊ] *(AE, infml)* privately owned flat in a shared appartment buildung
³⁴ **to stockpile** to keep a large supply of sth
³⁸ **fickle** always changing one's mind
³⁹ **mercurial** changing one's mood quickly

IKEA store in China

Zusatzmaterial WB
Task 2: Conjunctions
Task 5: Speaking
Task 15: Mediation

4 COMPREHENSION State the reasons for IKEA's success according to the text.

5 ANALYSIS Analyse how the author uses stylistic devices to grab the reader's attention at the beginning of the text. → S4, S10.2 →△3
Diff (help with): Vorgabe möglicher Stilmittel in einer Tabelle

6 EVALUATION Discuss whether IKEA is synonymous with Western culture.

7 EVALUATION Assess the effects of global consumer trends mostly following Western culture.
Hinweis: Auch als schriftliche Hausaufgabe geeignet

B Global production and its consequences

1 BEFORE YOU READ *When you go shopping, do you pay attention to where the clothes are produced? Does it influence your choice?*

Textile workers in Bangladesh

The web documentary Planet Money makes a t-shirt *traces the global manufacturing processes behind an ordinary t-shirt. One chapter focuses on the thousands of textile workers in Bangladesh.*

They're part of a global wave that goes all the way back to the
5 Industrial Revolution in England, when the first textile factories were created. In China in the 1980s, South Korea in the 1970s, America in the 1800s, and many other countries over the years, workers – mostly women – left subsistence farms to work in factories.

[…] Earlier this year, more than 1,000 workers were killed when
10 the Rana Plaza factory building in Bangladesh collapsed. Huge protests around the country followed, and Western companies that buy clothes in Bangladesh faced increasing pressure to improve working conditions and wages.

That pressure led the country to almost double its minimum wage, from $39 a
15 month to $68 a month. Still, that's far below the $104 a month the workers were asking for. […]

Factory owners worry that if the minimum keeps going up, the garment industry will find someplace else to make T-shirts. That's what's happened for decades: When labor costs rose in one country, Western buyers found someplace cheaper,
20 and prices for clothes continued to fall.

In the case of the Planet Money T-shirt, the buyer is Jockey. The company told us that the pattern of pulling out when wages rise may be coming to an end for now, because there's no country that's ready to replace Bangladesh as the cheapest place in the world to make clothes.

25 Wages in Bangladesh are going to rise, Marion Smith, a senior vice president at Jockey, told us. "That's good news from a humanitarian point of view."

But the long-run picture for Bangladeshi garment workers is less clear.

In China, South Korea and Japan, to name just a few countries, the textiles and apparel industry brought with it investment and manufacturing knowledge, which
30 those countries used to expand into higher-wage industries like electronics. As economies grow and countries move into other, more lucrative industries, textiles and apparel become less important. But the same may not happen in Bangladesh.

NPR website, 2013

Women working in a Bangladeshi clothes factory

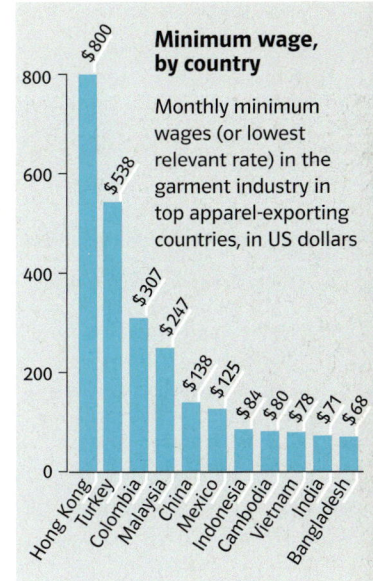
Minimum wage, by country
Monthly minimum wages (or lowest relevant rate) in the garment industry in top apparel-exporting countries, in US dollars

2 COMPREHENSION *Describe the process that made the textile industry move to Bangladesh. What role did the developed world play in this?* →▲4
Diff (after): Interpretation des Diagramms

L2/2 **3 LISTENING** *Listen to a report about two Bangladeshi women working in a clothes factory. Describe their living conditions and explain how their work has changed their lives.*

4 EVALUATION *Exploitation or opportunity? Discuss the garment industry's effect on poor people in Bangladesh.* **Zusatzmaterial KV 3:** Fairtrade-Kampagne
Geeignete Methode: Fish bowl discussion

8 **subsistence farm** farm that produces food mainly for the family living there
17 **garment** *(fml)* piece of clothing
27 **long-run** *here:* future
29 **apparel** *(fml)* clothing

Zusatzmaterial WB
Task 3: Synonyms
Task 4: Statistics

Texts

Hinweis
Die Erstbegegnung mit dem Text als Hörverstehen gestalten

VIP FILE

Ray Bradbury (1920–2012) was an American writer best known for his numerous science fiction novels and short stories. His most famous work is the dystopian novel *Fahrenheit 451*.

C Limited resources

L2/3

The Aqueduct

It leapt over the country in great stone arches. It was empty now, with the wind blowing in its sluices; it took a year to build, from the land in the North to the land in the South.

"Soon," said mothers to their children, "soon now the Aqueduct will be finished. Then they will open the gates a thousand miles North and cool water will flow to us, for our crops, our flowers, our baths, and our tables."

The children watched the Aqueduct being built stone on solid stone. It towered thirty feet in the sky, with great gargoyle spouts every hundred yards which would drop tiny streams down into yard reservoirs.

In the North there was not only one country, but two. They had rattled their sabers and clashed their shields for many years.

Now, in the Year of the Finishing of the Aqueduct, the two Northern countries shot a million arrows at each other and raised a million shields, like numerous suns, flashing. There was a cry like an ocean on a distant shore.

At the year's end the Aqueduct stood finished. The people of the Hot South, waiting, asked, "When will the water come? With war in the North, will we starve for water, will our crops die?"

A courier came racing. "The war is terrible," he said. "There is a slaughtering that is unbelievable. More than one hundred million people have been slain."

"For what?"

"They disagreed, those two Northern countries. That's all we know. They disagreed."

The people gathered all along the stone Aqueduct. Messengers ran along the empty sluiceways with yellow streamers, crying, "Bring vases and bowls, ready your fields and plows, open your baths, fetch water glasses!"

A thousand miles of filling Aqueduct and the slap of naked courier feet in the channel, running ahead. The people gathered by the tens of millions from the boiling countryside, the sluiceways open, waiting, their crocks, urns, jugs, held up toward the gargoyle spouts where the wind whistled emptily.

"It's coming!" The word passed from person to person down the one thousand miles.

And from a great distance, there was the sound of rushing and running, the sound that liquid makes in a stone channel. It flowed slowly at first and then faster, and then very fast down into the Southern land, under the hot sun.

"It's here! Any second now. Listen!" said the people. They raised their glasses into the air.

Liquid poured from the sluiceways down the land, out of gargoyle mouths, into the stone baths, into the glasses, into the fields. The fields were made rich for the harvest. People bathed. There was a singing you could hear from one field to one town to another.

"But, Mother!" A child held up his glass and shook it, the liquid whirled slowly. "This isn't water!"

"Hush!" said the mother.

"It's red," said the child. "And it's thick."

"Here's the soap, wash yourself, don't ask questions, shut up," she said. "Hurry into the field, open the sluicegates, plant the rice!"

In the fields, the father and his two sons laughed into one another's faces. "If this keeps up, we've a great life ahead. A full silo and a clean body."

---

² **sluice** [sluːs] artificial passage for water with a gate for regulating the flow
⁸ **gargoyle spouts** *Wasserspeier*
¹¹ **saber** *(AE)* heavy sword with a curved blade
²⁴ **streamer** long, thin flag
²⁶ **slap** *here:* the sound of feet hitting the ground
²⁸ **crock** pot or jar, usually made of clay

"Don't worry," said the two sons. "The President is sending a representative North
to make certain that the two countries there continue to disagree."
"Who knows, it might be a fifty-year war!"
They sang and smiled.
And at night they all lay happily, listening to the good sound of the Aqueduct, full and rich, like a river, rushing through their land toward the morning.

Ray Bradbury, *The Aqueduct*, 1979

Zusatzmaterial WB
Tasks 6–8: Listening

1 COMPREHENSION Hinweis: Auch als Hausaufgabe geeignet
  a) Describe the aqueduct and its significance for the people in the South.
  b) Give a detailed account of the Southern people's hopes with regard to the aqueduct and their reactions after the 'water' comes.

2 ANALYSIS Explain which single effect Bradbury's story creates for you. To do so it is helpful to look at the typical features of a short story and the imagery used in the text. → S5

3 ANALYSIS Hinweis: Auch als Hausaufgabe geeignet
  a) Which parallels with present-day conflicts do you see?
  b) Analyse the symbolic meaning of the aqueduct and the 'water'.
  Geeignete Methode zur weiteren Analyse: Freeze frame

4 EVALUATION
  a) Do you think the people in the South are justified in trying to profit from the war in the North? Write a comment. → △5 **Diff** (help with): Vorgabe von Aspekten
  b) Exchange your text with a partner. Read it and give feedback. → S33

5 VISUALS Describe and analyse the cartoon. Do you agree with its message?

6 SPEAKING In groups of four create a placemat for the following questions: What can be done in general to reduce the consumption of water and other finite resources? What can you personally do?
First read the fact file below and note down your ideas in your segment, then read what the other members of the group have written. Discuss the ideas and write down the ones you all agree on in the centre.

FACT FILE

Water scarcity

The United Nations have formulated a human right to water: sufficient, safe, acceptable, physically accessible and affordable water for everyone. However, more than one billion people worldwide lack sustainable access to clean drinking water and many more face water scarcity at least some time in the year. With current climate change and continuing population growth, almost half the world's population will experience water stress by 2030.

Safe drinking water is essential for hygiene and sanitation, but also for many industrial processess and for agriculture. This makes water both a necessity for human life and health and a major economic factor. In dry ('arid') regions, water disputes and conflicts are on the rise, e.g. over how much of a river's water one country may use before the river enters a neighbouring country.

Advanced texts

D NGOs, civil society and global players

Working for an NGO

FACT FILE

Medair is an emergency relief organisation based in Switzerland. It focuses on helping the world's most vulnerable and difficult to reach people so that they can recover and rebuild their lives after a crisis. Medair aims to have helped a total of 50 million people by 2025.

⁴ **relief** *here:* help, support
⁵ **onset** beginning
¹¹ **shelter** safe place to live
¹³ **resilient to sth** capable of withstanding sth
²⁹ **to restrain sth** to prevent sth from getting too large
³³ **contractor** *Vertragspartner*
³⁶ **by default** automatically
³⁷ **governance** the way a country or organisation is governed/managed

Zusatzmaterial WB
Task 16: Gapped texts

What are Medair's goals? What work does the organisation do?
Our biggest priority is on life-saving activities. Our focus is not only on emergency response, but also on rehabilitation and recovery after the emergency. We provide relief in response to natural disasters anywhere in the world, whether they are rapid-onset disasters, like earthquakes and floods, or slow-onset disasters, like famine. We also help people in conflict situations anywhere in the world: in war, civil war, ethnic or tribal conflict and in post-conflict crises.

Why are you working for Medair? What do you want to achieve?
My motivation for my current work at Medair is that I'm constantly striving to improve ways of helping a rapidly increasing number of disaster victims in our country programmes. We need to give these people culturally appropriate shelter and infrastructure solutions that will help to transform their communities and make them more sustainable and resilient to crises in the future.

Do you believe criticism towards international non-governmental organisations (INGOs) to be justified?
A very large number of lives are saved by the effort of INGOs, but the 'humanitarian space', or the arena in which organisations can provide help, is constantly getting smaller and more dangerous to work in. For example, relief work is problematic in countries where the host government is not fully cooperative, such as North Korea. It can also be difficult if INGOs stay longer in a country than necessary; or if the scale of a disaster cannot easily be solved with the relatively limited resources available, as we saw in Haiti. Unfortunately, a small number of less professional efforts by charitable organisations, or poorly-resourced organisations, are seized on by the press as representative of all the work being undertaken.

Which changes are needed in our globalised world to make the NGOs' work more effective?
Firstly, a recognition that some countries are under-developed and need assistance to reach a certain level, but that others are over-developed and need to restrain their use of global resources. This means we need to redefine fair-trade agreements to give us all a 'level playing field' not weighted to industrialised countries.

Then we definitely need less 'tied aid', as in "We will give you money for a dam if you use our engineering companies and contractors".

Thirdly, the national governments of poor countries with very high debts need to be encouraged to take responsibility for the welfare of all their citizens including those in opposition – and not pass this over to NGOs to deal with by default. Of course, this will require transparency and good governance, and a recognition that the donor countries also have some problems in these areas, for example if we look at US involvement in Latin America, the Middle East or Southeast Asia.

Interview with Mark Wooding from Medair by Hartmut Klose, 2014

1 COMPREHENSION
   a) *Describe the tasks Medair is pursuing in your own words.*
   b) *Outline the problems NGOs encounter.*

2 EVALUATION *With regard to the tasks and the problems NGOs face every day, would you like to be actively employed by such an NGO? Justify your position.*
   Hinweis: Auch als schriftliche Hausaufgabe geeignet

Are NGOs fit for their purpose?

The World Social Forum, which begins in Tunis today, is an important reminder of the pivotal role civil society organisations have often played in major social and political transformation.

The anti-slavery movement played a crucial part in bringing about legislation
5 to end slavery in the 19th century. Across the world, the trade union movement has been the lynchpin behind achieving basic labour rights and improvements in working conditions. The anti-apartheid movement brought about the downfall of the racist apartheid regime in South Africa in the 1990s. [...]

Civil society and NGOs have long been key to challenging systems that would
10 favour the few over the many, and give a voice to the voiceless, but is this the case today? Are they still fit for purpose?

There are many reasons why one might think that NGOs have never been better equipped to advocate and campaign. Dedicated campaigning and fundraising departments; professional, qualified, experienced and media-savvy staff now fill
15 advocacy roles. And thanks to better and cheaper telecommunications, social media and the internet, even small, previously obscure charities are able to quickly access information, images, stories from the field, turn them into campaigns and connect with their audiences. [...] But has this made today's campaigners more effective? Is it all enough?

20 Let me suggest some reasons why we should be concerned that this may not be enough. More than being a result of polished campaign strategies, the achievements of past movements can be attributed to highly driven, passionate participants, who exhibited a high degree of solidarity rooted in a shared set of beliefs, values and visions. They were largely independent from governments: they
25 neither took nor sought government funding. They were often subject to state surveillance; any engagement with government was highly strategic.

This contrasts with NGOs today which resemble more professional, technocratic bureaucracies, housing experts with well-honed functional and technical skills, providing opportunities for internship and career development. Employees jump
30 from one NGO to another – today working on environmental issues, tomorrow on children. Maybe in Rwanda and then in Vietnam. The modern NGO campaigner can also move neatly into government or business, and back into an NGO [...].

The close working relationship with government – where NGOs seek state funding, becoming co-producers of welfare, development and security – also raises
35 issues about autonomy and political positioning. [...] The sector must answer questions such as: at what point does intense competition among NGOs for commercial or government funding risk compromising key values and agendas? To what extent does the scramble for resources pit one NGO against another rather than fashion solidarity and collective campaigning? And to what extent does this
40 come at the expense of broader commitments to protect minorities and to defend the spaces of civil society? As co-producers of welfare, development and security, NGOs now have maybe more to lose. [...] Indeed, their very relevance may be at stake.

Jude Howell, *The Guardian*, 2013

FACT FILE

Non-governmental organisations (NGOs) do not belong to a government or a for-profit corporation. Many of the best-known NGOs such as Amnesty International, Greenpeace, Oxfam or Doctors Without Borders focus on human rights, ecology and health.

² **pivotal** ['pɪvətl] very important
⁶ **lynchpin** essential element
¹³ **fundraising** *Spendensammlung*
¹⁴ **media-savvy** knowing a lot about media
¹⁵ **advocacy** *here:* consultancy
¹⁶ **obscure** *here:* not well-known
²⁸ **to hone** to improve (a skill)
³⁷ **to compromise** *here: aufs Spiel setzen*
³⁸ **scramble** struggle
³⁸ **to pit sb against sb** to make sb fight against sb else

---

3 COMPREHENSION Sum up the differences between social movements of the past and NGOs today.

4 ANALYSIS Examine the author's line of argument and use of stylistic devices.
Hinweis: Auch als Hausaufgabe geeignet

5 EVALUATION Do NGOs still play a crucial role in a global civil society? Can you think of other ways of protesting which are more efficient? Discuss.
Geeignete Methode: Think – Pair – Share

Advanced texts

Starbucks celebrates record revenues

Starbucks reported record revenues on Thursday as the company avoided comment on British prime minister David Cameron's attack on the company's tax bill. The company's "busiest holiday season ever" drove revenues 11% higher to $ 3.8bn in the first three months of its fiscal year compared to the same period last year, executives told analysts. Profits were 13% higher at $ 432.4m. The news comes as Starbucks faces protests in the UK over its tax bill after admitting it paid just £8.6m in corporation tax over the past 14 years.

Cameron took a swipe at the firm at the World Economic Forum in Davos on Thursday. "Companies need to wake up and smell the coffee, because the customers who buy from them have had enough," he told business leaders. Cameron called for an international clampdown on corporate tax evasion. "In the UK we've already committed hundreds of millions into this effort – but acting alone has its limits. Clamp down in one country and the travelling caravan of lawyers, accountants and financial gurus just moves on elsewhere. So we need to act together at the G8," he said. […]

Last November Michelle Gass, Starbucks' European president, said the company had "never avoided paying taxes". A month later the company offered to pay £10m a year in corporate taxes in Britain for two years as it sought to defuse mounting protests. […] In 2013 Starbucks plans to open 1,300 new stores. Some 600 will be in the US, another 600 in China and the Far East and 100 in Europe, Middle East, Russia and Africa. "Starbucks has never been better positioned to achieve the goals we have set for ourselves around the world and I have never been more optimistic about our future," [chief executive] Schultz said in a statement.

Dominic Rushe, *The Guardian*, 2013

³ **revenue** income
⁴ **fiscal year** Geschäftsjahr
⁷ **corporation tax** tax companies pay on their profits
⁸ **to take a swipe at sb** (infml) to criticise sb
¹¹ **clampdown** increased effort to enforce a law or regulation

Capital has a nationality

Despite the increasing 'transnationalisation' of capital, most national companies in fact remain national companies with international operations, rather than genuinely nationless companies. They conduct the bulk of their core activities, such as high-end research and strategizing, at home. Most of their top decision-makers are home-country nationals. When they have to shut down factories or cut jobs, they usually do it last at home for various political and, more importantly, economic reasons. This means that the home country appropriates the bulk of the benefits from a transnational corporation. Of course, their nationality is not the only thing that determines how corporations behave, but we ignore the nationality of capital at our peril.

From: Ha-Joon Chang, *23 Things They Don't Tell You About Capitalism*, 2012

¹ **transnationalisation** process involving actions beyond national borders
³ **genuinely** truly, really
⁷ **to appropriate sth** (fml) to take possession of sth without permission
⁷ **bulk** largest part
¹⁰ **peril** risk, danger

6 COMPREHENSION
a) Outline why the British Prime Minister Cameron calls for an international clampdown on tax evasion and describe Starbucks's reaction to the protests they are facing. **Hinweis:** Auch als Hausaufgabe geeignet
b) Point out why international companies are not truly 'nationless' according to the second text.

7 SPEAKING
a) Write a short speech for or against placing stricter rules on large international companies. Partner A writes from the perspective of an NGO opposing corporate power. Partner B writes as a company representative.
b) Give your speeches to each other. Be prepared to give feedback.

E Developing and developed world

1 BEFORE YOU READ Why and how often do you buy new mobiles and other electronic devices? How do you dispose of the old ones?

West African nations pay a price for EU e-waste

Europeans are barred from exporting hazardous electronic waste to other countries, yet research shows there is a flourishing export market of such junk to Africa. Efforts are underway to strengthen the EU's rules – the Waste Electronic and Electrical Equipment Directive – on disposal of old appliances, televisions,
5 mobile telephones and computers. Barely one-third of such items are recycled at home, researchers say, while the bulk goes into landfills. But thousands of tonnes of electronic goods are exported where second-hand computer components and recycled metals are lucrative commodities for poorer countries. "A lot of this export is illegal or in an illegal grey zone," said Andreas Manhart of the Öko Institute for
10 Applied Ecology in Germany, who collaborated on a recent study – 'Where are WEEE in Africa' – produced by the UN Environment Programme. […]

The UN study says some 220,000 tonnes of electrical and electronic goods were shipped from the EU to West Africa in 2009. In Ghana alone, 30% of imports of allegedly second-hand products were useless, skirting EU efforts that call for
15 electronic goods to have some reusable value. Overall, the UN report shows that some 85% of containers arriving in Ghana with electrical and electronic goods came from Europe and 4% from Asia.

In August 2011, Europol warned that illegal waste dumping was on the rise within Europe – in abandoned mines and gravel pits – and in exports to Africa
20 from ports in Italy and northern Europe. "Criminals are exploiting the high costs associated with legal waste management and are making substantial profits from illegal trafficking and disposal activities, circumventing environmental legislation," the European police agency said in a statement. Reusing second-hand computer and other electronics or cycling components is becoming a major business in parts
25 of Africa, where environmental standards are much lower than in Europe or poorly enforced. Imports from Europe had been rising in the past decade, but declined in 2009 – coinciding with the economic decline – UN statistics show.

But the business comes with a price. Manhart cited severe human health risks and environmental impact from burning off electrical cord casings to get to
30 copper that can then be sold for recycling. The UNEP says discarded refrigerants and computer displays contain toxins or pollutants that can pose profound risks to people, as well as air and water quality. Some of the leading pollutants from e-waste are lead, mercury and endocrine disrupting substances such as brominated flame retardants. There is also concern that many of the workers engaged in
35 scrap metal and e-waste yards are children – some as young as five, the UN says. The UNEP has called for better controls in Africa, where the home-grown e-waste problem is growing.

Timothy Spence, EurActiv website, 2012

[1] **hazardous** dangerous
[6] **bulk** largest part
[6] **landfill** Müllhalde
[8] **commodities** goods that can be traded
[14] **allegedly** said to be true but not proven
[14] **to skirt sth** umgehen
[19] **gravel pit** Kiesgrube
[22] **trafficking** illegal buying and selling
[29] **cord casing** Kabelummantelung
[30] **UNEP** United Nations Environment Programme
[30] **refrigerant** Kühlmittel
[33] **endocrine disrupting substances** substances that may cause cancer or fertility problems by influencing hormones
[33] **brominated flame retardant** bromhaltiges Brandschutzmittel (krebserregend)

Avoiding mistakes
Wortschatz
[34] **engaged** tätig in etw
NICHT engagiert

Zusatzmaterial WB
Task 17: Prepositions

2 COMPREHENSION Sum up what happens to European e-waste and which consequences this has for people in Africa.

3 CREATIVE TASK Design an online petition to put public pressure on companies to guarantee complete recycling of their electronic products. →△6
Diff (instead of): Diskutieren, wie man zur Lösung des Problems beitragen kann
Geeignete Methode zur Präsentation und Auswertung: Gallery walk

Advanced texts

FACT FILE

Outsourcing is the process of letting another company do one aspect of your business (that you've previously done yourself).

Offshoring means relocating one aspect of your business to another country.

For example, if an American company contracts out customer support to a different company in India, it is both outsourcing and offshoring.

---

⁴ irrigation *Bewässerung*
¹³ to allow for sth to consider sth
¹³ intangible not able to be measured or defined
²⁶ excavator *Bagger*
³⁰ to soar to rise quickly

Avoiding mistakes
Aussprache
¹⁷**doubtless** [ˈdaʊtlɪs]

Reshoring manufacturing: Coming home

In 2005, a start-up company from California called ET Water Systems decided to move its manufacturing operations to China. At the time there was a general exodus to Asia in search of lower costs, recalls Mark Coopersmith, the firm's chief executive. ET Water Systems, which builds sophisticated irrigation devices for businesses, quickly started losing money, not least because it had so much capital 5 tied up in big shipments of goods which took weeks to cross the oceans. Innovation suffered from the distance between manufacturing and design, and quality became a problem too.

When five years later Mr Coopersmith investigated the difference between the total cost of production in China and America, including the cost of shipping, 10 customs duties and other fees, he was amazed to find that California was only about 10% more expensive than China. And that was just on the immediate numbers, without allowing for the intangible benefits of making the devices almost next door. ET Water Systems' new manufacturing partner, General Electronics Assembly, is in San Jose. […] 15

The number of firms known to have "reshored" manufacturing to America is well under 100. Doubtless many more are doing so quietly. Examples range from the tiny, such as ET Water Systems, to the enormous, such as General Electric, which last year moved manufacturing of washing machines, fridges and heaters back from China to a factory in Kentucky which not long ago had been expected to close. […] 20

The reshoring movement has to be kept in proportion. Most of the multinationals involved are bringing back only some of their production destined for the American market. Much of what they had moved over the past few decades remains overseas. And for many of the biggest firms the amount of work that they are still sending abroad outweighs the amount that they are bringing back onshore. 25 Caterpillar, for example, is opening a new factory in Texas to make excavators, but has also just announced that it will expand its research and development activities in China. […]

The crucial change that has taken place over the past decade or so is that wages in low-cost countries have soared. According to the International Labour 30 Organisation, real wages in Asia between 2000 and 2008 rose by 7.1–7.8 % a year. Pay for senior management in several emerging markets, such as China, Turkey and Brazil, now either matches or exceeds pay in America and Europe, according to a recent study by the Hay Group, a consulting firm. Pay in advanced economies, on the other hand, rose by just 0.5% to 0.9% a year between 2000 and 2008, says the 35 McKinsey Global Institute. In manufacturing, the financial crisis actually reduced pay: real wages in American manufacturing have declined by 2.2% since 2005.

The Economist, 2013

4 COMPREHENSION
 a) Define 'reshoring' in your own words.   **Hinweis:** Auch als Hausaufgabe geeignet
 b) Outline the reasons why some American companies are reshoring their operations to the US.

5 VIEWING
 a) Watch the video. Which products are being produced in the UK again?
 b) What additional advantages of reshoring are mentioned in the film?

6 EVALUATION How important is the origin of a product to you? Is it the same for every kind of product? Discuss in small groups.

Global learning

Time zones away from the quads of Cambridge, Mass., and Palo Alto, Calif., there's a curious educational evolution happening.

Though the modern massive open online course movement (MOOCs) originated in North America, two-thirds of their users live abroad – in places like Rwanda, China, and Brazil.

Foreign users are adapting the courses produced at Harvard, MIT, and Stanford to fit their local communities and cultures. And in the process, they're creating an entirely new education model. Instead of toiling at MOOCs alone with the dim light of a laptop, communities around the world are combining screen time with face time. In these small-group, informal, blended-learning environments, students work with the support of peers and mentors and compete online on a level playing field with the new elite of the world. "It gave me a taste of what is first world education," said Alejandra B., a 21-year-old studying business at a Catholic university in La Paz, Bolivia, and a MOOC participant in such a setting, told me. […]

Sixty-eight percent of Coursera's users come from outside the United States, with India, China, Brazil, and Mexico all in the top 10. In these countries, enrollment in tertiary education is growing by leaps and bounds. Public systems aren't equal to the demand, and private for-profit options are seen as offering a subpar product. MOOCs are being welcomed as a free resource and adapted to local contexts, whether for a single course or for entire degree programs, some of which charge tuition. […]

All of this activity aimed at extending access to learning is encouraging, but it's important not to be so carried away by techno-exuberance that we lose sight of some of the potential opportunity costs involved. The danger in overreliance on global MOOCs is that they don't build local capacity for education, research or knowledge creation in the education sector.

For example, Kepler, a U.S.-based endeavor, announced its intention to offer an education superior to any available at a Rwandan university for a lower cost. This may benefit a small group of Rwandans in the short term, but it does not assist President Paul Kagame's struggle to improve education and technology in that country over the long term.

It's easy to imagine a future in which the educational equivalent of reruns of Baywatch – a limited menu of glossy American fare – comes to dominate the cultural landscape in developing countries around the world, making it more difficult for cash-starved universities in those countries to pursue scholarship relevant to local contexts. This potential undermining of local education becomes especially problematic when the U.S. government takes an official role in promoting the use of MOOCs as a form of public diplomacy.

The trick going forward is to figure out how MOOCs can enhance, instead of just compete with, existing national education systems.

Anya Kamenetz, New America Foundation website, 2013

1 **quad** inner court of a university
8 **to toil** to work very hard
15 **Coursera** commercial MOOC platform
17 **tertiary education** university or equivalent education
18 **subpar** (AE) below usual standards
21 **tuition** Studiengebühr
23 **techno-exuberance** enthusiasm for technology
24 **opportunity costs** here: negative Nebeneffekte
27 **endeavour** here: company
33 **Baywatch** American TV series from the 1990s about beach lifeguards, starring David Hasselhoff
33 **fare** here: food

7 COMPREHENSION In your own words define what a MOOC is and describe how learners outside the US have adapted the model.

8 ANALYSIS Examine the positive and negative effects of online courses on developing countries.   **Hinweis:** Auch als Hausaufgabe geeignet

9 SPEAKING With a partner discuss which benefits you could gain from taking part in MOOCs. What do you think about critics fearing a commercialisation of education by the use of MOOCs? → **S23**   →△**7**   **Diff** (instead of): Vor- und Nachteile von MOOC
Geeignete Methode: Speed dating

Zusatzmaterial WB
Task 18: Present tenses

Advanced texts

F The individual in a global world

Over the mountains my true love waits

Tashi, a famous Bhutanese actor, has just returned from Hollywood.

"Tashi!" Karma was grinning. "The world traveler returns to the Hub Bar!" He called to the bartender and ordered two Hit beers. "For the international film star!"

Tashi sighed.

"You must tell me everything." Karma pulled up a stool and sat close by and started to devour Tashi's masala, spooning the oily, spicy peanuts and chopped onions into his mouth in between questions. "Was it like the song?"

"What song?" This launched Karma into a rendition of "Californication" by the Red Hot Chili Peppers, repeating the line *dream of Californication* four painful times. The bartender was smiling. "Well, was it?"

"Yes," said Tashi, taking a long swill of beer.

"Did you meet Beyonce?"

"No."

Karma frowned and peered into his friend's eyes. "What's wrong, Tashi? Didn't they like the movie?"

"They liked the movie. In fact, they will screen it in more cities."

Karma rubbed his hands together, and excitement beamed from his eyes. "Great, Tashi! Great! You will be the first Bhutanese film star known in the world! And Chencho will be the famous director! Maybe as famous as Khyentse Norbu even! This is great for our country!"

Tashi turned up the corners of his mouth for Karma and reflected his smile. "Chencho is very happy. His future in film is certain, now. He won't ever have to work in the import/export shop again, you know, he can really make enough money with his films. And even go abroad, if he keeps playing his cards right. He is very happy about everything."

"But you are not very happy," observed Karma.

"No."

"Did something bad happen?"

Tashi thought over the past two weeks. The long ride from Paro to Bangkok to Seoul to Los Angeles, the delirious mechanical hum. The hotel beside the freeway with its insects and slimy eggs and stale toast; the heat which made him feel dirty, as if his body was absorbing filth with each breath of stagnant air. He had tried to walk outside of the hotel but encountered only cars, and buildings, and people ignoring him or glaring at him; he spent most of the time inside the hotel with the dazzling array of glitzy, stupid television channels. There had been the screening, and the party afterwards, and another party, with a swimming pool, and so many people with their heavy floral smells and strangely altered faces. But there was the ocean, stretching out to infinity, and once he learned the way to the ocean, it had been manageable. Except for that one night, the night he pushed so far towards the edges of his mind, as if in hopes it would fall off and never bother him again. That night was none of Karma's concern. "No, I can't say that anything especially bad happened."

Karma clapped him on the back. "Well, cheer up! It's not so bad, being back in little ancient Bhutan."

Tashi looked up sharply. "Karma, I'm glad to be home." [...]

Tashi sighed and said, "I'm going for a walk." He stood up.

Thimphu river, Bhutan

6 **to devour** to eat very fast
14 **to frown** to make a disapproving face
19 **Chencho** film director in the story
19 **Khyentse Norbu** famous Bhutanese film director

Globalisation

It was still early, and though the sun had dropped behind the mountains, the sky still glowed with soft blue light. Tashi decided to walk along the river. He made his way between the shops and houses, noticing all over again things he never
50 usually noticed, the most ordinary things: strings of dried cheese hanging in the shop windows, deep red chillies drying on the rooftops, hand-lettered names of shops […]. Dogs yapped in the distance. The street sloping down to the river was streaked with paan-spit, and trash clotted the little stream that fed the water, but the Thimphu river itself was clear and cold. He remembered telling Mark, Chencho's
55 contact in Los Angeles, about the Thimphu river, and declaring that he wanted to see the Los Angeles river. Mark had laughed, and then had taken a detour from the restaurant they were heading towards. Tashi had stared in horror at the concrete channel. Power lines parsed out the steel sky overhead. The water was entirely trapped. It could not even be water anymore, Tashi thought, without the ability to
60 flow and carve the earth and make sounds and nurture fish and animals. He had realized at that moment that he wanted nothing to do with Los Angeles.

Shaking his head fervently, Tashi took a deep breath of the chill air, and stepped onto the covered wooden bridge. The bridge's windhorse prayer flags fluttered red, yellow, green, blue, white in the breeze, thousands of them, encasing the walkway
65 in a tapestry of sacred color. He listened to the hollow sounds of his footsteps on the worn boards. A raven came to sit on the railing, watching him with silent black eyes. […]

Tashi climbed the opposite bank, striding through the weeds and grasses to stand upon a ridge where he could overlook the city. White tattered prayer flags
70 hung serenely on wooden poles, protecting the world below. The national stadium lay on the opposite bank, and it was silent this evening, but Tashi knew exactly how it looked when it was full of citizens in their ghos and kiras, gathered for an archery or football match, a warm mass of colourful dots melting together. He looked up, to the chortens and the houses; white shapes with twinkling lights, places of home
75 … stately crumpling buildings with dragons and tigers painted on the walls, or the new green roofed government buildings positioned as mandated by the Thimphu structural Plan, buildings where bureaucrats devoted to the Principals of Intelligent Urbanism lived and worked. Yet the twinkling buildings did not reach very high up upon the mountains. He was surrounded by the black shapes of trees, solemn in
80 the distance, stretching to the peaks in every direction. Thimphu was a little world contained in a little valley. Tashi had left the city and the country before, of course – left to film in Arunachal Pradesh, left for the arduous inconvenient journey to Delhi to get his US visa – but leaving to cross the ocean was different, it left him different, he had left and now he was left somewhere else. He did not feel entirely
85 returned; he did not feel like he was wholly inside this little valley anymore.

From: Holly Jean Buck, "Over the mountains my true love waits", 2012

52 **to yap** to bark in high, quick sounds
53 **paan-spit** the remains spat out after chewing paan (Hindi for 'betel'), a stimulating leaf
58 **to parse out** *here:* to separate into different parts
60 **to nurture** to feed
63 **windhorse** figure symbolising the human soul in Asian tradition
72 **gho** traditional dress for men in Bhutan
72 **kira** traditional dress for women in Bhutan
74 **chorten** cultic building of Tibetan Buddhism
82 **Arunachal Pradesh** state in Northeast India

Los Angeles river, Los Angeles

1 COMPREHENSION
a) *Summarise what Tashi and Karma are talking about.*
b) *Describe Tashi's feelings after he has returned.*

2 ANALYSIS
a) *Characterise Tashi.* → **S7** **Hinweis:** Auch als Hausaufgabe geeignet
b) *Examine the descriptions of Los Angeles and Thimphu. How do these descriptions contribute to the atmosphere of the text?*
Geeignete Methode zur weiteren Analyse: Hot seat

3 EVALUATION
"He did not feel like he was wholly inside this little valley anymore" (l. 85). *Discuss whether experiencing different cultures and lifestyles in a globalised world enriches one's life or inevitably leads to a loss of identity.* → ▲8
Diff (after): Präsentation über die Einführung des „Bruttonationalglücks"
Geeignete Methode: Mobile debate

TIP

Direct characterisation means explicitly describing a person's character.

Methods of **indirect characterisation:**
- telling the reader about the character's actions and feelings
- using a certain language
- describing the character's surroundings

Spot on language

> **Hinweis**
> Selbstevaluation für Schüler über Green Line-Code

Improving texts

1 *Read the statements about globalisation and make them more dynamic by filling in the appropriate words from the list below.*

---
steady • worrying • immediately • fierce • more and more • appropriately • increasing • dramatically • exciting • ongoing • completely • than ever

- Globalisation provides **1** opportunities for young people as the world is getting smaller.
- New means of communication and transport connect people faster **2** .
- The worldwide flow of capital results in **3** economic growth.
- The developing nations profit from **4** technological advancement.
- Changes in one country affect other ones **5** and force them to react **6** .
- The gap between rich and poor is widening **7** .
- **8** competition for cheap labour leads to poor working conditions.
- The **9** process of outsourcing results in job losses in countries of the developed world.
- Another **10** development is that large corporations are gaining **11** power.
- Native cultures are in danger of losing their cultural identity **12** .

Using rhetorical devices effectively

2 a) *You can use rhetorical devices to make your texts more effective and convincing. Give a short definition for each of the following devices.* → **S10.2**

---
1. direct address
2. anaphora
3. enumeration
4. parallelism
5. metaphor
6. contrast
7. repetition
8. hyperbole
9. rhetorical questions
---

b) *Focus on either the chances or the challenges of globalisation. Then choose five rhetorical devices and write example sentences using these devices.*

Using connectives

3 a) *Decide which connective fits best to link the following sentences or sentence parts.*

---
1. Large international companies earn huge profits. **(Similarly/Moreover/Since)**, they endanger the sovereignty of elected parliaments.
2. Fair trade ensures fair prices. **(In particular/Finally/Unless)** it helps small farmers to earn a living.
3. Local farmers should cooperate **(even if/as well as/instead of)** competing with each other.
4. This deal grants corporations even more power. **(Yet/Therefore/Above all)** every citizen should oppose it.
5. The CEO said that revenues had fallen drastically. **(Also/Equally/Then)** he announced a new corporate policy to stimulate growth.
---

b) *What is the function of the correct connectives in the sentences in a)? Use the descriptions given below.*

---
showing a sequence • adding information • showing cause and effect • contrasting • emphasising
---

c) *For each function, add 3–5 more connectives you can think of.*

4 *What is your attitude towards globalisation? Write a short statement using the connectives from Task 3 to make your text coherent and logical.*

Mediation

5 During your internship at an international news agency you have to write an article about the speech President Gauck delivered to the winners of the 'Global economy prize 2012'. Focus on his views on the interdependence of globalisation, freedom and responsibility. Write about 200 words.

Globalisierung am Scheideweg

Und wie hat sich diese Welt nun verändert in den letzten 20 Jahren! In vielen Ländern haben Menschen politische und wirtschaftliche Freiheiten errungen. In anderen sind sie dabei. Wir haben in den letzten Monaten voller Spannung in den Mittelmeerraum geschaut und voller Sorge schauen wir nach Syrien. Die Menschen dort haben Bevormundung und Einschüchterung zum Teil abgeschüttelt, zum Teil wollen sie sie abschütteln. Sie haben Grenzen geöffnet. Und im Osten Europas, wo das früher geschehen ist, konnten erstmals viele an Freiheit und Wohlstand teilhaben und am Fortschritt mitwirken. Kräfte wurden freigesetzt. Fleiß und Ideen konnten sich neu entfalten.

In vielen anderen Ländern ringen aber die Menschen noch um mehr politische und wirtschaftliche Freiheiten. Und das betrifft auch eine wirtschaftliche Ordnung, von der wir erwarten, dass sie Millionen Menschen weltweit nicht niedergeschlagen macht, sondern ihnen einen eigenständigen Weg aus Armut eröffnet, sie zu aktiven Menschen macht, mit Mut und aufrechtem Gang.

Für viele ist, was sie erhoffen, also Wirklichkeit geworden, frei denken, frei leben zu können und materiell für sich und andere zu sorgen. Aber eben nicht für alle. Und „alle" in den Wohlstand mitnehmen zu können, das war das Versprechen der sozialen Marktwirtschaft, das noch heute Hoffnung macht. Bei dieser Gelegenheit lassen Sie mich sagen, dass der schlichte Gebrauch des Wortes Kapitalismus für so unterschiedliche Formen von Wirtschaft, wie wir sie in Europa und weltweit erleben, einfach leichtfertig ist. Also: Alle diese Chancen, die wir hier in Deutschland, die wir auch in Skandinavien gesehen haben, die müssen wir nun mit dem Stichwort Globalisierung verbinden.

Wenn wir das Gefühl haben, dass die Grundrichtung unserer Zeit dort stimmt, wo wir die Zunahme von Freiheit und Verantwortung erleben – dann wissen wir doch auch, dass es kluge Leute gibt, die sagen: Diese Globalisierung von Freiheit und Verantwortung steht in unseren Jahren am Scheideweg.

Mancher Mut – das haben wir erlebt – sinkt. Wirtschaftliche Probleme führen zu Rückzugstendenzen – auch in Ländern, die sie sich gerade erst ihre Freiheit erkämpft haben.

Und es gibt Menschen, die laut „Aber!" rufen.

Weltweit wächst der Wohlstand – aber eben nicht für alle. Die Armut nimmt ab, aber die Unterschiede zwischen Armen und Reichen werden größer und gefährden mancherorts den sozialen Frieden. Noch nie gab es einen so blühenden und ausgedehnten Welthandel. Aber Ökonomen weisen auf Schieflagen hin. Unternehmer nutzen Chancen – aber nicht alle haben verstanden, dass ein dauerhafter Erfolg nicht allein auf Niedriglöhnen und laxen Vorschriften für Arbeits- und Umweltschutz gründet. Arbeitnehmer stellen sich einem erhöhten Wettbewerbs- und Leistungsdruck. Aber oft genug erleben sie, dass Tätigkeiten in andere Länder verlagert werden – zu schlechteren Arbeits- und Umweltbedingungen.

Wir alle sind für den Schutz unserer Lebenswelt verantwortlich. Aber nach wie vor sind die Warnungen berechtigt, dass die Folge unseres Lebensstils das Klima verwandelt, dass lebensnotwendige Wälder abgeholzt werden und Landmassen erodieren.

Gerade auch junge Menschen auf dieser Welt empfinden diese Spannungen verstärkt. Sie sagen: „Globalisierung gefällt mir, aber da ist noch etwas, was mir wichtig ist!"

Und wenn ich, der Nichtökonom, dann die Ökonomen frage, was sie dazu beitragen können, dass wir optimistisch auf die Globalisierung und ihre Chancen sehen, dann höre ich oft: Nicht die Offenheit der Märkte sei das Problem, sondern ihre oft noch unzureichende Ordnung! Nicht der Markt sei schlecht, sondern ein ungeordneter Markt sei schlecht.

Wenn die Globalisierung heute am Scheideweg steht, dann deshalb, weil wir eine weltweit überzeugende Ordnung der Freiheit und des Friedens erst noch erringen müssen.

Joachim Gauck, 2012

Spot on vocabulary

Finding core vocabulary

1 *Create a mind map to collect the most important vocabulary for the different aspects of globalisation. Use the mind map below as a starting point.*

2 a) *Complex nouns often seem to be difficult since they are made up of additional parts at the beginning (prefix) and the end (suffix). These words become a lot easier when reduced to the main root. Make complex nouns by adding the necessary prefixes and/or suffixes to the root words in the box below.*

b) *Pick five root words and note as many new words (not just nouns) you can make from them as possible.*

prefix	root word	suffix
dis- • un- • mis- • under- • inter- • non- • in- • trans-	possess • aware • manage • product • prosper • develop • depend • govern • agree • equal • employ • sustain • nationalis(e)	-ion • -ness • -ment • -ivity • -ity • -ence • -ability • -ation

Talking about globalisation

3 *Prepositions give phrasal verbs a new meaning (e.g. to come across = to find). Complete the following sentences, then explain the meaning of the phrasal verbs in your own words.*

> for • about • out • for • down • to

1. It is the internet and other technologies that bring ▢ change.
2. Experts attributed their problems ▢ cultural misunderstandings.
3. The new movement pushes ▢ equal rights.
4. The journalist and international observers had to pull ▢ when the conflict escalated.
5. The Prime Minister called ▢ stricter legislation.
6. The company had to shut ▢ several unprofitable factories.

4 *Complete these collocations with the correct preposition. Use them to write five sentences about global civil society action.*
Zusatzmaterial KV 4: Brain28/Touch-Turn-Talk

1. to be appealing ▢ younger/older people
2. to ask ▢ better living/working conditions
3. to take responsibility ▢ sth
4. to focus ▢ a topic
5. to be optimistic ▢ the future
6. to be ▢ the rise
7. to pose a risk ▢ sb/sth
8. to strive ▢ freedom/equal opportunities

TIP

⊙ First work on the vocab sheets; then test yourself here!

Topic task

Globalisation 9

Code
7wi6zu

Creating a special issue of the school newspaper

It's time to prepare your annual special issue of the school newspaper, which is created together with your partner school in the UK or the US and written entirely in English. For this year's issue you decided on the topic of globalisation.
To prepare your part of the newspaper, which will be titled "A German take on globalisation", follow the online code. There you will find texts reflecting German views on different aspects of globalisation. You may also do your own research to find alternative texts.

STEP 1 — Forming groups and assigning roles

In groups of three or four, decide who will work on which topic.
There will be one newspaper page for each of the following topics:
- public opinion on globalisation in Germany
- culture and lifestyle
- ecology
- politics
- economy, technology and communication

Then distribute the following special roles:
- chief editor (coordinates the work)
- designer (responsible for the layout)
- two students who write an editorial introduction explaining how globalisation affects your personal, everyday lives → **S17**

STEP 2 — Writing your contributions

🌐 Follow the online code and read the texts which are relevant for your topic. Mediate the text(s) in a short, informative article, keeping in mind the following points:
- Which aspects are the most important ones for your readers (= pupils, parents and teachers at your partner school)?
- Are there any German terms or concepts that need explanation?
- Use your own words, but do not include your own views.

If you need further tips, consult the Core skill workshop section or the skills section.
→ **S26.1**

TIP

Dealing with critical comments

If there are any critical or offensive comments (e.g. on the role of the US), either leave them out (if they are not really important) or make it clear that they do not reflect your own view.

STEP 3 — Creating your newspaper pages

Determine the final layout of your part of the newspaper:
- Add photos or graphs if appropriate.
- Decide on an eye-catching cover.
- Use a (standard) word processing programme to neatly arrange your texts and pictures.

Proofread each other's texts and correct any mistakes. → **S20**

STEP 4 — Presenting the newspaper

Present your newspaper pages in class and discuss them. Then decide which pages should be included in the final version of the special issue.

10 India
Introduction

Code
bq83i8

The Gateway of India in Mumbai harbour was built between 1911 and 1924. It was the ceremonial entrance to India for British colonial governors until Indian independence in 1947.

5000 "dabbawallas" carry an estimated 200,000 home-cooked lunches to offices in Mumbai each day. It is claimed that only one in 6 million deliveries goes wrong.

India's IT services industry has grown massively since the 1990s and is still seen as a major factor in the nation's further economic development. Bangalore and Chennai are its most important centres.

1 BRAINSTORMING What do you already know about India? Make a list of keywords and places.

2 SPEAKING Examine the photos and texts on this page and then compare them with your results from the first task. Which aspects would you add to the page and where on the map would you place them?

Holi, the Hindu festival of colours, marks the beginning of spring. It is celebrated all over India and in recent years has gained global popularity.

The Indian railway network is one of the largest in the world, providing long-distance travel as well as suburban trains connecting the vast cities with the surrounding areas. There are more than seven billion passengers each year.

The majority of Indians still live in rural, predominantly agricultural regions, where tradition and caste are still very strong. Many try to escape rural poverty by moving to the large cities to find work.

With around 22 million inhabitants Delhi is the largest city in India, closely followed by Mumbai and Kolkata. The metropolitan area of Delhi also contains New Delhi, the seat of government.

3 RESEARCH *Find pictures for three of the additional aspects of India that you've found. Then write a short descriptive text for each of them.*
Geeignete Methode zur Präsentation und Auswertung: Gallery walk
4 SPEAKING *In class discuss what themes particularly interest you and explain why.*

Spot on facts

India – an overview

Colonisation and Independence

In 1858 India became a colony of the British Empire and in 1876 Queen Victoria took on the title of Empress of India. India remained a colony for almost a century until 1947. Before 1858 India had
5 been colonised and ruled by the Portuguese, the French and the British East India Company, a trading company with its own private armies. Rebellion against European colonisation occurred again and again throughout India's colonial history. Many
10 Indians had hoped that their loyalty to Britain in World War I in 1914 would be rewarded with Indian self-rule, but they were disappointed. Inspired by the leadership of Gandhi, the Indian National Congress continued Indian resistance to British rule in the interwar years. On 18th July 1947 King George VI signed the India Independence Act in London and the partition of the Indian subcontinent was sealed. It was divided up into two states with a Hindu and a Muslim majority: India and Pakistan, comprising East and West Pakistan. East Pakistan later separated
20 in 1972 to become Bangladesh with West Pakistan becoming today's Pakistan. The border between India and Pakistan is still disputed and the 'Kashmir problem' (i.e. whether Kashmir belongs to India, to Pakistan or should become an independent state) is
25 still unresolved.

1 RESEARCH In a group of four choose one of these topics: The British East India Company – Gandhi – Partition – the 'Kashmir problem' and find out more about it. Then write a short report of about 150 words on your topic. → **S32**   **Geeignete Methode:** Group puzzle
Zusatzmaterial KV 1: Hilfestellung für die Erstellung und Durchführung eines Kurzreferats (Short talk)

A sense of place

Geography: With an area of 3.3 million km² (over nine times the size of Germany) India is the
5 7th largest country in the world. The mountainous Himalayan region and the Ganges Plain are in the north whereas most of the southern and central
10 parts of the country belong to the Deccan plateau region. India also has three major river systems: the Indus, the Ganges and the Brahmaputra rivers. India is separated from the rest of Asia by mountains and the sea, which make the country a distinct
15 geographical entity.

The **climate** is also varied but is tropical in the south and mainly temperate in the north. The southwest or summer monsoon from June to September accounts for 70 % of India's rainfall.

20 **Politics:** The Republic of India is the world's largest democracy with New Delhi as its capital. Based on the British system, the parliamentary form of government has a lower (Lok Sabha) and an upper house (Rajya Sabha). The head of government is the
25 Prime Minister, usually the leader of the majority party in the lower house.

The Indian flag

Economy

Economy	Share of total employment, 2012	Share of GDP*, 2012	Share of GDP*, 1990
Agriculture	53 %	29 %	18 %

Traditional small village farming is still what the vast majority of Indians do for a living, but its importance in the country's economy is shrinking. More modern large-scale agriculture is needed if Indian farmers are to become more productive to feed a growing population and compete in export markets.

| Services | 21 % | 44 % | 56 % |

As a symbol of India's economic progress, the technology sector with its call centres employs less than half the number of people employed by Indian Railways, the country's largest employer.

| Industry | 19 % | 26 % | 27 % |

The manufacturing industry (e.g. textiles, food processing, petroleum, chemicals, cement, steel, mining and computer software) has the potential to create great wealth and new jobs, but it hasn't yet realised its full potential.

*GDP (Gross Domestic Product) *Bruttoinlandsprodukt*

Based on figures from the International Monetary Fund, *World Economic Outlook Database*, 2012

Population

Figures at a glance (based on census of India 2011)

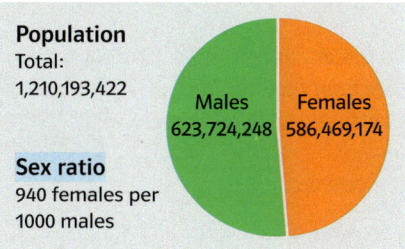

Population
Total: 1,210,193,422
Males 623,724,248
Females 586,469,174

Sex ratio
940 females per 1000 males

Population aged 0–6
Persons: 158,789,287
in % of total population: 13 %

Density of population
382 per km²

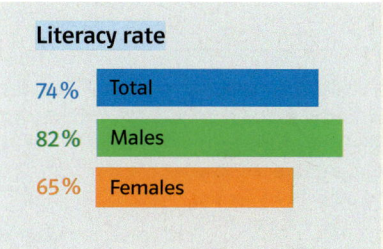

Literacy rate
74 % Total
82 % Males
65 % Females

2 SPEAKING Use the map at the beginning of the topic and the information here to give a talk summing up the most important information on India in two minutes. Use your own words and speak without looking at your notes. → S22

3 ANALYSIS The last Indian census was held in 2011. What questions or comments have you got concerning the census figures?

Hinduism: The main religion in India

India's people are about 80 % Hindu, 14 % Muslim, 2.5 % Christian, 2 % Sikh, <1 % Buddhist and <1 % Jain. Tensions between different religious groups are not uncommon, particularly between Hindus and
5 Muslims. Hinduism is the oldest living religion, with more than 900 million believers worldwide. A central concept is reincarnation (samsara) which is governed by one's actions and their effects (karma). Hinduism is not based on a single founder or scripture. It has a complex and diverse notion of God that involves many different aspects and incarnations of a supreme being. The three most important of these are Brahma, Shiva and Vishnu.

The Hindu triumvirate

Shiva – the destroyer
Shiva's role is destruction. He destroys the universe in order to recreate it and make it better for humankind. Shiva is therefore seen as a source of both good and evil.

Brahma – the creator
Brahma is the first god in the Hindu triumvirate or trimurti. His job was the creation of the world and all creatures.

Vishnu – the preserver
Vishnu's function is preservation. He returns to the earth in troubled times and restores the balance of good and evil. So far he has been incarnated nine times, but will be reincarnated one more time.

4 ANALYSIS Point out the main differences between Hinduism and what you know of the other major religions worldwide. **Hinweis:** Auch als Hausaufgabe geeignet

Core skill workshop

Analysing an extract from a novel

Part A Characters, setting and plot

When reading a fictional text, the reader is like a literary detective looking for text evidence to find information about different aspects of the story:
- Where and when do these things occur? (the **setting** – time and place)
- What happens? (the action/events and the development of the **plot**)
- Who is involved? (the **characters** and their relationships)

Characterisation can be explicit/**direct** when the reader is told what a character is like by the narrator, another character or by the character himself/herself. The information can also be implicit/**indirect**. Here, the reader must ' infer what characters are like from what they do (behaviour), say (dialogue) or think. What people wear – their physical appearance, the faces they pull or the gestures they make and also their surroundings can convey information about a character.

TIP

What makes the reader interested in a story? In some texts narrative passages create tension/suspense with an exciting plot, or there is a surprise. In others there are slower, more descriptive passages giving details or, perhaps, creating a particular atmosphere.

1 **COMPREHENSION** *Record text evidence from Extract A below about the Who?, What?, Where? and When? of the story. Compare your results with a partner and speculate about the plot.* → S5

2 **COMPREHENSION** *Now record text evidence from either Extract B or C from The Hungry Tide. Your partner must work with the other extract.*

3 **ANALYSIS** *The two extracts describe the scene on the platform from different angles. Characterise Kanai and Piya and speculate about how their relationship might develop.* → S7

Extract A (from Vikas Swarup, *The Accidental Apprentice*, 2013)
In life you never get what you deserve: you get what you negotiate. That was the first lesson he taught me.
   For the last three days, I have been putting that guidance into practice, negotiating frantically with my prosecutors and persecutors in a desperate bid to stave off the death penalty, which they all believe I deserve.   5

Extract B (from Amitav Ghosh, *The Hungry Tide*, 2005)
Kanai spotted her the moment he stepped onto the platform: he was not deceived, neither by her close-cropped black hair, nor by her clothes, which were those of a teenage boy – loose cotton pants and an   10
oversized white shirt. Winding unerringly through the snack vendors and tea-sellers who were hawking their wares on the station's platform, his eyes settled on her slim, shapely figure.   15

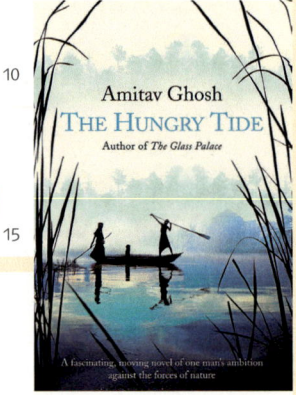

Extract C (from Amitav Ghosh, *The Hungry Tide*, 2005)
'Oh, I'm so sorry!' Piya was mortified: of everyone in the compartment, this was the last person she would have chosen to scald with her tea. She had noticed him while waiting on the platform in Kolkata and she had been struck by the self-   20
satisfied tilt of his head and the unabashed way in which he stared at everyone around him, taking them in, sizing them up, sorting them all into their places.

---

² **to negotiate** to try to reach an agreement
⁵ **frantically** quickly, in a disorganised way
⁵ **prosecutor** person who charges sb with a crime
⁵ **persecutor** person who treats sb in a cruel and unfair way
⁶ **to stave sth off** to delay sth
⁹ **to deceive** to make sb believe sth that is not true
⁹ **close-cropped** cut very short
¹² **unerringly** *here*: zielsicher
¹³ **vendor** sb who sells things
¹³ **to hawk sth** *here*: to sell
¹⁷ **mortified** extrem peinlich berührt
¹⁹ **to scald** [skɔːld] verbrühen
²¹ **unabashed** not embarrassed

160

4 BRAINSTORMING *Would you rather carry on reading* The Accidental Apprentice *or* The Hungry Tide*? Give your reasons and exchange ideas with others in your group.* **Geeignete Methode:** Think – Pair – Share

Part B Narrative perspective

When authors write a fictional text they have to choose someone to tell the story. It can be done through the eyes of a character or characters in the story or from the perspective of an observer. That's the **narrator**. **Narrative prose** can have an **unlimited** or a **limited narrative perspective**:
- A **first-person narrator** is **limited**. The narrator tells the story from his or her perspective, either as the protagonist or simply as a witness, an observer.
- A **third-person narrator** can be **limited**. He/She may know everything about one character or is just an observer. Third-person narrators can be **subjective** or, if they don't report on a character's thoughts or feelings, **objective**, also called **impersonal**. In a novel, but not in a short story, the author may choose to move the narrator from one character to another. This is called a **shifting point of view**.
- A **third-person narrator** can also be **unlimited**. This is an **omniscient** or 'all-knowing' narrator who may know everything about several characters' thoughts and feelings and may even comment on a character's behaviour.

5 ANALYSIS Look at extracts A, B and C again and ask yourself these questions to determine the type of narrator:
– Is the story told in the first or the third person?
– Is the narrator a character in the story?
– Is the narrator an observer of the events?
– Does the narrator know what the characters are thinking?

6 ANALYSIS *Examine how the different narrative points of view influence the way the reader experiences the story in these extracts and then swap ideas with another member of your course.* → S8

7 CREATIVE TASK Choose one of the extracts and rewrite it from another narrative perspective. **Hinweis:** Auch als Hausaufgabe geeignet

Part C Writing your analysis

> **Extract from *The Accidental Apprentice***
> It is Friday, 10 December, and traffic on Baba Kharak Singh Marg is the usual chaotic snarl of heat and noise. The road is jammed with lumbering buses, honking cars, whining scooters and spluttering auto-rickshaws. The sky is
> 5 cloudless but the sun is invisible behind that toxic cocktail of smog that smothers the city every winter.
>   I am wearing a grey cardigan over a demure, sky-blue salvar kameez, having prudently changed from my work uniform. It is a routine I follow every Friday, slipping out of the showroom during the lunch hour to make the short walk
> 10 across the marketplace to the ancient temple dedicated to the monkey god, Hanuman.
>   Most people go to temples to pray; I go to expiate. I have still not forgiven myself for Alka's death. Part of me will always think what happened to her

TIP
The author writes, the narrator speaks and a character takes part in the story.

USEFUL PHRASES

Narrative point of view
to see sth. through the eyes of sb
to identify with a character
to experience how sb feels about sth/sb's emotional involvement
to know what sb thinks about sth
to have limited/unlimited knowledge
to be a neutral/impartial observer
to be subjective/objective
to be reliable/unreliable

² **Baba Kharak Singh Marg**
  a street in central Delhi
³ **snarl** the angry noise a dog makes
⁷ **demure** modest
⁷ **salvar kameez** loose trousers and a long shirt
⁸ **prudent** sensible and careful
¹² **to expiate** ['ekspɪeɪt] büßen

Core skill workshop

14 mandir Hindu temple	
15 perpetually constantly	
16 to hedge one's bets auf der sicheren Seite sein	
20 Goddess Durga wife of Lord Shiva	
21 to redeem to make better	
21 distress great worry, unhappiness	
25 scrum Gedränge	
30 darshan blessing from the deity	
32 to accost sb to speak to sb in a rude and threatening way	
34 street loafer sb who wastes their time hanging around on the streets	
35 kurta pyjama loose shirt and trousers	
38 vermilion bright red colour	
38 tika/bindi forehead mark	
42 clipped here: clear and fast	

was my fault. Since that horrific tragedy, God is my only refuge. And I have a Hanuman Mandir.

Lauren Lockwood, my American friend, is perpetually fascinated by the fact that we have 330 million gods. 'Jeez, you Hindus sure like to hedge your bets,' she says. That's probably an exaggeration, but every temple worth its salt does have shrines to at least half a dozen deities.

Each of these deities has some special powers. Goddess Durga is the Invincible One who can redeem situations of utmost distress. After Alka's death, when my life was a dark tunnel of sorrow, pain and regret, She gave me strength. She is always with me whenever I need her.

The temple is unusually crowded for a Friday afternoon and I am caught up in the ceaseless scrum of devotees jostling to get to the sanctum sanctorum. The marble floor feels cool under my bare feet and the air is heavy with the intoxicating blend of sweat, sandalwood, flowers and incense.

I get into the ladies' queue, which is considerably shorter and manage to make my communion with Durga Ma in less than ten minutes.

Having finished my *darshan*, I am about to go down the stairs when a hand drops on my shoulder. I whirl around and discover a man gazing at me intently.

When an unknown adult male accosts a young woman in Delhi, the instinctive thing to do is to reach for that bottle of pepper spray one always keeps handy. But the stranger looking at me is no street loafer. He is an elderly man, dressed in an off-white silk kurta pyjama, with a white pashmina shawl draped casually across his shoulders. Fair and tall, he has an aquiline nose, a hard, resolute mouth and a head crowned by a shock of backswept, snowy-white hair. A vermilion tika adorns his forehead. His fingers are loaded with rings glinting with diamonds and emeralds. But it is his penetrating brown eyes that unsettle me. They seem to catch me with a directness I find slightly intimidating. This is a man who likes to be in control.

'Could I have a word with you?' he asks in a clipped tone.

From: Vikas Swarup, *The Accidental Apprentice*, 2013

Zusatzmaterial WB
Tasks 10–15: Reading and writing

8 COMPREHENSION Give a brief summary of the main events.
Zusatzmaterial KV 2: Feedback sheet für Kurzreferate

9 ANALYSIS
   a) Characterise the narrator, taking into account direct and indirect characterisation.
   b) Analyse the point of view and the narrator's role in the story.

10 ANALYSIS Examine how the author uses details to present a typically Indian setting. **Hinweis:** Auch als Hausaufgabe geeignet

11 ANALYSIS Examine how suspense is created here. Would you like to continue reading the story? Explain why. → S9

12 CREATIVE TASK
   a) With a partner decide on what you think the man wants to discuss with the narrator.
   b) Write the dialogue that follows from this scene. Try to make both voices sound authentic and 'in character'.

A A nation of entrepreneurs

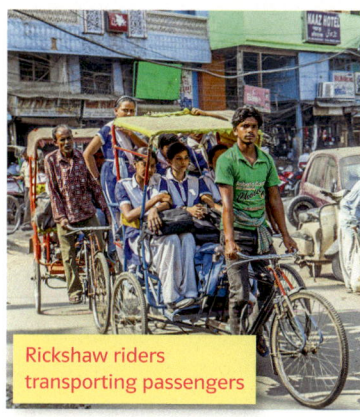
Rickshaw riders transporting passengers

Street market in India

Indian train vendor

Street-smart

Indians have had little option but to be street-smart about making money. Indeed, the street is the biggest employer in the country. India has a veritable army of 'footpath businessmen': small shopkeepers, tea stall owners, dhabawallahs, artisans, kabadiwallahs and rickshaw pullers. It is estimated that ten million men and women
5 work as street hawkers and vendors, and more than sixty million people are directly dependent on this trade. The organized sector of the economy – private, public and corporate – employs only 3 per cent of the workforce. The overwhelming majority – almost nine out of ten people – are self-employed, squeezing out an income in conditions of work that can hardly be imagined by a businessman in the developed
10 world. In Europe, 90 per cent of the working population work in the formal sector; they are productive and controlled and predictable environments where the safety net is visible. By contrast, the 'footpath businessmen' of India work on a razor's edge; every day is a new challenge, and almost no coordinate can be taken for granted. In spite of this, almost 60 per cent of India's gross savings comes from the unorganized sector.
15 Business is, indeed, the livelihood of a great many of the poor.

Pavan K. Varma, *Being Indian*, 2005

² **veritable** *here:* real
³ **dhabawallah/ dabbawalla** person delivering lunch boxes (tiffins) in Mumbai
³ **artisan** *Kunsthandwerker*
⁴ **kabadiwallah** junk or scrap dealer
⁵ **street hawkers and vendors** people who sell their wares on the street
¹² **razor** *Rasierklinge*

1 COMPREHENSION *Choose another title for the text and make a list of the most important points.* **Hinweis:** Auch als Hausaufgabe geeignet

2 VISUALS *Use vocabulary from the text to describe one of the street scenes shown in the photo in a diary entry you make on a trip to India.* → **S28.1**
Zusatzmaterial WB Task 1: Talking about footpath businessmen

3 VIEWING
   a) *Watch the film about the tiffin box delivery system and make notes of what you learn about the dabbawallas.*
   b) *Analyse how the film makers try to convey an authentic image of Mumbai.*
      → **S29**   → △**1**   **Diff** (help with): Vorgabe von Leitfragen

4 EVALUATION *Assess the chances of a similar home-cooked food delivery system in a large German city.*

Texts

A competitive edge

Globally, India is now sometimes portrayed as having a competitive edge over more sluggish developed countries that have abandoned thrift, given up on saving and refuse to postpone gratification. Values that are embedded in an Indian way of life appear to have unexpected relevance. A friend, Niranjan, forwarded me an email. It caught the idea that people like himself had a distinctive way of operating, and their lateral approach presented them with a new advantage. Like other Indians, Niranjan was taking pleasure in the possibility that citizens of his country were highly motivated, and no longer perceived only as victims of famine or superstition.

"An Indian man walks into a bank in New York City and asks for the loan officer. He tells the loan officer that he is going to India on business for two weeks and needs to borrow $5,000. The bank officer tells him that the bank will need some form of security for the loan, so the Indian man hands over the keys of a new Ferrari parked on the street in front of the bank. He produces the title and everything checks out. The loan officer agrees to accept the car as collateral for the loan.

The bank's president and its officers all enjoy a good laugh at the Indian for using a $250,000 Ferrari as collateral against a $5,000 loan. An employee of the bank then drives the Ferrari into the bank's underground garage and parks it there. Two weeks later, the Indian returns, repays the $5,000 and the interest, which comes to $15.41.

The loan officer says, 'Sir, we are very happy to have had your business, and this transaction has worked out very nicely, but we are a little puzzled. While you were away, we checked out and found that you are a multi-millionaire. What puzzles us is, why would you bother to borrow $5,000?

The Indian replies: 'Where else in New York can I park my car for two weeks for only $15.41 and expect it to be there when I return?'
Ah, the mind of the Indian!"

With its overlap of extreme wealth and lavish poverty, its mix of the educated and the ignorant, its competing ideologies, its lack of uniformity, its kindness and profound cruelty, its complex relationships with religion, its parallel realities and the rapid speed of social change – India is a macrocosm, and may be the world's default setting for the future.

Patrick French, *India – A Portrait*, 2011

2 **sluggish** very slow
2 **thrift** being careful with money
3 **gratification** Belohnung, Erfüllung
5 **distinctive** easy to see/recognise
6 **lateral approach** using your imagination to see a problem in a new way and then to solve it
9 **loan officer** (AE) person responsible for lending a sum of money (a loan)
12 **security** here: valuable item given to the bank as a guarantee
13 **title** (AE) here: registration document (for a car)
14 **collateral** sth valuable given as security for a loan
18 **interest** here: Zins
26 **lavish** abundant

Avoiding mistakes
Wortschatz
¹⁶**employee** so who is paid to work for a person or company
employer person or company that pays people to work for them

5 COMPREHENSION Outline the author's view of the contemporary Indian economy and its relevance for the world's economy. **Zusatzmaterial WB** Task 2: Writing
Geeignete Methode zur weiteren Analyse: Hot seat

6 ANALYSIS Explain the function of the joke forwarded by the author's Indian friend. Do you think it is effective and appropriate in this context?
Hinweis: Zur weiteren Analyse können die Schüler einen Sprechblasentext zum Bild verfassen

7 LISTENING Listen to the beginning of the novel *The White Tiger* by Aravind Adiga. Take notes on the following questions: → **S21** → △2
Diff (help with): Geschlossene Aufgaben zu Hörtext (True/False)
1. Who is the narrator and why is he telling the story?
2. What is so special about entrepreneurship in India?
3. How does he see India's role in the world compared to developed Western countries and to China?

8 RESEARCH Find information about a successful Indian businessperson and present him/her in a short talk. Then compare your results with the humorous example in the text and the businessman portrayed in the audioclip. → **S32**

B The rich-poor divide

Slums in Vakola

Bumping into people, she ran. Pushing cycles and carts, she ran.
Past Vishram Society, past the Tamil temple, past the construction site where the two towers were coming up, and into the slums; passing narrow lane after narrow lane, dodging stray dogs and roosters to run into the open wasteland beyond. A
5 plane soared above her. Finally she reached the *nullah*, a long canal of black water, on whose banks a row of blue tarpaulin tents had risen.
  Her neighbours were chopping wood; a rooster strutted round the huts; children played on rubber tyres tied to the trees.
  'No one is coming here, Mary,' her neighbour told her in Tamil. 'It was a false
10 alarm.'
  Slowing down, breathing deeply, Mary came to her tent, and looked inside its blue tarpaulin cover, held aloft by a wooden pole. Everything intact: cooking oil, cooking vessels, her son's school books, photo albums.
  'They won't come till after the monsoons,' her neighbour shouted. 'We're safe till
15 then.'
  Mary sat down and wiped her face.
Among the patchwork of fully legal slums, semi-legal slums and pockets of huts in Vakola, this row of tents next to a polluted canal, the *nullah* that cut through the suburb, led the most precarious existence. Because they had come here after
20 the last government amnesty for illegal slums, and because the canal could flood during a heavy monsoon, the squatters had not been granted the identification cards which 'regularized' a slum-dweller's existence and gave him the right to be relocated to a *pucca* building if the government bulldozed his hut. Municipal officials had repeatedly threatened the dwellers by the *nullah* with eviction, yet
25 someone had always intervened to save them, usually a politician who needed their votes at the next municipal election. Mrs Rego had come down to explain to them that things had changed. It was now a season of willpower in Bombay: the coalition of corruption, philanthropy, and inertia that had protected them for so long was disintegrating. A new official had been put in charge of clearing the city's
30 illegal slums. He has smashed miles of huts in Thane and promised to do the same in Mumbai. Every day their slum survived should be considered a miracle.

From: Aravind Adiga, *Last Man In Tower*, 2012

FACT FILE

Bombay was renamed **Mumbai** in 1996. With more than 18 million inhabitants it is the most populous city in India.

Vakola is a suburb in the north of Mumbai where new high rise blocks are being built as land for building in the centre becomes scarce.

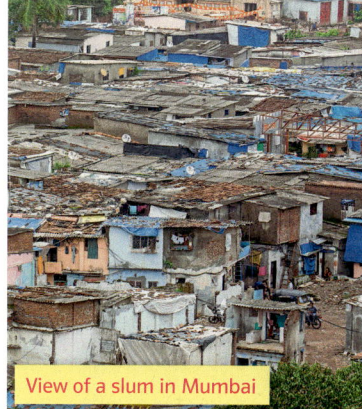
View of a slum in Mumbai

2 **Vishram Society** a block of flats where Mary works as a cleaner
2 **Tamil** ethnic group from the south of India and Sri Lanka; also the name of their language
6 **tarpaulin** *Zeltplane*
17 **legal/semi-legal slums** slums tolerated by the city authorities due to the need to house people, however primitively
19 **precarious** not safe
23 **pucca** Hindu word meaning solid, permanent; very good
24 **eviction** forcing sb to leave a house or land
28 **inertia** [ɪˈnɜːʃə] *here:* lack of desire to change things
30 **Thane** a city to the northeast of Mumbai

1 **COMPREHENSION** Outline what happens in this extract and explain why Mary is so afraid. → S13   **Hinweis:** Auch als Hausaufgabe geeignet

2 **VOCABULARY** Make a mind map on the topic of slums using vocabulary from the text.

3 **ANALYSIS** Examine the style and tone of this excerpt. How does it reflect Mary's emotions? → S10 → △3 **Diff** (help with): Auswahl an Adjektiven, Strukturierungshilfe
Zusatzmaterial WB Task 3: Indirect characterisation

4 **SPEAKING** Mary talks to a local politician about the need to legalise her slum. Write a script (just notes), practise the dialogue and then do the role play with a partner. → S12.2
Hinweis: Vorbereitung auch als Hausaufgabe geeignet

Zusatzmaterial WB
Task 16: Mediation

Avoiding mistakes
Wortschatz
²⁴**yet** nevertheless (conjunction)

Texts

Poor family in India

India has one third of the world's poorest, says World Bank

While new figures show that the number of those in extreme poverty around the world – surviving on 82 pence per day or less – has declined significantly, India now has a greater share of the world's poorest than it did thirty years ago. Then it was home to one fifth of the world's poorest people, but today it accounts for one third – 400 million.

The study found the number of extremely poor people had declined from half the world's population in 1981 to one fifth in 2010, but voiced concern at its increase in Sub-Saharan Africa and continuing high level in India.

World Bank president Jim Yong Kim said while the overall decline was "remarkable progress", the remaining 1.2 billion people living in extreme poverty was "a stain on our collective conscience." His colleague, World Bank chief economist Kaushik Basu, who until last year was economic advisor to Indian prime minister Dr Manmohan Singh, said the figures called for the world's wealthier countries to do more.

"We have made strides in cutting down poverty, but with nearly one-fifth of the world population still below the poverty line, not enough. Directing investment towards the poor will require coordinated effort by the Bank, our country partners, and the international development community; and will, let's face it, entail sacrifice on the part of those who are fortunate enough to be better off," he said.

The scale of continuing extreme poverty in India, despite its economy nudging growth rates of nine per cent in recent years, highlights what government strategists have called its "ticking time bomb." Its population is expected to reach 1.5 billion and become the world's largest nation by 2026 but its economy is not growing fast enough to create the 20 million new jobs per year they will need to prevent poverty increasing further.

Its problems are compounded by poor health services, child malnutrition and inadequate education and training. Almost half of pupils drop out of school by the age of 13 and only one in ten people have received any form of job training.

The perception of India as a fast-growing economy however has seen developed countries significantly reduce their aid. The United States has announced a 16 per cent reduction while Britain has announced it will end its £280 million per year aid programme.

Thomas Chandy of Save The Children said 200 million people had been lifted from poverty in the last two decades but the recent economic growth had left one third of the population untouched. "India's status has gone down despite the economic growth, inequality has widened which makes the poor poorer. In child mortality, infant mortality and maternal mortality, India seems to have the largest populations in all these categories. We would like to see focused interventions [because] the most difficult areas remain untouched," he said.

Daily Telegraph, 2013

---

10 **remarkable** unusual, surprising
11 **a stain on our collective conscience** *here:* sth is wrong which we are all responsible for
15 **to make strides in doing sth** to make progress/improvement in doing sth
17 **effort** ['efət] attempt to do sth
18 **to entail sacrifice** to involve going without sth/giving sth up
19 **fortunate** lucky
20 **scale** size, extent
20 **nudging** getting near
26 **to be compounded by** to make sth bad even worse
26 **malnutrition** not having enough of the right food
37 **infant** baby or very young child
37 **mortality** *Sterblichkeit*
37 **maternal** of a mother

Avoiding mistakes
Wortschatz
¹**figures** Zahlen
¹**number** Anzahl

Zusatzmaterial WB
Tasks 6–7: Speaking
Tasks 8–9: Listening

5 COMPREHENSION
a) In your own words outline how the number of people in extreme poverty has developed in India and in the world.
b) List the problems facing India in the fight against poverty.
Zusatzmaterial WB Task 4: Statistics

6 EVALUATION Discuss the following statement: "The cure to extreme poverty in India is faster economic growth." → S14 → ▲4 **Diff** (instead of): Erstellung eines Plans zur Armutsbekämpfung
Geeignete Methode: Thinking hats

C Popular culture

Cricket – India's national sport

Cricket is, in the words of sociologist Ashis Nandy, "an Indian game accidentally discovered by the British". India's most popular sport was introduced to the subcontinent by sailors of the East India Company in the 18th century. Although it was played by the British colonial elite, Indians quickly made it their own. Today, India
5 boasts a highly successful national team, a booming domestic league and more players than the rest of the world put together.

But what makes cricket so ideally suited to the Indian national character? For one thing, India is a complex country with infinite possibilities, just as cricket is a complex game with unlimited variations. Those who have ever tried to understand
10 the rules of the game will know how true this is. The caste system defines a person's role in society, just as a player's role is defined in his team, for example as a hard-hitting batsman or a spin bowler. The most famous cricketers like Sachin Tendulkar are worshipped as national heroes.

Most importantly, however, the players in the Indian national cricket team and
15 in the teams of the Indian Premier League enjoy fanatical support regardless of whether they are Hindus, Muslims, Sikhs or Christians. It is the unifying effect of the game in a country which is otherwise divided by caste, creed or colour which truly makes cricket India's national sport.

1 COMPREHENSION Explain why cricket is said to be "an Indian game".
Zusatzmaterial WB Task 5: The passive voice
2 RESEARCH Prepare a short oral report on either Sachin Tendulkar or the Indian Premier League. → S22
Zusatzmaterial KV 3: Regeln des Cricket-Spiels

VIP FILE

Sachin Tendulkar (born in 1973) is recognised as one of the greatest cricketers of all time. He retired from cricket in 2013. His fans say: "If cricket is religion, Tendulkar is a god".

Bollywood

[3rd May 2013 marked] the 100th anniversary of the first Bollywood film. It has been a century since the first wholly Indian-produced film was released in Bombay. D. Phalke's *Raja Harishchandra* was a black and white, silent film premiered in 1913 while India was still under the control of the British Empire. Indian cinema has
5 come a long way since. Bollywood is now the largest film industry in the world, having overtaken Hollywood in the 70s. Below are four facts celebrating the 100 years of Bollywood existence:
1. The nickname Bollywood refers to the origins of Indian cinema in Bombay and Hollywood.
10 2. Indian films are often referred to as the spice mix masala as they have a mixture of singing and dancing, romance, comedy and action.
3. Typical Bollywood conventions include star-crossed lovers, angry parents, family ties, sacrifice, corrupt politicians and kidnappings.
4. Bollywood produces an estimated 1,000 films every year.

Mirror, 2013

3 RESEARCH Use this text as the starting point for doing research to prepare a short report called: 'A hundred years of Bollywood'. **Hinweis:** Auch als Hausaufgabe geeignet
4 RESEARCH Choose a successful Bollywood film and do some research on its plot and the reasons for its success. Present the film in class. → S32

FACT FILE

Bollywood is sometimes called **Hindi cinema**. The films are mostly musicals with a lot of song and dance integrated in the film script. The success of a Bollywood film depends a lot on the quality of the music. Most Indian actors are excellent dancers, but not all of them can sing. Playback singers are often used and are very popular themselves.

Advanced texts

D Hinduism and India's caste system

1 **VIEWING** Watch the video clip, and make notes about the Indian caste system.

2 **BEFORE YOU READ** Use these notes to prepare an 'Info spot': Make a few notes on a card and talk freely on Hinduism and the caste system for two minutes. If you need help, you can check the fact file on the next page.
Hinweis: Auch als Hausaufgabe geeignet

Traditional wedding ceremony

Interview with Tarquin Hall

How did this story develop?
I'd heard of the Love Commandos, a real life charity that works with young people from different castes and religions who want to marry against the wishes of their families. At the same time I wanted the fourth book to be set in rural India and to explore the caste issue. So, bingo, the two ideas came together and I came up with the love story idea: a boy from an untouchable family running off with a high caste girl with the Love Commandos helping them out. Then I read an article about how researchers have been mapping the human genome here in India and how fascinating the findings are proving because you've had different endogenous groups of people living in the same communities as one another and never mixing – that is for centuries. So that became a big part of the plot, too. Basically that's how I work – I find what I want to talk about, so that each book tells you more and more about India, and then I try to come up with a decent plot.

How would you summarize what it is about?
It's basically about how caste continues to dominate Indian society and politics – less so in the cities, but to be honest even in a place like Delhi it's a big factor in most communities. It's an extraordinary thing, caste, unlike any other system that exists in any other society I've come across. If you're unfortunate enough to have been born into a low caste the chances are you will still end up doing the most menial of tasks. It is changing slowly. And there are many, many exceptions. But generally speaking that's still the case.

Tell me more about the "Love Commandos" ...
I spent quite a bit of time with the Love Commandos seeing how they work, and met run away couples in safe houses here in Delhi. These couples were on the run from their parents. Some of them were worried that they would be killed if they were found, that their relatives would do anything to stop them marrying someone from another caste or religion. You have to remember that 99% of all marriages in India are arranged. So the parents and the rest of the family have to give their consent.

Where do you stand on the topic of arranged marriage? Why did you decide to include the debate over the topic in this book?
It's definitely better to have choice in my opinion, to be able to have a say and decide for yourself. And obviously sometimes arranged marriages can be absolutely terrible, with people locked into an awful situation with someone they don't

---

VIP FILE

Tarquin Hall is a British author and journalist who lives in Delhi. His series of books about the Indian detective Vish Puri are very popular crime novels. In this interview he talks about his book *The Case of the Love Commandos*.

¹ **commando** specially trained soldier
¹ **charity** organisation helping people in need
⁹ **endogenous** [ɪnˈdɒdʒənəs] *here:* einheimisch
²⁰ **menial** [ˈmiːniəl] unskilled, lowly
²⁹ **to give one's consent to sth** to agree to sth

168

love – or worse with someone who persecutes them. That said, I have seen a lot of arranged marriages that work very, very well. People get on, learn to love one another and when times get tough I think sometimes it helps to feel this sense of commitment to not only your husband or wife but the rest of the extended family. […]

I found fascinating the explanations of the caste system and the Yadavs and the Brahmins. Can you explain it to our readers and talk about why you decided to include that topic in this book?

Well, as I show in the book, the power and position of the different castes has shifted in the past 60 or so years. Traditionally the Brahmins, the priestly caste, have been at the top. But nowadays that's not always the case. Not all Brahmins are necessarily priests and even if they are they're not necessarily that well off. Because of the affirmative action system set up after India gained its independence from Britain, there have been government job quotas for the lower castes. So that's empowered some of them and in some areas – it's hard to generalize – altered the local power structure. Democracy has also played a big part in bringing change. The lower castes have become powerful politically as they represent big vote banks. The Yadavs, whom I write about in the book, are a good example of this.

Blogcritics website, 2013

35 **to persecute** to treat in a cruel and unfair way
38 **extended family** *Großfamilie*
49 **to empower** to give power and rights
49 **to alter** to change
51 **vote bank** a loyal group of people who always vote for a certain candidate or political party

3 COMPREHENSION
a) Explain what the 'Love Commandos' are.
b) Summarise the aspects of caste Tarquin Hall mentions in the interview.
Hinweis: Auch als Hausaufgabe geeignet

4 VIEWING Compare the view of the caste system today as given in the film clip with the one in the interview.

5 EVALUATION Assess to what extent modern India has overcome the caste system. → S14.2 **Zusatzmaterial WB** Task 17: Structuring

6 EVALUATION List Hall's arguments for and against an arranged marriage. Then discuss how you would react if your parents decided whom you should marry.

FACT FILE

The caste system in India

Castes divide society into groups of people with different functions and status. The original Hindu caste system based on ancient religious texts defined four castes according to their spiritual and physical development and did not explicitly exclude movement from one caste to another.
Later the four castes were linked inseparably to the function individuals had in society: The highest caste, the **Brahmins**, were the intellectual and spiritual guides, priests and philosophers. Second were the **Kshatriyas**, the caste of warriors and rulers. Then came the **Vaishyas**, associated with trading and commerce, and the lowest caste were the **Shudras**, labourers and craftsmen. For fear of pollution, higher castes had to avoid any contact with the '**untouchables**', people who ranked below all others and did the dirty work. While the higher castes managed to strengthen their position the lower ones were denied any power. Infringement of caste rules of conduct led to severe punishment.
Since **1949** the **Constitution of India** has granted all its citizens **equal rights**, but changes have been gradual. The **Industrial Revolution** and today's **economic boom** have done much more to weaken the caste system. It has become possible for people to improve their status through professional and financial success. Especially in the cities, caste is losing influence.
The majority of the former untouchables, who now call themselves **Dalits** (the oppressed), are still underprivileged, but as their numbers are strong (18–20% of the population), democracy has equipped them with more power to fight for their rights.

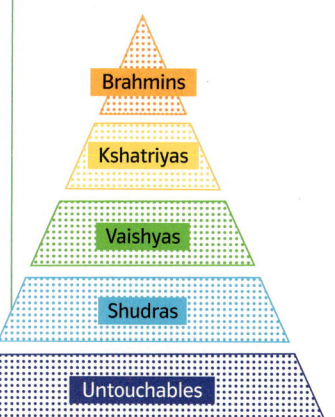

Advanced texts

E Tradition and gender roles

FACT FILE

The **Ramayana** is one of the two great Hindu epics. It portrays ideal characters, like an ideal king, husband or wife. It tells the story of **Rama** or Lord Ram, an avatar of Vishnu, and his wife, **Sita**.

Ravana is Lord Ram's antagonist in the Ramayana. He kidnaps Sita, but she is rescued.

Rama and Lakshmana look on as Sita undergoes the trial of fire to prove her faithfulness, one of the most dramatic episodes in the Ramayana. However, the docile and soft Sita may not be a role model for most women today.

1 BEFORE YOU READ What do you know about the role of women in India and the problems they face? **Geeignete Methode:** Speed dating

trial of fire exhausting or painful test
docile quiet and easy to control

India dishonoured?

Lord Ram spoke to his wife in front of the court:
O Sita, you are the embodiment of tolerance and forbearance. Moreover, you represent purity at its highest. But you have lived under the shelter of Ravana. I know the fire of your chastity has prevented Ravana from even touching your nail. But I have my own limitations. As a king I am answerable to my people, and therefore, I would like you to prove your purity in front of all so that in future people on this earth would not cast doubt – dare not put any blame – of infidelity on your noble character.

Sita turned to her husband's brother, Lakshman:
Agonised by these false rumours, I cannot bear living. I shall enter a blazing fire, the only course left for me now that I have been rejected in a public gathering by my husband who is not pleased with my qualities.

To understand the origins of most cultural practices in India requires going back to centuries-old religious mythology. The Ramayana, within which this exchange takes place, is known to almost every Indian child from a young age. This epic tale of kings and queens, family duty and promises, love and war, tradition and honour is a key part of the Hindu religious canon. Lord Ram is held up as the epitome of a dutiful son, a good husband and an honourable king who will do anything to rescue his wife Sita from the clutches of the evil Ravana. Sita is portrayed as the archetypal woman: kind, righteous, strong but obedient.

The story of Sita's fate is important not just because the Ramayana is so highly regarded but because the above exchange, narrated near the end, illustrates the significance given to a woman's 'honour'. There are several versions of the Ramayana, narrated by different sects of Hinduism across different parts of the

² **embodiment** person or thing representing a typical idea or quality
² **forbearance** quality of being patient and sympathetic to others
³ **under the shelter of** *here*: in the house of
⁴ **chastity** Keuschheit
⁸ **infidelity** act of not being faithful to your wife or husband
¹⁰ **agonised** having great pain
¹⁸ **epitome** perfect example
¹⁹ **from the clutches of** aus den Fängen von
²⁰ **obedient** doing what you are told to do
²¹ **highly regarded** thought of in a very positive way

170

country. In most versions Sita accepts the trial of fire and walks through unharmed.
However, in other versions she rejects the trial and calls on the Earth to consume her and spare her the indignity. The Mahabharata, another popular epic tale, has a similar tale to tell about the duty of men and women, the importance of tradition and the different roles of men and women. These religious texts undoubtedly shape popular perceptions on how women should act.

Salil Tripathi, a writer and columnist for the *Mint* newspaper in India, says texts such as the Ramayana and Mahabharata reinforce the underlying message that "if you want to be a good person, these are the role models to follow."

For many of India's Hindus (around 80% of the population), Muslims (14%), Christians (2.5%), Sikhs (2%), Buddhists (1%), Jains (>1%) and other minorities religion is a way of living and celebrating, not just a matter of attending a place of worship once a week. It can be extremely difficult to draw a line where religion ends and culture begins; the two have been intricately inter-woven over centuries. […]

Many Indians say that culture places men and women in different but complementary roles and that rather than subscribing to Western ideals of feminist equality Indian women are in fact put on a pedestal. During one very popular Hindu and Sikh festival for example, Rakhee, sisters tie a thread around their brothers' wrists, who in turn pledge to protect them for life.

This symbolism of Indian culture that puts women on a pedestal is very real – but it is also in fact the problem. Tradition requires that girls be brought up to be good daughters and later obedient wives, not independent women who should be encouraged to do what they wish. If she is judged to have brought 'shame' upon herself, she is seen as bringing shame on the entire family and even the community. Her role is reduced to remaining honourable until she can get married, produce children and run the household. In effect, by putting women on a pedestal, they are placed in a trap where they have to constantly live up to the expectations of others.

From: Sunny Hundal, *India Dishonoured – Behind a nation's war on women*, 2013

26 **to consume** *here*: to kill/destroy
27 **indignity** a state of feeling ashamed/embarrassed
30 **perception** way of seeing sth
32 **to reinforce sth** [ˌriːɪnˈfɔːs] to make sth stronger
38 **intricately inter-woven** *here*: very closely linked together
41 **complementary** *sich ergänzend*
41 **to subscribe to** to agree with
42 **pedestal** the base that a statue stands on
43 **thread** *here*: a thin string of cotton
44 **to pledge sth** to promise sth
48 **shame** dishonour, loss of respect
52 **trap** *Falle*

2 COMPREHENSION State the problem Lord Rama has in the extract from the Ramayana and what his wife, Sita, decides to do.

3 VOCABULARY 👥 **Hinweis:** Auch als Hausaufgabe geeignet
 a) Go through the text and collect adjectives and nouns describing the qualities expected of women.
 b) For each of these words try to find nouns, adjectives or verbs from the same word family. Use a dictionary if necessary. → **S3**
 Zusatzmaterial WB Task 18: Talking about gender stereotypes

4 COMPREHENSION Describe the traditional picture of the ideal woman and how it relates to modern India according to the text.

5 ANALYSIS Compare it with your picture of women in contemporary German society.

6 EVALUATION Discuss the following statement from the text: "This symbolism of Indian culture that puts women on a pedestal is very real – but it is also in fact the problem."

7 RESEARCH Find out more about the storyline in the Ramayana and give a short presentation in class. → **S22, S32**

Advanced texts

Cartoons for change in the New Delhi metro

Cartoons can make a difference, and Delhi metro commuters can attest to that fact. Between September and December 2011, commuters travelling between 21 metro stations along the Red Line of the Delhi Metro saw 12 cartoons by leading cartoonists such as Sudhir Tailang, Neelabh Banerjee and Jayanto Banerjee. The National Commission for Women (NCW) and UN Women supported the campaign to create greater awareness about women's empowerment in India.

Placed strategically along the 26 kilometer-long crowded Delhi Line, the cartoons provide visual relief to commuters, while also informing them about basic issues. "Seeing the cartoon, I was inspired to reflect upon my own actions at home. I will ensure that I do a background check of the groom before marrying my sister," said Rajesh, who commutes every day to Tis Hazari Metro Station. On seeing the cartoon on domestic violence, Rajesh felt that every family should ensure that the women of the family feel extremely safe and secure.

The cartoons went with the tag line: "It's time to change your attitude towards women."

"Almost 17 lakh people use the Delhi Metro every day. So these informative cartoons attract attention and serve as public service messages, rooted in the daily experiences of women across India. They will help people reflect about things that they don't reflect upon or take for granted," said Anne Stenhammer, Regional Programme Director, UN Women South Asia.

UN Women website, 2012

---

[1] **to attest to sth** to affirm that sth is true/correct
[6] **empowerment** being given power or rights
[10] **groom** *Bräutigam*
[16] **1 lakh** 100,000 (written 1,00,000 in the Indian numbering system)
[19] **to take sth for granted** to accept sth without question

---

8 VISUALS Your partner analyses one cartoon and you analyse the other. Then present your cartoon to your partner. → S28.2
Zusatzmaterial WB Task 19: Improve your style

9 EVALUATION The text claims that cartoons can make a difference. Assess whether cartoons like this can change attitudes towards gender equality.
Zusatzmaterial KV 4: Role play cards

10 ANALYSIS In the light of the ideas expressed about women in the text *India dishonoured?*, explain Rajesh's reaction to the cartoon on domestic violence.
→ △5 **Diff** (help with): Vorgabe von Aspekten

11 SPEAKING "The discrimination of women does not fit India's self-image as a modern democracy and a rapidly developing country." Discuss. → S24

F The history of India

The sun sets on the British Empire

On a warm summer night in 1947, the largest empire the world has ever seen did something no empire had done before. It gave up. The British Empire did not decline, it simply fell; and it fell proudly and majestically on its own sword. It was not forced out by revolution, nor defeated by a greater rival in battle. Its leaders
5 did not tire or weaken. Its culture was strong and vibrant. Recently it had been victorious in the century's definitive war.

When midnight struck in Delhi on the night of 14 August 1947, a new, free Indian nation was born. In London, the time was 8.30 pm. The world's capital could enjoy another hour or two of a warm summer evening before the sun literally and finally
10 set on the British Empire. […]

Inside the chamber of the constituent assembly [in Delhi], 2000 princes and politicians from across 1.25 million square miles that remained of India sat together on parliamentary benches. Yet amid all the power and finery, two persons were conspicuous by their absence. One was Mohammad Ali Jinnah, the leader of the
15 Muslim League, who was in one of those parts of the Empire that had just become Pakistan. His absence signified the partition of the subcontinent, the split which had ripped two wings off the body of India and called them West and East Pakistan (later Pakistan and Bangladesh), creating Muslim homelands separate from the predominantly Hindu mass of the territory. The other truant was Mohandas
20 Karamchand Gandhi, who was sound asleep in a smashed-up mansion in a riot-torn suburb of Calcutta.

Gandhi's absence was a worrying omen. The seventy-seven-year-old mahatma, or 'great soul', was the most famous and the most popular Indian since Buddha. Regarded as little short of a saint among Christians as well as Hindus, he had
25 been a staunch defender of the British Empire until the 1920s. Since then, he had campaigned for Indian self-rule. […]

In the chamber the dignitaries fell silent as the foremost among them, Jawaharlal Nehru, stepped up to make one of the most famous speeches in history. At fifty-seven years old, Nehru had grown into his role as India's leading statesman.
30 His last prison term had finished exactly twenty-six months before. The fair skin and fine bone structure of an aristocratic Kashmiri Brahmin was rendered approachable by a ready smile and warm laugh. Dark, sleepy, soulful eyes belied a quick wit and quicker temper. In him were all the virtues of the ancient nation, filtered through the best aspects of the British Empire: confidence, sophistication, and charisma.
35 'Long years ago,' he began …

From: Alex von Tunzelmann, *Indian Summer*, 2007

1 COMPREHENSION
a) Explain what was so special about the end of British rule in India.
b) Jinnah and Gandhi were absent at the constituent assembly. Explain why.
c) In your own words, describe how Nehru is presented in the final passage.
Hinweis: Auch als Hausaufgabe geeignet

2 ANALYSIS
Examine the author's attitude towards the British Empire.
Zusatzmaterial WB Task 20: Stylistic devices

3 LISTENING
a) Listen to the beginning of Nehru's famous speech and how Mark Tully, a British journalist living in India, comments on the events. Explain why India's independence was a cause for joy as well as sadness.
b) What does Tully's family show us about the relationship between British colonial officers and India?

VIP FILE

Mahatma Gandhi (1869–1948), on the right, was against Partition and campaigned for self-rule for a united India with non-violent demonstrations.

Jawaharlal Nehru (1889–1964), on the left, became India's first Prime Minister. He was, with Gandhi, a key figure in the Indian Independence Movement.

Muhammad Ali Jinnah (1876–1948) was leader of the separatist All-India Muslim League until Pakistan's independence in 1947 when he became Pakistan's first Governor-General.

5 **vibrant** lively; full of life and energy
11 **constituent assembly** meeting of representatives to draft and adopt a constitution
13 **amid** in the middle of
13 **finery** elegant clothes
14 **conspicuous** [knəˈspɪkjuːəs] easy to notice
19 **truant** *here*: missing person
25 **staunch** firm, loyal, strong
27 **dignitary** important person
32 **to belie** to give a false impression of
32 **wit** ability to say clever and amusing things
33 **virtue** [ˈvɜːtjuː] Tugend

Advanced texts

Train to Pakistan

In this historical novel Kushwant Singh tells the story of Partition in the summer of 1947 through the eyes of Sikhs and Muslims living in the fictional village of Mano Majra on the border of India with Pakistan.

The strangers took off their shoes and came inside the large hall. The lambardar and Meet Singh followed them. Men sat up and tied their turbans. Women put their children in their laps and tried to rock them to sleep again.

One of the group, who appeared to be the leader, motioned the others to sit down. Everyone sat down. The leader had an aggressive bossy manner. He was a boy in his teens with a little beard which was glued to his chin with brilliantine. He was small in size, slight of build and altogether somewhat effeminate; a glossy red ribbon showed under the acute angle of his bright blue turban. His khaki army shirt hung loosely from his round drooping shoulders. He wore a black leather Sam Browne: the strap across his narrow chest charged with bullets and the broad belt clamped about his still narrower waist. On one side it had a holster with the butt of a revolver protruding; on the other side there was a dagger. He looked as if his mother had dressed him up as an American cowboy.

The boy caressed the holster of his revolver and ran his fingers over the silver noses of the bullets. He looked around him with complete confidence.

'Is this a Sikh village?' he asked insolently. It was obvious to the villagers that he was an educated city-dweller. Such men always assumed a superior air when talking to peasants. They had no regard for age or status.

'Yes, sir,' answered the lambardar. 'It has always been a Sikh village. We had Muslim tenants but they have gone.'

'What sort of Sikhs are you?' asked the boy, glowering menacingly. He elaborated this question: 'Potent or impotent?'

No one knew what to say. No one protested that this was not the sort of language one used in a gurdwara with women and children sitting by.

'Do you know how many trainloads of dead Sikhs and Hindus have come over? Do you know of the massacres in Rawalpindi and Multan, Gujranwala and Sheikhupura?

What are you doing about it? You just eat and sleep and you call yourselves Sikhs – the brave Sikhs! The martial class!' he added, raising both his arms to emphasize his sarcasm. He surveyed his audience with the bright eyes daring anyone to contradict him. People looked down somewhat ashamed of themselves.

'What can we do, Sardarji?' questioned the lambardar. 'If our government goes to war against Pakistan, we will fight. What can we do sitting in Mano Majra?'

'Government!' sneered the boy contemptuously. 'You expect the government to do anything? A government consisting of cowardly bania moneylenders! Do the Mussalmans in Pakistan apply for permission from their government when they rape your sisters? Do they apply for permission when they stop trains and kill everyone, old, young, women and children? You want the government to do something! That is great! Shabash! Brave! He gave the holster on his side a jaunty smack.

'But, Sardar Sahib,' said the lambardar falteringly, 'do tell us what we can do.'

'That is better,' answered the lad. 'Now we can talk. Listen and listen very carefully.' He paused, looked around and started again. He spoke slowly, emphasizing each sentence by stabbing the air with his forefinger. 'For each Hindu or Sikh they kill, kill two Mussalmans. For each woman they abduct or rape, abduct two. For each home they loot, loot two. For each trainload of dead they send over, send two across. For each road convoy that is attacked, attack two. That will stop

---

FACT FILE

Sikhism was founded in the Punjab region in the 15th century. Most of the 30 million Sikhs worldwide still live there. Sikhs were classified by the British as a martial, i.e. warlike, class and many served in the British Army.

---

³ **Mano Majra** the name of the village
⁴ **lambardar** village official or headman
⁹ **brilliantine** hair oil
¹⁰ **effeminate** like a woman
¹² **a Sam Browne** a wide leather waist belt with a narrow shoulder strap
¹⁷ **to caress** to touch gently
¹⁸ **insolently** ['ɪnsələntli] showing a lack of respect
²³ **tenant** person paying rent to use a room, building, land
²⁷ **gurdwara** a Sikh church
²⁹ **Rawalpindi etc.** cities in the Punjab
³⁵ **Sardarji** a title for a chief or leader
³⁸ **bania** trader or merchant in Indian business caste
⁴² **shabash** bravo
⁴⁴ **Sardar Sahib** see Sardarji
⁴⁴ **falteringly** unsteadily, showing a lack of confidence
⁴⁵ **lad** young man
⁴⁸ **to abduct** to kidnap
⁴⁹ **to loot** to steal things from shops after a riot

the killing on the other side. It will teach them that we also play this game of killing and looting.'

He stopped to gauge the effect he had created. People listened to him with rapt open-mouthed attention. Only
55 Meet Singh did look up; he cleared his throat but stopped.

'Well, brother, why do you keep quiet?' asked the lad, throwing a challenge.

'I was going to say,' said Meet Singh haltingly, 'I was going to say,' he repeated, 'what have the Muslims here
60 done to us for us to kill them in revenge for what Muslims in Pakistan are doing. Only people who have committed crimes should be punished.'

The lad glared angrily at Meet Singh. 'What had the Sikhs and Hindus in Pakistan done that they were
65 butchered? Weren't they innocent? Had the women committed crimes for which they were ravished? Had the children committed murder for which they were spiked in front of their parents?'

Meet Singh was subdued. The boy wanted to squash
70 him further. 'Why, brother? Now speak and say what you want to.' […]

From: Kushwant Singh, *Train to Pakistan*, 1956

Indian refugees crowd onto trains as a result of Partition, Muslims fleeing to Pakistan and Hindus fleeing to India, resulting in one of the largest migrations in history.

4 COMPREHENSION *Describe the scene from the novel putting it in its historical context (see fact file).* **Zusatzmaterial WB** Task 21: Writing

5 ANALYSIS *What impression of the boy do you get from the text? Compare this with the way the villagers in the gurdwara react to him.* → **S7**
Hinweis: Auch als Hausaufgabe geeignet

6 ANALYSIS *Illustrate the use of anaphora in the boy's speech.*

7 EVALUATION *Think of recent international violent conflicts between religious or ethnic groups and compare them with ideas expressed in the text.*

8 CREATIVE TASK *If you were Meet Singh, how would you respond to the boy's demand at the end of the extract?* → **S12.2** → ▲**6** **Diff** (instead of): Brief von Meet Singh an dessen Bruder schreiben
Geeignete Methode: Think – Pair – Share

53 **to gauge** [geɪdʒ] to check
54 **rapt** very interested in, concentrated
58 **haltingly** unsteadily, hesitantly
60 **revenge** Rache
63 **to glare at sb** to look at sb angrily
66 **ravished** raped
67 **spiked** *here:* killed
69 **to subdue** made quiet
69 **to squash** *here:* to defeat, to crush

Avoiding mistakes
Aussprache
65**to butcher** [ˈbʊtʃə(r)]

FACT FILE

Partition and the Punjab
The Punjab region, located in today's northern India and eastern Pakistan, was divided between the two new countries during the Partition of 1947. The western half, which was to become part of Pakistan, had a Muslim majority, but of course many Muslims lived in the east and many Sikhs or Hindus lived in the west. Everybody feared persecution or displacement. In this atmosphere of anxiety and unrest, religious fanatics on both sides started a vicious circle of violence which ultimately killed between 200,000 and two million people and forced more than ten million to migrate.

Spot on language

Hinweis
Selbstevaluation für Schüler über Green Line-Code

Being aware of persuasive strategies

1 *Travel catalogues and brochures are both informative and persuasive. Study these typical persuasive strategies. Then examine the short text below and find examples.*

- Catalogues combine **desire and fulfillment messages**: You know you want to visit this country and, with us, you can.
- **Vivid descriptive passages** are often supported by glossy photos. Look for adjectives and also references to features typical of the location.
- Choice of words
  - with **connotations** of, for example, adventure/education/entertainment/relaxation
  - referring to friendliness, uniqueness and other **alluring expressions**
  - giving **emphasis** and, perhaps, exaggerating
  - **contrasting** the routine of home with the excitement/foreignness of the travel location
- Extensive use of **superlatives**.
- Use of the **imperative** and exclamation marks.
- Use of **rhetorical questions**, implying that the answer will be found by going on the trip.
- **Argumentative structures** and the use of evidence to convince and persuade the reader.
- **Emotional manipulation** by using references to sight, sound, smell and touch.
- Dialogue with the reader by using "you/we" creates a feeling of **intimacy and trust**.

India holidays

- India is a destination that really sinks into your soul. It's a country of extremes, which will dazzle your senses and leave you with memories that last a lifetime.
5 • The beauty of India is twofold. While the beaches of Goa are no doubt world-class, with soft sands meeting the warm waters of the Arabian Sea, India keeps its best secrets safe for those adventuring away from the shorelines.
10 • Submerge yourself in the hustle and bustle of the hot streets and bazaars, where the dust and aromas jostle for dominance. In the markets, you'll come across rows upon rows of ochre spices, and merchants will compete for your attention, offering bargains galore.
15 • There are certain sights that you simply cannot miss on holidays in India. The capital city of Delhi is one, but brace yourself for a mind-boggling experience, where ancient ruins and modern luxury sit side by side.
- The Taj Mahal in Agra is an altogether different wonder, which took 22 years to build and where peace and tranquillity reign, even during the busiest times. A good camera is an essential for holidays to India – don't
20 forget to get a snap of the famous lotus pool bench with the Taj in the background.
- What makes India such a fantastic holiday destination is the fact that for all of its heady chaos and mind-bending beauty, it also boasts beautiful sweeping beaches. […]

Taj Mahal

Thomas Cook website, 2014

2 *Point out what you really learn about India from this text in a summary of no more than 100 words.*
Hinweis: Auch als Hausaufgabe geeignet
3 *Choose a sight or travel destination in India and write your own travel brochure text for it.*

Mediation

4 *An English friend is about to take his/her final exams at the same time as you. You have decided to go on a trip together after the exams – to India. You have only got about two weeks so you want to go on an organised trip. Your friend's German isn't very good, but you have found a very promising offer in a German travel brochure. Make some notes on the most important points and then act out the phone call with a partner.* → **S26.1**

Here's what you want to tell him/her about:
- tour dates
- accommodation
- price
- meals
- itinerary
- trip highlights
- travel arrangements
- travel documents
- other things you should know

15 Tage Indien   ab 1599 €
Rajasthan – Das Land der Könige

Entdecken Sie die faszinierende Vielfalt und Farbenpracht Rajasthans! Auf den Spuren der Maharadschas finden Sie prachtvolle Paläste und kühne Festungen, die Sie in Fantasien von Tausendundeiner Nacht entführen. Ob im Palast der Winde in Jaipur, im Seepalast Jag Niwas in Udaipur, der als James-Bond-Kulisse diente, oder in den Festungsanlagen von Jaisalmer und Bikaner – überall ist die reiche Geschichte und Kultur Indiens unmittelbar zu erleben. Wir ermöglichen Ihnen einzigartige Begegnungen beim Besuch einer alten Karawanenstadt inmitten der Wüste oder Ihrer privaten indischen Tanzstunde. Zum Abschluss der Reise wird sich in Agra der erste Blick auf das Taj Mahal, den „Stein gewordenen Seufzer", für immer in Ihr Gedächtnis einbrennen – lassen Sie sich verzaubern!

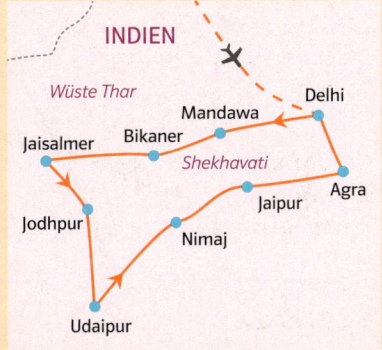

15 Reisetage ab

Jan	Feb	März	April	Mai	Okt	Nov
29	19	5	12	1	3	5
					18	19

Reisepreis ab €

Doppelzimmer	1599	1739	1849	1999
Einzelzimmerzuschlag	399	429	439	449

Abflugsorte und Zuschläge ab €
Je nach Verfügbarkeit der angegebenen Buchungsklasse Aufpreis möglich. Kerosinpreisänderungen vorbehalten.

Basel	249	Graz	99	München	39
Berlin	39	Hamburg	39	Wien	39
Dresden	39	Hannover	39	Zürich	249
Frankfurt	0	Leipzig	39		

Zuschlag Business-Class
einfach ab 1280 €   hin und zurück ab 2560 €
CO_2 Ausgleich Flüge ab 55€

Zusätzlich buchbare Extras

Rail & Fly 2. Kl. einfach	35 €
Visagebühren und -beantragung	70 €
Abendprogramm Jaisalmer	30 €
Stadtbesichtigung Udaipur	23 €
Exklusive Kathak-Tanzstunde Jaipur	59 €

Ihre Hotels (Änderungen vorbehalten)

Stadt	Nächte	Hotel	Landeskategorie
Delhi	2	Krishna	*** (*)
Mandawa	1	Mandawa Resort	***
Bikaner	1	Gaj Kesri	****
Jaisalmer	2	Desert Castle	****
Jodhpur	1	Karni Bhawan	****
Udaipur	2	Rajputana Palace	*** (*)
Nimaj	1	Nimaj Tulip	***
Jaipur	2	Mansingh Palace	****
Agra	1	Royal Plaza	*** (*)

Kleine Gruppen
- Höchstteilnehmerzahl: 20 Gäste
- Mindestteilnehmerzahl: 10 Gäste

Im Reisepreis enthalten
- Linienflug (Economy) nach Delhi und zurück; Abflugsorte und Zuschläge s. Tabelle, je nach Verfügbarkeit
- Transfers, Ausflüge und Rundreise mit guten, landesüblichen, klimatisierten Bussen und Taxis
- Unterbringung im Doppelzimmer mit Dusche/Bad/WC und Klimaanlage in den genannten Hotels
- Mahlzeiten wie im Tagesprogramm spezifiziert (F=Frühstück, M=Mittagessen, A=Abendessen)
- geführte Dünenwanderung
- Klimaneutrale Bus-/Jeep-/Bahnfahrten (mit dem Bau von Biogasanlagen in Indien)
- Reiseliteratur (ca. 15 €)
- Deutsch oder Englisch sprechende Reiseleitung

Spot on **vocabulary**

Synonyms and opposites

1 Find a synonym for the words in **A** and the opposite of the words in **B** using the vocabulary sheets on your CD or a dictionary.

> **A** presented • slow • (to) put off • satisfaction • working • confused • kindness • choice • craftsman • very big • difficult task • part of the economy

> **B** variety • wealth • educated • microcosm • independent of • private • unseen

Organising vocabulary for a talk

2 a) Make a mind map on India using points you have come across in this topic. You can use the mind map below as a starting point.

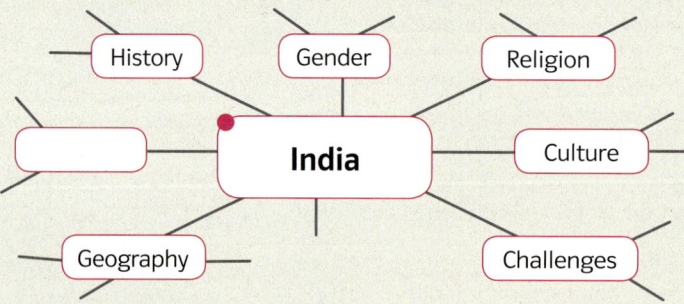

b) Prepare a short talk using your mind map. Think about the structure of your talk. Put the ideas in the order you want to talk about them.

Phrasal verbs

3 Combine the verbs and prepositions to form phrasal verbs you can find in this topic. The preposition gives the verb a new meaning. Write five sentences about India with them. Use passive constructions if necessary.

> up on • out • for • down • out of • into • up • off • around • on with • on • up for

1. to give ▭ (saving)
2. to squeeze ▭ (an income)
3. to account ▭ (one third of the population)
4. to call ▭ (wealthy countries to do more)
5. to cut ▭ (poverty)
6. to drop ▭ (school)
7. to bump ▭ (people)
8. to give ▭ (= stop trying)
9. to force ▭ (by revolution)
10. to step ▭ (to make a speech)
11. to grow ▭ (a role)
12. to take ▭ (shoes)
13. to dress ▭ (as a cowboy)
14. to look ▭ (a room)
15. to hold sb ▭ (as the epitome of a good husband)
16. to bring sb ▭ (to be an obedient wife)
17. to get ▭ (living)
18. to play ▭ (the entire cycle of life)
19. to keep ▭ (turning)
20. to speak ▭ (your rights)

TIP

First work on the vocab sheets; then test yourself here!

Topic task

India 10

Organising an Indian literature festival

In this topic you have come across a number of fictional text extracts written in English by Indian authors such as Amitav Ghosh or Vikas Swarup. The history and culture of India is brought to life in the characters of these stories.
In 2005 the Jaipur Literature Festival was founded. Each January readers and writers make a pilgrimage to Jaipur for five days of readings and dialogue.
Now organise your own small festival of Indian literature in your English course.

STEP 1   Choosing a novel
Perhaps one of the extracts you have read in this topic has made you curious and you would like to read the whole novel, or you have other novels about India you would like to read and present.

STEP 2   Choosing what to present
Decide what it is that you would like to present to your audience about the novel you have read. Choose a short passage from it to read aloud. Note down why you have chosen this extract and what it tells the reader about India. Perhaps it illustrates an aspect of one of the themes you have worked with here, or you simply want to talk about the story, its characters and the way the story is told.

STEP 3   Planning your contribution
As a speaker you have ten minutes to present your novel, read a passage aloud and maybe give the audience an opportunity to ask questions. You could also have a discussion with a partner about a novel you have both read. Whatever you do, plan and structure your contribution with the time limit in mind. Prepare notes to assist you in each part of your presentation.

STEP 4   Entering your contribution in the festival programme
You must enter the title, give a brief description of what you are going to do and choose a time slot (ten-minute intervals).
The class will be divided up into two groups and two talks will take place simultaneously so you will have to choose which talk you wish to attend when the programme is finalised.

STEP 5   Rehearsing
Rehearse your contribution at home or with a partner. While rehearsing, keep a watch or timer at hand and check whether your talk is the right length.

STEP 6   Holding your literature festival
Hold your Indian Literature Festival in your English course. One student opens the festival and another holds a closing speech on 'How can fiction help to develop intercultural understanding?' which will be followed by an open discussion. Here it will help to look back at what you have learnt about India while working on this topic.

Hinweis
Anschließend kann die Lektüre eines englischsprachigen Werks aus Indien erfolgen

11 The media
Introduction

Code
2ta7fs

Commuters reading the newspaper on their way to work on a train

Passer-by taking a photo of an accident

Photographers trying to take a photo of an important person

"The media's the most powerful entity on earth. They have the power to make the innocent guilty and to make the guilty innocent, and that's power. Because they control the minds of the masses."

Malcolm X (1925–1965),
African American minister and human rights activist

"The question isn't, 'What do we want to know about people?', it's, 'What do people want to tell about themselves?'"

Mark Zuckerberg (born 1984),
US computer programmer and founder of Facebook

1922 the BBC (British Broadcasting Company) is formed and the first radio broadcasts are given

1923 *Time Magazine* launches in the US, the first news magazine

1936 the BBC Television Service opens, the first broadcaster in the world to produce a high definition television service

1953 Queen Elizabeth II's coronation is watched by over 20 million people on live television across Europe – the Age of Television is ushered in

1971 first e-mail sent between two computers

1973 first cell phone

1980 CNN launches the first 24-hour news station

1 VISUALS *Describe each picture and say what aspect of media consumption or what trend they represent.* → S28.1 **Geeignete Methode:** Group puzzle

2 ANALYSIS
a) *Explain why the milestones marked along the timeline are important in the development of the media.*
b) ***Think:*** *Find other important milestones.* ***Pair:*** *Brainstorm your ideas with a partner.* ***Share:*** *Discuss your ideas in class.*

Typical family life in the past

Skydivers using a camera, a smart watch and a tablet PC

Astronaut taking a self-portrait

"What the mass media offers is not popular art, but entertainment which is intended to be consumed like food, forgotten, and replaced by a new dish."

W.H. Auden (1907–1973), Anglo-American poet

"You are what you share."

Charles Leadbeater, leading authority on innovation and creativity

1985
Live Aid, a rock concert to raise money for famine relief in Ethiopia, is one of the largest-scale satellite link-ups and TV broadcasts of all time – with around 400 million viewers in 60 different countries

1993
the World Wide Web is made available to everyone

1997
there are one million websites; blogging begins

2001
Wikipedia launches

2004
Facebook launches

2005
YouTube goes live

2006
Wikileaks starts

2007
Apple releases first iPhone (smartphone)

2011
activists organise an uprising in Egypt with the help of social networking sites

2012
the London Olympics – first 3D Games with live coverage available in HD, on tablets, mobiles, radio and TV

2013
social media is a major source of information about the Boston Marathon bombing

3 LANGUAGE In pairs, create a tag cloud around the word "media". Compare your results in class. **Geeignete Methode** zur Präsentation und Auswertung: Gallery walk

4 CREATIVE TASK Imagine you had to give up using your phone and the internet for a day. Describe how this would change and impact your daily routine.

5 SPEAKING
a) Read the quotes above and explain in your own words what is meant.
b) Choose the quote that you find the most interesting, and say why this is the case.

Zusatzmaterial WB
Task 1: Collocations
Tasks 6–7: Listening

181

Spot on facts

Developments in the media

Media in the twentieth century

In the twentieth century people kept up with the news by reading print media such as newspapers and periodicals, listening to the radio or watching the news on television. Newspapers came in two main formats: 'broadsheets', generally quality newspapers, and 'tabloids', mainly popular newspapers. Quality newspapers tended to have longer, more in-depth articles and presented information in a factual, less sensational manner.

The tabloids were known for their scandalmongering, celebrity gossip and subjective style. They used attention-grabbing headlines, often using puns, and had more visual content. However, most of the quality newspapers in the UK are now published in a tabloid format, and the differences in the journalistic style are not as pronounced as they used to be.

Television was one of the most important inventions of the twentieth century, as it was not only an important source of news and information but also entertainment. In the beginning there were only a few channels, but cable TV, then satellite TV greatly increased their number, giving people more freedom of choice, such as live coverage of sporting events, current affairs programmes, documentaries, popular science programmes, dramas, soaps and sitcoms, panel games, quiz shows and reality TV shows.

Traditional news sources, such as TV, radio and print newspapers, are increasingly being replaced by digital and online news sources. In fact, more Americans now access the news via the latter and often no longer turn to traditional sources.

The changing face of the media

The beginning of the twenty-first century saw great changes in the media landscape, as the rise of digital technologies has fundamentally changed how we communicate with each other. Online and perhaps more importantly mobile media have created new opportunities for us to become actively involved in sharing, remixing, and creating new content, so-called user-generated content. We are now able to participate in the news gathering process and can help to spread stories around the world. Stories are now often broken on social media websites and people give eyewitness reports from hotspots around the world. Directly after the Boston marathon bombings in 2013, ordinary people continually updated the world on what was going on, using their smartphones to take and post photos on social-networking sites. Journalists and news agencies can also now use crowdsourcing to ensure that they have access to all kinds of personalised content. One of the dangers with this approach is the lack of control regarding copyright, especially as some people seem unaware that infringing copyright or even committing piracy is a crime.

Where people got news yesterday (in millions)

- Watched news on TV — 55
- Any digital news — 50
- Read a newspaper — 39
- Listened to radio news — 33
- Got online/mobile news — 29

PEW Research Center for the People and the Press

"It's a newspaper! Bought it online for me dad's birthday. Apparently it's the forerunner of the tablet."

1 ANALYSIS Where did you get your news yesterday? Do a quick survey of the people in your class and compare your findings to those presented in the graph above. → S27

Social media and politics

Social media has gained importance as a forum for politics and political activism. Platforms such as Twitter, YouTube and Facebook have dramatically changed the way elections are run in many countries. They provide new ways for politicians to reach out to the electorate, especially to younger voters. By analysing the information collected on such platforms, a campaign can be customised to address the needs of a particular target group. In addition these platforms also offer politicians immediacy, so they can instantaneously find out how people respond to certain ideas or even controversies. One of the main advantages is that politicians no longer have to solely rely on the mass media to get their message to the people as they can connect with them directly in a more personal and faster way. An advantage for the public is that like-minded voters and activists can now easily share news and information with each other on Facebook or on Twitter.

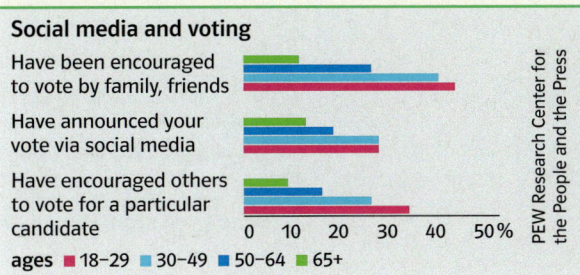

Social media platforms have also enabled people to draw attention to politically charged situations. In some cases when governments have tried to block democratic processes and banned journalists from entering their country during times of unrest, local citizens have continued to share their stories in real-time via social networking sites.

"Whatever technology comes and goes, the ability of a candidate or, for that matter, a brand to connect with people and show the people that they respect them and are about them and want to empower them is going to be increasingly important to the outcome because people aren't going to tolerate anything less. There's going to be a competitor who does respect that stuff and who does get that stuff."

Teddy Goff, Digital Director for President Obama's 2012 election campaign

Advertising

Advertising has been around for centuries. People are used to seeing adverts on billboards, on television or in newspapers. Increasingly, however, consumers are being bombarded with emails and online adverts that have been specially customised according to the user's search history and digital footprint. Viral marketing and crowdsourcing are now popular with advertisers as they can get consumers to spread the message and share their experiences. They also often recruit celebrities to endorse products or to mention them on their social media sites.

Advertisers are always looking to find interesting and innovative ways to advertise their products without doing so overtly, so-called covert advertising. One way is through infotisement: articles that seem to provide readers with news or information but that are really trying to sell a product or brand related to the story. Crucially these articles are written by advertisers and not by journalists. Advertainment combines advertising with entertainment and includes product placement in films or TV shows, but also specially developed short films by film directors around a product. In some cases they are also using transmedia storytelling (across different media) to connect with consumers in a more engaging and immersive way.

2 VISUALS Describe and analyse the cartoons. Explain their relevance to the topic. → S28.2 → △1
Diff (help with): Vorgabe von Stichwörtern   **Hinweis:** Auch als Hausaufgabe geeignet

Core skill workshop

Analysing visuals

There are many different kinds of visuals: photographs, cartoons, advertisements, infographics, diagrams, paintings and drawings. Yet they all have one thing in common: A visual can either accompany a text or stand alone and seek to convey a message. It is often more effective than a text, as it can provoke an immediate emotional response. Like a text, a visual can also be analysed and interpreted. Before you start talking, have a close look at the visual and collect your thoughts.

Part A Photos → S28.1

La Fallas, Valencia

There are many different kinds of photographs. Some are staged, others are snap shots and so seem more natural. Others document something as realistically as possible. When you do a task with a photograph, think about whether the visual is effective; if so, what can account for its effect? Is it timeless or does it speak to a particular group of people at a particular point in time?

FACT FILE

Las Fallas is a traditional festival in Valencia that takes place in March every year. The high point is the burning of the 'fallas' (large puppets made by local artists which are burned on a massive bonfire). There are also firework displays.

Zusatzmaterial WB
Task 2: Describing visuals

1 VISUALS Look at the photo and the fact file. Then read through the following description and rewrite it. Focus on the most important aspects first and add details to make it sound more interesting. Use suitable connectives.

> There is a building in the background. There are flames and sparks. On the left there is a big puppet. There are people holding mobile phones in the air. They are filming something. We cannot see the people's faces, only arms and hands. There is a lot of smoke and it is nighttime.

2 ANALYSIS Decide which statement best answers each question. Justify your answer.

1. What message is conveyed by the photo?
   a) The photographer is making a statement about the prevalence of mobile phones in our society today.
   b) The photographer is documenting an important local tradition.
2. Is it aimed at a particular target group?
   a) The photograph will appeal to people who are interested in travel.
   b) The photograph will interest people who take photos with their phones, especially young people.

3 EVALUATION Answer the following questions:

1. Does the photo succeed in getting its message across? Why (not)?
2. Which elements contribute to its success or failure?
3. Where might you expect to see a photo like this?

Part B Cartoons → S28.2

A cartoon is a witty drawing that criticises and pokes fun at a current event, a person, an institution or a development in society or politics. It often also has a title, caption or speech bubble, so make sure you take the combination of text and drawing into account. The following devices are often used to get the message across: exaggeration, irony, puns, symbols or a marked contrast between the picture and text. Consider the context in which it was made (i. e. when it was drawn, whether it is connected to a particular event or person, where it first appeared) and any associations it evokes. Remember, cartoons are not always funny, or not everyone will find them amusing. If you do not think it is, you should say so but always justify your opinion!

4 VISUALS *Order the following sentences describing the cartoon in a manner that makes sense. Decide whether you think all of the sentences provide necessary information.* **Geeignete Methode:** Think – Pair – Share

- It is a nice day as the sky is blue.
- The man holding the e-reader is wearing a green shirt and purple trousers.
- The man with the e-reader is asking the other man how the story ends because his e-reader's battery is dead.
- The men have their backs to each other, although the man with the e-reader is turning his head towards the other man.
- The print book has a red cover.
- The cartoon deals with the issue of print books versus e-books.
- The man with the print book seems to be engrossed in what he is reading.
- The man holding the print book is wearing grey trousers and a white shirt.
- Both men are wearing glasses.
- They are both reading: one man is reading a print book, the other one is holding an e-reader.
- Two men are sitting on either end of a bench in a park.

USEFUL PHRASES

Talking about cartoons

The cartoon is from … (source, if given) and deals with … (theme)

The cartoonist is poking fun at/making fun of …

The cartoon ridicules/mocks …

The speech bubble/thought bubble …

On a superficial/deeper/figurative level …

The style is realistic/tongue-in-cheek/humorous/sarcastic …

Zusatzmaterial WB
Task 5: Speaking

5 ANALYSIS *Create a grid like the one below and add the missing information.*

What is being criticised?	…
Which details contribute to this?	…
What devices are used?	…
Target group?	…
Do you agree with the message? Give reasons.	…

Core skill workshop

Part C Advertisements → S31

USEFUL PHRASES

Talking about visuals with text

The text was not what I expected…

The message is clear/ veiled/surprising/unusual/ confusing…

The font colour is the same as that of the logo. This creates a … impression.

The layout is very straightforward/unusual/ eye-catching.

The different elements are visually pleasing/ juxtaposed to create a sense of …

The advertisement/poster is trying to shock/ is very memorable/ is eye-catching because …

Advertisements usually combine a striking image with a slogan and/or text to persuade the viewer to buy a product or support a particular cause. When analysing an advert it's important not only to take the individual elements into account but also the layout and the way they complement each other.

6 VISUALS *Deal with the following points to come up with a description of the advert.*

1. Identify the organisation behind the advertisement and briefly state what it does.
2. How are the different elements (text, picture) arranged? What is the viewer's eye drawn to first?
3. State how the picture and text are related.
4. Point out any similarities between the text and the logo.
5. Describe the picture – what kind of shot is used and what elements does it contain?
6. Explain how colour is used in the advertisement and its significance.
7. Examine the way in which white space is used in the advert and what effect this creates.
8. What kind of language is used? Is it straightforward and informative, or is it persuasive and trying to create an emotional response in the viewer, or does it combine elements of both?
9. What information does the advert provide about its 'product'?

7 ANALYSIS

a) *Decide which of the following statements best sums up the message of the advertisement and say why.*

1. UNICEF is not a fan of Facebook and needs money to be able to vaccinate children.
2. UNICEF wants people to donate money and not merely "likes" so it can carry out its work.
3. A "like" on Facebook does not generate any money so UNICEF is not able to carry out its work.

b) *Collect ideas under the following headings: Target group? Effect the advert is meant to have on the viewer? How is this effect achieved?*

8 EVALUATION

a) *Discuss whether you think the advert has the intended effect or not.*
b) *Decide whether one particular element is responsible for its success or failure, and why.* → ▲2   Diff (after): Erstellen eines Werbeplakats für UNICEF

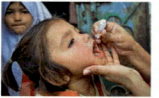

Texts The media 11

A Reality TV

1 BEFORE YOU READ
  a) Comment on the cartoon. → S28.2
  b) 👥 In pairs make a list of reality TV programmes you have seen or heard about. Briefly state the aim of each one. Compare your list with that of another pair.
  c) Discuss what all of these programmes have in common.

Reality TV: a ghastly plague upon modern society

The following blog post was written by James McLennan, a student at Reading University in Britain.

Reality TV made its first appearance in 1948 in the form of the show "Candid Camera". It was relatively harmless, merely showing people as themselves when
5 put into mildly comical situations, for example trying to work a broken water pump. Such good-natured humour left participants momentarily embarrassed but with their privacy and dignity intact. However, by 1973 with the production of a show called "An American Family" reality TV began to head down the road that's taken it to where it is today. PBS brought cameras into the home of Pat and Bill Loud,
10 filming them as they went about their daily lives for seven months. During this time viewers were able to live vicariously through the families' ups and downs, including when their son first declared himself gay.
  Today there are countless reality TV shows; from "Survivor" to "Big Brother", prime time television is plagued by an onslaught of voyeuristic TV. Some shows
15 are clearly more deplorable than others. "Joe Millionaire" for example puts a construction worker on dates with 20 women, all of them thinking he is a multimillionaire, the objective being to see if money really does matter. MTV, a channel that used to be associated with music videos, now fields more reality TV shows than most other channels. […]
20 It would seem that unlike in previous generations where TV shows such as "Father Knows Best" spoon-fed young people good morals, today's generation is instead getting an unhealthy dose of bad morals from the TV it watches. However, some would argue that today's young people are more media-savvy than their parents and know how to handle such exposure while not becoming overly
25 influenced by it. Nevertheless, young people are naturally impressionable and I find it hard to believe that they can be exposed to such extremes in culture at such a young age and not be affected. […]
  Perhaps one of the sicker ways that reality TV is shown is when a show becomes an extreme "voyeur-fest" of judgmental viewing. "Made" has young
30 people with dreams of greatness attempt to reach their goals through training with professionals while being filmed by a crew that tracks their progress. Sounds good, right? It would be if the producers would actually pick capable people to take part. Instead they choose those who are bound to fail so that we, the audience, may laugh at them. Apparently watching an obese girl trying to become a star
35 basketball player and then breaking down when she finds she can't, is good TV.
  With reality TV only soaring in popularity, people are set to think more about who should get voted off of Big Brother rather than who should get voted into Parliament. So what is it that compels people to watch these shows? Some researchers say that watching reality TV is a way for people to feel better about
40 their own lives. Supposedly they make one think, "I may be having a bad day, but

"I just hope I don't get voted off first."

11 **vicariously** experienced through the actions or feelings of another person
15 **deplorable** extremely bad

Texts

Still from a reality TV show

life is going better for me than for that bloke eating bugs." Others brand reality TV as "discomfort TV" rather than "comfort TV". They say that people merely welcome the opportunity to feel discomforted by what they see on the screen. I watched some myself before writing this article and found that reality TV is now such a big part of our society that knowing what's going on with the subjects on the show is a conversational boon between peers. One almost needs to know what's happened to the latest celebs on "Survivor" so as to take part in everyday conversation.

But just how real is reality TV? Cast members of "Survivor" have revealed that producers guided their statements during confessionals, controlled their consumption for product placement reasons, and refused to interfere even when violence became a concern. How much is scripted and controlled in these shows to produce dramatic effect? Sometimes it's obvious, but one is often left wondering just how much they script and yet pass off as real.

Reality TV allows us to look at others stuck in troublesome situations and judge them for ourselves. Sometimes those we see are just being put on the TV so that we may laugh at them. There is something fundamentally wrong with this idea. When I watch a comedy show I know it's OK to laugh when misfortune befalls a character because it's a comical situation that isn't really happening. But when I watch reality TV and witness laughter at the contestant who is encountering genuinely upsetting misfortune, I can't help but wonder if TV, and its viewers, has sunk to an all new low. Sadly, TV probably won't be rising above its newfound low anytime soon. Reality TV is not a fad like many had hoped, and will continue to be a success for many generations to come until, in all likelihood, something far worse replaces it.

James McLennan, *OpinionPanel* website, 2013

46 **boon** sth that is helpful, beneficial
50 **product placement** a kind of indirect advertising, when a company that makes a product pays to have it featured in a TV programme or film

2 COMPREHENSION
a) Would you 'share' or 'like' this blog post? Explain briefly why (not).
b)  Make a list of the criticisms that the author levels at reality TV programmes. Decide which of them you agree with and which of them you don't. Share and discuss your decisions with a partner.

3 ANALYSIS Examine the rhetorical devices the author uses to get his point across. → S4.2, S10.2 → ▲3 **Diff** (after): Analyse und Bewertung der Argumentationskette
Hinweis: Auch als Hausaufgabe geeignet

4 EVALUATION
Think: What motivates people to take part in reality TV shows? Note down your ideas.
Pair: Compare your ideas with your partner's.
Share: Discuss your ideas with the rest of the class.

5 CREATIVE TASK  You are producing a new reality TV show, for which you will need to cast certain 'types' of people to make it interesting.
a) In small groups decide what your show is about, then think of at least five different types that you will cast.
b) Write a short profile for each one, including character traits. → S7
c) Think of an attractive and interesting way to present your show and its cast to the rest of the class.
d) Organise a gallery walk – be prepared to answer questions and justify your choices. **Zusatzmaterial KV 1:** Evaluation sheet

Zusatzmaterial WB
Task 3: Synonyms

B The meaning of reality

1 BEFORE YOU READ *The following two extracts from contemporary novels deal with the topic of sharing in our digital society. Before you read them, brainstorm ideas with a partner about what information you share with other people and where you do so.* **Geeignete Methode:** Speed dating

Sharing is caring

The Circle *is a* dystopian *novel about a tech company with over a billion users that combines elements of Google and Facebook. Customers have one online identity, the 'TruYou', which links to a central operating system controlling their social media accounts, personal emails, banking and shopping. The idea behind this is*
5 *to create* transparency *and* civility *amongst users and to control and* monitor *their actions. In this extract, Mae, a young employee, is on the stage at a company meeting with Eamon Bailey, co-founder of the corporation. She is '*confessing*' to having stolen a kayak and gone sailing to Blue Island in the San Francisco Bay without telling anyone …*

10 "What did you see on this last trip, Mae? I understand it was quite beautiful."
"It was, Eamon. There was an almost-full moon, and the water was very calm, and I felt like I was paddling through liquid silver."
"Sounds incredible."
"It was."
15 "Animals? Wildlife?"
"I was followed for a while by a sole harbor seal, and he dipped above and below the surface, as if he was curious, and also urging me on. I'd never been to this island. Very few people have. And once I got to the island, I climbed to the top, and the view from the peak was incredible. I saw the golden lights of the city, and the
20 black foothills toward the Pacific, and even saw a shooting star."
"A shooting star! Lucky you."
"I was very lucky."
"But you didn't take a picture."
"No."
25 "Not any video."
"No."
"So there's no record of any of this."
There were audible groans from the audience. Bailey turned to the audience, shaking his head, indulging them.
30 "Okay," he said, sounding as if he were bracing himself, "now this is where we get into something personal. As you all know, I have a son, Gunner, who was born with CP, cerebral palsy. Though he's living a very full life, and we're trying, always, to improve his opportunities, he is confined to a wheelchair. He can't walk. He can't run. He can't go kayaking. So what does he do if he wants to experience something
35 like this? Well, he watches video. He looks at pictures. Much of his experiences of the world come through the experiences of others. And of course so many of you Circlers have been so generous, providing him with video and photos of your own travels. When he experiences the SeeChange view of a Circler climbing Mount Kenya, he feels like he's climbed Mount Kenya. When he sees firsthand video from
40 an America's Cup crew member, Gunner feels, in some way, that he's sailed in the America's Cup, too. These experiences were facilitated by generous humans who have shared what they saw with the world, my son included. And we can

16 **seal** *Robbe*
28 **groan** a low sound expressing pain, despair
29 **to indulge sb** to allow sb to enjoy sth
30 **to brace oneself** to get ready (for sth unpleasant)
41 **to facilitate sth** to make sth possible

189

Texts

VIP FILE

Dave Eggers (born 1970) is a US writer, editor and publisher. His work *A Heartbreaking Work of Staggering Genius* was a finalist for the renowned Pulitzer Prize in 2001 (general non-fiction).

46 **to deprive sb of sth** to prevent sb from having or enjoying sth
67 **aberrant** not what you would usually expect, unacceptable

only extrapolate how many others there are out there like Gunner. Maybe they're disabled. Maybe they're elderly, homebound. Maybe a thousand things. But the point is that there are millions of people who can't see what you saw, Mae. Does it feel right to have deprived them of seeing what you saw?"

Mae's throat was dry and she tried not to show her emotion. "It doesn't. It feels very wrong." Mae thought of Bailey's son Gunner, and thought of her own father.

"Do you think they have a right to see things like you saw?"

"I do."

"In this short life," Bailey said, "why shouldn't everyone see whatever it is they want to see? Why shouldn't everyone have equal access to the sights of the world? The knowledge of the world? All the experiences available in this world?"

Mae's voice was just above a whisper. "Everyone should."

"But this experience you had, you kept it to yourself. Which is curious, because you do share online. You work at the Circle. Your PartiRank is in the T2K. So why do you think this particular hobby of yours, these extraordinary explorations, why hide these from the world?"

"I can't quite figure out what I was thinking, to be honest," Mae said.

The crowd murmured. Bailey nodded.

"Okay. We just talked about how we, as humans, hide what we're ashamed of. We do something illegal, or unethical, and we hide it from the world because we know it's wrong. But hiding something glorious, a wonderful trip on the water, the moonlight coming down, a shooting star …"

"It was just selfish, Eamon. It was selfish and nothing more. The same way a child doesn't want to share her favorite toy. I understand that secrecy is part of, well, an aberrant behavior system. It comes from a bad place, not a place of light and generosity. And when you deprive your friends, or someone like your son Gunner, of experiences like I had, you're basically stealing from them. You're depriving them of something they have a right to. Knowledge is a basic human right. Equal access to all possible human experiences is a basic human right."

From: Dave Eggers, *The Circle*, 2013

Second-hand experiences

In the thriller Gone Girl *Nick and Amy Dunne have moved from New York to the small Midwestern town of North Carthage. One day Amy disappears, and it is not clear whether Nick has killed her or not. The town used to be dominated by a large mall, but the* recession *has meant it has* gone bankrupt.

The downfall of the mall basically bankrupted Carthage. People lost their jobs, they lost their houses. No one could see anything good coming anytime soon. *We never get to see the end*. Except it looked like this time Go and I would. We all would.

The bankruptcy matched my psyche perfectly. For several years, I had been bored. Not a whining, restless child's boredom (although I was not above that) but a dense, blanketing malaise. It seemed to me that there was nothing new to be discovered ever again. Our society was utterly, ruinously derivative (although the word *derivative* as a criticism is itself derivative). We were the first human beings who would never see anything for the first time. We stare at the wonders of the world, dull-eyed, underwhelmed. Mona Lisa, the Pyramids, the Empire State Building. Jungle animals on attack, ancient icebergs collapsing, volcanoes erupting. I can't recall a single amazing thing I have seen firsthand that I didn't immediately reference to a movie or TV show. A fucking commercial. You know the awful singsong of the blasé: *Seeeen it*. I've literally seen it all, and the worst thing, the

7 **Go** Margo, Nick's sister
8 **psyche** [ˈsaɪki]
10 **blanketing malaise** vague feeling of being ill, covering everything
11 **derivative** [dɪˈrɪvətɪv] made or formed from sth else without critical reflection

thing that makes me want to blow my brains out, is: the second-hand experience
20 is always better. The image is crisper, the view is keener, the camera angle and the soundtrack manipulate my emotions in a way reality can't anymore. I don't know that we are actually human at this point, those of us who are like most of us, who grew up with TV and movies and now the Internet. If we are betrayed, we know the words to say; when a loved one dies, we know the words to say. If we want to play
25 the stud or the smart-ass or the fool, we know the words to say. We are all working from the same dog-eared script.

It's a very difficult era in which to be a person, just a real, actual person, instead of a collection of personality traits selected from an endless automat of characters.

And if all of us are play-acting, there can be no such thing as a soul mate,
30 because we don't have genuine souls.

It had gotten to the point where it seemed like nothing matters, because I'm not a real person and neither is anyone else.

I would have done anything to feel real again.

From: Gillian Flynn, *Gone Girl*, 2012

Zusatzmaterial WB
Task 4: Relative clauses
Tasks 8–13: Reading and writing
Task 14: Mediation

25 **stud** (*infml*) sexually attractive man
25 **smart-ass** (*AE, infml*) sb who behaves in an annoying way, trying to show how clever they are

Leopard

The Pyramid of Cheops (also known as the Great Pyramid of Giza or The Pyramid of Khufu)

Volcanic eruption

Empire State Building, New York City

2 COMPREHENSION
a) Read through both extracts. Say which one you enjoyed most, and why.
b) Sum up each text in a few sentences.
c) Which of the following statements about the extract from *Gone Girl* are true? Find the relevant passage in the text to back up your answer. → ▲4
Diff (after): Analyse von Nicks Einstellung bezüglich der Welt, in der er lebt
- Nick is bored because he thinks that he will never see anything through fresh eyes.
- Nick thinks that seeing things through other people's eyes is better than reality.
- Life is better as we know how to behave because we have experienced similar things on the internet and on TV.

3 ANALYSIS   **Hinweis:** Auch als Hausaufgabe geeignet
a) Analyse the way in which Mae is characterised. → S7
b) Examine the narrative perspective of both texts. → S8

4 LANGUAGE Choose one of the texts and examine the style and language used. Make notes and present your findings to the class. → S10 → △5
Diff (help with): Vorgabe von Impulsfragen und Zitaten

5 EVALUATION Using the two texts as a starting point, discuss the pros and cons of sharing experiences online.   **Geeignete Methode:** Fishbowl discussion

6 SPEAKING Hold a mobile debate on the following quotation from *The Circle*, "Equal access to all possible human experiences is a basic human right". → S24

FACT FILE

Mobile debate
In this kind of debate, you move from one side of the classroom to the other to show which side you support. First write the motion (topic) on the board with 'for' on the left and 'against' on the right. Now decide whether you are 'for' or 'against' the motion and move to the appropriate side of the room. After this, you each present arguments to support your side. If an argument is particularly persuasive, you may change sides.

Advanced texts

Zusatzmaterial WB
Task 15: Paraphrasing

⁶ **paywall** part of a website that can only be accessed by paid subscribers
⁷ **commitment to sth** strong belief in sth
¹² **to bash in** (*infml*) to knock down
¹² **Occupy** international protest movement against social and economic inequality
¹³ **swine** pigs
¹⁴ **to frame sb** to make it look as if sb is guilty (of a crime)
¹⁵ **mortgage** [ˈmɔːgɪdʒ] Hypothek

FACT FILE

The *Three Little Pigs* is an English fairy tale, in which the pigs are threatened by a "big, bad wolf". So they each build a house: one of straw, another of sticks and the other of bricks. The wolf is able to blow down the first two houses but not the last one. So he tries to get in through the chimney, but ends up in a pot of boiling water.

C Journalism in the twenty-first century

1 BEFORE YOU READ Discuss what the term 'open journalism' might mean.

Open journalism

If there is one newspaper that has stood apart from the crowd in terms of its eagerness to embrace a digital-media world, it is the *Guardian* in Britain. The paper was one of the first to make user-generated content – and crowdsourcing – a key part of its business, and it was also one of the first to try to turn itself into a truly open platform for data sharing. Now, in what appears to be a response to the wave of paywall-ism that is sweeping the newspaper industry, editor Alan Rusbridger has launched a new campaign aimed at reinforcing the *Guardian's* commitment to "open journalism," an approach that he says is the only real option for media in the digital era.

The centerpiece of the campaign is a great video that reimagines the story of the *Three Little Pigs* as a modern morality tale, from the opening scene – in which riot police bash in the door of the third little pig's row house – to the Occupy-style street demonstrations in support of the swine, and ultimately a courtroom battle that sees the pigs admit to destroying their own homes in an attempt to frame the Big Bad Wolf, because they were unable to make their mortgage payments. Throughout the clip there are people commenting on Facebook, posting to Twitter with hashtags and uploading videos.

Mathew Ingram, *Gigaom*, 2012

2 COMPREHENSION   **Hinweis:** Auch als Hausaufgabe geeignet
a) Describe how the *Guardian* has made use of new technology.
b) How does the *Guardian* use a fairy tale to sell its idea of 'open journalism'?

3 CREATIVE TASK 👥 The pictures below are stills from the commercial for the newspaper mentioned above. How might the story unfold? Brainstorm your ideas in pairs.

11 The media

Citizen journalists

There are three key reasons that we should be wary about what citizen journalists write, publish and upload.

    Firstly, bias. As someone that studied history, I know that bias is evident in anything we say, write or do – whether we know it or not. Professional journalists are trained to understand both sides of a story and (as much as possible) divorce bias from what they are writing. It is why the majority of stories have quotes for and against a subject in them, even if the overall tone is slanted to left or right. Citizen journalists don't have this training and may well have an axe to grind – potentially making their reports unreliable, whether consciously or not.

    Second, the law. […] Again, journalists are trained to understand libel law and what can and can't be said. Reddit's coverage of the Boston Marathon bombing demonstrated what can happen when citizen journalists are given an unpoliced platform. The site's Find Boston Bombers thread wrongly accused several people of being involved in the atrocity, leading to harassment of their families and potentially slowing down the police investigation. In today's instant news cycle, where an unsubstantiated tweet can be front-page news in seconds, there's a real issue with potentially malicious or unthinking reports quickly making it into the mainstream news.

    Finally, there's the area of copyright. Lots of news sites now actively encourage you to upload your pictures, video and text to give added perspective on news and features. The latest, the *Guardian's* Witness site, provides the chance to contribute to live news and other content through a smartphone app. Content is vetted before going onto the site, with stories and videos made available to journalists for potentially developing into bigger pieces. All great, except that as soon as you post your prized video, the *Guardian* gets an unconditional, perpetual and worldwide licence to use it as it sees fit. You may still retain the copyright, but the paper can commercially exploit the content however it wants.

    Controlling how news is reported and disseminated is inextricably linked to power. Hence why dictatorships have always censored or removed the free press and run state TV stations with a rod of iron. While much of the western world has moved on from that, media is often controlled by a certain group, making citizen journalism a vital part of the opening up of reporting to everyone. But if it is to truly make a lasting impact for good, citizen journalists need to understand their own responsibilities when it comes to bias, the law and copyright and act accordingly.

Chris Measures, *Measures Consulting*, 2013

---

3 **bias** (unfair) prejudice for or against one person or group
5 **to divorce sth from sth** to separate sth from sth else
8 **to have an axe to grind** to have a strong personal reason for doing sth
10 **libel** *Verleumdung*
11 **Boston Marathon bombing** in 2013 two bombs exploded near the finishing line of the race, killing 3 people and injuring over 260 others
12 **unpoliced** not checked to make sure that sth is done correctly
14 **atrocity** cruel and violent act
14 **harassment** act of systematically annoying or worrying sb
17 **malicious** unkind and seeking to hurt sb
22 **to vet** to thoroughly check
25 **unconditional** total, without any restrictions
25 **perpetual** eternal, everlasting
26 **to retain** to keep
27 **to exploit** *here:* to make the best use of
28 **to disseminate** to spread
30 **with a rod of iron** very strictly

---

4 COMPREHENSION
  a) Does the author generally support or reject citizen journalism? Justify your answer. **Hinweis:** Auch als Hausaufgabe geeignet
  b) Point out the arguments presented against citizen journalism.

5 ANALYSIS With a partner examine the means the author uses to present his arguments. Then discuss your findings with the whole class. → S4.2

6 VIEWING Watch the interviews with Ian Katz and Becky Gardiner. In your own words explain how they say open journalism works.

7 EVALUATION Write a short essay (300–400 words) on the following topic: "Citizen journalists will soon replace professional journalists." → S14
Zusatzmaterial KV 2: Hilfestellung durch die Vorgabe von Kriterien

Zusatzmaterial WB
Task 16: Vocabulary building

Advanced texts

Avoiding mistakes
Wortschatz
[19] **caution** alertness in order to avoid danger or mistakes NICHT ~~Kaution~~

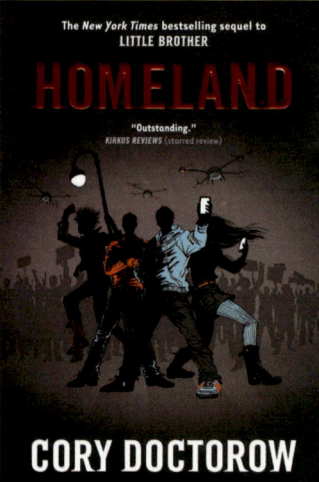

FACT FILE

Homeland is the sequel to *Little Brother*, which is set in San Francisco in the near future. Following a terrorist attack, the city is turned into a police state by the Department for Homeland Security. Marcus, a 17-year-old hacker, and his friends Darryl, Van and Jolu fight against this, and Marcus becomes a hacker hero.

[12] **Barbara Stratford** *a journalist who helped Marcus in* Little Brother *when he was kidnapped by Carrie Johnstone*
[13] **darknet** *website that is anonymous and those who use it also remain anonymous*
[16] **muckraking** *looking for and finding real or supposed corruption, scandal or wrongdoing*
[16] **journo** *(sl) journalist*
[17] **my folks** *(infml) my parents*
[41] **to slurp** *to drink noisily, here: to assimilate*

D The whistle-blower

Hinweis
Die Erstbegegnung mit dem Text als Hörverstehen gestalten

1 BEFORE YOU READ Look at the cover for Cory Doctorow's novel *Homeland*. What do you think the novel might be about? Does the cover make you want to read the book? Why (not)?

L2/12 **Marcus's dilemma**

In Cory Doctorow's novel Homeland *California's economy has collapsed and Marcus Yallow, the 19-year-old narrator and a former hacktivist, is a webmaster for a politician seeking election and promising reform. Masha, a girl from Marcus's past, gives Marcus a thumbdrive full of corporate secrets and incriminating evidence against the government. If she goes missing, he is to make the information public. After Masha has been kidnapped, Marcus is faced with a problem: He has to leak the information, but he can't admit to doing so, as that will cost his employer the election. In this extract he is discussing the problem with his girlfriend Ange, and friends Darryl, Van(essa), Jolu, and Jolu's colleague Kylie.*

"So what do you propose?" Darryl said. [...]
  "We tell it to the press. Mail a link to Barbara Stratford, anonymously, tell her how to access the darknet. Of all the journalists in the world, she's probably the most likely to be able to figure out how to use a Tor darknet site. And if she can't figure it out, she'll know lots of hairfaces who can help her out." Barbara Stratford was a muckraking journo who wrote for the *Bay Guardian*. She was an old friend of my folks', and had led the effort to spring me from the clutches of Carrie Johnstone's torturers. But she was a traditional print journalist with a lot to lose, and she moved with a lot of plodding caution.
  "That sounds *slow*," Darryl said. "What's she going to do, read all those docs, call up a second source to corroborate them, run it past legal, write a story, and file it for publication in next week's issue? We need this stuff to go live *now*."
  Ange opened her mouth to argue, but Jolu held a hand up. "No reason we can't do both. We tell your reporter friend about it, but we also post the darknet address where anyone can find it."
  "How?" I said. I'd been thinking about this. How do you publicize something while staying anonymous?
  Jolu shrugged. "Create a new Twitter account, use it from behind IPredator. Create a new Wordpress blog, do the same thing. Make a new Facebook identity, put it there, too."
  I shook my head. "That'll never work. Who pays attention to a Twitter account that's just been created?"
  "Well, you could retweet it, you've got thousands of followers. Or I could."
  "Yeah, and I could just make a blinking EL wire sign that says 'That anonymous account? It's really me.'"
  "Good point," Darryl said. "So we find someone we trust, and ask that person to ask *their* friends to big it up, link to it, retweet it, friend it, whatever. Make it hard to trace it back."
  Now Jolu was shaking his head. "Sorry, dude. Remember that they'll be doing this on social networks -- you know, places where they've conveniently laid out lists of all their friends for the whole world to see. All you do is, slurp up all those contacts, check to see which contact *they* have in common, and there you go, a convenient list of high-probability suspects to spy on or assassinate with your aerial drones."

Darryl shut up and glared at the table. Jolu stayed cool. "Sorry, man, but you
45 know, it's just *reality*. It's not convenient, but it's real."
Through this all, Van had been hanging back a little, not really seeming to be engaged with us. Now she said, "Kylie, Jolu says you're the smartest person he knows, and he's a smart guy. So what do you think we should do?"
"Well, let me start by saying this is a hard problem. Maybe *the* hard problem
50 today. You've got the same problem anyone who wants to attract attention to a product or a cause has. This is what every politician faces, everyone who makes soda-pop or opens a restaurant, everyone who wants to sell a record or get people to come to their little league games. It's the reason that ad agencies and marketing companies exist, it's the basis for billions of dollars in business every year. And
55 you've got the additional complications of wanting to make this stuff happen in a hurry, and of not wanting anyone to know who's behind it. What I mean to say here is, you're doing something *hard*.
"Now, all that said, there's at least two important things going for you here: First, you're *good*, you know a lot about computers and networks and people and
60 technology. And second, you've got a great 'product' to 'sell.' I've been in those docs, I know the kind of dynamite you're sitting on. You're not trying to get people to give a damn about yet another flavor of sugar water. You want to tell people about a trove of some genuinely explosive material, a pile of information plutonium that you've dug up in the government's backyard. There's a certain intrinsic interest
65 in this stuff, you know, and it's the kind of thing that people might enjoy telling each other about.
"I think our best strategy is going to be sending out messages from our new account, messages to anyone we can think of with any political clout or a lot of followers or a big platform of some description. Your basic, 'Hey, mister, look what
70 I've got,' message. Most of these people are going to ignore us, initially at least, because they get a bazillion of these every day, from con artists and spammers and PR people and nutcases. But we've got to think like dandelions here."

From: Cory Doctorow, *Homeland*, 2013

VIP FILE

Cory Doctorow (born in 1971) is a Canadian-British science-fiction author, activist, journalist and blogger, as well as being the co-editor of *Boing Boing*, an online magazine "devoted to the weird, wonderful and wicked things to be found in technology and culture".

⁵³ **little league game** baseball game for young people
⁶⁸ **clout** weight
⁷¹ **bazillion** a large indeterminate number
⁷¹ **con artist** a person who exploits others
⁷² **dandelion** Löwenzahn

TIP

A **whistle-blower** is a person who informs on an individual, organisation or government that they believe is engaging in illegal or immoral activities. They might also publicly disclose these activities.

2 COMPREHENSION
 a) *Describe the problem Marcus is facing.* **Hinweis:** Auch als Hausaufgabe geeignet
 b) *Outline the solution the friends come up with, and the reason behind it.*

3 LISTENING
 a) *Speculate on the meaning of the dandelion image at the end.*
 ⓒ L2/13
 b) *Listen to the recording and explain what Kylie means.*

4 ANALYSIS *Examine the language and style of the extract.* → S5.2, S10
Geeignete Methode zur weiteren Analyse: Freeze frame

5 SPEAKING *The extract questions the role of journalists. In small groups discuss the following topic: "Journalists no longer have an important role to play in modern society – they have been replaced by bloggers".* → △6
Diff (help with): Vorgabe von möglichen Aspekten

6 VISUALS *Look at the cartoon on the right and analyse the point of view it represents.* → S28.2

7 EVALUATION *Write an argumentative essay on the following topic: "Whistle-blowers make the world a safer place."* → S14.1
Hinweis: Zitat kann auch als Ausgangspunkt für eine mündliche Diskussion dienen

THE WHISTLE BLOWER'S WHISTLE

Zusatzmaterial WB
Task 17: Reported speech

Advanced texts

E Etiquette, ethics and the media

1 BEFORE YOU READ Has anyone ever annoyed you with their mobile phone use? Describe the situation to a partner and discuss how best to react.

Mobile phone use by many is outrageously rude

Seriously. If you want to come round and visit me, put your bloody phone away. I'm not sitting here checking my email, replying to it, or chatting with people on Facebook – or even worse, answering phone calls – whilst you're here, so I would appreciate it if you could mind your manners and actually act like you appreciate being with me for a while.

And if you say, "I'm not doing any of those, I'm just sending a few texts", it amounts to the same damned thing. It'll piss me off because it's rude and I've got better things to do than sit here and wait for you whilst you keep interrupting our conversation because you think it's more important for you to communicate with others.

I have set aside time to sit and talk with you, to hear what's going on in your life, and if you're remotely interested in what's going on for me, you can ask and I'll tell you. I did not invite you over or agree to spend time with you so I could watch you play with your bloody phone.

I promise, the Earth will not stop revolving and you will not die if you put that stupid thing away or shut it off whilst you are in my company. That doesn't mean put it on silent so it vibrates and you can keep checking every time some text or other lets you know it's arrived. Do you think I'm blind and I can't see you glancing at your phone? Are your other friends more important whilst you're with me? Is what you're texting/emailing/Facebooking about more important than I am at that time? If so, go home and quit wasting my time. If not, turn the bloody thing off and let's talk.

What the hell did people do before emails and texting and mobiles anyway? Do you think everyone shrivelled up and died when they went to visit someone for a couple of hours and people couldn't get in touch with them?

I'm insanely busy. I have tons of stuff to be doing. My time is valuable and if I'm giving you my undivided attention, the least you can do is respect that and show me the same courtesy. If you don't think I deserve the same respect from you, then stay home.

Liberty Forrest, *Huffington Post UK*, 2014

Wortschatz
³**whilst** *formal, especially BE* while

2 COMPREHENSION Outline what the author is upset about.

3 ANALYSIS
  a) Examine the style and tone of this blog post, the effect the author is trying to create and how successful she is. → S4.2, S10.1
  b) Speculate about the target group she is writing for.

4 CREATIVE TASK
  a) In groups think of five 'golden rules' for using your mobile phone. Choose your target group and then decide how best to get your message across: in an amusing, serious or maybe tongue-in-cheek manner. **Geeignete Methode:** Placemat
  b) Design a poster, an online advert or a short spot to present your "golden rules for mobile phone use".
  Geeignete Methode zur Präsentation und Auswertung: Gallery walk

Zusatzmaterial WB
Task 18: Conditionals
Task 19: Describing the tone of a text

Phubbing

Online safety

5 ANALYSIS
  a) Look at adverts 1 and 2 and explain the term 'phubbing'. **Hinweis:** Auch als Hausaufgabe geeignet
  b) Describe and compare the adverts. Which one do you find more effective?

6 SPEAKING Hold a mobile debate on the following topic: "Mobile phones should be banned in public places." → S24

7 ANALYSIS Compare the two adverts 3 and 4 in terms of their message, content and effectiveness.

8 SPEAKING Discuss what other advice you would have on how to behave online.

Zusatzmaterial WB
Task 5: Speaking

Advanced texts

F The power of transmedia

The death of a friend

> **Avoiding mistakes**
> Wortschatz
> ⁸**eventually** after a long time, finally
> **NICHT** eventuell

Anna Heath was the mother of three children and a brilliant languages professor. She was also a fictional character – part of the game *Perplex City*, which was a two-year-long treasure hunt developed by UK games company Mind Candy that attracted tens of thousands of players and sold more than a million puzzle cards.

One night in late June 2006, Anna disappeared. Her colleagues desperately tried to put together the pieces of where she had last been seen and by whom. Her husband appealed to the public for something, anything, that would ensure her safe return home. But it was all for nothing. The search for Anna eventually turned up her body in the catacombs beneath the city. She had been brutally tortured and murdered while investigating a series of thefts from the academy where she was employed.

The audience was devastated by her loss. They reported feeling as if they'd been punched in the gut, that they hadn't seen it coming, that they were surprised at the depth of grief they felt for an imaginary person.

Heartfelt condolence emails to all the other characters in the game flooded in. Players even cast about for a real-world way to honour Anna's memory. Together, some audience members folded 333 origami cranes (a number that had special significance in the world of *Perplex City*), and a group of them personally delivered the cranes to Mind Candy's London office.

Characters die in fiction all the time, of course, and audiences are often devastated by it. But in this case, their grief was made deeper by the feeling that Anna was a friend, not just a character. After all, they'd read her website and seen puzzles she had designed for her children to solve. They'd emailed her, and she had responded to them. Even worse, in the days leading up to her death, they had helped her to investigate a deadly secret society called the Third Power, and had even urged her to keep up her efforts. And, worst of all, they were the ones who had unwittingly sent her to her death that night.

They weren't merely sad – they felt personally responsible, because they had been complicit in her death. As Juxta on the online community Unfiction said, "That aching and seemingly bottomless little hole which has appeared, unbidden in the depths of your stomach as you heard this news? That would be guilt."

Any single-medium work can in theory make an audience laugh or cry. But make an audience feel directly involved in the events of a story? Whether we're talking about responsibility for sending a woman to her murder, or perhaps instead saving her life or introducing her to her future partner, you just can't evoke that feeling with a book or a movie.

This is the power of transmedia.

From: Andrea Philips, *A Creator's Guide to Transmedia Storytelling*, 2012

¹² **devastated** very shocked and upset
¹³ **to punch sb in the gut** to hit sb in the stomach
¹⁴ **grief** extreme sadness
²⁷ **unwittingly** not consciously or deliberately
²⁹ **complicit** involved in or knowing about sth bad (e.g. a crime)
³⁰ **unbidden** unexpectedly

1 COMPREHENSION
  a) Briefly describe the difference between the power of transmedia and that of a book or movie.   **Hinweis:** Auch als Hausaufgabe geeignet
  b) Note down everything we learn about the game *Perplex City*.
  c) How was the audience made to feel directly involved in the story? → ▲7
     Diff (after): Comment zu folgender Fragestellung: Should people get involved in virtual realities to such a degree as shown in the game *Perplex City*?

Transmedia and marketing

In the past, marketing campaigns delivered the same message across different media. But with the rise of digital and social media, a more effective way for advertisers to get their message across is through transmedia marketing campaigns. Today's consumers are attracted by adverts that feel like a story or
5 *game, so advertisers are creating new experiences for different platforms and tailoring them to their individual strengths. Campaigns are thus more complex, allowing more so-called points of entry, and this enables stronger emotional connections to be made with the target audience. The Wharton School of the University of Pennsylvania has an online business analysis journal, Knowledge@*
10 *Wharton. They interviewed Andrea Philips about transmedia. Here is an extract.*

WHARTON **We often see transmedia used in marketing campaigns, where the transmedia material is essentially an advertisement for another core product. Why is this a common approach to transmedia?**

PHILIPS I think that it has to do with an interesting shift happening in marketing
15 and advertising. There's a lot of talk about the attention economy, where we're in a flat-out war for attention. Marketers have cottoned to the idea that people aren't going to look at marketing just because you put it in front of them. People simply don't notice banner ads. Calling [the impact of a banner ad] an "impression" is a terrible lie, because it isn't making
20 an impression on anybody. You just tune it out. It might as well not exist. Marketers have started to realize they need to create content people will seek out because it has value to them, independent of the value to the marketer.

The Wharton School, University of Pennsylvania, 2012

16 **to cotton to sth** (AE, infml) to begin to like sth
18 **banner ads** small advertisements found on websites

2 COMPREHENSION Sum up the advantages of using transmedia for marketing.

3 RESEARCH The fantasy TV series *Game of Thrones* used a transmedia marketing campaign to create a pre-launch buzz around each season. Collect information about these campaigns. Share your findings in class and discuss how effective you find this kind of strategy.

4 CREATIVE TASK Think of a film or TV series that you have enjoyed. To what extent could a transmedia marketing campaign have made sense? Jot down your idea and then form small groups. Present your ideas to the group and be prepared to justify them. → **S22**

Spot on language

Hinweis
Selbstevaluation für Schüler über Green Line-Code

Using the definite and indefinite article

1 a) *The use of the definite and indefinite article is sometimes different in English and German. Complete the following rules concerning their usage in English. Find an example for each rule.*

1. ▨ is used when talking about professions and nationalities.
2. Institutions and means of transport are used ▨, unless a specific building or vehicle is meant.
3. If uncountable nouns (e.g. abstract nouns) are used in a general sense, ▨ is used.
4. Before singular names, even if there is an adjective before the name, there is ▨.
5. The indefinite article is placed ▨ words such as *half, what, quite* and *such*.
6. The definite article is placed ▨ words such as *half (of), both of, all (of)* and *twice*.

b) *Now read the following dialogue and correct any mistakes.*

A: What are you going to do when you leave the school?
B: I'm thinking of doing a course in media studies because I'd like to be journalist. What about you?
A: Well, I'm going to do work experience for a half year and then travel for a bit.
B: That sounds exciting. Whereabouts?

A: I'm going backpacking and travelling around India with the bus – I've always wanted to go there, ever since I saw a documentary about the life there. But I think it'll be a quite culture shock! And I'll also miss my friends!
B: Thank goodness for the smartphones! It's much easier to stay in contact with the people in the today's world.

Identifying adverbs and adjectives

2 a) *Briefly state the difference between adjectives and adverbs in English.*
b) *Draw up a grid and sort the following words according to whether they are adjectives or adverbs. In some cases the words are both, so write them in both of the columns:*

friendly • good • hard • late • ugly • unexpectedly • quite • early • well • often • quick • just • suddenly • always • long • obviously • lively • daily

c) *Choose five words and write a sentence with each of them, showing how the adjective or adverb is used in each case.*

3 *Look at the following pairs of adjectives and adverbs. What do you notice about them? What is the German equivalent of each word?*

hard – hardly • near – nearly • high – highly • late – lately • even – evenly • short – shortly

4 a) *Choose the correct word in each of the following sentences.*

1. Even though I live **near/nearly** my school, I **near/nearly** arrived too **late/lately** this morning as I was reading the latest news about the disaster.
2. **Late/Lately** I've noticed that adverts for certain products seem to be following me around the web.
3. I **hard/hardly** ever watch TV – I often just find it **hard/hardly** to find the time – but there's a new reality show in the US that's **high/highly** recommended. It's due to be broadcast in Germany **short/shortly**.

b) *Write two sentences of your own and give them to a partner to answer.*

Mediation

5 A British friend of yours has just written you an email telling you that he/she wants to take part in the casting show *Britain's got talent*. You have just read this article. Now write back, outlining the dangers as presented here. → **S26.1**

Zusatzmaterial KV 3: Vorlage für einen Fragebogen zu einer Umfrage in der Klasse

Du steckst in einer Seifenblase

Berühmt, dann bedeutungslos: Was Castingshows mit ihren Teilnehmern anstellen. Die langfristigen psychischen Auswirkungen auf Jugendliche wurden nun erstmals in einer Studie untersucht.

Ein Jugendlicher tritt bei „Deutschland sucht den Superstar" auf. Er singt ein paar Sekunden lang, dann unterbricht ihn Dieter Bohlen: Das, sagt er, sei „sehr, sehr, sehr, sehr, sehr schlecht" gewesen. Als sich der Junge anschließend verzweifelt auf den Boden wirft, setzt Bohlen nach, er solle jetzt nicht so ein Theater machen. Schließlich lässt er ihn abführen: Mitarbeiter greifen ihm unter die Arme, die Kamera filmt den Weg zum Ausgang.

Wie sich die Teilnahme an einer Castingshow langfristig auf die Psyche Jugendlicher auswirkt, haben nun erstmals das Internationale Zentralinstitut für das Jugend- und Bildungsfernsehen (IZI) sowie die Landesanstalt für Medien Nordrhein-Westfalen (LfM) in einer gemeinsamen Studie untersucht. Neunundfünfzig ehemalige Teilnehmer an Castingshows erhielten einen Online-Fragebogen. Ihre Antworten zeigen, wie die psychische Belastung empfunden wird. Behnam Moghaddam, der bei „The Voice of Germany" im Jahr 2011 den fünften Platz belegte, erklärt etwa, er habe zum Schluss der Show „die Grenze nicht mehr gezogen bekommen, wann bin ich flexibel und wann verbiege ich mich". Als der zeitliche Druck zwischen den Liveshows zugenommen habe, sei es zunehmend schwieriger geworden, „mir selbst und meinen Überzeugungen treu zu bleiben. In dieser Zeit bist du wie in einer Seifenblase, wie hermetisch entkoppelt von vielen Dingen." […]

Je nachdem, wie die Befragten die Castingshow-Erfahrung im Hinblick auf ihr späteres Leben einordnen, teilt sie die Studie in verschiedene Gruppen ein. Immerhin etwa ein Drittel der Befragten konnte die Show als professionelles Sprungbrett für die weitere Karriere nutzen. Ein weiteres Fünftel deutet die Show-Erfahrung positiv, als herausragende „Chance zur Selbstentwicklung". Die dritte Gruppe zeigte sich nach gutem Beginn über ihre Stigmatisierung als Verlierer enttäuscht, während eine vierte genau diese negative Inszenierung in heimlicher Komplizenschaft mit den Machern der Show auskostete. Alle weiteren

waren enttäuscht über den Umgang mit ihrer Person, entwickelten aber unterschiedliche psychologische Verarbeitungsstrategien, die von krampfhafter Selbstaffirmation bis hin zur zeitweisen Selbstaufgabe reichten.

Dabei wissen die Produzenten der Castingshows selbst sehr genau, was sie den Teilnehmern möglicherweise zufügen, und sichern sich vertraglich gegen etwaige physische und psychische Folgen ab. Zudem treten die Teilnehmer dem jeweiligen Sender nicht nur alle Verwertungsrechte an den Filmaufnahmen ab, sie sichern ihm auch das Recht auf Verfremdung zu. Seit „Popstars" im Jahr 2000 erstmals im Fernsehen lief, ist es gang und gäbe, Bilder und Töne zu manipulieren, Szenen herauszuschneiden oder nachzudrehen, wenn sie nicht dramatisch genug erscheinen.

Verblüffend aber ist, dass den meisten Teilnehmern und Konsumenten der Inszenierungsgrad von Castingshows offenbar kaum bewusst ist. Ein Großteil der jugendlichen Castingshow-Zuschauer, immerhin achtzig Prozent der Mädchen und sechzig Prozent aller Jungen, glaubt laut Maya Götz, der Leiterin des IZI, dem dokumentarischen Gestus der Sendungen. […] Maya Götz fordert deshalb, die Medienkompetenz der Jugendlichen auch im Schulunterricht gezielt zu verbessern. Nur so könnten sie erkennen: „Es handelt sich bei Castingshows um eine gezielte Inszenierung."

Morten Freidel, *Frankfurter Allgemeine*, 2013

Hinweis: Text kann als Grundlage für eine Diskussion, Rollenspiel oder Essay dienen

Spot on vocabulary

Talking about TV, print and digital media

1 a) *Sort the following words according to whether they have to do with TV or print media. Some of the words will fall into two groups. In each case, give the German equivalent.*

documentary • casting show • circulation • panel game • commercial • section • sitcom • headline • drama • cable • article • editorial • prime time • channel • column • broadsheet • tabloid • live coverage • reader • viewer • to syndicate (a column)

TV		Print	
English	German	English	German
…	…	…	…

b) *Choose six of the words used above and write a definition for each in English. Then get together in groups of four. Take it in turns to read a definition to the others (without letting anyone else see it) and see who can guess the meaning of the word first.*

c) *Now collect words regarding digital media. Find a way of organising them that will help you to learn them. The Spot on facts pages at the beginning of this topic are a good starting point.*

Collecting positive, neutral and negative adjectives

2 *Find adjectives that can be used to describe what news articles and headlines might be like. Group them according to whether they are positive, negative or neutral words. A few adjectives have been given to get you started.*

engaging • biased • opinionated • well-written • …

Collocations to do with the media

3 a) *Match each noun on the left with one on the right to form six collocations concerning advertising.*

advertising • brand • market • product • target • advertising		launch • campaign • group • loyalty • research • budget

b) *Complete the following text using the collocations from above.*

When a company develops a new product, they have to do **1** to determine their **2** and what it wants and needs. Once these questions have been answered, the business has to decide on an **3** and the goals for the **4**. A date also has to be set for the **5** so that the campaign can be planned around it. If the product is part of an existing brand, it is important to continue to build **6**. It's not an easy process!

4 *Write down the English equivalent of each of these phrases. Be careful, they are similar to the German expressions but not exactly the same!*

übers Internet • im Internet surfen • mit dem Internet verbunden sein • Cyber-Mobbing im Internet • einen Blogeintrag kommentieren • persönliche Daten • Zugang zu Informationen haben

TIP

First work on the vocab sheets; then test yourself here!

Topic task

The media | 11

Creating a marketing campaign

You are going to create a marketing campaign either for your reality TV show (see *section A, Task 5*) or for a film adaption of the novel *The Circle* (see *section B: Sharing is caring*). Your campaign must include an eye-catching logo, a poster and one other element of your choice.

STEP 1 Identifying the target group and goal

In small groups decide which product will be the focus of your marketing campaign. Then discuss who your primary target group will be. Once you have decided, discuss the goal of your marketing campaign. Should it be a teaser campaign to arouse curiosity or an informative campaign? Make a note of which aspects of the show or film you will focus on – you should think about what will appeal most to your primary target group and what will help you to achieve your goal.

STEP 2 Designing a logo

Find logos for reality TV shows or films that you like or dislike. Discuss why you find them appealing and effective or not. Brainstorm ideas about what your logo should look like. Decide whether you are going to create it by hand or using a computer. Then make sketches and think about tone and colour. Remember a logo is not just meant to look good; it has to reflect the brand. It must also not look too similar to other logos for similar shows or films.

STEP 3 Designing a poster

Depending on the type of campaign you are doing, decide what information needs to be presented and how best this can be done. Think about the relationship between text and visuals, the use of 'empty space' and the significance of colour. Make sure that the poster will appeal to the target group! Sketch different designs and decide which one is the most suitable.

STEP 4 Choosing another marketing element

What other element would add weight to your campaign? A social media initiative or a short advertising film, for example? Consider other ideas you may have come across and decide on what would be best for your campaign.

STEP 5 Gallery walk

Organise a gallery walk to present your logo, poster and extra marketing element. Be prepared to answer questions and to explain your decisions.

12 The arts
Introduction

Code
mn6bv5

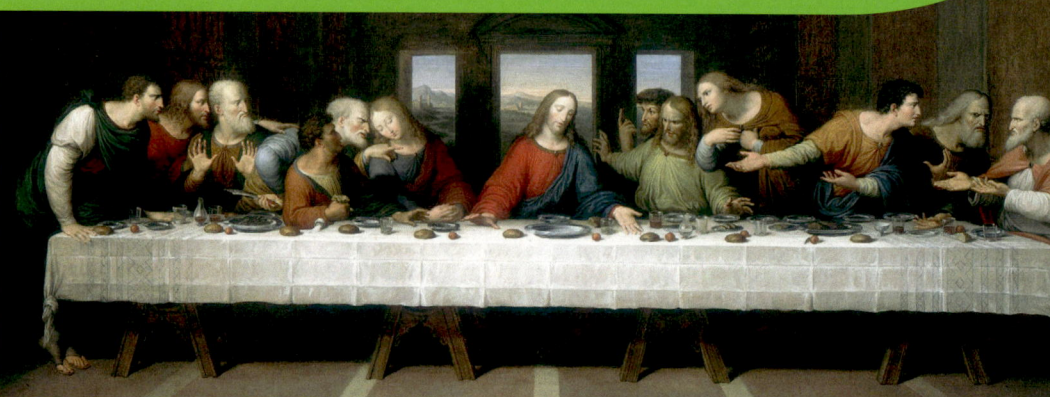

"There should be something revelatory about art. It should be totally creative and open doors for new thoughts and experiences."

Leonardo da Vinci, *The Last Supper* (c. 1495–1498)

Henri Matisse, *The Dessert* (1908)

Tracey Emin, *My Bed* (1998)

"Poor is the pupil who does not surpass his master."

"I don't paint things. I only paint the difference between things."

USEFUL PHRASES

Talking about art
emotional response
form (design, materials etc.) and content (idea, intention, meaning)
functional or decorative
to provoke a reaction

1 SPEAKING
a) The above works of art are from different periods. Describe each and speculate on what the artist was aiming to achieve. → **S28.1**
b) Read the quotations and decide which artist said what, giving your reasons.
c) Discuss what constitutes "art"; then formulate your own definition.
Geeignete Methode: Placemat

2 BRAINSTORMING Think of other art forms, e.g. film, music, dance, acting, photography, architecture etc. What forms of art do you enjoy? What 'good'/'bad' examples of art are there in the place where you live?

Texts
The arts | 12

A Combining visual art and music

1 BEFORE YOU LISTEN Look at this screen shot from the music video "Diane Young" by the American rock band Vampire Weekend. Compare it with Leonardo's Last Supper.

L1/1 Diane Young

You torched a Saab like a pile of leaves /
I'd gone to find some better wheels / Four, five
meters running round the bend / When the
government agents surround you again
5   Chorus: If Diane Young won't change your
mind, / Baby, baby, baby, baby right on time

Out of control but you're playing a role / Do
you think you can go till the 18th hole / Or will
you flip-flop the day of the championship? /
10 Try to go it alone on your own for a bit

Irish and proud, baby, naturally / But you
got the luck of a Kennedy / So grab the
wheel, keep on holding it tight / Till you're
tottering off into that good night
15 Nobody knows what the future holds /
And it's bad enough just getting old / Live
my life in self-defense / You know I love
the past, 'cause
I hate suspense …

Words: Rostam Batmanglij, Ezra König

¹ **torch** to set fire to
⁸ **18th hole** "finishing line" in a game of golf
⁹ **flip-flop** to change one's mind
¹² **Kennedy** Irish-American dynasty (President John F. Kennedy and Senator Robert F. Kennedy both assassinated)

"Whenever I see popular blog posts and online articles about something in pop culture that references something historical, I always wonder if the … ahem, younger generations know the origin of the original and how many other interpretations had been created prior to the one they tweeted, tagged, posted on digg' or shared on facebook."
Anonymous blog writer, 2013

issue *here:* child
citation quotation

"Any text is a new issue of a citation." Roland Barthes, *The Pleasure of the Text*, 1975

L1/1 2 LISTENING Listen to the song and attribute these themes to the song's parts: the fifty-fifty chance – dying young – no future – trapped by circumstances – desperate pride

3 ANALYSIS
   a) Analyse the images created in the text. Do you think they form a coherent theme? Try to agree on an interpretation.
   b) Comment on the band's choice to refer to Leonardo's Last Supper in their song. How do the Last Supper and the song relate to each other?   **Hinweis:** Auch als Hausaufgabe geeignet

4 SPEAKING In groups discuss the statements by the blogger and Barthes. Think of examples of art quoting (or being strongly influenced by) other art. How original can any work of art be? → S24 →△1
Diff (help with): Hinweis, dass viele Songs Vorlagen aus anderen Songs, Filmen, Comics oder Cartoons verwenden

Texts

> **Avoiding mistakes**
> Betonung/Aussprache
> ²**photographer** [fə'tɒɡrəfə(r)]
> ³**photograph** ['fəʊtəɡrɑːf]
> ¹⁷**photography** [fə'tɒɡrəfi]

A musician as a portrait photographer

Bryan Adams is a rock star who has also made a name for himself as a photographer. The following is an extract from an interview with him.

What is your idea of a great portrait photograph?
Something that makes you stop for a second and look again.

And what qualities do you most value in a subject?
Naturalness. […]

From your work it's clear that you are very good at persuading people to lose their inhibitions in front of the camera. In what ways do you think your own experience as a performer helps in that regard?
I think music and photos are intertwined. I recently met up with another photographer, David LaChapelle, who before dinner did a fantastic impromptu dance/mime of Etta James singing 'Groove Me'. Afterwards I sat there thinking David is more of a rock star than most rock stars, yet he's a photographer. […]

Your portrait of the Queen has an almost casual atmosphere. Did she mind the wellies being in shot?
I think she liked the wellies in the shot, it's what made her smile.

You've said that photography feeds into your music – could you tell us a little bit more about that?
Actually what I said was one feeds the other, it was in reference to taking a break from one to do the other. It helps to come back to things refreshed.

To what extent can you design and plan for how things go on a shoot, and to what extent do you enjoy improvising or happy accidents?
Being open for things too, and making things happen are the most crucial things to being a photographer. Both improvising and happy accidents are imperative. […]

When you are known very widely in one artistic sphere, how hard is it to establish yourself in a wholly different creative medium?
It's always hard to do one thing while the other thing is happening, but as long as your work is strong and you don't care what people say about you, you'll be OK.

Olivia Cole, *Spectator Life*, 2013

Billy Idol, Los Angeles, 2008 (photo by Bryan Adams)

The Queen (photo by Bryan Adams)

¹² **Etta James** American blues, gospel and jazz singer (1938–2012)
¹⁵ **wellies** rubber boots

The Queen (painted by Nicky Philipps)

5 COMPREHENSION What is Bryan Adams' approach to portrait photography?

6 ANALYSIS
  a) Speculate on Olivia Cole's reasons for beginning her feature with this photo of Billy Idol.
  b) Do you think that Bryan Adams' portrait of Queen Elizabeth II lives up to his own standards in terms of what "great" photography is?
  c) Analyse how he links the two arts of music and photography.
  Geeignete Methode: Think – Pair – Share

7 EVALUATION Painting is the more traditional approach to portraiture. In 2012 Nicky Philipps was commissioned to paint a portrait of the Queen for the stamp series celebrating the 60th Anniversary of her coronation. The result was very controversial. Do you think the criticism is justified? Write your own blog entry. → **S14.2** **Hinweis:** Auch als Hausaufgabe geeignet

The arts 12

B Art in various locations

1 BEFORE YOU READ What landmarks (buildings or structures) have particular significance for your town or region? What do you think of them?
Geeignete Methode: Speed dating

A controversial work of art

The Watts Towers are an unexpected landmark in an out-of-the-way part of Watts, a poor black suburb south of downtown Los Angeles and one of the city's problem areas. They were built by Italian immigrant Simon Rodia between 1921 and 1954. On the triangular plot of land on which his cottage stood, Rodia constructed 17
5 tower-like structures, two of which are over 99 feet (30m) tall. He used all kinds of steel pipes, tying them together with wire and covering them with cement and thousands of tiles, seashells and pieces of coloured glass.

Rodia kept himself to himself and was treated with suspicion by his neighbours, some of whom allowed their children to vandalise his work. He never explained
10 what the intention behind his masterpiece was, except to say, "I had in mind to do something big and I did it." Although he had no religious status, he is said to have performed baptisms and weddings there.

In 1955 Rodia gave away his property and spent the last ten years of his life in northern California, never returning to Watts.
15 In 1959, city officials said that the towers were not stable enough and decided to have them pulled down. By this time, however, the site had achieved some fame as an example of folk art and protest campaigns were started within the community and outside. Two former art students bought the property. To
20 demonstrate the solidity of the towers, a 10,000-pound truck-mounted crane was attached through a steel cable and it pulled on the tallest tower – but the tower wouldn't budge!

In the following decades not even earthquakes were able to destroy the site since Rodia's use of wiring to tie the steel
25 together instead of welding or bolting the structure had made it extremely flexible.

In 1990 the Watts Towers were declared a "National Historic Landmark". Today, computer-monitored sensors are there to detect the slightest changes in the structure due to heat, wind and vibrations.

Watts Towers in Los Angeles, California

Detail with mosaic

⁴ **triangular** a space with three corners
⁸ **suspicion** a feeling of mistrust
¹¹ **religious status** official position within a church
²⁵ **to weld** schweißen
²⁵ **to bolt** (ver)schrauben

2 COMPREHENSION The Watts Towers are described as an "unexpected landmark". Collect information from the text and photos which might justify this description. → S11   **Hinweis:** Auch geeignete Videos können hier gezeigt werden (z. B. Dokumentationen, Musikvideos …)

3 CREATIVE TASK Imagine the L.A. tourist office wants to include an entry about the Watts Towers in their travel brochure. Write the entry of about 100 words.
Hinweis: Auch als Hausaufgabe geeignet

4 SPEAKING
a) In groups develop a similar art project to create a new landmark for your own town or city. Prepare a presentation for your fellow students.
→ S22
b) Vote on the best project. → S33   **Geeignete Methode:** Gallery walk

Zusatzmaterial WB
Task 2: Mediation

5 BEFORE YOU READ Is it right for large companies to sponsor art, or should their profits be spent on social programmes for their employees? Discuss.
Geeignete Methode: Fishbowl discussion

Anger at Walmart heiress's $1.4bn gallery as art market becomes focus for protests

Crystal Bridges Museum for American Art is built at vast expense in rural Bentonville as supermarket giant cuts benefits for workforce.

When Alice Walton, heiress to the Walmart supermarket fortune and the 10th richest woman in the United States, opened a spectacular fine art museum in her home town, she might have expected plaudits and gratitude. It hasn't quite worked out that way.

The long-awaited opening of the Crystal Bridges Museum for American Art in Walton's home town of Bentonville, Arkansas, has provoked mixed reactions. Some have celebrated the unveiling of a significant new private art institution, but many have criticised the decision to spend $1.4bn of company and family foundation money as the retail colossus cuts back its workers' benefits.

The museum, which opened last weekend and features a survey of American art has also come under criticism from within the art establishment for both inflating values and buying masterpieces from impoverished art institutions without giving local institutions a chance to match Walton's offer.

While historians point out that this is little different from 19th-century robber barons such as Henry Clay Frick and Andrew Carnegie amassing vast collections of European art and bringing it to America, the prospect of hundreds of masterpieces in rural Bentonville, two hours' drive from Tulsa, is still controversial.

Walton, at 62 the youngest of Walmart founder Sam Walton's four children, started buying specifically for the project in 2005. The Moshe Safdie-designed institution, which sits in 120 acres of dogwood trees and trails minutes from downtown Bentonville, already has 440 works on display and 800 in storage. "We set market records for very few pieces that we purchased," says curator, David Houston. "But there is latent criticism from an east coast elite that bringing a famous painting like Thomas Eakins's [$68m] *Gross Clinic* to Arkansas is itself an act of cultural vandalism. We're bringing art to the public, but it's a different kind of public, and there are social and political connotations to that."

In the week since Crystal Bridges opened, it has already seen 5,000 registered visitors. "Sheer curiosity and hunger for an institution like this bears out Alice Walton's vision," Houston says.

Ben Waxman, spokesman for the union-affiliated Making Change@Walmart, said: "Opening a huge, opulent museum in the middle of nowhere while the company is cutting health insurance for its employees is troubling. It sends the message Walmart doesn't care about them."

Edward Helmore, *The Observer*, 2011

⁵ **plaudit** praise and admiration
⁹ **unveiling** removal of a cover
¹¹ **retail colossus** a huge retail store
¹⁴ **impoverished** having very little money
¹⁷ **H. C. Frick** (1849–1919), **A. Carnegie** (1835–1919) wealthy industrialists and patrons of the arts
¹⁷ **to amass** to collect a large amount of sth.

Crystal Bridges Museum of American Art in Bentonville, Arkansas

6 COMPREHENSION Summarise the pros and cons of the new museum and discuss the wider issues it raises. **Hinweis:** Auch als Hausaufgabe geeignet

7 ANALYSIS Analyse the strategies the author uses to suggest that his attitude towards the museum is at least ambivalent. → S4 →△2
Diff (help with): Vorgabe von Aspekten und Strukturierungshilfe

8 SPEAKING Simulate a town hall meeting on Walmart's museum. This meeting will include representatives from all the groups mentioned in the text. (Prepare suitable role cards.) → S24 →▲3
Diff (instead of): Interview zwischen Journalist und einem Unterstützer oder Gegner des Museums vorbereiten
Zusatzmaterial KV 1: Hinweise zur Erstellung von role cards;
KV 2: Hinweise zur Durchführung der Simulation

Street art: Beauty or Beast?

Banksy is the pseudonym of an England-based artist whose graffiti has been featured on walls, buildings and bridges throughout the world.

Local Amenities for Children, part of the series of street installations entitled *Little Big World*, created and photographed by Slinkachu.

Dalston House, created in east London by Argentinian artist Leandro Erlich, is an interactive art project that lives through the participation of its visitors.

Yarn bombing (or urban knitting) is a kind of street art that decorates objects with colourful pieces of knitting.

9 VISUALS Describe the examples of street art and speculate on the artists' motivation. → **S28.1** **Geeignete Methode:** Group puzzle

10 CREATIVE TASK Choose one of these works of art and write an interview between its creator and a local journalist. → **S12** →△**4** **Diff** (help with): Vorgabe von Stichpunkten
Hinweis: Auch als Hausaufgabe geeignet

11 SPEAKING Discuss which is more effective: art in museums, galleries and private collections, or art that is outside in public places? → **S24.1**
Geeignete Methode zum Austausch von Argumenten: Placemat; **Zusatzmaterial WB** Task 1: Adding emphasis

13 The Englishes
Introduction

Code g77e4v

Woman with a veil teaching English in an African country

Poster promoting a Salsa dancing event in Beijing

Sign in Malaysia written in four languages (Malay, Chinese, Tamil and English)

Passenger reading an English language newspaper in India (The Times of India)

private property *Privatbesitz*
trespasser *Unbefugte(r)*
to prosecute to take to court

1 **VISUALS** Describe the photos and newspapers. What do they say about the role of English in the world? → S28   **Geeignete Methode:** Think – Pair – Share

2 **SPEAKING** In which international contexts have you already used English (e.g. on holiday, on the internet, with exchange students etc.)? Interview at least three different partners.   **Zusatzmaterial KV 1:** Interview sheet
Geeignete Methode: Speed dating

3 **ANALYSIS** Explain the pie chart about Global English Speakers. What is the difference between the Global English speakers in the US and the UK and those in India, the Philippines and Nigeria? → S27

Poster informing passenger of the opportunity to learn English on the train

People travelling to holiday destinations

Global English Speakers (in millions)

- **15 %** United States (270)
- **7 %** India (125)
- **5 %** Philippines (90)
- **5 %** Nigeria (80)
- **3 %** United Kingdom (60)
- **65 %** Rest of the World (1175)

Diagram pointing out the distribution of English speakers worldwide

4 RESEARCH

a) Look at the cartoon. What does it say about the English spoken by people from Glasgow? → **S28.2**

b) The three recordings were made by speakers from Glasgow, Pakistan and Nigeria. Can you pick out the speaker from Glasgow?

c) Find out about the varieties of English spoken by native speakers around the world. → **S32**   **Hinweis:** Auch als Hausaufgabe geeignet

5 PRESENTATION
English is an official language in 88 states around the globe. In groups, prepare a poster about the role of English in one of these countries. Do some research about the role of English in this country and explain why it has become an official language. → **S22, S32**

Geeignete Methode zur Präsentation und Auswertung: Gallery walk
Zusatzmaterial WB Task 5: Speaking

Spot on facts

English

English – a timeline

- **Pre-Old English (before AD 500)**
  - Latin, Greek
  - Celtic
  - Old Norse (Danish)
  - Anglo-Saxon
  - **449 AD** After the Romans leave Great Britain, the Angles, Saxons and Jutes (Germanic tribes from the north of Germany, Denmark and the Netherlands) begin to settle in the south and east of Britain. Celtic tribes are forced to the northern and western parts of England, to Wales, Ireland and Scotland.

- **Old English (c. 500–1150)**
  - **789** The Vikings invade and settle large parts of the north and east of England bringing their language with them.
  - Norman French
  - **1066** The Normans invade England and French becomes the official language for more than 300 years.

- **Middle English (c. 1150–1450)**
  - **1337–1450** The 100 Years War between England and France – French is now the language of the enemy.

1 **COMPREHENSION** Explain the influences of important historical events on the development of the English language. Share your ideas with a partner.

2 **PRESENTATION** Divide into groups. Each group watches one or more of the ten video clips *The History of English in Ten Minutes* and notes down in which ways the events presented in each clip helped to form Modern English. Then each group presents its results to the rest of the class. → S22

3 **VOCABULARY** Make a mind map of the factors which have contributed to the success of English as a world language. **Hinweis:** Auch als Hausaufgabe geeignet

4 **COMPREHENSION** Describe in your own words the different kinds of English in the world today.

The Englishes

In the UK and Ireland regional varieties of English exist with differences in pronunciation (accent) and sometimes with moderate differences in vocabulary and grammar (dialect). These differences are sometimes attributed to influences from other languages such as Gaelic (Scotland/Ireland) or Norwegian (Northeast England).

The varieties of English around the world that first come to mind are those that have developed in North America, Australasia and South Africa. The differences between American, Australian and British English are due to the different ways the languages have developed. American English, for example, retains in pronunciation and vocabulary elements of British English in the 16th century – the time the first settlers from Britain went to North America. However, every country under British rule or influence during the centuries of Empire has produced its own brand of the product, some regarded as pidgin, creole or hybrid languages with vocabulary, grammar and pronunciation that differ greatly from standard forms of English and which have been taken over from one or more other local languages. Others, such as Indian English or Philippine English, are varieties on a par with American or Australian English, the difference being the presence of one or more other languages, usually spoken as a first language by the majority of the population. For these people, English is a second language, used as a lingua franca to communicate with fellow countrymen who have a different first language. In such cases English often has the status of an official language.

The Englishes 13

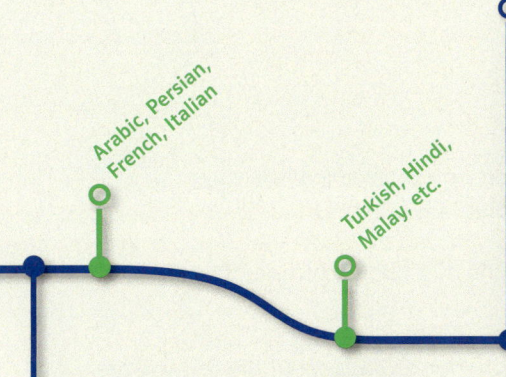

Modern English (c. 1700–
- **1755** Samuel Johnson publishes his *Dictionary of the English Language*.
- **1763** Canada becomes part of the British Empire.
- **1776** American War of Independence: The United States of America become the first country outside Britain to use English as its principal language.
- **1799** A British penal colony is founded in Australia.
- **1821** British presence is consolidated in British West Africa.
- **1840** New Zealand becomes a British colony.
- **1858** India becomes a British Crown colony.
- **1928** The *Oxford English Dictionary* is published.
- **1972** The first email is sent.

Early Modern English (c. 1450–1700)
- **1558** Queen Elizabeth I begins her 45-year reign as queen of England, usually regarded as the main period of the English Renaissance.
- **1600** The East-India Company is established in order to promote trade with India, paving the way for eventual British rule there.
- **1607** Jamestown, the first British settlement in America, is established.
- **1609** The settlement of Bermuda is the beginning of British presence in the Caribbean.
- **1611** The *King James Bible* is published.

○ **American English, Canadian English, Australian English, British English, Irish English, Scottish English**

○ **Chinglish** (Chinese English)

○ **Hinglish** (Hindi English)

○ **Singlish** (Singaporean English)

English as a global lingua franca

At the height of the British Empire in the 19th century it covered one fifth of the global landmass and included a quarter of the world's population. English was used throughout the Empire as the language of
5 trade, education administration and communication. Not only did it enable communicaton between the countries of the Empire, but it also facilitated communication within countries such as Nigeria whose population speaks hundreds of different
10 languages. With the rise of another English-speaking nation (the US) to world superpower status in the 20th century, the role of English as a global lingua franca was sealed. English, for example, is the official language for aeronautical and maritime
15 communications. 80% of the information stored in the world's computers is in English. More than half of the world's technical and scientific periodicals are in English, and English is used as the primary medium of instruction in places where international students
20 study.
　English is, however, not the most spoken language in the world – it comes second place to Mandarin Chinese. Although more and more people are travelling to places all over the world, the overall number of encounters with native English speakers 25
is declining. Research from the World Tourism Organisation shows that English has become the preferred language for communication between non-native speakers of English. This clearly underlines the growing importance of English as a global lingua 30
franca.

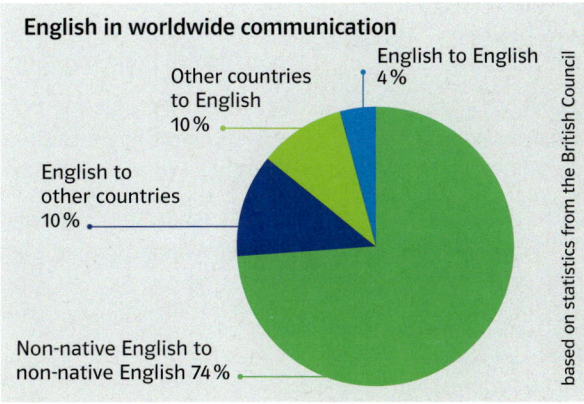

5 RESEARCH *Do some research to find out more about the current role of English as a lingua franca. Find other examples where English is used as means of communication in international contexts.* → **S32**

Zusatzmaterial WB
Task 1: Statistics; Task 2: Improve your style

213

Core skill workshop

Analysing a listening text

Part A Preparation

Before you hear a listening text you can prepare yourself in these ways:
- What do you already know about the topic?
- What type of text are you expecting?
- What additional clues do you get from the title, photos, pictures, fact files and the task?

1 BEFORE YOU LISTEN Gather all the information you can about the text you are going to hear. Sum up the general message in one sentence.

Part B Listening for gist and for detail

The first time you hear the text you should concentrate on the general message and keywords and phrases. This is called 'listening for gist'. → S21

◎ L1/6 2 LISTENING The radio interview is about British English phrases that have found their way into American English. Listen to the radio interview and take notes. Finally, share your notes with a partner. **Zusatzmaterial KV 2:** Listening strategies

When you listen to the text the second time, try to understand more of the information provided. This is called 'listening for detail'. → S21
Some of the following strategies might help you:

> **Inferring:** Guess the meaning from the context.
>
> **Predicting:** Often you can predict what might be said next. Some words help you to predict what is going to come next (e.g. words like but, although, moreover, additionally, finally, before/after). The speakers' intonation also often shows their attitudes and intentions.
>
> **Answer the wh-questions:** who? what? where? when? why? What information is still missing?
>
> **Structuring:** The task may require you to find out information under various headings. Use them to make a grid. A mind map is another very useful tool to organise the information you have just heard.

◎ L1/6 3 LISTENING Listen to the radio interview again and take notes on the details. Look at the tip box. The following questions might help you: → S21

1. What British phrases have entered into American English? (BE)
2. What equivalents for these Britishisms can be found in American English? (AE)
3. In which ways do the two dialects differ? In which ways are they converging? (AE/BE)
4. What are the attitudes of speakers in the UK towards Americanisms? (BE)
5. What attitudes do Americans show towards British words in American English? (AE)

TIP

One-way listening situations
In real-life contexts, pure listening situations are limited to radio programmes, music and announcements. You only hear the speakers' voices so you have to rely on their intonation to interpret what they are saying. Combined listening and viewing situations involve audiovisual media such as television or the cinema, so watching the speakers' body language as well as cinematic devices help to understand what is being said.

TIP

Graphic organisers can help you to take down notes while listening, by providing a visual representation of the information you are listening to. A typical graphic organiser is a Venn diagram, which helps you to compare information.

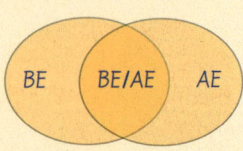

Draw the Venn diagram on a sheet of paper and put the information from the interview in it.

Part C Dealing with closed and half-open tasks

Tasks with a closed or half-open format require you to listen both for gist and for detail. Read through the tasks carefully to see where the focus is on general information in the text and where it is important to find out details in the text.

4 BEFORE YOU LISTEN You are going to hear a short radio interview about the relevance of English as a lingua franca (ELF) for global communication.
a) What do you already know about the use of English in global contexts? Read the fact file about the programme.
b) There are closed and half-open tasks on the CD-ROM. Choose one of the tasks and read it carefully to prepare you for listening to the text.
Hinweis: Auch als Hausaufgabe geeignet

> *The closed task starts like this:*
>
> Listen to the text. Then tick (✔) the correct answer (a, b, c or d) and fill in the grid below. Only one answer is correct.
>
> 1. English as a lingua franca (ELF) is
>   a) ☐ a variety spoken by people in New Zealand.
>   b) ✔ a global form of English used for communication in situations where no party is a native English speaker.
>   c) ☐ a variety of Indian English used in communication with people from other parts of the world.
>   d) ☐ a variety with a totally different pronunciation.

> *The half-open task starts like this:*
>
> Listen to a short radio interview about the relevance of English as a lingua franca (ELF) for global communication. While listening, fill in the table below, using key phrases.
>
> 1. What is English as a lingua franca?
>
>   <u>A form of English used for communication between non-native speakers</u>

FACT FILE

Word of Mouth is a weekly BBC radio programme about English.
In this edition called "English as a lingua franca" the host, Chris Ledgard, talks to language expert Jennifer Jenkins, chair of Global Englishes at the University of Southampton about how English has evolved around the globe.

TIP

Time limits
Normally there are time limits for the various parts of these tasks.
- For reading the tasks, e.g. two minutes.
- For completing the task after listening the first time, e.g. three minutes.
- For finishing the task after listening the second time, e.g. five minutes.

5 LISTENING Listen to the text and complete as much of the task as you can.

6 LISTENING Listen to the text a second time and finish the task. Before you start listening, think about the relevant information that is still missing. Create a mind map or graphic organiser that helps you to focus on the relevant information. Typical structures are:

1. **a herringbone technique**
   with key questions

2. **a layered hierarchy**
   with three different layers

3. **a concept map**
   with different sub-structures

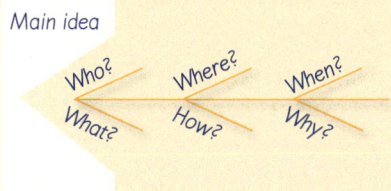

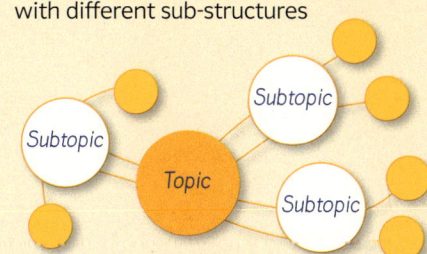

Core skill workshop

FACT FILE

"**21st century flux**" is a dub poetry song written and composed by Dizraeli, a British rapper, writer and poet from Bristol. Dub poetry is a form of performance poetry which emerged in the West Indies and which is heavily influenced by the rhythms of reggae music.

TIP

Taking notes
You probably won't understand everything in the song so it is important just to note down everything you understand in connection with the part of the message you have to deal with.

TIP

Listening
You may need to listen to the song more than twice. Every time you listen to it, check your notes and complete them.

TIP

The tasks here are open tasks. As an alternative you will find a closed task and a half-open task on the CD-ROM.

Hinweis
Weiterführend können die Schüler in Gruppenarbeit Hörverstehensaufgaben zu den eigenen Lieblingssongs entwerfen und den Kurs bearbeiten lassen

7 BEFORE YOU LISTEN Have a close look at the following word cloud for the song "21st century flux". With a partner speculate on what the song might be about. What does the title tell you?

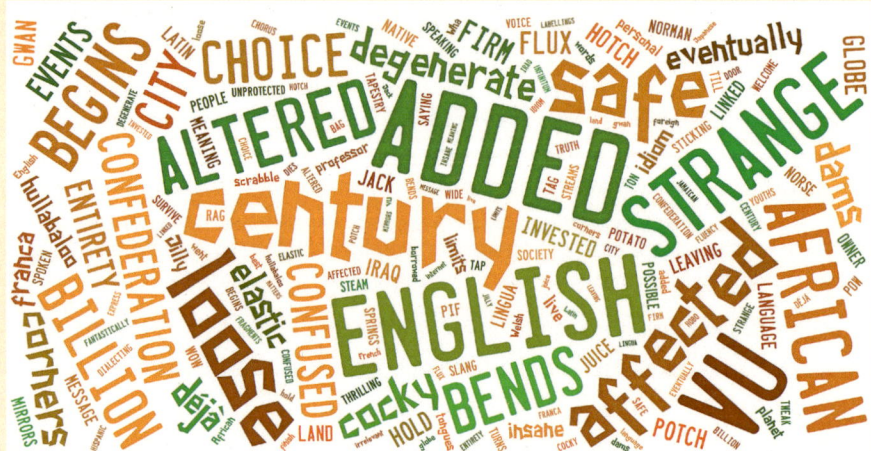

8 LISTENING Listen to the song the first time and in your own words summarise the three main points made in the chorus.

9 LISTENING
a) When listening the second time, find examples of the three points throughout the song. Work in groups of three and make a grid for your notes.
b) Answer the following questions:
• Why is English a new disease? →△1 **Diff** (help with): Vorgabe von Schlüsselwörtern
• What is the professor's criticism and how does the narrator respond? →▲2
• What is the consequence of English being a lingua franca? **Diff** (instead of): Analyse der Sprechweise

10 LANGUAGE
a) A line from the song contains these words. Find out where they come from and what they mean.
1. shampoo
2. juggernaut
3. moolah
4. hullabaloo
5. ad infinitum
6. pow-wow
7. kudos
8. déjà vu
9. wonton
10. billabong
11. wha gwan
12. wigwam

b) Explain why the poet uses these words in his poem.

11 ANALYSIS → S6
a) Explain the meaning of "English isn't English, it's an elastic patchwork".
b) Why did Dizraeli choose this music to go with his poem? How does the music fit with its message? **Hinweis:** Auch als Hausaufgabe geeignet

12 CREATIVE TASK Create your own poem about your individual experiences with English as a foreign language. What role does English have for you? (e.g. a second identity • a stumbling block • a connector, etc.)

13 EVALUATION Interpret the sentence "English is the language of choice … let it be said you added your voice". What does the poet want to express? → S6
Hinweis: Auch als Hausaufgabe geeignet

Zusatzmaterial WB
Tasks 6–7: Listening

13 The Englishes

A The global spread of English

1 BEFORE YOU READ With a partner make a list of your personal top ten songs. How many of these songs are performed in English? How many of the singers/bands are not from the US or the UK?

English – the global language of pop music?

In the last three years there has been a rise in the number of French artists choosing to sing in English, despite quotas requiring at least 40% of music played on radio stations to be in French. […] The internet, which is used by growing numbers of young people as a medium for listening to music, is cited as a reason
5 why English-language acts have become more popular. "Thanks to the internet, our generation has grown up listening to much more music than previous ones – especially English-language music," singer Jil Bensenior of folk-rock act Jil Is Lucky told Billboard magazine.

While singing in English may be a hindrance to getting airtime in France, it can
10 be a help in breaking the American market, as rock band Phoenix have done with their latest album Wolfgang Amadeus Phoenix, which has sold more than 400,000 copies. […]

Jim Hollington, deputy director of the British Council in France, said that not only had the French government made a huge commitment to raising standards
15 of English, with a foreign language being taught in all primary schools, he also believed that there had been a shift in attitudes over the last 15 years towards English: […] "People are stimulated by things that are relevant to their culture – they can understand lyrics. And as they get better in English, they want to sing in English," he said. The increased confidence in bands choosing to sing in English
20 breeds more confidence as it spills over into classrooms. […]

For the bands themselves, it seems unlikely they were thinking of helping their country's English fluency rates when they crafted their lyrics. Thomas Mars, vocalist for Phoenix, said international success was not a consideration when the band started writing lyrics in English. "When we write songs we do it for us and not to
25 gain international recognition. I don't believe you absolutely need to sing in English to gain that – but you need good music for sure," he said.

He didn't make a conscious choice to compose in English but enjoys the leap of expression between the two languages. "Even if it is not my first language I feel there are more unexplored territories thinking in French and writing in English,
30 than to write in French," he said.

Genevieve Roberts, *The Guardian weekly*, 2010

FACT FILE

French foreign language policy forces French radio stations to play a minimum of 40 per cent of its songs in French, half of them from new artists. The *Toubon* law, which was introduced in 1994, aims at promoting the role of French as the official language in France. Despite this linguistic censorship, the number of French artists performing exclusively in English is rapidly increasing.

⁴ **to cite** to name
⁸ **Billboard** American music magazine
⁹ **hindrance** obstacle
⁹ **airtime** the music played on the radio
¹⁴ **commitment** investment
¹⁶ **shift** change
²⁰ **to breed** to cause
²⁰ **to spill over** to reach
²² **to craft** to write
²⁷ **leap** *Sprung*

2 COMPREHENSION Outline the reasons for French artists to perform their songs in English.

3 ANALYSIS Find out more about French foreign language policy. Explain the reasons for the use of quotas on the radio.

4 EVALUATION Discuss whether a similar radio music quota in Germany would be helpful to promote German pop music. → S23   **Geeignete Methode:** Mobile debate

5 CREATIVE TASK Imagine you are a music producer who wants to promote mulitlingual pop music. Write a short entry for your internet blog in which you explain why you see a future for non-English pop songs in Germany. →△3
Diff (help with): Vorgabe möglicher Aspekte   **Hinweis:** Auch als Hausaufgabe geeignet

French rock band Phoenix

Texts

6 BEFORE YOU READ Make a list of five commonly used Anglicisms in German. Then share your ideas in class.

Why diet is a four-letter word in Germany

A new advertising campaign that urges consumers to "fuck the diet" has enraged German-language purists – and, surprisingly, not with its profanity. Cosmopolitan Germans have long flaunted their worldliness by littering their speech with Anglicisms, whether striking a deal over "ein Business-Lunch" or discussing the threat of "ein Cyberkrieg". Now, a brand of low-fat foods has jumped on the bandwagon, urging German customers to "fuck the diet". 5

The profane slogan is being used to flog Unilever's *Du darfst* (literally: you may, or you're allowed) range of allegedly healthy products. The new advert tells German women – in their native tongue – that the range is for "those who don't want to hold back, those who want to eat until they are full." Accompanying images of beautiful women with excellent teeth slurping low-fat spaghetti bolognaise, the voiceover says, "You can't be bothered to count calories? Then don't! With *Du darfst*, you can enjoy yourself without worrying – *Du darfst* means above all that you don't have to do anything. Just help yourself: fuck the diet!" 10

It hasn't gone down too well with some of the target group, with women taking to the official *Du darfst* Facebook page to deride the slogan "as neither big nor clever" and ask "who did you pay to come up with this?" 15

Every time the creep of "Denglisch" hits the headlines, there is much soul-searching over whether the language of Goethe and Schiller will soon be consigned to history. When the verb "leaken" was voted Anglicism of the year in 2011 in the aftermath of the Wikileaks furore, the German Language Association (Verein Deutsche Sprache), moaned to the Guardian: "There seems to be this attitude that English is somehow 'better' than German, that German somehow sounds old-fashioned, particularly for a certain group of people." 20

Holger Klatte, a spokesman for the VDS, noted back then that there was already a perfectly good alternative to leak – *durchsickern*, which means to percolate. In the name of keeping the German language alive, here's the German for *Du darfst*'s new catchphrase: "Scheiß auf Diät!", literally "Shit on the diet!". Hmm. You can kind of see why they didn't go for that one. 25

Helen Pidd, *The Guardian*, 2012

Young women eating spaghetti

four-letter word vulgäres Wort
[1] **to urge** to persuade
[1] **to enrage** to make very angry
[2] **profanity** vulgärer Ausdrück
[3] **to flaunt** protzen
[3] **to litter** to put in frequently
[5] **threat** Bedrohung
[5] **to jump on the bandwagon** to take part in sth fashionable
[7] **to flog** (infml) to sell
[8] **range** collection of sth
[8] **allegedly** supposedly
[11] **to slurp** (infml) to suck into one's mouth
[16] **to deride** to make fun of sth in a critical way
[18] **creep** slow invasion
[19] **to consign sth to history** etw. Geschichte werden lassen
[21] **aftermath** time immediately after
[21] **furore** Aufruhr
[29] **to go for sth** to decide on sth

Zusatzmaterial WB
Task 3: Adjective or adverb
Tasks 8–12: Reading and writing

7 COMPREHENSION Outline Unilever's advertising campaign and explain why it has caused an uproar not only among German language purists. → **S4.2**

8 ANALYSIS Analyse how the author uses language to support her position. Consider some of the following aspects:

1. **The structure of the article (coherence and line of argumentation)** → **S4.2**
Is there a logical structure of the article? Does the text make use of logical connectors? Does the text develop a logical pattern (e.g. generalisation, cause and effect, comparison/contrast, process or chronology of events?)

2. **Language and choice of words** → **S10.1**
What register of English is being used (formal/informal English, academic or colloquial/slang)? What sort of vocabulary is used (e.g. denotations/connotations, keywords, figurative meaning/literal meaning, euphemisms, synonyms)? What tone does the author use (e.g. is he/she serious, critical, cynical, humorous, sarcastic, ironic)? **Hinweis:** Auch als Hausaufgabe geeignet

9 EVALUATION Comment on the statement that German might be fully replaced by English in the near future. **Hinweis:** Auch als mündliche Diskussion geeignet

13 The Englishes

B Language and cultural identity

Learn English online: How the internet is changing language

Online, English has become a common language for users from around the world. In the process, the language itself is changing [...] There are now thought to be some 4.5 billion web pages worldwide. And with half the population of China now online, many of them are written in Chinese. Still, some linguists predict that within
5 10 years English will dominate the internet - but in forms very different to what we accept and recognise as English today.

That's because people who speak English as a second language already outnumber native speakers. And increasingly they use it to communicate with other non-native speakers, particularly on the internet where less attention is paid
10 to grammar and spelling and users don't have to worry about their accent [...].

Users of Facebook already socialise in a number of different "Englishes" including Indian English, or Hinglish, Spanglish (Spanish English) and Konglish (Korean English). While these variations have long existed within individual cultures, they're now expanding and comingling online. [...] "While most people don't speak English
15 as their first language, there is a special commercial and social role for English driven by modern forms of entertainment," says Robert Munro, a computational linguist and head of Idibon, a language technology company in California. "The prevalence of English movies in regions where there is not much technology other than cell phones and DVDs makes English an aspirational language. People think
20 it's the language of the digital age." [...]

The increasing prevalence of the internet in everyday life means that language online is not a zero sum game. Instead, it allows multiple languages to flourish.

"Most people actually speak multiple languages – it's less common to only speak one," says Mr Munro. "English has taken its place as the world's lingua franca, but
25 it's not pushing out other languages."

Instead, other languages are pushing their way into English, and in the process creating something new.

Jane O'Brien, BBC NEWS Magazine, 2012

1 COMPREHENSION Which three statements sum up what the article is about?

1. Chinese will dominate the internet within 10 years as more Chinese people come online.
2. Because most people who use the internet can speak more than one language, this influences the English they use.
3. As everyone uses it, It's easy to learn English on the internet.
4. English is used in modern technology to force people to learn English.
5. Experts believe the English used on the internet in the future will be different to today's English.
6. People feel English is the language of the modern age.

2 ANALYSIS Explain why Mr Munro thinks that English as the lingua franca of the internet will not necessarily replace other languages.
Hinweis: Auch als Hausaufgabe geeignet
3 EVALUATION Do a survey in class. What is your experience of English on the internet? When you do use it? When don't you use it? Is Mr Munro right in his assessment of the role of English? → **S30** **Zusatzmaterial KV 3:** Class survey

---

FACT FILE

Internet users
Recent figures show that currently more than 565 million people use the internet in English, compared to 510 million users in Chinese. Currently, just over 40 percent of the population in China use the internet (compared to more than 80 percent in the UK and the US). Accordingly, experts believe Chinese will overtake English as the dominant language of the internet within the next few years.

---

14 **to expand** to become bigger
14 **to comingle** to mix
18 **prevalence** dominance
19 **aspirational** sth one wants to have
22 **to flourish** to grow well

Avoiding mistakes
Wortschatz
9 **on the internet**
im Internet
NICHT in the internet

Zusatzmaterial WB
Task 4: Gerunds
Task 13: Mediation

Texts

Hinweis
Die Erstbegegnung mit dem Text als Hörverstehen gestalten

4 BEFORE YOU READ Most of the asylum seekers detained in centres in the UK come from Pakistan, India, Bangladesh, Afghanistan, Nigeria and China. Think about what role language plays for these people.
Geeignete Methode: Think – Pair – Share

◎ L1/9 ## The other hand

In the following extract from a novel Little Bee, a young girl from Nigeria held in a detention camp in England, has been spending her time preparing for a better future. One day she is released due to an error.

I am only alive at all because I learned the Queen's English. Maybe you are thinking, that isn't so hard. After all, English is the official language of my country, Nigeria. Yes, but the trouble is that back home we speak it so much better than you. To talk the Queen's English, I had to forget all the best tricks of my mother tongue. For example, the Queen could never say, *There was plenty wahala, that girl done use her bottom power to engage my number-one son and anyone could see she would end in the bad bush*. Instead the Queen must say, *My late daughter-in-law used her feminine charms to become engaged to my heir, and one might have foreseen that it wouldn't end well*. It is all a little sad, don't you think? Learning the Queen's English is like scrubbing off the bright red varnish from your toenails the morning after a dance. It takes a long time and there is always a little bit left at the end, a stain of red along the growing edges to remind you of the good time you had. So, you can see that learning came slowly to me. On the other hand, I had plenty of time. I learned your language in an immigration detention centre, in Essex, in the south-eastern part of the United Kingdom. Two years, they locked me in there. Time was all I had.

But why did I go to all the trouble? It is because of what some of the older girls explained to me: to survive, you must look good or talk even better. The plain ones and the silent ones, it seems their paperwork is never in order. You say, they get repatriated. We say, *sent home early*. Like your country is a children's party – something too wonderful to last forever. But the pretty ones and the talkative ones, we are allowed to stay. In this way your country becomes lively and more beautiful.

I will tell you what happened when they let me out of the immigration detention centre. The detention officer put a voucher in my hand, a transport voucher, and he said I could telephone for a cab. I said, *Thank you, sir, may God move with grace in your life and bring joy into your heart and prosperity upon your loved ones*. The officer pointed his eyes at the ceiling, like there was something very interesting up there, and he said, *Jesus*. Then he pointed his finger down the corridor and he said, *There is the telephone*.

So, I stood in the queue for the telephone. I was thinking, I went *over the top* with thanking that detention officer. The Queen would merely have said, *Thank you*, and left it like that. Actually, the Queen would have told the detention officer to call for the damn taxi himself, or she would have him shot and his head separated from his body and displayed on the railings in front of the Tower of London. I was realising right there, that it was one thing to learn the Queen's English from books and newspapers in my detention cell, and quite another thing to actually speak the language with the English. I was angry with myself. I was thinking, You cannot afford to go around making mistakes like that, girl. If you talk like a savage who learned her English on the boat, the men are going to find you out and send you straight back home. That's what I was thinking.

5
10
15
20
25
30
35
40

From: Chris Cleave, *The Other Hand*, 2009

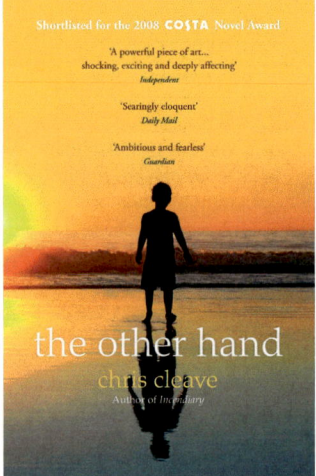

FACT FILE

Immigration Removal Centres

The UK Border Agency runs 12 detention centres, where asylum seekers are kept as long as their case is being decided. In 2012 more than 2,800 people were detained in removal centres; 240 of them were children under 18 and were kept in conditions similar to prisons.

8 **plenty wahala** a lot of trouble
13 **varnish** *Nagellack*
14 **stain** *Fleck*
28 **cab** taxi
28 **grace** *Gnade*
29 **prosperity** wealth
30 **ceiling** *Decke*
37 **railings** *Eisengeländer*
41 **savage** *Wilde(r)*

220

5 COMPREHENSION *Outline the living conditions and the social status of illegal immigrants as described in the text.*

6 COMPREHENSION *Work with a partner and complete the sentences with information from the text.* **Hinweis:** Auch als Hausaufgabe geeignet

1. The Queen's English …
   a) is an old form of the language that has been spoken by the British monarchy for centuries.
   b) is the official language of Nigeria.
   c) describes the standard type of English as used in books and newspapers.

2. According to Little Bee, compared to Nigerian English the Queen's English …
   a) has all the best tricks.
   b) is a bit sad.
   c) takes a long time to learn.

3. According to Little Bee, in order not to get repatriated, female asylum seekers have to …
   a) make a phone call.
   b) be either pretty or talkative.
   c) be rather plain and silent.

4. Little Bee is angry with herself because …
   a) she didn't tell the detention officer to call for a cab.
   b) it was wrong to thank the detention officer.
   c) she used the wrong kind of language to thank the detention officer.

5. Little Bee realises that …
   a) her English isn't very good.
   b) she needs to practise speaking to English people.
   c) she learned to speak English on the boat to England.

7 COMPREHENSION *Why is learning 'the Queen's English' important for Little Bee?*

8 ANALYSIS *Little Bee uses the expression 'the Queen's English' to describe two kinds of English. How do they differ from each other?* → △4 **Diff** (help with): Vorgabe möglicher Aspekte
Geeignete Methode zur weiteren Analyse: Hot seat

9 EVALUATION *Compare the sentence in Nigerian English about Princess Diana with how the Queen would say the same thing. Assess Little Bee's claim that Nigerian English is better than the Queen's English.* **Geeignete Methode:** Think – Pair – Share

10 CREATIVE TASK *Write a letter in which Little Bee tells her mother about her experiences in the immigration detention centre. Use Standard English.* → **S18.4**
Hinweis: Auch als Hausaufgabe geeignet

11 DISCUSSION *Work with a partner and discuss the two quotations below, which were both made by two former US presidents. What are the implications of the two quotes for a multicultural society?*

1. **THEODORE ROOSEVELT**
   "Every immigrant who comes here should be required within five years to learn English or leave the country."

2. **LYNDON B. JOHNSON**
   "The land flourished because it was fed from so many sources – because it was nourished by so many cultures and traditions and people."

Advanced texts

C Dialects of English

Voices from Britain → S21

In the following interview Rob Conley from Stepney, London, talks about Cockney, the local dialect in the East End of London.

FACT FILE

Cockney is a regional dialect spoken by working-class Londoners in the East End (within the sound of Bow Bells, i.e. in a local area around St. Mary-le-Bow, a 16th century church in the city of London). Apart from its disctinctive pronunciation and vocabulary, Cockney also makes use of rhyming slang (e.g. to have butcher's = to have a look. The rhyme is *butcher's hook = look*)

○ L1/10 **1 LISTENING**
  a) Describe the changes Rob Conley has noticed in the language. →△5 **Diff** (help with): Vorgabe einer Tabelle
  b) Examine the reasons for this change.

2 EVALUATION Do some research about Estuary English and the future role of Cockney. Present your results and discuss whether Cockney will become extinct within the next 50 years.

In the following interviews, different speakers of regional varieties talk about their dialects and explain the meaning of local vocabulary.

○ L1/11 **3 LISTENING** Make a list of the local vocabulary they talk about and what it means.

4 ANALYSIS Explain the role of regional vocabulary by referring to local German words in your area. Do you use words that differ from Standard German and are linked to a regional variety?

The history and future of British dialects → S21

The history of British dialects dates back to the early Anglo-Saxon settlers and the various invaders that came to the country over the centuries. They have all not only shaped the English language, but have also contributed to regional varieties. However, the last decades have seen a rapid decrease in the popularity of regional dialects. Will regional dialects all become extinct?

○ L1/12 **5 LISTENING** Explain the use of local words in Yorkshire dialects and compare them to their German equivalents. Can you see similarities?

○ L1/13 **6 EVALUATION**
  a) Describe what role regional varieties played at school.
  b) Discuss the future of regional dialects in view of language policies that aim at standardisation (RP English, Queen's English). → S14.1
  Hinweis: Auch als schriftliche Hausaufgabe geeignet

○ L1/14 **7 EVALUATION** Explain what role the media will play in protecting regional varieties.

Mind your language → S21

In 2011 the Newcastle-born pop singer Cheryl Cole was fired as a judge from the US talent show "The X-Factor USA" and replaced by another female judge because American audiences reportedly struggled to understand her strong Geordie accent.

8 BEFORE YOU LISTEN How important is it for people in the media to speak in a standard accent? Which TV presenters in Germany speak a regional dialect?

○ L1/15 **9 COMPREHENSION** Voice coach Elspeth Morrison makes three suggestions as to how Cheryl Cole could be better understood in America. What are they?

10 EVALUATION Should Cheryl Cole drop her Newcastle accent in order to be understood better in the US and keep her role on "The X-Factor USA"? → S14.2
Hinweis: Auch als schriftliche Hausaufgabe geeignet

Cheryl Cole

D Linguistic imperialism

1 BRAINSTORMING *What does the term 'imperialism' usually refer to? Collect ideas about what it could mean in connection with a language.*

2 BEFORE YOU READ *Imagine the Council of Europe decides that English is the only official language throughout Europe. What consequences would this have for your everyday life?* **Geeignete Methode:** Think – Pair – Share

Linguistic imperialism – Just speak English?

How should the European Union manage its multilingualism? The 28 partner countries speak an unwieldy 23 languages. [...] Many argued that it would be far more practical if all European matters were simply conducted in English. Why not let the most popular language spread to every corner of Europe – and, indeed, the
5 rest of the world?
   [...] But mandating English might also serve to undermine loyalty to the EU. There are too many Europeans who would rather not have English dominate political affairs. The continent has more native German-speakers, including four countries where German is an official language. French has as many native-
10 speakers in Europe, too, and is official in three countries (not to mention Europe's de facto capital, Brussels). Native English-speakers make up less than a fifth of the EU's population. And, awkwardly, English is the official language of the one country that will soon hold a referendum on whether to quit the EU entirely.
   But the real reason not to adopt a "mainly English" language policy involves
15 the EU's promise to its members, under the official motto "united in diversity". No country joined the union in order to be crushed under a homogenising wheel. Important laws are made at the EU level, and Europeans have a right to be able to understand them. [...] Recognising the importance of all languages big and small may seem romantic. But when it comes to arguments about language, as with
20 trade, emotion often trumps reason. Hard facts may be a good reason to, say, shut an old steel mill that cannot withstand competition. But a language is not a steel mill. There is far more at stake: not just people's livelihoods, but their identities and cultural diversity itself. The continent's proliferating anti-EU parties would throw themselves a party if the EU foolishly tossed aside national exceptionalism for an
25 English hegemony.
   Telling 26 of 28 EU countries that of course they can keep their cute little languages, but that all serious stuff (business, academic work, legislating) must be done in English, is asking them to accept second-class linguistic citizenship. Languages that are not used for science or business fail to develop the up-to-date
30 vocabulary and style needed to do so. Over time, if neglected, they shrink to fewer and fewer domains. In the long run, they may be spoken only at home or between intimates, like Swiss German or Scottish Gaelic.

R.L.G., *The Economist*, 2013

2 **unwieldy** not easy to deal with
6 **to mandate** to order, to make law
12 **awkwardly** unfittingly, unhelpfully
16 **to crush** *zerdrücken*
20 **to trump** to get the upper hand
22 **at stake** at risk, in question
22 **livelihood** *Auskommen, Lebensunterhalt*
23 **to proliferate** to become more numerous
24 **to toss aside** to throw away
25 **hegemony** *Vorherrschaft*
30 **to neglect** to not take care of
30 **to shrink** to decrease in size
32 **intimates** people who know each other well

3 ANALYSIS *Why are people afraid of the dominance of the English language within the EU, and what are the reasons that speak against English as the only official language of the EU?* →▲6 **Diff** (after): Analyse der Haltung des Autors zur Vormachtstellung des Englischen innerhalb der EU

4 PRESENTATION *Do some research about the diversity of languages within the EU and prepare a one-minute presentation about multilingualism in Europe.*
→ S22   →▲7 **Diff** (instead of): Letter to the editor, in dem die Ausdehnung der Vormachtstellung der englischen Sprache kritisiert wird

Zusatzmaterial WB
Task 5: Speaking

Advanced texts

E All the Englishes

1 BEFORE YOU READ
a) Which language(s) did you learn from your parents? Was German one of them?
b) What do you understand by the expression 'mother tongue'? How else could it be interpreted?
c) 👥 Explain to your partner: What different forms of German do you use every day and in which situations? Can you give examples of these different forms of German? **Geeignete Methode:** Speed dating

Mother Tongue

I am a writer. And by that definition, I am someone who has always loved language. I am fascinated by language in daily life. I spend a great deal of my time thinking about the power of language – the way it can evoke an emotion, a visual image, a complex idea, or a simple truth. Language is the tool of my trade. And I use them all – all the Englishes I grew up with.

Recently, I was made keenly aware of the different Englishes I do use. I was giving a talk to a large group of people, the same talk I had already given to half a dozen other groups. The nature of the talk was about my writing, my life, and my book, *The Joy Luck Club*. The talk was going along well enough, until I remembered one major difference that made the whole talk sound wrong. My mother was in the room. And it was perhaps the first time she had heard me give a lengthy speech, using the kind of […] standard English that I had learned in school and through books, the forms of English I did not use at home with my mother.

Just last week, I was walking down the street with my mother, and I again found myself conscious of the English I was using, the English I do use with her. We were talking about the price of new and used furniture and I heard myself saying this: "Not waste money that way." My husband was with us as well, and he didn't notice any switch in my English. And then I realized why. It's because over the twenty years we've been together I've often used that same kind of English with him, and sometimes he even uses it with me. It has become our language of intimacy, a different sort of English that relates to family talk, the language I grew up with. […]

You should know that my mother's expressive command of English belies how much she actually understands. She reads the Forbes report, listens to Wall Street Week, converses daily with her stockbroker, reads all of Shirley MacLaine's books with ease – all kinds of things I can't begin to understand. Yet some of my friends tell me they understand 50 percent of what my mother says. Some say they understand 80 to 90 percent. Some say they understand none of it, as if she were speaking pure Chinese. But to me, my mother's English is perfectly clear, perfectly natural. It's my mother tongue. Her language, as I hear it, is vivid, direct, full of observation and imagery. That was the language that helped shape the way I saw things, expressed things, made sense of the world.

Lately, I've been giving more thought to the kind of English my mother speaks. Like others, I have described it to people as "broken" or "fractured" English. But I wince when I say that. It has always bothered me that I can think of no way to describe it other than "broken," as if it were damaged and needed to be fixed, as if it lacked a certain wholeness and soundness. I've heard other terms used, "limited English," for example. But they seem just as bad, as if everything is limited, including people's perceptions of the limited English speaker.

5

10

15

20

25

30

35

Avoiding mistakes
Aussprache
⁸**dozen** [ˈdʌzn]

VIP FILE

Amy Tan is an Asian-American writer who mainly writes about family relationships and her own experiences of growing up as a first-generation Asian American. Her first novel, *The Joy Luck Club*, became a commercial success and was adapted into a feature film.

³ **to evoke** hervorrufen
⁶ **keenly** strongly
¹⁸ **switch** change
²¹ **intimacy** a close relationship
²³ **command** ability to speak
²³ **to belie** widerlegen
²⁴ **Forbes** American business magazine
²⁴ **"Wall Street Week"** an investment news programme
²⁵ **Shirley MacLaine** American actress and author
³⁰ **vivid** expressive
³⁴ **fractured** damaged
³⁵ **to wince** zusammenzucken
³⁷ **to lack** to be without
³⁹ **perception** Wahrnehmung

13 The Englishes

Los Angeles

Chinatown, Los Angeles

Stock exchange, New York

I know this for a fact, because when I was growing up, my mother's "limited" English limited my perception of her. I was ashamed of her English. I believed that her English reflected the quality of what she had to say. That is, because she expressed them imperfectly her thoughts were imperfect. And I had plenty of empirical evidence to support me: the fact that people in department stores, at banks, and at restaurants did not take her seriously, did not give her good service, pretended not to understand her, or even acted as if they did not hear her.

My mother has long realized the limitations of her English as well. When I was fifteen, she used to have me call people on the phone to pretend I was she. In this guise, I was forced to ask for information or even to complain and yell at people who had been rude to her. One time it was a call to her stockbroker in New York. […] I had to get on the phone and say in an adolescent voice that was not very convincing, "This is Mrs. Tan."

And my mother was standing in the back whispering loudly, "Why he don't send me check, already two weeks late. So mad he lie to me, losing me money."

And then I said in perfect English, "Yes, I'm getting rather concerned. You had agreed to send the check two weeks ago, but it hasn't arrived."

Then she began to talk more loudly. "What he want, I come to New York tell him front of his boss, you cheating me?" And I was trying to calm her down, make her be quiet, while telling the stockbroker, "I can't tolerate any more excuses. If I don't receive the check immediately, I am going to have to speak to your manager when I'm in New York next week." And sure enough, the following week there we were in front of this astonished stockbroker, and I was sitting there red-faced and quiet, and my mother, the real Mrs. Tan, was shouting at his boss in her impeccable broken English.

We used a similar routine just five days ago, for a situation that was far less humorous. My mother had gone to the hospital for an appointment, to find out about a benign brain tumor a CAT scan had revealed a month ago. She said she had spoken very good English, her best English, no mistakes. Still, she said, the hospital did not apologize when they said they had lost the CAT scan and she had come for nothing. She said they did not seem to have any sympathy when she told them she was anxious to know the exact diagnosis, since her husband and son had both died of brain tumors. She said they would not give her any more information until the next time and she would have to make another appointment for that. So she said she would not leave until the doctor called her daughter. She wouldn't budge. And when the doctor finally called her daughter, me, who spoke in perfect English – lo and behold – we had assurances the CAT scan would be found, promises that a conference call on Monday would be held, and apologies for any suffering my mother had gone through for a most regrettable mistake. […]

Avoiding mistakes
Aussprache
⁴⁹**guise** [gaɪz]
⁶⁷**benign** [bɪˈnaɪn]

⁴⁹ **guise** role
⁴⁹ **to yell** (infml) to shout
⁵¹ **adolescent** of a teenager
⁵⁸ **to cheat** betrügen
⁵⁹ **to tolerate** to accept
⁶² **astonished** amazed
⁶³ **impeccable** perfect
⁶⁷ **benign** not dangerous
⁶⁹ **to apologize** sich entschuldigen
⁷⁰ **sympathy** Mitleid
⁷¹ **anxious** concerned
⁷³ **appointment** Termin
⁷⁴ **to budge** (infml) to move
⁷⁵ **lo and behold** und siehe da
⁷⁶ **assurance** promise
⁷⁷ **apology** Entschuldigung

Advanced texts

Fortunately, for reasons I won't get into today, I later decided I should envision a reader for the stories I would write. And the reader I decided upon was my mother, because these were stories about mothers. So with this reader in mind – and in fact she did read my early drafts – I began to write stories using all the Englishes I grew up with: the English I spoke to my mother, which for lack of a better term might be described as "simple"; the English she used with me, which for lack of a better term might be described as "broken"; my translation of her Chinese, which could certainly be described as "watered down"; and what I imagined to be her translation of her Chinese if she could speak in perfect English, her internal language, and for that I sought to preserve the essence, but neither an English nor a Chinese structure. I wanted to capture what language ability tests can never reveal: her intent, her passion, her imagery, the rhythms of her speech and the nature of her thoughts.

Apart from what any critic had to say about my writing, I knew I had succeeded where it counted when my mother finished reading my book and gave me her verdict: "So easy to read."

From: *Touchstone Anthology of Contemporary Creative Nonfiction*, 2007

82 **draft** *Entwurf*
83 **for lack of** *aus Mangel an*
88 **to seak – sought** to look for
92 **to count** to be important
93 **verdict** *Urteil*

2 COMPREHENSION
  a) *Decide which headline from the list below goes with which section of the text (note the lines numbers), then put the headlines in the right order.*
  1. Mrs Tan's "limited" English
  2. Mother and daughter tongue
  3. The real Mrs Tan
  4. The power of language
  5. Critical praise
  6. Mrs Tan won't budge

  b) *Complete the following sentences about the text.*
  1. Because Amy Tan is a writer, language …
  2. For Amy's mother the kind of English Amy Tan used in her speech about her book …
  3. The English Amy Tan uses with her mother and husband is …
  4. For Amy Mrs Tan's English is not limited since she …
  5. To get things done, Mrs Tan soon realised that …
  6. As soon as the doctor called, Amy …
  7. In her stories Amy wanted to capture …

Zusatzmaterial WB
Task 14: Past tenses
Task 15: Register

3 ANALYSIS
  a) *What role does language play in the relationship between Amy Tan and her mother?*
  b) *How does Amy Tan describe the variety of English used by her mother? What words does she find for it? What other terms are often used in this context?* **Hinweis:** Auch als Hausaufgabe geeignet

4 CREATIVE TASK
  a) *Write a dialogue between Amy and her mother in which Amy explains why she has imagined her mother as the audience for her fiction.* → S12.1 →▲8
  b) *Exchange your dialogue with a partner's. Give him or her feedback.*
  c) *Choose one of the dialogues and act it out in class.*
  zu 4a) **Diff** (instead of): Erörterung der Frage, ob Amys Zögern, das Englisch ihrer Mutter als broken/limited English zu bezeichnen, gerechtfertigt ist

TIP

You can try to imitate the language Amy Tan and her mother use to speak to each other if you wish.

13 The Englishes

F English worldwide

Code g77e4v

Six countries

1 **BEFORE YOU LISTEN** Talk to your partner about English around the world. Have you ever met (or listened to) English speakers from countries outside the UK and the US? What were your own experiences with their variety of English?

L1/16–21 2 **LISTENING** These audios present some of the varieties of English from different countries around the world. In groups listen to one of the audios and do the tasks for that audio. Finally present the results of your tasks to the rest of the class. Which country are the speakers from? Sum up in a sentence what it is about.

TIP

The **six audios** are on the teacher's CD. Alternatively each group can hear the chosen audio by following the Green Line code.

Nigeria · Pakistan · Jamaica · Canada · India · Singapore

L1/16 Audio 1
1. Which accent does this accent remind you of?
2. Listen carefully to the way the speakers pronounce the word 'about'. Does it rhyme with 'shout', 'boat' or 'bite'?
3. What is different to British English about the way the speakers pronounce the end of the words 'popular' and 'texture'?

L1/19 Audio 4
1. Listen carefully to the way the speakers pronounce the end of the words 'available', 'beautiful', and the 'r's' in 'world', 'girls' 'empowered', 'are'. What do you notice?
2. What do you notice about the way the last speaker pronounces 'came', 'take', 'place' and 'available'?

L1/17 Audio 2
1. Listen carefully to the 'l' sound in the words 'full', 'also' and 'health'. What do you notice?
2. What is the difference between the way the first two speakers and the last speaker pronounce 'th'?

L1/20 Audio 5
1. Listen carefully to the way the third speaker pronounces 'melting pot'. Does 'pot' rhyme with 'lot' or 'cat'?
2. What do you notice about the way nationalities are pronounced?

L1/18 Audio 3
1. Listen carefully to the way the speakers pronounce the first part of the word 'country'. Does it rhyme with 'contact', 'counter' or 'canter'?
2. How does the second speaker pronounce 'th' in 'the'?
3. What do you notice about the way the third speaker pronounces the end of 'million'?

L1/21 Audio 6
1. Listen carefully to the way the first speaker pronounces the vowel in 'taste' and the 't' in 'item'. How are they pronounced differently from Standard English?
2. Listen to the way the last speaker says 'former prime minister of UK' and 'most'. What difference do you notice to Standard English?

USEFUL PHRASES

Talking about pronunciation

the speaker pronounces the word … like …

the pronunciation of the word … reminds me of/is similar to the pronunciation of the word …

the word … rhymes with …/the intonation of the word … is similar/is different to …

The way the speaker uses the word … is different from the standard pronunciation of the word …

Advanced texts

G The future of English

English will die out like Latin

While English still ranges among the top three world languages (with Chinese and Spanish), the British linguist Nicolas Ostler claims it may very soon die out as a world language and be replaced by 'machine translation', allowing people to communicate using their mobile phones and other hand-held devices.

Speaking at 'The Telegraph Hay Festival', Nicolas Ostler said English will decline just as Sanskrit, Persian, Greek and Latin died out as world languages before it. The author of 'The Rise and Fall of World Languages' explained that all 'lingua francas' rely on economic, cultural, administrative and military dominance. As Europe and North America lose economic power and are replaced by emerging nations like China, India, Russia and Brazil, English will become "the last lingua franca".

Dr Ostler, who speaks 26 languages, said English will actually be dominant for a relatively short time, compared to the ancient languages. It has been the lingua franca for just a couple of hundred years compared to the millennia that Latin ruled the world. But rather than Chinese or another language becoming dominant, he said the world will no longer need a 'linga franca' in the machine-dominated world.

"One day English too, the last lingua franca to be of service to a multi-lingual world, will be laid down. Thereafter everyone will speak and write in whatever language they choose and will understand." Dr Ostler said machine translation like Google translate or translation apps like Siri are improving all the time. Eventually he predicted that it will become easy to translate written documents quickly and use hand-held devices to translate speech and signs in real time.

"The most plausible future for English is it will continue to be spoken as a mother tongue (in English-speaking nations) but its position as lingua franca will be overtaken by technology as more and more people live their lives electronically." Half of the world's languages are so endangered they will die out by the end of this century. Dr Ostler, who is Chairman of the Foundation for Endangered Languages, said machine translation will mean fewer people bother to learn languages.

But it could protect languages as people will be able to speak their own languages, whilst also being able to communicate with other people through machines. He also urged young people to take an interest in foreign languages as there is nothing like speaking face to face. "It means the learning of a foreign language will become a specialist endeavour but it already is in this country," said the former Government adviser.

Dr Ostler said English is already in decline and may become more of a 'text language' before dying out completely as a dominant language. "It is conceivable that the nature of lingua franca English will become text talk," he said.

Nicolas Ostler, *The Daily Telegraph*, 2012

[1] **to range** *here:* to be placed
[4] **device** *Gerät*
[20] **eventually** in the end
[23] **plausible** likely
[28] **to bother** to take the trouble
[33] **endeavour** task
[35] **'text language'** language of text messages
[36] **conceivable** possible

1 COMPREHENSION Sum up what Dr Ostler thinks about the future of English.
Hinweis: Auch als Hausaufgabe geeignet

2 ANALYSIS Compare and contrast the information here with what you have learned about the role of English in other texts in this topic. In which ways do the predictions about the future of English differ from another?

3 RESEARCH Find out about the development of the global or colonial use of Latin, French or other languages. What factors played a role in their dominance and decline? Speculate on whether English will go the same way. →△9
Diff (instead of): Diskussion, ob die Kunst der Konversation zerstört wird, wenn Englisch als Lingua franca von Text talk abgelöst wird

English on the internet

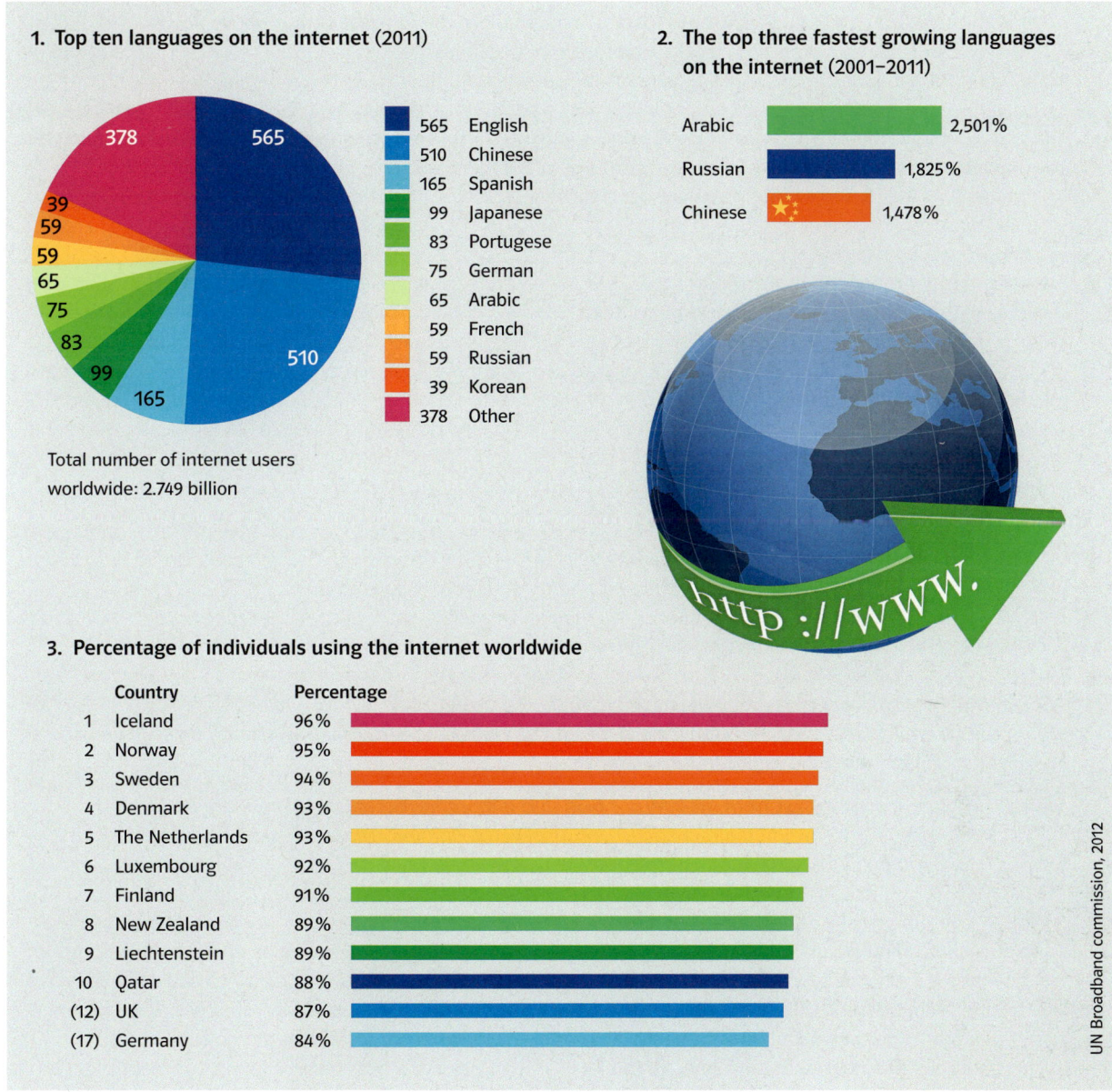

4 COMPREHENSION What do diagrams 1 and 3 reveal about the importance of languages and the percentage of people using the Internet per country? Explain both diagrams in your own words. → **S27**

5 ANALYSIS Can you find statistical support for Dr Ostler's position that English will soon decline as a world language?

6 COMMENT Do you believe that machine translation will make the learning of foreign languages redundant? → **S14.2** **Hinweis:** Auch als mündliche Diskussion geeignet

7 PRESENTATION Prepare a one-minute talk about the facts and figures presented on this page. What can you say about the role of English in the digital world? Is English still the lingua franca of the internet? → **S22** **Hinweis:** Auch als Hausaufgabe geeignet

Zusatzmaterial WB
Task 16: Statistics

Spot on language

Hinweis
Selbstevaluation für Schüler über Green Line-Code

Improving your English

The role of English as a lingua franca has lead to an increase in the number of non-native speakers of English. However, many learners of English tend to overuse words such as 'get', 'think', 'good', and 'bad' although there are more precise and suitable words to express the same meaning.

1 a) *Improve the text by finding alternatives to the overused words (highlighted). Share your results with a partner and discuss which alternatives you find more suitable. Use a dictionary whenever necessary. (Note: sometimes the word can just be replaced; sometimes the sentence structure has to be changed as well.)*

English has got more and more important as a means of communication in international contexts. Some people say this is bad for other languages, but others say it's good that people have a common language for communication. While some non-native speakers say that the use of English limits their ways of saying things, others say that they now can say the same idea in different ways. More and more anglicisms get into the German language year after year, which isn't good. Young people think it's cool to use English words; they think English is more cosmopolitan, so companies think young people will notice products if they are advertised in English. This is very interesting because older people often don't understand the slogans, which is bad as the message doesn't get to them.

b) *With the help of a dictionary (or the internet) create a list of synonyms, which can also be phrases, for one of the overused words in the text and present your results in class.*

Writing: Formal and informal English

2 *Formal English is generally considered to be more appropriate and tactful while informal English is often more direct. Note down three situations in which you would use informal English and three in which formal English would be appropriate.*

3 a) *Turn the following text from an internet blog into a more formal essay, using more appropriate language (e.g. by avoiding direct speech, phrasal verbs and informal expressions, and by making it more impersonal).*

Wow, the Internet really has changed my life! We now can communicate worldwide, can't we? But what we really need for this is a common language, a lingua franca. So some guys put forward this idea that Esperanto should be the global lingua franca, because it's neutral. But we have to think that over. In the EU, less than 0.02 per cent of the folks speak Esperanto. But more than 50 per cent of Europeans speak English.
   My dad was always like this, "We don't need to learn French or other languages. Lots of people worldwide already speak English, don't they?" He also went, "People who can't speak English will have a hard time. They won't get around in a globalised society, will they?" I think that's all crap – there are tons of other languages worldwide which all have got their own cultural value and are spoken by a lot of people. A global lingua franca could put people off learning other languages – so these languages and cultures could disappear altogether.
   Hey, what you know? I found out that Chinese, for example, is spoken by more people worldwide than English. So, folks: get learning Chinese pretty quickly!
   And what's more, loads of people who speak English as a foreign language say that they can't fully express their feelings and thoughts in English. So I think we gotta be fluent in at least two languages. Only then can we really be a part of the scene in international contexts.

b) *Share your results with a partner. What similarities and differences can you spot?*

Mediation

For a school project you and your partner at an English school (who unfortunately can hardly speak any German) are doing some research using the internet on the influence of English on German and vice versa. You have found the following text, which seems to contain quite a lot of anglicisms, but is nevertheless incomprehensible for your partner. He asks you to tell him what the text is about.

4 a) *Tell him what Denglish is and why it is problematic.* → **S26.1**

Warum Denglish Sprachmüll ist

In Funk und Fernsehen, in der Alltagssprache und in Zeitungen ist immer häufiger Denglisch zu vernehmen oder zu lesen. Das Wort bezeichnet jenes Kauderwelsch, in dem deutsche und englische
5 Wortbestandteile zu einem holprigen Neusprech zusammengerührt werden. Denglisch bezieht sich einerseits auf Wortschöpfungen, um die es in dieser Kolumne geht, aber auch auf Redewendungen – damit wird sich die nächste Sprachkolumne be-
10 schäftigen.

Als Begriff hat es Denglisch sogar schon in den „Duden" geschafft. Dort wird er so erklärt: „Abwertend für deutsch mit (zu) vielen englischen Ausdrücken vermischt." Das erste Wort der Definition sagt
15 bereits alles: abwertend! Denglisch ist also etwas Negatives, das es zu vermeiden gilt.

Trotzdem taucht es immer wieder in Zeitungsberichten auf. Mal werden Flüge gecancelt und leere Weinflaschen recycelt, mal ist Maybritt Illner eine
20 besonders toughe Moderatorin, mal wird der Nachwuchs gepampert und eine Datei downgeloadet, mal ist die Hotelbar total spacig durchdesignt und mit hippen Möbeln eingerichtet.

Solche Wortschöpfungen, in denen das englische
25 Original deutsch gebeugt wird, klingen grauenhaft, und sie sorgen für unnötige Verwirrung. Weil der englische Stamm des Wortes auch für des Englischen Kundige oft gar nicht auf den ersten Blick erkennbar ist – bei spacig könnte man genauso gut einen Tippfehler vermuten und sich fragen, ob es nicht 30 richtigerweise „spaßig" heißen müsste, gecancelt wiederum lässt an das deutsche „abgekanzelt" denken, was aber etwas völlig anderes bedeutet. Und müssen nicht Wörter, die deutsch dekliniert sind, eigentlich auch deutsch geschrieben werden? Dann 35 hieße es gezanzelt und rezützelt, aber was mag sich dahinter verbergen?

Derlei Probleme lassen sich ganz einfach umgehen: Indem der Autor auf denglische Wortschöpfungen verzichtet – und zwar auch dann, wenn sie im 40 „Duden" stehen (wie tough, chillen, hippe, cancelen, recyceln). Und indem er stattdessen auf deutsche Wörter zurückgreift. Schon stolpert kein Leser mehr, weil der gecancelte Flug nunmehr „gestrichen" ist, weil die recycelte Flasche genauso gut „wiederver- 45 wertet" werden kann, weil die toughe Moderatorin eigentlich bloß „durchsetzungsfähig" ist, weil die gepamperten Kinder „verwöhnt" werden (und nicht etwa Windeln verpasst bekommen, was man bei diesem kruden Denglizismus auch vermuten könnte), 50 weil die downgeloadete Datei auch einfach „heruntergeladen" werden kann, weil die spacige Hotelbar „futuristisch gestaltet" und mit „modernen, zeitgemäßen" (statt hippen) Möbeln ausgestattet ist. Wir sehen: Zum Sprachpansch gibt es durchaus eine 55 sinnvolle Alternative – die deutsche Sprache.

Sönke Krüger, *Die Welt*, 2007

b) *Write a comment on the question: Should we avoid anglicisms in German and use German words instead?* → **S14.2**

Spot on vocabulary

Writing about English and its varieties

1 *Create a table with words belonging to the same word family. Start by putting the words below into the correct column and then fill in the missing forms, using a dictionary if necessary. (Sometimes there may be more than one alternative.)* → **S3**

prosperous • intention • confident • compete • communicative • committed • variety

noun	verb	adjective
aspiration	aspire	aspirational
…	…	…

2 *Find the false friends in the following sentences and correct them.*

1. In their announcement the German brand "Du darfst" used a slogan that raised criticism not only among language purists.
2. The actual form of English is heavily influenced by a number of languages, including Latin, German, French, Norse, Dutch and many others.
3. Most multinational concerns have started to use English as means of communication.
4. Many German speakers of English make the same failures with respect to the use of tenses, word order and prepositions.
5. Handys have become an intrinsic part of modern life, so that owning the latest products has become a status symbol.
6. Some people think Chinese will become a lingua franca, but this meaning isn't generally accepted.
7. In countries like Sweden or the Netherlands nearly all the programmes show English and American films in English.
8. There is a lot of critic when German firms use English for their advertising slogans.

3 *Use the following vocabulary from this topic to complete the text:*

aspire • competitive • confident • dialects • dominant language • endangered • misunderstanding • native speaker • prevalence • proficiency • RP English • varieties • variety

English is no longer the global lingua franca according to a French business expert. Jean-Paul Nerrière, the author of the book *Don't Speak English, Parlez Globish* is quite **1** that within the next few years Globish will become the **2** of international business communication.

In his book, he describes how in a business meeting with colleagues from around the world he and the other non-native English speakers used a simplified version of English that was different from **3** and was completely understandable to them, but became a problem for the **4**, who was simply ignored because his language was too subtle and complex for the others. The **5** of English used by Nerrière and his colleagues has become popular as Globish, a new form of English used by people for whom it is their second language. According to Nerrière, everybody can easily **6** to achieve **7** in Globish which only uses 1,500 words and does without aspects of language that might lead to **8** and confusion, like humour, or idiomatic expressions.

Nerrière received a good deal of criticism for his proposal, especially from France where there is concern that the **9** of Globish in international business communication could pose a threat to **10** languages, while others, like French or Spanish might lose their global influence in this **11** process. Globish, Nerrière stresses, was "designed for trivial efficiency, always, everywhere, with everyone." He argues, it is far more advisable to learn Globish instead of struggling with the different **12** and **13** of English. His globalised version of English has already become so common that he urges Britons and Americans to learn it too.

> **TIP**
> First work on the vocab sheets; then test yourself here!

Topic task

The Englishes 13

Creating a podcast

Create your own podcast about the history and the future of the English language. In your podcast (which should last at least 5 minutes) you should cover some of the following aspects that are dealt with in this topic:

- The history of English
- English varieties and dialects
- English as a lingua franca
- Linguistic imperialism
- The future of English

STEP 1 Doing background research

In your group discuss which aspect (or which aspects) you would like to cover in your podcast. What do you think it would be interesting to talk about? What information surprised you? What aspects would you like to find out more about? Then do some further background research. → **S32**

STEP 2 Brainstorming first ideas and assigning roles

After your reseach, report back to the group and discuss which aspects you would like to focus on. Make sure that you assign roles (e.g. scriptwriter, presenter, interview partner(s), technician, editing expert) so that every group member can actively contribute to the podcast production.

STEP 3 Planning and scripting your podcast

As a group, develop and discuss your script, which should at least include an introduction (stating the title, giving a brief overview and introducing the presenter and his interview partners), a body and a conclusion (which includes a summary and conclusion of the topic and references and copyright where necessary). Furthermore, you should also find appropriate music for the beginning and conclusion. → **S20**
When writing the script, make sure that you use clear language and avoid words that you have difficulties in pronouncing. Your sentences should be in the present tense wherever possible. Try to avoid long and complex sentences.
Finally, do a rehersal of the podcast before recording it. Make sure that you can read the text freely without hesitating or stammering.

STEP 4 Recording and editing your podcast

Try to record your podcast under the best possible conditions (e.g. at home, in the school's computer lab) and make yourself familiar with the recording equipment beforehand. The internet offers a range of tutorials for computer recording software. Moreover, many smartphones enable the direct recording and editing of podcasts. Other tools for the recording and broadcasting of your podcast can be found on the internet.

STEP 5 Presenting your podcast

Finally, present your podcast in the classroom and give feedback on your classmates' podcasts. **Zusatzmaterial KV 4:** Feedback sheet

14 Shakespeare
Introduction

 Code
h4e4bt

This film version of Shakespeare's famous play *Romeo and Juliet*, written around 1590, was directed by Baz Luhrmann. Shakespeare didn't only write his plays, but often played small parts himself and directed the production. This is the reason why there are so few stage directions in his plays.

Elizabethan actors wore elaborate and very expensive costumes. These were usually contemporary. In Shakespeare's play *Antony and Cleopatra*, for instance, Cleopatra looked a lot more like an Elizabethan lady than the Queen of ancient Egypt.

Some of the actors in Shakespeare's day, like Richard Burbage, were real stars and became quite rich.

Expressions we owe to Shakespeare

- fight fire with fire
- the naked truth
- love is blind
- green-eyed monster
- foul play
- brave new world
- cold comfort
- heart of gold
- my own flesh and blood

Shakespeare had an enormous influence on the English language. We still use words and expressions he coined, for example when we say that "there is something rotten in the state of Denmark". This is a line from *Hamlet, Prince of Denmark*.

1 BRAINSTORMING What do you know about Shakespeare and his time, the Renaissance? Take a few minutes to think about it and start a mind map.

2 VIEWING → △1 Diff (help with): Vorgabe von Schlüsselwörtern

a) Watch the first part of the clip. What do you learn about the Globe and education in Shakespeare's day? Take notes and add to your mind map.

b) Watch the second part of the clip and comment on the changes mentioned. To what extent was 16th century society a modern one? How is this reflected in Shakespeare's plays?

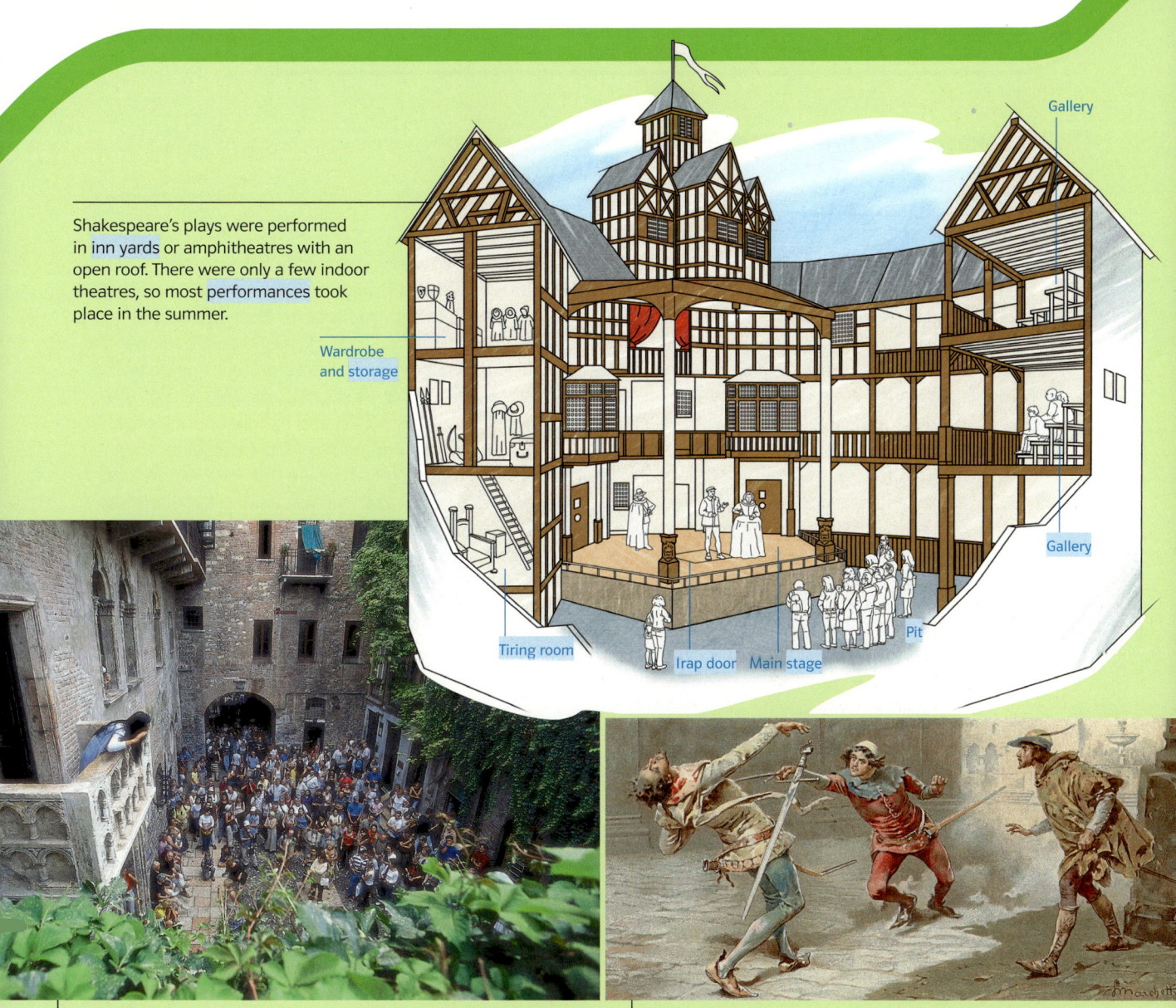

Shakespeare's plays were performed in inn yards or amphitheatres with an open roof. There were only a few indoor theatres, so most performances took place in the summer.

Wardrobe and storage
Gallery
Gallery
Pit
Tiring room
Trap door
Main stage

Romeo and Juliet is based on the medieval tale of two Veronese lovers who married against their parents' wishes. This is said to be the balcony of Juliet's house in Verona. Shakespeare took most of his ideas for plays from old stories or books – plagiarism was not an issue!

Since theatre companies travelled a lot, props had to be small and simple. Actors used swords for fight scenes like the one in *Romeo and Juliet*, where Mercutio is killed with a sword.

3 SPEAKING Describe the pictures on these two pages and use the information to talk about William Shakespeare and the Elizabethan theatre. What parallels and differences do you see to our times and our forms of entertainment? **Geeignete Methode:** Speed dating

4 LANGUAGE Which of the expressions we owe to Shakespeare can you explain? Choose one quote and invent a context for it. Who said it, and why? **Geeignete Methode:** Placemat

5 RESEARCH Choose one of Shakespeare's plays and find out what story it tells. Give a brief summary to the class. → S22 **Hinweis:** Auch als Hausaufgabe geeignet

Spot on facts

Shakespeare's life and times

The Renaissance

The Renaissance was a period of immense cultural change that has its roots in Italy in the late 14th century and extended to the early 17th century in England. It was a time of great learning and great art. Many inventions provided people with new insights and shook the foundations of society. One such invention was the telescope, which dealt a deathblow to geocentric cosmology; another one was the printing press, which made it possible to provide the masses, and not just a select few, with information and literature. Travel reports in particular were eagerly read and inspired British adventurers like Sir France Drake and Sir Martin Frobisher to follow the lead of the Spanish, Portuguese and French explorers. At the same time, outbreaks of highly infectious diseases like the plague killed thousands of people and made the lives of the survivors miserable. Shakespeare and other writers of the time met the demands of the people to be distracted and to hear about foreign places by choosing these as the settings for their plays. Although more people than ever before had access to books and learning, many old beliefs and superstitions continued to prevail, as the references to witchcraft and the appearances of ghosts in Shakespeare's plays show.

The Elizabethan Age

Queen Elizabeth (1533–1603) ruled over England for almost fifty years – most of Shakespeare's life. Her long reign was marked by prosperity and achievements in the arts, but also by various conflicts.

Religion played a dominant role in most people's lives, thus a lot of conflicts were caused by religious passions. Elizabeth's father, Henry VIII, a very headstrong and despotic monarch, broke with Rome and established himself as the head of the Protestant Church of England (also known as the 'Anglican Church'). His successors either tried to return England to Catholicism (like Mary), or to complete the Protestant Reformation (like Elizabeth). Either way, adherents of the 'wrong' religion were relentlessly persecuted.

Conspiracies and conflicts with other nations, especially with their Catholic rivals Spain and France, were another threat to stability. A tight network of spies and informants helped to find Catholics suspected of plotting against the Queen. They died either in the torture chambers or on the scaffold. Executions were public and frequent: Between 1,500 and 2,000 took place every year, several hundreds of them in London, and together with bear baiting they constituted the most gruesome form of public entertainment. It is small wonder then that shows of violence are frequent in Shakespeare's plays.

View of London in Shakespeare's day

Nevertheless, the Elizabethan Age is considered a "golden age" due to its relative stability, economic growth and the flowering of theatre, literature and music. Elizabeth succeeded in securing her position in England and abroad. She strengthened the English navy, sent adventurers to faraway countries, welcomed the idea of planting colonies there and encouraged privateers to attack Spanish merchant ships that were bringing gold from South America. The successful defeat of the Spanish Armada in 1588 was one of the most glorious moments of her reign and helped secure England's position as a leading sea power. When Elizabeth died heirless in 1603, everything had been arranged for a smooth transition of power to James of Scotland.

> **Avoiding mistakes**
> Aussprache
> ¹Renaissance [rɪˈneɪsns]

Shakespeare: an extraordinary life

William Shakespeare was born in Stratford upon Avon in April 1564. The exact date is not certain, but as he was baptised in the parish church on April 26th and it was customary to baptise children soon after birth, many think it is a safe guess to say that he was born on April 23rd – the same day on which he died in 1616. Little is known about Shakespeare's youth. His father was a glover who had managed to climb the social ladder by marrying a member of the landed gentry, Mary Arden of Warwickshire. It can be assumed that William Shakespeare attended the grammar school in Stratford and that it was here that he first became acquainted with classical ancient literature, one of the great sources of inspiration for his plays. The next hard fact in his life is his marriage to Anne Hathaway in November 1582 – he was 18, she 26, their daughter Susanna was born in May 1583. Two years later Anne gave birth to twins, Judith and Hamnet. There is not much information available on the next years in Shakespeare's life, either. He may have travelled to Italy, as the detailed knowledge of such Italian towns as Verona or Venice suggests, or he might have toured the country together with the Queen's Men, a theatre company that visited Stratford in 1586–1587. By 1592, however, he had become a person of interest in London. In a pamphlet, a rival playwright wrote unfavourably about Shakespeare, the actor turned playwright who believes that, although he lacks a university education, he can compete with such highbrow writers as Christopher Marlowe and Ben Jonson.

All the world's a stage ...

Theatre was as new to the Elizabethans as the internet to your parents, and probably equally fascinating. The first custom-built theatre was erected in London in 1567. Until then, plays were performed wherever theatre groups found a venue. Basically, there were three types of theatre: amphitheatres with an open roof (like the Globe, where Shakespeare's theatre company, the Lord Chamberlain's Men, performed), smaller indoor playhouses, where plays could also be staged in winter (like the Blackfriar's), or inn yards (like the Bull or the White Hart). It is in such inn yards that the theatre companies would perform when they travelled the country. In London alone there were more than 30 play venues. The big amphitheatres like the Globe or the Rose easily held 2,500 to 3,000 people, and the companies performed up to five different plays a week. Considering the number of places where plays were performed, and the fact that in Shakespeare's day about 200,000 people lived in London, we can assume that the theatres were immensely popular. Elizabethans loved a good play and they were ready to pay admission fees of nearly a day's wage. The plays were mass entertainment; competition was stiff, and the demand for new material very high. Shakespeare was highly prolific: he wrote more than 30 plays (comedies, tragedies, history plays), 154 sonnets, and several long poems. His stories have provided for great entertainment for four hundred years and have even been turned into operas. To this day he is the most frequently played and – with about 420 movies – the most filmed author worldwide. Shakespeare seems to be adaptable to almost any setting – the plays are as timeless as their characters and themes.

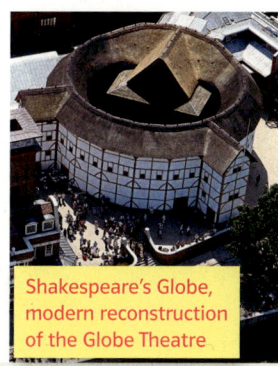

Shakespeare's Globe, modern reconstruction of the Globe Theatre.

1 **LISTENING** Listen to what two actors say about Shakespeare. Why is he still so fascinating? → S21

2 **COMPREHENSION** Complete your mind map from Task 1 on the Introduction pages with the information from the texts above.

3 **SPEAKING** Research one of these topics to find out more about it and give a short talk.

Zusatzmaterial WB
Task 13: Mediation

Core skill workshop

Analysing a scene from a play

Part A Examining the context

Drama is different from any other literary genre because of its multimedia character. Whereas in a short story or novel all the relevant information can be found in the text itself, in drama much of it is conveyed through acting. This means content can be provided both verbally and non-verbally. So when analysing a scene from a play that you read, you should first determine the relationship between the characters. Who is on the stage? What emotional situation are they in? Are there stage directions to tell the actors what to do, or to describe the scene?

USEFUL PHRASES

Talking about moods

to be in high/low spirits/in an exuberant mood

to be outraged/furious/angry

to be depressed/melancholic/pensive

1 VISUALS Describe the photos at the top of this page. What might be the relationship between the characters? What mood are they in?
Zusatzmaterial WB Task 1: Talking about moods and relations

Scene 1: The Taming of the Shrew

BIANCA Is it for him you do envy me so?
Nay then you jest; and now I well perceive
You have but jested with me all this while:
I prithee, sister Kate, untie my hands.
KATHERINA (*Strikes her*) If that be jest, then all the rest was so.   5
Enter **BAPTISTA**
BAPTISTA Why, how now, dame! Whence grows this insolence?
Bianca, stand aside. Poor girl! she weeps.
(*He unbinds her*)
Go ply thy needle; meddle not with her.   10
For shame, thou hilding of a devilish spirit,
Why dost thou wrong her that did ne'er wrong thee?
When did she cross thee with a bitter word?
KATHERINA Her silence flouts me, and I'll be revenged.
(*Flies after* **BIANCA**)   15

The Taming of the Shrew, Act II, Scene i

² **you jest** you are joking
² **to perceive** to realise
⁴ **I prithee** please
⁷ **whence grows this insolence** where do you get the nerve
¹⁰ **ply thy needle** do some sewing
¹¹ **hilding of a devilish spirit** evil monster
¹⁴ **to flout** to anger, to offend

Scene 2: A Midsummer Night's Dream

LYSANDER How now, my love! why is your cheek so pale?
How chance the roses there do fade so fast?
HERMIA Belike for want of rain, which I could well
Beteem them from the tempest of my eyes.

A Midsummer Night's Dream, Act I, Scene i

² **how chance** why is it that
³ **belike** maybe
³ **want of** lack of
³ **I could well ... my eyes** I could give them by crying

Shakespeare 14

L3/10

Scene 3: Much Ado About Nothing

BEATRICE	Good Lord, for alliance! Thus goes every one to the world but I, and I am sunburnt; I may sit in a corner and cry "Heigh-ho for a husband!"
DON PEDRO	Lady Beatrice, I will get you one.
5 BEATRICE	I would rather have one of your father's getting. Hath your grace ne'er a brother like you? Your father got excellent husbands, if a maid could come by them.
DON PEDRO	Will you have me, lady?
BEATRICE	No, my lord, unless I might have another for working-days:
10	your grace is too costly to wear every day.

Much Ado About Nothing, Act II, Scene i

[1] **alliance** *here:* marriage
[2] **but I** except me
[6] **your father got** your father's sons would make

2 COMPREHENSION *Read the scenes and match them with the photos. Give reasons for your choice. Then talk about the characters. Copy this grid:*

	Scene 1	Scene 2	Scene 3
Characters	Bianca, …	…	…
Stage directions	Strikes her (Katherina);	…	…
Relationship	…	…	…
Mood	…	…	…
Action	…	…	…

Part B Understanding the language

When examining the language of a scene, pay particular attention to
- rhythm (Is there a regular metre? Where does the stress pattern change?)
- rhetorical devices → **S10.2**

L3/9

3 LISTENING → △2 **Diff** (help with): Übung zu Rhythmus und Metrum
 a) Listen to Scene 2 and describe the specific rhythm of these lines.
 b) Get together in groups of ten. Line up and read the lines out loud, with each person reading one syllable. How does the rhythm affect you?
 c) Explain the meaning of these lines.

L3/8–10

4 LISTENING Now listen to the other dialogues and point out the differences in rhythm you notice. What is the effect achieved?

5 LANGUAGE
 a) *Practise the short dialogues with one or two partners. Think of ways of expressing emotions non-verbally (gestures and facial expression) and verbally (tone and emphasis).*
 b) How can non-verbal information change the meaning of the lines? Experiment with different ways of acting out the dialogues and discuss the effects achieved.
 c) Scan the text for clues that will help you to interpret the lines correctly.
 d) Shakespeare often uses metaphors in his work. Find some in the scenes.
    → **S10.2**

6 CREATIVE TASK *What might be the stories behind the lines? Work with a partner to collect ideas and write a story for one of the scenes.*
 Hinweis: Auch als Hausaufgabe geeignet

TIP

Shakespeare's plays are for the most part written in **blank verse**. There are no rhymes, but a particular rhythm called **iambic pentameter**, in which an unstressed syllable is followed by a stressed syllable five times per line. Some lines are written in prose (no regular metre, no rhymes).

Core skill workshop

Part C Interpreting a scene

Othello: Planting the seeds of doubt
🔊 L3/11

Othello (a "noble Moor") is a black Venetian general. After talking with his beloved wife Desdemona, he speaks to Iago, one of his most loyal soldiers – or so Othello thinks. But Iago is full of hatred for Othello because the general has promoted Michael Cassio to be his lieutenant instead of Iago.

OTHELLO	Excellent wretch! Perdition catch my soul,	5
	But I do love thee! and when I love thee not,	
	Chaos is come again.	
IAGO	My noble lord –	
OTHELLO	What dost thou say, Iago?	
IAGO	Did Michael Cassio, when you woo'd my lady,	10
	Know of your love?	
OTHELLO	He did, from first to last: why dost thou ask?	
IAGO	But for a satisfaction of my thought;	
	No further harm.	
OTHELLO	Why of thy thought, Iago?	15
IAGO	I did not think he had been acquainted with her.	
OTHELLO	O, yes; and went between us very oft.	
IAGO	Indeed!	
OTHELLO	Indeed! ay, indeed: discern'st thou aught in that?	
	Is he not honest?	20
IAGO	Honest, my lord?	
OTHELLO	Honest! ay, honest.	
IAGO	My lord, for aught I know.	
OTHELLO	What dost thou think?	
IAGO	Think, my lord?	25
OTHELLO	Think, my lord! By heaven, he echoes me,	
	As if there were some monster in his thought	
	Too hideous to be shown. Thou dost mean something:	
	I heard thee say even now, thou likedst not that,	
	When Cassio left my wife: what didst not like?	30
	[…] if thou dost love me,	
	Show me thy thought.	
IAGO	My lord, you know I love you.	

Othello, Act III, Scene iii

A scene from the film *Othello* (1995)

⁵ **wretch** *here:* girl
⁵ **perdition catch my soul** God help me
¹⁰ **to woo** to try to gain the love of sb in order to marry them
¹⁹ **discern'st thou aught** [ɔːt] do you find anything wrong
²³ **for aught I know** as far as I know
²⁸ **hideous** ['hɪdɪəs] terrible

USEFUL PHRASES

Talking about aims and effects

to aim at sth
to try to achieve sth
to cause a change
to feel the effect of sth
to produce an effect on sb
to effect a change in sb
the desired effect
manipulation/ manipulative behaviour
to manipulate sb

7 COMPREHENSION
a) Use the grid from Task 2 to determine the context of the scene.
b) Write a summary of the scene, using your notes from a).
Hinweis: Auch als Hausaufgabe geeignet

8 ANALYSIS Explain the aim Iago pursues and how he achieves it. How does his last line contribute to this aim?

9 CREATIVE TASK At what moment does Othello's mood change? How can you show this through gestures and facial expressions? How does Iago react? With your partner work on two freeze images: one showing Othello and Iago at the beginning, a second at the end of the dialogue.

10 EVALUATION Imagine Othello meets Desdemona after his conversation with Iago. Write the dialogue between them. → S12
Hinweis: Auch als Hausaufgabe oder als Partnerarbeit geeignet

Texts — Shakespeare — 14

A On the stage

1 BEFORE YOU READ *Why do people become actors? Create a mind map.*

It was hard being an Elizabethan actor

The golden age of theatre lasted only about the length of a good human lifetime, but what a wondrously prolific and successful period it was. Between the opening of the Red Lion in 1567 and the closing of all the theatres by the
5 Puritans seventy-five years later, London's playhouses are thought to have attracted fifty million paying customers, something like ten times the entire country's population in Shakespeare's day. To prosper, a theatre in London needed to draw as many as two thousand spectators
10 a day – about 1 per cent of the city's population – two hundred or so times a year, and to do so repeatedly against stiff competition. To keep customers coming back, it was necessary to change the plays constantly. Most companies performed at least five different plays in a week,
15 sometimes six, and used such spare time as they could muster to learn and rehearse new ones.

A new play might be performed three times in its first month, then rested for a few months or abandoned altogether. Few plays managed as many as ten performances in a year. So quite quickly there arose an urgent demand for
20 material. What is truly remarkable is how much quality the age produced in the circumstances. Few writers made much of a living at it, however. […] Even Ben Jonson, who passed most of his career in triumph and esteem, died in poverty.

Plays belonged, incidentally, to the company, not the playwright. A finished play was stamped with a licence from the Master of the Revels giving permission for its
25 staging, so it needed to be retained by the company. It is sometimes considered odd that no play manuscripts or prompt books were found among Shakespeare's personal effects at his death. In fact it would have been odd if they had been.

For authors and actors alike, the theatrical world was an insanely busy place, and for someone like William Shakespeare, who was playwright, actor, part owner
30 and probably *de facto* director as well (there were no formal directors in his day), it must have been nearly hysterical at times. Companies might have as many as thirty plays in their active repertoire, so a leading actor could be required to memorize perhaps fifteen thousand lines in a season as well as remember every dance and sword thrust and costume change. Even the most successful companies
35 were unlikely to employ more than a dozen or so actors, which meant a great deal of doubling up. *Julius Caesar*, for instance, has forty named characters, as well as parts for unspecified numbers of "servants", "other plebians" and "senators, soldiers and attendants". Although many of these had few demanding lines, or none at all, it was still necessary in every case to be fully acquainted with the relevant props,
40 cues, positions, entrances and exits, and to appear on time correctly attired. That in itself must have been a challenge, for nearly all clothing then involved either complicated fastenings – two dozen or more obstinate fabric clasps on a standard doublet – or yards of lacing.

In such a hothouse, reliability was paramount. Henslowe's papers show that
45 actors were subjected to rigorous contractual obligations, with graduated penalties for missing rehearsals, being drunk or tardy, failing to be "ready apparelled"

---

[21] **Ben Jonson** (1572–1637) playwright, poet and actor
[22] **esteem** admiration, respect
[24] **Master of the Revels** official censor
[26] **prompt book** text of a play used to help actors who forget their lines during a performance
[34] **sword thrust** a push with a sword
[40] **cues** words or actions in a play signalling other actors to come on stage
[40] **attired** in costume
[42] **fastening, clasp** *Schließe*
[43] **doublet** short, tightly fitting jacket for men
[43] **lacing** cord or string to fasten a garment
[44] **paramount** most important
[44] **Philip Henslowe** (1550–1616) theatrical manager
[46] **tardy** unpunctual, late
[46] **apparelled** in costume and with the correct prop

Texts

Zusatzmaterial WB
Task 2: Talking about the theatre
Task 3: Adverbs
Tasks 5–6: Speaking
Tasks 7–12: Reading and writing

USEFUL PHRASES

Talking about theatre productions

a traditional/modern-dress production

to have a good/poor/limited view of …

the scenery shows …

the director uses special effects/sounds to …

to play the classic villain/hero

to come onto/go off the stage/to be on stage

---

at the right moment, or – strikingly – for wearing any stage costumes outside the playhouse. These last were extremely valuable, so the fine was a decidedly whopping (and thus probably never imposed) £40. But even the most minor infractions, like tardiness, could cost an actor two days' pay.

Shakespeare appears to have remained an actor throughout his professional life […]. It can't have been easy to have been an actor as well as a playwright, but it would doubtless have allowed him (assuming he wished it) much greater control than had he simply surrendered a script to others, as most playwrights did.

From: Bill Bryson, *Shakespeare*, 2008

2 COMPREHENSION   Hinweis: Auch als Hausaufgabe oder als Partnerarbeit geeignet
   a) Outline the tasks an Elizabethan actor had to accomplish.
   b) Describe how playwrights fared in Elizabethan times.

3 EVALUATION Contrast the situation of actors and playwrights in Shakespeare's time with that of today. Use your ideas from Task 1 and the fact file below to do so. Consider film as well.

4 VISUALS How do different ways of presentation influence the impression an audience gets of a play? Use the pictures below to compare the experiences of audiences in Shakespeare's time with those of people seeing Shakespeare in the theatre or in film today. Think of perspective, setting, sound, atmosphere etc. → **S28.1**   **Geeignete Methode:** Think – Pair – Share

An Elizabethan performance of *Romeo and Juliet* | *Romeo and Juliet*, Maxim Gorki Theatre, Berlin | A scene from the film *Romeo + Juliet* (1996)

FACT FILE

Shakespeare's theatre

The best places in the theatres were not in the pit, close to the stage, but up in the galleries. For Elizabethans hearing every line was more important than seeing the action. That is why the actors – by the way, men only – often say what is going on, as in *Romeo and Juliet*: Mercutio comments on his own death for a full 17 lines. The interaction between spectators and actors was very different, too: If the audience did not like an actor, they might jeer or even throw objects at him. There were no breaks, so food vendors would circulate the audience with food and drinks. This caused unrest in the audience, of course – and since the plays were performed in broad daylight, everyone was constantly aware of their surroundings. So for the actors on stage, it was much harder to make the audience forget where they were and imagine nighttime in a castle in Denmark, as in the opening scene of *Hamlet*, or a shipwrecked boat, as in *The Tempest*.

Shakespeare 14

B The way to success

1 **BEFORE YOU READ** What is it that keeps your attention in a film or book? What makes you go on watching after the first few scenes, or go on reading after the first page? Work with a partner to write a list of elements that are important in a good story.

Macbeth: The opening scene

Zusatzmaterial WB
Task 4: Speaking

hurly-burly turmoil, riot
ere before
Graymalkin/Paddock cat's/toad's name (cats and toads were considered companions of witches)

From: *Macbeth: The Graphic Novel*, 2008; Script adaption: John McDonald

Texts

○ L3/13 **Othello: The opening scene**

Venice. A street at night.
Enter **RODERIGO** *and* **IAGO**.

RODERIGO Tush, never tell me, I take it much unkindly
That thou, Iago, who hast had my purse
As if the strings were thine, shouldst know of this. 5
IAGO 'Sblood, but you'll not hear me.
If ever I did dream of such a matter,
Abhor me.
RODERIGO Thou told'st me thou didst hold him in thy hate.
IAGO Despise me if I do not: three great ones of the city, 10
In personal suit to make me his lieutenant,
Off-capped to him; and by the faith of man,
I know my price, I am worth no worse a place.
But he, as loving his own pride and purposes,
Evades them with a bombast circumstance, 15
Horribly stuffed with epithets of war,
And in conclusion,
Non-suits my mediators. For "Certes," says he,
"I have already chosen my officer."
And what was he? 20
Forsooth, a great arithmetician,
One Michael Cassio, a Florentine,
A fellow almost damned in a fair wife,
That never set a squadron in the field,
Nor the division of a battle knows 25
More than a spinster, unless the bookish theoric,
Wherein the togèd consuls can propose
As masterly as he. Mere prattle without practice
Is all his soldiership. But he, sir, had the election,
And I, of whom his eyes had seen the proof 30
At Rhodes, at Cyprus, and on other grounds
Christian and heathen, must be lee'd and calmed
By debitor and creditor; this counter-caster,
He, in good time, must his lieutenant be,
And I, God bless the mark, his Moorship's ancient. 35

Othello, Act I, Scene i

⁶ **'sblood** damn
⁸ **to abhor** to hate
¹¹ **in personal suit** appealing to him in person
¹² **off-capped** took their hats off as a mark of respect
¹⁵ **a bombast circumstance … epithets of war** long talks about military achievements
¹⁸ **to non-suit** to refuse
¹⁸ **certes** certainly
²¹ **forsooth** in fact
²³ **almost damned in a fair wife** always in trouble because he is a lady-killer
²⁴ **squadron in the field** a group of soldiers in battle
²⁵ **division** strategical placing of soldiers
²⁶ **spinster** old unmarried woman
²⁶ **bookish theoric** theory
²⁷ **toged** wearing a toga
²⁸ **prattle** chatter, foolish talk
²⁹ **had the election** was chosen
³² **I must be lee'd** my career must be cut short
³³ **debitor and creditor, counter-caster** here: bookkeeper (Michael Cassio)
³⁵ **ancient** low military rank *(Fähnrich)*

2 COMPREHENSION *Summarise each opening scene in just a few sentences.*

3 ANALYSIS *Compare your list from Task 1 with the two opening scenes. Which elements of good storytelling can you find in these scenes that are also on your list?* → **S6.2**

4 ANALYSIS *Examine the two scenes for topics the plays might deal with.*
Hinweis: Auch als Hausaufgabe geeignet

5 EVALUATION
  a) *How effective are the scenes in catching the audience's attention?*
  b) *Comment on the special devices of the graphic novel. How do they contribute to conveying meaning and creating suspense?* → **S28**
  c) 👥 *Get together in groups of three or four, pick one scene and discuss ways of presenting it on stage.*
  Zusatzmaterial KV 1a–d: Vier verschiedene Eröffnungsszenen

C Shakespeare in film

Shakespeare in Love

EXT. The Curtain Theatre. Day. Hundreds of people are converging on the theatre. Among them is the Puritan Makepeace, vainly exhorting the crowds to run away from sin.

MAKEPEACE Licentiousness is made a show, vice is made a show, vanity and pride
5 likewise made a show! This is the very business of show.
But Makepeace is being carried inexorably through the main doors of the theatre.

INT. The Curtain Theatre. Backstage. Day. The Admiral's Men are all in costume, and are in a buzz of nervous excitement. Alleyn, dressed for "Mercutio," is giving last
10 minute instructions to Peter. James and John Hemmings are arguing about the timing of their entrance. Fennyman in his apothecary's cap is agonising over his lines. Wabash is stuttering over his. Alone in his dejection in the midst of all this, is Will, dressed for "Romeo." Fennyman approaches him, apothecary's cap in hand.

15 **FENNYMAN** Is this all right?
Will nods, miserable. Sam has found a private corner. He is gargling into a basin. He looks worried and furtive.

INT. The Curtain Theatre. Auditorium. Day. The audience is gathering.

EXT. The Curtain Theatre. Day. Word has got around. Even rich people are coming.
20 They arrive by carriage and by palanquin. Some of them are cloaked and hooded, slumming incognito. A cannon booms from the Curtain. The flag of the Admiral's Men flutters above.

EXT. The Curtain Theatre. Entrance. Day. Lambert and Frees are taking the entrance money.

25 **INT.** The Curtain Theatre. Auditorium. Day. The auditorium is now packed. Among them, sheepish, is Makepeace.

From: Marc Norman/Tom Stoppard, *Shakespeare in Love: A screenplay*, 1998

1 COMPREHENSION Describe the atmosphere these six film scenes convey.
Hinweis: Auch als Hausaufgabe geeignet

2 ANALYSIS Collect all the information the script contains for cameramen, sound technicians, actors and costume designers. Start like this:

Scene	Camera	Sound	Actors	Costume
1	Outside, focus on Makepeace	Crowd noises (shouting, shuffling)	Makepeace: agitated, probably gesticulating	Puritan clergy costume, distinctive in the crowd

3 VIEWING Now watch the film version. Analyse how it transports the information from the script and explain possible differences. → S29

4 EVALUATION
a) Watch the continuation of the film, which shows the opening scene of Romeo and Juliet. Compare this scene with the opening scenes of Macbeth and Othello. What influence does the medium of presentation (film, graphic novel, plain text) have?
b) Choose one of the opening scenes and write a film script for it. Decide on a setting and actors that you would like to cast. → S29.3 → ▲3
Diff (after): Überlegung zum Einsatz von filmischen Mitteln für einen spannenden Filmauftakt
Geeignete Methode zur Präsentation und Auswertung: Gallery walk

---

FACT FILE

Shakespeare in Love is a 1998 movie telling the fictitious love story of Will Shakespeare and Viola, a rich merchant's daughter, who goes against all conventions and plays Juliet in *Romeo and Juliet*. The scene takes place on the day of the premiere.

[1] **Int. (Interior)/Ext. (Exterior)** scene filmed inside/outside a building
[2] **vainly** unsuccessfully
[2] **to exhort** [ɪɡˈzɔːt] **sb** to urge sb to do sth
[4] **licentiousness** immoral behaviour
[11] **to agonise over** to worry
[12] **dejection** grief, misery
[15] **to gargle** to wash inside of throat and mouth
[16] **furtive** hoping not to be noticed
[25] **sheepish** looking embarrassed

USEFUL PHRASES

Describing atmosphere

an atmosphere of … is created

the atmosphere is charged with …

the action/lines contribute to the atmosphere

the audience can sense a … atmosphere

Advanced texts

D Insights into the human mind

Macbeth: Power and ambition

Macbeth has learned from three witches that he is to be the future king of Scotland and told his wife about this prophesy in a letter. He then hurries home from the battlefield to prepare a banquet in honour of the present king, Duncan. Duncan is Macbeth's relative and has just granted him the title 'Thane of Cawdor' for his faithful service and great bravery in a battle. 5

MACBETH	How now? What news?
LADY MACBETH	He has almost supped. Why have you left the chamber?
MACBETH	Hath he asked for me?
LADY MACBETH	Know you not he has?
MACBETH	We will proceed no further in this business. 10
	He hath honoured me of late, and I have bought
	Golden opinions from all sorts of people,
	Which would be worn now in their newest gloss,
	Not cast aside so soon.
LADY MACBETH	Was the hope drunk 15
	Wherein you dressed yourself? Hath it slept since?
	And wakes it now to look so green and pale
	At what it did so freely? From this time,
	Such I account thy love. Art thou afeard
	To be the same in thine own act and valour, 20
	As thou art in desire? Wouldst thou have that
	Which thou esteem'st the ornament of life,
	And live a coward in thine own esteem,
	Letting "I dare not" wait upon "I would," […]?
MACBETH	Prithee, peace. 25
	I dare do all that may become a man;
	Who dares do more is none.
LADY MACBETH	What beast was't then
	That made you break this enterprise to me?
	When you durst do it, then you were a man. 30
	And to be more than what you were, you would
	Be so much more the man. […] I have given suck and know
	How tender 'tis to love the babe that milks me:
	I would, while it was smiling in my face,
	Have plucked my nipple from his boneless gums 35
	And dashed the brains out, had I so sworn
	As you have done to this.
MACBETH	If we should fail?
LADY MACBETH	We fail?
	But screw your courage to the sticking-place, 40
	And we'll not fail. When Duncan is asleep –
	Whereto the rather shall his day's hard journey
	Soundly invite him – his two chamberlains
	Will I with wine and wassail so convince
	That memory, the warder of the brain, 45
	Shall be a fume, and the receipt of reason
	A limbeck only. When in swinish sleep

Zusatzmaterial KV 2
Erproben von Überzeugungs- bzw. Ablehnungsstrategien

Patrick Stewart and Kate Fleetwood in the 2010 film version of *Macbeth*

13 **worn in their newest gloss, not cast aside so soon** enjoyed while the feeling is fresh, not thrown away
20 **valour** great courage
22 **to esteem** to regard as
22 **ornament of life** *here:* the most valuable thing in life (the crown)
24 **to wait upon** *here:* to follow
25 **prithee** please
29 **to break this enterprise** *here:* to reveal this plan (killing Duncan)
30 **durst** past of dare
35 **boneless** toothless
40 **screw your courage to the sticking-place** be as courageous as possible
42 **whereto the rather** *here:* to which
44 **wassail** drinking toasts
45 **that memory, … a limbeck only** that they will forget everything

Shakespeare 14

		Their drenchèd natures lie as in a death,
		What cannot you and I perform upon
50		Th'unguarded Duncan? [...]
	MACBETH	Bring forth men-children only,
		For thy undaunted mettle should compose
		Nothing but males. [...] I am settled and bend up
		Each corporal agent to this terrible feat.
55		Away, and mock the time with fairest show:
		False face must hide what the false heart doth know.

Macbeth, Act I, Scene vii

48 **drenched** drunken
52 **undaunted mettle** fearless spirit
54 **each corporal agent** every part of me
55 **to mock the time** to deceive the world

1 COMPREHENSION Summarise this scene.

2 ANALYSIS Briefly describe the relationship between Macbeth and Lady Macbeth. What do we learn about the two characters? → △4 **Diff** (help with): Vorgabe von Leitfragen

3 VIEWING Watch the scene played by TNT. To what extent is the acting (body language, intonation, …) and the setting convincing? → S29.2
Geeignete Methode: Speed dating

Othello: Manipulation

Iago hates Othello and wants to destroy him. He first makes sure that Othello's lieutenant Michael Cassio falls from grace, then advises Cassio to ask Desdemona, Othello's wife, to help him regain Othello's esteem.

	IAGO	And what's he then that says I play the villain?
5		When this advice is free I give and honest,
		Probal to thinking and indeed the course
		To win the Moor again? [...] How am I then a villain
		To counsel Cassio to this parallel course,
		Directly to his good? Divinity of hell!
10		When devils will the blackest sins put on,
		They do suggest at first with heavenly shows,
		As I do now. For whiles this honest fool
		Plies Desdemona to repair his fortune,
		And she for him pleads strongly to the Moor,
15		I'll pour this pestilence into his ear:
		That she repeals him for her body's lust;
		And by how much she strives to do him good,
		She shall undo her credit with the Moor.
		So will I turn her virtue into pitch,
20		And out of her own goodness make the net
		That shall enmesh them all.

Othello, Act II, Scene iii

TIP

In a **monologue**, a person gives a speech adressing other people.
In a **soliloquy**, someone talks to him-/herself to reveal his/her inner thoughts and feelings.

Kenneth Branagh as Iago

6 **probal to thinking and indeed the course** plausible and the best way
9 **divinity of hell** here: satanic argumentation
13 **to ply** to keep asking sb
15 **pestilence** poison
16 **she repeals him** she takes his side
17 **to strive** to try hard
19 **to turn her virtue into pitch** to make her look very bad
21 **to enmesh** to catch as in a spider's web

4 COMPREHENSION Outline the plan Iago reveals in his soliloquy.
Hinweis: Auch als Hausaufgabe geeignet
5 ANALYSIS Compare Iago's plans for manipulation with Lady Macbeth's approach. → ▲5 **Diff** (after): Analyse des Verhaltens von Lady Macbeth und des Vorgehens Iagos mit Blick auf die Rolle der Frauen
6 EVALUATION "Shakespeare is the master of metaphor and psychology". Comment on this statement, based on the two excerpts. → S14.2 → △6
Diff (help with): Vorgabe von Übungen und Tipp zu Metaphern
Zusatzmaterial KV 3: Vortragen des Monologs von Iago

Advanced texts

Avoiding mistakes
Wortschatz
⁴**idle** *here:* without purpose, killing time; *also:* lazy, inactive, useless
NICHT: ~~eitel~~

⁴ **to scribble** to write randomly, with no purpose
⁴ **jottings** notes
⁶ ***Love's Labour's Lost*** a comedy written by Shakespeare
⁶ ***The Rape of Lucrece*** a long Shakespeare poem

The First Folio

VIP FILE

Ben Jonson was Shakespeare's rival both as an actor and a playwright, but also a good friend. When Shakespeare's former colleagues published the *First Folio* – the first collection of his plays – in 1623, Jonson contributed an affectionate poem "To the memory of my beloved, the author Mr. William Shakespeare".

E Shakespeare – fame and fortune?

1 BEFORE YOU READ Have you ever wondered what it might feel like to be famous? What would change in your life?

Writing Shakespeare

Around 1598, still relatively early in Shakespeare's career, a man named Adam Dyrmonth, about whom next to nothing is known, set out to list the contents of a collection of speeches and letters that he had transcribed. Evidently, his mind began to wander, because he began to scribble idly. Among the jottings that cover the page are the words "Rychard the second" and "Rychard the third," along with half-remembered quotations from *Love's Labour's Lost* and *The Rape of Lucrece*. Above all, the scribbler repeatedly wrote the words "William Shakespeare." He wanted to know, as it seems, what it felt like to write that particular name as one's own. Dyrmonth might have been the first to be driven by this curiosity, but he certainly was not the last.

As Dyrmonth's scribblings suggest, Shakespeare was famous in his own lifetime. Only a few years after Shakespeare's death, Ben Jonson celebrated him as "the wonder of our stage" and "the star of poets." But at the time such literary celebrity did not ordinarily lead to the writing of biographies, and no contemporary seems to have thought it worthwhile to collect whatever could be found out about Shakespeare while his memory was still green. As it happens, more is known about him than about most professional writers of the time, but this knowledge is largely the consequence of the fact that England in the late sixteenth and early seventeenth century was already a record-keeping society and that many of the records survived, to be subsequently combed over by eager scholars. Even with this relative abundance of information, there are huge gaps in knowledge that make any biographical study of Shakespeare an exercise in speculation.

From: Stephen Greenblatt, *Will in the World*, 2004

2 ANALYSIS Compare the attitude towards famous people in Shakespeare's time with that of today. What differences and what parallels do you see?

3 SPEAKING
Think: If Shakespeare was alive today, how would he be treated by fans and the media?
Pair: Exchange your ideas with a partner.
Share: Present one of them in detail to the class.

4 CREATIVE TASK Choose one of the following options:
 a) Create a Facebook account for Shakespeare. Who are his friends? What advertisements pop up when you visit his page? What news and pictures does he post?
 b) Imagine you had the chance to interview William Shakespeare in a TV show. Prepare a brief introduction and questions for the interview. → **S25**
  Hinweis: Auch als Hausaufgabe geeignet

5 EVALUATION Biographies of famous people often become bestsellers. What are the reasons for this interest in the lives of the famous? Discuss. → **S14.1**
Hinweis: Als mündliche Diskussion oder als schriftliche Hausaufgabe geeignet

6 BEFORE YOU READ Whereas the plays reveal only little information about Shakespeare himself, his sonnets are considered to be a more reliable source of information on Shakespeare as a person. What could be an explanation for this? **Geeignete Methode:** Think – Pair – Share

Sonnet 91

Some glory in their birth, some in their skill,
Some in their wealth, some in their bodies' force,
Some in their garments, though new-fangled ill,
Some in their hawks and hounds, some in their horse;
5 And every humour hath his adjunct pleasure,
Wherein it finds a joy above the rest:
But these particulars are not my measure;
All these I better in one general best.
Thy love is better than high birth to me,
10 Richer than wealth, prouder than garments' cost,
Of more delight than hawks or horses be;
And having thee, of all men's pride I boast:
   Wretched in this alone, that thou mayst take
   All this away and me most wretched make.

> **TIP**
> The **speaker** is not identical with the poet. The way a speaker acts and thinks, however, is often influenced by the poet's personal experiences.

3 **new-fangled ill** trendy and weird
5 **humour** temperament
5 **adjunct** corresponding
8 **to better** to surpass
13 **wretched** miserable, sad

7 LISTENING Listen to the sonnet and say in one sentence what it is about.

8 COMPREHENSION
  a) What Elizabethan status symbols does the sonnet list? Which ones can you detect in the paintings?
  b) Point out the speaker's attitude towards these status symbols.
  c) What would be equivalent status symbols today?
  d) Discuss: How important are status symbols today? What role do they play in your life?

9 ANALYSIS Analyse the structure of the sonnet and explain how this structure supports its main thesis. → S6.1

10 CREATIVE TASK Turn the sonnet into a short speech (about 100 words) about what should matter in life. Use modern English and modern status symbols.
Hinweis: Auch als Hausaufgabe geeignet

Henry, Prince of Wales, with Sir John Harington (1603)

Zusatzmaterial WB
Task 14: Analysing poetry

FACT FILE

The sonnets
Most of Shakespeare's 154 sonnets are written in iambic pentameter. They usually consist of fourteen lines that are divided into three quatrains (four lines of verse) and a couplet (two concluding lines). Shakespeare adressed the first 126 of his sonnets to a young man. This "fair youth" was presumably Henry Wriothesley, Earl of Southampton, who was at the time Shakespeare's patron and to whom Shakespeare dedicated two lengthy poems. Such patronage was advantageous for both sides – wealthy noblemen liked to create for themselves an image of culture and power, and poets relied on their support for financial and creative survival. Sonnets 127–152 are adressed to the "Dark Lady", whose identity is still unknown, but has given great cause for speculation.

Henry Wriothesley ['raɪzli] (1573–1624)

Advanced texts

◉ L3/17 **Fear no more**

Fear no more the heat o' the sun,
Nor the furious winter's rages;
Thou thy worldly task hast done,
Home art gone, and ta'en thy wages:
Golden lads and girls all must,   5
As chimney-sweepers, come to dust.

Fear no more the frown o' the great;
Thou art past the tyrant's stroke;
Care no more to clothe and eat;
To thee the reed is as the oak: 10
The sceptre, learning, physic, must
All follow this, and come to dust.

Fear no more the lightning flash,
Nor the all-dreaded thunder-stone;
Fear not slander, censure rash;   15
Thou hast finished joy and moan:
All lovers young, all lovers must
Consign to thee, and come to dust.

No exorciser harm thee!
Nor no witchcraft charm thee!   20
Ghost unlaid forbear thee!
Nothing ill come near thee!
Quiet consummation have;
And renowned be thy grave!

Cymbeline, Act IV, Scene ii

7 **frown** angry look
10 **reed** *Schilfrohr*
11 **sceptre, learning, physic** *here:* kings, scholars, doctors
14 **all-dreaded** much feared
14 **thunder-stone** *Donnerschlag*
15 **slander** damaging sb's reputation by telling lies
15 **rash** hasty and thoughtless
16 **moan** sound expressing unhappiness or pain
18 **to consign to sb** to commit oneself to sb
21 **to forbear** [fɔːˈbeə] *here:* to spare sb
23 **consummation** making sth complete or perfect
24 **renowned** [rɪˈnaʊnd] famous and honoured

11 COMPREHENSION
a) What is the general theme of the poem? Who is it addressed to?
b) Sum up each stanza in one sentence.

12 ANALYSIS Analyse the rhyme scheme and metre of this poem. What is the effect of the shift in metre in the final stanza? In what way does the poem's structure differ from the sonnet on the preceding page? → **S6.1**

13 CREATIVE TASK Unlike Shakespeare's sonnets, this poem is part of a play about mischievous plots against two lovers, Posthumus and Imogen, at the British court in Roman times. Imagine a situation in which this poem – a funeral song – might be sung, and write a brief story about it.
Hinweis: Auch als Hausaufgabe geeignet

14 EVALUATION
a) *Cymbeline* was presumably written in 1610. Assess to what extent it reflects the ideas of life and death people had in Shakespeare's time.
b) 1610 was also the year in which Shakespeare retired from his active career as a playwright and actor in London. Do you think there is a connection between the poem and this event? What might the poem tell us about the way he viewed his life until then?

15 CREATIVE TASK Find pictures to create a slide show for the song and music to accompany it.

Shakespeare 14

How could a commoner write such great plays?

For about 150 years people have doubted Shakespeare's authorship – among them such famous individuals as Sigmund Freud, Mark Twain or Orson Welles. In his film Anonymous, *Roland Emmerich picks up on the idea that William Shakespeare cannot have been the author of the famous plays, but that he must*
5 *have been someone well acquainted with politics and the court.*

First things first. The film's premise is that the plays and poems commonly attributed to William Shakespeare are actually the work of Edward de Vere, 17th Earl of Oxford. This notion, sometimes granted the unwarranted dignity of being called a theory, is hardly new. It represents a hoary form of literary birtherism
10 that has persisted for a century or so, in happy defiance of reason and evidence. The arrival of "Anonymous" has roused Shakespeareans more learned than I to the weary task of re-debunking – in the past two weeks *The New York Times* has published [two articles] opposing the Oxfordian position – and to their cogent arguments I can offer only a small corrective. This is a Roland Emmerich film. (At
15 least I assume it is, though I guess, in the spirit of the enterprise, I should be open to other possibilities. Joe Swanberg? Brett Ratner? Zhang Yimou? It all seems eerily plausible, once you start to think about it.)

My point is that it might be a mistake to suppose that the director of "10,000 B.C." – to mention only the most salient example – should be taken as a reliable
20 guide to history. Perhaps he [...], rather than advancing the case for Edward de Vere, set out to undermine it by exposing the absurd prejudices and fallacies on which the hypothesis rests. These can be boiled down to a sentimental and reactionary fantasy of class. How could Shakespeare, the half-educated son of an unlettered provincial glove maker, have written all those masterpieces? Surely it is
25 more plausible to suppose that they were the work of one of his betters.

A. O. Scott, *The New York Times*, 2011

16 COMPREHENSION Summarise the author's attitude towards the authorship question.

17 ANALYSIS Explain Scott's claim that the authorship debate rests on a "sentimental and reactionary fantasy of class". → S4.2

18 LANGUAGE Analyse the use of rhetoric devices, and explain what effect is achieved by them. → S10

19 EVALUATION Does class membership or social background still play a role in our modern society? How much has changed since Shakespeare's day? Discuss.
Hinweis: Als mündliche Diskussion oder schriftliche Hausaufgabe geeignet

20 SPEAKING
a) Apart from Edward de Vere, the main candidates for the authorship of Shakespeare's works are Christopher Marlowe (playwright and poet) and Sir Francis Bacon (philosopher, politician and author). Choose one of these candidates and find arguments that support their claim.
b) Prepare a TV show in which you defend either your candidate or Shakespeare as author of the plays. → S24

FACT FILE

The **authorship debate** began in the 19th century when Shakespeare rose to the status of greatest writer of all time. His humble origins and lack of an academic education have led to the supposition that he cannot have originated the plays. 'Oxfordians' believe that the Earl of Oxford really wrote the plays.

6 **premise** basic assumption
8 **unwarranted** unjustified
9 **hoary** so old that it is no longer of interest
9 **birtherism** theory that Obama is not a US-born citizen, and thus ineligible as President
10 **defiance** refusal to accept
12 **to re-debunk** to show again that an idea is wrong
13 **cogent** ['kəʊdʒənt] convincing
16 **Joe Swanberg, Brett Ratner, Zhang Yimou** film directors
19 **salient** most noticeable
21 **fallacy** a false idea

251

Advanced texts

F Not for an age, but for all time

Much Ado About Nothing, set in Delhi

Julius Caesar as political thriller in modern Africa

Shakespeare: A life on stage

Shakespeare's birthday on April 23 will be marked by an extraordinary relay. Over 24 hours, 60 groups of youngsters from New Zealand to Hawaii will enact excerpts from his plays. As part of this project, a Serbian youth group will perform *Romeo and Juliet*. How will they respond in a country so scarred by its own history of tribal divisions? Life has taught me a hard lesson about the power and impact of that play: my father, who died in 1970, banished me from his life because I played Juliet in a school production that dared to confront the prejudices of my people.

I was born in Kampala, Uganda. My ancestors had moved there from India, part of a wave of migration that began in the 1880s, when the British brought over Indian indentured laborers to build the East African railway. They were followed by Indian entrepreneurs and the impoverished, all hoping to make good in that fecund land. British imperialists set the migrants up to be a bulwark between themselves and "barbaric" blacks. Class and race divisions were institutionalized and internalized. Asian settlers saw indigenous Africans as Calibans – as crude, lascivious and untrustworthy as *The Tempest's* half-man, half-demon. Africans, in turn, detested the brown interlopers. To them, Asian merchants were like Shylock: usurers and exploiters.

In 1965, our English teacher decided to stage *Romeo and Juliet* and make it a metaphor of our divided lives. By acting as young lovers on stage, John Abwole, the African Romeo, and I breached the wall separating us. My family and community reacted with appalling cruelty. Papa never spoke to me again.

Shakespeare captivates audiences in the West, and resonates profoundly in postcommunist nations. But he is most alive for people of color. South Asians and Arabs and their diasporic peoples are Elizabethans still. In their world, children are parental possessions, marriages arranged, personal autonomy frowned upon. Strong women like Beatrice in *Much Ado About Nothing* or Katherine the shrew must be tamed. Countless Juliets are bullied, beaten, even killed if they refuse to be despatched to a chosen bridegroom. They hear their own fathers in Capulet's warning to his rebellious daughter:

An you be mine, I'll give you to my friend; / An you be not, hang, beg, starve, die in the streets, / For, by my soul, I'll ne'er acknowledge thee …

---

1 **relay** *here:* series of events
4 **scarred** marked with scars
4 **tribal divisions** fights between tribes
10 **indentured laborers** slaves
11 **impoverished** poor
12 **fecund** fertile, prospering
12 **bulwark** [ˈbʊlwək] defence, protection
14 **indigenous** native
14 **Caliban** character in *The Tempest*
15 **lascivious** [ləˈsɪvɪəs] showing sexual desire
16 **interloper** intruder
16 **Shylock** character in *The Merchant of Venice*
17 **usurer** [ˈjuːʒərə] money-lender who charges unfairly
24 **diasporic** living outside their home country
25 **to frown upon** to disapprove
26 **Katherine the shrew** refers to the rebellious main character in *The Taming of the Shrew*
30 **An you be mine …** *Romeo and Juliet*, Act III, Scene v

Shakespeare speaks directly to those suffering wars and oppression. Some of the real-life tragedies I have witnessed over the years echo Shakespeare. Bharti, a young Hindu, used to take refuge in our house in Kampala to escape her oppressive
35 father; he tried to force her into a marriage and she killed herself. My chemistry teacher, also a Hindu, fell in love with a Muslim woman; her family whisked her off to Pakistan and he swallowed acid in the school laboratory, dying for love. A distant relative in Tanzania was charged with hiring killers to murder her oldest son, his wife and their babies because her husband threatened to disown her favorite
40 younger boy. The papers called her "Lady Macbeth"; she fled to Pakistan and died alone.

When Julius Nyerere became the first President of independent Tanzania in 1964, he translated *Julius Caesar* into Swahili, then sent actors into villages to perform it and discuss the dangers of overweening power.

45 Today, Arab and African exiles across Europe imagine a bloody vengeance against their leaders, those tribal Macbeths and oil-rich Caesars. As Kenya descended into violence last January, Leo, a Rwandan exile in London, rang me. One day, he said, the citizenry will bear this no longer, just like the citizens of 15th century England who rebelled against their aristocratic rulers, tired of
50 the bloodletting and power struggles. He had just seen the Royal Shakespeare Company's (RSC) production of *Henry VI*. During its run, actors David Oyelowo and Chuk Iwuji – both of African origin – have been superb Kings, inhabiting the past and the present, and conveying through old conflicts the anguish of the strife now ravaging African nations, as well as the defiant optimism that may yet save them.

55 And in places where censorship reigns, Shakespeare can say what others cannot. Kuwaiti director Sulayman Al-Bassam uses him for subversive ends. "If you are an Arab theater maker looking to take a pop at authority, Shakespeare is your perfect bedmate, co-conspirator and alibi," he has said. Such is the yearning for catharsis in the Middle East that, when he took his *Richard III* to Egypt, it provoked
60 a near riot among people who couldn't get tickets.

I have turned the Romeo and Juliet tragedy in my own life into a theatrical piece commissioned by the RSC. After the show, I am often asked if I regret playing Juliet. No, I say. Shakespeare was worth the sacrifice – rather him than the love of a father. The playwright knows and serves me better.

Yasmin Alibhai-Brown, *Time*, 2008

39 **to disown** to accept no longer as member of the family
44 **overweening** too self-confident and proud
53 **anguish** great pain
53 **strife** conflict
54 **to ravage** to damage badly
57 **to take a pop at** (infml) to aim a punch at
59 **catharsis** releasing strong feelings as a way of providing relief from suffering or anger

©2008 Time Inc. All rights reserved. Reprinted/Translated from TIME and published with permission of Time Inc. Reproduction in any manner in any language in whole or in part without written permission is prohibited.

1 **COMPREHENSION** Outline the relevance of Shakespeare for Yasmin Alibhai-Brown's life and the lives of her family and friends.
Hinweis: Auch als Hausaufgabe geeignet

2 **RESEARCH** Work in groups to make a list of the Shakespeare plays mentioned in the text, and find out what they are about. In what way do they help to support the text?

3 **ANALYSIS** Analyse the author's opinion on the relevance of Shakespeare today. What different aspects of life does she refer to? How does she illustrate her point of view? **Zusatzmaterial WB** Task 16: Language awareness

4 **EVALUATION** Yasmin Alibhai-Brown says that she preferred Shakespeare to the love of a father. Analyse this statement and comment on it. → **S14.2**

5 **CREATIVE TASK** Choose one play in this chapter. Think of situations – national, global or private – which reflect the themes of the play, and use them as a starting point for writing a short essay on Shakespeare's relevance today.
→ **S14.1**

Zusatzmaterial WB
Task 13: Mediation
Task 15: Using -ing forms

Spot on language

Understanding Shakespeare's English

Characteristics of Elizabethan English

There is no reason to be afraid of Shakespeare's English. Of course some of the words he used have changed their meaning or are no longer in use, and some seem strange, but on the whole his language is not so far removed from the English we speak today. English was in flux then. Old forms like **thee** [ðiː]/**thou** [ðaʊ], **thy/thine** co-existed with the newer **you** and **your**, and we find all these forms in Shakespeare's plays. Some verb endings still existed which we do not use anymore, like **-st** (2nd person singular) or **-th** (3rd person singular). Another obvious difference is the rare use of the auxiliary "do" and its derivatives: they simply were not yet very common in Elizabethan days. Hence the sometimes strange word order in Shakespeare's sentences.

Queen Elizabeth I

1 *Change these sentences from Shakespearean English into modern English.*

1. Hath your grace not a brother like you?
2. Where grows this flower?
3. Thou hast it now.
4. Be not afeared!
5. Seest thou this letter?
6. She stayed not long.
7. What looked he like?
8. Thou canst see with thine own eyes.
9. Wherefore didst thou this?
10. Thou likedst not that.

2 *In Shakespeare's day, the subjunctive (e.g. "the Lord be praised") was used more often than it is today. It was used to express a wish or an intention and also in conditional clauses.*
Turn the following lines from Shakespeare plays into modern English by using forms of "want to" or "wish" or an if-clause + present tense. Modernise other words, too, if necessary (e.g. in sentence 1, "method" means "system").

1. Though this be madness, yet there is method in't.
2. Wilt thou be gone? It is not yet near day.
3. If this be known to you, then we have done you wrong.
4. Where will you that I go to answer this charge?
5. Wake Duncan with thy knocking! I would thou couldst!
6. I would there were no age between sixteen and three-and-twenty!

3 *Shakespeare invented or at least popularised a great number of phrases that have found a permanent place in the English language. Here are some – explain them and find other ways of saying the same thing.*

1. The team has lost three times in a row – I'd say the coach **is in a pickle**.
2. I love babies, but triplets are **too much of a good thing**.
3. Mandy should be more careful what she says. She **wears her heart on her sleeve**.
4. After the second own goal he **was the laughing stock** of the team.
5. He **broke the ice** by complimenting her on her dress.
6. My children came home for the weekend – they have **eaten me out of house and home**.
7. We found out the truth. **The game is up**!
8. After the bank's bankruptcy the manager **melted into thin air**.
9. He was **snatched out of the jaws of death** by the surgeon who operated on him.
10. Like many other investors, he **played fast and loose**.

> **Hinweis**
> Selbstevaluation für Schüler über Green Line-Code

Mediation

4 A friend from your partner school in England tells you about a Shakespeare project that the theatre group plans to perform at their school. They are complaining that their school is going to use the original text of the play, which they think is boring and far too difficult. They would prefer to perform Shakespeare in a modernised version. Based on the article from Die Welt, write an email to your friend and explain why there is a point in using original versions.

Shakespeares „Homies" reden jetzt Jugendslang

Romeo und Julia, Hamlet und Konsorten müssen Jugendsprache lernen: Der britische Satiriker Martin Baum hat Werke von William Shakespeare in Jugendslang „übersetzt". Schüler verstehen das elisabethanische Englisch kaum. Ziel des Satirikers ist nun, Jugend für Weltliteratur zu begeistern.

Vor ewig langer Zeit gründete ein französischer Jazzpianist eine Gruppe, die sich „Play Bach Trio" nannte. Diese Gruppe spielte tatsächlich Werke von Johann Sebastian Bach, aber modern, verjazzt, mit Schlagzeug und allen Schikanen. Eine ganze Generation von Schülern wurde damit traktiert – fortschrittliche Lehrer hofften allen Ernstes, sie könnten ihre Zöglinge durch diesen Trick verführen, sich freiwillig Barockmusik anzutun. Unter uns: Es war grässlich, eine Zumutung. Vor allem klang Bach in der aufgemotzten Version unglaublich langweilig. Mittlerweile deckt Staub die Erinnerung an das „Play Bach Trio", während der Meister selbst trotz Dreifachkinn und Puderperücke munter weiterlebt.

Nun hat Martin Baum, ein englischer Satiriker, 15 Stücke von Shakespeare in heutigen Jugendslang übersetzt – nicht in irgendeine Jugendsprache, sondern jenen proletarischen Jargon, der sich ans Cockney anlehnt, das Londoner Gegenstück zum Berlinerischen (oder zum Hamburger „Missingsch").

„De Happy Bitches of Windsor"

Hamlet verliert auf diese Weise ein H und wird zu „Amlet". „Die lustigen Weiber von Windsor" mutiert zu „De Happy Bitches of Windsor". „Viel Lärm um nichts" heißt jetzt „Much Ado about Sod All". Es ist sehr lustig – und man braucht allerhand Verrenkungen, um im Deutschen wiederzugeben, was daran eigentlich lustig sein soll. Martin Baum hat seinen Schlegel, seinen Tieck halt noch nicht gefunden. Hamlets berühmter Monolog hebt bei ihm an mit den geflügelten Worten: „To be or not to be, innit?" Also ungefähr: „Sein oder nich' sein oder was?"

Die Ausgangssituation von Shakespeares berühmtester Liebestragödie hört sich bei Martin Baum näherungsweise wie folgt an: „In Verona ham sich zwei Familien gekloppt, die Montagues und die Capulets. Und weil die dauernd gekämpft haben und so, hat der Prinz von Verona ihnen gesacht: Hört auf mit dem Scheiß, denn wenn ihr weiterkabbelt, hau ich euch zu Matsch."

Echter Shakespeare moderner

Das tragische Ende jenes Dramas aber packt Martin Baum in die Formel: „And they all lived in peace and harmony except for Romeo and his bitch Jools, who was both well dead."

Sagen wir's so: „Und sie lebten alle glücklich und zufrieden weiter, bis auf Romeo und seine olle Jule, weil die war'n ganz schön hinüber."

Zugegeben: Die modernisierten Versionen des Martin Baum kommen nicht ganz so betulich daher wie der verschlagzeugte Bach von anno dunnemals. Dennoch sei die Prophezeiung gewagt, dass sich der echte Shakespeare als haltbarer, moderner (häufig auch: witziger) erweisen wird als die hochgejazzte Nachahmung.

Hannes Stein, *Die Welt*, 2008

5 Have a closer look at the modernised quotes in the article. Do you think Martin Baum was successful in transforming Shakespeare's English into modern teenage slang? Is this also true of the German translations?

Spot on vocabulary

Talking about theatre and drama

1 a) *Complete these sentences by choosing the correct word.*

1. Shakespeare's (**dramedies/dramas/dramatics**) are still popular today.
2. The reason for this popularity is that their themes are still (**actual/acute/topical**).
3. When you watch a Shakespeare play, you can easily imagine action and scenes – even if there are only very few (**prompts/props/proms**).
4. Elizabethans loved a good laugh, so Shakespeare invented many (**hysterical/humorous/laughable**) characters, such as Sir John Falstaff.
5. In some plays, the Fool is an important character. His jokes often hide a painful (**trust/true/truth**).

b) *Explain the meaning of the words that do not fit and find example sentences for them.*

2 *Get together in groups of four. Copy the words below on cards, and turn them face down on the table. Take turns in picking one of the cards without letting the others see which word you have. Now either paraphrase, act or draw the word. The others must guess which word it is.*

playhouse • venue • prop • stage • blank verse • iambic pentameter • sonnet • quatrain • rehearsal • actor • balcony scene • costume • monologue • soliloquy • sword thrust • prompt book • metaphor • censorship

Talking about the Elizabethan stage

3 *Use the English equivalents of these German words to complete the text below.*

Publikum • Tragödie • Schauspieltruppe • anziehen • Regieanweisung • durch das Land reisen • Dramatiker • Requisite • Komödie • Regisseur • aufführen • Bekanntschaft machen mit

In Shakespeare's time, plays **1** a large **2**. They were mostly **3** in London's permanent theatres, but there were also travelling theatre companies that played in inn yards. This is probably how young Will Shakespeare first **4** the theatre. He was an actor before he became a **5** and wrote his famous **6** and **7**. Maybe he **8** with The Queen's Men, a **9** that visited Stratford when Will Shakespeare was in his early twenties. There are very few **10** in his plays, so the **11** of the play – often an actor himself – had to tell the other actors what **12** to bring on stage, or how to act.

4 *Work with a partner. Write the following words on a card, then put them face down onto the table. Turn one over and write down all the words and expressions that you can use to talk about it. Stop after 60 seconds and exchange your results. Then turn over the next card.*

atmosphere • a villain • mood • a hero • Shakespeare's language • Globe theatre • Elizabethan England

5 *Use all of the vocabulary given below to write a paragraph about entertainment in Elizabethan England.*

bear baiting • public executions • violence • (travelling) theatre companies • indoor playhouses • open-roofed theatres • admission fees • gallery • pit • food vendors • stamp of approval • Master of the Revels • censorship

TIP

First work on the vocab sheets, then test yourself here!

Topic task
Shakespeare 14

Filming a scene from Shakespeare

Create your own clip for the annual competition "Filming Shakespeare". Choose an interesting scene, write a script for your performance and film it.

STEP 1 — Choosing a scene from a play

Discuss what you want to show (action or inner feelings, monologue or dialogue?) and decide on a scene. You can pick one of the scenes in this chapter or choose a different scene, e.g.:
- Hamlet sees the ghost of his father (Act I, scene v)
- Macbeth's reaction after murdering King Duncan (Act II, scene ii)

STEP 2 — Forming expert groups

Decide which part of the film production you want to focus on:
- directing
- writing the script
- designing costumes and scenery
- acting
- sound and lighting

When doing the next steps, discuss the relevant points together and take notes for the film script. → S29.3

STEP 3 — Creating your own interpretation

Think of ways to make your Shakespeare scene relevant to the audience:
- **Setting:** Do you want to show an Elizabethan setting or transport the story into modern times or to a different historical period? What props, costumes and scenery will help you indicate place and time?
- **Text and language:** Do you want to act out the whole scene or leave parts out? Do you want to use the original text or modernise it?

Collect ideas on how the actors can contribute to making the audience understand the lines and the relationship between the characters. Think of:
- **Mime** (movements, gestures, facial expressions)
- **Intonation** (tone of voice and emphasis)

STEP 4 — Using cinematic devices

Decide which cinematic devices can make your scene "come to life":
- **Camera movement:** Use close-ups or zooming/tracking to highlight particular actors or items. → S29
- **Light:** Is it a day or night scene? Do you need spotlights?
- **Sound:** Use sounds or music to create a realistic/dreamy atmosphere or to highlight certain aspects of the scene/a character.

STEP 5 — Filming the scene

Before you film the scene, make sure that your film script contains all the relevant information and that all necessary props are at hand. Rehearse the scene several times.

Finally, film your scene, e.g. using the camera of a mobile/smartphone, and present it to your classmates.

> **TIP**
>
> Watch one of the numerous **Shakespeare film versions** to get ideas. *Hamlet* has been filmed in modern day New York; *O* shows Othello as a high school basketball star and in the series *ShakespeaRetold* Macbeth kills the chef of the Scottish restaurant in which he works.

> **TIP**
>
> **Film scripts** vary greatly, but usually they contain lines of dialogue and stage directions (compare the script in Section C). The more details (instructions for the actors, information on camera movements etc.) you note, the better prepared you'll be for your performance.

Diff pool

Topic 1 The individual and society

1 BRAINSTORMING 👥 △ → *help with Core skill workshop/Task 1c*
The following elements are part of a film and/or a literary text such as a novel or a short story. Make a list of the ones that refer to film, literary texts or both. Then compare the elements and decide whether they are similar. If possible, add more.

director • chapter • scene • author • sound • narrative • paragraph • lighting • sequence • characters • camera movement • point of view • setting • plot

2 CREATIVE TASK ▲ → *instead of Core skill workshop/Task 11*
At the end of the film Mason looks at the basket of apples and realises that he has been tricked. What are his thoughts and feelings? Write an interior monologue to show them, keeping in line with your findings about his character.

3 ANALYSIS ▲ → *instead of Texts A/Task 4*
Change the narrative perspective for lines 5 to 17 to an omniscient narrator and analyse the effect on the reader's view of the situation. Compare it with the original version. → **S8**

4 COMPREHENSION △ → *help with Advanced texts D/Task 2*
Read the following summaries which describe the nature of SoulSearch. Then decide which is the correct one. Give reasons for your choice.

1. SoulSearch is a new online search tool which can find runaways quickly. For this search a computer presents a runaway's picture and personal information, which is shown to an audience named 'the Circle'. As soon as the audience has been informed, the search begins. It is a race against the clock, but it is never lost. During this search the audience posts comments and pictures to reduce the number of picks until the runaway is the only one who remains.
2. SoulSearch is the latest online search tool which is able to find criminals within a very short period of time. The computer randomly chooses a criminal. After it has made its choice, a picture of the person and some personal data are presented on a screen. This information is made available to a large audience called 'the Circle' and it is the signal for the audience's participation. In the course of the search comments and pictures are posted by the audience, and the information provided limits the choices until the criminal is finally found. This search is a race against the clock because possible obstacles mean the outcome can never be predicted for certain.

> **TIP**
>
> **Omniscient narrator**
> An omniscient narrator knows and tells about the feelings and thoughts of the characters and their past and future. For Task 3, add information which an omniscient narrator might mention.

5 ANALYSIS → *help with Advanced texts D/Task 3*
To present the search for Fiona Highbridge, the author uses words referring to numbers, time and geographical places. Analyse the effects these words might have on the reader.

6 EVALUATION ▲ → *instead of Advanced texts D/Task 5*
Discuss whether it is justified to use social media to track down criminals. Consider human rights – e.g. the fact that every individual should be able to live in dignity and justice – and the right of society to be protected from crime.

Topic 2   The United Kingdom

1 ANALYSIS ▲ → *after Texts B/Task 3*
Analyse Jim's reaction to Lionel's attitude.

2 CREATIVE TASK △ → *instead of Texts B/Task 5*
Later that day Jim talks to his wife about his encounter with Lionel. In this dialogue he critically assesses it. What does he say and how does his wife react? Write the dialogue.

3 EVALUATION △ → *instead of Texts C/Task 3*
Imagine there is going to be a referendum on whether the UK should leave the EU. As a UK expatriate living in one of the member states of the EU, you are strongly opposed to this idea. Write a letter to the editor of about 100 words putting forward your arguments against the idea.

4 EVALUATION △ → *help with Texts D/Task 3*
Compare London with Berlin. Consider the following aspects and comment on the situation with regard to Berlin and the rest of Germany:

historical background • geographical position • political status • population size: about 3.4 million • house/apartment prices in the better areas • economy based on research and technological development, tourism and the media • other major cities in Germany: Frankfurt, Cologne, Hamburg or Munich

⊙ L3/21 **5** LISTENING △ → *help with Advanced texts E/Task 6*
Listen to the following programme in which several reasons are given to support the idea of a revival of the North. Not all of the reasons presented below are mentioned. Which of them are not named?

exciting opportunities for holidays • scientific and technological progress, for example in computing • great breakthroughs in engineering • increase in comparatively smaller mills • interesting job offers • rise in new buildings equipped with new technology • relatively low land prices • most attractive location for foreign direct investment by Japanese business • boost in the manufacturing business

Diff pool

6 ANALYSIS ▲ → *after Advanced texts F/Task 2*
Analyse the way the Royal Family is portrayed. Take the author's line of argument and his use of language into account.

7 SPEAKING → *help with Advanced texts F/Task 10*
The working woman and the jobless woman Cameron uses as an example meet in a pub. Work with a partner. One of you takes the role of the working woman and tries to convince the jobless woman to get a job. Your partner takes the role of the jobless woman who tries to justify her situation. The following ideas might be helpful. Add more if you like:

Working woman:
enjoy financial independence • get recognition • find satisfaction • save up for retirement • through taxes support community • not be a burden on the state

Jobless woman:
no stress • flexible • enjoy life • live for the moment • a different concept of life • independent from parents • learn to do with less

8 CREATIVE TASK ▲ → *instead of Advanced texts G/Task 3*
You are Lucy Skilbeck's son Duncan. Write a feature story for a broadsheet newspaper about your experiences growing up in Hackney.

Topic 3   Regional identities

1 LISTENING △ → *help with Texts A/Task 3*
Listen to another part of the song and decide whether the following statements about Tommy Thompson, Peggy White and Davy Harrison are true or false. Then listen again and correct the wrong statements.

1. Tommy Thompson is a member of the trade union.
2. He wants to negotiate for better working conditions.
3. Peggy White is a specialist doctor.
4. She has been able to cure the workers' different injuries because all the necessary medication is available to her.
5. Davy Harrison has never been sober in his life.
6. For him, being drunk is the only way to bear it.

2 ANALYSIS △ → *help with Texts A/Task 4a*
When examining the music, focus on tune, rhythm and the use of instruments. The following words can help you.

Tune: popular • sad • traditional • lively • catchy • solemn • depressing
Rhythm: fast • slow • steady • irregular • fierce • pounding • dance
Instruments: bass • fiddle • drums • guitar • violin • keyboard

3 SPEAKING → *after Texts A/Task 8*

"Language is our means of communication. Instead of promoting regional languages in a globalised world, it would be better to create a universal language." Discuss this issue with your partner. Partner A supports the idea of a universal language, Partner B is against it.

Topic 4   The US then and now

1 SPEAKING → *instead of Introduction/Task 5*

Find a biography of a person in the US that reflects your notion of America. Present it to the class and justify your choice.

2 CREATIVE TASK → *help with Core skill workshop/Task 9*

Write a speech on a topic that interests you and deliver it to the class. Use the following grid to structure it. The useful phrases can help you with your delivery.

	Structure of speech	Useful phrases
Introduction	Greet the audience and establish contact.	Good evening, ladies and gentlemen. …
	Refer to the occasion and the topic of your speech.	We've gathered here …
Main part	Keep the audience's attention by structuring your ideas, e. g. from the least to the most important ideas.	(It) is good/desirable …/ (It) is important/significant …/ (It) is necessary/urgent/vital …
	Link your ideas. Repeat the most important ones for emphasis.	Moreover/However/ Consequently … … has to be stressed/restated …
Conclusion	End your speech in a convincing way, e.g. by calling for action or making promises.	Therefore we have to …/need to … I assure/guarantee …
	Thank the audience.	Thank you for your attention …

3 ANALYSIS → *after Texts A/Task 6d*

In the text a few different ethnic groups are mentioned. Analyse their attitude towards each other. What does this attitude reveal about American society?

4 SPEAKING → *help with Texts A/Task 8*

Is it harder for first- or second-generation immigrants to be successful in a foreign country? The following aspects may give you some ideas for your discussion. Add your own ideas to this list.

language • traditions • relations • job qualifications • religion • norms and values

Diff pool

5 EVALUATION △ → help with **Texts A/Task 13**
When writing a comment, you should structure it well for effect.
Start with an introductory sentence and present the topic:
The question whether … is a controversial/debatable topic/issue.

In the main part present arguments both in favour of and against the idea and structure the points.
starting: To start with/First of all, people should be aware of the fact that building a mosque in Germany is …
adding: In addition/Moreover, proponents/opponents of mosques in Germany point out that …
giving examples: For example/For instance, the construction of the mosque in Cologne shows that …
contrasting: In contrast to/In comparison with Muslims, Christians favour …
emphasising: Most importantly/Above all, religious freedom …
making concessions: However/In spite of this/On the other hand, building a mosque in Germany is …
drawing a conclusion: Therefore/As a result, building a mosque in Germany should …

6 EVALUATION △ → help with **Advanced texts D/Task 3**
Before you can comment on this statement, you should be aware of the meaning of 'cross-cultural' and 'cross-ethnic'. The following explanations might help you:

1. 'Cross-cultural' refers to a comparison of behaviour of members of different cultural groups.
2. Accordingly, 'cross-ethnic' is related to a comparison of members of different ethnic groups.
3. Whereas 'culture' comprises elements such as learned and shared beliefs, values, language etc. 'Ethnicity' also includes culture, but is generally also linked to race.

Topic 5 International relations

1 ANALYSIS △ → help with **Introduction/Task 3b**
Examine the role of international organisations such as NATO, the UN, or the EU in conflict resolution. Take the organisations' aims, their members, their flexibility in decision-making and their overall acceptance into account.

2 SPEAKING ▲ → instead of **Texts A/Task 6**
UNICEF has launched a programme called "Learning for Peace". The goal of this programme is to encourage peace-building policies and practices in education. Participants include govermental representatives from the Netherlands and 14 other countries. Discuss whether a similar programme on the European level should be implemented which would turn the EU into the world's peacemaker instead of the world's policeman.

3 MEDIATION △ → help with **Texts C/Task 3**
Read this first draft of an email to your exchange student. The introduction and the conclusion are fine, but the main part needs some work. Reorganise

the text and cut out any unnecessary information. Finally, add any important passages which may be missing.

Dear …,

I found an interesting article about German-American relations that I'd like to share with you. As we know, the recent relationship (after WWII) between Germany and the US has been marked by a series of ups and downs ranging from profound gratitude in the aftermath of WWII to open resentment during the Iraq War and the Bush administration. Most recently, however, anti-Americanism seems to have dominated public and sometimes even political discourse.

Tobias Jaecker, writing for the *Die Zeit* newspaper, reports that the federal government of Germany wants to invest in an anti-spy program, which would have been unimaginable up until a few years ago. In the meantime many are asking for an open break with the US, especially after the release of embarrassing details of a phone conversation, in which an American diplomat, Victoria Nuland, said "Fuck the EU". A journalist for *Spiegel Online*, Jakob Augstein, argues in favor of more competencies for the European Parliament to strengthen Europe's position against America. This is anti-Americanism at its height and only serves to create a European identity that simply does not exist. Augstein concedes that democracy in Europe has its shortcomings, too.

All of this harks back a long time with the degenerate, materialistic and hypocritical United States on the one hand and cultured Europe on the other. This kind of anti-Americanism is very dangerous because it makes the Europeans feel good about themselves yet leaves their shortcomings uninspected, resulting in static nations unwilling to change. Such a position is anything but critical; instead, it is conformist and reactionary.

As a result, the underlying rationale behind anti-Americanism is, as with any 'anti-ism', an oversimplification of complex realities. This oversimplification is hyped by the media and results in a "we're good; they're bad" attitude, which is nothing short of hypocrisy and hubris.

I think Mr Jaecker has a point here, doesn't he? I look forward to hearing from you again.

All the best,

…

Topic 6   Migration and diversity

1 BEFORE YOU READ △ → *help with Texts A/Task 1*
'Diversity' can refer to various fields of life. Create a mind map to illustrate where this term applies. The following ideas might inspire you.

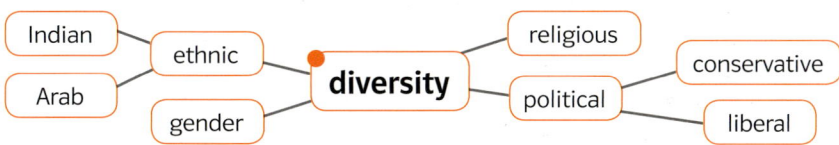

2 CREATIVE TASK △ → *instead of Texts A/Task 6*
You want to initiate a project day to celebrate diversity at your school. To get your fellow students' support for this project you need to win them over. Therefore you would like to deliver a short speech at the next student council meeting. Write this speech and deliver it to the class.

263

Diff pool

3 CREATIVE TASK ▲ → *instead of* **Texts B/Task 5**
After six months in Mexico, Cándido and his wife make a second attempt to cross the border from Mexico to California illegally. This time they are successful. Now picture one day of their life in California. Where are they staying? Do they have jobs? If so, what kind of jobs? Include these ideas and add more. Write a diary entry describing one day in their new life. You can write from either Américas or Cándido's perspective.

4 VISUALS 👥 △ → *help with* **Texts B/Task 7**
When analysing your poster, pay special attention to the following points:
1. **the characters shown** – what ethnicity are they, how are they dressed?
2. **the characters' facial expressions** – do they look threatening, anxious, hopeful, despairing, watchful etc.?
3. **the use of colours** (esp. in *Crossing Over*; think of the American flag) and **of light/darkness**
4. **the information in the title and subtitle** (esp. in *Sin Nombre*, consider the title's language and the letters themselves)

5 COMPREHENSION 👥 △ → *help with* **Advanced texts C/Task 3**
In his speech Fox shows positive and negative aspects of immigration. The following keywords may help you to identify them.

willingness/unwillingness to integrate • difference/commonality • number of immigrants • skilled/unskilled • economic independence/dependence • to maintain/to lose national identity • favouring existing citizens/neglecting potential citizens

6 CREATIVE TASK ▲ → *instead of* **Advanced texts C/Task 6**
As a journalist at a major English newspaper you have to interview Liam Fox shortly after he has given this speech. You question the validity of his arguments whereas Fox is eager to defend his proposal. Write the interview taking the characteristics of each role into account.

7 ANALYSIS △ → *instead of* **Advanced texts E/Task 4**
Analyse the portrayal of each group of immigrants and the welcome they receive. Focus on the use of negative or offensive language.

Topic 7 Faith and religion

1 EVALUATION △ → *help with Spot on facts/Task 3*
To structure the main part of your answer, focus on the following aspects:

- **US:** reasons for the introduction of the First Amendment • consequences of the First Amendment today
- **UK:** founding of the Church of England • members of the House of Lords

2 SPEAKING ▲ → *instead of Texts A/Task 6*
Compare the statistics on the composition of religious groups in the US and in the UK (see Spot on facts). Comment on your findings.

3 ANALYSIS △ → *help with Texts B/Task 5*
To examine the writer's attitude towards the AFA, focus on the following:

her use of irony • her use of rhetorical questions • how she contrasts the behaviour of the AFA and Christian values

Topic 8 Political systems

1 ANALYSIS △ → *after Spot on facts/Task 1*
For a better understanding, add the German political system to your comparison. For example, does the German chancellor or the president of Germany have similar duties to an American president or a British prime minister? How do the voting systems differ?

2 ANALYSIS △ → *help with Texts B/Task 2b*
Find English equivalents or paraphrases for these German phrases:
frischer Wind • volksnah • Vetternwirtschaft
Think about how they relate to the American change-of-office characteristics. Use your ideas to write three sentences describing advantages of the American change-of-office system.

3 SPEAKING ▲ → *after Texts B/Task 5b*
Group 1: Read the following quotation by Mark Twain, a US author and humorist: "Facts are stubborn things, but statistics are more pliable."
Group 2: Read the following quotation by the former British Prime Minister Winston Churchill: "The best argument against democracy is a five-minute conversation with the average voter."
Interpret the quotation within your group and decide (Group 1) whether open data based on statistics is the solution to better information management, or (Group 2) whether this is an argument for more or less open participation. Give reasons for your decision and share your ideas with the rest of the class.

Diff pool

Topic 9 Globalisation

1 CREATIVE TASK ▲ → *after* **Texts A/Task 1**
A New Guinea Highlander is asked by his grandson how life in New Guinea was different when he was a child. Write a dialogue using the information given in the text.

2 EVALUATION △ → *instead of* **Texts A/Task 3**
Would you rather live in traditional or modern New Guinea? Write a comment.

3 ANALYSIS △ → *help with* **Texts A/Task 5**
To help you analyse stylistic devices at the beginning of the text, copy the grid and fill it in.

Stylistic device	Example/line	Effect
Metaphor	…	…
Rhetorical question	…	…
Direct address	…	…
Parallel structure	…	…
Repetition	…	…

4 VISUALS ▲ → *after* **Texts B/Task 2**
Take a look at the graph on the right. What might happen if the minimum wage rose to $104 a month in Bangladesh? Discuss.

5 SPEAKING △ → *help with* **Texts C/Task 4a**
In what way do countries in different parts of the world profit from a war going on in another country? Think of sales of weapons, exploitation of resources etc.

6 EVALUATION △ → *instead of* **Advanced texts E/Task 3**
Discuss what you can do to help to solve the e-waste problem.

7 EVALUATION △ → *instead of* **Advanced texts E/Task 9**
Assess the pros and cons of your English class taking part in a MOOC. Mention at least three of these aspects:

authenticity • virtual learning situation • native speaker • personal touch • intercultural awareness • distractions • costs

8 RESEARCH ▲ → *after* **Advanced texts F/Task 3**
Bhutan has implemented the Gross National Happiness in contrast to the Gross National Product (GNP) or the Gross Domestic Product (GDP). Collect some information about it and give a short presentation.

Topic 10 India

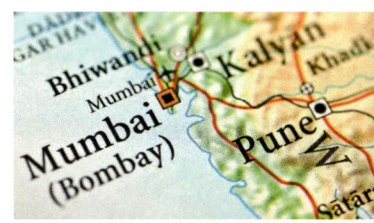

1 VIEWING △ → help with **Texts A/Task 3b**
When analysing how a film suggests authenticity, focus on narrative and cinematic devices. For narrative devices consider who and what is shown and what happens. Was the film shot in a studio or on location? For cinematic devices consider the camera movement, field size and perspective, sound and music etc. Is the production very 'clean' and highly polished or is a shaky hand-held camera used and are there unfiltered background noises?

2 LISTENING △ → help with **Texts A/Task 7**
Listen to the beginning of the novel *The White Tiger* and decide whether the following statements are true. Then correct the wrong ones.

1. The narrator is telling the story because China's Prime Minister is visiting Bangalore the following week and wants to talk to Indian entrepreneurs in order to learn about their success story.
2. Indian entrepreneurship is exclusive and requires formal training.
3. According to the narrator India and China will overtake the developed Western countries in the future with India being more advanced than China.

3 ANALYSIS △ → help with **Texts B/Task 3**

a) Choose the adjective which describes Mary's emotions in the first six lines best:
worried • desperate • concerned • disappointed • distressed • dejected • unhappy • displeased • annoyed • anxious

b) How is Mary's movement expressed in the language used in the first 16 lines? Make notes about a) the syntax, b) the use of the -ing form (gerund) and c) contrast.

c) Choose another adjective from this list to describe how she feels in line 16:
relieved • delighted • happy • satisfied • grateful • nice • comfortable • euphoric • at ease • relaxed

d) Explain how Mary's emotions change in the first part of the text and why. (ll. 1–16)

USEFUL PHRASES

Saying when
At first …
In the opening sentence/line/passage …
When she sees/hears that …
Having seen/heard/realised that …

4 SPEAKING ▲ → instead of **Texts B/Task 6**
Set up a plan which shows the steps India has to take to overcome the problem of extreme poverty. Include short-term, medium-term and long-term goals. Present your plan to the class.

5 ANALYSIS △ → help with **Advanced texts E/Task 10**
To explain Rajesh's reaction, focus on the following two aspects: On the one hand, violence against women, including domestic violence, is a real problem in India. Moreover, the bride traditionally moves in with the groom's family. On the other hand, as "India dishonoured?" points out, there is generally a problematic attitude towards women.

6 CREATIVE TASK ▲ → instead of **Advanced texts F/Task 8**
The evening after this scene Meet Singh writes a short letter to his brother, who lives in a nearby village, telling him of his encounter with the boy and of his fear of the conflict escalating even more.

Diff pool

Topic 11 The media

1 VISUALS △ → *help with* **Spot on facts/Task 2**
The following keywords will help you to describe the developments of the media and to analyse the cartoons:

Twentieth century: print media • broadsheet newspapers • tabloids • radio • television
Twenty-first century: digital technologies • active involvement • crowdsourcing • copyright
Social media: platforms for political activism • immediacy • spreading news
Advertising: customising • viral marketing • crowdsourcing • covert advertising

2 CREATIVE TASK ▲ → *after* **Core skill workshop/Task 8b**
You work for the advertising agency that UNICEF has entrusted with creating a new advertisement. Its aim is to encourage people to donate money for medical treatments of children in developing countries. Brainstorm ideas for this advert. Then design it and present it to the class.

3 ANALYSIS ▲ → *after* **Texts A/Task 3**
Examine the author's line of argument. Do you think it is effective? Give reasons.

4 ANALYSIS ▲ → *after* **Texts B/Task 2c**
Analyse Nick's attitude towards the world he lives in.

5 LANGUAGE △ → *help with* **Texts B/Task 4**
The following tasks and questions will help you to analyse the style and language used in the extracts.

Sharing is caring
1. How is nature described in ll. 11–20? Which atmosphere is created by this?
2. What 'activity' in the text is associated with words such as "deprive others of something", "unethical", "selfish"? Find more examples in the text and describe the effect of this choice of words.

Second-hand experiences
3. Describe the style and language of the following quotations: "Our society was utterly …" (ll. 11–12); "a fucking commercial" (l. 17); "smart-ass" (l. 25).
4. What stylistic devices does the narrator use in ll. 20–26 and to what effect?

6 SPEAKING △ → *help with* **Advanced texts D/Task 5**
The following ideas will help you to discuss the relevance of journalists and bloggers.

pace of spreading information • checking of sources/facts • providing a balanced/biased view • vast/specialist audience • interaction with audience

7 EVALUATION ▲ → *after* **Advanced texts F/Task 1c**
Should people get involved in virtual realities to such a degree as shown in the game *Perplex City*? Write a comment.

Topic 12 The arts

1 SPEAKING → *help with Texts A/ Task 4*
To discuss how original art can be, think, for example, of songs that use samples of other songs, or films based on other films, (graphic) novels or cartoons. Examples of frequently used sources are:

famous pieces of music • Shakespeare • fairy tales • biblical stories • Greek/Roman mythology • etc.

2 ANALYSIS → *help with Texts B/Task 7*
To analyse the author's attitude, focus on how he describes the museum's opening and WalMart as a company. Then examine the opinion expressed in each paragraph and the structure of the arguments.

3 SPEAKING → *instead of Texts B/Task 8*
Prepare and act out an interview between a journalist and a supporter (e.g. Alice Walton, the curator, an enthusiastic visitor) or an opponent (e.g. a former WalMart employee, a historian, a director of another art institution) of the museum.

4 CREATIVE TASK → *help with Texts B/ Task 10*
Partner A is the local journalist. You have to meet the expectations of a readership which likes to be well-informed.
Partner B is the street artist. You see this interview as an opportunity to become known to a wider range of people.
Consider the following ideas for the interview. Add more if possible.

start • inspiration • aim • support • training • earnings • recognition • future

Topic 13 The Englishes

1 LISTENING → *help with Core skill workshop/Task 9b (first question)*

a) Listen to the song for a second time. Pay special attention to the first ten lines (to "… survive unprotected"). How does the songwriter compare English to a disease? Focus on the following words and phrases taken from the song.

pours out of • sticking on • nothing's safe • it begins to spread • it dominates • it reigns/rains • altered • confused • everyone's affected • will not survive unprotected

b) What effect is created by these words? Explain.

2 LISTENING → *instead of Core skill workshop/Task 9b (second question)*
In part of the song a professor (starting with "Pif! …") and the narrator (starting with "Prof! …") exchange views. Listen to their rate of speaking, their intonation and, if applicable, the way they speak. Analyse whether – and if so how – these aspects underline the professor's critical attitude and the narrator's reaction to it.

Diff pool

3 CREATIVE TASK △ → *help with Texts A/Task 5*
As a music producer you want to promote non-English pop music in Germany. To spread this idea you write a short entry for your blog in which you argue for your plan. Use the following words and phrases for inspiration. Add more ideas if possible.

live in a globalised world • origin of immigrants in Germany • cultural enrichment • promotion of bands which otherwise would have remained (relatively) unknown

4 ANALYSIS △ → *help with Texts B/Task 8*
In this excerpt Little Bee gives us an example of how she imagines the Queen speaks. How does this differ from the normal Queen's English (i.e. Standard English)? Focus on sentence structure, choice of words, style and tone.

⊙ L1/10 **5 LISTENING** △ → *help with Advanced texts C/Task 1*
Use the grid to describe the changes Rob Conley has noticed in the language. Note examples for these changes and add the reason when given.

Change	Example	Reasons
…	brahn – brown	…
…	…	influences from immigrants
rhyming slang	…	…

6 ANALYSIS ▲ → *after Advanced texts D/Task 3*
Analyse the author's attitude towards the dominance of English within the EU. Take his line of argument and his use of language into account.

7 CREATIVE TASK ▲ → *instead of Advanced texts D/Task 4*
As a reader of *The Economist* and a proponent of multilingualism in Europe you write a letter to the editor in which you criticise the growing dominance of the English language. At the same time you stress the necessity of maintaining linguistic diversity. Consider the ideas presented in this newspaper article and the knowledge you have gained in the course of this topic.

8 EVALUATION ▲ → *instead of Advanced texts E/Task 4a*
Amy Tan hesitates to call her mother's English "broken English" (l. 34) or "limited English" (l. 38). Discuss whether this hesitance is justified. Refer to the text and your personal experience or general knowledge.

9 EVALUATION △ → *instead of Advanced texts G/Task 3*
If English as a lingua franca is replaced by text talk, it will ruin the art of conversation. Discuss.

Topic 14 Shakespeare

1 VIEWING △ → *help with Introduction/Task 2*
Before watching the clip, make sure you understand these keywords.

Part 1: replica of the old Globe; original Elizabethan techniques; melting pot of Elizabethan London; Shakespeare's modern mind; grammar school education in Stratford; the great classical writers

Part 2: 16th century Renaissance; to question the ancient knowledge; a world of horizons pushed back; a cosmopolitan state of mind

2 LISTENING △ → *help with Core skill workshop/Task 3*

a) Copy the following lines. First try tapping and counting them, then mark the stressed (/) and unstressed (_) syllables.

Example: _ / _ / _ / _ / _ /
           If only I could find the pattern here.
           _ / _ / _ / _ /
           Let's count the lines and find the rhymes.

1. "How now, my love! why is your cheek so pale?" *(A Midsummer Night's Dream)*
2. "Those lips that Love's own hand did make
   Breathed forth the sound that said 'I hate'" *(Sonnet 145)*

b) Read the following line. Is there a pattern?

"No, my lord, unless I have another for working-days."
(Much Ado About Nothing)

c) Frequently used feet are iamb (unstressed-stressed: "Now don't forget what I have said") and trochee (stressed-unstressed: "Speak no more of rhymes, they bore"). Identify the metre in these Shakespeare lines.

1. "Through the forest have I gone. / But Athenian found I none"
   (A Midsummer Night's Dream)
2. "But soft! What light through yonder window breaks?" *(Romeo and Juliet)*
3. "Give me your hands, if we be friends, / And Robin shall restore amends."
   (A Midsummer Night's Dream)

> **TIP**
>
> **Metre** is often described as the mathematical part of poetry, but this should not put you off. Remember: A **foot** is a unit of stressed and unstressed syllables. So first find the pattern, then count how often it is used in one line. It is best to read out the line, tap your feet while you do so and count how often you tap (use your fingers for that): Five repetitions (feet) – pentameter, four – tetrameter etc.
> The **stress pattern** can vary and sometimes there is no regular pattern.

3 CREATIVE TASK ▲ → *after Texts C/Task 4b*
Cinematic devices help catch and hold the audience's attention, such as music, sound effects, lighting and camera movements. Which of these devices would you use to turn your film script into a gripping start for the film? → **S29**

4 ANALYSIS △ → *help with Advanced texts D/Task 2*
The following questions can help you find out more about the two characters and their relationship to one another.

a) Look at these phrases from the text. Who says them? What do they mean?

When you durst do it, then you were a man.	I dare do all that may become a man.	False face must hide what the false heart doth know.	Live a coward in thine own esteem.	But screw your courage to the sticking-place.
He hath honoured me of late, and I have bought golden opinions from all sorts of people.	From this time, such I account thy love.	If we should fail?		Art thou afeard to be the same in thine own act and valour, as thou art in desire?

Diff pool

  b) *Note the keywords used in the phrases. What do the two focus on?*
  c) *What does this tell us about their personalities and their relationship?*
  d) *Find more quotes in the text to support your findings.*

5 EVALUATION ▲ → after **Advanced texts D/Task 5**
Considering the role of women in Elizabethan times, which of Lady Macbeth's tactics were most shocking to Elizabethans? Do you think that Iago's schemes for Desdemona would work equally well today?

6 EVALUATION △ → help with **Advanced texts D/Task 6**
  a) *Look at the metaphors below. Rephrase them, using everyday language, and compare the effect. Why do you think are metaphors so common?*

  You are the sunshine of my life. • You have a heart of stone. • She broke his heart. • My father is a couch potato. • That computer is a dinosaur.

  b) *Explain the meaning of these Shakespeare quotes. Which ones are metaphors, which ones similes?*

  "Juliet is the sun" • "All the world's a stage" • "They are a as gentle as zephyrs" (zephyr = milder Westwind) • "Life's but a walking shadow" • "Sometime too hot the eye of heaven shines"

  c) *Psychology is about how the human mind works, how it influences behaviour and how others can influence us. In order to understand the role psychology plays in these scenes, consider the following questions:*

  Macbeth (Power and ambition): What thoughts and feelings make it hard for Macbeth, who could kill enemies in a battle, to kill Duncan under his own roof? At what point in the scene might he try to avoid looking his wife in the eye? Why does Lady Macbeth talk so much about manliness? What feelings and reactions does she intend to provoke in her husband?
  Othello (Manipulation): Do you think the relationships between Othello and Desdemona, Othello and Cassio, Cassio and Desdemona are based on trust? Are they strong relationships?

> **TIP**
>
> **Metaphors** are words or phrases that imply a comparison without directly saying so (if 'as' or 'like' are used, we use the word **simile** instead). Metaphors are very common in everyday language.

Intercultural communication

Introduction

Intercultural communication and intercultural competence

To communicate successfully in an English-speaking country it's not enough just to be able to speak English. Once you speak English to an American, Australian or a British person, this person automatically assumes you are aware of the cultural conventions and will expect you to behave the same as an English-speaking person.

Intercultural competence is about being aware of these conventions and responding accordingly. This does not mean that the manners or conventions in Anglo-Saxon countries are more polite or better than in your own country. They are simply different, and when you are in an Anglo-Saxon country, you should adapt to the system there. Of course, there are some cultural differences among English-speaking countries; however, most of them use the same conventions.

Describing differences in cultural conventions is tricky because in some situations there are American or British people who tend to act more the way a German would and German people whose behaviour is similar to British or American people.

Don't forget the saying: "When in Rome, do as the Romans do."

1 *Take a look at some of these conventions in English speaking countries and talk to your neighbour about what is usual in Germany:*

1. Acknowledge other people around you. For example:
   a) Greet them when you pass them in the street.
   b) Have a short conversation with them when you are on a train or a plane.
   c) Talk to someone while waiting in a queue.

2. Always excuse yourself if you get too close to another person. You say, "Excuse me" politely even if someone bumps into you. In that case the other person also apologises.

3. Stand in a queue and wait for your turn in any situation, not just at the grocery store or the bus stop. Even if the person in front of you is looking at the chewing gum display or reading a sign, you patiently wait your turn.

4. Give the other person their personal space by keeping your distance. This is usually in every situation at least an arm's length from the other person.

5. Be prepared to share with others. If you see a stranger standing and you are sitting on a bench, move over to let others sit down. Reserving seats for your family or friends is frowned upon.

6. If you can't say anything nice, don't say anything at all. For example, do not give someone your honest opinion about their awful new shirt even if they ask you.

7. Facial expressions: Smile when you see and talk to people, but do not stare at anyone.

There are also verbal conventions about the way you say things. The following pages will give you the opportunity to practise ways of asking questions and expressing requests and opinions in English. Have fun learning how to create a pleasant atmosphere for small talk and learn how to negotiate properly in English so that you will feel at home in an English-speaking country.

TIP

All the audio files, role cards and solutions are on the CD in this book.

Intercultural communication

Asking politely

Is 'please' enough?

1 👥 Look at the illustrations and discuss with a partner what they say about English and German stereotypes.

2 a) You have just arrived at your host family's house and the father asks you if you'd like something to drink. Which of these answers is the most polite and which is the least polite?

1. Do you think I could have a cup of coffee, please?
2. I'd like a cup of coffee, please.
3. Could I have a cup of coffee, please?

b) 👥 Share your ideas with a partner.

3 a) Practise asking politely for something in these situations.

1. You want to borrow a friend's laptop.
2. You're in a colleague's office and need to use the phone.
3. You want to know how to get to the bus station.
4. You didn't hear something and ask someone what was said.
5. You're carrying a big parcel and can't open a door.

b) 👥 Consider with a partner how you would formulate these requests in German. Are there any differences?

TIP

Making polite requests

It is typical to make requests particularly politely in English, but a common misconception is that you just have to add 'please'. It may seem exaggerated to use so many words for a simple request, but you will find that this is common practice.

USEFUL PHRASES

Asking for something

I wonder if I/you could …/ might be able to …

I was wondering if I could …/might be able to …

Do you think I/you could …/might be able to …?

Asking politely

Saying 'yes' and 'no'

4 a) *Listen to these short dialogues and note which of the responses to the requests are inappropriate.*

b) *For the dialogues with the inappropriate responses, think of polite ways of refusing.*

5 a) *Look at the following requests and choose the better response for each situation.*

1. Do you think you could keep an eye on my rucksack?
   a) Yes. But only for a few minutes.
   b) Yes, of course. Are you going to be away for long?

2. I wonder if I could sit at your table.
   a) No, it's reserved.
   b) No, I'm sorry, I'm expecting company.

3. I was wondering if you could give me a lift to the station.
   a) Yes, of course. I'm going right past it anyway.
   b) Yes. The bus doesn't go there from here.

4. Do you think I could have a glass of water?
   a) Yes. Here's a glass and there's the tap.
   b) Of course, it's so hot at the moment, isn't it?

b) *Would you make the same choice in a German context?*

c) *It is usual to make a polite comment when someone replies to a request. Practise the dialogues in **a)** with a partner and choose a **polite** comment from the box.*

> - Thanks, I was suddenly so weak from the heat.
> - Oh, good. And maybe you could go past the post office too.
> - Oh, that's really a shame. Thanks anyway.
> - But this glass is dirty!
> - Thank you so much. I promise I'll only be a couple of minutes.
> - Well, there's no one sitting there now.
> - Are you sure? I wouldn't want to put you to any trouble.
> - And could you make sure no one sits on that chair?

6 *You're on one of the famous London double-deckers with a friend. It's a bit crowded but there might be a couple of seats for you. Mediate back and forth. Remember what you have learnt so far.*

1. *Frag doch mal den Mann da, ob er nicht ein wenig rücken könnte, damit wir auch mal sitzen können.*
   You: …
2. *Yes, of course. It's a bit of a squeeze but there's room for two more.*
   You: …
3. *Na endlich. Ich konnte einfach nicht mehr stehen.*
   You: …

7 *Practise making requests and responding politely using the role cards on the CD. Be ready to perform your scenes in front of the class.*

USEFUL PHRASES

Refusing politely
I'm really/very/awfully terribly sorry, but …
I'd like to help you, but (unfortunately) …

TIP

Mediating requests
To achieve your aim, you need to be polite and adapt to the circumstances. Consider the necessary differences in register and style depending on who you are talking to (stranger, friend).

Intercultural communication

Opinions and criticisms

Saying what you think

"If you can't say anything nice, don't say anything at all." Some non-native speakers consider it dishonest if an American or British person doesn't express their true opinion in such a situation, but English speakers generally dislike making criticisms. Even when invited to give their opinion, they will give a neutral reply.

1. a) Listen to these two conversations. Two German girls are on work placements in Britain and get the chance to speak to the managing director (MD) of the firm. With a partner compare how their opinions come across by making notes like this.

MD's question	Sophie's statement
Enjoying time at Barlow's?	…

   b) What impression does the MD get of each girl as summed up in his last sentence?

2. Here are some questions you may be asked in an English-speaking context. Your immediate thoughts are in brackets. But generally speaking, English speakers won't make a comment which could hurt another person's feelings. Consider the situation in each case and complete the sentence to make a suitable reply.

   1. COLLEAGUE Do you like fish and chips?
      [You think that kind of food is very unhealthy.]
      YOU Well, I've haven't really tried it yet, but …
   2. BOSS What did you think of the meeting this morning?
      [You were bored and didn't understand half of what was going on.]
      YOU It was really interesting, but …
   3. HOST Did you have a good weekend at the seaside?
      [It rained and there was a cold east wind.]
      YOU It's such a beautiful part of the country but …
   4. FRIEND Hey, what do you think of my new trainers?
      [You hate that brand and the colour is almost blinding.]
      YOU The colour is really unusual but …
   5. FRIEND You'll love the local folk music group at the festival.
      [You can't stand that sort of music and amateurs are usually awful]
      YOU They must be really good …

Opinions and criticisms

3 👥 *Generally speaking English-speakers won't make a comment on anything if it could hurt another person's feelings. Look at these situations and think of ways of replying that won't offend the other person.*

1. Your American host family takes you to "The German Heritage Bakery" after church on Sunday. It all seems very American, the cheesecake doesn't look anything like what is sold in Germany and a real German bakery wouldn't sell doughnuts. Your host asks you what you think of the bakery.
2. You are working as an assistant at an American school for a year. The students' German is not very good. The German teacher at the school asks you how you learned to speak English so fluently. You think it's because the German school system is so much better. What are you going to say?
3. At your American high school there's going to be a dance. Your American friend asks you to come round to see the very short black skirt she has specially bought for it. It makes her legs look extremely fat. What are you going to say?
4. As a treat for their German guest your American family is making s'mores. These consist of toasted marshmallows with a layer of chocolate on graham crackers. The whole family simply loves them. You have only ever eaten marshmallows that are cold and are a little unsure. Your host makes a s'more just for you.

4 *You're visiting the US with your father, who can't speak much English. He has quite strong views on many things. Mediate for him in this conversation with an American you meet on your travels.*

AMERICAN	Well, how are you enjoying America so far?
YOU	…
FATHER	Ich finde, dieses amerikanische Bier schmeckt nach nichts.
YOU	…
AMERICAN	This one's our favorite.
YOU	…
FATHER	Deutschland hat das beste Bier der Welt.
YOU	…
AMERICAN	Yes, we've heard a lot about the Oktoberfest!
YOU	…
FATHER	Amerikaner kauen ständig Kaugummi.
YOU	…
AMERICAN	Yes, it keeps your breath fresh all the time.
YOU	…
FATHER	Überall wird man freundlich bedient, aber die Restaurants haben nur dieses Fast-Food.
YOU	…
AMERICAN	Yeah, there are so many you don't know which one to choose!
YOU	…
FATHER	Wo sind dann die richtigen Restaurants?
YOU	…
AMERICAN	Oh, yes, but you'd have to go downtown for that.
YOU	…

🔊 5 👥 *Practise expressing and reacting to opinions using the role cards on the CD. You can perform these scenes in front of the class too.*

USEFUL PHRASES

Reacting politely

That sounds really interesting/delicious/nice/unusual/good

I wonder if maybe …

That's very nice of you (to say so) …

Oh, that'll be interesting …

TIP

Feedback

When you perform in front of the class, your classmates can give you feedback: Were the dialogues credible? Where did you run into trouble?

Intercultural communication

Making a complaint

Complaining politely

TIP

Complaining politely is done indirectly by using the passive voice, by asking a polite question or by using:
There seems to be/have been…
I'm afraid…
I was wondering…
I think…

1 A common misconception about complaining in English is that people think all you need to do to make a complaint polite is to add "Excuse me," "Pardon me" or "Sorry to bother you" to it.

a) Read the direct complaints. Then match them to a better version.

Direct complaint	Better version
1. Sorry to bother you but no one told me about the meeting.	a) Pardon me. Did you have any problems getting here this morning?
2. Excuse me, why didn't you answer the e-mails I sent you?	b) Excuse me, but I was just wondering whether you received the e-mails I sent you last week.
3. Sorry, but you haven't paid me for the work I did last month.	c) Sorry to bother you, but I don't seem to have been given the information about the meeting.
4. Pardon me, but you are sitting on my seat.	d) Sorry, but there seems to have been a mix-up somewhere. I'm afraid I haven't been paid yet for the work I did last month.
5. Pardon me. You're late! We've been waiting for 30 minutes.	e) Excuse me. I'm afraid something might have gone wrong here. Do you think it would be possible for me to have the bagel I ordered?
6. Excuse me, this isn't what I ordered. I wanted a bagel and not this toast.	f) I'm sorry to bother you, but there seems to have been a misunderstanding. On my ticket it says carriage 14, seat 25.

b) Talk to a partner and think about how you would complain in your home country in these situations. What is appropriate and expected here?

2 Sometimes we have to complain in order to get what we need or ordered. Listen to the speakers and find out how they complain effectively.

Scene	Customer's polite phrases	How does the employee feel?
1.	…	…

a) Copy the chart above.
b) Write down the phrases the customer uses at the beginning of his or her complaint.
c) How do you think the employee feels when the customer uses these polite phrases?

Making a complaint

3 *Practise complaining politely. Help the tourists to complain politely by altering the text in the speech bubbles. You may use phrases from Tasks 1 and 2 and from the box on the right.*

- Can we order now, please?
- Excuse me, but this check is wrong! We didn't eat fish!
- Excuse me, but I didn't order that!
- Pardon me. What do you mean, you don't accept credit cards?
- Sorry, ma'am. The food is way too salty!
- Ma'am! Excuse me! Where is our food? We've been waiting for 30 minutes now!

USEFUL PHRASES

Polite complaints

I'm afraid …

I'm terribly sorry to have to ask you this …

Would you mind helping me with this issue …

I'm afraid there might have been a misunderstanding.

Could I ask you to take a look at this again?

We see that you're very busy, but do you think you could …

Excuse me, ma'am, but this meat isn't quite the way …

4 *Now read these dialogues, looking for examples of polite and impolite behaviour.*

1. **CUSTOMER 1** Excuse me, I bought this T-shirt yesterday, and it seems to be the wrong size.
   ASSISTANT 1 Did you buy the wrong size or is the label wrong?
   CUSTOMER 1 Oh, I see. Well, I usually take size M but this is way too small for me.
   ASSISTANT 1 Well, you should have tried it on before you bought it.
   CUSTOMER 1 I'm afraid I don't understand why this should be a problem. Could I talk to your supervisor, please?
2. **CUSTOMER 2** This T-shirt's the wrong size.
   ASSISTANT 2 No problem, sir. Would you like to exchange it or have your money back?
   CUSTOMER 2 I'm sure it's got the wrong label in it.
   ASSISTANT 2 Well, the best thing to do would be to look on the rack over there and see if there's a larger size.
   CUSTOMER 2 And if that's too big?
   ASSISTANT 2 Perhaps this T-shirt has got the wrong label. There may be another in size M on the rack for you to try on as well.
   CUSTOMER 2 OK, thanks. I'll see what I can find.

a) Explain who is being unhelpful in the first dialogue and how the polite partner reacts.

b) Identify who is causing problems in the second dialogue and how the polite partner deals with that.

5 *Using the role cards, practise complaining with a partner. One of you is the guest and one is the hotel receptionist. Decide whether you are going to be helpful or difficult!*

Intercultural communication

Register

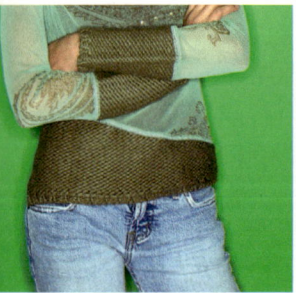  

How formal do you need to be?

When people talk about 'register' in a language, they are referring to the level of formality. Just as with your native language, you should vary the level of your English to suit the social occasion and the person you are talking to, as well as adjust the language according to your intention. If you were asking a British professor for an extension on a term paper, you would use extremely polite language to fit the situation in order to get your extension, which is your intention.

1. 👥 *Just as you choose your clothes to fit the occasion, you change the formality of your language to fit the situation as well. Look at the cartoon and talk to your partner about why the inappropriate register makes the cartoon funny.*

"Don't you find the ringing of one's mobile phone most annoyingly irritating Terence my good fellow?"

2. Some words or phrases are considered to be more polite than others. Decide whether the following phrases are formal or informal. You should keep a list of these phrases in your folder.

   1. Can I borrow your pen, please?
      Would you mind lending me your pen for a second, please?
   2. That is a lovely dress you are wearing!
      I really like that dress. Is it new?
   3. Should you require further assistance, please don't hesitate to contact me, sir.
      Just call me if you need any help!
   4. The flight will be departing shortly, ma'am.
      We're going to be leaving soon.
   5. These cameras over here are rather inexpensive.
      Let's look at those cheaper cameras.
   6. To finish this task, we still need more input from you.
      If you don't start working, we'll never get this job finished.
   7. She would really appreciate it if you could stop making so much noise.
      Stop talking, please!
   8. Please read this book by tomorrow!
      This book should be read by tomorrow.

3. 👥 *Look at your list and explain which of the following aspects made one phrase more formal than the other:*
   - the structure of the sentence
   - and/or the choice of words

> **TIP**
>
> **"Excuse me, sir!"**
> Using 'ma'am' and 'sir' can be quite confusing for some people. To be safe, you should address someone with 'ma'am' or 'sir' when talking to an older man or woman as well as with someone you don't know. Here are some possible situations when you would need them:
> - asking someone for directions
> - talking to a complete stranger
> - talking to your boss or to a professor

Register

4 *Talk to a partner and think about how you vary your language in German. Look at the phrases again and think about which ones you'd use in German and on what occasions.*

5 a) *Listen to the dialogues and match them to the pictures. Then decide whether the speaker was using the right register.*

USEFUL PHRASES

Asking politely

I wonder if it wouldn't be too much trouble to ask you to …

Could I ask you to do me a favour, please?

(Sir,) Do you think it would be possible for me to …

Excuse me, I'm sorry to bother you, do you think you could tell me …

b) *If the register was wrong, change the dialogue so the register is correct.*
c) *Ask the people in the pictures for the following information using the correct register. You can use the useful phrases box to help you.*

1. You'd like to know where the restrooms *(AE)*/toilets *(BE)* are.
2. You are looking for the main office.
3. You are wondering whether this person saw your classmate walk by. She's tall and has got red hair.
4. You need to know what time it is.

Formal and informal situations

6 *Your friend wants to go to a musical in London. You're helping by calling the box office. Mediate between your friend and the booking clerk.*

FRIEND	Frag mal, ob wir Karten für heute Abend bekommen können?	YOU	…
YOU	…	CLERK	Well, sir, I could offer you tickets for tomorrow's matinée.
CLERK	I'm afraid the only tickets available for this evening are with restricted view.	YOU	…
		FRIEND	Klasse! Dann nehmen wir zwei Karten für den Nachmittag.
YOU	…	YOU	…
FRIEND	Und morgen Abend?	CLERK	I can offer you two seats together in the middle of row 7.
YOU	…	YOU	…
CLERK	I'm sorry, sir, but tomorrow evening is completely sold out.	FRIEND	Die nehmen wir!
YOU	…	YOU	…
FRIEND	Wir sind aber nur heute und morgen hier. Kann man da nichts machen?		

7 *Using the role cards on the CD, make dialogues to match the formality of the situation.*

Intercultural communication

Small talk (I)

You actually talk to strangers?

English-speaking people often talk to each other even if they don't know each other. It is considered rude and unfriendly not to get involved in such a conversation.

1 a) *Look at the situations below and decide whether you would normally start or carry on a conversation with the other people.*

1. You and several strangers are waiting for a bus to arrive.
2. You are on a very full train on the way to school. None of your friends are there that morning, but there are people sitting next to you.
3. You are taking the lift to the third floor and there are three other people in it.
4. You are waiting in line to pay for jeans you just tried on in a store.
5. A complete stranger walks by and comments on your T-shirt.

b) *Do you talk to strangers? Do you greet strangers in the street? Do you talk to people you don't know in trains? If not, why not? With a partner think about situations in which you might talk to strangers in Germany.*

2 a) *Listen to the two conversations. Note the reactions of the German people.*
b) *How could the German people have replied more appropriately? Practise with a partner.*

3 *Discuss how the general atmosphere changes if people talk to each other rather than ignoring each other in public places.*

Ice-breakers

Getting a conversation going often depends on the situation. Someone who is good at small talk adapts the conversation to the scene.

4 *With a partner look at the situation and decide how you could start a conversation. Practise getting the conversation going. The useful phrases may help you.*

1. You are at the airport waiting to board the plane. Boarding has been delayed due to the storm. What could you say to the man or woman sitting next to you?
2. It's September and you are about to go on a year abroad to teach children in a foreign school. All of the volunteers have just met for the first time. A young Chinese woman has just walked up with a cup of tea and is standing in front of you.
3. You are eating breakfast in a youth hostel in Spain. A British person has just sat down across from you.
4. You are at a party and decide to go and get something to eat. What are you going to say to the host who is standing next to the buffet?
5. It's registration time at the university. As you stand in line waiting to pick up your papers, what could you say to the American in front of you?

USEFUL PHRASES

Ice-breakers

At this rate we'll never get …

How long have you been sitting here?

Are you enjoying your tea?

Do you usually eat this for breakfast at home?

This queue is going to last forever …

I'm glad it's not so crowded/busy/hot/cold here today. It was so … yesterday.

What a cool T-shirt! You must be a … fan!

Small talk (I)

What can you talk about if you don't know the person?

5 *These brief encounters are exactly that – short. People don't get into deep meaningful conversations in a lift or in a queue. Look at the list below and decide which of the topics would be appropriate for small talk.*

Situation	Topic
in a train	the rainy weather
in a line at a clothing store	the great sales
waiting for the Tube	the inefficiency of the London Underground
in a line at a grocery store	Too many people are overweight nowadays.
waiting in line at the registration office of your new college	classes that will be offered next semester
at your first meeting for international volunteers	The German health system is better than the American health system.
You have just met the other people who will be in your dorm at college.	What they like to do in their free time.

> **TIP**
>
> **Topics unsuitable for small talk**
> 1. Health problems and diseases
> 2. Religion
> 3. Politics
> 4. The Government
> 5. The War
> 6. Unfavourable comparisons between your country and the one you're visiting.
> 7. Things that don't function well in the country you're visiting, even if the other person mentions them.

6 *Think of other appropriate topics for the situations in the chart in Task 5. Then come up with a list of good topics for small talk.*

7 *Now it's time to practise starting a conversation with these people. Use the situations in Task 5 and perform your scene for others in your class.*

Keeping small talk small

8 *It can happen. You're chatting to someone in a queue and suddenly it's there – an inappropriate remark, such as the ones you noted in Task 5. Listen to the dialogues and note how small talk is kept small.*

9 *Practise keeping small talk small. Find ways of changing the subject when faced with these remarks:*

1. "Of course the euro is totally overvalued."
2. "From Germany? That's the country where you're still at school when you're twenty."
3. "To my way of thinking the government just pays people not to work."
4. "People should live their lives according to the Lord's word in the Bible."
5. "Young people these days spend all their time chatting on the internet and tweeting."
6. "Well, it seems to me Germany just wants to dominate the EU."
7. "All these immigrants who flood in! Most of them are here illegally."
8. "Well since you ask, I just can't get over the flu I had and I'm so tired all the time."

> **TIP**
>
> **Changing the subject**
>
> You can make a neutral reply such as, "Well I don't know much about that." Then pick up on one word or phrase to steer the conversation away from a controversial topic or one inappropriate for the small talk situation.

10 *Practise keeping small talk small using the role cards on the CD.*

283

Intercultural communication

Small talk (II)

How to keep the conversation going

Successful small talk is like a ball bouncing – Person A says something (usually ending with a question) that encourages Person B to respond. Person B answers, and then bounces the conversation back to Person A (again usually with a question) etc. Be supportive: don't block the conversation by just saying 'no', or giving a similarly negative response. It would be extremely rude to say nothing at all to a person who is trying to talk to you.

1 a) *Listen to the two dialogues and decide which of them is a good example of small talk. How did the speakers keep the balls bouncing?*
  b) *Small talk doesn't usually take up much time, but sometimes it can open doors for you. How did getting involved in small talk help the German in the second dialogue?*

USEFUL PHRASES

Question tags can be quite helpful when trying to keep a conversation going.

You're from Germany, aren't you?

The weather is quite nice today, isn't it?

It's really hot in here, isn't it?

We're really having to wait a long time today, aren't we?

This theatre seems very popular, doesn't it?

2 *Keeping small talk going is something that can be learned. Look at the chart and develop the dialogue with a partner.*

Situation: waiting in line for your American driver's license.

Partner A	Partner B
– long line!	– always long – first time America?
– two weeks – from Germany	– where in Germany?
– Cologne – know it? – been to Germany?	– no, ancestors from Germany – grandmother – German cookies – still bake them in Germany?
– Christmas – grandmother's cookies – kind?	– *Lebkuchen, Springerle.* – know them?
– Lebkuchen, yes – Springerle, South Germany – regional cookies in USA?	– yes – my turn for license – nice talking to you – good luck with license

3 *Read the start of this conversation. Then choose one of the topics on the list to go on. It should be something that fits in with what has gone before. After a few exchanges your partner does the same. If none of the topics on the list fit, choose something else.*

– So you're new on Mrs McGuire's team?
– Yes, I'm on a work placement from Germany.
– Hey, good old Germany. Whereabouts?
– Munich. Do you know it?

holidays • placements • weather • public transport • food and drink • parties • school • big cities • sport

Small talk (II)

4 *Practising small talk – keeping the ball bouncing:*
  a) First make cards with small talk situations on them. For example: waiting in a queue, on a bus, in a cafeteria, waiting for a game to start …
  b) With a partner take a card and think for a minute about topics for small talk for the situation.
  c) Practise spontaneous small talk with the situations on your card. The partners that can keep their 'ball bouncing' (i.e. the conversation going) the longest win.

How can I end the conversation or tell when the conversation is over?

It isn't polite to ignore signals that your partner wants to end the conversation. Non-verbal signals are important too. Many English speakers smile in most situations. It doesn't always mean they're still interested in continuing a conversation. If someone really wants to meet up with you again, he or she will probably ask for contact details immediately. If this doesn't happen, don't press it.

5 *Look at each dialogue and decide which conversation ended successfully.*

  1. **A** Well, it's been nice talking to you. I have to be making a move.
     B Oh, which way are you going? Maybe you could show me the way to the bus station.
     A Sorry, I really have to dash now.

  2. **A** Well, it's been nice talking to you. I have to get back to the office.
     B Yes, I have to go, too. I need to see if I can find the bus station.
     A Have a good rest of your trip!

  3. **A** Well, it's been nice talking to you. That's my bus.
     B Oh, that's a shame! We were having such a nice chat.
     A Yeah, well, have a good trip.

  4. **A** Well, it's been nice talking to you. I have to check whether anyone's been trying to get in touch with me.
     B Yes, and I need to get to the bus station. Bye.
     A See you.

6 *"We must meet up sometime." Listen to the dialogues, decide in which one it is most likely they will meet up again and note how this is achieved.*
(L4/14)

7 *Use the cards you made for Task 4. After the ball has bounced back and forth for some time, one of you signals verbally that the conversation is coming to an end. End the conversation successfully, keeping in mind the strategies you learnt in Tasks 5 and 6.*

8 *Small talk and everyday life: We are not always in a good mood or healthy, but we have to remain polite and friendly. Play the improvisation small talk game in class. Print out the sheets with the role cards on the CD. Then cut the cards and place them in three piles: Situation (1), Partner A (2) and Partner B (3). Write the number of the pile on the back of each card. With a partner draw a situation card, a card for Partner A and a card for Partner B. Look at your setting and mood. Decide how you are going to handle the situation. Be prepared to act this out in front of the class.*

TIP

Small talk ball game

Each pair has a small rubber ball (e.g. a tennis ball). Every time you ask a question, bounce your ball to your partner and vice versa. If one of you forgets to ask a question, the ball stops bouncing and the round of small talk is over.

USEFUL PHRASES

Ending small talk

For a start:
Well, it's been nice talking to you.

And then:
I have to get back to my desk/go to my next class.

I think this is my stop/my bus.

Oh, the queue's moving at last/it looks like it's stopped raining.

I need to check if I have any messages/check the time the bus leaves.

I think a colleague is/my parents are looking for me.

Enjoy your stay!

I hope you manage to settle in well.

Good luck with your placement/on your first day.

Intercultural communication

Negotiating

The fine art of negotiation

Being able to negotiate in any language is a very important skill because it allows people to solve conflicts in a peaceful manner. Of course, negotiating is strongly linked to the business world. However, negotiating starts long before you have your first job. Most children learn at an early age how to negotiate for a better allowance or for more free time to surf on the internet. One thing is for certain – good negotiators usually get what they want more often than others.

1 Why didn't the boy in the photostory get what he wanted?

2 In which of the two dialogues does the person get what they want? Explain why by completing these sentences on a separate piece of paper.
   1. The boy in the first dialogue presents the matter as …
   2. The attitude of the girl in the second dialogue is …

Negotiation tactics

In order to be successful in negotiation, you need work on your negotiation tactics.
1. **Preparation:** Decide how you are going to present the point you want to negotiate. You need to get the other person into the mood for talking about the matter.
2. **Bidding for more than you want:** As you may have to make compromises, it might be a good idea to start with the maximum solution, so that what you really want, which is less than that, seems acceptable.
3. **Arguments:** Go through your arguments carefully and be prepared for …
4. **Counter arguments:** If you know what the arguments from the other side could be, it will help you present your…
5. **Compromise:** Be realistic in deciding what compromises you can offer. It's helpful if you can …
6. **Make the compromise attractive:** If the other person feels they are gaining something from the compromise, they'll be more likely to agree.

3 Good negotiation is also about language. With a partner match the appropriate phrases to the tactics above.

a) A possible solution would be to …
b) There seems to be a problem here.
c) If I understand you right, you agree …
d) I don't know how you feel about it, but …
e) I understand/I see that that might be …
f) Perhaps I could… and then you could …
g) Well, that's a nice idea/would help, but …
h) We could try it out and see how it goes.
i) Would it be possible to …?
j) Something is puzzling me.
k) I wouldn't go that far.
l) I've noticed that …
m) That wouldn't be necessary.
n) I'm not sure how to put this.
o) An alternative would be to …

Negotiating

4 Listen to the dialogue and note how the tactics above were used. Make a note of the language used in these tactics too.

Language for negotiation

5 Tactically, it is better to avoid direct statements in negotiations. Look at the chart below and match each direct demand with a more polite request.

Direct demand	Polite request
1. I need to borrow the car this evening.	a) Do you think it would be OK if I went to the movies with my friends this weekend?
2. We want to go to the movies on Saturday.	b) Excuse me, Mr. Smith. I'm afraid we've already got three tests next week. Do you think we could postpone it for a week?
3. We can't have a test next Tuesday. We've already got three next week!	c) I was just wondering if I could use the car this evening, if it wouldn't be too much trouble.
4. I'd like my friends to come over for a party on my birthday.	d) Pardon me for asking, but I've heard that some of the other students are getting a bit more money for working here.
5. That room you gave me is too full. There's only one bed free in there. Give me another room.	e) Sorry to trouble you again, but it would be great if I could switch rooms. Have you got any other available rooms in your hostel?
6. That's not enough money for me.	f) Are we planning anything special for my birthday next week? Would it be OK if my friends came over?

USEFUL PHRASES

Negotiating

I'd rather not … if at all possible.

Would it be too much trouble to ask you whether …

I agree with you, but don't you think we should look at other aspects?

We have established that we both agree on …

As I understand it, you would feel comfortable …

How would you feel about … working …

I see your point. Could we just try to look at this from another angle?

6 With a partner rephrase these direct demands. The polite requests in Task 5 can help you.

> I have to help my friend in Biology class in the next period. She needs help with her presentation.

> We don't want any homework this weekend!

> We need to leave class five minutes earlier to make an announcement.

> I can't take the test next week because I've got a doctor's appointment.

7 With a partner work on your negotiating skills. Follow the role cards.

Intercultural communication

Watch your English!

Bad influences and false conceptions

1 *The way British or American celebrities dress and talk in the media sometimes gives people the wrong impression of the English-speaking world.*

   ⊚ S
   ⊚ L4/17

   a) Listen to these short dialogues and note the bad influences from the media and other false conceptions that are inappropriate in everyday life.

   b) Write down the sentences used to apologise or get out of an embarrassing situation.

   c) 👥 Think about German manners. Discuss rules of politeness that are common knowledge here in Germany. What would you tell an English-speaking person about German manners?

English as a lingua franca

You've practised all of the topics in this section of the book and know how to behave and speak when you meet English speakers around the world. But not all of your conversations in English will be with people for whom English is their mother tongue. Will they understand the subtleties of polite English? Will they understand your small talk?

> **TIP**
>
> **Promoting understanding**
>
> When you notice that someone isn't familiar with the way English is used in very polite or indirect ways, you need to use a simpler, more direct language, but don't forget to keep it polite and use '… *please*', '*sorry, but …*' etc.

⊚ S
⊚ L4/18

2 a) Listen to the dialogues and find examples of polite phrases and how they've been misunderstood.

   b) How was the problem solved in each of the dialogues?

3 Match these very polite phrases with more direct alternatives.

Very polite	Alternative
I was wondering if I could possibly have …	If we don't see each other again, goodbye.
I'm not sure if that's such a good idea.	Can you give me …, please?
I'm afraid, it would be rather inconvenient for me next week.	Sorry, but I don't want to do that.
I'm sure we'll see each other before you leave at the end of the month.	I'm sorry, but I haven't got time then.

4 a) Other non-natives may have strong accents or may not speak very good English, which makes it hard for you to understand them. How do you deal with this situation? Discuss the advantages and disadvantages of these options:

   1. Correct their English; otherwise they'll never learn it properly.
   2. Ask them to repeat it, as you're not sure you understood what they said.
   3. Ask them to say it another way.
   4. Say what you think they said and ask them if you understood it correctly.

   b) Note down what you can say when you don't understand what someone has said.

Watch your English!

Adjusting to the situation

With a group of people all from different countries, some will speak English better than others. Make your English clear and simple so that nobody feels left out.

5 *With a partner choose one of these four situations and write a dialogue text. Choose words which everyone in the group would understand easily. Include some of the strategies you have learned in this chapter.*

 **SITUATION 1**

You are taking part in a European sports championship in Berlin and running against young competitors from nine different countries.

You want to know:
- where they are staying
- if their team coaches allow them to meet up in the evenings and
- if so, whether they want to come to a restaurant (what food do they like?)
- and later, to go out to a club and dance

They want to know:
- what the choice of restaurants is
- how old they have to be to get into the club

 **SITUATION 2**

You are doing an internship at the United Nations base in Geneva, Switzerland, with other interns from Kenya, Sweden, America and Italy.

You are the newest intern, and you want to know:
- whether the other interns like the work they are doing
- tips they could give you about work
- where you could go in your free time
- who you can ask about getting a travel pass for the city

They want to know:
- where you come from
- why you decided to try an internship here

 SITUATION 3

You join an international team of young people working as volunteers in Sri Lanka, building a new school.

You want to know:
- where they come from
- whether they have problems with the food, the sanitation or the working conditions
- if so, how they deal with them
- what good experiences they have had here

They want to know:
- where you come from
- how long you will be working with them
- whether you have done volunteer work before

 **SITUATION 4**

You are taking part in an international debating tournament in Athens, Greece, and competing against teams from all over the world.

You want to know:
- where they come from and whether they are staying in the same accommodation
- how and where they learned how to debate
- topics they will be speaking on
- what the social evening programme includes

They want to know:
- where you come from
- your favourite debating topics
- who else is in your team

Skills

Table of contents

Word skills
- **S1** Learning vocabulary with vocabulary sheets
- **S2** Guessing new words
- **S3** Working with a dictionary

Text skills
- **S4** Dealing with non-fictional texts
  - **S4.1** Understanding non-fictional text types and typical features
  - **S4.2** Analysing non-fictional texts
- **S5** Dealing with narrative texts
  - **S5.1** Understanding narrative text types and typical features
  - **S5.2** Analysing narrative texts
- **S6** Dealing with poetry and drama
  - **S6.1** Analysing poetry
  - **S6.2** Analysing drama
- **S7** Characterisation
- **S8** Narrative perspectives
- **S9** Narrative techniques
- **S10** Style and stylistic devices
  - **S10.1** Style, tone and register
  - **S10.2** Stylistic devices
- **S11** Skimming, scanning and taking notes
  - **S11.1** Skimming and scanning
  - **S11.2** Taking notes

Writing skills
- **S12** Creative writing
  - **S12.1** Free writing
  - **S12.2** Material-based writing
  - **S12.3** Diary entry
- **S13** Summary
- **S14** Essay
  - **S14.1** Argumentative essay
  - **S14.2** Comment
- **S15** Speech
- **S16** Review
- **S17** Newspaper article
- **S18** Letter
  - **S18.1** Writing a formal letter/letter to the editor
  - **S18.2** Writing an application
  - **S18.3** Curriculum Vitae – CV
  - **S18.4** Personal letter or email
- **S19** Term paper and quoting
  - **S19.1** Term paper
  - **S19.2** Sources
  - **S19.3** Quoting
- **S20** Paragraphs, editing and checking
  - **S20.1** Writing paragraphs
  - **S20.2** Editing and checking

Listening skills
- **S21** Listening comprehension

Speaking skills
- **S22** Presentation
- **S23** Dialogue
- **S24** Discussion and debate
  - **S24.1** Debate
  - **S24.2** Chairing a discussion or talk show
  - **S24.3** Taking part in a discussion or talk show
- **S25** Interview

Mediating skills
- **S26** Mediating and translating skills
  - **S26.1** Mediating
  - **S26.2** Interpreting and translating

Special skills
- **S27** Statistics, diagrams and maps
- **S28** Working with visuals
  - **S28.1** Pictures
  - **S28.2** Cartoons
- **S29** Working with films
  - **S29.1** Film types and cinematic devices
  - **S29.2** Analysing films
  - **S29.3** Making a film
- **S30** Making a survey
- **S31** Advertising
  - **S31.1** Advertising strategies
  - **S31.2** Working with advertisements
- **S32** Doing research
- **S33** Peer evaluation
- **S34** Dealing with exam tasks (with *Operatoren*)

Word skills

S1   Learning vocabulary with vocabulary sheets

Learning vocabulary is essential to language learning: The more words and collocations or connections between words you know, the better you will be able to communicate your ideas and succeed in your exams. The vocabulary files on the accompanying CD-ROM can help you to learn and revise vocabulary. Find out which way of working with the files suits you best and try to apply the words you learn wherever possible.

The **CD-ROM** contains **text-based vocabulary files**, comprising the most important words and phrases from the book. They are listed in the order in which they occur in the texts. There is one vocabulary file for each text.

The files can be edited with a word processor, so you can easily add new words and phrases.

Three-column files
- **Left-hand column:** word or phrase to be learned (notes on pronunciation or stress can be added).
- **Middle column:** German translation.
- **Right-hand column:** information that helps you remember the word/phrase and how to use it, e.g.
  - words from the same word family
  - paraphrases, synonyms, antonyms, false friends
  - example sentences and collocations

What you can do with them:
- Use the files for homework and exam preparation (on the screen or printed out).
- Reduce, rearrange or add to the lists.
- Be creative: Turn them into mind maps, vocabulary tests or quizzes for a partner etc.

Symbols and abbreviations

adj	adjective
adv	adverb
AE	American English
↔	antonym
BE	British English
coll	collocation
esp	especially
≠	false friends
fml	formal
Fr.	French word with the same meaning
hum	humorous
infml	informal
≈	nearly the same meaning
Lat.	Latin word with the same meaning
n	noun, substantive
!	Pay attention to pronunciation or usage.
pej	pejorative
pl	plural
sg	singular
sb	somebody
sl	slang
sth	something
=	synonym
v	verb
vlg	vulgar
→	from the same word family

Green Line Oberstufe • The US then and now • Vocabulary sheet

Introduction

Word/phrase	Translation	Usage/memory aid
to put up with sth	sich mit etw. abfinden; etw. ertragen	■ If there's a situation you don't like but can't avoid, you have to put up with it. ■ to put up with = to accept
inequality	Ungleichheit	■ I recently read a utopian novel about a classless society without any social inequality. ■ inequality → equal (adj) → unequal (adj)

Skills

S2 Guessing new words

Here is a list of guessing techniques that can be applied to texts containing new words. There will always be some words you don't know, but this should not prevent you from understanding the most important points from the texts.

Guessable words

- words that are used in a German context:
  boycott, clown, laptop, track, …
- words that are similar to German words – but watch out for false friends!
  campaign, globalisation, lyrical, province, …
- words that are similar to words you know from another foreign language (French, Latin, Spanish, Italian, Greek) – but watch out for false friends!
  capital, community, destruction, dignified, minor, mural, phase, to renounce, to suspend, …
- compounds of words you already know:
  knowledge-based, passer-by, postcolonial, …
- words from a word family you already know:
  applicant, beneficial, entrepreneurial, …
- words you already know, but with a different meaning (which is guessable from the context):
  a large retail **company** *– a new theatre* **company**
- words whose meaning you can guess from the context: *The riots, then, he says, were partly about turning the tables on* **despised** *representatives of authority. "It was to give them a taste of their own medicine".* In this example you guess that *despised* must be a negative adjective (*despised = hated*).

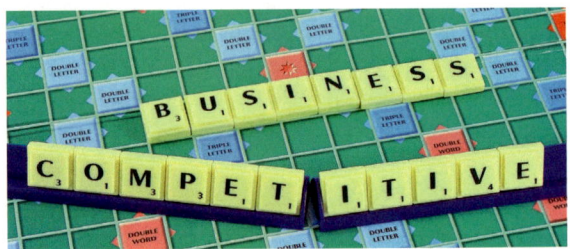

S3 Working with a dictionary

Use the information on word category, register, collocations and usage given in dictionaries to find the word that fits the context best. An **English–German, German–English dictionary** is best suited for the purpose of **translation**, whereas an **English–English dictionary** helps you get to know the **usage** of words.

Here is an example from the Cambridge Advanced Learner's Dictionary:

- pronunciation
- word category/part of speech
- style/usage
- idioms
- frequency (information on the relative importance of a word: E=Essential; I= Improver; A= Advanced)

- grammatical details ([I] = intransitive verb)
- different meanings with definitions and examples showing typical usage
- collocations

Text skills

S4 Dealing with non-fictional texts

S4.1 Understanding non-fictional text types and typical features

Non-fiction is a term for several text types whose main purpose is giving truthful information about facts and opinions. Some types try to influence the reader or use fictional elements to make a more interesting read. It is important to understand the purpose of the text, what effect it should have on the reader, and how the author uses a particular structure, language and style to achieve this purpose.

Text types are:
- **expository texts:** news article/news report, essay, interview, scientific paper, …
- **descriptive texts:** feature story, biography, travel writing, …
- **argumentative/persuasive texts:** argumentative essay, comment, editorial/leader, letter to the editor, review, speech, …
- **instructive texts:** manual, recipe, …

Tasks often ask you to **analyse** or **write** a certain type of non-fictional text, e.g. a news article or review. Therefore it is essential to know the differences. Here are some important text types and their features:

Text type and purpose	Structure	Language and style
broadsheet newspaper article (quality paper) neutrally informing the public	• **headline:** main information • **lead:** most important point • **body:** starts with the most important information (wh-questions), then further details	• objective style, e.g. avoiding strong adjectives → **S17** • clear, to the point, no repetitions • uses dates, examples, quotes from experts etc. to illustrate or prove facts
tabloid newspaper article (popular paper) informing the public in an exaggerated manner	• **headline:** sensationalised, as short and snappy as possible • **lead:** most exciting point • **body:** short, simple and superficial	• narrative style: vivid description of events; can centre on a person presented as a hero, victim or criminal • often mixes fact and opinion • emotive/exaggerated language: e.g. adjectives, colloquial language
newspaper comment and leader/editorial influencing the reader's opinion on a current topic	• **introduction:** outline of the theme • **body:** presents pros and cons leading to a 'logical' conclusion – the author's position • **conclusion:** sums up the author's opinion, inviting the reader to form his/her own opinion	• clear, concise style • uses valid arguments/examples to illustrate the author's position • choice of words indicating praise or criticism • frequent use of contrast, comparison, rhetorical questions etc. → **S10.2, S14.2**
review personal comment on a book, film, theatre performance, …	• **introduction:** catchy, states what is being reviewed • **body:** summarises content, gives background facts, comparisons **conclusion:** sums up the author's opinion, often with a recommendation/warning	• fairly objective or highly subjective style, depending on the purpose and target group → **S16** • aims at convincing and entertaining the reader • frequent use of arguments, examples, comparisons etc. → **S10.2**
speech informing the audience and/or influencing their opinion	• **introduction:** example or question illustrating the topic • **body:** logical order of arguments • **conclusion:** sums up main point(s), calls for action	• clear, addressee-oriented style • logical order of arguments • keywords repeated for emphasis • uses rhetorical devices to convince listeners → **S10.2, S15**

293

Skills

S4.2 Analysing non-fictional texts

STEP 1 Preparation
- Skim the text to identify the topic and the main arguments.
- Find out about the intention/purpose of the text, using your knowledge of the typical features. Considering background information (historical context, source, author, target group) can be helpful.
- Secure your comprehension of the text by looking for keywords and making notes.

STEP 2 Writing
- Briefly sum up the main points/the author's intention.
- Examine the relationship between style and content. Look at each section of the text and describe effects created by the structure of the text, its language, register, style and tone. → S10
- Sum up your findings. If asked, give your personal impression of the text.

STEP 3 Editing and checking → S20.2

> **TIP**
>
> **Writing about non-fictional texts**
> - Answer questions on the text precisely and to the point. Do exactly as you are told when you are asked to **analyse**, **examine**, **compare** or **interpret** things. → S34
> - Explain everything in your own words, but use quotations to support your statements, marking them clearly as quotations and giving line references. → S19.3
> - Clearly distinguish between facts and your interpretation.
> - If asked, state your opinion separately, after discussing the facts, and with reasons.
> - Avoid repetition.

USEFUL PHRASES

Giving information on the text

The (article) was written by … and published in (source) on (date).

It shows/deals with/provides insight into …

Talking about the structure

In the first paragraph the author/writer presents …

In the next section the reader's attention is drawn to …

The next paragraphs provide more details on/examples of … Thus, the author illustrates …

The author supports his/her views with strong/valid arguments.

The author's line of argument starts off with … and culminates in …

Connectives/structuring devices → S20.1

Talking about language and style

The author strictly separates between/often mixes fact and opinion.

The repetition of …/The use of words such as … emphasises/underlines …

The quotation/The detailed description of … evokes …/ makes the reader feel …

Summing up/Conclusion

All in all, the author gives an unbiased/rather biased account of the situation/the events.

The text presents all facts in a clear and objective/in a very subjective way.

The author convincingly shows/proves …

This enables the reader to draw their own conclusions.

Text skills

S5 Dealing with narrative texts

S5.1 Understanding narrative text types and typical features

The novel has become the most successful literary genre, flexible and entertaining, with many subgenres for different reader interests. Authors can parody or mix sub-genres. Short stories have special characteristics.

Characteristics of the novel

Function	• tells a **fictional story**, which transports the reader into a fictional world (which can be close to real life or fantastical) to entertain and sometimes educate the reader
Focus	• able to give large amounts of detail because length is unlimited • can focus on any number of **characters/protagonists** and show developments over time; different **narrative perspectives** possible → S7, S8 • may cover several **events** or **locations** • can focus on a long period of **time**, sometimes over several generations • time settings could be historical, contemporary or futuristic
Structure	• long, informative **introduction** or direct start 'in the middle of things' *(in medias res)* • **order of the plot** can be chronological or written with narrative techniques such as frame story, flashbacks, back story or foreshadowing → S9 • mainly separated into **chapters** • cliffhangers (exciting endings to chapters, making the reader want to read more) • **ending** can be closed, open, predictable or unexpected
Language and style	• always in the genre of **prose** (following the flow of natural speech) • can be written in many different **styles**, may be artful → S10 • contains descriptive sections, reported speech and direct speech

> **TIP**
>
> **Important sub-genres of the novel with examples**
> • **coming-of-age:** *To Kill a Mockingbird* by Harper Lee
> • **crime:** *Sherlock Holmes* by Arthur Conan Doyle
> • **dystopia:** *Fahrenheit 451* by Ray Bradbury
> • **family saga:** *White Teeth* by Zadie Smith
> • **fantasy:** *Lord of the Rings* by J.R.R. Tolkien
> • **fictional diary:** *Adrian Mole* by Sue Townsend
> • **Gothic or horror:** *Frankenstein* by Mary Shelley
> • **historical:** *The Eagle of the Ninth* by Rosemary Sutcliffe
> • **philosophical/psychological:** *The Ambassadors* by Henry James
> • **romance:** *Sense and Sensibility* by Jane Austen
> • **science fiction:** *Cloud Atlas* by David Mitchell

Characteristics of the short story

Function	• gives a short glimpse of a life-changing event or revelation • captures an important moment or an important feeling
Focus	• single event, single setting, short time span • only one or two characters
Structure	• direct beginning, little or no introduction • central turning point or surprising 'twist in the tale' near the end
Language	• often elliptical (details or sentence parts left out) • one distinctive language or style choice

Skills

S5.2 Analysing narrative texts

STEP 1 Preparation
- Read carefully. Note keywords or unusual words and the overall effect of the text.
- Check what you have been asked to do: e.g. **analyse**, **examine**, **compare**, **interpret**. → S34
- Make notes about author and background; note if the text belongs to a particular sub-genre.
- Who and/or what is the main subject of the text?
- Collect evidence for the effect of the text, using notes on structure, characterisation, narrative perspective/technique, style, register etc.
  → S7–S10

STEP 2 Writing
Use the **checklist** to choose what is important for your task and write a structured answer:

Introduction
- Include general information about the text. Don't forget: author, title, text type and theme!

Body
- Each paragraph should make one point to support your argument/interpretation. → S20.1
- Always connect the author's choice (stylistic devices, characters, location, time etc.) with its effect. Look for possible reasons why the author made these choices.
- Explain everything in your own words, but use quotations from the text to support your statements, marking them clearly as quotations and giving line references. → S19.3
- Clearly distinguish between facts and your interpretation!

Conclusion
- End your answer with a short summary, or (if asked) a comparison of this text with other works, or with your own experience, or your personal impression of the text.

STEP 3 Editing and checking → S20.2

> **TIP**
>
> **Checklist for tasks on narrative texts**
> - type and context: genre, author
> - plot: what happens; theme
> - setting: time, place, atmosphere
> - protagonists: relationships, direct/indirect characterisation
> - narrator and point of view
> - narrative techniques: chronology, frame story, suspense, descriptions, comments
> - plot structure: character introduction, turning point, surprising turn of events
> - language: word choices, register, style
> - effect created by the relationship between style and content

USEFUL PHRASES

Introduction

The text is (not) a typical example of a (sub-genre) novel/short story/…
It is a … but it also contains elements of a …
It was written in … by …
In the … century … were very popular because … The author is famous for …

Talking specifically about the plot, setting and characters

The text tells the story of … from the point of view of …
It is set in …(time or place)
The narrator is …
The main character(s) is/are …
We get to know … by …
His/Her relationship with … is …
There is a conflict between … and …
He/She is faced with the dilemma of …
The author uses the narrative perspective of … to …
Narrative techniques used include …

Talking about the structure

At the beginning, … Later he/she learns/changes …
The turning point is … At the end, …
There is a surprising turn of events when …
The development of … is mirrored/paralleled by …

Talking about language and style

The detailed description of … evokes … / makes the reader feel … /creates an atmosphere of …
The repetition of … /The use of words such as … emphasises/underlines …
It is striking that …
The author makes use of/combines … in order to …
Suspense is created by …

Summing up/Conclusion

The way … is presented reminds the reader of …
This text is a good example of …
The reader is left with the impression that …
In conclusion, the most important aspect is …

S6 Dealing with poetry and drama

S6.1 Analysing poetry

- **Formal poetry types:** ballad, elegy, epic poem, haiku, ode, sonnet, …
- **Free verse:** No rhyme or fixed rhythm pattern, sounds like natural speech. Often used in the 20th/21st century to express strong feelings or concentrate on unusual words/thoughts/ associations.
- **Enjambement** (run-on line): connects lines and content, increases flow or tension.

> From **Poem in October**
> [...] Pale rain over the dwindling harbour
> And over the sea wet church the size of a snail
> With its horns through mist and the castle
> Brown as owls [...]
>
> Dylan Thomas, 1945

> **Making cocoa for Kingsley Amis**
> _ / _ /   _ / _ /
> It was a dream I had last week   a
> And some kind of record seemed vital. b
> I knew it wouldn't be much of a poem   c
> But I love the title.   b
>
> Wendy Cope, 1986
> (Kingsley Amis: English novelist and poet)

- **Style:** A poem can be lyrical, song-like, descriptive, narrative, comparative, humorous, reflective, …
- **Title:** Don't forget: The title can be part of the poem!
- **Metre (rhythm):** pattern of accented or stressed (/) and unaccented (−) syllables
- **Rhyme:** Words are labelled with letters to show the rhyme scheme.

STEP 1 Introduction
- State in your own words: the poem's main theme • its message or the story it tells • who the speaker is (if there is one) • who he/she is addressing.

STEP 2 Examining the formal elements
- Look closely at **structure** and **form** (stanzas, rhyme scheme, rhythm/metre, any changes) and **language** (simple/complex, repetitions, comparisons/contrasts, images/symbols).
- Describe how these formal elements are used to create a certain atmosphere/feelings; explain how they support the message of the poem.

STEP 3 Additional points and conclusion
- Say (if asked) whether you find the poem convincing, or describe your own feelings.
- When **interpreting songs**, answer the following question: Do the musical genre, melody, vocals or accompanying instruments support the lyrics?
- Conclude with the main effect/impression.

> **TIP**
> In a poem, **every single word** is important. Reading the poem several times (aloud) will help you to understand it.

USEFUL PHRASES

Introduction/Main theme

The poem/sonnet "…" by … deals with/is about …
The speaker describes/reflects on … in order to …
The title makes the reader think of/that …

Talking about structure and form

The poem is divided into … stanzas/sections/lines.
The poem follows/does not follow a clear rhyme scheme.
Lines x and y rhyme/do not rhyme at all.
The arrangement of the rhymes is (aabb).
The poem is an example of free verse.
The poem is based on a regular metre.
It has a flowing/monotonous/staccato rhythm.

Talking about language

The poet uses complex imagery/emotive language/ ambiguity/contrasts/unusual associations in order to …
The words (mainly) belong to the word field/area of …

Form and function

The poem conveys/creates a feeling/atmosphere of …
The repetition of the word "…" stresses/emphasises …
The change of (rhythm) in line x indicates …
The run-on line (ll. x-y) intensifies the feeling of …

Conclusion

The poem is convincing/moving/special because …
… the reader can identify with the speaker/situation.
The reader is left with the impression that …

S6.2 Analysing drama

A play is presented to the audience through direct speech, by the actors and actresses, on a theatre stage or in a film/radio play. The setting gives the audience or reader clues about action and atmosphere. The action can be on stage or off-stage. Actors move, interact with each other, exit and enter the stage. Stage directions in the text give the actors instructions on how to present an action or feeling. A director can decide to change the original setting, in order to change the focus of the play or connect it to current events.

Types of plays
- **Comedy** has a happy ending.
- **Tragedy** has a sad or catastrophic ending.
- **Tragicomedy** is a mixture of both.
- **One-act or short plays**, like short stories, concentrate on one important moment/event.

Setting (what you can see/hear and where)
- Acts and scenes can be set in different **places**, indoor and outdoor settings.
- The **scenery**/backdrop is detailed or minimal.
- **Costumes**, **sound**, **lighting** and **props** (chairs, beds, bags, letters, swords, etc.) contribute to action and atmosphere.
- The **time setting** can be modern/historical; e.g. set in ancient Rome/modern America/the 1960s.
- The **time of action** can be long or short, with time leaps or gaps.

Classic 5-act structure of the plot
- The **exposition** introduces characters and theme.
- The **rising action** increases tension/complications.
- The **climax/turning point** starts a downfall (tragedy) or a turn for the better (comedy).
- The **falling action** increases problems (tragedy) or works towards solving them (comedy).
- The **dénouement** closes the play, with a catastrophe (tragedy) or a happy/open ending.

Characters/Protagonists
- **Major characters** can be heroes/antiheroes – or heroines. Antagonists are enemies or opposites.
- **Minor characters** can introduce major characters or reflect the main action in a subplot.
- **Extras** don't have a speaking part – they may play servants, crowds, armies etc.

STEP 1 Introduction
- Sum up the **main theme** and/or message of the excerpt/the whole play.

STEP 2 Examining the formal elements
- Look at the elements of each **character** (typical? changing?), their effect on other characters or the audience,
- **place/time setting**, atmosphere, director's interpretation if describing a performance,
- and the **language** (speech type: crowd scene, dialogue, monologue or soliloquy), characteristic words/register, emotions), e.g. *The playwright/dramatist uses … to show sb's feelings/plans/to express a dilemma.*
- What causes the **action**/feelings in this part? What are the effects of the action here? Does the audience/a character find out something new?
- Describe **how these elements combine** to create a certain atmosphere/feelings/effects, e.g.: *Dramatic irony appears when a character thinks … but the audience knows that it's not true* or *Comic relief is when humorous scenes with minor characters break up tension in a tragedy.*

STEP 3 Conclusion
- In the conclusion comment on the main effect or impression on the reader/audience, comparisons/contrasts with other scenes/plays and give a personal response if required.

RADIO *(without preamble, having been switched on by Mrs. Drudge)* We interrupt our programme for a special police message. *(Mrs. Drudge stops to listen)* The search still goes on for the escaped madman who is on the run in Essex.

MRS. DRUDGE *(fear and dismay)* Essex!

RADIO County police led by Inspector Hound have received a report that the man has been seen in the desolate marshes around Muldoon Manor. *(Fearful gasp from Mrs. Drudge)* The man is wearing a darkish suit with a lightish shirt. He is of medium height and youngish. Anyone seeing a man answering to this description and acting suspiciously, is advised to phone the nearest police station. *(A man answering this description has appeared behind Mrs. Drudge. He is acting suspiciously. He creeps in. He creeps out. Mrs. Drudge does not see him)*

Tom Stoppard, *The Real Inspector Hound*, 1968

S7 Characterisation

When dealing with a novel, film or play, you will often be asked to analyse or examine a certain character and his/her behaviour, relationship with others etc. To write a characterisation, you need basic vocabulary:

Types of characters
- **protagonist/hero/heroine** (main character)
- **antagonist** (another important character who is in conflict with the protagonist)
- **flat character** (does not change, has no depth)
- **round character** (changes, is presented in detail)

Types of characterisation
- **direct characterisation:** The narrator or a character tells the reader explicitly what a character is like.
- **indirect characterisation:** The reader interprets a character by what the character thinks, says, feels or does, and how he/she interacts with others.

STEP 1 Preparation
Collect any relevant information given in the text about the character:
- personal data (name, age, gender) and appearance;
- what the character says/does/thinks (main traits, behaviour, mood, views, language, …);
- what others say (or the narrator says) about him/her.

What do your findings reveal about the character and his attitude towards others? Do his/her characteristics or the reader's view of him/her change in the story? Draw conclusions and use evidence from the text (quotes and lines). → S19.3

STEP 2 Writing
Introduction
- Briefly present the character (basic personal data and outward appearance).
- Say what his/her function/role in the story is and how he/she relates to the other characters.

Body
- Describe the character's traits, behaviour and development, providing details from your notes
- Do not forget to use examples and quotes to support your statements.

Conclusion
- Sum up the most important traits.

STEP 3 Editing and checking → S20.2

USEFUL PHRASES

Personal data
The protagonist is a young/middle-aged/elderly/a 38-year-old single/married person/widow(er)/child of … origin.

Outward appearance
He/She is described as being tall/small • good-looking/handsome/ugly • obese/stocky/slim • healthy/sickly.
He/She has a bony/wrinkled/square/round/oblong face • bright/dull eyes • long/flat/pointed nose • matted/straight/curly hair • … is bald.
He/She has tattooed/weather-beaten/leathery/smooth/freckled/scarred skin • a loud/coarse/sonorous/soft voice.

Positive character traits
He/She is/seems to be amiable • cheerful • open-minded • modest • decent • good-natured • honest • trustworthy • generous • gentle optimistic • self-confident • sympathetic • considerate • sensitive • reasonable • ambitious • determined • brave • courageous.

Negative character traits
He/She is/seems bad-tempered • cheeky • showy • rude • violent • narrow-minded • gloomy • spiteful • deceitful • unfeeling • stingy • inconsiderate • ruthless • dishonest • unreliable • anxious • pessimistic • shy • lazy • conceited • insecure, because he/she …

Drawing conclusions about a character
The body language/This action reveals that …
X's statement "…" (l. x) shows/proves that he/she …
X appears to be/is portrayed as …

Talking about relationships
to build up/continue/break off a relationship
Their relationship is characterised by deep affection/hostility/suspicion/feelings of …
The difficult/poor/close/casual relationship changes in the course of the story/remains unchanged until the end.

Skills

S8 Narrative perspectives

The effect of a story on the reader is strongly influenced by the **point of view**, or **perspective**, from which it is told. Narrative types can be mixed and the point of view can change in the course of the story.

> **TIP**
>
> Check for **"he/she"** or **"I"** in the narration (not in the parts in direct speech!) to find out whether it is written in the third/first person. Don't confuse narrator and author!

Third-person omniscient narrator
- This narrator is not visible in the story and tells the story from the outside, but knows everything (is omniscient) about the characters' thoughts and feelings as well as the background of the story.
- Sometimes the narrator will comment on the characters' behaviour, the events coming later in the story, or even on the writing itself.
- This style of narration is mainly neutral and more distanced than first-person or single perspective narration.

> Emma Woodhouse, handsome, clever, and rich, with a comfortable home and happy disposition, seemed to unite some of the best blessings of existence; and had lived nearly twenty-one years in the world with very little to distress or vex **her**. […] The real evils, indeed, of Emma's situation were the power of having rather too much **her** own way, and a disposition to think a little too well of **herself**; these were the disadvantages which threatened alloy to **her** many enjoyments.
>
> From: Jane Austen, *Emma*

Third-person limited narrator
- This type of narrator tells the story from the outside, but only describes feelings and thoughts from the perspective of one particular character in a story.
- The narrator is not identical with this character.
- We sympathise more easily with the character we are told most about.

> It affected **him** on the spot as a move in a game, and **he** was even then not without the sense that that wasn't the way Jeanne should be married. But **he** quickly showed **his** interest, though – as quickly afterwards struck **him** – with an absurd confusion of mind. "You? You and – a – not Chad?" […] Yet didn't it seem the next minute that Monsieur de Vionnet was after all not in question? – since **she** had gone on to say that it was indeed to Chad **she** referred.
>
> From: Henry James, *The Ambassadors*

First-person narrator
- A character narrates the story from his/her own perspective. ("I …") We only know what this character thinks, knows, sees or hears.
- The first-person narrator is often, but not always, the main protagonist.
- We understand and sympathise most easily with this type of narrator.

> **I** give Pirrip as **my** father's family name, on the authority of his tombstone […]. As **I** never saw **my** father or **my** mother, and never saw any likeness of either of them (for their days were long before the days of photographs), **my** first fancies, regarding what they were like, were unreasonably derived from their tombstones. The shape of the letters on **my** father's gave me an odd idea that he was a square, stout, dark man, with curly black hair.
>
> From: Charles Dickens, *Great Expectations*

USEFUL PHRASES

Writing about narrative perspective

The story is told by a … narrator.

The neutral description of … lets the reader judge … for him/herself.

The biased description of … shows why/how we are expected to judge him/her.

The narrative perspective is limited, because the reader only sees …

We immediately share the experiences/feelings of the first-person narrator.

Therefore we understand best why/how the character deserves sympathy.

S9 Narrative techniques

Structure
- The **plot** (what happens) can be told directly to the reader, or by one character to another in the story.
- The **exposition** is the first part of the narrative. It gives basic information about setting, characters and plot.
- There is often a development in the main part, in which a conflict escalates (**rising action**). After the **climax** or turning point, we speak of **falling action**.
- The ending may be surprising, abrupt or open. A classic **dénouement** is the resolution of a conflict or solution to a mystery, making the ending happy or tragic.
- A **frame story** presents a story within a story.

Chronology
- A **back story** gives the history of characters, objects, places or other elements in the story.
- In a **flashback** the narrative is taken back in time (a popular film technique).
- In a **flash-forward** future events are revealed.
- **Foreshadowing** means that there are clues early in the story that hint at a future development. This is typical of crime and mystery stories, or tragedies.

Narrative situation
- The **point of view** of the narrator shows his/her attitude to the characters and can limit what the reader knows.
- An **unreliable narrator** does not tell the whole truth to the reader.
- **Suspense** is created by not giving away too much information; typical of crime or adventure stories.
- **Tense** influences the distance between reader and characters. If the narrator uses present tense, you feel close to the action.
- **Irony** can be used as a distancing effect by the narrator.
- Narration can vary between **dialogues** (direct speech), **description** and **comments**.
- More distance is created when the narrator uses **indirect speech** to report what the characters are saying and thinking.
- **Stream of consciousness** represents, as exactly as possible, what the character is thinking, and seems unstructured, chaotic and very close to the reader.

Frame story
from: Nathaniel Hawthorne, *The Scarlet Letter*
But, one idle and rainy day, it was my fortune to make a discovery of some little interest. Poking and burrowing into the heaped-up rubbish in the corner, unfolding one and another document […] I chanced to lay my hand on a small package […] There was something about it that quickened an instinctive curiosity, and made me undo the faded red tape that tied up the package, with the sense that a treasure would here be brought to light. […] They were documents, in short, not official, but of a private nature.

Foreshadowing
from: John Green, *Paper Towns*
The way I figure it, everyone gets a miracle. Like, I will probably never be struck by lightning, or win a Nobel Prize, or become the dictator of a small nation in the Pacific Islands, or contract terminal ear cancer, or spontaneously combust. But if you consider all the unlikely things together, at least one of them will probably happen to each of us. […] My miracle was this: out of all the houses in all the subdivisions in all of Florida, I ended up living next door to Margo Roth Spiegelmann. […] Margo always loved mysteries. And in everything that came afterward, I could never stop thinking that maybe she loved mysteries so much that she became one.

Stream of consciousness
from: Virginia Woolf, *Mrs Dalloway*
She had often wanted to write to him, but torn it up, yet felt he understood, for people understand without things being said, as one realises growing old, and old she was, had been that afternoon to see her sons at Eton, where they had the mumps, to be quite frank, then, how could Clarissa have done it? – married Richard Dalloway? a sportsman, a man who cared only for dogs. Literally, when he came into the room he smelt of the stables. And then all this? She waved her hand.

Skills

S10 Style and stylistic devices

S10.1 Style, tone and register

Style is the typical way of writing or speaking used by a person; their choice of tone, grammar and narrative techniques.
Tone is the general mood, feeling or attitude being expressed; it is the emotional content of a text rather than the devices used.
Register is the choice of words, style and grammar used in a certain social context; reflects social status; situations often have rules for appropriate register.

> **TIP**
> - **Style**, **tone** and **register**, difficult to separate, are mainly considered together.
> - It is useful to note the way a character speaks.
> - Don't forget: Form follows function. Comment on the way these devices are used to convey an impression.

Situation	Features	Examples
formal: in a formal speech or letter; addressing someone unknown or higher in a hierarchy	• respectful, neutral, detached style • complete and complex sentences • formal expressions • foreign/specialist words	*After analysing the evidence, the hypothesis was concluded to be correct.* • *I would be grateful for your advice on this.*
informal: used in spoken rather than written language, when speakers know each other well	• more personal and familiar style • simple sentences, can be incomplete or ungrammatical, dialect or slang • vivid, colloquial or vulgar expressions	*Morning all!* • *How's things? Fancy a cuppa?* • *Gotta go get a donut.* • *Ain't you got brains? C'mon, stupid.*
literary: used mainly in written literary texts	• eloquent/elevated style • complex sentences • rich vocabulary • use of stylistic devices • can combine registers for various effects	*"So we went on in the quiet, and the twilight deepened into night. The clear blue of the distance faded, and one star after another came out."* (Wells, *The Time Machine*)

S10.2 Stylistic devices

Here are some of the most important stylistic devices, used to make a text more interesting and effective.

alliteration: bold, bright and beautiful
anaphora: I didn't like his hairstyle. I didn't want to tell him. I didn't think I ought to be unfriendly.
antithetical phrase/contrast: a fire-and-ice relationship; a white star in the dark sky
enumeration: old, grey, suave, majestic
hyperbole: an absolutely fantastic book
irony: Well, that was clever! Now it's broken.
parallelism: It's a great for me, for you, for everyone.
personification: Huge cities never sleep.
repetition: "March for your rights!" he cried, and we marched and marched.
rhetorical question: Wouldn't we all like a holiday?
simile/metaphor: … like a bull in a china shop. She's a little monkey.
synecdoche: I need a new set of wheels. (= a car)

USEFUL PHRASES

Describing style, tone and register

The author/speaker makes use of/combines …	An atmosphere of … is created by using …
… everyday/colloquial/informal/vulgar language.	… a humorous/ironic/serious/critical/positive tone.
… formal/literary/archaic/slang expressions.	… vivid/animated/exaggerated language.
… a concise/witty/eloquent/clear/impersonal style.	… a polite/blunt/rude way of addressing sb.

Text skills

S11 Skimming, scanning and taking notes

S11.1 Skimming and scanning

Skimming
Skimming means going through a text quickly and getting the gist. This technique is useful either when you first look at a text before you analyse it in detail, or when there is no chance to look at the text in detail.

> **TIP**
> Look out for **headings, pictures** and **keywords**. They give you an idea of what to expect from a text. Don't read every word; concentrate on beginnings and ends of paragraphs as well as keywords.

Scanning
Scanning means going through a text quickly and finding particular details. This technique is useful either when only part of the text is relevant because you have to answer particular questions on it, or when you have to compare only some aspects in different texts.

> **TIP**
> What **questions** do you want to answer using the text? Guess relevant keywords and look out for these when scanning the text. Stop when you find one and read that part of the text carefully. Underline or mark the text if possible. Take notes if necessary.

S11.2 Taking notes

STEP 1 Deciding what you need
Depending on what you want to do with your notes later, decide what you want to note down, i.e. just skimming for the gist (for a summary or to prepare a talk) or scanning for particular details (e.g. for a comparison).

STEP 2 First reading
Read the text and underline or mark it, if possible. Use systematic markings, symbols and abbreviations you will recognise when you look at them later on.

STEP 3 Taking notes
Skim or scan the text to extract the important headings (or questions) and keywords from the text. Write them down and add your own comments. You can use mind maps, grids, flow charts or other ways of collecting and visualising information if you like.

STEP 4 Adding more points
If you need more detailed information for some aspects, you can add these points to your list from Step 3 after scanning the text. Add comments if necessary.

> **TIP**
> - Use **simple language** for your notes and avoid copying words without understanding them properly.
> - **Structure** your notes by writing them in hierarchical order with headings and by using numbers, bullets (•) or dashes (–) to list subordinate points.

Gist (skimming):
– after car stolen, Delaney gets another
– meets Kyra in restaurant, feels depressed
– Kyra sees dog locked in sb's car, angry
– D. wants to calm down and go for hike
– but then stays watching car for thieves
– K. sees Mexican jobseekers, angry
…

Details (scanning):
Contradictions:
– Delaney anti-racist but scared of immigrants, ashamed of feelings of hate
– D. knows hiking would calm him but stays, paranoid, watching new car
– Kyra wants to protect her dog and others but no sympathy for suffering immigrants

Example from: T.C. Boyle, *The Tortilla Curtain*; Part 2, Chapter 1

Skills

Writing skills
S12 Creative writing

S12.1 Free writing

The first step in free writing about a topic is to brainstorm ideas and organise them in a mind map.

STEP 1 Preparation
- Decide who you are writing the text for, the purpose of the text and the text type or genre.
- Consider how you can express your ideas best and which techniques are the most suitable for your story. Look at → S8 and → S9 for point of view and narrative techniques, and → S7 for characterisation.

STEP 2 Writing
- If you decide to tell a story, cover these points: Who? When? Where? What? How? Why? The first four can be used in an exposition to introduce the main characters, setting and theme.
- In the main part write about the main action and finish up with an interesting conclusion. → S5

STEP 3 Editing and checking → S20.2

- On the right is an example of a dialogue between a mother, her son and the son's school headmaster. Note the use of style, tone and register → S10 to show the relationship between the three characters.

  Mother: alternates between informal/familar with son and formal/respectful with headmaster

  Son: informal, colloquial

  Headmaster: formal, polite

TIP

Your free writing text
- Your text needs to develop logically, so use structuring devices and connectives. → S14, S20
- Your style should be consistent. → S10
- If you are writing a poem, remember that the form is very important. Choose formal elements which suit what you want to convey. → S6.1
- If you are writing a dialogue, consider stage directions to support the spoken text. → S6.2

Outside the headmaster's office
MOTHER When we're in there, just be polite and behave yourself!
SON It wasn't just my fault. Mr Smith started it.
MOTHER I don't care who started it. Don't make it worse. Just say you're sorry, or you'll get kicked out of school, and you can forget your exams, and how will you get a good job then?
SON Stop nagging, Mum! It wasn't that bad.
Mother and son go into the office, glaring at each other.
HEAD Good afternoon, Mrs Beecher. I'm so glad you could come. I think it's important that we have this little talk to clear up the matter of James's bad behaviour.
SON Not just mine.
Mrs Beecher interrupts quickly.
MOTHER Thank you so much, Mr Clarkson. I've spoken to James and he says he regrets the way everything got so out of hand. He would like to apologise for the whole incident. It was completely his fault.
SON *whispers angrily to his mother* What do you mean, I never said that! (*to headmaster*) Mr Clarkson, I am very sorry for throwing my book at Mr Smith and breaking the test tube rack, but I would also like to complain about Mr Smith's behaviour. He shouldn't have called me a blasted idiot …
HEAD I'm sure Mr Smith didn't mean it the way you took it, James.

S12.2 Material-based writing

Your creative writing can be based on a printed text or on audiovisual material – an audiotext, a video or film, a cartoon, a photo or a picture.
- **Printed texts:** Your task may be to tell a part of the story that is not in the text, write about a different subject using the same text type, to change the point of view, or to tell the same story using a different text type.
- **Audiovisual material:** You may be asked to relate what happened before/after the situation shown, or do a similar task to printed texts.

> **TIP**
> - When asked to **write something based on a text**, first make sure you have understood the text properly.
> - Then use what you know about text types and features to create a new text that matches the original. → S5–S10

For example, the outcome of Shakespeare's *Othello* is presented here as a newspaper report:

Army general kills wife in night of bloodbath
Was this a racially motivated act or simply jealousy?

CYPRUS. Last night a terrible crime was committed in the castle lodgings of Venetian general Othello (42), a dark-skinned gentleman famous for fairness and courage until today. His wife Desdemona (18) was found dead in her bed after screams and shouting had woken the neighbours.

Lieutenant Cassio (25), quickly on the scene, expressed his shock and horror at the terrible act. Othello had smothered his own wife, Cassio claimed, and then stabbed himself to death.

Our reporter W. Shakespeare asked how this could have happened to the beautiful white lady. Could racial tension have had something to do with it?

But Cassio attributed this murder to another, more scandalous cause. Othello had apparently been fooled by his ensign Iago (28), making the general so jealous that he killed his wife in a blind rage. A handkerchief seems to have convinced Othello of his wife's infidelity. "I mourn for my good friend Othello that he was forced into this madness by such a villain", Cassio said.

The incident closely followed an alarming brawl between said Cassio and fellow Venetian Roderigo (27), in which the latter was killed and Cassio injured. Brigands may have been involved in the fight, but if so, they have disappeared without trace.

The dead lady's father, Senator Brabantio (49), said to reliable sources, "I knew that violent Moor, that foul thief, was not to be trusted!" Cassio has replaced Othello as leader of the Venetian forces in Cyprus in the war against the Ottomites.

Rumour has it that this was not the only death in the Cyprus castle last night. More news to come in our evening edition.

S12.3 Diary entry

Another creative task can be to write a diary entry for a fictional character in a story. Here's an example of a diary entry Iago could have written (Shakespeare, *Othello*):

> *Second day in Cyprus*
> *Here in the castle, far away from Venice, where the mood is warlike and men are easily angered, I have come very close to fulfilling my plot against Othello. His dearest Desdemona seems even more beautiful now. Why did she marry him? They will all be punished for it!*
> *I have planted the seeds of jealousy in the Moor's brain. Desdemona has pleaded with her husband to forgive Cassio for injuring Montano last night; I suggested that Cassio has been spending too many hours alone with her, that he loves her overmuch. Playing the honest man, I have encouraged his suspicion, and now he is certain she is untrue. I have stolen her handkerchief. Cassio will die! And a few others with him ...*

> **TIP**
> - **Diary entries** are not normally meant to be read by anyone but the writer.
> - Characteristic contents of a diary are memories, feelings, fantasies, thoughts, emotions, recollections, daydreams or ideas, which can be connected with an experienced event.
> - When writing, follow the original style of the text and characters as much as possible.

Skills

S13 Summary

When you write a summary, you have to briefly restate the author's main ideas (non-fictional texts) or retell a story in your own words (fictional texts). Your summary should be much shorter than the original, usually about a quarter to a third of the length of the original text.

STEP 1 Preparation (NON-FICTIONAL text)
- Read the text carefully to find out the main idea (thesis). Underline it.
- Read the text again and highlight ideas, facts or arguments (words and phrases rather than whole sentences) that support the thesis.

OR

STEP 1 Preparation (FICTIONAL text)
- Read the text carefully and underline the main characters and setting.
- Divide the text into sections. When there is a new aspect or development, underline keywords, main points and the turning point in the plot.

STEP 2 Writing, for both types of text
- In the first sentence mention author, title, text type and the main idea/theme of the text.
- Write short paragraphs summing up the major arguments (non-fiction) or what happens, who contributes to the action, and how the events are connected (fiction). Follow these rules:
  - Use your own words as often as possible.
  - Use the present tense.
  - Leave out non-essential information (e.g. examples, descriptive details, direct quotes).
  - Do not include your own ideas and opinions.

STEP 3 Editing and checking → S20.2
- Check and if necessary revise your summary. You can do this best if you imagine you are a reader who knows nothing about the topic.

Excerpt from the original text

[…] it must have been nearly hysterical at times. Companies might have had as many as thirty plays in their active repertoire, so a leading actor could be required to memorize perhaps fifteen thousand lines in a season as well as remember every dance and sword thrust and costume change. Even the most successful companies were unlikely to employ more than a dozen actors, which meant a great deal of doubling up. Julius Caesar, for instance, has forty named characters, as well as parts for unspecified numbers of "servants", "other plebians" and "senators, soldiers and attendants".

Example of a summary of a non-fictional text:
Bill Bryson writes, in this excerpt from his biography *Shakespeare* (2008), that the 'golden age' of theatre in Shakespeare's time was extremely difficult for both actors and writers, who had to work very hard. He says that theatre companies had to perform around five different plays every week for about two thousand spectators a day to make a good profit.

Because a play may only have been performed ten times a year, there was also a great demand for new plays. Yet writers struggled to make a living, as plays then belonged to the company.

Actors' lives were hard too. They doubled in several roles and had to learn thousands of lines, as well as managing all the acting instructions, dress changes and dances.

Being reliable was essential, according to Bryson. Actors were fined heavily if they were late or wore expensive costumes outside the playhouse. Shakespeare, a multi-talented playwright, actor and part-owner of a playhouse, may have had more control over his plays than others.

USEFUL PHRASES

Non-fictional texts

According to the author, …

The author says/writes/claims/states that …

In addition/conclusion, the author argues that …

Fictional texts

X makes an important discovery/decision here.

The relationship between X and Y takes a turn for the worse/better.

There is a change in … which causes … to …

S14 Essay

S14.1 Argumentative essay

An argumentative essay (or composition) presents a controversial topic from opposing points of view in a clear and logical way. Typical tasks will ask you to **discuss**, **assess** or **evaluate** a topic or statement.

STEP 1 Preparation
Collect ideas and information about the topic; note arguments for and against it. Use mind maps or lists. **Make an outline** of what you are going to write and in which order. For the body of your essay choose a logical structure which fits the topic/task best:

- **Dialectical approach:**
  - Present all of the negative points first, then the positive or alternate between arguments and counter-arguments for each aspect.
  - Arrange points, e.g. from weakest to strongest.
- **Other approaches:**
  - chronological order
  - comparative: deal with similarities first, then differences
  - enumerative ('list' form): neutral sequence of paragraphs

Decide if you want to persuade the reader to agree with you or if you want to remain neutral.

STEP 2 Writing
Introduction
Present the issue and attract the reader's attention, for example using background facts about the problem and its relevance today; a suitable quotation or short anecdote or question(s) that you will give answers to in the essay.

Body
Based on your outline, present each point in a separate paragraph. → S20.1 (paragraph writing) Support your points with evidence (examples, statistics, personal experience etc.).

Conclusion
Give a short summary of what you have written, but do not introduce any new ideas here. You may: give an outlook on further consequences/future developments/possible solutions; state your own opinion/give a recommendation or appeal to the readers to reach their own conclusion.

STEP 3 Editing and checking → S20.2

USEFUL PHRASES

Presenting aspects and examples
… consists of (two) aspects.
It is a … rather than a … problem/issue.
… should also be considered/mentioned.
… is relevant/completely irrelevant to …
There are various reasons why …
This also raises questions about …
Some researchers say … / Studies show …
Proponents/Opponents say/point out …

Using connectives → S20.1

Talking about developments and results
… can/will/should lead to/cause/result in …
The main/short-term/long-term consequences are …
… could have serious/far-reaching consequences for …

Summing up/Conclusion
Therefore,/Consequently,/ As a result, people should/might/must …
In other words, …
And here's what really (matters/happens/is at stake): …

Skills

S14.2 Comment

A comment is a type of essay in which you give your opinion on a topic. It usually deals with a controversial issue or statement, which can be based on a text.

STEP 1 Preparation
- Form your opinion on the topic.
- Collect all the material (arguments and examples) you can to support your opinion.
- Think of possible counterarguments. Refuting them can be a good way to convince the reader.
- Make an outline to structure your material. It is a good idea to start with the weakest argument and end with the strongest.
- To make your text convincing, plan stylistic devices, e.g. rhetorical questions or hyperbole. → S10.2

STEP 2 Writing
Introduction
Present the issue and attract the reader's attention. When commenting on a given text, briefly summarise the point the author makes.

Second part
State your opinion and outline reasons for your view.

Third part
Present your arguments in one paragraph each.
→ S20.1

Conclusion
Summarise your opinion and give an outlook on further developments or possible solutions. Do not introduce any new ideas here.

STEP 3 Editing and checking → S20.2

Example of a comment
Peace and wealth

The author claims that competition is the key to global peace and wealth. There are a few aspects which would support this view, but can it really be true that this behaviour, essentially a battle between opponents, can produce peace and riches?

　It is true that healthy competition between businesses prevents corruption, monopolies and over-inflated prices. Large-scale corruption and poverty makes people dissatisfied with leaders or managers. This could lead to riots.

　Maybe the author also assumes that competition increases productivity, which does indeed raise short-term profits for employers and employees.

　I find it hard to believe, however, that competition is the most important factor. Concentrating on a supportive social atmosphere instead of on competition makes people less stressed, more secure and more productive. Companies who care for their workers earn more money in the long run.

　World peace is obviously much more affected by violence, crime and terrorism. I disagree with the author; good government, diplomacy and education are certainly the key to global peace, and hard work in a cooperative environment is the real key to wealth.

USEFUL PHRASES

Expressing your opinion/Convincing people	Countering arguments
Those who advocate …, often argue that …	I agree/do not agree at all with …
It might be argued that …	However, I agree with … only to a certain extent.
We have to bear in mind, however, that …	Certainly, the author has a point. Yet/Nevertheless …
With this in mind you can better understand why …	This sounds good, right? However, …
So what is it that (makes people do sth… /leads to …)?	I would like to mention the fact that …
So why …?	I strongly question/support/object to …
I believe/suppose …	I find it hard to believe that …
I am sure/convinced/certain that …	Instead of adopting this (simplistic) stance, we should …
As far as I can see …	There is something fundamentally wrong with this idea/point of view.
Looking at … from this/their point of view, you have to admit that …	
It is quite obvious that … / There is no doubt that …	Summing up/Conclusion → S14.1

S15 Speech

Three elements are often mixed in a speech, but depending on the purpose, one of them is dominant:
- **informative:** telling people what you know about a topic
- **explanatory:** showing people how something works or why it is effective
- **persuasive:** trying to win people over and persuade them to take action

STEP 1 Preparation
- Check your purpose. Is your main intention to inform, explain or persuade? Should the speech be entertaining or serious or both?
- Think about your audience. Does the topic interest or affect them? What do they know about it already?
- Organise points logically using connectives to link the sections.
- To make your speech convincing, find suitable rhetorical devices. → S10.2

STEP 2 Writing and making the speech
Introduction
- Greet the audience politely. Thank them for the invitation. State your topic and its importance.
- Catch your listeners' attention, for example with: *a surprising fact or trend • a new discovery • an eye-opening experience • a provocative statement or question • an anecdote/joke/quotation.*
- State your aim and outline your speech structure.

Body
- Hold your listeners' attention. Develop your ideas step by step, e.g.: *in chronological order • from the least to the most important idea • all arguments against and then for your idea • alternating pros and cons • connecting problems with solutions.*
- Support your statements with facts, statistics or examples of personal experience.
- Clearly link the sections of your speech. → S20.1
- Repeat and emphasise important ideas.

Conclusion
- Round off your speech with one of the following: *a short summary • a rhetorical question • a quotation • a promise • an appeal • a call for action • a vision of this topic in the future*
- Ask whether anyone has any questions.

TIP

Public speaking
- Introduce yourself.
- Announce what you're going to talk about. Then say it. Then sum up what you have said.
- Speak in a slow, clear, natural way, using cue cards.
- Stress important words to emphasise key points.
- Pause at the end of each sentence.
- Make sure you don't talk for too long. Most people start to lose concentration after ten minutes.
- Rehearse your speech. Ask someone to listen and give you feedback.
- Do you need to allow time for questions? Have you prepared more information for your answers?

USEFUL PHRASES

Dealing with problems
… is a serious/pressing/urgent problem.
We can overcome this difficulty/settle the conflict/make a compromise/negotiate an agreement/promote reconciliation by …

Looking into the future
In the near future/short term/long term/long run, …
A short/long term solution would be to …
I am hopeful/confident that …
We should work towards …

Taking action
We have to ensure/see to it that …
We should take care not to …
I am prepared/determined to …
We should adopt a resolution to …

Special rhetorical devices for speeches
direct address enumeration • anaphora • imagery
rhetorical questions • hyperbole • alliteration • contrast
repetition • appeal to the audience

Skills

S16 Review

Reviews range from short, informal opinions to well-planned, complex reviews written by professional critics, depending on their purpose and target group. Even if the review is negative, you should aim to entertain and use strategies to hold the reader's interest. Most reviews show the following characteristics:

STEP 1 Introduction
- a joke, quote or anecdote to catch the reader's interest
- the writer's first reaction
- clear statement of what is being reviewed
- title and main theme

STEP 2 Body
- outlines the plot and comments on characters/actors or short quote(s), without giving away too much about the ending
- writer's opinion of central aspects, supported by facts and examples

STEP 3 Conclusion
- writer's view is summed up
- usually includes a recommendation or a warning
- may compare what is being reviewed to another example of its type
- often rated, e.g. 'four stars out of five'

Film review
- Mention genre: comedy, gangster, adventure, action, drama, Western, romance, epic, thriller?
- Does the film fit/expand/change the genre?
- Comment on actors: appropriate/convincing?
- How do the technical elements (editing, lighting, special effects, sound, camerawork) contribute to the overall effect of the film?
- Comment on director, compare with other films.
- If based on a novel/a remake, give details of earlier version(s) and compare aspects. → S29

Theatre/live performance review
- Include the location and date of performance for concerts, shows and plays.
- It is important to name and comment on the author, director, actors or performers.
- Comment on the director's interpretation, special effects, stage and costume design, music, setting, style and language. → S6.2
- Compare with earlier versions or original work.
- Write on feelings during/after the performance.

Book review
- Give information about the author: who he/she is, what he/she has written before; are they famous?
- Mention genre: crime novel, historical novel, short story, non-fiction, fictional novel set in …
- Comment on protagonists, setting, time or plot.
- Mention the effect of language and style, narrative perspectives and techniques, concentrating on the most marked/interesting aspects. → S5, S7–S9
- Compare this book with others/your experience.

Review of an internet website
- Purpose of the website clear? (Information, advertising, selling, publicity or appeal?)
- Comment on the home/start page: suitable impression, clear message, illustrations?
- Navigation logical, easy to use or confusing?
- Quality of information: regularly updated, sources named, trustworthy?
- Quality of language and text length suitable?
- Overall impression: effective, convincing?

USEFUL PHRASES

Good phrases for reviews

Who would have thought that …	… was the best/worst/funniest most … performance/book/version/website/ … I have ever watched/read/reviewed.
Although I had initially expected …	
… has made an outstanding debut as … in …	The best thing about … was …
… was most/least convincing/impressive/ … in the opening/closing/ … scene, because …	… was absolutely amazing/fantastic/hilarious.
My favourite moment was in… /at the point when …	… made me cry/laugh/wish I was …
I found … hard to believe/difficult to follow.	I would recommend this … to anyone who loves …
I didn't understand …	Don't watch/read this … if you hate …

S17 Newspaper article

There are three basic types of news articles: **reports** (news), **features** (news and background) and **comments** or **leaders/editorials** (including the writer's opinion). News reports inform the public about interesting and important events in an unbiased way. As total objectivity is not possible, they should at least be fair, with all the relevant points included, even if the writer does not agree with them.

STEP 1 Preparation
- Research the topic and make sure you can answer the wh-questions: Who? What? When? Where? Why? – and sometimes How? or So what?
- Remember the ABC of news writing: Accuracy (be exact, all the facts have to be correct), Brevity (keep it short and to the point), Clarity (make sure everyone understands).

STEP 2 Writing
- Attract the reader's attention with the headline and the lead (usually the first sentence or paragraph) which contains the most important or exciting point and makes the reader want to go on reading. → S4.1, S20.1
- The structure of a newspaper article is an inverted pyramid with the most important aspect at the top. More facts and additional details follow, with the least important ones at the end, so readers can stop reading when they feel they have enough information. If the story is written well, however, he/she will read on.

STEP 3 Editing and checking → S20.2

TIP

Using the right style
- Good news style is objective. Stick to the facts and do not give your opinion.
- Be informative, active (avoid passive sentences) and to the point, with nothing repeated and no unnecessary information.
- Keep everything logical and easy to understand.
- Quotes, examples and anecdotes are often used in news writing. Make sure quotes match the speaker's intention. Without the right context, they may be misunderstood. Only use quotes to make a point clearer.
- In a tabloid report, however, use emotive language and include vivid descriptions. → S4.1

Here is an example of the same story as reported by a quality newspaper (above) and a tabloid (below).

British backpacker Sam Woodhead missing in Australian outback

A British backpacker has disappeared after he set out on a run in the Australian outback.

Sam Woodhead was reported missing from a cattle station after he failed to return from a jog two days ago. Local authorities launched a hunt for him amid fears he may have lost his way in a hot, isolated region of central Queensland.

His mother is understood to have urged police to widen the search on the grounds that her son, an experienced long-distance runner, could have travelled some way from his base, near the town of Longreach.

His sister, Rebecca, issued an anxious plea for news on Facebook. "If anyone hears from my brother, please contact me ASAP," she wrote. In another posting, she added: "Thanks so much for all your messages regarding Sam. Still no further news, but we have the helicopter going out again in the morning, Aus time, and hundreds of people going on a voluntary search party. Will keep you all posted."

Brit teen lost in 40°C outback: Hunt for backpacker who vanished on gap year

A British teenager has gone missing while out running in searing 40°C heat in the Australian outback.

Student Sam Woodhead, 18, was last seen on Tuesday when he left the Queensland cattle farm where he was working as a ranch hand on his gap year tour. He is feared to have got lost, overcome by heat or even bitten by a snake. Rescuers have mounted a huge search involving planes, helicopters and heat detectors.

Speaking from the family home in Richmond, South West London, his dad Peter said today, "It is very difficult, and obviously we're trying to be supportive and strong. Although we haven't had any news regarding the search, we remain upbeat." Choking back tears, he added: "We're not going to give up until we hear something either way, hopefully positive. We will do everything we can, physically, mentally, emotionally and financially, to try to bring him home safe and well."

Skills

S18 Letter

S18.1 Writing a formal letter/letter to the editor

This is the type of letter you write to businesses, government offices or companies, or also to the editor of a newspaper to express your opinion about an article. The style is formal, factual and respectful, even if you are complaining about something.

Writing
- In the reference line, clarify the letter's topic.
- If you do not know the name of the person, write: *Dear Sir or Madam*, and if you do know their name: *Dear Mr/Ms/Dr Jones,*
- The first line begins with a capital letter.
- Summarise the most important point at the end.
- Finish a *Sir* letter with *Yours faithfully*, and a *Dear Ms (Name)* letter with *Sincerely,/Yours sincerely*, (or less formally, *Best/Kind regards*), then sign it and type your full name.
- If you have enclosed a document, write after your typed name *Enclosures/Encl.:* with its title or a description.

Exceptions for a letter to the editor
- In the reference line, say exactly which article you are referring to (e.g. *Immigration Attitude Turnaround*, 30 November 2013).
- Write *Sir*, or *Madam*, and not *Dear*.
- Make the letter short, to the point and polite, even if you are criticising the article.
- Use strategies to make your opinion convincing.
  → S14.2
- End the letter with your name and where you live. Do not use *Yours faithfully/sincerely*.

Creative Concepts Ltd.
62 Denmark Street
London WC5 10B
England

Daniel Borchert
Alleenstrasse 42
35396 Giessen
Germany

24th March 20…

Your invitation to an interview

Dear Mr Jones,

Thank you very much for your letter. I am writing to accept your invitation to the interview for the position of Director's Assistant.

Please find enclosed a new reference from my last employer, which I received yesterday.

Thank you for giving me this opportunity. I am looking forward to discussing this matter with you on the 10th of April.

Should you have any further questions, please do not hesitate to contact me.

Yours sincerely,

Daniel Borchert

Daniel Borchert

Encl.: Reference from Lloyds Bank

TIP

Tips for writing formal letters
- Use formal and polite style.
- Introduce your theme and say why you are writing.
- Points and structure should be exact and clear.
- Offer the recipient the option to contact you at the end of the email.

USEFUL PHRASES

Starting the letter	**In a letter to the editor**
I am writing regarding/to ask about/to thank you for …	With reference/I am referring to your article of …
In last week's/In reference to your letter dated …	In his/her article dated/from …, the author stated that …
Middle of the letter	After carefully studying the article, I am sorry to say that/ would like to express doubts about/to add that …
I appreciate/apologise for/would be grateful if …	I definitely support/agree with the author's opinion on …
Please send me/Would you please be so kind as to …	I am very glad that this topic has finally been …
Ending the letter	I was hoping for a more impartial treatment of/would appreciate more objectivity when …
Please feel free to contact me if you have any questions.	In my experience …
Thank you very much in advance for your help/advice.	An option the author did not consider would be to …
I am looking forward to meeting/hearing from you soon.	Undoubtedly, it would be more acceptable if …
For your convenience I have enclosed …	

S18.2 Writing an application

In a letter of application, which is usually accompanied by a CV *(BE)*/resume *(AE)*, you are expected to provide certain information in a certain order.

Laura Borchert
Oberfeldstrasse 20
35396 Giessen
Germany

Ms L. Johnson
Creative Concepts Ltd.
62 Denmark Street
London WC5 10B
England

19th February 2015

Application for work placement

Dear Ms Johnson,

I am a pupil at a grammar school in the town of Giessen in Germany. This summer I would like to gain work experience at Creative Concepts and enhance my proficiency in English, IT and marketing skills in an international business environment.

As you will see from the enclosed CV, I have visited the USA, South Africa and the UK with my family, and I can speak and write English fluently. I will complete my studies in a year's time when I take the *Abitur* exams, which are similar to the British A-levels. My aim is to study information science in the UK after that. You will also see that I have already had some work experience in my father's web applications company here in Giessen.

I am particularly interested in working in London as it is one of the most creative centres for web design and applications in the world. Your firm was recommended to me by my brother, Daniel Borchert, who spent three weeks doing work experience with Creative Concepts in 2011, enjoyed it immensely and gained valuable experience, especially in the customer development department.

I am keen to gain practical experience and learn about the services your company offers. I have good computer skills and would be able to carry out general office duties, but I would really be interested in working in the customer development department.

I am sure that I would make a valuable contribution to your organisation. If you think that I might fit into your firm for a few weeks this summer, I would very much look forward to hearing from you.

Yours sincerely,

Laura Borchert
Laura Borchert

Encl.: CV

- You can – but you don't have to – put your name above the address.

- For German words, write ß as ss and ä, ö and ü as ae, oe and ue.

- *BE*: placement
  AE: internship

- Include a reference to show what the letter is about.

- Introduce yourself in the first paragraph and say why you are writing the letter.

- In the second paragraph, mention important points from your CV (*AE: resume*).

- Say why you want the job, what you know about it and what you think you can bring to it.

- End with a friendly sentence which looks forward to a reply.

- Print your name under the signature and mention what you are enclosing.

Skills

S18.3 Curriculum Vitae – CV

Here is an example of a CV (*BE*). For a resume (*AE*), present the information in short sentences.

Curriculum Vitae

Personal details
Name: Laura Borchert
Address: Oberfeldstrasse 20, 35396 Giessen, Germany
Contact: Tel.: +49 (0)641-34838
Email: laura.borchert@….de
Nationality: German
Date of birth: 10th January 1998

Profile
I am creative, skilled with computers and hard-working.
I would love to experience the innovative and inspiring environment at Creative Concepts.

Education
Since 2008   Herderschule (grammar school), Giessen
To be completed in 2016 with the Abitur (corresponding to British A-levels)

Work experience
2014 (summer)   Work placement at Borchert Website Solutions
– Helped with written correspondence
– Dealt with telephone inquiries
– Carried out routine office duties

Language skills
German: native speaker
English: fluent in speaking and writing (C1)
French: good working knowledge (B1)

Interests
Computers – programming and blogging
Sport – handball, tennis, swimming, skiing
Travel – trips to South Africa (2007), the US (2008) and the UK (2012, 2014)

References available upon request

- Include a short profile describing skills and motivation.
- Don't include a photo, your marital status, religion or information about your family. In a resume (*AE*), leave out nationality, date and place of birth.
- Order the events chronologically or start with the most recent.
- Explain but don't translate names of schools, companies and qualifications.
- Describe what you did in your job. Don't just give your job title.
- Give your language level on the Common European Reference scale (A2, B1, etc.) if you think your reader knows the scale.
- Use your interests to describe your personality.
- Don't forget to check your CV for mistakes before you send it.

S18.4 Personal letter or email

Features of personal correspondence
The language used in personal letters is your choice. You can use:

short forms:	I'm • we're • there's • they didn't
question tags:	don't you? • couldn't they? • aren't we? • ok?
colloquial terms:	Hi … • No way! • guy • I'm fed up with …
Start like this:	Dear Ben, • Hi Jenny, …
First line:	Start with a capital letter!

Finish like this: Best wishes, • All the best, • Best regards, • Love, • See you soon, • Miss you, • Take care, • Hope to see you/hear from you soon, Tim/Lea (first name only).

Check emails with the automatic spell check, or for other mistakes or sentences which can be misunderstood, before you press *Send*.

S19 Term paper and quoting

S19.1 Term paper

A term (or research) paper records research you have done on a particular subject. Follow these steps:

STEP 1 Choosing a subject
- You may be given a list of subjects, or you may be able to make suggestions yourself. Choose the subject you like most.
- Don't choose a subject that is too general. Answer concrete, relevant questions in logical steps, using facts to prove or support what you say.

STEP 2 Finding sources
- Don't use sources more than twenty years old unless you are working on historical aspects.
- Use books, newspapers, magazines and the internet. Using several different sources is best.

STEP 3 Organising your search
- Make a list of keywords and phrases you might need in your search for material.
- Start a file card for each source: subject, author, title, publishing information, relevant pages.

STEP 4 Taking notes
- Skim through sources to find what is useful for answering your question(s), then read carefully.
- Write down notes and quotes and make a note of page numbers/key headings you need to use for footnotes or to find the information again.
- Do not misrepresent the author's meaning.
- Collect material which supports and opposes your thesis to write a well-balanced text.
- Collect facts, not just opinions. Comment on authors' statements and why they are important.

STEP 5 Planning
- Check that your task can be answered in your own words using the material you have found.
- Sort your notes into groups under headings you can use in the steps/sections of your paper.

STEP 6 Writing
- **Introduction:** Present the topic of the paper and the question(s) which will be answered.
- **Body:** Write points or answers in logical sections and paragraphs supported by quotes and reasons.
- **Summary and conclusion:** Summarise/comment on important research results or conclusions.

STEP 7 Editing and checking → S20.2
- Read the whole paper as if you were reading it for the first time. Reading aloud will help you.
- Check spelling, phrasing and sentences.
- Check there is a footnote for each quote and that every source was cited correctly. → S19.3

STEP 8 Formatting and documenting sources
- Format your text with consistent font style/sizes, spacing, margins, footnotes and page numbers.
- Create a contents page, checking sections for correct headings and page numbers, and a front page with the following information: name, class, subject, teacher, task, date.
- List your different sources in alphabetical order in a list of references at the end. → S19.2
- Include a signed statement of authorship, e.g.: *This term paper is my own work and no sources have been quoted without due reference.*

Skills

S19.2 Sources

You must document all of the sources you have used for longer texts or written work, e.g. a term paper. Making notes while researching and writing your paper makes writing a complete list at the end easier. Ways of listing details can vary, but they are all based on the same principle: the most important detail is the author or original source; other details show publishing rights, dates and how to find the text.

Making footnotes and citing sources
- The **first footnote** for a source should list the full details. Use your software's automatic function.
- If you quote the **same source again**, it can be written in a short form like the Harvard system: **author, year and page number** in a footnote or in brackets in the text: *Smith 2014: 37*, or: *ibid., p. 3*, if you keep quoting from the same text.
- For more than one book by the same author, add a short form of the title.

> Bill Smith analyses migration problems in Britain.[1]
> [1]Smith, Bill, *Real Life in the UK,* London: Brown, 2014, p. 3.
>
> Smith writes that real life is about integration.[2]
> [2]Smith 2014: 23.
>
> Smith exposed problems we had not thought about before (Smith, *Real Life,* 2014: 37 ff.), but in his next book, he suggested solutions (Smith, *What Next?* 2016: 3).

Creating a list of references (titled References or Bibliography)
- Write your list in alphabetical order of authors' surnames. References can be in sections, e.g.: Books • Articles • Internet sources • Other sources (your photographs, interviews).
- Include the following details: *author's surname • forename • title (cursive) • place of publication • publisher • publication year*

> Adiga, A., *The White Tiger,* London: Atlantic, 2008.
> Eggers, Dave, *The Circle.* New York: Knopf, 2013.
> Jones, Owen, *London riots – one year on,* in: *The Independent,* 24 July 2012, p. 5.

- If you read just one chapter, add Chapter x.
- For a newspaper/internet article or a text from a compilation or journal, write author, title, then in: newspaper, date and page number or in: website 'online' with date or in: first editor's name, (ed.), book title, and publishing details.

> Stone, Daniel, *This Land Is Your Land,* in: *National Geographic* online, 23 April 2014.
> Turner, J., *'Romance' and the Novel,* in: Nash (ed.), *Review of English Studies* 258, Oxford: OUP, 2012.

S19.3 Quoting

Always make a clear difference between text you wrote yourself and text or facts written by others. You can cite a text **directly**, with quote marks: "…", or **indirectly**, paraphrasing in your own words. Use […] to add to or leave words out of a direct quote, **l.** for line, **ll.** for lines, **p.** for page and **ff.** for following pages/lines. Use '…' for direct speech in a quote, and cite from a poem or play with **/** between the lines:

> In her poem 'Life', Emily Dickinson uses the metaphor of a bird: "Hope is the thing with feathers / That perches in the soul" (ll. 1–2). It "sings the tune […] and never stops at all"; and in contrast to poetry itself, hope works "without the words" (ll. 3–4), which presents it as a universal emotion not connected to language.

USEFUL PHRASES

Direct quotation (whole sentence):
In his/her book/article …, X states: "…" (p. 7 ff.).

Direct quotation (built into your sentence):
The advantage is that "the … are …", claims X (l. 6).
X presents … as "…", which … (p. 12).

Indirect quotation (paraphrasing)
X claims/reports/writes in … (title) that …
According to X … is/has/was/could … (ll. 7–9).
In X's article there is a good description of …, which is based on/gives reasons for/explains why … (l. 4).
While X argues against …, Y gives reasons for …

S20 Paragraphs, editing and checking

S20.1 Writing paragraphs

Writing compact paragraphs helps the reader to recognise the structure and understand your text better. An introductory paragraph catches the reader's interest with a question you can answer in steps and come back to in your conclusion. Most paragraphs state, support and comment on one aspect, argument or idea:

Ideal paragraph structure
- **The topic sentence** (the first sentence of the paragraph) is a 'mini-thesis' which states one main idea, clearly and without detail.
- **Supporting sentences** have a connecting word or phrase to the topic sentence and give facts, details or examples which support the main idea.
- **Paragraph conclusions** comment on the information and round off the paragraph.

> **TIP**
>
> **Writing good sentences**
> - Use different **sentence structures**. Highlight aspects by putting them at the beginning of a sentence.
> - Vary **adverbs of comment**:
>   (un)fortunately • frankly • naturally • probably • sadly
> - Use **adverbs of degree**:
>   almost • drastically • most of all • rarely • rather • really
> - **Link sentences** with connectives:
>   although • as … as • as well • even if • for example • however • in order to • in spite of • not until • since • therefore • unless • whereas • while
> - **Link paragraphs** with structuring devices:
>   first of all • secondly • on the one/other hand, … • furthermore • consequently • finally • last but not least

Rainforests are disappearing rapidly. **Naturally**, problems arise when these unique tropical forests are cut down. But which of them are most urgent?
  Sadly, one result of deforestation is that more than half of the world's animals are endangered. The tree kangaroo and the jaguar are **almost** extinct. Animals play an important role in the forests, **for example** the spider monkey for seed dispersal. So if these animals die, not only the food chain, but also plants will be affected.
  Furthermore, food from plants like avocados, bananas or pineapples can no longer be harvested in these forests. Medicines and other products are made using plants from the forests **as well**. We lose valuable resources if we clear forest areas.
  The **most** worrying effect **of all, however**, is that when logging companies cut down these trees, they are cutting away their great ability to absorb carbon dioxide. According to the WWF, 15 % of all greenhouse gas emissions are a result of deforestation. We can't afford to lose more trees.
[…]

S20.2 Editing and checking

- Make time to read through your draft and check for mistakes. Take a break before, if possible.
- Check for your most frequent mistakes first.
- Concentrate on one aspect, then read again for the next. Read aloud to check the flow of the text.
- Make overly complex sentences simpler or shorter.
- Check for correct content and logical structure. Is an important point missing?
- Check for spelling, grammar, punctuation mistakes and variety in words and sentences.
- If possible, ask someone else to check too.
- In an exam write a neat and tidy final version.

Example: The first draft of the paragraph highlighted **above.**
Logic: no link to last paragraph: add *however*
Content: they – *who*?;
worrying – link content to last paragraphs: *most w. effect of all*
Sources: 15 % – quote from …?

A worrying effect of cutting down trees is they cut the trees' ability to absorb carbon dioxide. 15 % of all greenhouse gas emissions, is a result of deforestation. Trees are important.

Spelling: absorp – *absorb*
Vocabulary: cut – better: *cut away*;
important – better to use vivid phrase: *can't afford to lose*
Grammar: is – mistake: *are*
Punctuation: no comma here

Skills

Listening skills

S21 Listening comprehension

In everyday life, one-way listening situations can be radio programmes, speeches, presentations, songs and announcements. Purely listening tasks in lessons and exams are the same. You don't have to reply; you just have to understand them. First, you will understand the gist, then the details.

Combined listening and viewing situations can also be one-way, such as TV programmes or films in the cinema, or experiencing presentations using visual media. Here you can observe the speaker's body language, visual clues, and tone to help you understand what is being said.

STEP 1 Preparation for note-taking while listening
- Write down the task title, situation and information you already know; for example who is speaking. If a checklist helps, use one.
- For a particular task, write suitable headings to give you a frame for collecting important information. Make these as simple as possible.

```
World without media London 2015
 — Mr Smith's opinion: no real loss
   less loneliness, more personal contact
 — Reason 1: more time to talk
 — Reason 2: fewer distractions
```

STEP 2 Listening for the first time: gist
Make notes while you listen:
- If the text is important and you are able to take notes, first write down **keywords and phrases** which sound important. Listen for stresses on certain words or the repetition of words to help you find them.
- Leave space between your first notes for more notes when you listen again.
- Write down **names**, **dates**, **numbers**, **times and places** when you hear them, with one or two words to explain them. They may be very useful later.

STEP 3 Using the break between listening times
- Read through the words you wrote and look at the task again.
- Check what you easily understood to see if it still seems logical.
- Write an answer to the first task(s) if necessary.
- Check what you still need to listen for.

STEP 4 Listening again for more detail
- Concentrate on what you still need to know.
- Listen for grammatical signs to help you understand the meaning. Present, future or past tense? Singular or plural?
- Listen for connecting words (*and*, *but*, *because*, *on the other hand*, …) which help you to understand how the information is being used.

> **TIP**
>
> **Strategies for understanding quickly**
> - **Don't panic** if you don't hear or understand every word! You will probably still understand the most important information.
> - **Intonation patterns** will help you to recognise a speaker's attitude or intention. Does what the speaker says sound like a question, criticism, suggestion, statement, agreement, ironic statement, or a joke?
> - Use **anticipation** to help you. What do you think they are going to say?
> - Remember **words you know** for the topic.

USEFUL PHRASES

Coping in two-way listening situations (telephone call, conversation, debate)

I'm sorry, I didn't quite catch what you said.

Could you say that again, please?

Could you please repeat that?

Sorry, I don't understand the word '…'. What does it mean?

Can you spell that for me, please?

Did I understand you right when you said …

I never heard that word before. Could you please explain what you mean by '…'? Does it mean …?

I think you said … Am I right?

Could you possibly speak just a little bit more slowly, please?

Speaking skills

S22 Presentation

STEP 1 Research and sources
- Collect information and material from different sources, including books. Check their quality.
- Document all sources and graphics. → **S19.2**
- You can also use statistics/interviews/surveys.
- Use at least two sources for every aspect of the presentation. It makes your statements reliable.

STEP 2 Preparation
Making notes
- Plan and visualise the structure on a mind map.
- Write keywords and notes for each section on different cards. Don't read from a complete text; one prompt card for each section is good.
- Note facts or details you find interesting, funny or surprising. Use them throughout the talk.
- Quote from experts/people with experience of an aspect of your topic.

Visuals (maps, photos, video clips, diagrams, PowerPoint presentation, flip chart, objects)
- Visuals should be big enough to see easily from the back of the room. Comment on the visuals.
- Use one main visual element for each section to help the audience to remember each aspect.
- Use little or no text; your talk is the text! Pictures help the audience to visualise what you say.

Language
- Choose the right register for your audience.
- Use short and simple sentences with examples.
- Use the phrases below, and adverbs of degree and comment → **S20.1** to make the talk lively.
- Repeat important points. Use rhetorical devices. Explain important/difficult words. → **S10.2, S15**

Handout
- Write only the most important points from your presentation, on just one page. Include sources.
- Include name, class, subject, teacher, task, date.

STEP 3 Making the presentation
- Test any equipment as early as possible. Check all you need and give handouts to the audience.
- Smile, interact with the audience and be friendly, polite and self-confident. You are the expert!
- Speak loudly, clearly; not too fast or monotonously.
- Use the tips for public speaking. → **S15**
- Giving a brief outline of the talk at the beginning helps the audience to know what to expect.

USEFUL PHRASES

Introduction

Good morning/afternoon/evening, my name is … and my topic today is / I'm going to talk to you about …

I will begin by explaining/describing … and continue with a list of the most important … Finally I will …

Interactive and rhetorical questions

Have you ever thought/been in a situation where …

If you think about …, what comes to mind first?

Did you know that …?/I'm sure you will have …

Is there anybody here who has heard of … who/which …

Linking/summarising/repeating points → **S 20.1**

Therefore the advantages/disadvantages of … are …

Similarly/In contrast to …, recent developments in … have been surprisingly

Quotes

X once said that/X, an expert in …, stated that …

According to X …/Although X said …, Y …

Integrating and commenting on visuals

This is an example of a … which is/was used in …

X, who you can see in the picture, is/was a … who …

Conversational elements and troubleshooting

Can everybody hear me? If not, please let me know.

I'm afraid I lost my train of thought. Let me go back to …

Conclusion

So what we have learned today/the most important … is … /To summarise, then, the most important point …

I've now reached the end of my presentation. Thank you for listening. Does anyone have any questions?

Skills

S23 Dialogue

One part of your oral exam is often a dialogue. You discuss a topic with a partner and/or your examiner. (The first part is usually a monologue: talking alone on a topic/describing a text or a visual.)

STEP 1 Preparation
- Revise useful conversation phrases
- Check your topic knowledge.
- Choose the appropriate register. → S10.1

STEP 2 In dialogue
- Make arguments clear and logical.
- Give good reasons for your opinion and accept other people's perspectives. Be tactful and fair.
- Pick up on/support what your conversation partner(s) said, but make your points clear too.
- Show that you are listening carefully. Ask friendly questions.

Remember that non-verbal communication can be as important as what you say!

USEFUL PHRASES

Getting along in dialogue

Polite phrases instead of just saying yes or no

No, I'm afraid I don't think so. • Yes, that's partly true. • I agree, but to be honest/nevertheless, … • That's interesting, but what do you think about …?

Modals and softeners to sound less direct

Could I /May I/ Would you …? I'd like … • not really/ exactly • as a matter of fact • it's just • even so • maybe a little • well, actually …

Feedback phrases to keep up a friendly atmosphere

Oh, well • of course • I see • you know • I mean • really? • Are you sure? • I understand that … • I appreciate your concern about … • I hadn't seen it from that angle before. • You're absolutely right. • That's a good idea.

Encouraging agreement

I'm sure we both/all agree that … • Let's agree on/to … • So it's settled that …

S24 Discussion and debate

S24.1 Debate

All around the world there are debating societies and contests. A debate is a formalised discussion following clear rules. It is a contest between teams of speakers for (proposition) and against (opposition) a statement or 'motion' (e.g. "This house believes that …") which ends in a vote.

Taking part in debates can help you to express opinions and arguments clearly and improve your English. How about starting a debating club at your school?

STEP 1 The chairperson ('chair') introduces the issue and presents the motion to be voted for.

STEP 2 In the first round, four speakers speak alternately for and against the motion without being interrupted. The audience (called 'the floor') listens.

STEP 3 An open debating phase follows, in which the floor takes part, raising hands and, if allowed by the chair, making comments or asking questions.

STEP 4 In the second round, speakers summarise positions or make prepared 'rebuttal' speeches against the other party's arguments.

STEP 5 The chair calls for a vote by raising hands for/ against the motion and concludes the debate.

S24.2 Chairing a discussion or talk show

Your role as a chairperson
- Be neutral. Do not express your own opinion.
- Do not judge opinions expressed by others.
- Avoid dominance. Let the participants talk.
- Give all speakers an equal chance to talk.
- Ask open or provocative questions.

STEP 1 Preparation
- Note the topic's main aspects and vocabulary.
- Write prompt cards with keywords on important aspects. Note the order of the speakers.
- Make notes during the discussion to help you to refer to speakers' statements and sum up.

STEP 2 Introduction
- Greet the audience and participants and state the topic and its importance.
- State the question/controversy being discussed.
- Introduce the speakers.
- Ask all participants to sum up their opinions in an introductory statement.

STEP 3 Conducting and concluding
- Ask open, precise questions encouraging speakers to give a detailed answer (not just yes/no). See the useful phrases box below.
- Ask for closing statements, sum up, conduct a vote (in a debate) and thank speakers.

USEFUL PHRASES

Structuring the discussion

Introduction

Good morning and welcome to our discussion of/debate on the topic of …

The question now/The motion to be discussed today is …

To my right, I'd like to introduce … and …, who are …

I'd like to start with … and I would like you to make an introductory statement about where you stand on this issue/your opinion about …

Introducing a new aspect

Most of you argue that … This raises the question whether/if …

We haven't yet talked about the statistics, which show …

Does that mean/Would you all agree that …?

Conclusion

Time is almost up now. Could each of you briefly summarise your main point again, please?

What has become clear in our discussion is that …

Thank you for your attention.

Keeping order and involving all speakers

Avoiding digressions and repetitions

Can we please stay with … for the moment?

I would like to return to/Going back to …

Would you please come to the point?

Could you please answer …'s question?

Including everybody, dividing time fairly

Mr …, we haven't heard your opinion on … yet.

Ms …, what is your opinion of/how do you feel about …?

I have a number of people on my list who would like to say something about …

Ms …, would you like to reply to this?

Keeping order

Would you please let … finish his/her statement?

Would you please listen to …?

I have your name on the list; you'll have your turn in a minute.

If I could just stop you there – … would like to comment on your statement.

Skills

S24.3 Taking part in a discussion or talk show

Stating your case	Defending your case	Interacting with others
Beginning • I would like to start by asking/saying/telling … • Let me begin with … • As a start, …	**Defending your point** • That's not what I was trying to say. • My point is that … • I see your point, but I still feel … • That's not quite what I mean. • What I am saying is that …	**Picking up sb's statement** • I would like to comment on what X said about/come back to … • If I may just remind you of what X said about … • As we have just heard from …
Giving an opinion • In my opinion/view, … • To my mind, … • I am of the opinion that … • I am sure/convinced that …	**Making suggestions** • What about (+gerund)? • If I were you, I would … • I would suggest/recommend … • I call for/request …	**Interrupting politely** • May I interrupt you for a second? • Excuse me, could you explain that again please? • Sorry, can I just make a point?
Giving an example • For instance, look at … • Take …, for example. • Let me give you an example of what I mean by … • To illustrate this point, …	**Dealing with interruptions** • I haven't finished yet, if you don't mind. • If I might just finish … • I haven't got to my point yet. • Excuse me, could you just …	**Arguing against something** • I strongly criticise … • I completely disagree with you on … • I would question that argument.
Giving evidence • Statistics/surveys show … • Most scientists now agree/ There is strong evidence that … • I know this from first-hand experience./I'd like to draw your attention to the fact that …	**Balancing** • On the one hand …, (but) on the other hand … • Although …, we mustn't forget that … • That is certainly true, but at the same time it is obvious that …	**Disagreeing** • I'm sorry, but I don't agree at all. • I think you might be mistaken. • I'm not sure it is as simple as that. • I believe X was mistaken when he/she …/I'm afraid things are not as simple as X would have us believe.
Structuring • There are three points I would like to make. • First of all, … Secondly, … Thirdly, … Finally, …	**Playing for time** • To be quite honest, … • What I'm trying to say is … • So you mean that … • I'm glad you asked me that.	**Asking for an opinion** • How do you feel about this? • What is your view/position on …? • I would be very interested to hear X's opinion on this.
Adding • I'd like to add that … • It is also important to know … • Another reason is that …	**Giving in (to some extent)** • Even if that is so … • That's probably true, but … • Possibly/I agree in principle, but …	**Checking understanding** • Do you really mean to say …? • So, if I understand you correctly, … • What exactly do you mean by …?
Introducing a new point • I would like to raise another point. • What we haven't discussed yet is the question whether/if … • We should also discuss what this means for …	**Correcting misunderstandings** • I'm afraid there has been some misunderstanding. • What I actually said was … That's not quite what I meant by/ • Don't get me wrong. I meant …	**Supporting someone** • That's a good idea. • I fully support X's view. • I wholeheartedly support X's statement. • That sounds very convincing.
Emphasising • I would like to emphasise that … • Let me repeat what I said earlier. • What I strongly believe is that …	**Drawing conclusions** • That's why …/For this reason, … • The logical consequence is … • This leads to/implies that …	**Agreeing** • Absolutely/Exactly/I totally agree. • I can go along with that. • I think you're right to a point.

S25 Interview

An interview is a direct and simple way of getting personal stories and opinions, expert explanations or other answers to questions on all kinds of topics. Interviews can be read as a text, heard on the radio or viewed on podcasts, TV news or talk shows. For the best results, an interviewer (interviewing sb, conducting the interview) should prepare questions carefully, and the interviewee (being interviewed, giving the interview) should be ready and able to reply.

STEP 1 Initial preparation
- **Choose a topic**. Think what you want to know.
- Create simple, precise and **clear questions**.
- Sort them into **categories** in a systematic order.
- **Choose who** you will interview. Asking **more than one** person these questions helps to fill knowledge gaps, show reasons for different opinions, compare results or check facts/explanations, e.g. in research for written work.
  Or consider conducting a survey. → **S30**
- Choose **the interview method**: Will there be a video or audio recording, or will you take notes?

STEP 2 Before the interview

- **Contact** the interviewee in advance, so he/she has time to agree and think what to say.
- **Explain** the topic, give example questions. Ask for permission to make a recording/take photos.
- Say **how long** the interview will be to encourage the interviewee to give shorter, simpler answers.
- **Write questions** and framing phrases on cards.
- **Mark cards** which are most important and which are ok to leave out if time is running out.

USEFUL PHRASES

Phrases for interviewers
Starting the interview

Mr/Ms …, welcome to this interview and thank you for coming/agreeing to share your thoughts on …

The/Today's topic is … I'd like to find out/ask you why …

My name is … I'm a reporter from … May I ask you about your views on/some questions about …?

Statements to introduce aspects

Many people are saying at the moment/think that …

We have been talking about/discussing … in …

You might already have heard of … (an idea/person)

You did some research/wrote a report on …

Direct, open questions (Avoid yes/no questions!)

To start with, please tell us how/why/when/what …

What do you think about/is your opinion on …?

How do you feel about that? Do you agree/disagree?

How important is it for you to …/How does this influence you?

What advice would you give to somebody who …

What would you do/What would have happened if …?

When did you first …

Some people consider your views as … How would you respond?/What I'd like to know is why you …

It may be right that … but don't you think/wouldn't you agree that …? So would you prefer to …/Why did you …?

Structuring, connecting questions (Be flexible!)

You said/have argued that … Does that mean …?

We've heard about your experience of … It would interest me very much to hear/know …

Let's pick up on your last statement. Do/did you …?

Let's move on to/talk now about/ … I'd like to know …

I'd also be really interested to hear your views on …

Responding politely and neutrally (Don't judge!)

Really? That's interesting/surprising/… But …

That is certainly an unexpected/unusual answer. Are you …

I see/Good point/Thank you for that insight.

Ending the interview

Thank you very much for your time/(being here and) speaking to me/sharing your views on … with me/us.

I'm sorry to say our time's (nearly) up./We've come to the end of the interview. It's been great talking to you.

Phrases for interviewees
Gaining time/asking for help

That is a very good question. As a matter of fact, …

Let me think … How shall I put this?

I expected you to ask that/I'm not sure I understood that.

That's quite a difficult question to answer immediately.

Could you please repeat/rephrase the question?

Not answering or changing direction

This is a topic I'd prefer not to talk about. Actually …

I'm afraid I don't know enough about … to be able to …

I must admit I'm not an expert on …

That's probably a question an expert should answer.

I think it's more important to look at …

Skills

Mediating skills

S26 Mediating and translating skills

S26.1 Mediating

What is mediation?
- You provide the mediating **link** between two languages and normally also between two different text types or (cultural) situations.
- Mediation always starts with a **task**: You are given a **new situation** (context, text type, addressee, style, intention …). You should **pick out** particular information from an original text in an **original situation** (which is often very different) and **'repackage'** it for the new situation, following the task instructions.
- You **never** just translate every sentence of the original text exactly.
- Sometimes you need to summarise all of the important points, but more often you should go through the whole text to find all the information on just **one or more aspects**, like all of the advantages of something, or all of the reasons for something.
- In a mediation situation, **don't mix** the information with your own knowledge/opinion.
- However, idiomatic terms and cultural concepts may need explanation (e.g. CDU, FAZ, *Fernweh*). Use your skills in intercultural competence.
- You may add some **suitable text** before or after, e.g. if you have to write an email, greet the reader, say why you are giving him/her this information and end the email formally or informally, according to the situation.

Mediation techniques

STEP 1 Looking carefully at the task
- Check what relevant points you need to find. It will affect how you should read the text.

STEP 2 Reading the original text
- After reading/listening once for gist, note the text title, type and purpose, and if necessary, the author's/speaker's name, intention and tone, in order to pass the information on correctly. → S11

STEP 3 Preparing your mediation
- Check the new situation: text type and length, addressee, purpose, relationship between you and the addressee (for your text's register/style).
- Mark only task-relevant keywords in the original.
- Don't stop after finding one point you need (e.g. a reason). Check for more in the rest of the text.
- Leave out any information you don't need.

STEP 4 Writing your mediation text
- Use suitable language and 'packaging' sentences for the new task situation and mention the source.
- Sum up relevant points in your own words; for your purpose you may rearrange the order.
- Paraphrase/explain if you don't know the exact translation of a word or if idiomatic features like proverbs are not the same in the new language.
- Check for false friends, incorrect tense, spelling, prepositions, word order and style. Your text should sound natural in the new language.

S26.2 Interpreting and translating

Interpreting between people and languages

When interpreting is used
- Interpreting is used when a mixture of quick translation and spontaneous mediation is necessary. Professional instant interpreting is very difficult and has to be an exact translation. There is obviously more freedom in normal, everyday interpreting, which is described here.
- You may, for example, interpret between speakers during a conversation or explain what was in a listening text you heard only once.

Features of interpreting
- You have **little time** to think, so concentrate on the main points, purpose, tone or message.
- You can ask speakers to repeat or explain what they have said, or watch their body language to help you **interpret meaning**. Otherwise you have to guess meanings from the context. → **S2**
- You should always **remain polite** and friendly, even if the original speaker is rude or direct. This may require a change in register or tone, different words or idioms and using your intercultural competence.
- Always **consider the needs** of the recipient you are interpreting for. Explain or paraphrase unfamiliar concepts. Apply the correct register.
- However, **don't invent** completely different content or add too much of your own opinion or knowledge!

> **Example of interpreting** in a conversation between your teacher, yourself and your Canadian exchange student. Note the change in tone.
>
> **TEACHER** Bitte erkläre doch gleich deinem Gast, dass hier weder Jacken noch Essen, Getränke oder Kaugummi im Unterricht geduldet werden.
>
> **YOU** Michelle, you can come and sit here with me. But let's hang our jackets up outside first; that's what we always do here. It's normally too hot in here anyway. … I'm afraid the teachers are quite strict on keeping food, drinks and chewing gum out of the classroom too.
>
> **MICHELLE** Ok, that's fine by me. We can take drinks into lessons at home, but we're not allowed to eat in class either.

Translating

When translation is used
- Translation is needed in situations when you are asked to translate a text as exactly as possible and not leave anything out.
- Usually you are allowed to use a dictionary to look things up. → **S3**
- In translation, the original intention, style, tone and register should remain the same.

STEP 1 Preparation
- Context is important: The style in the output text must be the same level as in the input text.
- Read the input text carefully before translating.
- Use skimming/scanning to find important points and use strategies for guessing words if you don't have access to a dictionary. → **S2, S11**

STEP 2 Writing
- Translate every sentence. Split them up into two sentences if necessary in the output language.
- Check for false friends and be careful with differences between languages in tense, idioms, prepositions, word order and style.
- Paraphrase only if there is no suitable translation in the dictionary.
- Use the dictionary for dealing with meanings, idiomatic differences, examples of usage, and then for editing and polishing. → **S3**
- The output text should be a good and natural-sounding text in the output language. Check for this again after translation. Reading aloud helps.

Skills

Special skills

S27 Statistics, diagrams and maps

Diagrams visualise statistics and make them much easier to understand and analyse. Different diagram types are each best for presenting a particular type of data. Check for relevant details, clarity, up-to-date statistics and reliable sources to assess quality. Data visualisation is now a vital tool for working with the global flood of statistical information, e.g. in journalism, research, economics and politics.

> **TIP**
>
> Look for data visualisation on the internet to find or create your own imaginative graphic forms for projects and presentations, e.g.:
> - **Data maps** show what happens where, such as which parties won elections in which states.
> - **Word or tag clouds** highlight frequently used words or links, like keywords or news stories.
> - **Rectangular tree maps** show relative sizes of categories, e.g. areas of government spending.

USEFUL PHRASES

Bar chart, for comparing figures directly

The horizontal/vertical bar chart, from (source) in (year), shows how many … are/were/had … in relation to … The majority of … have …

The chart shows the proportion/amount/number of … from (year) to (year).

The horizontal axis represents …, and the vertical axis shows …

The first/last/longest/shortest bar shows that … ranks higher/lower than average.

The number of …dominates/is insignificant in comparison to …

The chart indicates/makes it clear that … is given more importance than …

Pie chart, for percentages or proportions

The pie chart published by … shows/represents the results/amounts of X in percent in/for … (year/country/election/institution/…). The list of … in the legend shows …

The segments show clearly that the amount/success/share of … is larger/smaller than … Surprisingly/obviously, nearly half/all/a third of … This could be a result of …

As you can see from the pie chart, … has the majority/biggest share/is minimal.

This relativises the media publicity given to …

Comparing the charts for … and …, the number/proportion/

percentage share of … has increased/decreased, whereas … has …

Line graph, showing developments and trends over time

The line graph from … shows the development of … from … to …

The vertical axis shows the number/percentage/amout of …

The horizontal axis shows the time from … to …

The red/blue/… line represents X, while the … line shows Y.

X reached its peak/highest point/lowest point in …, which was probably because …

The number of … increased/rose/remained constant/decreased/fell (gradually/steadily/rapidly/steeply/significantly) until …

Since then there has been a sharp/strong/marked …

The change was possibly caused by/surely had sth to do with …

… shows a similar/parallel/contrasting development/an upward/downward trend.

Thematic map, showing statistics by location

The map shows the distribution of …

The (green/…)-coloured areas show/stand for …

You can see that most of the … can be found in …

In …, however, the situation is very different: …

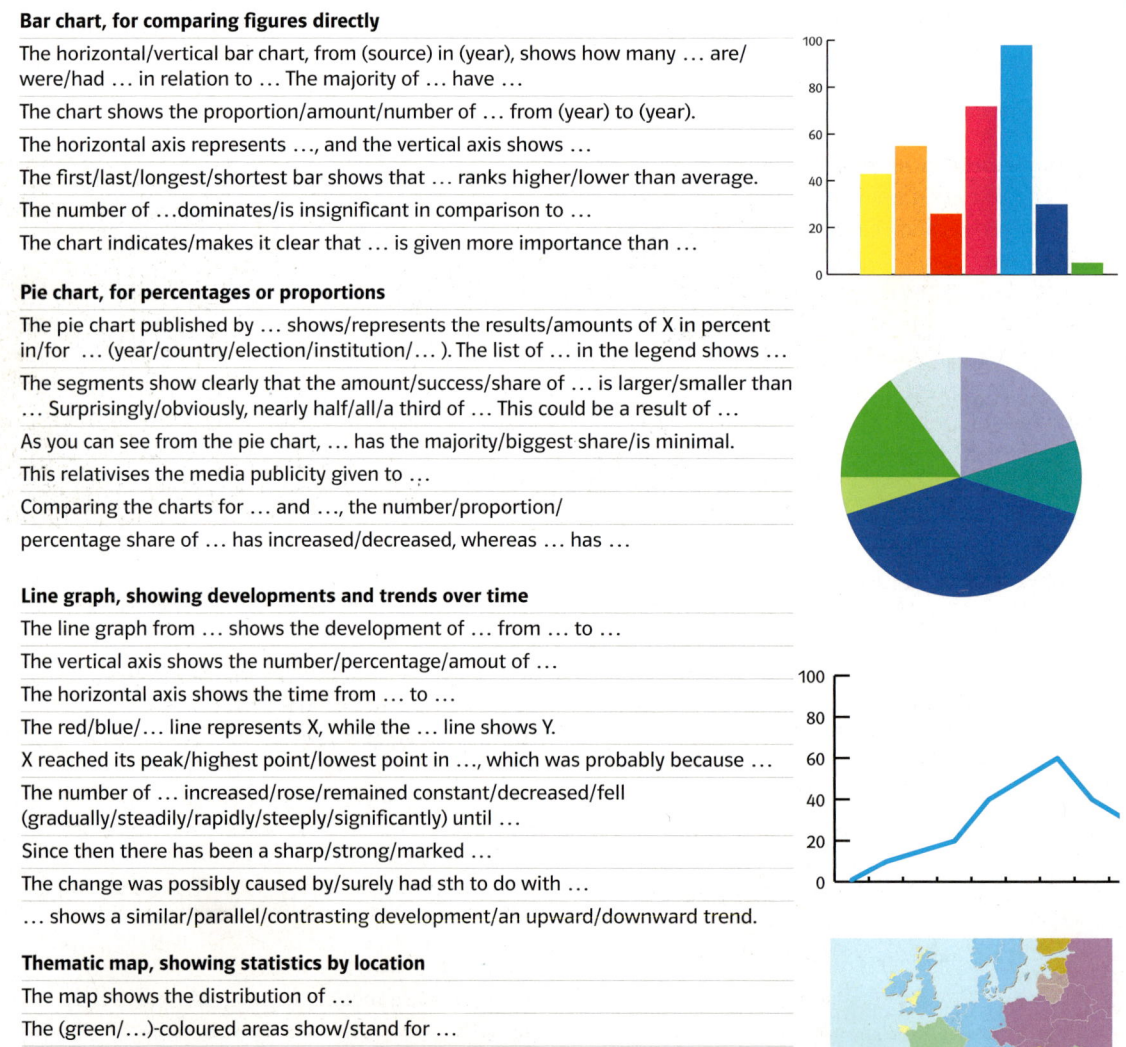

S28 Working with visuals

S28.1 Pictures

STEP 1 Introduction
- Note what the picture shows in one sentence.
- Add any information you know (creator's name, picture type; when/where/why it was created), your first reaction and emotions felt, if asked.

STEP 2 Description
- Describe the picture systematically. Imagine you are describing the picture to a blind person; what important elements and background are needed to explain the picture and its message?
- Use the **present progressive** to describe what people are doing in a picture, and the **simple present** to describe objects and the setting.
- Describe speech bubbles and captions, people's body language and facial expressions and their relationship with each other.

STEP 3 Analysis
- Describe the message conveyed by the picture. Is it aimed at a particular target group?
- Was the picture intended to have a certain effect on the viewer? If so, how is this achieved?
- Say how language, light, colours, focus and perspective are used to support the message.

STEP 4 Evaluation
- State whether the picture is effective and which elements are responsible for its success/failure.
- If it is a historical picture, compare the original effect it may have had with the one it has now.
- Give your personal opinion (if asked) or your thoughts on which topic the picture represents.

USEFUL PHRASES

Introduction

The photo/sketch/portrait/watercolour/still life/news photo/selfie/landscape/cartoon/oil painting was created by … and published in …	The perspective is from above/below/eye level/the side, in a close-up/medium shot/long shot field size.
In the picture we/you can see …	There is a contrast between … / … is clearly visible, whereas … does not stand out so much.
The main focus is on …	The eye is drawn to …/The artist presents … as …
The picture illustrates the topic of …	It is a black and white/(brightly-)coloured picture, which emphasises the contrast between/colours of …
It gives a detailed/realistic/shocking/dramatic view of …	
The picture was obviously composed to achieve the effect of …	The light/colours/position of elements of … create an … atmosphere/contribute to/give an impression of …
My first thought/assumption when I saw it was …	

Description and analysis/message

On the left-hand/right-hand side you can see …	**Interpretation and evaluation**
In the foreground/background/middle/centre there is …	The overall effect of the picture is … because/which …
In the top/bottom left/right-hand corner …	The picture reminds me of/is symbolic of/is a (non-)stereotypical view of… because …
	it is effective/moves me deeply because …

Skills

S28.2 Cartoons

A cartoon usually combines a drawing with a text. Cartoons often pick up on one current news event and criticise people, institutions or developments in society and politics.
Some cartoons may just be entertaining, often making fun of public figures, but others can make a serious and important critical point simply and clearly using visual means.

STEP 1 Introduction
- Give available information on the context (author, date and first publication source).
- Briefly state the issue or target group.

STEP 2 Description
- Describe the cartoon in detail. → S28.1
- Include the contents of captions, speech bubbles etc. and their relationship to the picture.

STEP 3 Analysis
- Examine the elements (characters, objects, text) and explain the message they convey. Pay attention to the function of characters (do they represent well-known people or a particular group?) and typical techniques (see tip box).

STEP 4 Evaluation → S28.1 (Step 4)

> **TIP**
>
> Cartoonists often use the following techniques:
> - highlighting prominent features/actions/events by **caricature** (exaggerating characteristic elements)
> - **exposing inconsistencies** (e.g. contrasting a statement with a picture showing the opposite)
> - **irony** (depicting the opposite of what is really meant)
> - making use of **puns** or **word play**
> - **symbolic** elements

USEFUL PHRASES

Introduction/First impression

The cartoon was drawn by … and it was published/appeared in (source) on (date).

It was created in response to …

It shows/deals with/refers to/comments on …

The cartoonist makes fun of …/criticises … for (doing sth).

Description

The cartoon consists of/is made up of (several) …/is divided into …

There is a (short/an ironic) caption/speech bubble/thought bubble in/on/next to …

The caption says/states that …/is a comment by …

Position of elements → **S28.1 (phrases/description)**

Analysis

The cartoon stands for/represents/is a caricature of …

The cartoon plays on the stereotypical view of …

… is exaggerated/stressed/symbolic for …

… reinforces the cartoonist's message that …

The humour lies in the discrepancy/contrast/parallels/misunderstanding between … and …

Evaluation

The cartoon (only partly) achieves its aim of (doing sth).

In my opinion, the cartoonist is (not) successful in presenting/criticising … because …

The cartoon appeals (does not appeal) to me. In my opinion, it is convincing/simplistic/confusing/unfair.

The cartoonist skilfully/effectively shows …

Unfortunately, it remains unclear whether … or …

S29 Working with films

S29.1 Film types and cinematic devices

Film types

Entertainment
- Anyone can post entertaining video clips on the internet; some become extremely popular.
- Music videos give visual atmosphere to songs. Feature films are full-length films made for presentation in the cinema or for home viewing. Feature films may correspond to, parody or mix typical genres such as action, adventure, animated, comedy, drama, epic, gangster, romance, thriller or Western films.

Presenting information
- Newscasts provide information on current events.
- Documentaries explain and guide through topics such as travel, history, science or wildlife.

Advice and education
- "How to" videos on the internet help you do anything from repairing a bike to learning Greek.

Selling products
- Commercial clips are one of the most successful forms of advertising. → S31

Cinematic devices: camera techniques

Field size	Effect
long/wide-angle/full shot	distancing, overall impression; a full, 'establishing' shot sets the scene
medium shot	complete view of whole body or object; focuses attention
close-up shot	closer view: body only – from the waist up; emphasises action and interaction
detail/extreme close-up	the viewer can see facial expressions and emotions clearly; concentration on an important detail

Camera angle	Effect
high angle, bird's eye	makes people look smaller, less significant
eye-level view	looks like a neutral, natural viewpoint
low angle, worm's eye	makes people look bigger, more significant
overhead shot	e.g. view from a tower; gives an overview, orientation
crane shot	shows a scene from all perspectives
reverse-angle shot	shows the person being talked to, not the person talking; shows reactions
over-the-shoulder shot	shows interaction between speaker and addressee; often used for interviews

Camera movement	Effect
static shot	no camera movement; calm, slow scene
zoom	camera static, but coming closer to (focusing on) detail by zooming in
panning/tilting shot	moving horizontally from a static position; pan left/right, tilt up/down to increase tension or move the focus slowly
tracking shot, hand-held camera	smooth movement along tracks or hand-held camera beside, behind or in front of moving person/object as if walking/running with them; emphasises movement
point-of-view shot	point of view of one character; viewer sees the scene through his/her eyes

bird's eye view

Skills

Cinematic devices: editing techniques

Editing	Effect
cut	film stop: instant change from one scene to another; increases pace (speed)
fade in, fade out	gradual appearance/disappearance at the beginning/end of a scene; calmer than a cut
crosscut	view alternates between two different scenes happening simultaneously; creates suspense, emphasises contrasts; audience knows what is happening in both places
flashback, flash forward	making cuts and changes in the storyline
slow motion, freeze frame	playing speed slows down or stops to intensify a movement or moment
fast motion, time lapse	fast sequence of shots exaggerates speed; time lapse taken over a long time, shows change, growth, development
soundtrack, subtitles	music, sound effects added later to enhance atmosphere; superimposed text to aid viewers' understanding/translate
voice-over	comments on action, like a third-person narrator in a story; or words spoken by characters not visible on screen

editing

slow motion

S29.2   Analysing films

STEP 1   Viewing for notes on detail and effect
Make a **viewing table** for your notes with spaces for details like action/story, characters/body language, space/setting, sound/music, camera techniques, mood (emotional/neutral?), editing/special effects, colours/lighting and language (speech/action ratio, style). View several times.
→ S6.2, S7, S10, S29.1

USEFUL PHRASES

Cinematic devices

In the establishing shot the audience can see …

This brings … close./This creates distance between …

The viewer sees … from above/below/behind/from a … perspective, which makes … look …

The tracking shot follows …/the movement of …

The shots follow each other quickly/slowly, creating a sense of …/Suspense is created by …

The camera pans/tilts from left to right/top to bottom, moving the focus from … to …

… is shown in slow motion, intensifying …

… moves the action forward/surprises the viewer.

The relationship between … is shown to be … by …

The characteristic/repeated use of … emphasises …

Action and language

There is more action than speech in the scene, which emphasises …

…'s body language/reactions show(s) that …

STEP 2   Writing/preparing a presentation
Choose from the notes what's important for the task.
Introduction
- Include general information about the film, e.g. director, scriptwriter, title, genre and theme, and the film's main function/effect.

Body
- Each paragraph should make one point to support your argument/interpretation. → S14
- Connect the choice of what goes into the film (characters, movements, location, music etc.) with the overall effect of the film. Explain how the effects are achieved, with examples.
- Comment on how a film script differs from the original literary text, if appropriate.

Conclusion
- End with a short summary, or (if asked) a comparison of this film with others, or with your own experience, or your personal impression.

STEP 3   Editing and checking → S20.2

TIP

- **For writing a review** → S16
- **For commercial clips (adverts):** Explain how the elements contribute to the chosen strategy. → S31
- **For a music video clip:** Interpret the song lyrics (→ S6.1); research the musical genre, the artist and fans. Does the artist or the song play the main part in the video?

S29.3 Making a film

STEP 1 Assembling a film crew
- Choose a director, a camera crew, scriptwriters and supporting/editing teams.

STEP 2 Preparation
- Find suitable actors, location(s) and setting.
- Decide on the use of light (bright, fading, …), colour (colours mainly dark, warm, …), space (interior or exterior, wide or narrow) and cinematic devices. → S29.2
- Then produce a film script and a storyboard.

STEP 3 Filming
- Follow your storyboard.
- Repeat takes if necessary.

STEP 4 Editing
- Use suitable editing techniques. → S29.2
- Add sound (music, dubbing, voiceover, effects).

Example of a film script (adaptation of the first scene from *The White Tiger* by Aravind Adiga)
Scripts are always typed in this Courier font and format, so that one page equals about one minute of film.

```
1 EXT. Beijing, Great Hall of the People -- DAY
     Fade-in to time lapse of PEOPLE of all kinds walking across Tiananmen Square past
     the façade, including businessmen and street vendors. Chinese music.

2 INT. Beijing, Premier Wen Jiabao's office -- SAME TIME
     Crosscut to Chinese PREMIER at desk, leaning back in chair, reading a printout
     letter (several pages). Secretary, nervous, stands waiting for reaction. Silence.
                    PREMIER
     (annoyed, irritated; speaks in Chinese. Subtitle in English appears)
            It's in English.
                    VOICEOVER BALRAM
     (Balram, speaking in English with an Indian accent)
            Mr Premier, Sir.
            Neither you nor I can speak English, but there are some things
            that can be said only in English.

3 INT. Bangalore, India, huge and shabby room, nearly empty, one large 70's chandelier;
  fan above, splitting up the light; radio -- NIGHT
     Fade-in to Balram cross-legged on floor with a silver laptop but talking, not
     typing. Dreamy look on his face.
                    BALRAM
            … and at 11:32 p.m. today, which was about ten minutes ago, when
            the lady on All India Radio announced, "Premier Jiabao is coming
            to Bangalore next week", I said that thing at once.
```

Example of a storyboard (Shot 3 from the film script above)

Audio	Near silence, voice fades in	Radio background: Indian music	Fade out radio. Balram louder
Video	*(illustration: bird's eye view of room with chandelier, Balram small in centre)*	*(illustration: Balram seated cross-legged with laptop and radio)*	*(illustration: close-up frontal portrait of Balram)*
Shot	Fade-in establishing shot: bird's eye view, chandelier to left, Balram small, centre	Move: slow crane zoom round back of Balram to front close-up at "announced"	Stop at: Close-up frontal shot Balram, from "I said that thing at once."

Skills

S30   Making a survey

Surveys are used to collect information from a set or large number of people. Carefully prepared questions make the results easy to record, collect, compare, interpret, visualise and present to other people.

STEP 1 Preparation
- Write down exactly what you want to find out.
- Decide how many people are needed for reliable and representative results.
- Choose the **target group**. You may want to ask different age, gender or interest groups.
- Note your **hypothesis**: a theory or assumption you can prove or disprove with the survey.

STEP 2 Writing questions
- Use your notes to choose the correct question types. Make all questions clear and simple.
- For simple, quick results use: **yes/no** for clear-cut questions, **multiple choice** for more alternatives, or **rating questions** to collect opinions or trends.
- If you want people to suggest a creative solution to a problem or describe personal experience in more detail, use **open questions**. Visualising these results is difficult. If you need short and precise answers, limit the answer space to a few lines.
- **Don't suggest 'facts'** in the questions or answers you want the respondents to write:
  Why do you think Fair Trade prices are too high?
  Do you want to save the world by buying organic?

STEP 3 Conducting the survey
- Distribute your survey and set a deadline.
- Collect the results in a chart or tally (Strichliste).
- Sort open answers into suitable **categories**.

STEP 4 Presenting the results
- State the survey topic and your expectations.
- Say if the hypothesis was proved right/wrong.
- Give the majority opinion or clearest result.
- Suggest reasons for surprising or interesting results, make a top ten list of popular answers, compare different answers and/or visualise findings in a chart or map. → S27
- Conclude with what you learned from the survey.

Example survey
Customer behaviour and global problems

Age group: ☐ under 25   ☐ 25–50   ☐ over 50 years old

1. **Which factors influence you most when you buy food and clothes?** (no more than 3 answers)
   ☐ visible quality   ☐ Fair Trade products
   ☐ popular food   ☐ fashionable clothes
   ☐ easy-to-prepare food   ☐ easy-to-wear/wash clothes
   ☐ organic/eco-friendly   ☐ non-allergenic products
   ☐ low prices, sales offers and bargains
   ☐ non-animal/vegetarian products

2. **Do you check where products come from before you buy them?**   ☐ yes   ☐ sometimes   ☐ no

3. **What would be the single best way to make Fair Trade and organic products more popular?**
   ☐ government subsidies for lower prices
   ☐ advertising campaigns by NGOs
   ☐ talking to family and friends about what to buy
   ☐ more news stories about bad conditions for labourers
   ☐ education about global problems in schools
   ☐ eating less meat so you can afford Fair Trade

4. **Rate the present effects of your customer behaviour.**
   Circle from 1 (I definitely contribute to global problems) to 10 (I actively contribute to reducing global problems).
   1   2   3   4   5   6   7   8   9   10

5. **Write up to two reasons for your rating here:**
   _____

6. **Do you think customer behaviour changes can help to solve global problems?**
   ☐ yes   ☐ no   ☐ not as much as …   ☐ only if …   ☐ with …
   _____

Thank you. Please return to … by the 29th November.

Examples for presenting results

- Present yes/no results using a **pie chart**:

- Present multiple choice results in a **bar chart**:

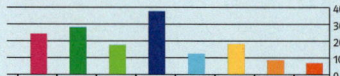

- Present ratings in a chart or as a **statement**:
  Most saw themselves as/Young people tend to …

- Present open answers in **categories**:
  Most respondents gave lack of information as a reason. Just one felt that …

Special skills

S31 Advertising

S31.1 Advertising strategies

The **AIDA** strategy consists of four steps. The advert
- first attracts immediate **a**ttention, e.g. with a surprising eye-catcher or ear-catcher
- arouses further **i**nterest in the next step, e.g. with a new slogan or unusual layout,
- then appeals to a special **d**esire or need, e.g. the need for health or comfort,
- and finally asks the target group to take a desired **a**ction, e.g. to buy the product or to donate money.

The **USP** strategy concentrates on a **u**nique **s**elling **p**roposition, i.e. a single message or piece of information about what is special or desirable.

The **KISS** strategy is good for all kinds of advert: **k**eep **i**t **s**hort and **s**imple.

The **PPPP** strategy says an advert should contain a **p**icture, a **p**romise, some **p**roof and a **p**ush to act.

The **SUCCESS** principles are for radio/film adverts:
- **s**implicity – find the core of your idea
- **u**nexpectedness – grab attention by surprising
- **c**oncreteness – the idea is graspable, memorable
- **c**redibility – make ideas believable and build trust
- **e**motion – make listeners respond emotionally
- **s**tories – use true to life and realistic messages
- **s**ound – build trust with a likeable voice

S31.2 Working with advertisements

Analysing printed advertisements

STEP 1 Introduction
Mention the following: advertiser, target group, what is being advertised (a product, brand, company, person, organisation) and what the main message is.

STEP 2 Body
Explain the strategy used (such as AIDA) and how the following elements contribute to the effect:
- layout (foreground/background, focus, text, …)
- textual elements (headline, slogan, statement)
- relationship of language to visual content
- photographic elements
- visual element design (size/type, colours, logo)

STEP 3 Conclusion
Comment on the quality and effectiveness of the advertisement.

STEP 4 Editing and checking → S20.2

TIP

Creating a radio or film commercial

Length
A radio or film commercial is usually exactly 30 or 60 seconds long, with around 75 words of text.

Script content
What image or message do you want to convey?
Who is your target group?
Which strategy will you use to make this clear? → S31.1

Structure
Divide the ad into parts: a beginning (e.g. sound or tune), a voice-over message, an ending (repetition of the main message and/or the tune).

Language
Use simple words, short sentences and rhetorical devices.

Recording
Make sure you keep to the set length. Adapt the script, the voice and tone and repeat if necessary. Use suitable film techniques if you are making a film commercial. → S29

USEFUL PHRASES

Describing advertisements

The advertisement consists of …	The way … is presented suggests that …
… is striking/prominent/obviously important.	The ad makes fun of/plays with/combines elements of …
Clearly, the … advertising strategy has been used.	The advert is informative/manipulative/provocative/shocking/moving/exaggerated …
The main emphasis/focus is on …	
The slogan uses alliteration/irony/wordplay/joke to …	The contrast between the picture and the text
The picture/film evokes/provokes …	… makes you feel/want (to) …
The colours/light create(s) an … atmosphere.	… creates a desire for/gives the impression that …

Skills

S32 Doing research

You will often have to research a topic before you can talk or write about it.
There are many different ways of finding out information.

STEP 1 Choosing sources
- Go to your school, local or state **library**.
- Look in **books**, **newspapers** and **magazines**.
- **Research online** (see tip box).
- **Write to an organisation** or an agency that might be able to send you brochures, posters or information sheets, e.g. tourist offices, museums, government agencies, NGOs (non-government organisations), or political parties.
- **Talk to someone** who knows a lot about the subject, e.g. English/American friends, exchange students at your school.
- Carry out an **interview** with an expert or do a **survey** and document the results. → S25, S30
- **Always note down your information sources and quote them correctly!** → S19.2, 19.3

STEP 2 Checking author and source quality
- **Don't believe everything you read!** Anyone can publish anything on the internet, especially in Wikipedia. Printed articles and books have normally been more carefully chosen and edited, but these can also be biased or too generalised and simple.
- Check up on the author or writing team. Avoid texts without a named author or team of authors.
- Is the source background serious, reliable and trustworthy? Was it written by a respectable journalist, professor, expert, institution or government agency? Are the survey results really representative? Or is the text trivial? Avoid sources generally known to be sensationalist and superficial, e.g. something written by a hobby historian, or something from the popular press.
- Is the source up to date or too old to be useful?

> **TIP**
>
> **How to find the best information**
> - Plan plenty of time to research, read through and check up on what you have found.
> - If you find that the quality of your sources is not good enough, go back and look again or ask for help!
> - Your local or state library will offer research tips, recommend specialist journals on the topic and explain how to use academic search engines.

STEP 3 Checking the quality of the contents
- Is the text **neutral** and **objective** or is the writer/speaker expressing a personal, biased opinion?
- Is what has been said or written just **hearsay**, without expert **proof** or **personal experience**?
- Does the source include reliable information on **both sides of a controversial topic** or is all of the information one-sided?
- Follow links to quoted sources to check their validity. You may find some good information there too. If not, don't trust the original text!
- Check the **sources of information** your text's author used. Are they listed? Are they good quality sources?

> **TIP**
>
> **Researching online**
>
> **Effective search engine use**
> - Enter the words you're looking for, e.g. 'solar energy projects Australia'.
> - Use as few words as possible. The more clearly you define your keywords, the better results you will get.
> - If you're looking for a set phrase, use inverted commas, e.g. 'Martin Luther King's speeches'.
> - You can use + (= require), or - (= exclude).
>
> **Troubleshooting**
> - If you get too many results, use more specific keywords.
> - If you don't get the right kind of results, think of other words to describe the subject.
> - If you still don't get the results you want, use your search engine's help support.
>
> **Finding information quickly on a website**
> - Many websites offer a search function. If not, use the search function in the edit ('Bearbeiten') menu or Strg+F to find certain words on the page.

S33 Peer evaluation

Giving feedback to your classmates and getting feedback yourself has several advantages.

- You get a quick response and immediate tips.
- Your classmates understand problems you have because they are at a similar learning level.
- You get the chance to speak more in English.
- Positive criticism is better than not knowing what you could do to improve your techniques.

It's important to follow these rules:
- Talk/write about several different aspects and don't forget to mention what was good; not all aspects of a talk or text will be bad.
- Criticise parts of the work if necessary, but not the person!
- Formulate criticism positively, e.g. as a tip.

You can give your feedback orally and/or use tables to write notes on different aspects.

Example table for quick feedback
Use this to give your classmate a better idea of what was good and what needs improvement:

Presentation feedback	☺+ Well done	☺ Good	☺ Satisfactory	☹ Needs improvement	☹– Biggest problem(s)
Preparation					
Quality of content					
Language skills					
Voice clear and loud					
Topic made interesting					
Easy to understand					
Media competence					
Time management					

Example table for dialogue task feedback

Content	You contributed well to the discussion.	0	1	2	3	4	5
	You showed understanding of the topic.	0	1	2	3	4	5
	You displayed knowledge and brought in your own ideas.	0	1	2	3	4	5
Communication	You showed interest in and reacted to what your partner said.	0	1	2	3	4	5
	You reacted appropriately when he/she didn't understand something.	0	1	2	3	4	5
Language	You spoke fluently.	0	1	2	3	4	5
	You used suitable topic vocabulary.	0	1	2	3	4	5
	You made few mistakes.	0	1	2	3	4	5
	You used good pronunciation and intonation.	0	1	2	3	4	5

USEFUL PHRASES

Positive feedback
I was impressed by/I really liked the way you …
You're really good at …

Positive criticism
… was really good, and I think your presentation/text would be even better if you …
Why don't you try this: …
I noticed that you often say …/make this mistake: … Correcting it is easy: concentrate on …
It's not a huge problem, but it could make a big difference in the overall impression if you …

Look out for … when you're writing …
It might help if you always check for …
When I do …, I often get the feedback that … Maybe it's the same for you.
It helped me when my teacher gave me this tip: …
I'm sure the reader would be impressed if you …
I'm afraid I didn't understand this paragraph. Could you explain what you meant? It might be better to break that long sentence up into shorter and simpler sentences.

Skills

S34 Dealing with exam tasks (with *Operatoren*)

When you are preparing for exams, you need to know all of the relevant information and check which strategies are important for each task type.

Typical exam task areas test the different skills mentioned in the European Reference Framework for language learning and the Abitur exam consists of a combination of these task areas:

Reading	→ S4–S11
Writing	→ S12–S20
Mediation	→ S26.1
Listening	→ S21
Speaking alone	→ S22–S24
Speaking with others	→ S22–S24

In your oral exam you may be asked to combine a monologue part (e.g. talking about visuals) with a dialogue part, discussing the topic with a partner. There are three **task sets** (*Anforderungsbereiche*) you should recognise when you read the task and see **key instruction words** (*Operatoren*).

Task types can be:
- **closed**: only one correct answer possible, checking a single piece of knowledge or a single skill
- **half-open**: structured questions expecting limited answers (e.g. in one sentence, one paragraph or in keywords)
- **open**: with more than one possible answer; combining a range of knowledge and skills with problem-solving strategies to show higher levels of understanding

Practising using mock written exams

Get hold of some mock (example) exams and take the time to do them in a situation like the real exam:

STEP 1 Working in the right setting
- Work in a quiet room and set yourself the exact time you will be given in the real exam.
- Don't use any material to help you which is not allowed in the real exam.

STEP 2 Planning how to write
- Make sure you know what you are expected to do for each task.
- Plan enough time to read the questions very carefully, plan, write and check your answers.
- Write a checklist of tasks/important things to remember.

STEP 3 Writing your answers
- Use separate paper for notes and first drafts.
- Write the task number/title above each answer.
- Write clearly and neatly. It is important that the examiner can easily read what you write.
- Check what you have written and write a clean copy if necessary. → S20.2

STEP 4 After writing the mock exam
- As soon as you have finished, write down: *how you feel • what difficulties you had • what you'd do differently next time • what you still need to learn*
- Use these notes to plan your work and time management for the final exam.

I Orientation, comprehension (understanding) and reproduction

Keyword	What you have to do	Example task
describe	Say what something or someone is like by giving details.	Describe the setting and the atmosphere in the story.
outline	Give the main features/structure of a topic.	Outline the author's views on social media.
point out	Find and explain certain aspects.	Point out the main differences in how the two characters are presented.
present	(Re-)Structure something and write it down.	Present the situation of the characters.
state	Specify something clearly.	State briefly the main developments in the family described in the text.
summarise, sum up	Give a concise account of the main points or events.	Summarise the information given in the text about the consequences of water pollution.

You may also be given (half-)closed tasks like multiple choice or matching exercises to test understanding.

Keyword	Example task	Key word	Example task
complete	Complete the sentences in no more than 10 words.	match	Match each paragraph with one of the headings (A-H) offered.
fill in/fill in the gaps	Fill in the gaps in the text with the right words.	tick (✔)	Tick the correct solution and give a quote from the text to prove your answer.
		quote	

II Analysis and restructuring

Keyword	What you have to do	Example task
analyse	Describe and explain in detail certain aspects and/or features of the text.	Analyse the opposing views on class held by the two protagonists.
characterise	Describe and examine the way a character is presented.	Characterise the two brothers in the story.
compare	Point out similarities and differences.	Compare how the characters are portrayed in the film and the novel.
contrast, juxtapose	Describe and examine differences between two or more aspects.	Contrast the author's idea of multicultural society with other theories you know of.
examine	Describe and explain in detail certain aspects and/or features of the text.	Examine the author's use of language.
explain	Describe something and give reasons.	Explain the cartoon's message.
illustrate	Explain/make something clear with examples.	Illustrate the author's use of imagery.
relate	Find connections between aspects of two different sources.	Relate the protagonist's principles to the article by x on y.

III Evaluation, discussion and/or text production

Keyword	What you have to do	Example task
assess	Consider in a balanced way the points for and against a topic using examples.	Assess how realistic the different characters in the story are.
comment (on)	Express your opinion on the topic in question, giving evidence to support your view.	Comment on the author's view.
discuss	Consider different sides of an issue by giving reasons for and against, with examples.	Discuss how the internet influences our communicating behaviour.
evaluate	Form an opinion after carefully considering and presenting advantages and disadvantages.	Evaluate the success of the campaign as presented in the text.
justify	Give adequate reasons for your decisions or conclusions.	Justify your answer.
interpret	Analyse the form and content of something and explain its meaning in a wider context.	Interpret the message of the poem.
Write a ...	Use your knowledge of a particular text type to produce a text, e.g. diary entry/interview script.	Write a letter to the editor expressing your opinion.

Appendix

Glossary of literary terms

Some of the terms are used to explain others. They are underlined.

act [ækt]	A major division in a play. Each act may have one or more scenes. In classical drama, we speak of rising action up to the climax, and falling action leading to the resolution.
action [ˈækʃn]	1. The main story of a play, short story, narrative, poem or novel etc. 2. The main series of events that form the plot.
alliteration [əˌlɪtəˈreɪʃn]	Alliteration is a figure of speech in which consonants, especially at the beginning of words, are repeated. E.g. "Betty Botter bought some butter."
allusion [əˈluːʒn]	A reference in a literary work to a character or theme found in another literary work.
anadiplosis [ˌænədɪˈpləʊsɪs]	The repetition of a prominent (and usually the last) word in one phrase at the beginning of the next.
analogy [əˈnælədʒi]	A comparison in which an idea or a thing is compared to another thing that is quite different from it.
anaphora [əˈnæfrə]	Repetition of words or phrases at the beginnings of neighbouring sentences or clauses for emphasis.
anecdote [ˈænɪkdəʊt]	A brief narration of or a story about an individual or an event.
antagonist [ænˈtægənɪst]	Opponent of the protagonist.
antithesis [ænˈtɪθəsɪs]	Antithesis is a rhetorical device in which two opposite ideas are put together in a sentence to achieve a contrasting effect.
association [əˌsəʊʃiˈeɪʃn]	Something that comes to your mind from memory or imagination when you look at or read something else.
atmosphere [ˈætməsfɪə]	The feeling created in a literary work using descriptions of the surroundings.
autobiography [ˌɔːtəbaɪˈɒɡrəfi]	Prose representation of parts or of the whole life of a person, written by him-/herself.
biography [baɪˈɒɡrəfi]	Prose representation of parts or of the whole life of a person, written by another person.
blank verse [blæŋk ˈvɜːs]	Unrhymed iambic pentameter. Shakespeare's characters often speak in blank verse.
chapter [ˈtʃæptə]	One of the sections a book is divided into.
character [ˈkærəktə]	A fictional person in a piece of literature. Flat characters are not very complex and do not change in the course of the action, whereas round characters are usually complex and go through a development.
characterisation [ˌkærəktraɪˈzeɪʃn]	Presentation of characters in a text. Direct characterisation: The narrator of the text tells the reader what a person is like. Indirect characterisation: The reader has to find out what a person is like through what this character does, says, thinks or feels.
characteristic [ˌkærəktəˈrɪstɪk]	A typical feature, or trait, of a person or character.
cliché [ˈkliːʃeɪ]	An expression or idea that has been used so often that it is no longer effective.
climax [ˈklaɪmæks]	The moment in a play, novel, short story, narrative or poem at which the suspense reaches its highest point. It is usually the turning point in the action.
comedy [ˈkɒmədi]	Originally, comedy was a genre of drama of ancient Athens. Comedies (as opposed to tragedies) usually have a positive ending. Since the 19th century comedy has been associated with humour.
conclusion [kənˈkluːʒn]	Last part of a literary work which sums up its content and finishes it.

Glossary of literary terms

conflict ['kɒnflɪkt]	The tension in a situation between characters usually in drama and fiction. Conflict may also occur between a character and his/her society or environment.
connotation [ˌkɒnəʊ'teɪʃn]	The connotation of a word or phrase is not its dictionary definition, but the emotional or thematic content associated with it.
content ['kɒntənt]	The term is used to refer to what is said in a literary work, as opposed to how it is said.
context ['kɒntəkst]	Those parts of a text which precede and follow any particular passage, giving it a meaning and making it more understandable than if it were read in isolation.
contrast ['kɒntrɑːst]	A way of creating a strong effect on the reader which puts two extremes in opposition, e.g. the features of two characters or the way they talk, or the atmosphere of two places.
dénouement [deɪ'nuːmɑ̃ŋ]	The part of a drama following the climax and leading to the resolution.
dialogue ['daɪəlɒg]	1. The speech of characters in any kind of narrative, story or play. 2. A literary genre in which characters discuss a subject at length.
diction ['dɪkʃən]	The choice of words used by a writer which determine the style of the passage: formal, informal, colloquial or slang.
drama ['drɑːmə]	The sort of fiction that is represented in performance on a stage.
dystopia [dɪs'təʊpɪə]	Opposite of utopia; describes an unpleasant imaginary world, usually of the future, e.g. *Nineteen Eighty-four* by George Orwell.
emotive language [ɪ'məʊtɪv 'læŋwɪdʒ]	Language used to create empathy through the use of words (usually adjectives or adverbs) that relate to or refer to emotions.
emphasis ['emfəsɪs]	The stress placed on certain words or passages that make them seem more important than other parts of the piece of writing. This can be achieved in many ways, e.g. by a difference in the typeface (type of print), repetition, use of imagery or punctuation.
enjamb(e)ment [ɪn'dʒæmbmənt]	This is the continuation of a sentence or phrase from one line of poetry to the next.
enumeration [ɪˌnjuːmə'reɪʃn]	A number of points set out in a list.
epic ['epɪk]	An epic is a long narrative poem about the deeds of warriors and heroes. It incorporates myth, legend, folk tale and history. Epics are often of national significance because they embody the history of a nation in a grandiose manner. The two kinds of epic are: a) oral epic, e.g. *The Iliad* and *The Odyssey* and b) literary epic, e.g. Virgil's *Aeneid*.
euphemism ['juːfəmɪzm]	More gentle expression used instead of the more direct one to express unpleasant, frightening or embarrassing facts, e.g. "The old dog was put to sleep (i. e. killed)."
exaggeration [ɪgˌzædʒər'eɪʃn]	Making something seem greater, better or worse than it really is.
exposition [ˌekspəʊ'zɪʃn]	The first part of a play or short story giving the information which is necessary to understand the conflict and events which follow.
fairy tale ['feəri ˌteɪl]	The fairy tale tends to be a narrative in prose about the fortunes and misfortunes of a hero or heroine who, having experienced various adventures of a more or less supernatural kind, lives happily ever after.
fiction ['fɪkʃn]	Fiction is the general term for invented stories. It is now usually applied to novels, short stories and related genres.
figurative language ['fɪɡjərətɪv ˌlæŋwɪdʒ]	Language using images and pictures that must be 'translated' to be understood. E.g. "The ground is thirsty and hungry."
flashback ['flæʃbæk]	Part of a film, novel or play in which the plot suddenly changes to events in the past.
foreshadowing [fɔː'ʃædəʊɪŋ]	Suggesting or showing what will occur later in a narrative.

Appendix

frame narrative ['freɪm ˌnærətɪv]	A story in which another story is enclosed.
genre ['ʒɑ̃:nrə]	Literary type or class. Some major genres include: tragedy, comedy, novel, short story, poetry, science fiction, drama etc.
hero/heroine ['hɪərəʊ]/['herəʊɪn]	The main male/female protagonist.
hyperbole [haɪ'pɜ:bəli]	A figure of speech that involves exaggeration in order to produce a more noticeable effect.
iambic pentameter [aɪ'æmbɪk pen'tæmɪtə]	The most commonly used type of metrical line in poetry and verse drama, this consists of five iambic feet with a short/long, or unstressed/stressed, pattern.
identification [aɪˌdentɪfɪ'keɪʃn]	The effect of bringing the reader very close to a character in a story.
imagery ['ɪmɪdʒri]	Use of language which represents objects, actions, feelings, thoughts, and ideas through the use of simile and metaphor.
inspirational poetry [ˌɪntspə'reɪʃnl ˌpəʊɪtri]	An inspirational poem reflects an experience in life perceived as a kind of revelation and tries to give you new ideas and encourage you to do something.
interpretation [ɪnˌtɜ:prɪ'teɪʃn]	The individual way you read the meaning of a work of art.
introduction [ˌɪntrə'dʌkʃn]	Can be the first part of a speech. It may also refer to the start of an essay which states the author's intention and gives the reader some idea of the theme and scope of work.
irony ['aɪərəni]	Using the contrast between what is said and what is meant in order to create humour.
legend ['ledʒənd]	A story, part fact and part fiction, about the life of a saint, folk hero or historical figure. It is handed down from generation to generation and is popularly accepted as being true.
metaphor ['metəfə]	One thing is represented by a word which normally describes something different, e.g. "All the world's a stage." Unlike a simile it contains no words of comparison ('like', 'as').
metre ['mi:tə]	The regular pattern of stressed and unstressed syllables in a poem, e.g. iamb (˘), trochee (˜), anapaest (˘˘), dactyl (˜˜) etc.
mirror ['mɪrə]	To mirror something is to reflect or represent something, to have similar features. A character's mood can be mirrored by the weather, for example.
monologue ['mɒnəlɒg]	A long speech spoken by one speaker in a play (see soliloquy).
mood [mu:d]	The feeling a literary work creates in the reader developed through setting, theme, tone and diction (see atmosphere).
motif [məʊ'ti:f]	One of the dominant ideas in a work of literature; a part of the main theme. Where an image, incident, or other element is repeated significantly within a single work, it is more commonly referred to as a 'leitmotif'.
narration/narrative [nə'reɪʃn]/['nærətɪv]	A story, prose or verse, involving events and characters.
narrator [nə'reɪtə]	The voice that tells a story.
non-fiction [ˌnɒn'fɪkʃn]	Non-fiction is a representation of a subject which is presented as fact (German: *Sachliteratur*).
novel ['nɒvl]	A long fictional prose text, often including a large number of characters, different settings and a complex plot.
novella [nəʊ'velə]	The novella is a fictional narrative restricted to a single event, situation or conflict, which leads to an unexpected turning point. The conclusion is surprising.
paradox ['pærədɒks]	A statement which, on closer inspection, reveals a kind of truth which at first seems contradictory, e.g. "Deep down he's really very shallow." Another example from Hegel is: "Man learns from history that man learns nothing from history."

Glossary of literary terms

parallel structures/ parallelism [ˈpærəlelˌɪzəm]	Using parts of a sentence that are grammatically the same or similar in their construction, sound, meaning or metre. Parallelism examples are found in literary works as well as in ordinary conversations.
parenthesis [pəˈrənθəsɪs]	An explanatory word, phrase, or sentence inserted into a passage from which it is usually set off by punctuation, e.g. brackets.
parody [ˈpærədi]	A literary work that imitates the style of another literary work. A parody can be simply amusing or it can be mocking in tone, such as a poem which exaggerates the use of alliteration in order to show the ridiculous effect of overuse of alliteration.
persona [pəˈsəʊnə]	First-person narrator in a poem. Also called the speaker.
personification [pəˌsɒnɪfɪˈkeɪʃn]	Attribution of personality to an impersonal thing, e.g. "The wind cries softly outside the window."
play [pleɪ]	A work designed to be presented on a stage and performed by actors.
plot [plɒt]	The sequence of events in a story as they relate to one another.
poem/poetry [ˈpəʊɪm]/[ˈpəʊɪtri]	Piece of writing divided into single lines. It often expresses the speaker's experiences. Most poetry makes use of four important poetic devices: metre, rhyme, rhythm and stanza.
point of view [ˌpɔɪnt əv ˈvjuː]	The perspective from which the narrator presents the story.
prose [prəʊz]	The kind of writing found in news articles, short stories, novels etc. as opposed to poetry.
protagonist [prəʊˈtæɡnɪst]	The main character in a work of fiction.
proverb [ˈprɒvɜːb]	A brief popular saying that expresses a belief that is generally thought to be true.
pseudonym [ˈsjuːdənɪm]	A 'false name' taken by a writer. Also known as pen name or *nom de plume*.
pun [pʌn]	A play on words, usually the humorous use of a word with two meanings or of different words that sound the same, e.g. "I'm always ill on Tuesdays," said Tom weakly.
quotation [kwəʊˈteɪʃn]	Something that a person has said or written.
register [ˈredʒɪstə]	The set of language characteristics that is appropriate for a particular situation involving people of a particular status.
repetition [ˌrepɪˈtɪʃn]	Single words or phrases that appear several times in one text, a way of creating emphasis.
resolution [ˌrezəˈluːʃn]	The part of a story which occurs after the climax and establishes a new state of affairs, e.g. the death of the two lovers in *Romeo and Juliet* or the marriage of Cinderella and the Prince.
review [rɪˈvjuː]	A short notice, discussion or a critical article about a text, a film, a play etc.
rhetorical device [rɪˌtɒrɪkl dɪˈvaɪs]	A stylistic device that is used intentionally to move the reader or listener.
rhetorical question [rɪˌtɒrɪkl ˈkwestʃn]	A question that need not be answered because the answer is either obvious or else it cannot be answered at all. It is mainly there for effect.
rhyme [raɪm]	Similarity of sounds in two or more words. This often occurs at the end of lines (end rhyme), e.g. t**eacher** – pr**eacher**. The pattern created is called a rhyme scheme.
rhythm [ˈrɪðm]	The sound pattern of a phrase. It is mainly based on metre.
satire [ˈsætaɪə]	Combines humour and criticism with the aim of making people laugh at the stupidity of individuals and institutions. It differs from comedy in that it seeks to correct or improve.
scene [siːn]	A subdivision of an act in a play or an opera or other theatrical entertainment. A scene normally represents actions happening in one place at one time.
science fiction [ˌsaɪəns ˈfɪkʃn]	Novels or short stories set in the future or another world, which often focus on imaginary technological developments. Science fiction may be utopian or dystopian.

Appendix

screenplay [ˈskriːnpleɪ]	The script of a film. It contains dialogue and/or narration with instructions for sets and camera positions.
script [skrɪpt]	Dialogue and/or narration with instructions for the staging of a play. A film script is also called a screenplay.
setting [ˈsetɪŋ]	The time and place that characterise a work of literature.
short story [ˈʃɔːt ˌstɔːri]	A fictional prose narrative that is too short to be published as a volume on its own. A short story normally focuses on a single event and setting with only one or two main characters.
simile [ˈsɪmɪli]	A comparison between objects or ideas, using 'like', 'as' or 'as if', e.g. "He fought like a tiger."
soliloquy [səˈlɪləkwi]	The monologue of a character who speaks his or her thoughts aloud when there is nobody else present.
speaker [ˈspiːkə]	First-person narrator in a poem. Also called the persona.
stanza [ˈstænzə]	The regular number of lines which form a unit of a poem.
stereotype [ˈsteriəʊtaɪp]	Fixed ideas about other people or things. They may be positive or negative prejudices.
stream-of-consciousness [ˌstriːm əv ˈkɒnʃəsnəs]	A technique of writing in which a character's perceptions, thoughts, and memories are all presented together in an apparently irregular form. It can appear as dreams, memories, imaginative thoughts or real perception.
structure [ˈstrʌktʃə]	The sum of the relationships of the parts with each other. We can speak of a structure of a word, a sentence, a paragraph, a chapter, a book and so forth. The formal structure of a play consists of its acts and scenes and their interdependent balance.
style [staɪl]	How a writer uses language. It is the tone and the 'voice' of the writer, often typical of a certain period or genre.
subplot [ˈsʌbplɒt]	A subordinate or minor collection of events in a narrative.
suspense [səˈspens]	Suspense results mainly from two factors: 1. the reader's identification with and concern for the welfare of a character, and 2. an expectation of violence.
symbol [ˈsɪmbl]	Something concrete which stands for an abstract idea, e.g. a rose is a symbol of love.
synecdoche [sɪˈnekdəki]	Synecdoche is a literary device in which a part of something represents the whole or it may use a whole to represent a part.
theme [θiːm]	The theme of a novel, poem, short story etc. is the central idea or message. It may be demonstrated by the use of symbols, repetition and statements.
thesis [ˈθiːsɪs]	Argument or proposition of a text. The thesis of a text is its abstract content and the proposition it argues for.
tone [təʊn]	The author's attitude towards his/her subject, characters and readers.
tragedy [ˈtrædʒədi]	A form of drama representing the downfall of a central character (protagonist). Shakespeare is famous for his tragedies, including *Macbeth*, *King Lear*, and *Hamlet*.
trait [treɪt]	A typical feature of a character.
turning point [ˈtɜːnɪŋ ˌpɔɪnt]	The moment in a story or a play when there is a change in direction which leads toward the end result. See also climax.
understatement [ˈʌndəsteɪtmənt]	An understatement is a figure of speech used to intentionally make a situation seem less important than it really is.
utopia [juːˈtəʊpiə]	The term is based on the Greek words for 'no place' and 'good place'. It refers to literature which describes an imaginary ideal society and political state (opposite of dystopia).
verse [vɜːs]	Another word for poetry, a single line of a poem, or a stanza.

Classroom methods

1 Think – Pair – Share

Use this method for • collecting ideas or preparing for a discussion/talk/…
STEP 1 • Work silently and alone on a topic or task and take notes.
STEP 2 • Share your results with a partner. Listen carefully and explain your ideas to each other. → S23
• Take notes and come to an agreement if required.
STEP 3 • Present your conclusions to a different pair of students, a small group or the rest of the class. Present results in a short talk or visually. → S22

2 Fishbowl discussion

Use this method for • training for speaking and active listening
• expressing and defending arguments for or against a topic
STEP 1 • Split into two groups. Select a chairperson and speakers in group 1 (the 'fish'). Group 1 speakers prepare statements/arguments for/against a set topic; one student prepares to chair the discussion. Group 2 (the 'observers') prepare criteria for feedback. → S24, S33
STEP 2 • Make a double circle: chair and debate speakers in the centre, observers in the outer circle. Hold the discussion. Each speaker makes their statement before general discussion starts. The observers keep quiet and make notes for feedback.
STEP 3 • After the set time, the inner circle is quiet while the observers give feedback and suggestions for arguments they might have used. → S33
Alternatives • For a second round, swap places: observers become speakers and vice versa.
• Observers swap with speakers during the discussion if they have better arguments.

3 Placemat

Use this method for • comparing ideas or thinking about new arguments
• agreeing on a joint solution
STEP 1 • Work in groups of four students sitting around a 'placemat': a large piece of paper divided into sections around a centre field (see the picture). Every group member notes their ideas on the set task in the section nearest to them.
STEP 2 • Turn the placemat clockwise and read what the other students have noted down. Repeat this step until you have all read every section.
STEP 3 • Then discuss the ideas in your group.
• Agree on the best idea(s)/answer(s) and write these in the centre of the placemat. → S24

4 Speed dating (or Double circle)

Use this method for • sharing results or discussing a topic
• reacting to different opinions and speakers in a short time
STEP 1 • Two students face each other sitting at one desk. Share your results/discuss a given topic with the student facing you.
STEP 2 • Switch desks three times as if you were switching partners in a speed date café. Take notes and come to an agreement if required. → S23
Alternative • Sit facing each other in a double circle of chairs.
• Those sitting in the outer circle move clockwise to new partners.

Appendix

5 Group puzzle (= Jigsaw puzzle)

Use this method for
- shared group work on complex topics

STEP 1
- Make home groups of four.
- Each student works alone on a different task or topic.
- Make notes and prepare for discussion. → **S24**

STEP 2
- Swap places so that each new group is made up of four 'experts' from each of the home groups on the same task/topic.
- Discuss the answers/results and come to a decision/agreement.

STEP 3
- Then go back to the home groups.
- Report about your task and discuss the results.

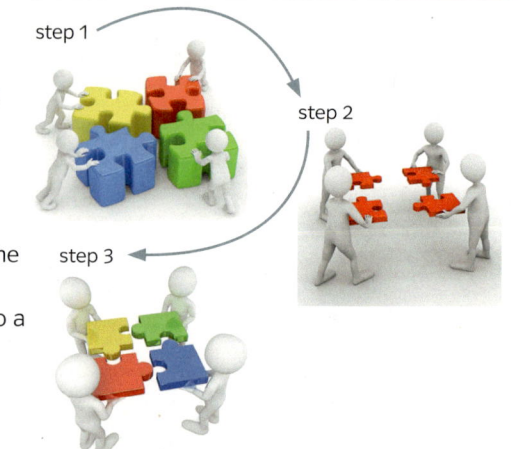

6 Hot seat

Use this method for
- using cultural, historical and character knowledge to present yourself as a different person
- practising interview techniques and defending positions using the correct register

STEP 1
- Some students are given a role (can be a fictional or non-fictional person).
- These students prepare to answer questions in role.
- The rest prepare questions to ask. → **S25**

STEP 2
- One role character sits in the 'hot seat' to be interviewed.
- Give plausible answers according to the role.

Alternatives
- Role players could improvise a debate before the audience asks questions.
- Other students play roles (journalist, judge, police investigator) when asking questions.

7 Gallery walk

Use this method for
- presenting results, sharing information and comments

STEP 1
- Prepare the results of a task/group work for visual presentation on one table/wall in the room. → **S22, S28**
- Choose one 'expert' to stand next to the visual presentation and explain/answer questions.

STEP 2
- All other students walk around the room, look at the presented results and make notes.
- You can ask the 'expert' to explain or answer questions.

8 Freeze frame (Standbild)

Use this method for
- understanding a character's point of view or role in a text/conflict
- understanding a (difficult) part of a literary text and recognising symbolic elements

STEP 1
- Work in groups and read the text extract.
- Choose a moment/event from the text as the basis for a freeze frame to represent what is important.

STEP 2
- Each of you represents one character. Decide together how you will create the freeze frame.
- Practise the freeze frame and prepare to explain why you chose these positions.

STEP 3
- Each group presents the freeze frame to the others.
- The viewers ask questions and give feedback. → **S33**

Text- und Bildquellenverzeichnis

Textquellen:
12 Quotes: (1) Quotation made by Margaret Thatcher, talking to *Women's Own magazine*, October 31, 1987; (2) John, F. Kennedy, quotation from *The Inaugural Address*, 1961; **13** Quotes: (2) Edward Snowden, quotation from an interview with Glenn Greenwald (US journalist), 2013; (3) Quotation made by Vince Lombardi; **19** www.bbc.com, BBC News UK, April 3, 2013 © 2013 BBC; **20–21** Text Copyright © 2011 by Veronica Roth; **22** From "I thought I'd be happy to be an old wrinkly - but no one told me how rude the young would be" by Fay Weldon, *Mail Online*, July 3, 2013; **24–25** From "Generation Boris", *The Economist*, London, June 1, 2013; **26** Poem written by Edwin Arlington Robinson, 1897 © public domain under US law from 2006; **27–29** Excerpt(s) from THE CIRCLE by Dave Eggers, copyright © 2013 by Dave Eggers. Used by permission of Alfred A. Knopf, an imprint of the Knopf Doubleday Publishing Group, a division of Random House LLC. All rights reserved. Any third party use of this material, outside of this publication, is prohibited. Interested parties must apply directly to Random House LLC for permission.; **30–31** From *The New York Times*, June 8, 2013 © 2013 The New York Times. All rights reserved. Used by permission and protected by the Copyright Laws of the United States. The printing, copying, redistribution, or retransmission of this Content without express written permission is prohibited.; **33** By Martin Klostermann, *Spiegel Online*, February 10, 2013; **36** Quotes: (1) Quotation from "Are we about to witness the end of Britain? by Dominic Sandbrook, *Mail Online*, January 29, 2012; (2+3) Quotations from "What does Britishness mean to you?" by Stephen Moss, *The Guardian*, London, February 5, 2012; (4) Quotation from "Can you be Scottish and British?" by James Walsh, theguardian.com, July 3, 2014; **37** Quotes: (1+2) Quotations from "What does Britishness mean to you?" by Stephen Moss, *The Guardian*, London, February 5, 2012; (3) Quotation from "Can you be Scottish and British?" by James Walsh, theguardian.com, July 3, 2014; (4) Quotation from a speech Bill Clinton (former US President) gave in a public forum in London, 2014; **40** (Broadsheet newspaper) From *The Guardian*, London, January 16, 2014; (Tabloid newspaper) From *Mail Online*, January 14, 2014; **41** Quotes: (1) blogs.ec.europa.eu; (2) Quotation by Helena Morrissey, *The Telegraph*, London, July 27, 2013; (3) By Max Evans, *The Daily Express*, London, January 2, 2014; (4) BBC News, bbc.co.uk – © 2013 BBC; **41–42** By Owen Jones, *The Independent*, London, July 24, 2012; **43** Excerpts from "What does Britishness mean to you?" by Stephen Moss, *The Guardian*, London, February 5, 2012; **44** © Craig Taylor, 2009, *A Million Tiny Plays About Britain*, Bloomsbury Publishing Plc.; **45.1** Winston Churchill, excerpt from his speech about the tragedy of Europe in Zurich on September 19, 1946; **45.2** From "Robin Cook's chicken tikka masala speech" by Robin Cook, theguardian.com, April 19, 2001; **45.3** © Crown copyright 2013. Reproduced with the permission of the Controller of Her Majesty's Stationery Office.; **46–47** BBC News, bbc.co.uk – © 2010 BBC; **48–49** From "Laura Barton: My north-south divide" by Laura Barton, *The Guardian*, London, July 12, 2010; **50–51** By Nicholas Wapshott, Reuters, New York, July 22, 2013; **52–53** © Crown copyright 2012. Reproduced with the permission of the Controller of Her Majesty's Stationery Office.; **54** Excerpt from "Mother" by Lucy Skilbeck, from *Londoners* by Craig Taylor, Granta Books, London, 2012 © 2011, 2012 by Craig Taylor; **55** From *Counting Eggs* by Peter Daniels, Mulfran Press, Cardiff, 2012; **57** By Christoph Driessen, *Mitteldeutsche Zeitung*, Halle/Saale, 3. März 2011; **60** Quotes: (1) *Letter to My Daughter* by Maya Angelou, Penguin Random House © Maya Angelou 2008; (2) Quotation from the song lyrics "Better Version Of Me" by Fiona Apple; **62** "Shipyard" Text: Lawry, John/Mathes, Robert Ballou/Sumner, Gordon Matthew/Sutton, Julian Michael/Tickell, Kathryn Derran/Tickell, Peter © Copyright Control Shares/FMI Blackwood Music Inc./Maybe I can Music/Steerpike (Overseals) Ltd, EMI Music Publishing Germany GmbH, Berlin; **63** By Allan Massie, *The Scotsman*, Edinburgh, October 15, 2013; **64–65** © 2012 The Atlantic Media Co., as first published in The Atlantic Magazine. All rights reserved. Distributed by Tribune Content Agency; **67** Quotes: (1) Fareed Zakaria, quotation from the television programme *The Global Public Square*, CNN, November 6, 2011; (2) Ari Shapiro, quotation from the radio programme *American Dream Faces Harsh New Reality*, National Public Radio, May 29, 2012; (3) James Truslow Adams, quotation from *The Epic of America*, Little, Brown and Co., Boston, 1931; (4) Quotation made by J. G. Ballard (unsourced); (5) Quotation made by Max Beerbohm, English essayist, parodist, and caricaturist; **71.1** Thomas Jefferson, quotation from *The First Inaugural Address*, 1801; **71.2** Abraham Lincoln, quotation from *The Gettysburg Address*, 1863; **71.3** John, F. Kennedy, quotation from *The Inaugural Address*, 1961; **71.4** William Jefferson Clinton, quotation from *The Second Inaugural Address*, 1997; **72** www.whitehouse.gov © The White House; **74–75** From NATIVE SPEAKER by Chang-Rae Lee, copyright (c) 1995 by Chang-Rae Lee. Used by permission of Riverhead Books, an imprint of Penguin Group (USA) LLC.; **76–77** www.nyc.gov © 2010 The City of New York; **78–79** Excerpt from pp. 231–4 [1119 words] from TO KILL A MOCKINGBIRD by HARPER LEE. Copyright © 1960 by Harper Lee; renewed © 1988 by Harper Lee. Foreword copyright © 1993 by Harper Lee. Reprinted by permission of HarperCollins Publishers.; **80** By Ronald Brownstein, *National Journal Magazine*, September 21, 2012 Copyright © 2014 by National Journal Group Inc; **82–83** From *The New York Times*, 16th December 2012 © 2012 The New York Times. All rights reserved. Used by permission and protected by the Copyright Laws of the United States. The printing, copying, redistribution, or retransmission of this Content without express written permission is prohibited.; **84** "As I Grew Older" by Langston Hughes © 1994 Estate of Langston Hughes published by permission of Harold Ober Associates, New York; **85** "stupid america" is reprinted with permission from the publisher of *Here Lies Lalo: The collected Works of Abelardo Delgado* by Abelardo Delgado, edited by Jarica Linn Watts (©2011 Arte Público Press- University of Houston); **87** By Heike Buchter, Thomas Fischermann, Angela Köckritz, ZEIT ONLINE, 29. August 2012; **92–93** From *The Washington Post*, January 23, 2103 © 2013 Washington Post Company. All rights reserved. Used by permission and protected by the Copyright Laws of the United States. The printing, copying, redistribution, or retransmission of this Content without express written permission is prohibited.; **94.1** Excerpt from "The EU: should Britain be in or out? - 'EU treatment of human rights is second to none'" by Baroness Shirley Williams (The Liberal Democrat), *The Observer*, London, January 18, 2014; **94.2** Excerpt from "The EU: should Britain be in or out? - 'If we left, we would get back our democracy'" by Mark Reckless (The Tory MP), *The Observer*, London, January 18, 2014; **95** By Tobis Jaecker, ZEIT ONLINE, 24. Februar 2014; **103** "Diverse City" Text & Melodie: Chris Stevens & Ivan Santiago & Toby McKeehan & Byron Chambers © 2004 Achtober Songs/Regisfunk Music/Universal Music – Brentwood Benson Songs. Für D, A, CH: SCM Hänssler, 71087 Holzgerlingen; **104** By Stephen Evans, *BBC News*, December 30, 2010 © BBC 2010; **105** By Lola Adesioye, the guardian.com, February 27, 2008; **106–107** Copyright © 1995 by T. Coraghessan Boyle. Permission by Mohrbooks AG, Zürich; **108–109** www.liamfox.co.uk, © 2014 Dr Liam Fox MP Member of Parliament for North Somerset. All rights reserved.; **110–111** © Ayad Akhtar, 2013, *Disgraced*, Bloomsbury Methuen Drama, an imprint of Bloomsbury Publishing Plc.; **112** From "Does lack of black models on cover of British Vogue amount ro racism?" by Tasny Hoskins, theguardian.com, August 12, 2014; **113** From A SHORT HISTORY OF IMMIGRATION © Geoff Page, 2011; **114–115** From "Zambian-born rapper Chansa releases epic song 'Immigrant'" by Lisa Evans, canadianimmigrant.ca, August 28, 2013 © 2013 Metroland Media Group. All rights reserved., **117** www.ruhr-guide.de, *Ruhr-Guide on-*

345

Appendix

line magazine, 2011; **122–123** ©2013 National Public Radio, Inc. NPR news report excerpt from a report titled "More Young People Are Moving Away From Religion, But Why?" by NPR Staff was originally published on NPR.org on January 15, 2013, and is used with the permission of NPR. Any unauthorized duplication is strictly prohibited.; **123** ©2013 National Public Radio, Inc. NPR news report excerpt from a report titled "On Religion, Some Young People Show Both Doubt And Respect" by NPR Staff was originally published on NPR.org on January 17, 2013, and is used with the permission of NPR. Any unauthorized duplication is strictly prohibited.; **124** From *The New York Times*, December 22, 2012 Copyright © 2012. The New York Times. All rights reserved. Used by permission and protected by the Copyright Laws of the United States. The printing, copying, redistribution, or retransmission of this Content without express written permission is prohibited.; **125** Copyright Guardian News & Media Ltd 2012; **127** By Erica DeMichiel, TheHuffingtonPost.com, February 2, 2013 © Erica DeMichiel; **130** From *The Negotiator* by Frederick Forsyth, Corgi Books/Transworld Publishers, a division of The Random House Group Ltd, London, 1989 © Frederick Forsyth 1989; **131** Quotes: (1) Quotation from the Open Knowledge Foundation website, https://okfn.org, *The Open Knowledge Foundation*, Cambridge, 2014; (2) From wordpress.com, quotation made by Prof. Dwayne Winseck, professor at the School of Journalism and Communication, Ottawa, Canada, 2012; (3) Marten Mickos, June 13, 2012. From opensource.com. Licensed under a Creative Commons Attribution-NoDerivatives 4.0 International License (CC BY-ND 4.0).; (4) From: http://blogs.gartner.com/andrea_dimaio/2011/07/14/the-case-against-online-participation-and-government-as-a-platform/ © Andrea Di Maio, reprinted with permission.; **136–137** www.fussball-lernen-global.org, © KICKFAIR e.V., Ostfildern; **138** www.kickfair.org, © KICKFAIR e.V., Ostfildern; **139** From THE WORLD UNTIL YESTERDAY: WHAT CAN WE LEARN FROM TRADITIONAL SOCIETIES? by Jared Diamond, copyright © 2012 by Jared Diamond. Used by permission of Viking Penguin, a division of Penguin Group (USA) LLC.; **140** Republished with permission of Business Insider, Inc., from *Business Insider*, Kim Bhasin, September 14, 2012; permission conveyed through Copyright Clearance Center, Inc.; **141** ©2013 National Public Radio, Inc. NPR news report titled "Workers In Bangladesh Are Getting A Raise" by Caitlin Kenney was originally published on NPR.org for "Planet Money Makes A T-Shirt" on December 2, 2013, and is used with the permission of NPR. Any unauthorized duplication is strictly prohibited.; **142-143** First published by the *Chicago Tribune* and reprinted by permission of Don Congdon Associates, Inc. © 1980 by Ray Bradbury; **145** By Jude Howell, *Guardian Professional*, London, March 26, 2013; **146** By Dominic Rushe, theguardian.com, January 25, 2013; **146** 111 words from 23 THINGS THEY DON'T TELL YOU ABOUT CAPITALISM by Ha-Joon Chang (Penguin Books 2010, 2011). Copyright © Ha-Joon Chang, 2010.; **147** By Timothy Spence, euractiv.com, March 13, 2012; **148** From *The Economist*, London, January 19, 2013; **149** From *The Weekly Wonk* by Anya Kamenetz, November 14, 2013 © 2013 New America Foundation; **150–151** From *Paradises and Dustscapes – Stories from the Heart of Globalisation*, by Holly Jean Buck © Holly Jean Buck 2012; **153** www.bundespraesident.de, © 2012 Bundespräsidialamt; **160** Extract A: Extracted from THE ACCIDENTAL APPRENTICE by Vikas Swarup. Published by Simon & Schuster UK; Extracts B+C: Reprinted by permission of HarperCollins Publishers Ltd. © Amitav Ghosh, 2004; **161–162** Extracted from THE ACCIDENTAL APPRENTICE by Vikas Swarup. Published by Simon & Schuster UK; **163** From *Being Indian* © copyright Pavan K. Varma, 2004.; **164** From *India - A Portrait* by Patrick French, Penguin Books, London, 2012 © Patrick French, 2011; **165** © Aravind Adiga, 2011, reprinted by permission of Atlantic Books Ltd; **166** By Dean Nelson, *The Telegraph*, London, April 18, 2013; **167** Excerpt from "Bollywood 100th anniversary: 100 fascinating facts to celebrate a century of Indian cinema" by Katie Imms, *Mirror Online*, May 03, 2013; **168–169** © 2014 Scott Butki; **170–171** From *India Dishonoured: Behind a nation's war on women* by Sunny Hundal, Guardian Books, London, 2013; **172** www.unwomensouthasia.org © UN Women. All rights reserved.; **173** From *Indian Summer: The Secret History of the End of an Empire*, by Alex von Tunzelmann, Simon & Schuster UK, London, 2007 © Alex von Tunzelmann, 2007; **174–175** From *Train to Pakistan* by Khushwant Singh, published by Penguin Books India, New Delhi, 2007 © Khushwant Singh; **176** http://www.thomascook.com/lp/1x6-en6umn/holidays-india/; **180** Quotes: (1) Quotation from a speech delivered by Malcolm X in 1963; (2) Quotation made by Mark Zuckerberg on the purpose of Facebook; **181** Quotes: (1) Quotation from "The Poet & The City" by W. H. Auden, from *The Dyer's Hand and other Essays*, Vintage Books, New York, 1962; (2) Quotation from *We Think: The Power Of Mass Creativity* by C. W. Leadbeater, Profile Books (GB), first published 2009; **183** (Quote) © 2014 Teddy Goff, republished by permission of The Big Think Inc.; **187–188** By James McLennan, www.opinionpanel.co.uk, March 15, 2013; **189–190** Excerpt(s) from THE CIRCLE by Dave Eggers, copyright © 2013 by Dave Eggers. Used by permission of Alfred A. Knopf, an imprint of the Knopf Doubleday Publishing Group, a division of Random House LLC. All rights reserved. Any third party use of this material, outside of this publication, is prohibited. Interested parties must apply directly to Random House LLC for permission.; **190–191** Excerpt(s) from GONE GIRL: A NOVEL by Gillian Flynn, copyright © 2012 by Gillian Flynn. Used by permission of Crown Books, an imprint of the Crown Publishing Group, a division of Random House LLC. All rights reserved. Any third party use of this material, outside of this publication, is prohibited. Interested parties must apply directly to Random House LLC for permission.; **192** By Mathew Ingram, Gigaom, March 1, 2012; **193** © 2013 Chris Measures http://measuresconsulting.wordpress.com/2013/05/01/the-rise-of-citizen-journalism/; **194–195** Reprinted by permission of the author and the author's agents, Scovil Galen Ghosh Literary Agency, Inc.; **196** © Liberty Forrest 2013; **198** © 2012 From *A Creator's Guide to Transmedia Storytelling: How to Captivate and Engage Audiences Across Multiple Platforms* by Andrea Phillips. Reproduced with permission from McGraw-Hill Global Education. All rights reserved.; **199** From Knowledge@Wharton, 7/3/2012 © 2012 Knowledge@Wharton. All rights reserved. Used by permission and protected by the Copyright Laws of the United States. The printing, copying, redistribution, or retransmission of this Content without express written permission is prohibited.; **201** By Morten Freidel, *Frankfurter Allgemeine*, Frankfurt/Main, May 12, 2013; **205** "Diane Young" Text: Batmanglij, Rostam/König, Ezra © Imagem Music GmbH, Berlin; **206** From "A Thousand Words" by Olivia Cole, *The Spectator*, London March 30, 2013; **208** By Edward Helmore, *The Observer*, London, November 2011; **217** From "French pop music finds its voice with English language lyrics" by Genevieve Roberts, *Gurdian Weekly*, September 14, 2010; **218** By Helen Pidd, *The Guardian*, London, April 10, 2012; **219** By Jane O'Brien, *BBC News Magazine*, December 14, 2012 ©BBC; **220** Excerpt from *The Other Hand* by Chris Cleave, Sceptre, an imprint of Hodder & Stoughton Ltd, London, 2009 © Chris Cleave 2008; **223** From "Johnson: Just speak English?", *The Economist*, London, September 17, 2013; **224–226** Copyright © 1989 by Amy Tan. First appeared in *The Threepenny Review*. Reprinted by permission of the author and the Sandra Dijkstra Literary Agency.; **228** From "Hay Festival 2012: English will die out like Latin, leading linguist claims", *The Telegraph*, London, June 6, 2012; **231** By Sönke Krüger, *Die Welt*, 19. November, 2007; **241–242** Excerpt from *Shakespeare: The World as a Stage* by Bill Bryson, Harper Perennial, An imprint of HarperCollins Publishers, London 2008, pp. 77-80 © Bill Bryson 2007; **245** © Marc Norman & Tom Stoppard; **248** From WILL IN THE WORLD by Stephen Greenblatt. Copyright ©2004 by Stephen Greenblatt. Used by permission of W. W. Norton & Comany, Inc.; **251** From *The New York Times*, October 27 © 2011 The New York Times. All rights reserved. Used by permission and protected by the Copyright Laws of the United States. The printing, copying, redistribution, or retransmission of this Content without express written permission is prohibited.; **252–253** ©2008 Time Inc. All rights reserved. Reprinted/Translated from TIME and published with permission of Time Inc. Reproduction in any manner in any language in whole or in part without written permission is prohibited.; **255** By Hannes Stein, *Die Welt*, 25.04.2008; **265** (Political systems, task 3) quotation made by Mark Twain, US author and humorist; quotation made by Winston Churchill (former British Prime Minister); **297** (S6.1) Excerpt from "Poem in October" by Dylan Thomas, from *Collected poems 1934-1952*, J. M. Dent & Sons, London, 1952; excerpt from "Making cocoa for Kingsley Amis" by Wendy Cope, from *Making cocoa for Kingsley Amis*, Faber & Faber, London, 1986; **298** (S6.2) From *The Real Inspector Hound* by Tom Stoppard, Faber & Faber, London, 1968; **300** (S8) Excerpt from *Emma* by Jane Austen, John Murray, London, 1816; excerpt from *The Ambassadors* by Henry James, Methuen, London. 1903; excerpt from *Great Expectations* by Charles Dickens, Chapman and Hall, London, 1861; **301** (S9) Excerpt from *The Scarlet Letter* by Nathaniel Hawthorne, Ticknor, Reed & Fields, Boston, 1850; from PAPER TOWNS by John Green, copyright © 2008 by John Green. Used by permission of Dutton Children's Books, a division of Penguin Group (USA) LLC; excerpt from *Mrs Dalloway* by Virginia Woolf, Harcourt, Brace & Co., London, 1925; **302** (S.10.1) Quotation from *The Time Machine* by H.G. Wells, William Heinemann, London 1895; **306** (S13) Excerpt from *Shakespeare: The World as a Stage* by Bill Bryson, Harper Perennial, An imprint of HarperCollins Publishers, London 2008, © Bill Bryson 2007

Bildquellen:
Cover Getty Images RF (Photodisc), München; **12.1** Ullstein Bild GmbH, Berlin; **12.2** shutterstock.com (wavebreakmedia), New York, NY; **12.3** Interfoto (Alinari/Maraini Fosco), München; **12.4** Getty Images (OJO Images), München; **13.1** Corbis (Peter Marshall/Demotix/Demotix), Berlin; **13.2** Getty Images (Hero Images), München; **14.1+2** Source: Pew Research Center; **14.3** David Simonds, Ealing London; **15.1** Pew Research Center, 2014/Pew Research Social & Demopgraphic Trends; **15.2** Source: Pew Research Social & Demopgraphic Trends; **16.1** Avenue Images GmbH (StockDisc), Hamburg; **16.2** iStockphoto (RF/Paul Piebinga), Calgary, Alberta; **16.3** Thinkstock (Jupiterimages), München; **16.4** Fotosearch Stock Photography (Digital Vision), Waukesha, WI; **16.5** Avenue Images GmbH (Fancy RF), Hamburg; **16.6** Getty Images RF (Digital Vision/Vicky Kasala), München; **16.7** Avenue Images GmbH (Fancy RF), Hamburg; **16.8** Klett-Archiv (Thomas Weccard), Stuttgart; **16.9** iStockphoto (RF/Andrei Tchernov), Calgary, Alberta; **17.1+2** © Lev Pakman 2014; **18.1–3** © Lev Pakman 2014; **19.1** Charles Griffin, Larnaca; **20.1** Getty Images (Axelle/Bauer-Griffin/FilmMagic), München; **21.1** tmg–Tele München Gruppe, München; **23.1** Thinkstock (Hemera), München; **23.2** shutterstock.com (ChaiyonS021), New York, NY; **23.3** shutterstock.com (Ollyy), New York, NY; **23.4** shutterstock.com (Dundanim), New York, NY; **23.5** shutterstock.com (Lisa F. Young), New York, NY; **25.1** Alamy Images (geogphotos), Abingdon, Oxon; **25.2** Social Research Institute, Ipsos Mori, London; **28.1** iStockphoto (Damir Cudic), Calgary, Alberta; **28.2** Thinkstock (iStock/Maciej Nowkowski), München; **29.1** www.CartoonStock.com (Larry Lambert), Bath; **30.1** Thinkstock (iStock/Tomas Banisauskas), München; **30.2** Getty Images (Taxi), München; **31.1** Getty Images (Charles Norfleet/FilmMagic), München; **32.1** Fotolia.com (Tatyana Gladskih), New York; **33.1** Thinkstock (Jupiterimages), München; **35.1** shutterstock.com (dmaster), New York, NY; **36.1** Thinkstock (Photodisc/Michael Blann), München; **36.2** shutterstock.com (hipproductions), New York, NY; **36.3** Reuters (Dwi Oblo), Frankfurt; **37.1** Picture-Alliance (empics), Frankfurt; **37.2** Thinkstock (iStockphoto), München; **37.3** Getty Images (Scott Barbour), München; **37.4** Corbis (Clifford Peeples/Demotix), Berlin; **37.5** shutterstock.com (Asta Plechaviciute), New York, NY; **38.1** Fotolia.com (Kaarsten), New York; **40.1** FOCUS (Martin Parr/Magnum Photos), Hamburg; **41.1** Picture-Alliance (EPA/Andy Rain), Frankfurt; **43.1** Picture-Alliance (Barry Batchelor/PA/empics), Frankfurt; **44.1** Getty Images (Peter Macdiarmid), München; **45.1** Getty Images (Horace Abrahams/Keystone), München; **45.2** Getty Images (Jeff Overs/BBC News & Current Affairs), München; **45.3** shutterstock.com (Frederic Legrand), New York, NY; **46.1** Thinkstock (iStock Editorial/hehague), München; **46.2** Getty Images, München; **47.1** Fotolia.com (rabbit75_fot), New York; **48.1** shutterstock.com (Tom Plesnik), New York, NY; **48.2** Getty Images, München; **49.1** www.CartoonStock.com (McKeough, Joe), Bath; **50.1** laif (Ian Jones), Köln; **51.1** Getty Images (Chris Jackson), München; **51.2** Picture-Alliance (Photoshot), Frankfurt; **52.1** Picture-Alliance (Photoshot), Frankfurt; **53.1** shutterstock.com (luxorphoto), New York, NY; **54.1** Mauritius Images (Photo Alto), Mittenwald; **55.2** Getty Images (Luis Enrique Ascui/Bloomberg), München; **59.1** Thinkstock (Stockbyte), München; **60.1** Getty Images (Photodisc), München; **60.2** Alamy Images (Jeremy Sutton-Hibbert), Abingdon, Oxon; **60.3+4** Alamy Images (Visions of America, LLC), Abingdon, Oxon; **60.5** shutterstock.com (Bikeworldtravel), New York, NY; **62.1** Getty Images (Hulton Archive), München; **62.2** Fotolia.com (Pookini), New York; **64.1** gemeinfrei ("USA-2000-population-density". Lizenziert unter Public domain über Wikimedia Commons – http://commons.wikimedia.org/wiki/File:USA-2000-population-density.gif#mediaviewer/Datei:USA-2000-population-density.gif); **65.1** Fotolia.com (Bettina Wehmeyer), New York; **65.2** shutterstock.com (Sean Pavone), New York, NY; **65.3** Thinkstock (Blulz60), München; **66.1** Getty Images (Taxi), München; **66.2** Fotolia.com (Brad Pict), New York; **66.3** gemeinfrei (PD); **66.4** Corbis (Bettmann/Corbis), Berlin; **67.1** Comstock, Luxemburg; **67.2** Kichka, Michel, Jerusalem; **67.3** f1 online digitale Bildagentur (Imagebroker), Frankfurt; **68.1** The Library of Congress (Archibald M. Willard), Washington, D.C.; **69.1** US Census; **69.2** iStockphoto (Nicole K. Cioe), Calgary, Alberta; **69.3** Fotolia.com (Darko Veselinovic), New York; **71.1** iStockphoto (HultonArchive), Calgary, Alberta; **71.2** Wikimedia Deutschland, Berlin; **71.3** Wikimedia Deutschland (Public Domain/Cecil Stoughton, White House), Berlin; **71.4** Corel Corporation Deutschland, Unterschleissheim; **72.1** Picture-Alliance (Kyodo), Frankfurt; **73.1** Ullstein Bild GmbH (Granger Collection), Berlin; **74.1** Ullstein Bild GmbH (Joker/Erich Haefele), Berlin; **74.2** Getty Images (OJO Images), München; **76.1** iStockphoto (Frankonline), Calgary, Alberta; **77.1** Picture-Alliance (dpa/EPA/Gino Domenico), Frankfurt; **77.2** Interfoto (Classicstrock/J. McGrail), München; **79.1** akg-images (Album), Berlin; **80.1** nach: Pew Research Center, Internet & American Life Project; **80.2** BigStockPhoto.com (Mikess5), Davis, CA; **80.3** nach: Pew Research Center, Internet & American Life Project; **81.1** Moms Demand Action, Zionsville; **81.2** Getty Images (George Frey/Bloomberg), München; **81.3** Fotolia.com (maconga), New York; **83.1** Granlund, Dave, Waconia MN; **84.1** Ullstein Bild GmbH (The Granger Collection), Berlin; **84.2** Thinkstock (Robert Dodge), München; **85.1** shutterstock.com (Ryan Rodrick Beiler), New York, NY; **87.1** iStockphoto (Amanda Rohde), Calgary, Alberta; **88.1** Thinkstock (Keith Levit Photography), München; **89.1** iStockphoto (clu), Calgary, Alberta; **90.1+2** shutterstock.com (ildogesto), New York, NY; **90.3** Action Press GmbH, Hamburg; **91.1** Avenue Images GmbH (Medio Images), Hamburg; **91.2** Reuters (Mihai Barbu), Frankfurt; **91.3** Fotolia.com (Henner Damke), New York; **92.1** Schrank, Peter, Aldeburgh; **94.1** DI Markus Szyszkowitz, arch. design + cartoons, Wien; **95.1** Getty Images (Chip Somodevilla),

Appendix

München; **96.1** Picture-Alliance (dpa), Frankfurt; **96.2** Thinkstock (Photawa), München; **96.3** Picture-Alliance (dpa/EPA/Glenn Hunt), Frankfurt; **96.4** Reuters (Jason Reed), Frankfurt; **97.1** shutterstock.com (Nando Machado), New York, NY; **97.2** Thinkstock (Oli Scarff), München; **97.3** Picture-Alliance (empics), Frankfurt; **97.4** www.CartoonStock.com (Fran), Bath; **100.1** www.CartoonStock.com (Campbell, Martha), Bath; **102.1** Picture-Alliance (Laci Perenyi), Frankfurt; **102.2** Imago (Gribaudi/ImagePhoto), Berlin; **102.3** Alamy Images (IS831), Abingdon, Oxon; **103.1** Getty Images (Rick Diamond/WireImage), München; **104.1** Alamy Images (RF Image State), Abingdon, Oxon; **105.1** Getty Images (Cindy Ord/WireImage), München; **106.1** Penguin Group (USA) Inc., New York, NY 10014; **107.1** Interfoto (NG Collection), München; **108.1** Corbis (Gideon Mendel), Berlin; **109.1** Getty Images (Iconica), München; **110.1** Getty Images (Bill Pugliano), München; **110.2** laif (Allan Tannenbaum/Polaris), Köln; **111.1** Picture-Alliance (AP/Erin Baiano), Frankfurt; **112.1** shutterstock.com (Ovidiu Hrubaru), New York, NY; **115.1+2** Copied with permission of Canada Post Corporation; **117.1** Picture-Alliance (Christian Hartmann/Handout/dpa/ef), Frankfurt; **118.1** Corbis (Steve Parkins/Demotix), Berlin; **119.1** Corbis (KevinN Lamarque/Reuters), Berlin; **119.2** ddp images GmbH (interTOPICS/Capital Pictures), Hamburg; **120.1** Thinkstock (Digital Vision), München; **120.2** Alamy Images (Oso Media), Abingdon, Oxon; **120.3** Getty Images (Universal Images Group), München; **120.4** Getty Images (Stockbyte), München; **120.5** Cagle Cartoons (Hajo de Reijger), Santa Barbara, CA; **120.6** Getty Images (Joe Raedle), München; **121.1** Klett-Archiv (Office for National Statistics), Stuttgart; **122.1** Corbis (Tim Clayton), Berlin; **123.1** Klett-Archiv (U.S. Census Bureau, Statistical Abstract of the United States: 2012), Stuttgart; **125.1** Avenue Images GmbH (StockDisc), Hamburg; **126.1** Getty Images, München; **126.2** nach: National Association for the Advancement of Colored People; **126.3** Getty Images (Bill Clark/Roll Call), München; **126.4** Parliamentary House of Commons, London; **126.5** Alamy Images (Mark Sykes), Abingdon, Oxon; **126.6** Klett-Archiv (http://www.civicyouth.org/CIRCLE/Young voters in the 2012 Presidential Election), Stuttgart; **127.1** shutterstock.com (Warren Goldswain), New York, NY; **128.1** Fotolia.com (kropic), New York; **128.2** shutterstock.com (fstockfoto), New York, NY; **128.3** Thinkstock (iStock/kropic), München; **129.1** Picture-Alliance (empics), Frankfurt; **129.2** Corbis (Jamie Wiseman/The Daily Mail/Pool/Reuters), Berlin; **129.3** iStockphoto (EdStock), Calgary, Alberta; **130.1** Getty Images (Keith Torrie/NY Daily News Archive), München; **132.1** Getty Images (Mandel Ngan/AFP), München; **132.2** laif (Sven Torfinn), Köln; **132.3–5** Fondation GoodPlanet (7 Billion Others), Paris; **133.1** Picture-Alliance (Imaginechina/Mo Weinong), Frankfurt; **133.2** Corbis (Carl & Ann Purcell), Berlin; **133.3** Getty Images (Frederic J. Brown/AFP), München; **133.4** laif (Xie Zhengyi/Imaginechina), Köln; **133.5–7** Fondation GoodPlanet (7 Billion Others), Paris; **134.1** www.CartoonStock.com (Hawkins, Len), Bath; **135.1** www.CartoonStock.com (Grizelda), Bath; **137.1** Getty Images (Lonely Planet), München; **138.1** Alamy Images (Yadid Levy), Abingdon, Oxon; **139.1** Imago, Berlin; **139.2** Mauritius Images (Alamy), Mittenwald; **140.1** Corbis (Imaginechina), Berlin; **141.1** laif (Kathrin Harms), Köln; **141.2** Source: International Labour Organization; **143.1** www.CartoonStock.com (Martirena, Alfredo), Bath; **143.2** Avenue Images GmbH (Corbis RF), Hamburg; **143.3** Fotosearch Stock Photography (Digital Vision), Waukesha, WI; **144.1** Medair (Andrew Robinson), Dortmund; **145.1** Logo, Stuttgart; **145.2** Amnesty International, Berlin; **145.3** Greenpeace Deutschland e.V.; **146.1** Thinkstock (Wavebreakmedia Ltd), München; **147.1** laif (Sandra Hoyn), Köln; **148.1** Video(s) supplied by BBC Worldwide Learning, London; **149.1** Fotolia.com (apops), New York; **150.1** shutterstock.com (Wout Kok), New York, NY; **151.1** iStockphoto (Halbergman), Calgary, Alberta; **155.1** Sandy Lohß, Chemnitz; **155.2** Imago, Berlin; **156.1** shutterstock.com (BasPhoto), New York, NY; **156.2** Mauritius Images (Alamy), Mittenwald; **156.3** shutterstock.com (Konstantin Sutyagin), New York, NY; **157.1** shutterstock.com (Alexandra Lande), New York, NY; **157.2** f1 online digitale Bildagentur (Pixtal), Frankfurt; **157.3** shutterstock.com (Steve Estvanik), New York, NY; **157.4** iStockphoto (Jeremy Richards), Calgary, Alberta; **158.1** Thinkstock (Stockbyte), München; **159.1+3** Fotolia.com (Malgorzata Kistryn), New York; **159.2** Thinkstock (Photos.com), München; **160.1** HarperCollins (© 2005, Amitav Ghosh), London-Hammersmith; **163.1** shutterstock.com (Jorg Hackemann), New York, NY; **163.2** shutterstock.com (Pawel Pietraszewski), New York, NY; **163.3** Alamy Images (John Oldham), Abingdon, Oxon; **164.1** laif (Hollandse Hoogte), Köln; **165.1** iStockphoto (VasukiRao), Calgary, Alberta; **166.1** shutterstock.com (Kaetana), New York, NY; **167.1** Corbis (Babu/Reuters), Berlin; **167.2** Corbis (Frederic Soltan), Berlin; **168.1** shutterstock.com (f9photos), New York, NY; **168.2** Klett-Archiv (Peter Kraus, Wäschebeuren), Stuttgart; **168.3** Getty Images (Ulf Andersen), München; **170.1** gemeinfrei; **172.1+2** UN Women/Neelabh Banerjee; **173.1** akg-images (Archiv Peter Ruehe), Berlin; **175.1** Corbis (Bettmann), Berlin; **176.1** Thinkstock (Byelikova Oksana), München; **179.1** Getty Images (Himanshu Vyas/Hindustan Times), München; **179.2** Dennis, Paul, Lahnstein; **180.1** Thinkstock (Darrin Klimek), München; **180.2** Corbis (Stringer/Pakistan/Reuters), Berlin; **180.3** shutterstock.com (cinemafestival), New York, NY; **181.1** Picture-Alliance (The Advertisi), Frankfurt; **181.2** NASA, Washington, D.C.; **181.3** News Syndication (The Sun), London; **182.1** nach: Pew Research Center for the People & the Press; **182.2** www.CartoonStock.com (McGeary, Ron), Bath; **183.1** Pew Research Internet & American Life Project; **183.2** Marketoonist LLC, San Anselmo, CA; **184.1** Corbis (Pablo Ortega/Demotix), Berlin; **185.1** www.CartoonStock.com (Hagen, Ralph), Bath; **186.1** ©UNICEF Sweden. Photo: UNICEF/Asad Zaidi; **187.1** www.CartoonStock.com (Proud, Bill), Bath; **188.1** Action Press GmbH (Rex Features Ltd.), Hamburg; **189.1** shutterstock.com Svetlana Chistyakova), New York, NY; **190.1** laif (Davide Lanzilao/Contrasto), Köln; **191.1** Corbis (Hans Strand), Berlin; **191.2** Mauritius Images (Doug Scott), Mittenwald; **191.3** Picture-Alliance, Frankfurt; **191.4** iStockphoto (Pierre Janssen), Calgary, Alberta; **192.1–4** The Observer, Guardian News & Media Ltd, London; **194.1** Bildzitat; **195.1** laif (Friedrich, Brigitte/SZ Photo), Köln; **195.2** www.CartoonStock.com (Lindsay Foyle), Bath; **196.1** Thinkstock (Jupiterimages/Polka Dot), München; **197.3** Fotolia.com (J. J.Brown), New York; **197.4** www.fuzion.ie, Cork; **197.1+2** www.stopphubbing.com (McCann, Melbourne), Melbourne; **198.1** shutterstock.com (Bennyartist), New York, NY; **199.1** laif (©2013 Stuart Isett. All rights reserved./Polaris), Köln; **199.2** laif (Hazel Thompson for The New York Times), Köln; **201.1** shutterstock.com (HP-photo), New York, NY; **202.1** iStockphoto (Govinda Jakosalem Trazo), Calgary, Alberta; **202.2** Klett-Archiv, Stuttgart; **203.1–3** shutterstock.com (conrado), New York, NY; **204.1** JupiterImages photos.com, Tucson, AZ; **204.2** Digital image © 2014 Succession H. Matisse, Issy-les-Moulineaux © Succession H. Matisse/VG Bild-Kunst, Bonn 2014 [Henri Matisse: Harmony in Red]; **204.3** Picture-Alliance (Photoshot), Frankfurt © Tracey Emin. All rights reserved/VG Bild-Kunst, Bonn 2014 [Tracey Emin: My Bed, 1998]; **205.1** Beggars Group, London; **206.1+2** Trunk Archive (Bryan Adams), New York; **206.3** Picture-Alliance (dpa/EPA/British Royal Mail), Frankfurt; **207.1** Corbis (Bettmann), Berlin; **207.2** shutterstock.com (Frances L Fruit), New York, NY; **208.1** Corbis (Walter Bibikow/JAI), Berlin; **209.1** Corbis (Ted Soqui), Berlin; **209.2** Slinkachu, London; **209.3** Action Press GmbH (Julian Makey/Rex Features), Hamburg; **209.4** Picture-Alliance (Victoria Bonn), Frankfurt; **210.1** Picture-Alliance (Wolfgang Langenstrassen/dpa), Frankfurt; **210.2** Thinkstock (szefei), München; **210.3** iStockphoto (pma2010), Calgary, Alberta; **210.4** iStockphoto (Andrew Wood), Calgary, Alberta; **210.5** Getty

Images (Raveendran/AFP), München; **211.1** Getty Images (Francois Nascimbeni/AFP), München; **211.2** Alamy Images (Art Directors & TRIP/Helen Rogers), Abingdon, Oxon; **211.4** www.CartoonStock.com (Goddard, Clive), Bath; **211.3** (Grafik) nach: Graddol, D. (2006). English next. London: British Council, p. 29.; **211.3** (Weltkugel) iStockphoto (Oleg Prikhodko), Calgary, Alberta; **216.1** Klett-Archiv (erstellt mit Tagxedo), Stuttgart; **217.1** Getty Images (Tim Mosenfelder), München; **218.1** Thinkstock (Stockbyte), München; **220.1** Hachette UK Ltd. (Author: Chris Cleave Publisher: Hodder and Stoughton), London; **222.1** dreamstime.com (Denis Makarenko), Brentwood, TN; **224.1** dreamstime.com (Sbukley), Brentwood, TN; **225.1** GOODSHOOT (Goodshoot), Annecy-Le-Vieux; **225.2** Estrada, Tiffany, Stuttgart; **225.3** Fotolia.com (svlumagraphica), New York; **227.1+2** Geoatlas, Hendaye; **227.3** shutterstock.com (Adam Golabek), New York, NY; **227.4** Fotolia.com (vospalej), New York; **227.5** Thinkstock (Hemera), München; **227.6** Geoatlas, Hendaye; **229.1** Fotolia.com (get4net), New York; **231.1** ddp images GmbH (Sebastian Willnow), Hamburg; **233.1** Klett-Archiv (Thomas Weccard), Stuttgart; **233.2** iStockphoto (jophil), Calgary, Alberta; **234.1** Wikimedia Deutschland (Public Domaine), Berlin; **234.2** Picture-Alliance (The Advertisi), Frankfurt; **234.3** Shakespeare's Globe (John Tramper), London; **235.1** Getty Images (Look), München; **235.2** Klett-Archiv (Christian Dekelver), Stuttgart; **236.1** interTOPICS GmbH (LMK Media), Hamburg; **237.1** Ullstein Bild GmbH (histopics), Berlin; **237.2** Corbis (Jason Hawkes), Berlin; **238.1** Ullstein Bild GmbH (Will), Berlin; **238.2** Klett-Archiv (Cornelia Kaminski), Stuttgart; **238.3** ddp images GmbH (Olaf Malzahn), Hamburg; **240.1** akg-images (album), Berlin; **240.2** Kramer, Angelika, Stuttgart; **241.1** Ullstein Bild GmbH (ArenaPAL/Norrington Nigel), Berlin; **242.1+3** ddp images GmbH, Hamburg; **242.2** Picture-Alliance (Tim Brakemeier/dpa), Frankfurt; **243.1** Classical Comics Ltd, Litchborough,Towcester; **244.1** shutterstock.com (Phant), New York, NY; **245.1** Interfoto (Mary Evans/MIramax Films/Universal Pictures/Ronald Grant Archive), München; **246.1** Getty Images (Chris Jackson), München; **247.1** akg-images (MPortfolio/Electa), Berlin; **248.1** gemeinfrei (Andreas Praefcke), **249.1** iStockphoto (MG & co), Calgary, Alberta; **249.2** gemeinfrei; **249.3** Ullstein Bild GmbH (The Granger Collection), Berlin; **250.1** PantherMedia GmbH (Stefan Balling), München; **250.2** shutterstock.com, New York, NY; **251.1** Imago, Berlin; **252.1** Shakespeare Birthplace Trust (Ellie Kurttz), Warwickshire; **252.2** Shakespeare Birthplace Trust (Kwame Lestrade), Warwickshire; **254.1** gemeinfrei (PD); **255.1** Thinkstock (Hemera), München; **256.1** Ullstein Bild GmbH (Granger Collection), Berlin; **257.1** Picture-Alliance (Süddeutsche Zeitung), Frankfurt; **257.2** Thinkstock (Digital Vision), München; **259.1** Fotolia.com (Pixelacts), New York; **259.2** iStockphoto (stevenallan), Calgary, Alberta; **261.1** shutterstock.com (Stuart Jenner), New York, NY; **262.1** Fotolia.com (Loic Le Brusq), New York; **264.1** iStockphoto (Arturo M. Enriquez), Calgary, Alberta; **265.1** MEV Verlag GmbH, Augsburg; **266.1** PantherMedia GmbH (Fabrizio Troiani), München; **266.2** iStockphoto (Eliza Snow), Calgary, Alberta; **267.1** Thinkstock (istockphoto), München; **267.2** shutterstock.com (Pete Niesen), New York, NY; **268.1** iStockphoto (Alberto Pomares), Calgary, Alberta; **268.2** iStockphoto (sellingpix), Calgary, Alberta; **269.1** shutterstock.com, New York, NY; **274.1** Picture-Alliance (dpa), Frankfurt; **274.2** www.CartoonStock.com (Neville, Ronnie), Bath; **274.3** iStockphoto (RF/Dmitry Bezkorovayny), Calgary, Alberta; **275.1** Thinkstock (iStockphoto), München; **276.1** Thinkstock (Dynamic Graphics), München; **276.2** Thinkstock (ariwasabi), München; **276.3** Fotosearch Stock Photography (PhotoDisc), Waukesha, WI; **276.4** Thinkstock (Jed Share/Kaoru Share), München; **279.1** Fotolia.com (MNStudio), New York; **279.2** Thinkstock (Photodisc), München; **280.1** Thinkstock (Ron Chapple Studios), München; **280.2** iStockphoto (RF/David Rehner), Calgary, Alberta; **280.3** Avenue Images GmbH (imageshop), Hamburg; **280.4** www.CartoonStock.com (Adey Bryant), Bath; **281.1** Fotosearch Stock Photography, Waukesha, WI; **281.2** Thinkstock (George Doyle), München; **281.3** Thinkstock (Wavebreakmedia Ltd), München; **281.4** Fotolia.com (Tupungato), New York; **282.1** Thinkstock (Mike Watson Images), München; **282.2** iStockphoto (BlackJack3D), Calgary, Alberta; **284.1** Fotolia.com (Picture-Factory), New York; **284.2** shutterstock.com (Pressmaster), New York, NY; **285.1** shutterstock.com (shipfactory), New York, NY; **286.1+2** Getty Images (Cultura), München; **287.1–4** Klett-Archiv (Thomas Weccard), Stuttgart; **288.1** shutterstock.com (PathDoc), New York, NY; **288.2** shutterstock.com (iordani), New York, NY; **289.1** shutterstock.com (Stefan Holm), New York, NY; **289.2** shutterstock.com (Martin Lehmann), New York, NY; **289.3** shutterstock.com (mangostock), New York, NY; **289.4** shutterstock.com (Monkey Business Images), New York, NY; **292.1** PantherMedia GmbH (keerati), München; **293.1** Fotolia.com (tdoes), New York; **293.2** Fotolia.com (svort), New York; **294.1+2** Thinkstock (iStock/gpointstudio), München; **295.1** shutterstock.com (pixmac), New York, NY; **295.2** Thinkstock (iStockphoto), München; **299.1** Bananastock, Watlington/Oxon; **299.2** Avenue Images GmbH (Stockbyte RF, George Doyle), Hamburg; **299.3** iStockphoto (RF/Amanda Rohde), Calgary, Alberta; **299.4** Thinkstock (iStockphoto), München; **299.5** MEV Verlag GmbH, Augsburg; **299.6** shutterstock.com (David Pereiras), New York, NY; **304.1** Thinkstock (Digital Vision), München; **307.1** Thinkstock (Stockbyte), München; **307.2** Avenue Images GmbH (Imgram Publishing), Hamburg; **307.3** Klett-Archiv (Thomas Weccard, Ludwigsburg), Stuttgart; **309.1** Klett-Archiv (Thomas Weccard), Stuttgart; **310.1** Thinkstock (BananaStock), München; **312.1** Klett-Archiv, Stuttgart; **313.1** Klett-Archiv, Stuttgart; **314.1** Klett-Archiv, Stuttgart; **315.1** shutterstock.com (Dean Mitchell), New York, NY; **315.2** iStockphoto (R. J. Seymour), Calgary, Alberta; **317.1** shutterstock.com (Krzysztof Wiktor), New York, NY; **318.1** Fotolia.com (Igor Mojzes), New York; **319.1** iStockphoto (clu), Calgary, Alberta; **320.1** Imago, Berlin; **321.1** iStockphoto (René Mansi), Calgary, Alberta; **325.1** Klett-Archiv (Thomas Weccard), Stuttgart; **326.1** Alamy Images (RF), Abingdon, Oxon; **327.1** Corbis (Visuals Unlimited), Berlin; **327.2** iStockphoto (Andrew Howe), Calgary, Alberta; **327.3** dreamstime.com (Eddy Van Ryckeghem), Brentwood, TN; **328.1** www.CartoonStock.com (Toles, Tom), Bath; **329.1** Mauritius Images (United Archives, © Warner Bros. Filmszene: Harry Potter und der Gefangene von Askaban), Mittenwald; **329.2** Getty Images (Chris Hyde), München; **330.1** shutterstock.com (Stanislav Popov), New York; **330.2** Thinkstock (Chalabala), München; **334.1** iStockphoto (Dean Mitchell), Calgary, Alberta; **344.1** Fotolia.com (fotomek), New York; **344.2** Fotolia.com (Martin Schumann), New York; **344.3** Fotolia.com (Texelart), New York; **350.1–351.1** Klett-Archiv (Klett-Archiv), Stuttgart

CD-ROM-Quellen:
Vocabulary sheets: Lektorat editoria, Fellbach; Anja Treinies, Düsseldorf
Videos: *Topic 6 Migration and diversity:* "European migration" video supplied by BBC Worldwide Learning; *Topic 13 The Englishes:* "The History of English in Ten Minutes" © The Open University

Every effort has been made to locate owners of copyright material, but in a few cases this has not proved possible and repeated inquiries have remained unanswered. The publishers would be glad to hear from any further copyright owners of material reproduced in this book.